The African American Years

The African American Years

CHRONOLOGIES OF AMERICAN HISTORY AND EXPERIENCE

GABRIEL BURNS STEPTO

CHARLES SCRIBNER'S SONS®

THOMSON

™

GALE

New York • Detroit • San Diego • San Francisco • Cleveland • New Haven, Conn. • Waterville, Maine • London • Munich

THOMSON
★
GALE ™

The African American Years

Gabriel Burns Stepto

Copyright © 2003 Charles Scribner's Sons. Charles Scribner's Sons is an imprint of The Gale Group, Inc., a division of Thomson Learning, Inc.

Charles Scribner's Sons™ and Thomson Learning™ are trademarks used herein under license.

For more information, contact
Charles Scribner's Sons
An imprint of The Gale Group
300 Park Avenue South, 9th floor
New York, NY 10010
Or you can visit our Internet site at
http://www.gale.com

ALL RIGHTS RESERVED
No part of this work covered by the copyright hereon may be reproduced or used in any form or by any means—graphic, electronic, or mechanical, including photocopying, recording, taping, Web distribution, or information storage retrieval systems—without the written permission of the publisher.

For permission to use material from this product, submit your request via Web at www.gale-edit.com/permissions, or you may download our Permissions Request form and submit your request by fax or mail to:

Permissions Department
The Gale Group, Inc.
27500 Drake Rd.
Farmington Hills, MI 48331-3535
Permissions Hotline:
248 699-8006 or 800 877-4253, ext. 8006
Fax: 248 699-8074 or 800 762-4058

Cover photographs reproduced by permission of Corbis-Bettmann (Harriet Tubman), Reuters/Corbis-Bettmann (Denzel Washington), Archive Photos, Inc. (The Cotton Club and Jackie Robinson), and AP/Wide World Photos (Dr. Martin Luther King Jr. with Malcolm X and Maya Angelou).

Since this page cannot legibly accommodate all copyright notices, the acknowledgments constitute an extension of the copyright notice.

LIBRARY OF CONGRESS CATALOGING-IN-PUBLICATION DATA

Stepto, Gabriel.
    The African American years / Gabriel Burns Stepto.
        p. cm. -- (Chronologies of American history and experience)
    Includes bibliographical references (p.) and indexes.
    ISBN 0-684-31257-3 (alk. paper)
        1. African Americans--History--Chronology. 2. African Americans--History--Sources.   I. Title. II. Series.
E185.S797 2003
973'.0496073--dc21

2002012869

Printed in the United States of America
10 9 8 7 6 5 4 3 2

Contents

Editorial and Production Staff

Project Editor
Mark F. Mikula

Senior Development Editor
Nathalie Duval

Editorial
Mark Drouillard, Gloria Lam, Matt Nowinski, Chris Romig, Tricia Toney, Ken Wachsberger

Indexing
Do Mi Stauber

Permissions
Margaret A. Chamberlain

Imaging and Multimedia
Leitha Etheridge-Sims, Lezlie Light, David G. Oblender, Luke Rademacher, Robyn Young

Product Design
Michelle DiMercurio

Composition
Evi Seoud

Manufacturing
Rita Wimberley

Publisher
Frank Menchaca

Preface

History is a set of interpretations of past events that historians and the reading public come to agree upon. It is a process in which we look back and try to give a name to what happened. These shared conclusions do not stay fixed through time; they change as people change.

Nowhere is flux and the reinterpretation of the past more alive, or for that matter, more critical, than in the history of the African peoples in the Americas. This history mixes widely accepted stories, wishful thinking, plain old ignorance (of both an active and a passive nature), and a propensity for error—for it is the history of a people whose arrival in the New World was marked by an attempt to erase the linguistic and cultural traces of its past.

Writing and reading the history of African Americans in the Americas, then, present a unique challenge. They are, in a sense, acts of interpreting an anti-history, an un-history, a history that was not meant to be told, a past that was forbidden to be named.

To write and read the story of African Americans, who for large parts of their experience in the United States were not treated even as human beings, much less citizens or people of record, we must turn to a wealth of sources. Memoirs, letters, family histories, newspapers, oral histories, city directories—these are just a few of the types of materials writers and readers must draw upon both to construct the past and to reconstruct prior interpretations of that past.

This volume presents such sources along with essays and a chronology of the African American experience.

These elements are meant to offer not another shared, fixed conclusion, but rather a set of tools enabling the student, the researcher, and the general reader to engage in his or her own construction and reconstruction. The timeline included at the front of this book intends to capture the sweep of African American history by pinpointing its key years and, within those years, recording significant events. The essays and sidebars in the second part of the book provide the context, the background for understanding the significance of events and relating them to the larger story of African American history. The primary sources constitute historical evidence. Think of these elements not as forming a monolith, telling an official story, but rather as a weave of distinct threads that, as a whole, provides an image of the African American past open to many readings and further investigations.

At the outset of the twenty-first century, it is a bold but altogether fair statement to say that African Americans have either created or been an integral part in the conception of most of the great literature, music, art, and culture the United States has produced. Regardless of how we judge the cultural or the technological impact of the United States on world culture, black Americans are a part of that impact. African American years are therefore America's years and these, at least to some extent, are the twenty-first century world's years. Critical interpretation and reexamination of the tranformations of these years can only enhance our understanding of our global community.

—Gabriel Burns Stepto

The African American Years: Chronology

1444

With the Portuguese advances in shipbuilding and the explorations of Henry the Navigator, a quantum leap in shipbuilding technology is achieved. This means that the caravels can stay out of port far longer, and can carry a greater cargo—and as a result, the slave trade explodes in the decades that follow. **SEE SIDEBAR** *The European Slave Trade Begins, p. 77*

1492

Christopher Columbus sails west to the Americas with a crew that includes one sailor, Pedro Alonso Niño, who may have been black. In the decades that follow, black sailors, soldiers, and explorers take part in most of the Spanish conquests in the New World.

1539

Estevanico, a black explorer, leads an expedition north from Mexico to discover for Spain the regions of present-day Arizona and New Mexico. **SEE ENTRY** *African Americans on the Frontier, p. 213*

1608

Matthew Da Costa, a black interpreter for the Portuguese and French courts, is present at the founding of Quebec City, the capital of New France, the fledgling French colony in North America. A free man in a position of respect and authority, Da Costa will come to be regarded as Canada's first black immigrant.

1619

Twenty Africans arrive in Jamestown Harbor aboard a Dutch slave ship. Statutory slavery does not exist yet, and they are sold as indentured servants, many of them gaining their freedom and land in the years that follow. But within twenty-five years, statutory slavery will be established in Massachusetts, and thereafter every colony will follow suit, making racial slavery a legal fact throughout the colonies. **SEE SIDEBAR** *Twenty Africans Arrive in Jamestown Colony, p. 71*

1628

Slavery in Canada begins when Olivier Le Jeune, an African child of six, is kidnapped and taken to New France, where he is sold as a slave. Le Jeune serves as a domestic slave until his death in 1654. African Canadian slaves who follow will serve primarily as household servants like Le Jeune, while native Canadian people, the Panis, will be used in agricultural slavery. Canadian slavery receives royal sanction in 1689, 1709, and again in 1760, when New France falls to the English.

1634

French Catholic missionaries in Louisiana begin to provide education for all workers, regardless of their race or status.

1638

Virginia passes legislation that requires a servant who escapes for a second time to be branded on the cheek or shoulder with the letter *R*.

Most scholars agree that the first Africans brought to America as slaves arrived in Virginia in 1619. Note the nudity of the captives, the Renaissance clothing of the white men, the elaborate pavilion, and the Dutch ship in the background. Early Virginia records suggest that at least some of the "twenty negars" of Jamestown went on to become free men and women, with property and slaves of their own. **THE LIBRARY OF CONGRESS**

1640

John Punch, an African indentured servant, is made a "slave for life" as punishment for an attempt to escape with two other servants. Of the three, Punch alone is black, and he alone is condemned to lifelong servitude. John Punch is the first person known to be enslaved in the North American colonies. This ushers in the age of racial slavery. **SEE SIDEBAR** *Acknowledging Permanent Slavery: The Escape and Capture of the Slave John Punch, p. 92*

1641

The first colonial slavery statute is adopted in the Massachusetts colony. Entitled "Liberties of Forreiners and Strangers," it guarantees the liberty of English settlers at the same time that it authorizes the enslavement of Indian prisoners of war and Africans captured and sold in the slave trade. **SEE PRIMARY SOURCE DOCUMENT** *The First Slavery Statute and First Anti-Literacy Act, p. 80*

1651

Anthony Johnson, probably one of the twenty Africans who arrived in Jamestown in 1619, receives a grant of 250 acres in Northampton County, Virginia, with the right to import five persons as labor. Other free blacks receive similar grants in Virginia during this decade.

1655

Elizabeth Key, a slave since birth, sues for her freedom and wins. She is born the daughter of an influential Virginia planter and a slave woman. Her suit is based on three arguments: (1) her father was a free man; (2) she had been baptized, the implication being that a Christian could not be a slave for life; and (3) she had been sold to another planter even after she had served nine years.

1661

The Virginia Assembly passes the Act on Runaways, which establishes a distinction between English and Negro servants. Runaway English servants are to have the time of their indentures lengthened as punishment. But if they run away with "Negroes who are incapable of making satisfaction by addition of a time"—that is, who are already slaves for life—then the English runaways are to be punished by having to serve the extra time for the masters of the Negro slaves. This is the colony's first legal recognition that some black servants are actually enslaved for life. **SEE PRIMARY SOURCE DOCUMENT** *The Runaway Slave Act, p. 92*

1662

The Virginia Assembly adopts the first statute making slavery an inheritable condition based on the mother's status, according to which all children born of enslaved women are deemed slaves for life. In the following year, Maryland enacts a law that also extends slavery to the children of freeborn Englishwomen who marry slaves. **SEE PRIMARY SOURCE DOCUMENT** *"An Agreement to Deliver 17 Negro Slaves," p. 79*

1663

Black slaves and white indentured servants join in the first recorded slave conspiracy in Gloucester County, Virginia, on September 13. Their plan is betrayed by an indentured servant.

Maryland enacts a law giving legal recognition to slavery. It reduces all Africans to slavery, regardless of their previous status, as well as white women who marry black slaves and the children of such marriages. In 1681, a portion of this law is repealed when Maryland declares that the children of indentured white women and enslaved black males are born free. **SEE ENTRY** *The First Africans to Arrive in the New World, p. 71*

1664

The first antimiscegenation law is passed in Maryland Colony on September 20, banning marriages between Englishwomen and blacks. It is followed by similar laws in Virginia (1691), Massachusetts (1705), North Carolina (1715), South Carolina (1717), Delaware (1721), and Pennsylvania (1725). Such laws remain on the books in several states until the mid-twentieth century.

1668

The Virginia Assembly adopts an act denying equality before the law to free blacks. This is the first of many laws passed throughout the colonies that establish legal and civil distinctions between black and white freemen. Despite attempts to drive out or enslave free black people, their numbers continue to grow slowly in all of the colonies.

1669

The Virginia Assembly passes an act acquitting masters of "felony murder" for the killing of slaves during the course of punishment. It is called "An Act about the Casuall Killing of Slaves." **SEE PRIMARY SOURCE DOCUMENT** *Virginia Passes the "Casual Slave Killing Act," p. 79*

1671

As more and more Africans become converts to Christianity, Maryland enacts a law stating that the Christian conversion of slaves does not in any way negate their slave status. Prior to this, the terms "Christian" and "free" had been used interchangeably.

1672

King Charles II of England charters the Royal African Company to trade in slaves. It quickly comes to dominate the Atlantic slave trade, bringing thousands of newly captured Africans to North America in the decades that follow. **SEE ENTRY** *The First Africans to Arrive in the New World, p. 71*

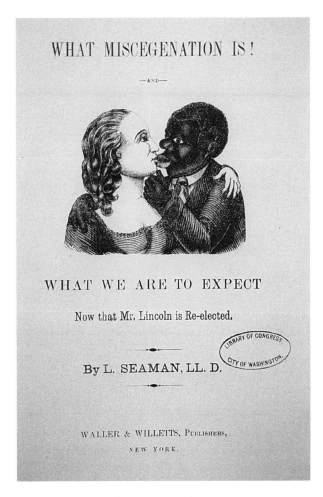

Much of the early anti-black sentiment was stirred up by the promise that without legislation banning their interaction, black males would be involved romantically with whites females. This brand of fear-mongering has a storied past and was used continually to discourage interracial relationships. **THE LIBRARY OF CONGRESS**

1676

Slaves, indentured servants, and small landowners join the wealthy planter Nathaniel Bacon in a rebellion against the policies of tidewater planters and the royal governor of Virginia, William Berkeley. Although Bacon's Rebellion is eventually quelled by English forces, it provides an example of political and military cooperation among Virginia's black and white servants.

1680

Repealing a 1670 law that made "Indians and others" free, the Virginia Assembly passes an act stating that all nonwhite, non-Christian servants, whether they come by land (Indians) or by sea (Africans), will be "adjudged, deemed, and taken to be slaves." The new law also states that for such persons, conversion to

Christianity will not be cause for their manumission from slavery. Though Virginia has already passed many laws governing the use and behavior of enslaved people, this is its first slavery statute.

1688

On February 18, the Mennonite Quakers of Germantown, Pennsylvania, meet to adopt a formal protest against slavery, the first known antislavery declaration in the Western world. In the Great Awakening of the mid-1700s, Quakers in England and the colonies will reaffirm their opposition to slavery and move to ban slaveholders and slave traders from their fellowship. In the 1820s, Quakers will leave the South in large numbers to create new settlements in the West. **SEE ENTRY** *The Debate over Slavery in the United States, p. 108*

1704

Elias Neau, a French immigrant from the Church of England's Anglican Society for the Propagation of the Gospel, opens a school for slaves in New York City. The school brings Christianity to slaves in the area.

1705

Virginia enacts the colonies' first comprehensive slave code. Among its provisions are laws that ban Negroes, mulattoes, and Indians from holding civil, military, or religious office and from bearing witness in a court of law. The code also condemns them to slavery for life except when they have been Christians in their own countries or free in a Christian country and declares them to be "real estate," exchangeable in the payment of debts. Under the code indentured women servants who bear illegitimate black or mulatto children are fined. Virginia's slave code becomes the model for other colonies' sexual, civil, and legal regulation of human property.

1712

The first major slave revolt occurs in New York City on April 6, when slaves gather to revenge themselves for abuses by their owners. They kill nine whites before they are overcome and arrested. In the wake of this revolt, twenty-one slaves are executed and six commit suicide. **SEE ENTRY** *The First Africans to Arrive in the New World, p. 74*

1731

Benjamin Banneker, astronomer, mathematician, surveyor, farmer, and city planner, is born in Maryland. **SEE ENTRY** *The African American Intellectual Experience, p. 404*

1739

Under the leadership of Cato, slaves in Stono, South Carolina, revolt on September 9, stealing arms and ammunition and marching south, hoping to reach the Florida border, and killing twenty-five whites who attempt to stop them. Most are eventually captured, and thirty are hanged.

1740

The first antiliteracy law is adopted in the South Carolina colony. It defines literate slaves as "great inconveniences" and prohibits teaching slaves to write and employing them in any task involving writing. It also establishes a penalty of "100 pounds, current money" for breaking the law. In the decades following, dozens of such laws will be enacted throughout the slaveholding South. **SEE ENTRY** *African American Newspapers and Periodicals, p. 228*

1741

Rumors of a slave conspiracy circulate in New York City following a series of arsonist fires. Although there is scant evidence that such a conspiracy was afoot, thirty-one slaves and five whites suspected of plotting with them are hanged. **SEE ENTRY** *The First Africans to Arrive in the New World, p. 74*

1746

Absalom Jones, leader during the black pioneer period, is born.

Lucy Terry, a sixteen-year-old African slave, composes the poem "Bars Fight" to commemorate the August 28 Indian raid on Deerfield, Massachusetts, and the murder of English settlers. It is the first poem by a black American poet and is passed down through oral tradition among the residents of Deerfield until 1855, when it is printed for the first time.

1750

Philadelphia Quakers, under the leadership of Anthony Benezet, establish the first free school for African Americans. At his death, Benezet wills a portion of his estate as an endowment for the school.

1770

Crispus Attucks, a fugitive slave, is the first patriot to die in the cause of American independence. He is shot by British soldiers, along with four other men, in what comes to be known as the Boston Massacre. In the trial that follows, the soldiers are found not guilty of murder, but two are convicted of manslaughter.

1773

David George establishes the first independent African American church in Silver Bluff, Georgia. George is among the black loyalists who leave with British forces following the American Revolution, resettling in Nova Scotia and later in Sierra Leone and founding Baptist churches in both places. The Silver Bluff church comes under the leadership of Jesse Galphin and is relocated to Augusta, Georgia, as the First African Baptist Church.

Phillis Wheatley's *Poems on Various Subjects, Religious and Moral* is published, the second book ever to be published by an American woman. Brought to America in a slave ship as a child of seven, Wheatley becomes in her lifetime one of the best-known poets of New England.

1775

The Pennsylvania Society for the Abolition of Slavery, the nation's first abolitionist society, is organized by Philadelphia Quakers on April 14. Five days later, African American minutemen fight in the battle of Lexington and Concord. On October 23, the Continental Congress bars African Americans from the army, and on November 7, Lord Dunmore, the former royal governor of Virginia, welcomes them into the British army, promising freedom in return for military service. On December 31, George Washington orders recruiting officers to accept free African Americans into the Continental army.

Black soldiers—Salem Poor, a free black, and Peter Salem, a slave—fight the British heroically at the Battle of Bunker Hill on June 17.

1776

The Continental Congress unanimously adopts the Declaration of Independence on July 4, stating that "all men are created equal." Language condemning the slave trade is struck out of the final document in deference to the delegates from South Carolina and Georgia.

1777

Sinai Reynolds, today the fifth great-grandmother of an African American family that traces its lineage back through eight generations, is born into slavery in Maryland. Her husband, Henry Reynolds, the fami-

This lithograph is based on a well-known engraving of Phillis Wheatley by an African American artist, Scipio Moorhead. Moorhead's identity might have remained unknown except for a notation about him that was discovered in a 1773 volume of Wheatley's poetry. **CORBIS-BETTMANN**

ly's fifth great-grandfather, is born in 1781 in North Carolina. They will meet and marry in North Carolina when Sinai is either sold there or brought there by her owners. Their first three children, all daughters, will be sold away from them, disappearing forever. **SEE SIDEBARS** *The Reynolds/Calhoun Family, pp. 354–367*

Vermont adopts the nation's first emancipation act, on July 2. Fourteen years prior to its becoming a state, Vermont's General Assembly becomes the first legislative body to take action against the establishment of perpetual slavery. The declaration guarantees the freedom of all males by the age of twenty-one and of all females by the age of eighteen, regardless of their place of birth. When slaveholders attempt to get around the law by selling their slaves out of state, the General Assembly in 1786 passes An Act to Prevent the Sale and Transportation of Negroes and Mulattoes out of This State.

1780

Black Massachusetts taxpayers, including Paul Cuffe, protest "taxation without representation" to the state legislature. In 1783, the legislature will grant taxpaying black citizens of the state the right to vote.

Inspired by revolutionary ideals and Quaker antislavery sentiment, Pennsylvania becomes the first slave state to abolish slavery. The Act for the Gradual Abolition of Slavery allows slaveholders to keep slave mothers' children born after March 1, 1780, until they reach the age of twenty-eight. Other northern states will follow with their own "gradual abolition" laws. **SEE SIDEBAR** *The Gradual Abolition of Slavery, p. 102*

1781

Los Angeles, California, is founded by forty-four settlers; twenty-six of them are of African descent.

1783

Following the colonial victory in the American Revolution, black loyalists, African American slaves who gained their freedom by fighting on the British side in the conflict, resettle in Canada's Maritime Provinces of Nova Scotia and New Brunswick. As many as thirty-five hundred black loyalists come north, joining other black immigrants who have already resettled in the Maritime Provinces. In 1792, many black loyalists will leave Canada for Sierra Leone, a British colony in West Africa.

1784

Poet Phillis Wheatley dies in Boston, Massachusetts.

Thomas Jefferson drafts an ordinance to govern the Northwest Territory, land lying north of the Ohio River and east of the Mississippi River in what is now the upper Midwest. Among other things, the ordinance excludes slavery from the territory after the year 1800. Congress adopts the Northwest Ordinance on July 13, 1787. The exclusion of slavery from the Northwest Territory draws many Canadian slaves south, some arriving by means of an early, southbound underground railroad.

1787

Prince Hall, Revolutionary War veteran and founder of the first African American Masonic lodge, petitions the Massachusetts legislature for equal school facilities for black children, on October 17.

The first free school for African American students is opened in New York City on November 1. Named the African Free School, it will provide education for Henry Highland Garnet, Alexander Crummell, Samuel Ringgold Ward, and a host of others. By

1834, seven African Free Schools will be operating in New York City.

In November, Absalom Jones and Richard Allen organize the Free African Society in Philadelphia, in response to the segregation of black congregants at St. George's Methodist Episcopal Church. Pulled from their knees while at prayer, Jones and Allen leave the congregation with many other African American members.

The Constitution of the United States is approved by delegates to the Constitutional Convention. Article I, Section 2 distinguishes between the free and the enslaved in apportioning representatives from the states to the House of Representatives, counting each slave as "three-fifths" of a person. The new Constitution also permits slaveholders to retrieve fugitive slaves across state lines and postpones the abolition of the slave trade until 1808.

1790

The first federal census shows a black population of 757,208 persons. Of these, 59,577, or approximately 8 percent, are free. Blacks, free and enslaved, constitute 19.3 percent of the U.S. population.

The Brown Fellowship Society is founded in Charleston, South Carolina, by free African American men. Only fifty memberships are available, at a cost of fifty dollars each.

1791

Because of his many talents Benjamin Banneker is asked to join the team surveying the Federal Territory, which would become the new capital.

In August, more than a hundred thousand slaves on the island of Santo Domingo rise up in revolt, murdering slaveholders and burning plantations. The French colonials are driven to the seacoast and beyond, many of them resettling in the American South and bringing with them tales of the slave-led revolution that terrify American slaveholders. When the English attempt to seize Santo Domingo for themselves, Toussaint L'Ouverture takes control of the rebel forces and defends the island. Haiti, the first black republic in the Americas, finally achieves independence in 1804.

1792

Benjamin Banneker publishes his first *Almanac*. During the previous year, he sent a copy of his manuscript to Thomas Jefferson, then secretary of state, along with a statement against slavery.

1793

Congress adopts the first fugitive slave law, on February 12. The Constitution had already allowed for the retrieval of fugitive slaves across state lines. The new law provides for the adjudication of masters' claims before local magistrates.

Lieutenant Governor John Graves Simcoe of Upper Canada—present-day Ontario—issues Canada's first emancipation proclamation, declaring that "no Negro or person brought to this Province shall be subjected to the condition of slavery." The General Abolition of Slavery in the British Empire, which is proclaimed in 1833 and takes effect on August 1, 1834, abolishes slavery elsewhere in Canada and throughout the British colonies.

A Haitian-born trader and trapper, Jean Baptiste Point Du Sable, establishes a trading outpost in the spot that will later become Chicago.

The Connecticut native and Yale graduate Eli Whitney invents the first cotton gin. Short-staple cotton can be grown anywhere, but its stubborn seeds make it an unprofitable, labor-intensive crop. While working as a tutor in Georgia, Whitney creates the prototype for a machine that easily separates the seeds from short-staple cotton, thus speeding up its production. In a few short years, cotton will become "king," expanding into the Mississippi Territory (Alabama and Mississippi) and the Louisiana Purchase states of Louisiana and Arkansas.

When a yellow fever epidemic sweeps through Philadelphia, members of the Free African Society help nurse the sick and dying and remove the dead. To refute charges of profiteering during the epidemic, the society's founders, Absalom Jones and Richard Allen, publish *Narrative of the Proceedings of the Colored People during the Awful Calamity in Philadelphia.*

1794

Richard Allen forms Bethel Church, a black Methodist congregation in Philadelphia, on June 10. In 1816, it will become the Bethel African Methodist Episcopal Church, the flagship congregation of the first black Protestant denomination, with Allen named its first bishop.

Under the leadership of Absalom Jones, the meetinghouse of Philadelphia's Free African Society is dedi-

cated as St. Thomas's African Episcopal Church on October 12, the nation's first black Episcopal church. Jones is named its pastor and in 1804 is ordained the first African American Episcopal priest.

1796

With the departure of the black loyalists from the Maritime Provinces, Canada's labor supply drops sharply, and six hundred Jamaican maroons are resettled in Nova Scotia. In 1800, given the opportunity to settle in Britain's West African colony of Sierra Leone, all but a handful will leave to join the black loyalists who have gone before.

1797

Sojourner Truth is born a slave in Hurley, New York. **SEE ENTRY** *The Debate over Slavery in the United States, p. 112*

1798

In a notice placed in the December 19 issue of the Baltimore *Intelligencer*, Joshua Johnston announces himself as "Portrait Painter," offering his services as "a self-taught genius" who has "experienced many insuperable obstacles in the pursuit of his studies." Johnston will paint many of the leading citizens of Baltimore and their families, but his name will be lost, and his unsigned portraits, though widely admired, will be known only as the work of the "brass tacks" painter. Not until the mid-twentieth century will art historians confirm the identity of this early African American artist. **SEE ENTRY** *The Art of African Americans, p. 435*

1800

An antislavery petition is presented by free blacks to Congress.

The black population is 1,002,037 (18.9 percent of the U.S. population).

Gabriel Prosser leads the best-planned and most nearly successful slave revolt in the nation's history. With thousands of other slaves enlisted in his cause, Prosser plans to attack Richmond, Virginia, on August 30 and establish a black state. Although the plan is betrayed, Prosser and his fellow insurgents prepare to move on Richmond and are prevented from doing so only by fierce rains that wash out the bridges. Forced to postpone the attack, Prosser is arrested with thirty-four other men, tried, and hanged.

Nat Turner is born in Southampton County, Virginia.

Zion African Methodist Episcopal Church is dedicated in New York City.

1803

The Louisiana Purchase nearly doubles the territory of the United States. Under the presidency of Thomas Jefferson, the United States acquires from France almost nine hundred thousand acres between the Mississippi River and the Rocky Mountains. Thirteen new states will eventually be carved out of the Louisiana Purchase, including Louisiana (1812), Missouri (1820), and Arkansas (1836). Slavery rapidly expands westward along the southern frontier in response to the demand for labor to clear the newly acquired lands. **SEE PRIMARY SOURCE DOCUMENT** *The Louisiana Purchase and the Missouri Compromise, p. 125*

1804

The Ohio legislature on January 5 adopts the first "black laws" to control the immigration of African Americans into the state. Other northern states will pass similar laws restricting the labor, education, and movement of African Americans in order to discourage the settlement of free Negroes and fugitive slaves within their borders.

1805

Benjamin Banneker dies in Maryland.

Prince Hall, activist and Masonic leader, dies in Massachusetts.

By this year, all of the northern states have either abolished slavery or passed laws providing for its gradual abolition. Small numbers of people will remain enslaved in the North for decades after, but the majority of black northerners are now free, although discrimination in training and employment keeps most of them in dire poverty. **SEE ENTRY** *Free African Americans in the United States, p. 91*

1808

The African slave trade to the United States is officially abolished on January 1, though it continues to deliver contraband captives to isolated offshore regions like the Sea Islands of South Carolina and Georgia. Elsewhere, with the end of slave importation, slaveholders begin to rely heavily on enslaved women to increase the number of slaves. Slaveholders in the upper South, especially Virginia, prosper through breeding and the sale of slaves to the South and West. **SEE ENTRY** *The Debate over Slavery in the United States, p. 110*

1810

The African Insurance Company of Philadelphia, the first insurance company managed by blacks, opens with Joseph Randolph as its president.

The black population is 1,377,808 (19 percent of the U.S. population).

1811

The Haitian-born slave Charles Deslandes leads a rebellion of slaves outside New Orleans. Federal troops put down the rebellion, which results in the death or execution of more than a hundred slaves.

Paul Cuffe, a shipowner and native of Cuttyhunk, Massachusetts, sails with a group of African Americans to Sierra Leone to develop trading ties and encourage colonization and missionary work.

1812

Andrew Jackson urges free blacks to rally in support of the War of 1812.

Martin Delany is born free in Charles Town, Virginia **SEE ENTRY** *The Debate over Slavery in the United States, p. 113*

Pennsylvania legislature considers a bill that would limit where free Negroes may live and require black citizens to report any black visitors within twenty-four hours of their arrival. It would also allow police officers to demand a registration certificate from any black person and to arrest newcomers unable to produce such a document. Those arrested would be subject to a fine, imprisonment, or sale into slavery. James Forten publishes a series of eloquent letters condemning the provisions of the bill, which does not pass.

1815

The composer and bandmaster Francis "Frank" Johnson (born in Martinique in 1792) organizes his first band in Philadelphia from members of the Third Company of Washington Guards, active during the War of 1812. Johnson will pioneer the popular American band concert, publishing his works in sheet music and traveling widely. In 1837, the Frank Johnson Band will become the first American musical group to perform abroad. **SEE ENTRY** *The History of African American Music, p. 332*

Henry Highland Garnet is born in Kent County, Maryland. **SEE ENTRY** *The African American Intellectual Experience, p. 405*

1816

The African Methodist Episcopal Church is organized at a convention in Pennsylvania. **SEE ENTRY** *The African American Religious Experience, p. 369*

The American Colonization Society, organized to transport free and emancipated Negroes to Africa, is founded by the House of Representatives on December 28. The issues of abolition and colonization will henceforth be combined, with many arguing in favor of abolition only if those emancipated are transported. African American leaders such as James Forten of Philadelphia vigorously oppose colonization. **SEE ENTRY** *The Debate over Slavery in the United States, p. 113*

1817

Captain Paul Cuffe, entrepreneur seaman and activist, dies.

Frederick Douglass is born in Tuckahoe, Talbot County, Maryland. **SEE SIDEBAR** *African American Intellectuals: Frederick Douglass (1817–1895), p. 112*

1818

Absalom Jones dies in Pennsylvania.

1820

The black population is 1,771,656 (18.4 percent of the U.S. population).

The new state of Maine adopts a constitution granting all male citizens, regardless of race, voting rights and access to public education. In the same year, Pennsylvania grants a portion of its education budget to free blacks, provided they are housed in separate schools. Adopting the Maine model, Rhode Island will amend its constitution in 1843 to provide for public schooling regardless of race. **SEE ENTRY** *The Education of African Americans, p. 274*

"Mayflower of Liberia," with eighty-six blacks, sails for Sierra Leone.

The Missouri Compromise is enacted on March 3 after Missouri petitions for admission to the Union as a slave state. In order to maintain a balance between free and slaveholding interests in Congress, the act admits Missouri as a slave state and Maine, formerly part of Massachusetts, as a free state. With the exception of Missouri, it also prohibits slavery in all

portions of the Louisiana Purchase territory north of thirty-six degrees, thirty minutes north latitude (the southern boundary of Missouri). The Kansas-Nebraska Act of 1854 will repeal the Missouri Compromise, leaving the question of slavery north of this line to popular vote. **SEE PRIMARY SOURCE DOCUMENT** *The Louisiana Purchase and the Missouri Compromise, p. 125*

1821

African Methodist Episcopal Zion Church becomes a national presence with its headquarters in New York City.

1822

While still being planned, Denmark Vesey's revolt in Charleston, South Carolina, involving as many as nine thousand slaves, is betrayed on May 30 by a slave. A literate carpenter who purchased his freedom in 1800, Vesey was inspired by the Bible and the 1791 Haitian Revolution. Following the betrayal of his plan to attack Charleston, 131 African Americans and 4 whites are arrested, and 37 are hanged. **SEE ENTRY** *The Final Century of Slavery in the United States, p. 156*

Hiram Revels, the first black senator, is born free in Fayetteville, North Carolina.

James Varick becomes first bishop of African Methodist Episcopal Zion Church.

1823

Alexander Lucius Twilight becomes the first known black college graduate, receiving his B.A. degree from Middlebury College.

1827

John B. Russwurm and Samuel Cornish publish the first issue of *Freedom's Journal,* the nation's first African American newspaper, on March 30. Cornish is a Presbyterian minister and vigorous opponent of the colonization movement. Russwurm is one of the nation's first black college graduates, having graduated from Bowdoin College in Maine the previous year. **SEE ENTRY** *African American Newspapers and Periodicals, p. 228*

Slavery is abolished in New York State on July 4.

1829

David Walker, a free African American who has moved from North Carolina to Boston, publishes his *Appeal*

This is a wood engraving of Nat Turner on October 30, 1831. Turner had eluded capture for more than two months by hiding out in a cave near Calvin Pond in Southampton County, Virginia. During that time, scores of black people in Virginia and elsewhere were attacked, and many killed, as whites exacted vengeance for Turner's August rebellion. **CORBIS-BETTMANN**

on September 28, calling for slaves to rebel. The pamphlet is clandestinely circulated throughout the South, where it causes great alarm. In the following year, Walker is found dead in his Boston shop, evidently the victim of poison. Thirty-six years later, his son, Edward G. Walker, will be elected to the Massachusetts House of Representatives. **SEE PRIMARY SOURCE DOCUMENT** *Preamble to* Appeal to the Coloured Citizens of the United States *by David Walker, p. 391*

A race riot in Cincinnati, Ohio, prompts thousands to leave for Canada.

1830

The black population is 2,328,642 (18.1 percent of the U.S. population).

The first national convention of African Americans meets on September 20 at Philadelphia's Bethel Church, with Richard Allen presiding, "to devise ways and means for the bettering of our condition."

James Augustine Healy, first black Roman Catholic bishop, is born.

The commencement of the abolitionist campaign and the establishment of the Underground Railroad bring thousands of African American freedom seekers north to Canada in the thirty years prior to the American Civil War. There they establish settlements in Canada West (present-day Ontario); found schools, churches, and other organizations; and start newspapers supporting the abolitionist cause. With the outbreak of the Civil War, many will return south to fight in the Union army and rejoin their families.

1831

William Lloyd Garrison publishes the first issue of the *Liberator* on January 1, with the financial backing of the African American businessman James Forten, among others. Later in the same year, Garrison joins others in founding the Massachusetts Anti-Slavery Society and the New England Anti-Slavery Society. The appearance of the *Liberator* is often regarded as heralding the beginning of the abolitionist movement. **SEE ENTRY** *The Debate over Slavery in the United States, p. 111*

Nat Turner's Revolt takes place in Southampton County, Virginia, on August 21 and 22. Beginning with Turner and seven others, the insurrection enlists other slaves as it progresses and results in the murder of fifty-seven whites. Turner escapes, but is captured on October 30, tried, and hanged. Following the insurrection, slave states pass new laws tightening controls over slaves and free blacks. **SEE ENTRY** *The Final Century of Slavery in the United States, p. 157*

1832

New England antislavery organization is founded in Massachusetts. **SEE ENTRY** *The Debate over Slavery in the United States, p. 111*

Sinai and Henry Reynolds are sold by Silas Reynolds to William Nimmons of Newnan, Georgia. Their new owner allows them to "hire their time" in town rather than live on the plantation, providing they pay for the expenses of their five remaining children. Through the bakery business they set up, they will in time save enough money to purchase themselves and two of their children. Two more will be manumitted by Nimmons in 1852. The remaining child, Nelley, born around 1810, will remain enslaved until emancipation. **SEE SIDEBARS** *The Reynolds/Calhoun Family, pp. 354–367*

1833

Prudence Crandall, a Quaker woman, advertises in the *Liberator* that she is opening a school in Canterbury, Connecticut, for "young ladies and little misses of color." Her fellow townspeople vigorously oppose her plan and push through the state legislature a "black law" banning the establishment of schools for, or the teaching of, "colored persons who are not inhabitants of this State." Crandall is arrested on June 27 and tried under the new law, and her school is later burned. **SEE PRIMARY SOURCE DOCUMENT** *Miss Prudence Crandall and the Canterbury School, p. 279*

The American Anti-Slavery Society is organized in Philadelphia on December 4, with the participation of black and white abolitionists from Philadelphia and New York City.

1834

On August 1, slavery is abolished throughout the British Empire. Some West Indian planters, unwilling to hire free labor, abandon their holdings and relocate to the American South.

1835

Abolitionist societies organize an antislavery mail campaign, sending thousands of pieces of antislavery literature south. In Charleston, South Carolina, their pamphlets are confiscated and publicly burned on July 29.

North Carolina disenfranchises its free black citizens, the last of the southern states to deprive free African Americans of their voting rights.

Noyes Academy in Canaan, New Hampshire, is mobbed and destroyed by white farmers on August 10, after opening its doors to African American students. Henry Highland Garnet and Alexander Crummell, who have come from New York City to study there, continue their education at the Oneida Institute in upstate New York. **SEE SIDEBAR** *African American Intellectuals: Henry Highland Garnet (1815–1882), p. 129*

1836

Alexander Lucius Twilight is elected to the Vermont legislature.

The American Anti-Slavery Society organizes a petition campaign to the United States Congress, which invokes the "gag rule" to suppress all debate on the slavery issue. The gag rule is opposed by many legislators, who condemn the limitations it imposes on

citizens' right to petition, but it remains in effect until December 1844.

1837

Colored American, the second major black newspaper, begins publication.

The abolitionist printer Elijah P. Lovejoy is murdered by a pro-slavery mob in Alton, Illinois, on November 7, after declaring his intention to establish an abolitionist printing press in the town. Lovejoy has already been driven out of Missouri, and his press there was burned, following his public denunciation of a lynching. Lovejoy's murder and Congress's use of the gag rule to suppress debate on slavery will serve to bring new support to the abolitionist movement. **SEE PRIMARY SOURCE DOCUMENT** *Excerpt from* The South since the War *by Sidney Andrews, p. 200*

1838

David Ruggles, a journalist and bookseller, publishes the nation's first African American magazine, the *Mirror of Liberty,* in June. The magazine opposes slavery, colonization, and segregation in churches and public services. **SEE ENTRY** *African American Newspapers and Periodicals, p. 228*

Charles Lenox Remond, the son of a West Indian immigrant to Salem, Massachusetts, and a member of the New England Anti-Slavery Society, becomes the first African American to lecture publicly against slavery. He is joined the next year by Samuel Ringgold Ward, in 1841 by Frederick Douglass, and in 1843 by Sojourner Truth. **SEE ENTRY** *African American Newspapers and Periodicals, p. 228*

Frederick Douglass escapes from slavery in Maryland on September 3, traveling north from Baltimore to New York. Within a few years, he will become one of the most powerful voices in the abolitionist movement, drawing large crowds wherever he appears. His speeches about his own enslavement become the basis for the first of his three autobiographies, the 1845 *Narrative of the Life of Frederick Douglass, an American Slave, Written by Himself,* a brief and powerful indictment of the slave system. **SEE PRIMARY SOURCE DOCUMENT** *"A Fugitive's Necessary Silence" by Frederick Douglass, p. 137*

1839

Under the leadership of Joseph Cinque, Mende slaves on board the slave ship *Amistad* revolt, killing all but a handful of the crew and demanding the return of the ship to the West African coast. The crew con-

Civil War hero Robert Smalls became a South Carolina official and Republican congressman after the war. During Reconstruction, he fought for education and civil rights. **THE LIBRARY OF CONGRESS**

trives to bring the ship into Long Island Sound, and Cinque and the other captives are arrested and confined for a year and a half in New Haven, Connecticut, until the U.S. Supreme Court rules that they are free. **SEE PRIMARY SOURCE DOCUMENT** *An Account of the* Amistad *Revolt, p. 123*

Robert Smalls, Civil War hero and Reconstruction congressman, is born.

White residents of Newnan, Georgia, file a formal complaint against Sinai and Henry Reynolds because they have been allowed by their owner, William Nimmons, to "hire their time." It is not known whether the Reynolds are subsequently forced to return to the Nimmons plantation. **SEE SIDEBARS** *The Reynolds/Calhoun Family pp. 354–367*

1841

Blanche Kelso Bruce, an early black senator, is born a slave in Virginia.

A slave revolt occurs on the *Creole,* a ship bound for New Orleans.

Solomon Northup, a free African American from upstate New York, lured to Washington, D.C., by the

promise of work is kidnapped there into slavery. Northup labors for the next twelve years on the Red River frontier of Louisiana before finally being rescued and returned to his family. Although he attempts to bring charges against his kidnappers, he receives no justice in the courts. In 1854, he publishes the narrative of his ordeal, *Twelve Years a Slave,* one of the most detailed accounts of American slavery in its later phase along the western frontier. **SEE PRIMARY SOURCE DOCUMENT** *Twelve Years a Slave by Solomon Northup, p. 143*

The U.S. Supreme Court frees Joseph Cinque and the *Amistad* rebels. **SEE PRIMARY SOURCE DOCUMENT** *An Account of the* Amistad *Revolt, p. 123*

1842

The capture of George Latimer results in the first fugitive slave court case.

1843

Isabella van Wagener renames herself Sojourner Truth and leaves New York City on foot, with her few belongings and twenty-five cents, on June 1. In the decades leading up to the Civil War, she crisscrosses the northern part of the nation, an itinerant, powerful spokeswoman in the cause of abolition and women's rights. **SEE SIDEBAR** *Sojourner Truth (1797–1883), p. 161*

Harriet Jacobs escapes to Philadelphia after seven years spent in hiding in her grandmother's attic, leaving behind a son and daughter whom she later brings out of slavery. In 1849, she moves to Rochester, New York, joining her brother John in the abolitionist movement. There she meets the abolitionist Amy Post, who encourages her to put her story in writing. Jacobs publishes her *Incidents in the Life of a Slave Girl, Written by Herself* in 1861, at her own expense. **SEE PRIMARY SOURCE DOCUMENT** *Tracing the Roots of African American Cultural Traditions in Early Slave Narratives, p. 80*

The Narrative of Frederick Douglass is published.

Henry Highland Garnet, called "the Thomas Paine of the abolitionist movement," addresses the National Convention of Colored Citizens in Buffalo on August 22, calling upon slaves to engage in open rebellion against their owners. By a single vote, the convention fails to endorse his proposal. **SEE SIDEBAR** *African American Intellectuals: Henry Highland Garnet (1815–1882), p. 129*

The first meeting of the Liberty Party, committed to the political abolition of slavery, is held in Buffalo, New

York, on August 30. The party is opposed by William Lloyd Garrison and other Boston abolitionists, who condemn any participation in a corrupt political process, but it is supported by many New York abolitionists, including Samuel Ringgold Ward and Henry Highland Garnet. **SEE ENTRY** *The Debate over Slavery in the United States, p. 112*

1847

Liberia is declared an independent republic on July 26, with Joseph Jenkins Roberts, a Virginia native, as its first president. Some slaves in the South are emancipated on the condition that they agree to emigrate to the new republic. Most northern and free African Americans continue to oppose colonization. **SEE ENTRY** *The Debate over Slavery in the United States, p. 113*

Breaking with William Lloyd Garrison and the American Anti-Slavery Society, Frederick Douglass publishes the first issue of his newspaper *North Star* on December 3. **SEE ENTRY** *The Debate over Slavery, p. 113*

National Black Convention convenes in Troy, New York.

1848

The Free Soil Party is organized in Buffalo, New York. The platform of the party includes supporting the abolition of slavery.

During the Christmas holidays, a young slave couple, William and Ellen Craft, escape by train from Macon, Georgia, disguised as servant and master. Escapes from the Deep South are rare, and the Crafts' daring run for freedom makes them celebrities among abolitionists. Pro-slavery forces, including President James K. Polk, vow to hunt them down and return them to slavery. The Crafts' escape helps bring about the passage of the 1850 Fugitive Slave Law two years later, but by then they have left for England. In 1860, William Craft publishes the story of their escape, *Running a Thousand Miles for Freedom; or, The Escape of William and Ellen Craft from Slavery*. **SEE PRIMARY SOURCE DOCUMENT** *"Reception and Treatment of Kidnappers," p. 168*

1849

Avery College is established in Pennsylvania.

On behalf of his daughter, Benjamin Roberts files suit in November against the city of Boston to end segregation in the public schools. The Massachusetts Supreme Court rejects his suit, laying the groundwork for the "separate but equal" doctrine of *Plessy v. Ferguson* half a century later. In 1855, separate schools for black and white children are abolished by Massachusetts state law. **SEE ENTRY** *The Education of African Americans, p. 276*

George Washington Williams, the first major black historian, is born in Pennsylvania.

Harriet Tubman escapes from slavery in Maryland, returning south at least nineteen times over the next decade to bring her family and hundreds of other slaves to freedom. During the Civil War, she works as a Union spy behind Confederate lines. **SEE SIDEBAR** *Harriet Tubman (1820–1913) and the Underground Railroad, p. 175*

1850

The black population is 3,638,808 (15.7 percent of the U.S. population).

In April, the black frontiersman James P. Beckwourth discovers a pass over the Sierra Nevada northwest of the present-day city of Reno and later leads the first wagon train of settlers through what is now known as Beckwourth Pass. **SEE ENTRY** *African Americans on the Frontier, p. 214*

Massachusetts Supreme Court establishes the "separate but equal" precedent that later becomes the foundation for the Supreme Court ruling in *Plessy* v. *Ferguson*. **SEE PRIMARY SOURCE DOCUMENT** *The Ruling in* Plessy v. Ferguson *and Justice John Marshall Harlan's Dissent, p. 263*

Under pressure from southern legislators, Congress on September 18 passes the Fugitive Slave Law, the second and harsher of two laws meant to facilitate the return of escaped slaves to their owners. It does away with free soil, making assistance to escaping slaves illegal, allowing federal marshals to search any house where they think a slave might be hiding, and denying fugitives the right to a jury trial. After passage of the law, thousands of fugitive slaves living in the North flee to Canada, and protests occur in Boston and elsewhere, initiating the final turbulent decade before the Civil War. **SEE SIDEBAR** *A Plan for Thwarting Slave Hunters, p. 115*

1851

Black abolitionists rescue a fugitive slave from Boston courtroom.

The soprano Elizabeth Taylor Greenfield gives her first recital before the Buffalo Musical Association and two years later debuts in Philadelphia to rave reviews. In 1854, she performs for Queen Victoria. Called "the Black Swan," Greenfield enjoys a successful career, paving the way for other black sopranos. But with the rise of Jim Crow, opportunities for

Under the Fugitive Slave Act, the court ordered escaped slave Anthony Burns back to slavery on June 2, 1854. An estimated 50,000 outraged citizens lined the streets of Boston as soldiers led Burns away in shackles. **ARCHIVE PHOTOS, INC.**

public performance before white or integrated audiences will die out, and for the next fifty years black singers will perform almost exclusively for black listeners. **SEE ENTRY** *The History of African American Music, p. 329*

On September 11, in Christiana, Pennsylvania, a slaveholder named Gorsuch, accompanied by federal marshals, attempts to retrieve fugitive slaves from the home of William Parker, a free African American. Parker and the slaves defend themselves with firearms, driving off the slave catchers and killing Gorsuch. The event becomes known as the Christiana Riot.

William Nell publishes the first history devoted to African Americans, *Services of Colored Americans in the Wars of 1776 and 1812*. It forms the basis of his extended study *Colored Patriots of the American Revolution* (1855).

1852

Harriet Beecher Stowe publishes *Uncle Tom's Cabin* on March 20, attacking slavery on religious and moral grounds and advocating the colonization of freed African Americans. The novel is widely read, selling three hundred thousand copies in its first year, and contributes to the gathering national storm over slavery.

Martin Delany publishes the first major statement of a black nationalist position: *The Condition, Elevation, Emigration and Destiny of the Colored People of the United States, Politically Considered.*

1853

The abolitionist and fugitive slave William Wells Brown publishes in England *Clotel; or, The President's Daughter: A Narrative of Slave Life in the United States*. It is the first novel by an African American, and purports to tell the history of the enslaved daughter and granddaughters of Thomas Jefferson. **SEE ENTRY** *The African American Literary Experience, p. 337*

1854

The Ashmond Institute, later renamed Lincoln University, is founded on January 1 in Chester County, Pennsylvania, for educating African American men.

The fugitive slave Anthony Burns is arrested in Boston on May 24 and remanded to slavery. An antislavery riot occurs in opposition to his return, and some two thousand federal troops are required to remove Burns from Boston.

John V. DeGrasse, physician, is admitted to the Massachusetts Medical Society.

Congress passes the Kansas-Nebraska Act on May 30, opening new territories to settlement and repealing the Missouri Compromise of 1820, which had attempted to establish congressional parity between slave and free interests. The new act leaves the question of slavery to popular vote. Free-soil interests easily prevail in Nebraska Territory, but a bloody local war between free-soilers and pro-slavery forces ensues in Kansas. By the time Kansas enters the Union as a free state in 1861, the South has seceded to form the Confederacy. **SEE ENTRY** *The Debate over Slavery in the United States, p. 114*

1855

John Mercer Langston, an Ohio lawyer, becomes the first African American elected official when he is elected clerk of Brownhelm Township in Lorain, Ohio. In 1888, he is elected to Congress from Virginia. **SEE SIDEBAR** *John Mercer Langston (1829–1897), p. 222*

Henry and Sinai Reynolds leave Georgia with four of their eight children to settle in Chicago. Their daughter Nelley remains behind in slavery, cook to the Andrew B. Calhoun family. Nelley's daughter Siny Catherine was born in 1830, and her granddaughter Catherine Felix in 1860, the child of Siny Catherine and her husband, Preston Webb. All three will remain as house slaves in the Calhoun family until emancipation. Although members of the Reynolds-Calhoun family are divided between Newnan, Georgia, and Chicago, Illinois, they remain in touch through letters. **SEE SIDEBARS** *The Reynolds/Calhoun Family, pp. 354–367*

1856

On January 1, Biddy Mason wins freedom for herself and her daughters in a California court of law. Mason had crossed the deserts of Nevada and Arizona with her three daughters and her Georgia owner to settle in San Bernardino. When her owner attempted to remove the family to Texas in order to evade California's constitutional prohibition against slavery, Mason sued. The judge who decides the case declares that "all men should be left to their own pursuit of freedom and happiness." Investing the money she earns as a nurse and midwife in Los Angeles real estate, Mason goes on to become one of California's wealthiest African Americans. **SEE ENTRY** *African Americans on the Frontier, p. 214*

In January, Margaret Garner escapes from slavery across the frozen Ohio River with her four children, her husband, and her husband's parents. When the group is overtaken by slave catchers, Garner slits the throat of her infant daughter and attempts to kill herself and her other children. Although Ohio authorities try to bring murder charges against her in order to expose the injustice of the Fugitive Slave Law, Garner is returned to slavery.

Booker Taliaferro Washington is born a slave in Virginia.

The Methodist Episcopal church founds Wilberforce University in Ohio on August 30, for the education of African Americans. The African Methodist Episcopal church later assumes direction of the school.

1857

The Supreme Court issues its decision in the case of *Dred Scott* v. *Sandford.* When Dred Scott sues for his and his family's freedom under the Missouri Compromise of 1820, claiming Missouri citizenship, the Court rules against him, arguing that he is not a citizen. Chief Justice Roger Taney goes even further, arguing that the framers of the Constitution, and hence the Constitution itself, held the Negro to have "no rights which the white man was bound to respect." *Dred Scott* v. *Sandford* also opens the new territories to slavery. **SEE PRIMARY SOURCE DOCU-**

MENT *Chief Justice Roger Taney's Majority Decision in* Dred Scott *v.* Sandford, *p. 253*

1858

The first African American play, *The Escape,* is published.

John Brown holds antislavery convention in Chatham, Canada.

1859

In January, Thomas Hamilton brings out the first issue of the *Anglo-African Magazine,* the most ambitious black publishing venture prior to the Civil War. Over the next few years, writers like Frances Ellen Watkins Harper, Martin Delany, Frederick Douglass, and William Wells Brown will appear in the pages of the *Anglo-African.* **SEE ENTRY** *African American Newspapers and Periodicals, p. 228*

Arkansas legislature requires free blacks to choose exile or enslavement.

Six hundred black Californians emigrate to Vancouver Island in British Columbia, in flight from worsening racial conditions to the south. As ranchers, businesspeople, and gold miners, they will achieve prosperity and economic independence.

John Brown and twenty-one others attack the federal arsenal at Harpers Ferry, Virginia, on October 16, in order to procure weapons and establish an outpost on slave soil from which to wage war on slavery. Ten men lose their lives in the attempt, and Brown and the remaining men are captured, tried, and hanged in December. The raid gains wide approval among those abolitionists who have come to feel that only violence can end slavery. **SEE SIDEBAR** *John Brown's Attack on Harpers Ferry, p. 148*

Two hundred and forty years after the arrival of the first twenty Africans at Jamestown and more than fifty years after the official abolition of the slave trade, the slave ship *Clothilde* delivers the last cargo of slaves to Mobile, Alabama. On the eve of the Civil War, the country's black population numbers some four and a half million persons, almost 90 percent of them in slavery.

1860

Abraham Lincoln is elected president on November 6, having promised to protect slavery where it already exists but oppose its extension into new territories. A month later, South Carolina secedes from the Union, and by March 1861, six more slaveholding states will have followed its lead, forming the Confederate States of America. With the April firing on Fort Sumter and the beginning of the Civil War, four more Southern states will secede. **SEE ENTRY** *African Americans and the Civil War, p. 170*

The black population is 4,441,830 (14.1 percent of the U.S. population).

The 1860 census reveals that Henry and Sinai Reynolds occupy a house on Griswold Street in Chicago's Third Ward, the city's developing black neighborhood. Black laws control where African Americans can live in the city, and housing is scarce. To help pay for their house, the Reynoldses take in boarders, a woman and a small child. **SEE SIDEBARS** *The Reynolds/Calhoun Family, pp. 354–367*

1861

On April 12, the Confederacy fires on Fort Sumter, South Carolina, and the Civil War begins. The war exacts a heavy price in human lives, among them 68,178 African Americans listed as dead or missing by the war's end, more than one-third of the participating black forces.

Congress passes Confiscation Act.

Major General Benjamin Butler declares slaves to be "contraband of war," authorizing their capture as property of the enemy. **SEE ENTRY** *African Americans and the Civil War, p. 171*

On September 25, the secretary of the navy authorizes the enlistment of slaves in the Union navy. Almost thirty thousand African Americans will serve as Union sailors during the war.

On November 7, the Union army captures Port Royal and liberates most of the South Carolina Sea Islands. The "Port Royal experiment" begins, bringing northern teachers south to aid and educate the Sea Island people. In the same month, the first Negro regiment in the Union army, the First South Carolina Volunteers, is formed under the command of Thomas Wentworth Higginson.

1862

President Abraham Lincoln submits a draft of Emancipation Proclamation to Congress.

The end of slavery in Washington, D.C., is announced on April 16.

On July 17, Congress authorizes the enlistment of African Americans in all branches of the Union military. At the time of the authorization, Negro volunteer units have already been formed: the South Carolina Volunteers on May 9 and the First Kansas Colored Volunteers on July 12. The First Regiment of

Louisiana Native Guards, formed from the free Negroes of New Orleans, becomes the first black regiment to be officially mustered into the Union army on September 27, 1862.

The first blacks to confer with a U.S. president meet with Abraham Lincoln.

The First Louisiana Native Guards become the first black regiment to receive official recognition.

Robert Smalls, an African American pilot in charge of the Confederate boat *Planter,* sails it out of Charleston Harbor with his family and other fugitives on board and, on May 13, presents it to the Union navy. Smalls rises to the rank of captain in the Union navy, the only African American to do so during the Civil War, and is elected to Congress from South Carolina in 1875. He serves until 1879 and again from 1881 to 1887.

Charlotte Forten, a twenty-four-year-old teacher and writer from Philadelphia, arrives on St. Helena Island on October 29 to begin her teaching career among the liberated people of the Sea Islands. In her journal, she records her daily impressions of the landscape and people and the progress of the war, and notes the Emancipation Day festivities at the camp of the First South Carolina Volunteers. **SEE ENTRY** *African Americans and the Civil War, p. 174*

Congress passes Second Confiscation Act, freeing all slaves belonging to rebels.

1863

Abraham Lincoln issues the Emancipation Proclamation. It frees all slaves held in the states of the Confederacy, declaring them "henceforward ... free." It does not free slaves in those slaveholding states and regions that remain in the Union: Maryland, Missouri, Kentucky, Delaware, thirteen Louisiana parishes, the forty-eight counties of West Virginia, or seven Virginia counties. **SEE PRIMARY SOURCE DOCUMENT** *The Emancipation Proclamation, p. 188*

The 54th Massachusetts Volunteers, the first Negro regiment in the North, is raised after the War Department authorizes the Massachusetts governor on January 26 to recruit among African Americans. On March 10, the 54th Massachusetts Colored Infantry captures the city of Jacksonville, Florida, without firing a single shot. (The city returns to Confederate control for another year after the 54th withdraws.) Under the command of Colonel Robert Gould Shaw of Boston, the 54th will distinguish itself in its July 18 charge on Fort Wagner, South Carolina, and Sergeant William Carney of Company C will belat-

Robert Smalls (1839–1915) became a sudden hero when he captured the Confederate ship *Planter* in 1862. As ship's pilot, Smalls boarded his family and several fugitive slaves and sailed the ship out of Charleston Harbor and into waters controlled by the Union navy. For his services, he was awarded the rank of captain, and continued in the service of the Union navy throughout the Civil War. He served as congressman from South Carolina from 1875 to 1879 and again from 1881 to 1887. **NATIONAL ARCHIVES AND RECORDS ADMINISTRATION**

edly receive the Congressional Medal of Honor for his actions.

On May 1, the Confederate Congress proclaims all African American troops and their officers criminals, thus condemning black prisoners of war to slavery or death. On July 30, President Lincoln responds, warning the Confederacy that, for every captured black soldier who is killed or enslaved, the Union will shoot or condemn to a life of hard labor one rebel prisoner of war.

Three regiments of Negro troops defeat Confederate troops from Texas at the battle of Milliken's Bend on June 7.

In response to Union army conscription, whites riot in New York City and elsewhere. Between July 13 and 17, white mobs rampage through New York City,

A group of freed slaves walk toward Union lines to freedom after the issuance of the Emancipation Proclamation in January of 1863, when the Union Army became an army of liberation. **THE LIBRARY OF CONGRESS**

killing African Americans and burning their houses and schools.

In November, Robert Smalls refuses to surrender the *Planter* to Confederate forces and earns his captaincy.

1864

On April 12, 1864, Confederate soldiers overrun Fort Pillow, Tennessee, garrisoned largely by black soldiers, and massacre everyone inside, including women.

The First Kansas Colored Volunteers storm the Confederate lines at Poison Spring, Arkansas. They suffer heavy casualties. Those who are captured are murdered. African American troops are not taken prisoner as their white counterparts are.

Nelley Calhoun, her daughter Siny Catherine, and her granddaughter Catherine Felix travel with their owner Andrew B. Calhoun to Atlanta when he goes to visit a son wounded in the war. They will all escape together when Sherman's army burns the city.

Congress orders equal pay, equipment, and medical care for African Americans in the Union army.

In June the *Kearsarge* and *Alabama* do battle off the coast of France, near Cherbourg. Joachim Pease, acting as loader for the No. 2 gun, is praised for his bravery under fire and earns both the Navy Medal of Honor and Congressional Medal of Honor.

Congressional Medal awarded to John Lawson for his efforts in the Battle of Mobile Bay.

John Lawson distinguishes himself as a crewman on the Union flagship, the USS *Hartford*, during the Battle of Mobile Bay in August. Despite being wounded by an enemy shell, Lawson remains at his post throughout the entire battle. For his valor he wins both the Navy Medal of Honor and the Congressional Medal of Honor.

On June 28, Congress repeals the fugitive slave laws.

Black soldiers participate in the ten-month siege started in Petersburg, Virginia. Grant wants a quick engagement to cut off rail supplies to Richmond, but Lee wants to prolong the siege hoping the North will tire of the casualties and accept a peace settlement. Twelve hundred of the sixty-three hundred casualties are black soldiers. The engagement ends one week before the final Southern surrender.

On July 7, Maryland amends its state constitution to abolish slavery. The state has been called "the cradle of Negro giants"—the birthplace of Frederick Douglass, Harriet Tubman, Benjamin Banneker, James Pennington, and Henry Highland Garnet, among others.

This photograph of a contraband camp at Richmond, Virginia, was taken by the renowned Civil War photographer Mathew Brady in 1865. Slaves who had escaped across Union lines were often housed in contraband camps. They were put to work for the Union Army, farming, cooking, building defenses, and performing a variety of other tasks essential to the war effort. **NATIONAL ARCHIVES AND RECORDS ADMINISTRATION**

William Tecumseh Sherman occupies Atlanta.

1865

Throughout the Civil War, the Confederacy has used slave labor in noncombatant work, but on January 11, with his forces hemmed in throughout the South, Robert E. Lee urges that the Confederate army use slaves as soldiers, stating that it is "not only expedient but necessary."

On February 18, Confederate troops abandon Charleston, South Carolina. Among the Union forces that subsequently take control of the city are members of the 54th Massachusetts Colored Infantry.

On March 13, Jefferson Davis, president of the Confederacy, signs into law an act authorizing the enlistment of slaves.

The Civil War ends when the Confederate general Robert E. Lee surrenders to Ulysses S. Grant at Appomattox Court House in Virginia. Within a week, the U.S. flag is raised once again over the ruins of Fort Sumter. Among those present at the ceremony are Captain Robert Smalls, William Lloyd Garrison, Major Martin Delany, and Robert Vesey, the son of

Denmark Vesey, executed for planning a slave insurrection forty-three years before.

Immediately following the surrender at Appomattox, Southern states begin to enact "black codes," to control the labor and movement of emancipated people. The codes stipulate what sort of work blacks may and may not do, and on what terms, and where they may and may not rent land. The codes also establish heavy penalties, including forced labor, for unemployment or refusal to work, defined as "vagrancy."

Congress establishes the Bureau of Refugees, Freedmen, and Abandoned Lands, or Freedmen's Bureau, on March 3, to assist emancipated people in the transition to freedom. During the seven years of its existence, the bureau will legitimize marriages between former slaves, adjudicate disputes in freedmen's courts, establish thousands of schools, and assist in the founding of several colleges and teacher training schools. When President Johnson begins pardoning Southern landowners and returning their property, the bureau will also attempt to force ex-slaves to return to plantation work.

The Thirteenth Amendment to the Constitution of the United States, abolishing slavery, is adopted following the Union's victory over the Confederacy. Henry

Highland Garnet is invited to deliver a memorial sermon in the U.S. House of Representatives commemorating passage of the Thirteenth Amendment.

Freed African Americans hold mass meetings throughout the South to demand equal rights and the vote.

On August 19, the African American sculptor Mary Edmonia Lewis leaves for Italy, where she will remain, except for brief return visits to the United States, until her death in 1909. Like many African American artists and musicians, Lewis will find a warmer reception for her work in Europe than at home.

Father Patrick Francis Healy becomes the first African American to receive a doctorate when the University of Louvain in Belgium awards him a degree in theology. Father Healy will go on to become the president of Georgetown University in 1873, serving in that position for ten years.

John S. Rock becomes the first black admitted to practice before the U.S. Supreme Court.

Shaw University and Atlanta University are founded.

1866

Fisk University is founded in Nashville, Tennessee, on January 9.

On February 5, Radical Republican Thaddeus Stevens proposes to Congress that abandoned lands in the South be divided up among freedmen in forty-acre lots. His proposal is defeated by a vote of 126 to 37.

African American Edward Walker is elected to Massachusetts Assembly from Boston.

A delegation of black leaders, including Frederick Douglass, meets with President Andrew Johnson. They present their views on the personal safety and protection of the rights of African Americans, and they solicit the president's views. Johnson is opposed to any federal laws to protect freed slaves and feels that the states have to solve problems within their own boundaries.

Congress passes the first Civil Rights Act over President Andrew Johnson's veto on April 9. The Act to Protect All Persons in the United States in Their Civil Rights and Furnish the Means of Their Vindication addresses Chief Justice Taney's opinion in *Dred Scott v. Sandford,* delivered in 1857, by conferring citizenship upon African Americans and giving them "the same right, in every State and territory," as whites. It fails to protect African Americans in the South, however, and is followed in 1868 by the Fourteenth Amendment.

In May and July, race riots occur in Memphis and New Orleans. Scores of African Americans and their white supporters are killed, and homes, schools, and churches are burned.

1867

Second Confiscation Act, giving land to freedmen, is defeated when voted on in Congress.

The first Acts of Reconstruction are passed by Congress on March 2, initiating the period of Radical or Congressional Reconstruction. These acts stipulate that each unreconstructed Southern state remain under military rule until such time as a popularly elected convention, with delegates from both races, has framed a new constitution.

Black voters constitute a majority in five southern states. Blacks vote in Alexandria, Virginia, but election commissioners refuse to count ballots. Blacks vote in Tuscumbia, Alabama, but the ballots are set aside pending "clarification."

The Fisk Jubilee Singers are formed under the directorship of George L. White. Consisting of eleven singers and a pianist, the group will go on tours to raise money for Fisk University's building fund, bringing the music of the spirituals to listeners in the United States and abroad.

Howard University, Talladega College, and Biddle Memorial Institute (which later becomes Johnson C. Smith University) are founded.

The Ku Klux Klan holds its first national meeting in April. In May, white supremacists organize the Knights of the White Camellia. **SEE SIDEBAR** *The Ku Klux Klan Holds Its First National Meeting, p. 235*

Monroe Baker is named mayor of St. Martin, Louisiana.

Morehouse College is established in the basement of the Springfield Baptist Church by the Rev. William Jefferson White, a Baptist minister and cabinetmaker. Its stated mission is to prepare black men for the ministry and teaching.

Congress passes several Reconstruction Acts to provide for political participation of blacks in southern state politics.

Southern states vote on constitutional conventions (Virginia, Georgia, South Carolina, Louisiana).

1868

The South Carolina Constitutional Convention convenes on January 14 to draw up a new state constitution.

JUBILEE SINGERS

MAGGIE PORTER.   E. W. WATKINS.   H. D. ALEXANDER.   F. J. LOUDIN.   THOMAS RUTLING.

JENNIE JACKSON.   MABEL LEWIS.   ELLA SHEPPARD.   MAGGIE CARNES.   AMERICA W. ROBINSON.

A chorus from Fisk University comprised of former slaves or children of slaves went on many singing tours to raise funds for the school. First assembled in 1867 and named for a biblical reference to a time where slaves were emancipated, the Fisk Jubilee Singers gave rise to several black choral groups and legitimized spiritual music as a serious form of expression worthy of the American stage. **CORBIS-BETTMANN**

The majority of its delegates, 76 of 124, are African American. When the General Assembly meets on July 6, 84 of the 157 representatives are African Americans. Whites retain control of the South Carolina Senate.

The Fourteenth Amendment to the Constitution is adopted on July 28, guaranteeing due process and equal protection under the law for African Americans. In its attempt to place African Americans on an equal legal footing with whites, it takes up where the Thirteenth Amendment abolishing slavery left off.

Arkansas Governor Powell Clayton declares martial law after Ku Klux Klan sponsors widespread acts of terrorism.

B. F. Randolph, senator and chairman of Republican Party, is assassinated in broad daylight in South Carolina.

Pinckney B. S. Pinchback and James J. Harris become the first African American delegates to attend a Republican convention.

Congress readmits North Carolina, South Carolina, Louisiana, Georgia, Alabama, Arkansas, and Florida.

Democrat conservatives and military overtake Florida convention drafting a new constitution placing power in hands of the governor. The black vote is effectively neutralized.

Thaddeus Stevens, architect of Radical Reconstruction, dies in Washington.

John Willis Menard is elected to Congress, but he is refused a seat by an election committee that rules that it is too early to admit a black member. Menard unsuccessfully asks to hold his office on the House floor in the course of the following year. Joseph H. Rainey will enter Congress as a representative from South Carolina in 1870 and serve for almost ten

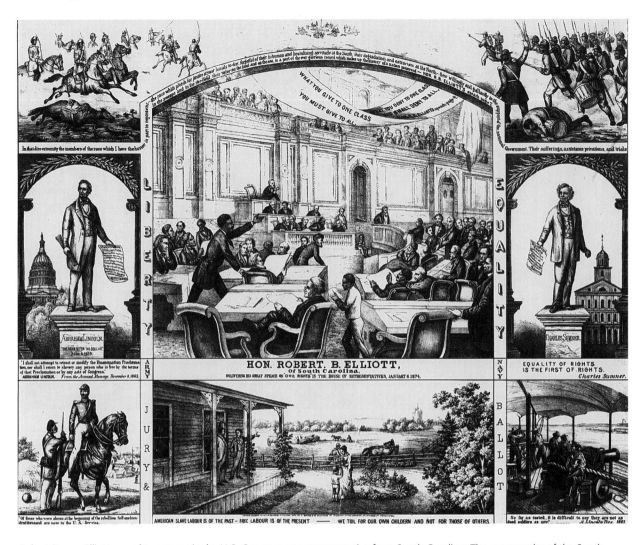

Robert Brown Elliott served two terms in the U.S. Congress as a representative from South Carolina. The commander of the South Carolina National Guard in the years immediately following the Civil War, Elliott became one of the first black congressmen when he was elected in 1871. In 1874, he spoke eloquently in favor of the Second Civil Rights Bill, memorialized in this lithograph. It became law in 1875 but was found unconstitutional in an 1883 Supreme Court decision. The Court argued that the bill, which had granted African Americans equal access to public transportation and accommodations, violated the property rights of others guaranteed under the Constitution. **THE LIBRARY OF CONGRESS**

years. Twenty African Americans will serve in Congress during the remainder of the nineteenth century, including Robert Brown Elliott of South Carolina (1871–1875), Robert Smalls of South Carolina (1875–1879 and 1881–1887), John Mercer Langston of Virginia (1889–1891), and George H. White of North Carolina (1897–1901).

Lower house of Georgia rules that blacks are ineligible to hold office and ejects them.

Ulysses S. Grant is elected president with southern blacks providing decisive votes.

South Carolina and Louisiana approve constitutions with black officials and anti-discriminatory language in place.

Southern states vote on constitutional conventions (Mississippi, Arkansas, Florida).

W. E. B. Du Bois is born in Great Barrington, Massachusetts.

The Hampton Institute is founded.

1869

On February 10, fifteen-year-old Nat Love leaves his family in Tennessee and heads west to Dodge City, Kansas. For the next twenty years, Love will drive cattle between Texas and Kansas. One of the most famous of the black cowboys and rodeo riders, he will earn the nickname "Deadwood Dick."

National Convention of Black Leaders meets in Washington, D.C. Frederick Douglass is elected president.

Nelley Callhoun, who remained behind in slavery when her parents and siblings went north, travels to Chicago to be with her dying mother, Sinai Reynolds, in her final days. **SEE SIDEBARS** *The Reynolds/Calhoun Family, pp. 354–367*

White conservatives capture Tennessee legislature in an election season marred by assassinations.

1870

The Fifteenth Amendment to the Constitution is adopted on March 30, giving African American men the right to vote. It is subsequently subverted throughout the South as white legislators adopt voting requirements that exclude black voters.

The black population is 4,880,009 (12.7 percent of the U.S. population).

Andrew B. Calhoun deeds Nelley, Siny Catherine, and Catherine Felix Calhoun a small plot of land in the town of Newnan, Georgia, in recognition of their faithful service to his family while they were held as slaves. Although they keep the land, they do not live on it, choosing to move to Atlanta instead. There, Nelley works as a laundress and Siny Catherine as a hairdresser. Nelley's grandchildren, including Catherine Felix, will attend Atlanta University during the 1870s. An African American family that has traced its lineage through these three women back to Henry and Sinai Reynolds remains in Atlanta into 2002. **SEE SIDEBARS** *The Reynolds/Calhoun Family, pp. 354–367*

Congress passes the first Enforcement Act to enforce the Fifteenth Amendment because terrorist tactics are being used throughout the South to keep blacks from voting.

Governor William Woods Holden of North Carolina declares various counties in a state of Klan insurrection.

Hiram R. Revels, Mississippi state senator and former Freedmen's Bureau agent, enters the United States Senate on February 25, elected to fill the vacated seat of the former Confederate president, Jefferson Davis. He will serve for one year. He and Blanche K. Bruce, elected from Mississippi in 1875, are the only two African Americans to serve in the U.S. Senate during the nineteenth century. P. B. S. Pinchback, elected to the Senate from Louisiana in 1873, is never seated. **SEE ENTRY** *African Americans in Political Office, p. 204*

White conservatives suppress the black vote in North Carolina, capturing the legislature.

1871

Klan trials begin in Oxford, Mississippi, and Columbia, South Carolina.

President Ulysses S. Grant declares martial law in nine South Carolina counties affected by the Klan.

Congress passes the Second Enforcement Act or the Ku Klux Klan Act—giving federal officers and courts control of voter registration and voting in congressional elections. The law is designed to enforce the Fifteenth Amendment.

Congress passes the Third Enforcement Act regarding Klan conspiracy as rebellion against the United States and giving broad powers to the president to suspend the writ of habeas corpus and declare martial law in rebellious areas.

1872

P.B.S. Pinchback is sworn in as governor of Louisiana after the sitting governor is impeached. In the same year, he is elected to the Senate after relinquishing the governorship. **SEE ENTRY** *African Americans in Political Office, p. 205*

Paul Laurence Dunbar, poet, is born in Dayton, Ohio. **SEE SIDEBAR** *The Poet Paul Laurence Dunbar (1872–1906), p. 338*

1873

The 43rd Congress convenes with seven blacks.

The Colfax Massacre occurs on Easter Sunday morning in Grant Parish, Louisiana, with the murder of more than sixty African Americans. Similar acts of violence will occur throughout the South in the 1870s, resulting in the use of federal troops. **SEE ENTRY** *African Americans in Political Office, p. 205*

1874

Sixteen blacks are lynched in Tennessee.

Armed Democrats seize Texas government and end Radical Reconstruction.

Blanche Kelso Bruce is elected to a six-year term in the Senate, Mississippi. **SEE ENTRY** *African Americans in Political Office, p. 204*

1875

The 44th Congress convenes with eight blacks.

Democrats suppress the black vote and take Mississippi election.

Former slave Blanche K. Bruce was the first African American to serve a full term in the U.S. Senate. In 1879, during a debate on a Chinese exclusion bill he opposed, Bruce became the first black senator to preside over a Senate session. **THE LIBRARY OF CONGRESS**

President Ulysses S. Grant sends federal troops to Vicksburg, Mississippi.

The Second Civil Rights Act is passed by Congress on March 1, granting African Americans equal access to public accommodations and transportation.

1876

Edward A. Bouchet becomes the first African American to earn a Ph.D. from an American university, when Yale University awards him a doctorate in physics. Bouchet, who is also the first African American initiated into Phi Beta Kappa, subsequently has difficulty finding employment commensurate with his training and achievements. For twenty-six years, he teaches chemistry at the Institute for Colored Youth in Philadelphia. **SEE ENTRY** *African Americans in the Sciences, p. 420*

Edward Bannister, one of the founding members of the Providence Art Club—now the Rhode Island School of Design—takes first prize for painting at the Philadelphia Centennial Exposition with a landscape painting, *Under the Oaks.* His depictions of the Rhode Island countryside earn him renown and respect in his adopted city of Providence and else-

where. Although *Under the Oaks* is now lost, many of Bannister's paintings survive today in museums around the country. **SEE ENTRY** *The Art of African Americans, p. 437*

President Ulysses S. Grant sends federal troops to South Carolina to restore order after widespread racial rioting and white terrorism erupts.

The Senate refuses to seat P. B. S. Pinchback.

1877

When racial harassment drives James Webster Smith to leave West Point, Henry O. Flipper becomes the first African American to graduate from the United States Military Academy on June 15. As the nation's only black army officer, Flipper is hounded by racial prejudice, charged with embezzlement, convicted of conduct unbecoming an officer and a gentleman, and dishonorably discharged. His name is finally cleared on May 3, 1977, thirty-seven years after his death.

The 45th Congress convenes with one black senator and three congressmen.

Rutherford B. Hayes appoints Frederick Douglass as marshal of District of Columbia.

John Mercer Langston is named minister to Haiti. **SEE SIDEBAR** *John Mercer Langston (1829–1897), p. 222*

1879

With the end of Reconstruction and the withdrawal of the last Union forces, white violence escalates against freed people in the South. In 1879, fearing the reestablishment of slavery and looking for better economic conditions, some twenty thousand African Americans emigrate from southern states to Kansas.

The 46th Congress convenes with one black senator.

1880

The black population is 6,580,793 (13.1 percent of the U.S. population).

The white southern journalist Joel Chandler Harris publishes the first collection of African American folktales, *Uncle Remus: His Songs and Sayings,* based on stories he has heard as a boy. Harris invents a black storyteller, Uncle Remus, who offers the folktales to a young white boy. Although the portrayal of Uncle Remus and his relationship to the boy is marred by Harris's racial attitudes, the tales themselves prove to be authentically African American. Some of them, like the story of Brer Rabbit and the Tar Baby, will become enduring classics of American storytelling.

1881

The 47th Congress convenes with two black congressmen.

Blanche Kelso Bruce is appointed register of treasury by President James A. Garfield.

Frederick Douglass is appointed recorder of deeds for District of Columbia.

Henry Highland Garnet is named minister to Liberia.

The Jim Crow era begins when Tennessee adopts a law segregating railway transportation. Similar Jim Crow laws will follow in Florida (1887), Mississippi (1888), Texas (1889), Louisiana (1890), Alabama, Kentucky, Arkansas, and Georgia (1891), South Carolina (1898), North Carolina (1899), Virginia (1900), Maryland (1904), and Oklahoma (1907). **SEE ENTRY** *Reconstruction and the Rise of Jim Crow, p. 197*

Spelman College is founded on April 11 in Atlanta, Georgia, as the Atlanta Baptist Female Seminary. It is the first school dedicated to the higher education of African American women.

Booker T. Washington founds Tuskegee Normal and Industrial Institute on July 4. Based on the model of Hampton Institute, Washington's alma mater, Tuskegee will devote itself to the moral and industrial training of African American youth and to the training of teachers for the public schools. **SEE ENTRY** *The African American Intellectual Experience, p. 406*

1882

Forty-nine blacks are reported lynched during the course of 1882.

George Washington Williams publishes his *History of the Negro Race in America from 1619 to 1880*. A monumental work in two volumes, Williams's *History* is the first comprehensive study of black America.

Between 1882 and 1892, the inventor Elijah McCoy is awarded more than twenty-five patents for lubricating locomotive engines and other machinery, earning his inventions the title "the real McCoy." In this same period, another African American inventor, Granville Woods, also obtains dozens of patents for a variety of electrical devices. **SEE ENTRY** *African Americans in the Sciences, p. 420*

Henry Highland Garnet dies in Monrovia.

This engraving of a portrait of Henry O. Flipper, West Point's first African American graduate, shows him shortly after he joined the Tenth Cavalry of "Buffalo Soldiers." Flipper was assigned to the western frontier shortly after leaving the Academy. He was the Army's sole black officer. In 1882, he was charged with embezzlement of company funds, and though cleared of this charge he was dismissed from the service for conduct unbecoming an officer and a gentleman. His name was not cleared until 1977. **FISK UNIVERSITY LIBRARY**

1883

The Supreme Court on October 15 overturns the Civil Rights Act of 1875 on the ground that it is unconstitutional. The Court rules that equal access to public accommodations for African Americans violates an owner's right to private property under the due process clause of the Fourteenth Amendment.

Fifty-three blacks are reported lynched during the course of the year.

Sojourner Truth dies in Battle Creek, Michigan.

Four blacks are killed in a race riot in Danville, Virginia.

1885

"Jelly Roll" Morton is born in Gulfport, Mississippi, as Ferdinand Joseph La Menthe.

The 49th Congress convenes with two black congressmen.

Jelly Roll Morton (1885–1941) was one of the early jazz greats and the first jazz composer to write his works down. By the age of twelve, he was making a living as a pianist in New Orleans. Photograph by Frank Driggs. **ARCHIVE PHOTOS, INC.**

Martin R. Delany, politician and black nationalist, dies. **SEE ENTRY** *The Debate over Slavery in the United States, p. 113*

1886

Seventy-four blacks are reported lynched.

Twenty blacks are killed in Mississippi's Carrollton Massacre.

1888

Capital Savings Bank in Washington, D.C., becomes the first black bank to open.

1890

One-hundred-thirteen blacks are reported lynched.

In the years following the Civil War, black publishing ventures proliferate throughout the country, and by 1890 there are 575 black newspapers nationwide, including the New York *Age,* the Washington *Bee,* and the California *Eagle.* Many offer broad coverage of social, religious, and cultural matters as well as reports on current political events and editorial commentary. **SEE**

ENTRY *African American Newspapers and Periodicals, p. 229*

The black population is 7,488,676 (11.9 percent of the U.S. population).

The Blair Bill, designed to promote literacy among free blacks, is defeated in the Senate.

The Mississippi Constitutional Convention adopts literacy and "understanding" tests in order to exclude African Americans from voting. The so-called Mississippi Plan becomes the model for depriving black voters of the ballot in North and South Carolina, Louisiana, Alabama, Virginia, Georgia, and Oklahoma. **SEE ENTRY** *Reconstruction and the Rise of Jim Crow, p. 196*

1891

Provident Hospital and Training School for Nurses is founded in Chicago by Daniel Hale Williams on January 23. It is the nation's first hospital administered by African Americans and the only nursing school for African Americans. Two years later, on July 9, 1893, Dr. Williams will perform the first open-heart surgery at Provident Hospital. **SEE ENTRY** *African Americans in the Sciences p. 420*

1892

Anna Julia Cooper publishes *A Voice from the South,* one of the early milestones in African American feminist thought. A vigorous advocate of education for African American women, Cooper will help to found the Colored Women's YWCA in 1905 and serve for many years as principal of Dunbar High School in Washington, D.C. **SEE ENTRY** *The African American Intellectual Experience, p. 406*

A record number of lynchings, 241, occur in this year, as Jim Crow practices take hold. Ida B. Wells-Barnett, a tireless crusader against lynch law, will meticulously record them in her 1895 book *A Red Record.* **SEE PRIMARY SOURCE DOCUMENT** *"The Case Stated" and "Lynch Law Statistics" by Ida B. Wells-Barnett, p. 233*

1895

Booker T. Washington delivers the "Atlanta Compromise" speech on September 18, at the Cotton Exposition in Atlanta, Georgia. The speech calls for economic progress among black Americans but affirms their social segregation and political disenfranchisement. A year later, the Supreme Court hands down its *Plessy* v. *Ferguson* decision, establishing the "separate but equal" doctrine. **SEE SIDEBAR** *Black Intellectuals: Booker T. Washington and the Atlanta Compromise, p. 414*

Abraham's Oak, a 1905 painting by Henry O. Tanner. Tanner gained fame for his painting of biblical and landscape scenes. **NATIONAL MUSEUM OF AMERICAN ART/ART RESOURCE, NY**

The National Conference of Colored Women holds its first meeting in Boston in the month of August, under the leadership of Josephine St. Pierre Ruffin. This will lead in 1896 to the founding of the National Association of Colored Women, whose first president will be Mary Church Terrell. **SEE ENTRY** *The African American Intellectual Experience, p. 408*

Frederick Douglass dies in Anacostia Heights, District of Columbia.

Three of Henry O. Tanner's paintings are exhibited at the Cotton States and International Exposition in Atlanta. Two are among Tanner's best-known depictions of black life, *The Thankful Poor* and *The Banjo Lesson,* which Tanner has exhibited in Paris. In Atlanta, Tanner's work is shown in the "Negro Building," while work of white artists, including Tanner's teacher, Thomas Eakins, is shown in the "art exhibit." **SEE ENTRY** *The Art of African Americans, p. 437*

1896

The poet Paul Laurence Dunbar publishes his *Lyrics of Lowly Life* to critical acclaim. Dunbar's poems, in both dialect and standard English, explore the experience of slavery and the trials of African American life in the post-slavery period. **SEE SIDEBAR** *The Poet Paul Laurence Dunbar (1872–1906), p. 338*

The Supreme Court issues a decision in the case of *Plessy* v. *Ferguson,* arguing that separate accommodations in travel, schooling, and other public facilities do not violate the Constitution's Thirteenth Amendment prohibiting slavery or the Fourteenth Amendment guaranteeing all citizens due process and equal protection under the law. *Plessy* v. *Ferguson* establishes the doctrine of "separate but equal" and becomes the legal foundation for Jim Crow segregation throughout the United States. **SEE ENTRY** *African Americans and the Law, p. 247*

1897

One-hundred-twenty-three blacks are reported lynched.

John Mercer Langston dies in Washington, D.C.

1898

One-hundred-one blacks are reported lynched.

Bob Cole, the friend and collaborator of James Weldon Johnson and his brother John Rosamund Johnson, stages the first black musical comedy, *A Trip to Coontown,* in New York in April. The play, produced and performed entirely by African Americans, departs from the minstrel tradition in offering a plotted story with musical numbers.

The 10th Cavalry, composed of African American soldiers, rescues Teddy Roosevelt's Rough Riders on July 1, in the charge of El Caney, in Santiago, Cuba. The Spanish American War results in the acquisition of the Philippines, Guam, and Puerto Rico by the United States. **SEE ENTRY** *The Ongoing Effort for Inclusion in the Military, p. 295*

Blanche K. Bruce dies in Washington, D.C.

Louisiana adopts constitution with "grandfather" clause barring black voters. **SEE SIDEBAR** *The Reconstruction Amendments, p. 263*

1899

Scott Joplin publishes his "Maple Leaf Rag," bringing ragtime music to the general American public. The piece will be recorded in 1903. **SEE ENTRY** *The History of African American Music, p. 324*

Eighty-five blacks are reported lynched.

Edward Kennedy ("Duke") Ellington is born in Washington, D.C.

1900

The black population is 8,833,994 (11.6 percent of the U.S. population).

Booker T. Washington is elected president of the National Negro Business League.

Daniel Louis Armstrong is born in New Orleans, Louisiana.

Pan-African Congress Meets in London; W. E. B. Du Bois attends.

1901

One-hundred-five blacks are reported lynched.

Alabama adopts a constitution with a "grandfather" clause that inhibits the black vote.

On invitation from President Theodore Roosevelt, Booker T. Washington dines at the White House. The event rankles members of Roosevelt's Republican Party who are not ready to accept African Americans as equal members of society and African Americans who think that Washington should have declined

the invitation because the government does not yet afford them equal opportunities.

Hiram Revels dies in Aberdeen, Mississippi.

George H. White, the last of the post-Reconstruction African Americans elected to Congress, leaves the House of Representatives on March 4. No African American will serve in Congress again until the election of Oscar DePriest, from Chicago, in 1929. **SEE ENTRY** *African Americans in Political Office, p. 205*

1902

Ma Rainey of the Rabbit Foot Minstrels sings blues for the first time in a professional show, to the delight of the audience. Ma Rainey will begin to specialize in the blues, making a number of recordings and becoming one of the legendary early blues women. **SEE ENTRY** *The History of African American Music, p. 325*

1903

W. E. B. Du Bois publishes *The Souls of Black Folk.* The book offers a wide-ranging appreciation of the accomplishments and lives of African Americans, great and small, and sharply criticizes the philosophy of Booker T. Washington. **SEE ENTRY** *The African American Intellectual Experience, p. 406*

As founder of the Saint Luke Penny Savings Bank in Richmond, Virginia, Maggie Walker becomes the first black woman to preside over a bank.

1904

Mary McLeod Bethune establishes the Daytona Educational and Industrial Institute for girls. It is the first black school in Florida to offer education beyond the elementary grades.

1905

The *Chicago Defender* begins publication on May 6 under the editorial direction of Robert S. Abbott, the son of former slaves. The *Defender* will circulate widely in the South during the years of the Great Migration, bringing African Americans north in search of jobs and a better life.

Henry Furness becomes the last black minister named to Haiti.

African Americans in Nashville, Tennessee, form their own bus service, the Union Transportation Company, when the city line institutes racial segregation in its streetcars but refuses to hire black drivers and conductors for the Jim Crow cars.

Fond of entertaining, President Roosevelt often had dinner guests. Booker T. Washington, after the success of his autobiography *Up From Slavery*, was invited to dine with the president one evening. After the White House released the guest list the next morning, the southern press and some northern papers harshly criticized Roosevelt, and it became the biggest news since the assassination of President McKinley. **CORBIS-BETTMANN**

W. E. B. Du Bois and William Monroe Trotter, editor of the *Boston Guardian,* meet with other African American intellectuals and professionals at Niagara Falls on July 11–13, to organize protests against the government's indifference to African American civil rights. The Niagara Movement, as it comes to be called, will lead to the founding of the National Association for the Advancement of Colored People (NAACP). **SEE ENTRY** *The African American Intellectual Experience, p. 406*

1906

Paul Laurence Dunbar dies in Dayton, Ohio.

Dr. John Hope, a graduate of Brown University and a member of Phi Beta Kappa, becomes the first black president of Morehouse College. He strives to create a vigorous intellectual environment. He challenges Booker T. Washington's contention that training for blacks should focus on vocational and agricultural skills.

The first African American Greek letter fraternity, Alpha Phi Alpha, is founded at Cornell University in Ithaca, New York.

1907

Jack Johnson defeats Tommy Burns in Sydney, Australia, to become the first black heavyweight boxing champion.

1908

Thurgood Marshall is born in Baltimore, Maryland.

This photograph, taken around 1910 in Meridian Hill Park, Washington, D.C., shows an African American woman in charge of two white children. Prior to World War I, one of the few job options for African American women was caring for the young children and families of upper middle-class white women. **NATIONAL ARCHIVES AND RECORDS ADMINISTRATION**

The first African American sorority, Alpha Kappa Alpha, is established at Howard University in Washington, D.C., just two years after the first African American fraternity was formed at Cornell University.

1909

Sixty-nine blacks are reported lynched.

The National Association for the Advancement of Colored People (NAACP) is founded on February 12, the 100th anniversary of Abraham Lincoln's birthday, following a bloody race riot in Lincoln's hometown of Springfield, Illinois. Over the next several decades, the NAACP will lead the fight for the strengthening of laws to protect the civil rights of African Americans. **SEE ENTRY** *The African American Intellectual Experience, p. 406*

Matthew Henson and Commander Robert Peary become the first men to reach the North Pole, on April 6. **SEE SIDEBAR** *Matthew Henson and the Journey to the North Pole, p. 421*

President Theodore Roosevelt recommends a committee to investigate problems in Liberia. In the following year, the committee recommends financial aid.

1910

The first city ordinance requiring white and black residential areas passes in Baltimore, Maryland.

Sixty-seven blacks are reported lynched.

The black population is 9,827,763 (10.7 percent of the U.S. population).

The *Crisis,* the official magazine of the NAACP, begins publication in April. Under the editorship of W. E. B. Du Bois, the *Crisis* will use art, humor, political analysis, and on-site reporting to keep the plight of African Americans in public view. **SEE ENTRY** *African American Newspapers and Periodicals, p. 229*

The second NAACP Conference is held in New York City.

1911

Sixty blacks are reported lynched.

Fearing that the newly opened prairie of present-day Manitoba, Saskatchewan, and Alberta will fall prey to American expansionism, the government opens it to homesteading on free 160-acre parcels of land. When African Americans and Asians come north to take part in the homestead movement, the government takes steps to exclude all but white settlers, including adopting an ordinance banning black settlement on the basis of "climatic unsuitability." Fourteen hundred African Americans settle on the prairie, among them John Ware, a former South Carolina slave.

The National Urban League is founded in October in New York City. Less radical in its demands and tactics than the early NAACP, the National Urban League focuses its attention on the plight of African Americans in cities.

Marcus Garvey forms the Universal Negro Improvement Association in Jamaica. The association, which takes as its motto "One God, One Aim, One Destiny," seeks to unite Africans around the world. It develops a mass following among working-class African Americans following Garvey's emigration to New York in 1915. **SEE SIDEBAR** *Marcus Garvey and the "Africa for Africans" Movement, p. 240*

William Lewis is appointed assistant attorney general of U.S.

1912

Sixty-one blacks are reported lynched.

James Weldon Johnson anonymously publishes his *Autobiography of an Ex-Coloured Man,* ushering in twentieth-century African American literature. The story of a light-skinned black man who decides to pass for white, the novel is considered a true autobiography until 1927, when Johnson reveals himself as the author. **SEE ENTRY** *The African American Literary Experience, p. 339*

A blues piece is written down for the first time when W.C. Handy, the "Father of the Blues," composes the "Memphis Blues" as a campaign song for a Memphis politician. **SEE ENTRY** *The History of African American Music, p. 325*

1913

Fifty-one blacks are reported lynched.

The conductor James Reese Europe leads an orchestra of black musicians performing symphonic music at Carnegie Hall, New York. Europe will become one of the early jazz orchestra leaders and the music director of the 369th Infantry Band during World War I.

The 369th Infantry, New York's Fifteenth Colored Regiment, attracted many famous people to its ranks. Among them was the bandleader James Reese Europe, shown here returning home in a War Department Staff photograph taken on February 27, 1919. **NATIONAL ARCHIVES AND RECORDS ADMINISTRATION**

Harriet Tubman dies in Auburn, New York.

President Woodrow Wilson begins to segregate working, eating, and lavatory spaces in federal government buildings.

1914

Ernest Just receives the first Spingarn Medal from the National Association for the Advancement of Colored People (NAACP) for his achievements as a biologist. A pioneer in the field of marine biology, Just will spend the last years of his life in Europe, where his work as a scientist is more highly respected than in his own country. **SEE ENTRY** *African Americans in the Sciences, p. 422*

U.S. signs a commerce treaty with Ethiopia.

1915

Fifty-six blacks are reported lynched.

Booker T. Washington dies in Tuskegee, Alabama.

Robert Smalls, Reconstruction congressman, dies in Beaufort, South Carolina.

On Thanksgiving Day, in Georgia, William Joseph Simmons, along with fifteen of his friends, revives the then-dormant Ku Klux Klan.

Louisiana's "grandfather" clause is defeated. **SEE SIDE-BAR** *The Reconstruction Amendments, p. 263*

The NAACP leads a protest against the showing of *Birth of a Nation,* a film that recounts both the Civil War and its aftermath from the point of view of southerners. The movie is criticized by many African Americans as a vehicle for the perpetuation of racist ideas. Demonstrations in Los Angeles and New York City are largely unsuccessful in keeping the movie-going public out of the theaters.

The Great Migration of African Americans to northern cities begins. Escaping racial violence and a lack of economic and political opportunity in the South and drawn by the hope of work in the burgeoning industries of the North, more than six million people will head for northern urban centers before the migration ends in the 1960s. In the 1970s and 1980s, as northern industry collapses, African Americans will begin to move south in greater numbers. **SEE ENTRY** *Migration, Industrialization, and the City, p. 315*

The Supreme Court issues its decision in the case of *Guinn* v. *United States,* finding unconstitutional Oklahoma's "grandfather clause," which exempts from state voting requirements any whose ancestors have voted prior to January 1, 1866. The grandfather clause, in use also in Maryland, allows whites who fail voting tests to vote anyway, while at the same time excluding African Americans.

1916

The first issue of the *Journal of Negro History* is published by Carter G. Woodson, the man who later originates Negro History Week (now Black History Month).

Fifty blacks are reported lynched.

The Spingarn Medal is given to Colonel Charles Young, the organizer of the Liberian constabulary.

1917

Chandler Owen and labor leader A. Philip Randolph begin publishing the *Messenger* in support of the organized labor movement and workers' rights. In the years following World War I, the U.S. Post Office will refuse to deliver the *Messenger* on the grounds that it contains seditious material. **SEE ENTRY** *African American Newspapers and Periodicals, p. 231*

Marcus Garvey begins publishing *Negro World,* reporting on events relevant to black people throughout the world. With its advocacy of Pan-African unification, *Negro World* anticipates the later philosophies of black power and Afrocentricity. **SEE ENTRY** *African American Newspapers and Periodicals, p. 231*

The New York City Fifth Avenue March takes place on July 28. Thousands of African Americans march in protest of lynchings and racial inequalities.

Thirty-seven blacks are reported lynched.

The United States enters World War I.

Henry Burleigh receives the Spingarn Medal for his contributions to the field of music.

Joe Oliver and Louis Armstrong, New Orleans jazzmen, arrive in Chicago, part of the "jazz migration" that brings the early innovators of jazz north. **SEE ENTRY** *The History of African American Music, p. 327*

In *Buchanan* v. *Warley,* the Supreme Court strikes down a Kentucky ordinance that restricts African Americans from moving into neighborhoods predominantly inhabited by whites.

1918

Sixty blacks are reported lynched.

World War I ends; records show that 370,000 black soldiers served in the war, with 1,400 holding officer ranks.

George White, last of the post-Reconstruction congressmen, dies.

A race riot in Philadelphia, Pennsylvania, leaves four African Americans dead and many injured.

W.C. Handy moves to New York City, where he records his music and founds a music company. **SEE ENTRY** *The History of African American Music, p. 325*

1919

Seventy-six blacks are reported lynched.

On February 17, the 369th Regiment—a black regiment formerly known as the 15th New York Infantry—marches up Fifth Avenue to Harlem, on its triumphal return from the European battlefields of World War I. Although the 369th was treated with abuse in Spartanburg, South Carolina, where it trained, it distinguished itself in combat, receiving the Croix de Guerre from the French government, as did the 371st and 372nd Negro regiments. More than 370,000 African Americans took part in the World War I effort as soldiers and officers. **SEE ENTRY** *The Ongoing Effort for Inclusion in the Military, p. 296*

On February 18, 1919, the New York Fifteenth Colored Infantry, otherwise known as the 369th Regiment, celebrated its victorious return from World War I with a march through the streets of New York. The 369th was the only army regiment to carry a state flag—the flag of New York—into battle. **CORBIS-BETTMANN**

The Pan-African Congress, organized by W. E. B. Du Bois, meets at Grand Hotel in Paris, France. **SEE SIDEBAR** *W. E. B. Du Bois (1868–1963), p. 413*

Twenty-six race riots occur in the "red summer" of 1919 in cities and localities throughout the North and South. Federal troops are needed to bring calm to Chicago, where rioting results in the death of fifteen whites and twenty-three African Americans.

1920

Fifty-three blacks are reported lynched.

The black population is 10,463,131 (9.9 percent of the U.S. population).

The National Negro Baseball League is organized by Andrew "Rube" Foster. The league is composed of six teams from midwestern cities with large African American populations. The league enjoys great popularity until it folds in 1931 during the Great Depression.

Charles Gilpin appears on Broadway in Eugene O'Neill's *The Emperor Jones* and is named one of the ten people who have done the most for the American theater by the Drama League of New York, the first African American so honored.

James Weldon Johnson becomes the first black executive secretary of the NAACP.

The national convention of Marcus Garvey's "Universal Negro Improvement Association" is held in Harlem.

1921

On May 31, a race riot erupts in Tulsa, Oklahoma, when an African American bootblack is falsely accused of raping a white woman. Death reports range from 36 to 175, and 11,000 blacks are left homeless when the black neighborhood is leveled by bombs.

The second Pan-African Congress is held in London, Brussels, and Paris.

Fifty-nine blacks are reported lynched.

Known for teaching chemistry to students at the Tuskegee Institute, George Washington Carver is shown here reading through letters.
CORBIS-BETTMANN

P.B.S. Pinchback, who held many offices during Reconstruction, dies.

1922

The House of Representatives on January 7 passes the Dyer Anti-Lynching Law, which dies in the Senate under the filibustering of southern Democrats and northern conservatives. No anti-lynching law is ever passed by the U.S. Congress.

The first all-black musical, Eubie Blake and Noble Sissle's *Shuffle Along,* opens. It is the first of a string of African American musicals that will play to audiences in New York City in the 1920s.

Fifty-one blacks are reported lynched.

1923

Bessie Smith's recording of "Downhearted Blues" is issued and sells over a million copies. From 1923 until her premature death in 1937, Smith will establish the blues as a national musical genre, composing and recording dozens of blues classics, including

"Backwater Blues," which is based on the Mississippi floods of the late 1920s. **SEE ENTRY** *The History of African American Music, p. 325*

Half a million African Americans leave the South during this year. In September, the governor declares Oklahoma to be in a "state of rebellion and insurrection" following widespread Ku Klux Klan violence.

Marcus Garvey, leader of the Universal Negro Improvement Association (UNIA), is sentenced to a five-year prison term on a single count of mail fraud. In this same year, Garvey's wife edits and publishes a volume of sayings and speeches titled *Philosophy and Opinions of Marcus Garvey.*

The Spingarn Medal is awarded to George Washington Carver for his contributions to agricultural science.

1924

"Dixie to Broadway," "the First Real Revue by Negroes," opens in New York City. The show features actress Florence Mills and music by Will Vodery, an African American with a long-time association with the Ziegfeld Follies.

Big-band pioneer Fletcher Henderson opens Roseland Ballroom on Broadway in New York City.

1925

Aaron Douglas Jr., an artist whose work is most often associated today with the Harlem Renaissance, arrives in Harlem from Topeka, Kansas, where he has been teaching high school art. **SEE ENTRY** *The Art of African Americans, p. 438*

The March issue of the magazine *Survey Graphic,* edited by Alain Locke, becomes a book called *The New Negro,* officially ushering in the Harlem or New Negro Renaissance. The Great Migration, which is bringing tens of thousands of black southerners north, and the "red summer" of 1919, which saw racial riots in northern cities, have contributed to the rise of a politically conscious class of urban intellectuals and artists. In cities across the North, especially in Harlem, their publishing and performance ventures have led to a rich flowering of African American art and thought. **SEE ENTRY** *The Art of African Americans, p. 437*

Louis Armstrong's Hot Five and Hot Seven groups make their first recordings, ushering in the jazz era and establishing Armstrong as the premier trumpeter of the new music. The groups, composed of New Orleans musicians and led by Armstrong, record in Chicago between 1925 and 1928. **SEE ENTRY** *The History of African American Music, p. 327*

Malcolm X is born in Omaha, Nebraska.

Marcus Garvey enters federal prison in Atlanta.

A. Philip Randolph founds the Brotherhood of Sleeping Car Porters on May 8, the first national black labor union. The brotherhood fights aggressively to better the wages and working conditions of its members, who come to be known as Pullman porters, and in 1937 finally negotiates a contract with the Pullman Palace Car Company. Because of their union's strength, the Pullman porters prosper even during the Great Depression, becoming a symbol of upward mobility for other African Americans. **SEE ENTRY** *African American Labor History, p. 429*

The Spingarn Medal is awarded to diplomat, author, and leader James Weldon Johnson.

Xavier University, the only historically black Catholic university in the United States is established in New Orleans by St. Katharine Drexel and the Sisters of the Blessed Sacrament.

Alain Locke, the father of the New Negro Movement. Locke urged African American writers and artists to explore their cultural heritage as a motif. In doing so, he helped to usher in the Harlem Renaissance, a period of unparalleled artistic creativity. **THE LIBRARY OF CONGRESS**

1926

Carter G. Woodson organizes the first Negro History Week, which later becomes Black History Month.

Mordecai Johnson is named the first black president of Howard University.

The Spingarn Medal is awarded to historian and scholar Carter G. Woodson.

1927

The fourth Pan-African Congress is held in New York City.

After serving 33 months in a penitentiary for mail fraud, Marcus Garvey's sentence is commuted, thanks to an extensive petition campaign. Garvey is deported to Jamaica upon his release.

Florence Mills, performer and singer, dies in New York City at the age of thirty-two.

Duke Ellington opens with his band at the Cotton Club in Harlem on December 4. Catering to white audiences, the Cotton Club is the premier dance and supper club spotlighting African American performers. Ellington will be the featured bandleader at the Cotton Club between 1927 and 1931, establishing a national reputation. **SEE SIDEBAR** *Duke Ellington and the Evolution of American Classical Music, p. 329*

A member of the Great Migration, sixteen-year-old Mahalia Jackson leaves New Orleans for Chicago, where, with Thomas A. Dorsey, she will popularize gospel singing and music. **SEE ENTRY** *The History of African American Music, p. 329*

1928

Bill "Bojangles" Robinson, the most famous of all African American tap dancers, appears on Broadway in the all-black revue, *Blackbirds of 1928,* tapping up and down a flight of stairs—a dance that would become his signature "stair dance."

The Spingarn Medal is awarded to critically acclaimed novelist Charles Chesnutt. **SEE ENTRY** *The African American Literary Experience, p. 338*

1929

The stock market crashes on October 29, ushering in the Great Depression. Blacks will be particularly hard hit by the Depression.

In the fall, black Chicagoans initiate a "Jobs for Negroes" campaign, organizing a boycott against stores that do not hire African Americans. Their motto is "Don't Buy Where You Can't Work." Similar campaigns are mounted with some success in Cleveland, New York, and Los Angeles.

Martin Luther King Jr. is born in Atlanta, Georgia.

Morehouse and Spelman Colleges become affiliated with Atlanta University.

Oscar DePriest, from Chicago, Illinois, is sworn into Congress.

1930

The black population is 11,891,143 (9.7 percent of the U.S. population).

James Weldon Johnson resigns as executive secretary of the NAACP.

The National Association for the Advancement of Colored People (NAACP) mounts a successful campaign to defeat President Herbert Hoover's nomination of a North Carolina judge, John J. Parker, to the Supreme Court. On April 21, the Senate refuses to confirm Parker, whose record of opposing black voting rights has been made public by the NAACP. The *Christian Science Monitor* calls the NAACP campaign "the first national demonstration of the Negro's power since Reconstruction days."

1931

On October 29, William Grant Still's first symphony, the *Afro-American* symphony, is premiered by the Rochester Philharmonic Orchestra, in Rochester, New York. A graduate of Wilberforce University, the Oberlin Conservatory of Music, and the New England Conservatory of Music, Still is a prolific composer in a variety of forms. Also in 1931, he becomes the first African American to lead a major symphony orchestra, when he takes over the direction of the Los Angeles Philharmonic. Still's opera *Troubled Island* will premiere at the New York City Opera in 1949. **SEE ENTRY** *The History of African American Music, p. 329*

Ida B. Wells-Barnett dies in Chicago, Illinois.

1932

The composer and pianist Thomas Dorsey, of the Ebenezer Baptist Church in Chicago, along with Sallie Martin and Willie Mae Ford Smith, found the National Convention of Gospel Choirs and Choruses to promote the singing of blues-based gospel music in churches throughout the nation. **SEE ENTRY** *The History of African American Music, p. 329*

On November 7, the Supreme Court issues its first decision in the case of the Scottsboro Boys. Taken up by the International Labor Defense, the case reaches the Supreme Court, which rules in *Powell* v. *Alabama* that the defendants had been denied due process in not receiving adequate legal counsel. When the defendants are again tried and found guilty and sentenced to death, the case comes once more before the Supreme Court, which rules on April 1, 1935, in the case of *Norris* v. *Alabama,* that the exclusion of Negroes from the juries is a violation of the defendants' rights of due process.

1934

Arthur Mitchell defeats Oscar DePriest to become the first black Democratic congressman. **SEE ENTRY** *African Americans in Political Office, p. 205*

Charles Houston is named director of the NAACP legal campaign.

W. E. B. Du Bois resigns from NAACP in a policy disagreement.

The Cotton Club, shown here in 1932, was in its heyday during the 1920s and 1930s. Performers such as Duke Ellington and Cab Calloway got their start at the world famous Harlem night club. **ARCHIVE PHOTOS, INC.**

The Southern Tenant Farmer's Union, a rare interracial labor organization, is formed in Arkansas when eleven whites and seven blacks meet to address the crisis facing tenant farmers in cotton agriculture. All agree that success against the planters can only be achieved if they preserve interracial unity.

1935

Joe Louis defeats Primo Carnera at Yankee Stadium.

On March 19, a riot erupts in Harlem when a false rumor spreads that a white shopkeeper has beaten a black boy for shoplifting. By the end of the riot, three blacks are dead, 200 are wounded, and damage is estimated at $2 million (mostly to white-owned property). Mayor Fiorello La Guardia appoints a biracial Mayor's Commission on Conditions in Harlem to investigate the event.

Langston Hughes's *The Mulatto* begins a long run on Broadway.

The National Council of Negro Women is founded in New York City on December 5, under the leadership of Mary McLeod Bethune, a teacher and civil rights activist. The child of South Carolina slaves emancipated at the time of the Civil War, Bethune began Bethune-Cookman College in a one-room building in Daytona Beach, Florida, in 1904, with a dollar and a half and five young pupils.

The American contralto Marian Anderson returns from a two-year tour of Europe to give her first major concert in the United States on December 30. **SEE ENTRY** *The History of African American Music, p. 329*

NAACP lawyer Charles H. Houston successfully represents Donald Murray in his suit to gain admission to the all-white University of Maryland Law School.

Like Charlie Parker, Dizzy Gillespie had an astonishing ability to play faster, better, and cleaner than many of his contemporaries in the jazz scene. The trumpeter helped originate the new jazz style known as bebop. **NANCY ANN LEE**

Murray becomes the first African American in the twentieth century to integrate a state university in the South.

The chemist Percy Julian successfully synthesizes physostigmine, a drug used in the treatment of glaucoma, a disease of the eye. While many African American scientists during this period teach in historically black colleges and universities, Julian will seek employment as a research chemist in the private sector, eventually founding his own company, Julian Laboratories, outside Chicago. **SEE ENTRY** *African Americans in the Sciences, p. 422*

The establishment of the Federal Art Project under the auspices of the Works Progress Administration provides employment during the Depression years for a number of African American artists, including Aaron Douglas Jr., Augusta Savage, Archibald Motley Jr., and Richmond Barthe. **SEE ENTRY** *The Art of African Americans, p. 438*

Jazz vocalist Ella Fitzgerald is discovered when she performs in an amateur competition at Harlem's Apollo Theater. Fitzgerald is hired by Chick Webb as vocalist for his band and she makes her first recording with them later that year.

DuBose Heyward and Ira and George Gershwin collaborate on *Porgy and Bess,* a folk opera centering on African American characters. The show, which opens during the year, features such songs as "Summertime," "I Got Plenty o' Nuttin,'" and "It Ain't Necessarily So." It will take several different revivals of the opera for the show to gain a following.

Charlie Parker and Dizzy Gillespie perform "be-bop." **SEE ENTRY** *The History of African American Music, p. 327*

1936

John Hope, president of Atlanta University, dies.

The American track-and-field star Jesse Owens wins four gold medals at the summer Olympic Games in Berlin. The son of an Alabama sharecropper, Owens set nine world records in 1935 and 1936, three of them at the Olympic Games.

Mary McLeod Bethune is named the director of Negro Affairs National Youth Administration.

The Spingarn Medal is posthumously awarded to educator John Hope.

Interviewers employed by the Works Progress Administration compile 2,194 interviews with former slaves. Taken together, these oral narratives provide the most complete record that exists of testimony about American slavery by those who lived through it, and continue to serve as a vast source of information and inspiration for scholars and artists.

1937

Zora Neale Hurston publishes *Their Eyes Were Watching God,* a novel of black southern life. Although a member of the Harlem Renaissance, Hurston concentrates in her work as both a novelist and ethnographer on rural black life in the South. **SEE SIDEBAR** *African American Women Writers: Zora Neale Hurston (1891–1960), Gwendolyn Brooks (1917–2000), and Rita Dove (b. 1952), p. 340*

Singer Bessie Smith dies after being left on the road after an auto accident in Mississippi. **SEE PRIMARY SOURCE DOCUMENT** *Last Affair: Bessie's Blues Song by Michael Harper, p. 318*

Joe Louis defeats Jim Braddock to become the boxing heavyweight champion, only the second black to become heavyweight champion and the first even permitted to fight since Jack Johnson lost the title in 1915.

The Pullman Company formally recognizes the Brotherhood of Sleeping Car Porters. **SEE ENTRY** *African American Labor History, p. 429*

William Hastie is confirmed as the first black federal judge, U.S. Virgin Islands.

1938

Crystal Bird Fauset is elected to the Pennsylvania legislature, becoming the first black woman elected to a state legislature.

Joe "King" Oliver, jazz pioneer, dies in Savannah, Georgia.

James Weldon Johnson dies of auto accident injuries in Maine.

The U.S. Supreme Court in *Missouri* ex rel. *Gaines* v. *Canada* orders the University of Missouri, which has no black graduate school, to admit African American student Lloyd Gaines, arguing that scholarships to out-of-state schools do not constitute equal admission.

1939

In New York City, Jane Bolin becomes the first black woman judge.

While working at Columbia Presbyterian Hospital in New York City, Dr. Charles Drew establishes the first blood bank and conducts pioneering research into the preservation of blood plasma. During World War II, he will establish a blood bank in Britain for the American Red Cross. Although his work will save many lives during the war and after, in 1950 Dr. Drew himself will bleed to death from injuries sustained in an automobile accident. **SEE ENTRY** *African Americans in the Sciences, p. 423*

The NAACP Legal Defense and Educational Fund incorporates under Thurgood Marshall. **SEE SIDEBAR** *Thurgood Marshall (1908–1993), Father of African American Legislative Rights, p. 208*

Hattie McDaniel becomes the first African American to win an Oscar for her performance as "Mammy" in the Civil War epic *Gone with the Wind.*

Opera contralto Marian Anderson is refused access for racial reasons to Constitution Hall for a Washington, D.C., concert by the Daughters of the American Revolution (DAR). Anderson responds by giving an Easter Sunday outdoor recital—introduced by Secretary of the Interior Harold Ickes—on the steps of the Lincoln Memorial before a crowd of 75,000. The scandal prompts Eleanor Roosevelt to resign her DAR membership. **SEE ENTRY** *The History of African American Music, p. 329*

In 1939, the contralto Marian Anderson gave an historic concert on the steps of the Lincoln Memorial, having been denied the use of Constitution Hall by the Daughters of the American Revolution. **CORBIS-BETTMANN**

1940

Hansberry v. *Lee*—the Supreme Court declares that it is illegal for whites to bar African Americans from white neighborhoods. The plaintiff in this case is Carl Hansberry, a prominent real estate broker who moved his family to an all-white neighborhood. His daughter Lorraine's play *A Raisin in the Sun* is based on this incident.

The Mississippi-born novelist Richard Wright publishes *Native Son,* an unflinching treatment of the degraded life of African American migrants in Chicago. The story's hero, Bigger Thomas, calls into question much of the philosophy of "racial uplift" that has been popular among black intellectuals since Reconstruction. Wright later moves to France, where he spends the remainder of his life. **SEE ENTRY** *The African American Literary Experience, p. 339*

Benjamin O. Davis Sr. is appointed brigadier general on October 16, the nation's first African American general. His son, Benjamin O. Davis Jr., commander of the Tuskegee squadron of black fighter pilots, will become the air force's first African American general on October 30, 1954. **SEE ENTRY** *The Ongoing Effort for Inclusion in the Military, p. 297*

The American Negro Theater is organized by Frederick O'Neal and Abram Hill.

President Franklin D. Roosevelt and representatives from the War and Navy Departments meet with three African American leaders: A. Philip Randolph, Walter White, and T. Arnold Hill. This meeting produces a policy of giving black servicemen better treatment and greater opportunity within the confines of racial segregation.

Marcus Garvey dies at age 52 in London, England.

1941

On January 16, the day after a Howard University student, Yancey Williams, sues government officials to force their consideration of his application to the Army Air Corps, the War Department announces the formation of a squadron for Negro cadets, to be trained at Tuskegee Institute in Alabama. African American pilots begin training at segregated facilities at Tuskegee Institute. The Tuskegee experiment produces a trained fighter unit, the 99th Pursuit Squadron, operated and maintained by African American pilots, mechanics, and clerks. This is the beginning of the celebrated Tuskegee Airmen, who will serve with distinction during World War II. **SEE ENTRY** *The Ongoing Effort for Inclusion in the Military, p. 296*

The twenty-three-year-old Jacob Lawrence paints *The Migration Series* in a rented studio, laying out sixty canvases on the floor and painting them together in order to produce a work that is unified in style and color. Although the Great Migration to northern cities has been going on for decades, it has somehow remained invisible and undiscussed in a nation that regards African Americans as a rural southern people and race relations as essentially a "southern problem." Lawrence's haunting images, displayed in museums and reproduced in magazines, bring the migration to light in the American consciousness.

In the May issue of the *Black Worker,* the labor leader A. Philip Randolph calls for a massive march on Washington on July 1 to protest discrimination in defense industry employment. At a meeting with President Franklin Roosevelt on June 18, he refuses to call off the march, and on June 28, in response to the threatened action, President Roosevelt issues Executive Order 8802, desegregating the nation's defense industries and other government programs. In the following month, he announces the formation of the Fair Employment Practices Commission (FEPC). **SEE ENTRY** *The Ongoing Effort for Inclusion in the Military, p. 298*

As part of the war effort, Charles Drew is named architect of the blood bank for the National Research Center. His procedures are later used as a model for the Red Cross.

"Jelly Roll" Morton, pioneer jazz pianist, dies. **SEE ENTRY** *The History of African American Music, p. 327*

The NAACP, with the help of Aline Black and Melvin Alston, two teachers from Norfolk, Virginia, successfully challenges the constitutionality of unequal pay for teachers based on race.

Dr. Robert Weaver is given the task of integrating blacks into national defense programs. **SEE ENTRY** *The African American Intellectual Experience, p. 409*

New York City bus companies agree to hire black drivers and mechanics.

The Spingarn Medal is awarded to novelist Richard Wright.

The Supreme Court rules that separate train facilities must be "substantially equal."

Untrained in the use of antiaircraft weapons, Dorie Miller, a messman aboard the battleship *Arizona,* shoots down several Japanese planes in the attack on Pearl Harbor on December 7. Miller is awarded the Navy Cross for his actions. He perishes with the crew of the carrier *Liscome Bay* when it is sunk by a torpedo on November 24, 1943.

1942

John H. Johnson, an Arkansas migrant to Chicago, mortgages his mother's furniture to raise money for his first publishing venture, *Negro Digest.* In the years that follow, Johnson will establish a vast publishing empire including such widely read magazines as *Ebony* and *Jet.* **SEE ENTRY** *African American Newspapers and Periodicals, p. 231*

The *Booker T. Washington,* the first U.S. merchant ship captained by a black person, is launched in Delaware with Hugh Mulzac at the helm.

The Congress of Racial Equality (CORE) is founded in June in Chicago by a biracial group of civil rights leaders committed to nonviolent direct action. CORE pioneers a variety of tactics, including the sit-in, that civil rights workers of the 1950s and 1960s will use to great effect. Following the 1946 Supreme

Dorie Miller, an African American navy ensign, became an unexpected hero when he shot down at least three Japanese planes at the bombing of Pearl Harbor in 1941. A cook on the *Arizona,* Miller took control of an anti-aircraft gun when the crew was incapacitated. He received the Navy Cross for his heroic actions and was pictured on a recruitment poster for the military. **NATIONAL ARCHIVES AND RECORDS ADMINISTRATION**

Court decision banning segregation in interstate buses, CORE sends the first integrated bus of freedom riders south on April 9, 1947, to challenge segregationist practices. **SEE ENTRY** *The Civil Rights Struggle: From Nonviolence to Black Power, p. 400*

1943

"Fats" Waller, legendary musician, dies.

George Washington Carver dies in Tuskegee.

Detroit Riot of 1943—many African Americans and whites move to Detroit seeking employment in defense industries. The city is unprepared to handle the influx, and racial tensions are exacerbated by competition for jobs and housing. Violence erupts

and quickly spreads throughout the city, and military police are finally brought in to restore order. A Fact-Finding Committee blames the riots on blacks' "militant appeals for equality." However, the mayor sets up an Interracial Committee—the first of its kind in the nation—with authority to investigate complaints and to use the courts to enforce antidiscrimination laws.

Bluesman and guitarist Muddy Waters (McKinley Morganfield) leaves Clarksdale, Mississippi, for Chicago, where he will take up the electric guitar and create what comes to be called "urban blues." A participant in the Great Migration, Waters will bring the blues of the Delta region of Mississippi to a generation of urban African Americans. **SEE ENTRY** *The History of African American Music, p. 326*

President Edwin Barclay of Liberia becomes the first African president to visit the White House.

The Spingarn Medal is presented to Judge William H. Hastie "for his distinguished career as jurist and as an uncompromising champion of equal justice."

Two African American scientists are recruited to the Manhattan Project, which is developing the atomic bomb for American war use. The chemist William Knox is a section leader of the project at Columbia University in New York, while the mathematician and physicist J. Ernest Wilkins works on the project at the University of Chicago. **SEE ENTRY** *African Americans in the Sciences, p. 423*

More than forty people are killed in various race riots in the Deep South, Texas, and Harlem.

William Hastie, civilian aide secretary of war, resigns in a protest of segregation.

War hero Dorie Miller dies aboard the carrier *Liscome Bay* when it is sunk by an enemy torpedo.

1944

Adam Clayton Powell Jr. of Harlem is elected as the first black congressman from the East. **SEE ENTRY** *African American Newspapers and Periodicals, p. 231*

Due to a shortage of troops after the casualties from the Battle of the Bulge, Lt. Gen. John C. H. Lee persuades Gen. Eisenhower to call for volunteers among the predominantly black service units to retrain as riflemen. Forty-five hundred African Americans sign up, undergo training, and serve in sixty-man platoons that join two-hundred-man white rifle companies. This improvised racial policy integrates the fighting but not the army.

Supreme Court declares an all-white Texas Democratic primary unconstitutional in *Smith* v. *Allwright*. The Court states that blacks cannot be barred from voting in the Texas Democratic primaries.

The United Negro College Fund is incorporated.

1945

One thousand white students participate in a walkout to protest integration in Gary, Indiana.

The first issue of *Ebony* magazine is published by John Johnson. **SEE ENTRY** *African American Newspapers and Periodicals, p. 231*

The Brooklyn Dodgers sign Jackie Robinson and send him to one of their farm teams.

World War II ends; statistics show that a total of 1,154,720 blacks were inducted during the war.

1946

Colonel Benjamin O. Davis assumes command of Lockbourne Air Force Base, Ohio. **SEE ENTRY** *The Ongoing Effort for Inclusion in the Military, p. 297*

In response to race riots in several American cities during the year, President Harry S. Truman establishes the President's Committee on Civil Rights to determine how law enforcement "may be strengthened and improved to safeguard the civil rights of the people." The committee's report, issued the following October 29 and entitled *To Secure These Rights*, condemns the nation's racial practices.

Poet Countee Cullen dies in New York City.

The Spingarn Medal is given to jurist Thurgood Marshall.

The Supreme Court bans segregation in the bussing industry.

1947

The Congress of Racial Equality (CORE) decides to test a court ruling that bans segregated interstate travel. In what is called the Journey of Reconciliation, sixteen men (eight white and eight black) travel by bus through the region challenging segregated seating arrangements that relegate blacks to the back of the bus. The arrest of four of the protesters in Chapel Hill, North Carolina catapults CORE and the Journey of Reconciliation to national attention.

Jackie Robinson joins the Brooklyn Dodgers on April 15. The first African American to play in the major leagues, Robinson coolly puts up with innumerable incidents of racial harassment by white spectators to become one of the game's greatest players as well as an enduring example of grace under pressure.

The NAACP presents "An Appeal to the World," a petition against racism, to the United Nations.

A presidential committee condemns widespread conditions of racial injustice.

1948

The California Supreme Court voids a statute banning interracial marriage.

Poet Claude McKay dies in Chicago, Illinois.

A. Philip Randolph tells a Senate committee that he will encourage African Americans to resist induction into the military as long as the armed forces are segregated. On June 26, he organizes the League for Non-

Benjamin O. Davis, Sr. became the first African American to be promoted to general in the Army in October 1940. He later served in the European Theater of Operations as an adviser to the Army on race relations during World War II. **AP/WIDE WORLD PHOTOS**

Violent Civil Disobedience against Military Segregation, and on July 26, President Harry S. Truman issues Executive Order 9981, declaring that "there shall be equality of treatment and opportunity for all persons in the armed services without regard to race, color, religion, or national origin." On October 21, 1951, the last of the Negro regiments, the 24th Infantry, is dissolved. **SEE ENTRY** *The Ongoing Effort for Inclusion in the Military, p. 298*

Ralph J. Bunche is appointed acting mediator for the U.N. Special Commission on Palestine after the assassination of Folke Bernadotte by Jewish militants. Bunche negotiates with both sides and arranges an armistice. His actions earn him the 1950 Nobel Prize for Peace.

The U.S. Supreme Court hands down its decision in the case of *Shelley* v. *Kraemer,* declaring that state courts may not enforce restrictive housing covenants designed to exclude African American residents. *Shelley* v. *Kraemer* is one of thirty-two cases that

Thurgood Marshall argues before the Supreme Court as an attorney for the National Association for the Advancement of Colored People (NAACP), among them *Smith* v. *Allwright,* which strikes down as unconstitutional white voting primaries in Texas and elsewhere, and *Brown* v. *Board of Education,* which invalidates the doctrine of "separate but equal." **SEE ENTRY** *African Americans and the Law, p. 249*

President Harry S. Truman urges Congress to adopt anti-lynching legislation.

1949

CORE organizes sit-ins at St. Louis lunch counters.

WERD in Atlanta, Georgia, begins broadcasting as the first black-owned radio station.

Joe Louis retires after holding heavyweight crown for twelve years.

Born to Alabama sharecroppers in 1914, Joe Louis became one of the great folk heroes of modern black America, defeating German Max Schmeling in 1938 and maintaining a heavyweight boxing title for twelve years. He joined the U.S. Army during World War II at the rank of sergeant. This war-time cartoon, titled "Champion of Champions," highlights his life and heroics. **NATIONAL ARCHIVES AND RECORDS ADMINISTRATION**

1950

During this decade of intensifying civil rights activity in the South, one and a half million African American southerners migrate to the North in the last major wave of the Great Migration. The second reconstruction of the South, as the Civil Rights movement is sometimes called, will lead to the creation of new economic opportunities in the nation's Sun Belt. That, and an accompanying deindustrialization in the North, will begin to draw black northerners south by the mid-1960s. **SEE ENTRY** *Migration, Industrialization, and the City, p. 317*

The black population is 15,042,286 (10 percent of the U.S. population).

Gwendolyn Brooks is awarded the Pulitzer Prize for her second volume of poetry, *Annie Allen*, on May 1. In language of stunning beauty and complexity, *Annie Allen* explores the inner life of an African American woman as she adjusts her youthful dreams of romance and success to the realities of inner-city poverty. **SEE SIDEBAR** *African American Women Writers: Zora Neale Hurston (1891–1960), Gwendolyn Brooks (1917–2000), and Rita Dove (b. 1952), p. 340*

The Korean War begins. Segregation still persists. The largest African American combat unit, the 24th Infantry, which traces its regimental lineage to the post–Civil War reorganization of the Army, goes to war in July 1950. Black troops share in the first American victory.

Carter G. Woodson, "Father of Black History," dies.

Charles Drew, developer of blood bank concept, dies.

Ralph J. Bunche, scholar and United Nations diplomat, is awarded the Nobel Peace Prize for his brilliant negotiation of an armistice in the Arab-Israeli War of 1948.

1951

Jet magazine is first published by Jack Johnson. **SEE ENTRY** *African American Newspapers and Periodicals, p. 231*

Paul Robeson and William L. Patterson present a petition to the United Nations, charging the U.S. government with genocide. It charges the United States with genocide by "deliberately inflicting on [African Americans] conditions of life calculated to bring about their physical destruction" through executions, lynchings, and terrorism.

Oscar DePriest, congressman, dies in Chicago.

A bomb explodes in Florida killing NAACP official Harry T. Moore.

In Washington, D.C., Mary Church Terrell, a prominent civil rights and women's rights activist for fifty years, joins the sit-ins challenging racial segregation in restaurants and public accommodations. Partially as a result of these sit-ins, the Municipal Court of Appeals outlaws segregation in restaurants in the District of Columbia.

1952

Fletcher Henderson, inaugurator of the Big Band Era, dies.

Ralph Ellison publishes the novel *Invisible Man*, the story of a black southern "innocent" who comes to Harlem after being expelled from college. Serious and hilarious by turns, *Invisible Man* earns critical acclaim and receives the National Book Award. **SEE PRIMARY SOURCE DOCUMENT** *Excerpt from* Invisible Man *by Ralph Ellison, p. 351*

Tuskegee reports that 1952 is the first year without lynchings in seventy-one years that statistics have been recorded.

The University of Tennessee admits its first black student.

1953

Bus boycotts begin in Baton Rouge, Louisiana.

President Dwight Eisenhower establishes a committee for non-discriminatory policy in government contract awards.

The movement of blacks into Trumbull Park housing in Chicago, Illinois, starts ongoing riots.

1954

The Supreme Court issues its first decision in the case of *Brown* v. *Board of Education*, abolishing segregation in public schooling and ordering the states to proceed with "all deliberate speed" to desegregate public schools. *Brown* v. *Board of Education* overturns the "separate but equal" doctrine established in 1896 in *Plessy* v. *Ferguson*. School integration begins in Washington, D.C., and Maryland schools. **SEE PRIMARY SOURCE DOCUMENT** *Excerpts from* Brown v. Board of Education *and* Bolling v. Sharpe, *p. 291*

Benjamin O. Davis Jr. is named the first black general in the U.S. Air Force.

President Dwight Eisenhower names J. Ernest Wilkins assistant secretary of labor.

The military announces the elimination of all segregated regiments in the armed forces.

Ralph Bunche is named undersecretary of the United Nations.

1955

The mutilated body of fourteen-year-old Emmett Till is pulled from the Pearl River in Money, Mississippi, on August 28. Till, in Mississippi on a visit from Chicago, was lynched for saying "Hey, baby" to a white woman. Till's mother is allowed to reclaim his body after promising she will bury him in a closed casket, but at his Chicago funeral she leaves the casket open. Black newspapers publish the story and continue to report on it for a full month before it is picked up by the white press. **SEE ENTRY** *The Civil Rights Struggle: From Nonviolence to Black Power, p. 399*

A Baltimore court bans segregated recreational facilities.

Charlie Parker, founder of modern jazz, dies at age thirty-four.

Perhaps no other musician inspires such awe as Charlie Parker. His talent and exhaustive approach to music contributed to the creation of bebop, and much of his technique is still incorporated in modern American music. Photograph by James J. Kriegsmann. **UPI/CORBIS-BETTMANN**

Mary McLeod Bethune, educator and civil rights leader, dies in Florida.

Marian Anderson makes her debut at the Metropolitan Opera House in New York City.

On December 5, Rosa Parks refuses to yield her seat to a white passenger on one of Montgomery's city buses, initiating the Montgomery Bus Boycott, which begins on December 21, bringing Martin Luther King Jr. to national prominence as the principal leader of the new civil rights movement.

1956

First International Conference of Black Writers and Artists is held in Sorbonne, Paris.

Following the Supreme Court's second decision in *Brown* v. *Board of Education,* the Louisville, Kentucky, public schools are integrated on September 10, but the National Guard is called out to control mob violence in Sturgis and Clay, Kentucky, and Clinton, Tennessee, and to provide protection for African American students. In Clinton, a New Jersey segregationist who has come south to stir up hatred among white parents is arrested and jailed. **SEE**

ENTRY *The Civil Rights Struggle: From Nonviolence to Black Power, p. 399*

Autherine Lucy enters the University of Alabama, four years after being accepted and then having her acceptance rescinded when the school administration discovered she is not white. In the wake of the U.S. Supreme Court *Brown* decision, the university is ordered by a federal district court to admit her. Following protests, she is suspended from the school on the grounds that her own safety is in jeopardy. The NAACP protests the suspension, and the federal court orders that the school reinstate her and undertake measures to protect her. Shortly thereafter, Lucy is expelled from the university on the grounds that she has maligned its officials by taking them to court. The NAACP, feeling that further legal action is pointless, does not contest this decision. In 1992 the University of Alabama names an endowed fellowship in her honor.

Birmingham blacks begin mass defiance of "Jim Crow" laws.

African American students enter Clay, Kentucky, public schools with National Guard protection.

Jazz pianist Art Tatum dies.

On January 30, the home of Martin Luther King Jr. is bombed in connection to the bus boycotts in Alabama.

Numerous federal orders and Supreme Court rulings during the year ban segregation in city transportation, and bus actions occur in Tallahassee as well as Birmingham. The Montgomery Bus Boycott ends a year after it began, on December 21, with the integration of the city's buses. **SEE ENTRY** *The Civil Rights Struggle: From Nonviolence to Black Power, p. 400*

The home of Reverend F. L. Shuttlesworth is bombed by Birmingham, Alabama, racial terrorists.

Singer Nat King Cole is attacked on stage in Birmingham, Alabama.

In some quarters white resistance to school integration grows. Segregationists use a variety of stratagems to circumvent court-ordered desegregation, including shutting down schools and forming private schools.

The Spingarn Medal is given to Jackie Robinson for his achievements in baseball and his role in opening the sport to other African Americans.

The Supreme Court refuses to review a lower court decision banning segregation.

The Tennessee National Guard quells mobs protesting school integration.

A white mob impedes black students from entering school in Texas.

1957

Congress passes the Civil Rights Act of 1957, the first such act since 1875. It gives the attorney general greater power to handle interference with the desegregation of public schools and establishes a new Civil Rights Commission. Most importantly, it provides that suits involving the denial of voting rights will be heard in federal rather than state courts, thus providing enforcement for the Constitution's Fourteenth Amendment.

The Southern Christian Leadership Conference is founded in New Orleans on February 14, under the leadership of Martin Luther King Jr. With the legal underpinnings of segregation all but destroyed, King advocates a combined strategy of nonviolent direct action, litigation, economic boycotts, and voter registration to challenge segregation.

In June, African Americans in Tuskegee, Alabama, begin an economic boycott of city stores to protest redrawing of city boundaries that deprives them of the right to vote in city elections.

On September 24, President Eisenhower orders federal troops to Central High School in Little Rock, Arkansas, to provide protection for nine African American students. The federal troops are withdrawn in November, but the National Guard remains in Little Rock until May 8, 1958. **SEE ENTRY** *The Civil Rights Struggle: From Nonviolence to Black Power, p. 400*

Tennis star Althea Gibson wins the women's singles championship at Wimbledon in England.

New York City passes the nation's first fair-housing legislation, the Fair Housing Practice Law, on December 5, banning housing discrimination on the basis of race or religion.

Martin Luther King Jr. is awarded the Spingarn Medal.

A Nashville, Tennessee, school is destroyed by a bomb that is planted to protest the enrollment of black students.

A prayer pilgrimage, held in Washington, D.C., is the largest civil rights demonstration to date.

1959

Lorraine Hansberry's play *A Raisin in the Sun* premieres on Broadway. The story of an extended African American family, it earns critical acclaim and the

Billie Holiday was perhaps the most influential jazz vocalist of the era. Her rise to stardom, however, was marred by personal troubles. Severe depression and drug addiction shortened her career. She died at age forty-four in the hospital where she was under house arrest for possession of narcotics. **ARCHIVE PHOTOS, INC.**

New York Drama Critics' Circle Award. **SEE ENTRY** *The African American Literary Experience, p. 340*

Benjamin O. Davis Jr. is promoted to Major General.

Billie Holiday, celebrated jazz singer, dies at age forty-four.

W. C. Handy, early blues composer and musician, dies.

Ernest Green graduates from Central High School in Little Rock, Arkansas, with six hundred white classmates. The school had become the center of national attention in 1957 when President Eisenhower called for federal troops to protect African American students.

Mack Parker is lynched in Poplarville, Mississippi.

Miles Davis begins historic *Kind of Blue* recording at Columbia Studios in New York City.

Rather than integrate its schools, Prince Edward County, Virginia, closes its public school system on June 26. On May 26, 1964, the Supreme Court will rule that the county cannot evade the Court's decision in *Brown* v. *Board of Education* by simply closing its schools and will order the county to reopen the schools on an integrated basis.

1960

Andrew Hatcher is named associate press secretary for John F. Kennedy.

Bishop Laurean Rugambwa is named the first black cardinal in the modern era.

With new immigration policies promulgated throughout the British Commonwealth, black immigrants from Africa and the West Indies settle in Canada in record numbers. Prior to this period, exclusionary Canadian immigration policy has kept the African Canadian population below twenty-five thousand.

The black population is 18,871,831 (10.5 percent of the U.S. population).

Richard Wright, novelist, political leader (Communist), and essayist, dies.

President Dwight Eisenhower signs the Civil Rights Act of 1960.

Elijah Muhammad, the leader of the Nation of Islam, calls for a Black State. **SEE ENTRY** *The African American Religious Experience, p. 373*

Fayette County, Tennessee, ruling ends restrictions to black voters.

Martin Luther King Jr., is arrested at a student initiated protest in Atlanta. Presidential candidate John F. Kennedy intervenes to secure his release from jail.

The student sit-in movement begins on February 1 in Greensboro, North Carolina. By the next week, sit-ins have been mounted in fifteen southern cities, with the support of the Congress of Racial Equality (CORE). The police become involved in demonstrations across the country. In Nashville, Tennessee, they arrest one hundred school demonstrators. In Florida, they use tear gas to break up student protests. During the year, some fifteen hundred students are arrested and mob violence occurs, but with the use of nonviolent direct action, the sit-in movement successfully desegregates lunch counters first in San Antonio and then throughout the South. At its national convention in July, the Democratic Party adopts a civil rights plank in support of school desegregation and sit-ins. **SEE ENTRY** *The Civil Rights Struggle: From Nonviolence to Black Power, p. 400*

1961

Atlanta Chamber of Commerce announces a plan for the desegregation of lunch counters.

The Freedom Riders, having announced their intention to ride buses through a range of southern states, receive numerous threats: that they will be pulled from the buses and lynched. With the Civil Rights movement gaining ground, it is clear that the Freedom Riders might well be harmed. Robert F. Kennedy, attorney general, sends U.S. Marshals to oversee the safety of the riders.

On May 4, James Farmer, the director of the Congress of Racial Equality, and an integrated group of freedom riders begin a bus trip through the South to test the region's compliance with desegregation rulings. Their bus is bombed in Anniston, Alabama, on May 14. Two weeks later, the Freedom Ride Coordinating Committee is formed in Atlanta, and by midsummer freedom rides are occurring throughout the South. **SEE ENTRY** *The Civil Rights Struggle: From Nonviolence to Black Power, p. 400*

Governor John Patterson declares martial law in Montgomery, Alabama.

President John F. Kennedy names Thurgood Marshall to U.S. circuit court of appeals.

Robert Weaver is appointed director of the U.S. Housing and Home Finance Agency, at the time the highest federal position ever held by an African American. **SEE ENTRY** *The African American Intellectual Experience, p. 409*

President John F. Kennedy appoints Clifton R. Wharton Sr. U.S. ambassador to Norway. He is the first black to attain this position by rising through the ranks of the foreign service.

Police use dogs and tear gas on demonstrators in Baton Rouge, Louisiana.

Purlie Victorious, a play by Ossie Davis, opens on Broadway.

The Supreme Court reverses the conviction of sixteen sit-in students arrested in Baton Rouge.

1962

A battle plays out on the nightly news each evening regarding the effort of James Meredith to enroll in the University of Mississippi. The court of appeals orders Governor Ross Barnett to admit Meredith to classes. The governor, largely in an effort to appease his constituents but also out of personal conviction, declares that he will defy the law in order to promote the values Mississippi holds dear. When Federal Marshals escort Meredith into classes at the university, the students begin to riot, along with family members and citizens. Governor Barnett uses the event as

On the day of the March on Washington in 1963, eleven civil rights leaders posed for a portrait at the base of the Lincoln Memorial. A. Philip Randolph, who first called for a march on Washington in 1941 to protest segregation in the defense industry, is at the center of the first row. Martin Luther King Jr. is to Randolph's left. **NATIONAL ARCHIVES AND RECORDS ADMINISTRATION**

a platform for his anti-integration beliefs. **SEE ENTRY** *The Education of African Americans, p. 276*

The Albany Movement is organized to abolish discrimination in all public facilities in Albany, Georgia. It is supported by the Southern Christian Leadership Conference, the Student Non-Violent Coordinating Committee, NAACP, and the Congress of Racial Equality and led by Martin Luther King Jr. Many of the demonstrators are beaten and jailed, including Dr. King, who leaves Albany without a victory.

Southern school news reports only 7.6 percent of black students attend integrated classes.

1963

James Baldwin, the son of southern migrants, publishes *The Fire Next Time,* a powerful prophecy of the coming chaos of racial violence and hatred. The stepson of a preacher and a preacher himself in his youth, Baldwin portrayed his early life in the black church in his first novel, *Go Tell It on the Mountain,*

published in 1953. The essays he writes during the civil rights struggles of the 1950s and 1960s, including *The Fire Next Time,* bring the African American tradition of the sermon into the political arena. **SEE PRIMARY SOURCE DOCUMENT** *Excerpt from* The Fire Next Time *by James Baldwin, p. 402*

Two black students are escorted into Alabama University over the protests of Governor George C. Wallace.

Nearly a quarter-million people boycott the Chicago school system to protest segregation.

Martin Luther King Jr. opens the desegregation campaign in Birmingham, Alabama, on April 3. Arrested along with two thousand other demonstrators, King addresses a "Letter from Birmingham Jail" to his fellow clergy, denouncing their calls for gradual change. **SEE SIDEBAR** *Martin Luther King Jr. (1929–1968) and the "Letter from Birmingham Jail," p. 400*

On June 12, President John F. Kennedy declares racial prejudice and segregation a "moral issue." He calls on Congress to strengthen voting rights and create job opportunities for African Americans.

Medgar Evers, field director of the National Association for the Advancement of Colored People (NAACP) in Mississippi, is assassinated outside his house in Jackson on June 12. The man charged with his murder is tried twice, with hung juries on both occasions. He is finally convicted at a third trial in 1994.

At the March on Washington on August 28, a quarter of a million people hear Martin Luther King Jr. deliver his "I Have a Dream" speech. On the same day, W. E. B. Du Bois dies in Ghana at the age of 95. Two weeks later, segregationists bomb the Sixteenth Street Baptist Church in Birmingham, killing four African American girls. **SEE ENTRY** *The Civil Rights Struggle: From Nonviolence to Black Power, p. 401*

1964

Blacks and Puerto Ricans boycott New York City schools to protest segregation.

Academy Award given to Sidney Poitier for his performance in *Lilies of the Field.*

The poet and playwright Amiri Baraka (Leroi Jones) establishes the Black Arts Repertory Theater School in Harlem, ushering in the black arts movement. In the same year, Baraka's *Dutchman* receives the Obie Award for the best off-Broadway play. **SEE ENTRY** *The African American Literary Experience, p. 341*

Congress passes the Civil Rights Act of 1964, further empowering the attorney general to protect citizens against discrimination. It forbids discrimination in public accommodations, denies federal funds to programs that engage in discrimination or segregation, and establishes the Equal Employment Opportunity Commission. **SEE ENTRY** *The Civil Rights Struggle: From Nonviolence to Black Power, p. 401*

The bodies of three civil rights workers are discovered in a shallow grave outside Philadelphia, Mississippi, on August 4, the victims of Ku Klux Klan violence. Michael Schwerner, James Chaney, and Andrew Goodman had been missing since June 21. By the year's end, the civil rights struggle in Mississippi will have resulted in three deaths, eighty beatings, more than a thousand arrests, and the bombing of more than sixty churches, homes, and other buildings.

John Conyers Jr. is elected to Congress as a representative from Michigan.

Malcolm X breaks with the Black Muslim movement. No longer bound by Elijah Muhammad's religious structures, he is free to develop his own philosophy of the black freedom struggle.

Martin Luther King Jr. is awarded the Nobel Peace Prize on October 15 for his work in the civil rights movement. It is a curious time because, while King's work on civil rights has been historically and socially popular, after the Nobel Prize he embarks on a course questioning the nature of the capitalist system, and the basic tenets of economic inequality, as opposed to racial inequality. Clearly, King's work in the last years of his life anticipated the social and economic woes of the following decades, including the state of "class discrimination" that characterizes life at the turn of the twenty-first century for many Americans—a sort of discrimination that cuts powerfully along racial lines, but that is accepted as the natural result of a society that applauds economic success. While King is celebrated as one of the great American leaders, few of the books and television programs that applaud Dr. King will discuss at length the ideas he put forward during this period.

Cassius Clay defeats Sonny Liston to take heavyweight crown.

Organization of Afro-American Unity is founded in New York City by Malcolm X.

Race riots occur throughout the country. In New York a demonstration against police brutality turns violent. The rioting spreads to Brooklyn's Bedford-Stuyvesant neighborhood. Race riots also erupt in Chicago, Jersey City, Rochester, and Philadelphia.

1965

First black student enrolled at University of Alabama, Vivian Malone, graduates.

Martin Luther King Jr. leads a successful voting rights campaign in Selma, Alabama. Demonstrations began early in 1965 and reached a turning point on March 7, when a group of demonstrators began a march from Selma to the state capitol in Montgomery. State troopers attack the marchers with tear gas and clubs on the outskirts of Selma. The police assault on the marchers increases national support. President Johnson reacts by introducing the Voting Rights Act of 1965.

President Lyndon Johnson signs into law the 1965 Voting Rights Act, authorizing federal examiners to register African Americans wherever state authorities have refused to do so. On March 7, 1966, the Supreme Court upholds the act, rejecting arguments by southern states that the right to determine voter qualifications is reserved to the states. On the following June 7, James Meredith is shot and wounded in Hernando, Mississippi, while leading a march to dramatize the voter registration drive. On July 12, he

Three attempts were made to march from Selma to Montgomery to call attention to voters' rights. State troopers attacked marchers with batons and tear gas during the first attempt on March 7, 1965, in what was dubbed Bloody Sunday. Martin Luther King, Jr., led the second march and troopers again turned the marchers away. With support from President Johnson, King finally led a successful march from Selma to Montgomery on March 25. **AP/WIDE WORLD PHOTOS**

leads a second march in Canton, Mississippi. **SEE ENTRY** *African Americans in Political Office, p. 402*

In one of the last of the major civil rights actions in the South, the Student Nonviolent Coordinating Committee leads a march of twenty-five thousand people from Selma to the steps of the capitol in Montgomery, Alabama, on March 25, after receiving authorization from a federal judge. This action follows a much smaller march, led by Martin Luther King Jr. and Ralph Bunche. Both marches are intended to dramatize the issue of voting rights.

Dorothy Dandridge is found dead in her apartment. While a great actor, Dandridge is emblematic of the struggles of African American male and female actors in Hollywood during this period. Black actors are offered only a small range of stereotypical roles, making it hard to earn a living, feel pride in their work, and gain official recognition for their artistry.

The mathematician and statistician David H. Blackwell becomes the first African American to be named to the National Academy of Sciences. **SEE ENTRY** *African Americans in the Sciences, p. 422*

Lorraine Hansberry, playwright and author, dies in New York City.

Black liberation leader Malcolm X is assassinated in the presence of his wife and children as he delivers a speech to the Organization of Afro-American Unity at the Audubon Ballroom in New York City. Malcolm founded the OAAU following his break with Elijah Muhammad and the Black Muslims. The question of Malcolm X's murder has never been solved. Some conspiracy theorists believe the FBI, which actively monitored and discredited civil rights leaders, organized the assassination. But the most likely explanation seems to be that the killing was ordered from within the Nation of Islam. The Nation and Elijah Muhammad, who viewed Malcolm X with a combination of jealousy and desperate concern, were being seriously compromised by Malcolm's militant stance and sophisticated manipulation of the media. He had become much larger than those he was supposed to serve and promote and was using the Nation of Islam as a platform for the effective overthrow of the racial status quo, rather than for building an Islamic faith organization with many committed members in its fold. **SEE**

ENTRY *The African American Religious Experience, p. 373*

Nat King Cole, singer and early black television performer, dies in California.

On April 11, members of St. Thomas Episcopal Church in Philadelphia, the nation's oldest African American Episcopal church, vote to annul their 1796 charter limiting the congregation to "Africans and descendants of African race."

Spingarn Medal is awarded to Leontyne Price.

Watts Riots break out in Los Angeles: 34 are killed, 1,032 are injured. Property damage amounts to more than 35 million dollars.

1966

More than 2,400 people attend a White House conference on Civil Rights.

Bill Russell is named the coach of the Boston Celtics. He is the first black to coach a professional team.

Huey P. Newton and Bobby Seale found the Black Panther Party for Self-Defense. The party expands from its base in Oakland, California, to become a national organization.

Rioting occurs in the Watts section of Los Angeles on March 16, and in African American neighborhoods of Chicago and Cleveland during July. While there were many riots in the previous years, the Watts riots usher in an age of violent confrontation within the inner-cities of America and bring them to national attention.

The Supreme Court rules on March 25 that Virginia's poll tax is unconstitutional, thus invalidating similar taxes in other states. Poll taxes have historically been used to deprive African Americans of the vote.

On July 1, delegates at the national convention of the Congress of Racial Equality (CORE) vote to endorse the concept of black power, first enunciated by a spokesman of the Student Nonviolent Coordinating Committee (SNCC), Stokely Carmichael. The outspoken, militant stance endorsed by the black power movement helps distance the SNCC from the more moderate approaches endorsed by the leadership of competing civil rights organizations. A few days later, the National Association for the Advancement of Colored People (NAACP) publicly disavows the concept. This is the beginning of the black power phase of the civil rights movement. It will attract younger African Americans who take issue with the nonviolent direct-action tactics of Martin Luther King Jr. and the Southern Christian Leadership Conference

(SCLC). In addition, it is a part of the trajectory established by Malcolm X, and many believe the presence of militant and violent race organizations forced the institutional powers to look at the demands of King and the NAACP as reasoned and worthwhile. As Malcolm X put it, "they could deal with him [Martin Luther King Jr.] or they could deal with me." **SEE ENTRY** *The Civil Rights Struggle: From Nonviolence to Black Power, p. 402*

Edward Brooke of Massachusetts becomes the first black senator since the Reconstruction Era.

Julian Bond is denied a seat on the Georgia legislature for his opposition to the Vietnam War.

On July 10 Martin Luther King Jr. opens his Chicago campaign to call attention to northern segregation in housing, jobs, and schooling. A few days later, rioting breaks out in the African American neighborhoods of Chicago's West Side. The campaign dramatizes the widening rift between the black power and nonviolent wings of the civil rights movement when King and other demonstrators are stoned in the white neighborhood of Gage Park on August 5.

National Guard is mobilized to quell various riots and disturbances.

Robert Weaver is named the secretary of housing and urban development, becoming the first black cabinet member.

1967

In a unanimous vote, the Supreme Court invalidates all remaining antimiscegenation laws on June 12.

Carl Stokes of Cleveland, Ohio, is elected the first black mayor of a major metropolitan city.

H. Rap Brown becomes Stokely Carmichael's successor as National Chairman of SNCC where he continues a militant stance.

Jimi Hendrix's "Foxy Lady" climbs the charts in U.S.

Major Robert H. Lawrence is named the first black astronaut. **SEE ENTRY** *African Americans in the Sciences, p. 424*

Martin Luther King Jr. announces his opposition to the Vietnam War, alienating some of his strongest allies in government, including President Lyndon Johnson.

Adam Clayton Powell Jr. is expelled from the House of Representatives. It is the first time since 1919 that the House had expelled one of its members. Powell vows to fight the case all the way to the Supreme

African Americans, able to vote for the first time, line up outside a local general store in rural Alabama in 1966. The signing of the 1965 Voting Rights Act ensured that African Americans would be registered to vote and rejected southern states' arguments that they could set voter qualifications. **CORBIS-BETTMANN**

Court. However, he wins a special election to fill his own vacant seat.

Muhammad Ali is convicted of violating the Selective Service Act. His stance on the Vietnam War causes him to be stripped of his heavyweight title, beginning a period of alienation and economic and social struggle for the boxer turned activist.

Thurgood Marshall becomes the nation's first African American associate justice of the Supreme Court in September, when the Senate confirms President Lyndon Johnson's nomination. A graduate of Lincoln and Howard Universities, Marshall joins the Court with an impressive array of legal victories behind him, most famously, *Brown* v. *Board of Education,* which led to the undoing of the "separate but equal" legal precedent that supported segregation policies during the first half of the twentieth century. During the twenty-four years he serves on the Court, Marshall will consistently vote to uphold affirmative-action programs and to oppose the death penalty, restrictions on women's reproductive rights, and restrictions on the First Amendment right of free speech.

1968

Arthur Ashe becomes the first black winner of the U.S. Open Tennis Championship.

Martin Luther King Jr. addresses poverty and the imbalances of capitalism in many speeches.

Martin Luther King Jr. is assassinated on April 4 in Memphis, Tennessee, where he has arrived to assist striking sanitation workers. Many speculate the assassination is the work of those organized within the government and the FBI. With his new targets of economic and social inequality, he was branded a "communist" and many feared if he had half the success he had had with civil rights, it would mean significant change for elements of government and, more importantly, the big businesses that rely on an inexpensive African American labor force to turn their profits. In the week that follows, rioting occurs in 125 American cities, including Newark, New Jersey, and Detroit, Michigan, with the loss of thirty-eight lives. Twenty thousand federal troops, and 34,000 National Guardsmen are mobilized to quell riots. **SEE ENTRY** *The Civil Rights Struggle: From Nonviolence to Black Power, p. 402*

At the 1968 Olympics, two medalists raise fists in the famous Black Power salute, which brought the cause of black Americans seeking to change society in the United States to an international stage. **AP/WIDE WORLD PHOTOS**

The Civil Rights Act of 1968 is passed on April 10, banning discrimination in most of the nation's housing. This is another victory for the members of the NAACP legal fund and its descendants. The movement that began with the challenge to the segregation of students in public institutions will over the following decades be applied again and again in all sectors of society. **SEE ENTRY** *African Americans and the Law, p. 250*

Athletes John Carlos and Tommie Smith display the black power salute on the medal stand at the Mexico City Olympics.

A record number of black congressmen (and the first black congresswoman, Shirley Chisholm of New York) are elected.

1969

Black Panther Party's clashes with police decimate party leadership. Fred Hampton and Mark Clark are killed in a raid. Eldridge Cleaver leaves for exile to avoid returning to prison. Bobby Seale is arrested for conspiracy to incite rioting at the 1968 Democratic Convention in Chicago. In May Connecticut officials charge Seale and seven other Panthers with murder in the slaying of party member Alex Rackley. In New York twenty-one Panthers are charged with plotting to assassinate policemen and blow up buildings. Nearly all the charges brought against Panther members either do not result in convictions or are overturned on appeal. The prosecutions absorb much of the party's resources.

James Earl Ray pleads guilty and is sentenced to 99 years in prison, but not the death penalty despite its wide application in Tennessee, for the murder of Martin Luther King Jr. Many fear that Ray is only the patsy for a conspiracy organized by government or government-related groups.

Moneta Sleet, a photographer whose work appears in *Ebony* magazine, becomes the first African American man to receive the Pulitzer Prize.

1970

In San Rafael, California, three Soledad Prison inmates, including George Jackson, are being tried for the murder of a prison guard when Jackson's brother Jonathan enters the courtroom, holds the room at gunpoint, and distributes weapons to the three defendants. A dramatic shootout results in four people getting killed, including a judge and Jonathan Jackson. During the investigation several of the guns are traced to Marxist activist Angela Davis, who is placed on the FBI's Ten Most Wanted List. Distrustful of the judicial system, Davis goes into hiding but is later arrested in New York City for unlawful evasion.

The black population is 22,600,000 (11.1 percent of the U.S. population).

Charles Godone is awarded the Pulitzer Prize for his play *No Place to Go.*

Benjamin O. Davis Sr. dies. A retired general, Davis climbed the ranks of the military like no African American before him—and few afterward.

Joe Frazier knocks out Jimmy Ellis for heavyweight title.

Painter Jacob Lawrence is awarded the Spingarn Medal.

Jimi Hendrix, an astonishing original rock musician and innovator, dies. In a world where the roles for black entertainers were limited to soul, gospel, and pop-related ventures, Hendrix became a superstar of the rock-and-roll movement. His performances, his stage antics, (including setting his guitar on fire), and

The inimitable Louis Armstrong (1901–1971) was perhaps the most innovative jazz musician of all time. As a trumpeter and as a singer, Armstrong left his mark on every song he took up and a tradition of excellence for other musicians who followed. **AP/WIDE WORLD PHOTOS**

his revolutionary approach to recording still serve as examples to nearly everyone who seeks to make a mark in entertainment. His accidental death by drug overdose is said to have robbed the world of a visionary whose work transcended the angry dialectic of race that dominated his time.

Voting Rights Act is extended by Richard Nixon.

1971

Richard Nixon rejects sixty demands of Congressional Black Caucus.

Jazz great Louis Armstrong dies.

Twelve congressmen boycott Richard Nixon's State of the Union address for his refusal to address black issues. In many ways, Richard Nixon's angry and non-participatory attitude toward congressional black leaders was the model used by Republican leaders in the decades that followed. Republican Presidents Reagan and Bush employed similar tactics, working to appease the public and black leaders while pushing legislation that would have devastating effects on the African American population.

Congressional Black Caucus is organized. **SEE ENTRY** *African Americans in Political Office, p. 207*

Ralph Bunche, Nobel Peace Prize winner, dies in New York.

Samuel Gravely Jr. becomes the first black admiral in the U.S. Navy.

Vernon E. Jordan is appointed executive director of the National Urban League.

1972

Angela Davis is acquitted by a white jury for her alleged role in a 1970 courtroom shooting in San Rafael, California, in which a judge and three others were killed.

Mahalia Jackson, gospel singer, dies in Illinois.

NAACP reports that unemployment of blacks is worse than at any other time since the Great Depression.

Eight thousand African Americans from every region of the Unites States attend the first National Black Political Convention in Gary, Indiana. The convention approves a platform that demands reparations for slavery, proportional congressional representation for blacks, the elimination of capital punishment, increased federal spending to combat drug trafficking, a reduced military budget, and a guaranteed income of $6,500 for a family of four.

Richard Nixon is reelected, despite a large black turnout for George McGovern, a reflection more of black mistrust of Nixon than black support for McGovern.

Forty years of medical experimentation on human subjects come to light and become the worst medical scandal in U.S. history. The Tuskegee Syphilis Experiment (1932–1972) was a study conducted by the U.S. Public Health Service. It involved observing the effects of untreated syphilis on several hundred black men living in rural Alabama. The study proceeded without the informed consent of the participants. The study is still ongoing in 1972 when a whistle-blower inside the PHS leaks the story to the press. Health officials try to defend their actions but public outrage silences them as they agree to end the experiment.

1973

Arna Bontemps, celebrated writer and educator, dies in Tennessee.

Thomas Bradley is elected mayor of Los Angeles.

1974

Two blacks sit on the committee deciding whether to impeach President Richard Nixon in the Watergate scandal.

Edward "Duke" Ellington dies. His work as a band leader, performer, and composer reflects a genius for organizing, composing, and melding a vast range of American musical traditions. His vision encompasses a "classical" reserve and appreciation for the thousands of pages of music that passed across his music stand. As musicologists begin to deal with the implications of jazz as an "American classical music," Ellington emerges as one of the great minds of the twentieth century. **SEE SIDEBAR** *Duke Ellington and the Evolution of American Classical Music, p. 329*

Hank Aaron breaks Babe Ruth's home run record. Although Aaron will come to be viewed as one of the all-time undisputed kings of baseball, he receives death threats and nasty letters intended to demoralize him in his quest for greatness.

Muhammad Ali defeats George Foreman in Zaire for the heavyweight boxing title.

1975

Elijah Muhammad, leader of the Nation of Islam, dies at age seventy-seven.

Josephine Baker, singer and performer, dies in Paris, France.

Frank Robinson becomes the first black to manage a major league baseball team when he debuts in April as player-manager for the Cleveland Indians.

1976

Seventeen black members of Congress are reelected.

Paul Robeson, singer and activist, dies in Philadelphia, Pennsylvania.

President Gerald Ford presents the Medal of Freedom to Jesse Owens for his "inspirational life" and for his contribution to the ideals of freedom and democracy. Owens won four gold medals at the 1936 Olympic Games in Berlin, upsetting his Nazi hosts (as well as racists on both sides of the Atlantic), and disputing Adolf Hitler's belief in Aryan racial superiority.

FBI documents reveal an extensive campaign conducted against civil rights leaders.

1977

Roots, the television miniseries dramatization of Alex Haley's novel of black history, is one of the greatest successes in the history of television. Close to 130 million Americans follow the 300-year saga chronicling the travails of African Americans in their trajectory from Africa to Emancipation.

Erroll Garner, jazz pianist and innovator, dies in Los Angeles.

1978

The U.S. Supreme Court rules in a 5 to 4 decision, in *Regents of the University of California* v. *Bakke,* that the University of California must admit Allan Bakke to its medical school. Bakke had charged that he was rejected because preference was given to minority students with lower scores. The Court rules that race *can* be considered in admissions decisions, but that schools cannot apply rigid quotas for minorities.

African American scientists Guion Bluford Jr., Frederick D. Gregory, and Ronald E. McNair become part of the nation's space program, joining the National Aeronautics and Space Administration (NASA) as astronauts in training. McNair, a laser physicist, will perish with the rest of the crew of the space shuttle *Challenger* in 1986, when the shuttle explodes after takeoff. **SEE ENTRY** *African Americans in the Sciences, p. 424*

More than nine hundred people, mostly black, die in Guyana in Jonestown mass suicide under cultist Jim Jones. He and many members of the religious community that he led, The People's Temple, moved from California to South America the year before.

1979

Arthur Lewis becomes the first black to receive a Nobel Prize in a category other than peace when he is honored for his work in economics.

The number of black women earning doctorates in mathematics, science, and engineering exceeds that of black men for the first time, a trend which has continued to the present day. **SEE ENTRY** *African Americans in the Sciences, p. 424*

The first raps are recorded in this year, when a Brooklyn group, Fatback Band, brings out "King Tim III (Personality Jock)" and the Sugar Hill Gang records "Rapper's Delight." Rapping has already been in existence for some three years when these songs are recorded. **SEE ENTRY** *The History of African American Music, p. 330*

Frank E. Petersen is named the first black general in the U.S. Marine Corps.

Ku Klux Klansmen kill five participants attending an anti-Klan meeting in Greensboro, North Carolina.

The Supreme Court rules that employers can use quotas to aid minorities in employment.

Charles Mingus, jazz bass player and American composer, dies.

1980

The black population is 26,500,000 (11.7 percent of the U.S. population).

Jesse Owens, winner of four gold medals in the 1936 Berlin Olympics, dies in Tucson, Arizona.

Joe Louis, who is regarded by many as the greatest heavyweight champion, dies in Nevada.

Labor Department announces black unemployment at 14 percent.

Ronald Reagan is elected president despite widespread protest from civil rights groups.

Vernon E. Jordan Jr., executive director of the National Urban League, is shot in the back. One suspect is

Hank Aaron surpasses Babe Ruth's record by hitting his 715th home run on April 8, 1974. Once thought of as an unbreakable mark, many baseball fans did not want to see it broken, especially by an African American. As he neared the record, Aaron was inundated by thousands of pieces of hate mail daily. **CORBIS-BETTMANN**

tried and acquitted on the charge of violating Jordan's civil rights, not attempted murder.

1981

Acquired Immune Deficiency Syndrome (AIDS) first receives national media attention. Although the disease is widely regarded as affecting mainly white gay men, it is clear by the end of the decade that African Americans can no longer deny the extent to which it is affecting their community. (Cultural taboos against homosexuality are often cited as the reason for the denial among blacks.)

After a meteoric rise, Jean Michel Basquiat carries the somewhat dubious honor of being the first black painter to succeed in white, largely European, art establishment, largely because of his race. Basquiat's success was also his undoing. Saddled with pressure to always outdo his last artistic success, Basquiat's origins as an angry adolescent, street waif and occasional

A piano player of the bebop period and beyond, Thelonious Monk had a curious touch and brilliant mode of phrasing. He composed pieces that have become among the most revered of jazz standards, such as "Rhythm-a-ning" and "'Round Midnight." He died in 1982. **AP/WIDE WORLD PHOTOS**

prostitute developed into a life of constant drug use, and cocaine and heroin dependency. He died of an overdose in 1989 at the age of 28. **SEE SIDEBAR** *The African American Urban Artist: Rap, Graffiti, and the Painting of Jean-Michel Basquiat, p. 441*

Vernon E. Jordan Jr. resigns as executive director of the National Urban League.

1982

The administration of President Ronald Reagan fights vigorously against a third extension of the Voting Rights Act of 1965. Nevertheless, the Act is not only extended, but it is also amended to address the wide range of strategies designed to circumvent it.

Jazz pianist and bebop innovator, Thelonious Monk, dies.

1983

Alice Walker's *The Color Purple,* the story of an abused black southern woman who learns to stand up for

herself, is published. Told in a series of letters, the novel receives the Pulitzer Prize for fiction. **SEE ENTRY** *The African American Literary Experience, p. 342*

Harold Washington is sworn in as the first black mayor of Chicago.

Jesse Jackson announces on the television program "60 Minutes" that he will run for the Democratic nomination for the presidency. He will garner an impressive 3.3 million votes out of the approximately 18 million cast.

President Ronald Reagan signs into law a bill making Martin Luther King Jr.'s birthday a national holiday.

Vannessa Williams becomes the first black woman to win the Miss America title. Her reign ends abruptly when nude photographs of her surface.

1984

Benjamin Hooks, executive director of the NAACP, leads a 125,000-person March on Washington to protest the "legal lynching" of civil rights by the Reagan administration.

The Cosby Show premieres on NBC in the fall. The show, which features Bill Cosby as Cliff Huxtable, an obstetrician living with his wife and four children in a brownstone in New York City, breaks new ground by representing the daily lives of an African American upper-middle-class family, which had been rarely seen on American television.

Bishop Desmond Tutu is awarded the Nobel Peace Prize for opposition to South African apartheid.

During the summer games held in Los Angeles, Carl Lewis wins four gold medals, becoming the first athlete to match Jesse Owens's domination of the track and field events at the 1936 Berlin Olympics.

Jesse Jackson formally withdraws from presidential race.

Singer Marvin Gaye is shot and killed by his father in Los Angeles.

In November, Randall Robinson and other activists begin an anti-apartheid vigil in front of the South African embassy in Washington, D.C. The vigil, which raises awareness about the evils of apartheid and expresses opposition to President Reagan's policy of constructive engagement, lasts over fifty-three weeks.

1985

In a final showdown with police, eleven members of the group MOVE are killed when a bomb is dropped on their headquarters in Philadelphia. MOVE's philosophy—rejecting the "man-made" or "unnatural" and refusing to subscribe to "man's laws"—brought its members into conflict with social workers concerned over children and with neighbors who complained of garbage and fecal odors and rat infestations.

Bernard Goetz, a white man who shot four New York City black youths, paralyzing one of them, is indicted on weapons charge. He is dubbed the "Subway Vigilante" during the trial that follows.

Patricia Roberts Harris, the first black woman ambassador and cabinet member, dies in Washington, D.C.

1986

Centers for Disease Control and Prevention reports that blacks constitute 25 percent of those taken by AIDS.

African American scientist-astronaut Ronald McNair is killed when the ill-fated space shuttle *Challenger* explodes shortly after liftoff on January 28. In February, the Massachusetts Institute of Technology names the building that houses its Center for Space Research after McNair.

Spike Lee's first film, *She's Gotta Have It,* is released and is a popular success. It is followed by several other successful films, including *Do the Right Thing* (1989) and *Malcolm X* (1992). Lee becomes the first black filmmaker to consistently treat themes of African American cultural identity and to do so with critical and commercial success.

The Supreme Court upholds affirmative action as a remedy for past discrimination by a 6-3 vote.

1987

August Wilson receives a Pulitzer Prize for his play *Fences.*

Bernard Goetz is found not guilty of attempted murder for the shooting of black New York City youths.

Colin Powell is named the White House National Security Adviser.

Novelist and activist James Baldwin dies. Baldwin's extraordinary career led him eventually to live a quiet life in the south of France where he felt, as a black man and as a homosexual, he could lead a more fulfilled existence.

1988

Romare Bearden, regarded as one of the greatest black painters of the century, dies.

Poet and scholar Sterling Brown dies. Brown, though not well known outside of literary circles, is one of the most important African American literary figures of the twentieth century. Like Paul Laurence

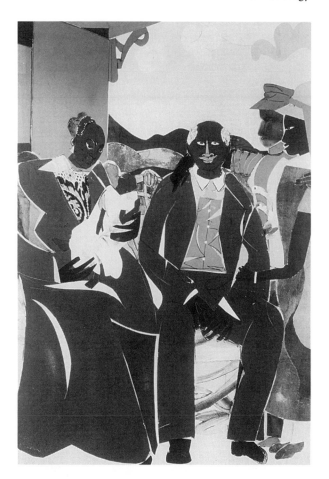

Family, a collage on wood, was inspired by artist Romare Bearden's childhood memories. **THE ESTATE OF ROMARE BEARDEN**

Dunbar before him, Brown focused on the formal elements of English language letters. Within the various sonnet and balladic traditions. Sterling Brown celebrated the African American vernacular, working southern and eastern black speech, humor, culture and identity into the shape of "English" letters, thereby creating an American literary tradition and forever inscribing African American letters into the trajectory set out by the likes of William Shakespeare, John Milton, Edmond Spenser, and John Donne. **SEE SIDEBAR** *Twentieth-Century African American Poet Sterling Brown (1901–1989), p. 353*

At the Seoul Olympic Games, track-and-field athlete Florence Griffith Joyner, popularly known as "Flo Jo," wins three gold medals, tying Wilma Rudolph's 1960 record. Her sister-in-law Jackie Joyner-Kersee wins the gold medal in the heptathlon—the most demanding event in women's track and field—making her "America's best all-around female athlete."

Sportscaster Jimmy "the Greek" Snyder is fired after making racist remarks.

One of the first ladies of rap, Queen Latifah opened the door for countless women trying to succeed in the male-dominated musical genre. **AP/WIDE WORLD PHOTOS**

Motown Records is sold to MCA/Boston Ventures for $61,000,000.

Novelist Toni Morrison wins the Pulitzer Prize for her novel *Beloved.* Morrison's novel deals with the legacy of slavery in the years following the Civil War.

Jesse Jackson makes a strong showing in the Democratic presidential primaries, coming in either first or second in thirty-one out of thirty-six primaries, and accruing almost seven million votes out of a total of twenty-three million cast.

For the first time, the Supreme Court reverses an affirmative action judicial policy. The ruling, based on the idea that affirmative action is a form of reverse racial discrimination, begins a process of reversals by the Supreme Court on matters of affirmative action. In universities, however, the presence of a diverse student body remains popular. So while these rulings slowly begin to undo the advances made, the concept and spirit of affirmative action hold in many public institutions and continue up until the end of the century to affect admissions policies for many private institutions.

1989

The Centers for Disease Control and Prevention report that in the United States African Americans are twice as likely as whites to contract AIDS; more than one-half of all women with the disease are African American; about 70 percent of babies born with the disease are African American; and nearly one-fourth of all males with the disease are African American.

Census Bureau reports black poverty at 31.6 percent versus 10.1 percent for whites.

Colonel Frederick Gregory is the first black put in charge of a space mission when he is named the commander for missions of the space shuttle *Discovery.*

Roy Eldridge, trumpet player, dies in Valley Stream, New York.

President George Bush names General Colin Powell chairman of the Joint Chiefs of Staff. Not only is Powell the first African American to hold this position, but he is also the youngest. His role in the Persian Gulf War will vault him to prominence and further his political career.

Labor Department reports black unemployment at 11.9 percent versus white unemployment at 4.3 percent.

Ron Brown is elected chairman of the Democratic Party, becoming the first black person to head a major party.

The Supreme Court rules that whites can seek redress in "reverse discrimination" suits.

1990

In the predominantly white neighborhood of Bensonhurst, New York, a group of whites shoots and kills black sixteen-year-old Yusuf Hawkins who has come to the neighborhood to look at a used car. Protest marches in the wake of the incident are plagued by violence between protesters and hostile residents of the neighborhood. Five whites are eventually convicted and sentenced for the killing.

The black population is 29,987,060 (12.1 percent of the U.S. population).

Sarah Vaughan, jazz vocalist, dies. Likely the greatest female jazz vocalist of the century beside Ella Fitzgerald, Vaughan's effortless range and grace may be heard on many great jazz recordings of the last seven decades.

Charles Johnson publishes the novel *Middle Passage,* the surreal tale of a black American who signs on with the crew of a slave ship. Critically acclaimed, *Middle Passage* receives the National Book Award. **SEE**

ENTRY *The African American Literary Experience, p. 343*

Dexter Gordon, jazz musician, dies in Philadelphia, Pennsylvania.

Entertainer Sammy Davis Jr. dies in Beverly Hills, California.

It is difficult to pinpoint the exact emergence of hip-hop to a specific year. However, this vocalese rhyming tradition that evolved out of the roots of rap music dominated much of the 1990s, and in the beginning of the next century began to be re-integrated back into various mainstream music, such as rock-and-roll, R&B, soul, and even gospel.

Washington, D.C., mayor Marion Barry is arrested for drug use. Barry is convicted of cocaine possession and serves a six-month prison sentence.

On the national front, the debate regarding affirmative action is beginning to heat up. President George Bush caves to conservative pressure, vetoing the 1990 Civil Rights Bill. He then reverses course and signs the 1991 Civil Rights Act.

1991

President George Bush lifts all sanctions against South Africa, stating that the country "had made progress."

President George Bush nominates Clarence Thomas, a right-wing African American conservative jurist, to the Supreme Court. After a bitter confirmation process in which Thomas is accused of sexual misconduct with a female colleague, Anita Hill, he is appointed to the bench.

Riots break out between blacks and Jews in Crown Heights, Brooklyn, when a young black boy is killed by a car driven by a Jewish driver.

Persian Gulf War breaks out; 24.5 percent of the servicemen engaged are black; 15 percent of the casualties are black.

Police officers in Los Angeles stop a car driven by an African American named Rodney King. The four officers proceed to kick and beat him with clubs, fracturing his skull and one of his legs. A witness records King's beating on videotape. The tape is broadcast throughout the country. Within two weeks the police officers are indicted on charges that include assault with a deadly weapon.

Thurgood Marshall, the first black justice, announces his retirement from the Supreme Court.

Perhaps the greatest professional basketball player ever to take the court, in the 1990s Michael Jordan astounded fans around the world by leading the Chicago Bulls to six championships in eight years. In 2001 he returned to the court in a different uniform, playing for the Washington Wizards. **©SCOTT WACHTER/CORBIS-BETTMANN**

Miles Davis, one of the most talented jazz horn players of the twentieth century, dies. **SEE SIDEBAR** *Miles Davis (1926–1991), Jazz Innovator, p. 334*

Whoopi Goldberg wins Academy Award for best supporting actress for her performance in *Ghost*.

1992

Bill Clinton is elected president. Clinton's election ushers in a new age of politics and a new image of government. During the following years, Clinton consistently takes symbolic stances on issues of historical importance to African Americans. Black voters provide the margin of victory in numerous states.

Vernon Jordan serves as the head of the transition team for President Bill Clinton.

Maya Angelou represents a new generation of female intellectuals, a literary and poetic superstar who has written countless essays and treatises on the condition of life in the United States for African Americans, including the powerful memoir *I Know Why the Caged Bird Sings.* AP/WIDE WORLD PHOTOS

Alex Haley, author of the Pulitzer Prize–winning *Roots,* dies.

Blues singer Willie Dixon dies in Burbank, California.

Poet Derek Walcott is awarded the Nobel Prize for Literature.

After an astonishing acquittal in the case of four officers who were recorded beating an unarmed Rodney King, mass rioting ensues across the nation. The event is one of a series of troubling racial events that unfold before the nation's eyes on the television screen. These riots and the O. J. Simpson case come to characterize the beginning of the era of the 24-hour news cycle, and also bring stories of racial injustice into a new sort of national forum. Some later argue that the coverage is part of a process of "unveiling" where racial inequality is concerned, and that it forces a new age of racial responsibility.

The Cosby Show ends its ground-breaking run on network television.

Mike Tyson, former heavyweight champion, is convicted of rape and sentenced to six years in prison.

Spike Lee releases his film *Malcolm X,* which is based on the autobiography of the slain civil rights leader.

1993

Bill Clinton asks poet Maya Angelou to compose and read a poem at his inauguration.

President Bill Clinton appoints a record number of African Americans in his new administration. Those positions include secretaries of energy, agriculture, and commerce; head of veterans affairs; and surgeon general.

Thurgood Marshall, Supreme Court Justice for twenty-four years, dies. His extraordinary contributions to American life are memorialized in an outpouring of popular grief and adulation.

Police Sergeant Stacey C. Koon and Officer Laurence M. Powell are found guilty of violating Rodney King's civil rights after being tried again in federal court.

"Dizzy" Gillespie, a seminal figure during the golden age of jazz, dies.

Rita Dove, winner of the 1987 Pulitzer Prize in poetry, is named poet laureate of the United States, the youngest person ever to be named to this position.

James Morgan, last of the Buffalo Soldiers, dies at the age of 100.

African American novelist Toni Morrison is awarded the Nobel Prize for literature. Among her works are *Song of Solomon,* a novel of the urban migration that makes use of the African American folktale of the flying Africans, and *Beloved,* a novel about slavery based on the true story of Margaret Garner, a fugitive slave mother who was willing to kill her children rather than see them returned to slavery. **SEE SIDE-BAR** *African American Novelist Toni Morrison (b. 1931), p. 343*

1994

President Bill Clinton's plan for universal health care, a focal point for the last two years of his term, is defeated in the legislature.

The Florida legislature agrees to pay up to $150,000 to each survivor of the Rosewood Massacre. On New Year's Day in 1923 a white woman claimed that she had been assaulted by a black man. A white mob marched to the small black community of Rosewood in search of the man. Failing to find him they proceeded to burn nearly every house. Many people fled the violence.

The Spingarn Medal is awarded to Maya Angelou for excellence in international literature.

Ralph Ellison, essayist and author of the *Invisible Man,* dies.

Cabel "Cab" Calloway, bandleader and jazz pioneer, dies.

1995

Louis Farrakhan of the Nation of Islam organizes the Million Man March as an opportunity for black men to take responsibility for their lives and communities. Many turn out for the march. It stimulates black voter registration and political activism.

The WB Network is launched, signaling a new, transformative age of programming among the major television networks. Instead of trying to fill quotas, networks begin to seek out the most popular entertainers they can find for their dollar—and increasingly those entertainers are black Americans.

The Spingarn Medal is awarded to John Hope Franklin, historian and African American studies scholar.

University of California votes to end affirmative action policies in admissions and hiring.

O.J. Simpson is found not guilty of two counts of murder in a heavily publicized trial in which he is accused of killing his ex-wife Nicole Brown Simpson and her acquaintance Ronald Goldman. The verdict results in widespread debate among Americans, with some believing that the acquittal is just recompense for the abuses committed against African Americans within the U.S. legal system. In 1997, he is found guilty of wrongful death in a civil suit.

1996

As a result of the buoyant economy and the beginning of Democratic Party efforts to decrease debt and balance the national budget, African Americans enjoy one of the best periods of prosperity in the course of the century.

African American women constitute 6.5 percent of the enlisted personnel in the armed services.

1997

In a significant gesture, President Bill Clinton offers an apology to the descendants of black Americans involved in the clandestine "Tuskegee Syphilis Experiment" between the years of 1932 and 1972. This is viewed as particularly important, as American presidents have always been careful not to apologize to African Americans for wrongs committed as a result of social attitudes of general inequality; the apology sets a precedent that many believe will have implications for the "reparations for slavery" movement.

Rapper Sean "Puffy" Combs (now known as P. Diddy) has parlayed his career into several ventures. As well as being an entertainer, he has produced other artists' records, has issued a line of clothing, and has formed a film production company.
AP/WIDE WORLD PHOTOS

1998

The FBI reports that crimes with race as a primary motivating factor declined during the course of the year to 4,710 from 5,396 in 1996.

The Spingarn Medal is awarded to Myrlie Evers Williams for four decades of civil rights service and leadership.

President Bill Clinton signs welfare reform, forcing tens of thousands off welfare rolls.

Michael Jordan wins his fifth championship with the Chicago Bulls. Jordan's return to basketball after a year spent playing baseball, and subsequent domination of the sport make him into one of the highest paid athletes in the history of American sport-particularly in the area of endorsements, where he earns an estimated 25 to 30 million dollars a year. In many ways, Jordan also single-handedly brings an image of the African American male as handsome, dominant, a fierce competitor, and a man of character to the American public.

Texaco settles a class action suit brought by its African American employees.

Denzel Washington has won two Academy Awards, one for his supporting role in the Civil War drama *Glory,* and one for his stunning portrayal of a corrupt police officer in *Training Day.* Photograph by Lee Celano. **REUTERS/CORBIS-BETTMANN**

1999

In February, Amadou Diallo, a young African immigrant, is shot and killed by four New York City policemen in the doorway of his Bronx apartment building. Forty-one shots are fired. Local residents protest over police brutality. Rallies are held everyday outside of police headquarters until the police officers are indicted for murder. Many prominent citizens are arrested daily, including David Dinkins, Carl McCall, Ossie Davis, Ruby Dee, and Susan Sarandon.

During the course of the 1990s figures like Tupac Shakur, Dr. Dre, Sean Puffy Combs, and Jay-Z emerge as international entrepreneurs, diversified among a range of entertainment and media-related industries. This stands in stark contrast to earlier generations that were often taken advantage of by their managers and record labels.

President Bill Clinton is impeached for lying in a court deposition regarding his affair with an intern and related issues. Insufficient votes in the Senate keep him from being removed from office.

Toni Morrison is awarded the Nobel Prize for Literature.

Milton "Bags" Jackson, jazz vibraphonist and founding member of the modern jazz quartet, dies.

2000

Tiger Woods becomes the youngest player to win all four major golf championships (the British Open, the Masters, the PGA Championship, and the U.S. Open).

The 2000 census makes various changes in semantics and the racial categories offered to participants. As a result, a dramatically different picture of America emerges. The number of Hispanics and other groups skyrockets, as well as those identifying themselves as of mixed ethnic origin. Many speculate that further changes, better clarifying or doing away with the "other" category, might mean another seismic shift in the nation's ethnic identity. The census suggests those identifying as simply "Caucasian Americans" will be another minority segment of the American ethnic diversity, perhaps by the year 2025.

Vashti Murphy McKenzie is appointed the first female bishop of the African Methodist Episcopal Church in its 213-year history.

In perhaps the most closely contested presidential election in the history of the United States, two-term Texas governor George W. Bush beats the sitting vice president, Albert Gore, by 763 votes in Florida to take its electoral votes and the presidency despite Gore's victory in the popular election by approximately a half million votes. The election is not decided until days after the final votes are cast, and hinges on a partial recount and the allowance of disputed overseas and absentee votes. The process is plagued by confusing voting cards that caused tens of thousands of votes from largely Democratic counties to be discounted. African Americans across the state are left off registration lists and a pattern of intimidation by state troopers and other officials of a state controlled by the challenger's brother, Jeb Bush, the governor of Florida, are widely reported. African Americans kept from polling places in Florida file legal challenges.

2001

President George W. Bush's cabinet member selections are confirmed by the Senate. Two of the conservative African Americans selected, Secretary of State Colin Powell and National Security Adviser Condoleezza Rice, served in Bush's father's administration. Dr. Roderick Paige is named secretary of education.

President George W. Bush's selection for attorney general, John Ashcroft, is confirmed by the Senate. Ashcroft's opposition to a school desegregation plan for St. Louis while he was Missouri state attorney general and his stance against affirmative action make him an unpopular choice among many African Americans.

Despite bad economic forecasts that began to appear in the last months of President Bill Clinton's second term in office, George W. Bush pushes for a tax cut, largely designed to give significant amnesty to the rich and large corporations. In the months following the cut, the forecasted budget surpluses disappear and shortly thereafter the nation is again in debt.

Michael Jordan returns to the basketball court to play for the Washington Wizards. His competitive fire and mature leadership help the Wizards improve, but not enough to return them to the playoffs.

The Reverend Jesse Jackson admits to having fathered an illegitimate child with a Rainbow Coalition staffer. Jackson apologizes and says he will step out of the public eye to spend time with his family.

With his win at the Masters, Tiger Woods holds all four major titles at once, the first golfer in more than fifty years to do so.

The United Nations conference against "racism, racial discrimination, xenophobia and related intolerance" takes place in Durban, South Africa. Organizers call it a "unique opportunity to create a new world vision for tackling all aspects of racism and prejudice in the 21st century." While the final declaration of the world conference on racism does not go as far as apologizing for slavery, the resolution states that countries have a moral obligation "to stop and reverse the lingering effects of slavery." It goes on to say that slavery and the slave trade "were a crime against humanity and should always have been so." United States representative Jesse Jackson makes a statement demanding a full apology and reparations for the enslaving of Africans by European countries.

Terrorists organized and funded by Osama bin Laden's Al Qaeda organization crash airplanes loaded with fuel shortly after take-off into the World Trade Center and the Pentagon. A fourth plane, believed to be headed for the White House, crashes as the passengers wrestle with terrorists. The attacks kill more than 3,000 Americans, immediately usher in a state of national alert, and give rise in the following months to a war mentality and economy.

In an attempt to capture Saudi Arabian terrorist Osama bin Laden, the United States launches an attack against the Taliban regime in Afghanistan. The war is dominated by the "smart weapon" air assaults used in the Persian Gulf War, and is over in a matter of months. However, bin Laden escapes and his terror organization, Al Qaeda, regroups internationally.

Veteran outfielder Barry Bonds hits seventy-three home runs for the San Francisco Giants, breaking Mark McGwire's record of seventy.

A federal judge commutes the death sentence of former Black Panther and journalist Mumia Abu-Jamal, who had become a cause of the anti-death penalty movement while in prison in Pennsylvania.

2002

Denzel Washington, who portrays a corrupt cop in *Training Day,* becomes the first black male since Sidney Poitier to win an Academy Award for best actor; while African American actress Halle Berry wins for her performance in *Monster's Ball,* marking the first time African Americans win both the best actor and best actress awards. It is an extraordinary moment, as the evening's top honors are garnered by black Americans, including a lifetime achievement award to Sidney Poitier. **SEE ENTRY** *The Close of the Twentieth Century and Beyond, p. 446*

Venus and Serena Williams are the first African American women to be simultaneously ranked number one and number two in tennis.

Lionel Hampton, the jazz percussionist and bandleader who brought the vibraphone to prominence and whose career spanned sixty years, dies on August 31. He recorded the first-ever vibraphone solo while playing with Louis Armstrong in 1930, and went on to perform and record with many of jazz's greatest musicians, including Benny Goodman, Charlie Parker, Charles Mingus, Illinois Jacquet, Dexter Gordon, and Dinah Washington. Also active in politics, Hampton campaigned for Richard Nixon, Ronald Reagan, and George Bush, Sr. He helped found the Gladys Hampton Houses, a low-income complex in Harlem named after his wife who died in 1971. In 1997, days after a fire destroyed his home and possessions-among them a collection of jazz memorabilia that included rare photographs and albums and his music scores-he received the National Medal of the Arts from President Clinton.

The Colonial Period
and the Revolutionary War

The historical moment that gave birth to the New World, that later led to the creation of the United States—and at the same time marked the beginning of the story of Africans in the New World—represents one of the critical moments in the story of humankind. In the period around the year 1492 (when Christopher Columbus "discovered" the North American continent), the Western world was changing in various and profound ways, and the story of civilization was in the process of accelerating, forever making the New World distinct from the Old one.

Perhaps most significant to the history of Africans in the New World and African Americans was the increasing importance of Europe and the Judeo-Christian tradition associated with it. During the Dark and Middle Ages advances in philosophy, the sciences, literature, and the arts were restricted to only a handful of monasteries and minds on the European continent while enjoying relative prosperity on the African continent and in the cultural centers of Islam and the Ghanaian Empire. The end of the fifteenth century, however, marked a turning point. The mercantile and religious zeal of the European nation-states found sud-

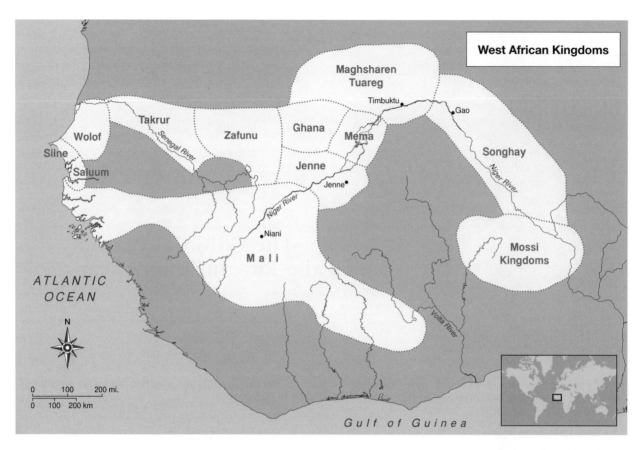

West African Kingdoms

Maghsharen Tuareg

Timbuktu

Gao

Takrur

Ghana

Wolof

Zafunu

Mema

Songhay

Siine

Saluum

Senegal River

Jenne

Jenne

Niger River

Niani

M a l i

Niger River

Mossi Kingdoms

ATLANTIC OCEAN

N

Volta River

0   100   200 mi.

0   100   200 km

Gulf of Guinea

The peoples of West Africa created great kingdoms centuries before the Italian Renaissance. The kingdom of Ghana, for example, was the site of a thriving civilization as early as A.D. 400. Many of the kingdoms pictured in this map are the ancestral origins of African Americans whose ties to Africa and histories were effectively broken during the Atlantic slave trade. (Map created by XNR Productions.) **THE GALE GROUP**

den and unprecedented expression and were in a state of constant evolution and export, thanks in great part to the coupling of these cultural phenomena with a handful of technological advances, such as the advent of the printing press, the astrolabe, and advances in shipbuilding.

The previous centuries had seen some European scientist-philosophers literally burned at the stake for their various visions. While that brand of religious superstition would remain a part of European culture for centuries to come, the European enthusiasm for all things pecuniary, religious, and technological was opening up, literally, a New World. In conjunction with this New World, a new, and disturbing, chapter began for many of the world's peoples of color—a chapter that would be particularly brutal for the peoples of Africa.

The final decades of the fifteenth century and the initial decades of the sixteenth century witnessed the invention of the printing press by Johannes Gutenberg; the decline of the Venetian shipping empire; and the turning back of the Ottoman Empire—and with it the Islamic faith—from the region of the Adriatic and from its incursion into the heart of the European continent.

These, however, were only brief blips on the radar compared with the events occurring on the Iberian Peninsula. If we think of the funding of the adventurer Columbus by the Spanish state (headed by Ferdinand of Aragon and Isabella of Castile) as the moment that first planted the seed of what would develop into the New World and the United States, we begin to gain some focus on this bit of history. The first journey around the southern tip of Africa was made, turning shipping commerce away from the overland eastern European and Arabian routes, away from the ships of Venice, and toward the Iberian Peninsula and its strategic command over the vast unknown of Atlantic off to the west. This was also the moment in which slavery developed into a new, much more efficient and more brutal, method of pillaging inland African villages for labor both inexpensive and relatively easy to capture.

Gutenberg's invention of the printing press meant that for the first time information could be disseminated on a massive scale; this invention almost single-handedly gave birth to the secular world (including the first "novels"—books relating the story of an "everyman" rather than of figures of laical significance), and with it a mod-

The first panel of *Aspects of a Negro Life: The Negro in an African Setting* by Aaron Douglas. Douglas painted four scenes, starting with freedom in Africa, to enslavement in the United States, to emancipation, and finally life in the modern city. The mural, completed in 1934, incorporated techniques that would become his signature such as concentric circles and silhouettes that lent to the dream-like aura of the painting. **PHOTOGRAPH BY MANU SASSOONIAN/ART RESOURCE, NY**

ernizing world. The presence of these new and secular fonts of information may have further stoked the zealotry of the European monarchs. The Spanish monarchy was obsessed with the consolidation of the Catholic faith under the yoke of their growing empire. The Moors, who had thrived on the Iberian Peninsula since the eighth century, creating grand caliphates, cities, as well as great art and science, were finally ejected from their last stronghold in Granada in 1492. The Jews, who were traditionally the scholars, cartographers, and intellectuals of Spain and Portugal, also had no place in the burgeoning vision of an Iberian Peninsula free of heretics.

In what was perhaps the precursor to the fascistic twentieth-century efforts of a Joseph Stalin or an Adolf Hitler, the Inquisition raged on in Spain, sanctioned by a series of fiats and papal bulls that were handed down by the Vatican and were enforced on the rack and in the burnings in the public squares. Some histories say that daily life in the Spanish capital included the regular smell of burning flesh, which hung in the air, serving as a reminder to people of the cost of questioning faith or allowing forms of heresy to go unreported. This culture was the figurative cargo of the *Santa María,* the *Niña,* and the *Pinta* when these ships of Columbus dropped anchor in 1492 somewhere off the coast of current-day Florida. And it was with a zealous drive for progress and wealth as a backdrop that the great ships turned into the ports of western Africa and the first shackled Africans were led from the holding pens into the cramped holds below deck. ■

The First Africans to Arrive in the New World

ADAPTED FROM ESSAYS BY ANTHONY MILES

THE BEGINNINGS OF THE SLAVE TRADE

The story of African Americans begins with these first Africans, who first came to America involuntarily through the Atlantic slave trade, which was conducted largely along the coast of West Africa and served to transfer blacks to European colonies in the Americas.

These Africans entered the slave trade in several ways. Europeans kidnapped blacks and shipped them overseas to be sold, and while Africans resisted this, often successfully, they also took part in the slave trade. The extent of their involvement continues to be debated, but it is clear that Africans sold into slavery captives taken in wars or raids on other tribes and kingdoms. In many African societies, slavery was also a punishment for crime, meted out through a variety of legal proceedings.

Whether Africans came to be enslaved through kidnapping, war, or traditional social mechanisms, most were eventually sold to European traders and wound up aboard slave ships bound for the Americas. The conditions on the Middle Passage, as the Atlantic voyage was called, were appalling. Packed and chained tightly together and made to lie on their sides, newly enslaved Africans en route to the Americas died at a rate of 16 percent—of disease, suffocation, and other causes, including suicide and despair.

Because they came from many ethnic groups and locations, transported Africans had different languages and cultures, a diversity that made communication among them difficult. Individuals from the same tribe, or with similar languages, might communicate with one another. But these connections often were torn asunder at the end of the Middle Passage, when they were sold to masters from different places throughout the New World.

Recalling his arrival in Virginia, Olaudah Equiano wrote: "All my companions were distributed different ways and only myself was left. I was now exceedingly miserable and thought myself worse off than any of the rest … for they could talk to each other, but I had no person to speak to that I could understand." Such feelings, experienced by Equiano in the eighteenth century, must have been even greater for the first group of twenty Africans brought to Virginia by a Dutch slaver in 1619.

By 1775, on the eve of the American Revolution, the number of African Americans in the population had grown to nearly five hundred thousand, making up almost 20 percent of the people in Britain's thirteen North American colonies. At the root of this population growth was the institution of slavery, a system of unpaid labor based on white ownership and domination of African Americans.

RACISM AND THE BEGINNINGS OF RACIAL SLAVERY

Whether slavery developed out of racism or racism developed out of slavery remains one of the major questions of the colonial period. Although it appears impossible to determine which came first, it is clear that both slavery and racism developed either at the same time or within a relatively short time of each other.

Eventually, American slavery came to be based on race, and its increasing prominence in the social and economic fabric went hand in hand with increased racism. As slavery grew, those who profited from it used notions of black inferiority to justify the institution. Racist ideas were slavery's lowest common denominator and were found in every region, regardless of differences in the nature of the institution itself.

Slavery existed in every colony, but it differed from region to region. Varying economies, labor needs, climates, and environments all helped to determine the numbers of Africans, native-born African Americans, and whites in any given area. All of these factors played a role in determining the nature of the slave system that developed in each colonial region.

THE CHESAPEAKE REGION IN THE EARLY YEARS

The Chesapeake region included the colonies of Maryland and Virginia, where Africans first arrived. The status of the first people put ashore in Virginia in 1619 remains unclear. For several years after their arrival, the colonists seem to have considered them indentured servants, listing them as such in the censuses of 1623 and 1624. However, they appear to have served for longer periods of time than white indentured servants.

In these early years, indentured blacks and whites often ate, worked, and slept in the same areas, in conditions that offered opportunities for interaction across racial lines. United in their work and leisure activities, they also joined together in escape and rebellion.

Conditions were difficult and dangerous. Black and white laborers worked long hours growing and preparing tobacco and were threatened alike by numerous diseases. "Seasoning," the process by which they adjusted to the climate and developed resistance to disease, was a hazardous business. Many did not survive, but for those who did, the dream was to finish out the terms of indenture and become farmers. Like their white counterparts, some black survivors of these early years eventually gained their freedom, purchased land, and became small planters. Some even came to own servants and slaves of their own. But the early promise of equal opportunity for African Americans quickly eroded.

SEE PRIMARY SOURCE DOCUMENT *Memoir of a Boy Sold into Slavery*

EARLY LEGAL RECOGNITION OF SLAVERY IN THE CHESAPEAKE REGION

It is impossible to tell exactly when racial slavery first began in Virginia, but the first legal recognition of it occurred in 1661, in a law that specified the punishment for white servants who ran away with black slaves. The 1661 law did not affect blacks who had already been granted their freedom, but it did make it clear that only blacks could be slaves. Another Virginia law defined as free the children of white or free black mothers. Its failure to distinguish between free and unfree whites provides further evidence that only blacks could be slaves.

In Maryland, slavery was not recognized under law until 1663. Unlike Virginia, Maryland sought to reduce even previously free blacks to slavery. In one of the clearest formulations of the connection between race and slave status, Maryland law also declared the mixed-race children of white women who married slaves to be "slaves as their *fathers* were."

As the 1600s drew to a close, the law was defining more and more sharply an inferior place for blacks within white colonial society. Eventually, the law came to regulate the majority of actions and relations between blacks and whites, usually at the expense of African Americans' rights. Most important among the rights lost was the right to hold property, for this offered the only means of economic and social advancement within the colonies.

Despite the early legal recognition of racial slavery, Chesapeake planters at first preferred white laborers and imported them in large numbers. But a variety of causes—including competition from other colonies, new opportunities for advancement in England, and declining opportunities in Virginia and Maryland—began to lessen the supply of new servants. What did not diminish was the need for labor. This, together with the chartering in 1672 of the Royal African Company, which made its profits from the slave trade, led to a substantial rise in the African American population.

SEE PRIMARY SOURCE DOCUMENT *"An Agreement to Deliver 17 Negro Slaves"*

CHANGES IN SLAVE LIFE IN THE CHESAPEAKE REGION

From 1695 onward, blacks were imported at the rate of more than a thousand per year. In Virginia the African American population grew from about 4,600 in 1680 to 13,000 by 1700. Around 1740, Virginia's black population began to sustain natural growth, and on the eve of the

---

Twenty Africans Arrive in Jamestown Colony

When the first twenty African slaves arrived in Jamestown harbor, statutory slavery did not yet exist. The first slaves were sold as indentured servants and many worked to buy their freedom and were in fact among the first founding members of the original colonies. Within twenty-five years however, statutory slavery would be established in Massachusetts, with every colony following suit and thereby creating the "racial slavery" that forever marked both the character of the young nation and every American generation that would follow. While slavery did not exist as a statutory institution in Virginia until the 1660s and 1670s, many Africans were imported as slaves well before then.

These original Africans to arrive in Jamestown are particularly significant because they clearly show that racial slavery was not the norm when the first settlers arrived in the New World and that among the pioneers who first set about taming the land, there were Africans—the first African Americans.

American Revolution it had reached almost 200,000. With the expansion of slavery and the explosion of the black population, work became much more limited and routine. Most blacks labored on large plantations, where they lived apart from whites in slave quarters. This provided opportunities for them to continue old social practices, and to develop new communities and hybrid cultural forms.

By the 1770s, African Americans made up almost 40 percent of the population of the Chesapeake region, virtually all of them slaves. In many communities, African Americans outnumbered whites, which led to fears of rebellion or insurrection. Such fears often resulted in increased repression, while some people argued for an end to the slave trade or expressed doubts about the wisdom of slavery itself. The fear of rebellion, as well as the effort to prevent it, would remain long after the revolution.

SEE PRIMARY SOURCE DOCUMENT *Virginia Passes the "Casual Slave Killing Act"*

THE LOW COUNTRY

The coastal regions of Georgia and the Carolinas made up the low country. Unlike Virginia, South Carolina had been envisioned from the beginning as a slave society, chartered by slave-owning Barbadian planters and members of the Royal African Company and first settled by slave-owning planters from Barbados. The colony of Georgia, originally founded to reform English criminals, at first banned slavery from its borders. The expansion of rice cultivation quickly brought slavery to the colony, however, and once there it expanded rapidly. By the 1760s, Georgia was importing slaves from South Carolina, and later directly from Africa. By 1775, Georgia's African American population was approximately equal to its white population of fifteen thousand. Slavery took firm hold along North Carolina's coast but developed intermittently in the more mountainous backlands, which were settled by people moving south from Virginia, Pennsylvania, and points farther north and by immigrants from northern England and Scotland.

Of the low-country colonies, South Carolina was by far the wealthiest and most productive, and African slaves were crucial to its economic development. In the beginning, the colonial proprietors encouraged planters to grow a variety of crops for export, and as a result, by the end of the seventeenth century, South Carolina had developed one of the most diversified colonial economies. In the region's early development, African slaves contributed their knowledge of tropical soil, farming, and husbandry to a number of early experiments with different crops, including indigo, sugarcane, and cotton. Some African groups had developed special techniques for raising livestock in tropical climates. Members of these groups were particularly valuable to South Carolina's early cattle industry, which supplied meat to Barbados.

The colonists soon discovered that rice was the ideal crop for their environment. They knew little, however, about cultivating it. Africans, on the other hand, had long experience growing rice, which formed a major part of their daily diet. Largely as a result of their expertise, rice became the driving crop of South Carolina's economy. Indeed, only after the widespread adoption of African growing techniques did rice production take off. The success of rice growing led to the development of large-scale plantation agriculture. Many plantations were owned by absentee planters who lived in Charleston or other places where they were less likely to be exposed to malaria. Rice was a labor-intensive crop, and many workers were required to produce it in exportable quantities. Thus, West African slaves, who enjoyed some resistance to malaria, were imported in large numbers to maintain the plantation labor force.

In the early years, the colonial proprietors also encouraged the importation of slaves by what was known as the headright system, whereby planters received a certain portion of land, or "headrights," for every laborer they imported. This led to large-scale importing of slaves, with the result that blacks outnum-

bered whites in South Carolina as early as 1715. By 1740, African Americans made up 90 percent of the population in some plantation areas.

LIFE FOR SOUTH CAROLINA'S BLACK MAJORITY

As in Virginia and Maryland, the concentration of large numbers of slaves helped to sustain African beliefs and traditions and promoted the development of new forms of distinctively African American culture. In coastal South Carolina, isolation intensified this process, allowing for the development of Gullah culture, which to this day retains elements of African tradition, belief, and language. With planters absent, overseers often organized work by tasks. Once their tasks were finished, African Americans had time to themselves. Many used the time to raise their own vegetables or help family members with work, in this way freeing up time they could spend together. This situation had negative consequences as well. As in the Chesapeake region, so too in South Carolina, the black majority aroused fears of rebellion. These fears were realized in the 1739 Stono Rebellion, which claimed the lives of thirty whites and forty-four African Americans and took several days to put down.

South Carolina's Fundamental Constitutions of 1669 had made it clear that the colony was to be supported by black labor but dominated and controlled by whites. Through the years, as the black population grew, repressive laws multiplied. These laws removed almost all power into the hands of whites, leaving blacks with few rights or means of expressing their grievances.

SEE PRIMARY SOURCE DOCUMENT *The First Slavery Statute and First Anti-Literacy Act*

NEW ENGLAND

In the New England colonies of Connecticut, Massachusetts, Rhode Island, and New Hampshire, slavery was practiced on a much smaller scale. These colonies produced a variety of exportable materials through whaling, fishing, and the raising of grain and livestock. Because their economies did not rely on labor-intensive commercial agriculture, they did not need a huge labor force. Moreover, as southern commercial agriculture grew, the price of slaves also rose throughout the colonies, making slave labor on a large scale unprofitable for northern slaveholders. For these reasons, fewer slaves lived in New England than in any other mainland region.

New Englanders also had a different sense of community. While most southern colonies were founded for profit, the New England colonies were founded as religious communities by Puritans seeking to escape persecution in England. These communities centered around the family. They also had a long tradition of apprenticeship, whereby a child as young as nine or ten would be "sent out" to another family in order to learn a trade or farming skills. Apprenticeship came to serve as a model for New England slavery.

While the status of the first Africans in Boston remains uncertain, it is clear that slavery soon became a legitimate institution in New England, its growth aided by the involvement of New England ship merchants in the slave trade. In the early days of the trade, merchants sent ships to the coast of Africa to take on slaves who would then be sold to planters in the Caribbean and southern mainland colonies. Those who could not be sold in these markets—the least healthy, or the most troublesome—often were brought to New England. As slavery became more institutionalized, New England slave owners began to place special orders with slave merchants. Some preferred small children, who could easily be reared within the apprenticeship system and who adopted their owners' values more readily than adults might.

Like apprentices, New England slaves lived and worked with their masters' families. This arrangement fostered intimacy, which led in turn to a milder form of bondage. And because Africans remained a small percentage of the New England population, there were not the fears of rebellion that made for harsh slave codes in the South. In fact, New England was known for the mild nature of its slave institution. Work remained the focus of slaves' lives, just as in the South, but the types of work differed dramatically. Under the apprenticeship model, New England slaves were not only agricultural laborers, but also bakers, shoemakers, blacksmiths, coopers, and sailors, to name just a few occupations. Although they remained property, New England slaves enjoyed many more rights than southern slaves. They could own property themselves and pass it on to their children. They could associate more freely with one another, without white supervision. Though widely scattered among the white population, they took advantage of their freedoms to develop and promote a common culture.

The factors that made New England slavery so mild produced negative results as well. Many New England masters preferred unmarried male slaves, in part because children were considered an extra expense, and not—as in the South—an increase in wealth. The resulting imbalance in the ratio of men and women, as well as the wide dispersion of the black population, made it much harder to form families than in the large plantation communities of the South. Then too, New England masters sometimes liberated slaves who were no longer productive, rather than continue to give them food and shelter, as happened in the South. Many slaves refused this treatment, saying, "Massa eat the meat; he now pick the bone."

Although slavery was milder in the North, racism was not. Assumptions about African American inferiori-

This broadside advertises a recent shipment of 250 "fine healthy Negroes, just arrived from the Windward and Rice Coast," to be sold in Charlestown, Virginia. Printed at the bottom of the sheet is the notice "N.B. Full one Half of the above Negroes have had the SMALL-POX in their own Country." Such information interested prospective buyers, who feared losing slaves to disease during the "seasoning" period, when they were adjusting to a new place and climate. "Seasoning" was especially brutal in the coastal, rice-growing regions of South Carolina and Georgia. **THE LIBRARY OF CONGRESS**

ty pervaded social as well as political arrangements. Ironically, racism also contributed to the decline of slavery as an institution in New England. Puritan communities that had a strong instinct for public charity were continually burdened with the expense of supporting old and infirm slaves who had been freed by their masters. As New England's white population grew, colonists also worried about vocational opportunities for whites and the need to support larger numbers of poor whites. Such concerns, along with slavery's lack of economic importance to the regional economy, contributed to its decline in the years before the revolution. Just as slavery was becoming more deeply entrenched as the chief social and economic institution of the South, it was on the verge of extinction in the North.

THE MIDDLE GROUND
Between New England and the Chesapeake region—in New York, New Jersey, Pennsylvania, and Delaware—there arose yet another form of slavery, an in-between form, both geographically and in terms of its nature and severity.

Slavery existed in the middle colonies in the 1630s, and the number of blacks in this region increased substantially after Britain took over New York from the Dutch.

Here, the British presence made slavery much harsher, diminishing the rights accorded to slaves. In Pennsylvania, on the other hand, the Quaker presence provided a strong opposition to slavery. But while each of the middle colonies had a different history of slavery, in all of them slave ownership became a symbol of status and wealth and this brought many blacks together in cities. The urban nature of slavery in the middle colonies was its most remarkable feature. While many middle-colony slaves, like those in New England, lived with families, they enjoyed greater independence than most of their nonurban counterparts, north or south. They also enjoyed a greater variety of work, which contributed to their greater anonymity.

As in the southern colonies, large concentrations of slaves produced great fears of insurrection. New York City experienced two insurrection scares, one in 1712 and the other in 1741. Although the evidence of slave conspiracy was questionable in the 1741 scare, it nevertheless resulted in the execution of thirty-one blacks and four whites and the deportation of seventy more African Americans. Both events provoked legislative responses. Yet it was difficult to control or restrict the movement of urban slaves. They moved freely among workplaces, made deliveries, and hired themselves out. As in New England, African Americans used their mobility and relative independence to build a distinct and supportive community and culture beyond the influence of whites.

AFRICAN AMERICAN CULTURE

From the first moment of their enslavement, Africans began adapting to their new situation through a process called *acculturation*. Learning a new language was a particularly important part of this process. The first Africans to arrive very likely communicated with their European masters through signs and gestures. These Africans had to learn English from whites. Those slaves who came later entered established black communities and usually learned English from other blacks. This allowed for the formation of different patterns of speech, in which English words were added to West African grammar.

Such developments were particularly pronounced among blacks living on the isolated rice plantations of South Carolina and Georgia. In the culture that developed there, known as Gullah, many African words were retained in addition to grammatical structures. The Gullah people of the South Carolina and Georgia Sea Islands continued in isolation through much of the twentieth century. Their language and culture appear to have changed very little and may thus provide the best means of understanding how African American culture developed.

How much of their African cultural heritage have African Americans retained? This question is still being debated. It seems clear, however, that Africans in America have retained and passed down much more of their African heritage than a few words and grammatical

structures. From Africa, slaves brought with them the knowledge of how to make traditional instruments, including drums and a three-stringed, guitar-like instrument now known as the banjo. They brought traditional music and dance forms, which they incorporated in their work, their free-time entertainment, and their burials and other ceremonies. As blacks became more acculturated, they also created their own celebrations around white holidays like election day, celebrations that incorporated elements of both cultures.

Africans also brought their concepts of participatory worship, magic, and death. These concepts had a dramatic impact on the development of evangelical and black Christianity. In the early years of American slavery, few blacks converted to Christianity. This was particularly true in New England, where the Puritan style of preaching did not appeal to those of African descent. Noting that blacks enjoyed singing in church, many ministers began to sing psalms with great fervor. By this and other means, they sought to convert slaves, and at the same time they altered white forms of worship.

The rise of evangelical Christianity around the turn of the eighteenth century is a testament to the power of African styles of worship. The communal and participatory practices of African worship became part of both black and white religious practices. In baptism and in certain distinctively African American forms of worship, like the ring shout, African Americans fused their various African traditions into a single culture.

Spirits also played a large role in African worldviews, which held that one joined the spirits of one's ancestors after death. Through their contact with white workers, children, and masters, blacks imparted these concepts to whites, which led to the now commonplace idea that families would be reunited in heaven. For blacks who converted to Christianity, heaven eventually replaced the African idea of an ancestral home one entered after death. Heaven became one's true home, an idea that helped blacks to endure and resist the conditions of their bondage.

SEE PRIMARY SOURCE DOCUMENT *Tracing the Roots of African American Cultural Traditions in Early Slave Narratives*

RESISTANCE AND REBELLIONS

Slavery was an institution of subjection and domination based on fear and force. African Americans resisted both the physical and the psychological oppression of slavery. In their attempt to create meek and docile servants, masters and white ministers often quoted biblical passages that laid out the obligations of servants to their masters. Afro-Christianity, on the other hand, emphasized those passages that dealt with liberation and triumph over oppression. Traditional African beliefs in magic and the

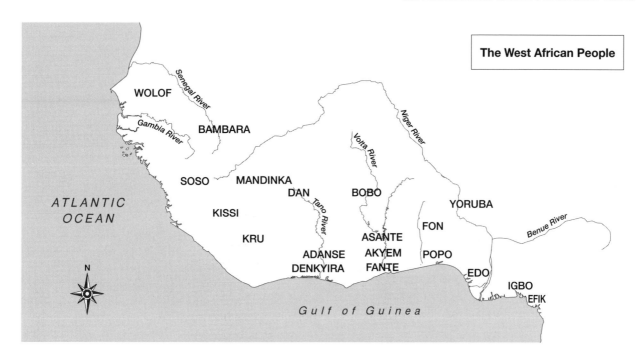

The vast majority of African Americans in the United States today come from various villages on the western coast of Africa. Some African Americans work to recreate their genealogy, thereby tracing their lineage back to one these West African peoples and the regions in which they lived. (Map created by XNR Productions.) **THE GALE GROUP**

powers of certain roots and herbs also played a part in slave resistance. Slaves often used charms created by medicine men or women known as *Obeah* to protect themselves against violence from a master or overseer.

Slaves resisted white domination by other means as well. Masters retained the authority to name slaves, including the slaves' children, but slaves often chose alternative names that were used only among themselves. And although they were not generally given or allowed to have last names, slaves developed them anyway as a means of resistance and passed them on to their children. Such names served to identify family members, even those who had been sold far from home.

The physical oppressions of slavery were great. Slaves were worked hard for long hours and often were underfed. In the South, they were also subject to whippings and beatings for a variety of minor offenses. Women were particularly vulnerable. In addition to facing the same physical dangers as men, they were also subject to sexual violence from masters, masters' sons, and overseers. Slave women were given little or no time off from work when they were pregnant or raising children.

Slaves developed a number of ways of resisting these conditions. They engaged in work slowdowns or stoppages, sabotaged equipment, and pretended to be ill. Often, they ran away as the huge number of advertisements for runaway slaves attests. Some escaped permanently into the wilderness, where they lived with Native Americans or formed their own *maroon* communities.

This occurred most often in the South, especially in South Carolina.

Slaves also resisted violently, either individually or in planned insurrections. Fear of slave revolt was widespread in all slave-holding communities outside New England. Whether or not slaves planned as many insurrections as whites feared remains an open question. Yet a number of insurrections did take place, often when the white community was distracted or divided by some other issue. The overwhelming force with which these insurrections were suppressed may well have served to limit the number of them. Religion played a strong role in slave insurrections, most of which were described and justified by their leaders in religious terms.

Both culturally and structurally, persons of African descent exerted an influence on slavery and the development of American culture. The African American experience in the colonial period provided a strong foundation for the further development of African American culture and a preparation for the experiences blacks would endure in the future. On the eve of the revolution, African Americans already had a century and a half of experience and tradition to rely upon. As slavery developed in the nineteenth century, they would continue to adapt their strategies of survival and to challenge white control.

A NOTE ON FREE BLACKS

Throughout the colonial era, a small number of blacks were free. Although the number grew, legislative attempts to restrict manumission reduced the opportunity for others to gain their freedom. Free blacks were never fully recognized as colonists, however, and had no real position within the colonial social order. As such, they were a threat to that order and suffered from a host of discriminatory laws and provisions.

Some free blacks, particularly in New England, became farmers and lived comfortably, respected by the white community. Venture Smith, who lived in eighteenth-century Connecticut, was a free black who eventually became a farmer and then a slaveholder himself. In New England, the homes of free blacks often provided gathering places for the black community. Free blacks were also heavily involved in planning a number of insurrections. Their reputation for this kind of activity earned them the special distrust of many legislators, who then took away even more of their rights. Thus, free blacks lived difficult lives. They had their freedom, but it was a poor freedom at best.

BIBLIOGRAPHY

Glasrud, Bruce A., and Alan M. Smith, eds. *Race Relations in British North America, 1607–1783.* Chicago: Nelson-Hall, 1982.

Higginbotham, A. Leon. *In the Matter of Color: Race and the American Legal Process: The Colonial Period.* New York: Oxford University Press, 1975.

Isaac, Rhys. *The Transformation of Virginia, 1740–1790.* New York: Norton, 1982.

Jordan, Winthrop. *White over Black.* Chapel Hill: University of North Carolina Press, 1968.

Morgan, Edmund. *American Slavery, American Freedom.* New York: Norton, 1975.

Mullin, Gerald W. *Flight and Rebellion.* New York: Oxford University Press, 1972.

Piersen, William D. *Black Yankees.* Amherst: University of Massachusetts Press, 1988.

Sobel, Mechal. *The World They Made Together.* Princeton: Princeton University Press, 1987.

Thornton, John. *Africa and Africans in the Making of the Atlantic World, 1400–1680.* New York: Cambridge University Press, 1992.

Wood, Peter H. *Black Majority: Negroes in Colonial South Carolina from 1670 through the Stono Rebellion.* New York: Norton, 1974.

Wright, Donald R. *African Americans in the Colonial Era.* Arlington Heights: Harlan Davidson, 1990.

PRIMARY SOURCE DOCUMENT

Memoir of a Boy Sold into Slavery

INTRODUCTION In this memoir, the *Narrative of Louis Asa-Asa,* a young boy recalls his capture in a French ship called the *Pearl,* and transport along the route of the infamous Middle Passage. The narrative is given as nearly as possible in the narrator's words, with only so much correction as is necessary to connect the story, and render it grammatical.

It is necessary to explain that Louis came to this country about five years ago, in a French vessel called the Pearl. She had lost her reckoning, and was driven by stress of weather into the port of St. Ives, in Cornwall. Louis and his four companions were brought to London upon a writ of Habeas Corpus at the instance of Mr. George Stephen; and, after some trifling opposition on the part of the master of the vessel, were discharged by Lord Wynford. Two of his unfortunate fellow-sufferers died of the measles at Hampstead; the other two returned to Sierra Leone; but poor Louis, when offered the choice of going back to Africa, replied, "Me no father, no mother now; me stay with you." And here he has ever since remained; conducting himself in a way to gain the good will and respect of all who know him. He is remarkably intelligent, understands our language perfectly, and can read and write well. The last sentences of the following narrative will seem almost too peculiar to be his own; but it is not the first time that in conversation with Mr. George Stephen, he has made similar remarks. On one occasion in particular, he was heard saying to himself in the kitchen, while sitting by the fire apparently in deep thought, "Me think,—me think——" A fellow-servant inquired what he meant; and he added, "Me think what a good thing I came to England! Here, I know what God is, and read my Bible; in my country they have no God, no Bible."

How severe and just a reproof to the guilty wretches who visit his country only with fire and sword! How deserved a censure upon the not less guilty men, who dare to vindicate the state of slavery, on the lying pretext, that its victims are of an inferior nature! And scarcely less deserving of reprobation are those who have it in their power to prevent these crimes, but who remain inactive from indifference, or are dissuaded from throwing the shield of British power over the victim of oppression, by the sophistry, and the clamour, and the avarice of the oppressor. It is the reproach and the sin of England. May God avert from our country the ruin which this national guilt deserves!

We lament to add, that the Pearl which brought these negroes to our shore, was restored to its owners at the instance of the French Government, instead of being condemned as a prize to Lieut. Rye, who, on his own responsibility, detained her, with all her manacles and chains and other detestable proofs of her piratical occupation on board. We trust it is not yet too late to demand investigation into the reasons for restoring her.

The Negro Boy's Narrative

My father's name was Clashoquin; mine is Asa-Asa. He lived in a country called Bycla, near Egie, a large town. Egie is as large as Brighton; it was some way from the sea. I had five brothers and sisters. We all lived together with my father and mother; he kept a horse, and was

The European Slave Trade Begins

The European slave trade began when the Portuguese prince Henry the Navigator sailed down the coast of Africa and took captive over 200 Africans. For many years, Arab slave traders had captured and transported Africans; however, with the advent of superior methods of capture and transport, the transatlantic slave trade began in earnest.

The years both before and after Columbus's expeditions to the New World saw an astonishing number of advances that changed the course of history, initiating the age of Europe's dominance over the seas. For example, the last decades of the fifteenth century saw the invention of the moveable type printing press, making possible the first mass-produced books. The craft of ship-building exploded forward; advances in hull and forecastle construction made it possible to build much larger ships that could take longer voyages. These new ships had bigger sails fixed to taller masts, and a navigator standing at the ship's highest point above the line of the horizon. Henry the Navigator was the first to use these advances, effectively ushering in an age of improved slave trading and transporting.

The arrogance of the colonial age was not limited to the capture and sale of people. The new technologies pitted Portugal and Spain against one another to conquer new territories. The nations essentially decided to divide up the world as they saw it. The agreement between the two nations promised to the Spanish throne all lands discovered 370 leagues west of The Cape Verdean Islands and to the Portuguese throne all lands found 370 leagues east of the islands. The Portuguese aimed to exploit the western coast of Africa, the trade routes to the east going around the horn of Africa, and any lands in Africa—the effect of which can be seen in the presence of the Portuguese language in Angola, Cape Verde, and numerous other locales of the region. The Spanish end of the bargain, however, was far more advantageous: they, in effect, had rights to all of the New World. These early decisions would mark all history to follow, creating languages, cultures, nations, and entire peoples with their own ethnic characteristics grown out of centuries of miscegenation.

respectable, but not one of the great men. My uncle was one of the great men at Egie; he could make men come and work for him: his name was Otou. He had a great deal of land and cattle. My father sometimes worked on his own land, and used to make charcoal. I was too little to work; my eldest brother used to work on the land; and we were all very happy.

A great many people, whom we called Adinyes, set fire to Egie in the morning before daybreak; there were some thousands of them. They killed a great many, and burnt all their houses. They staid two days, and then carried away all the people whom they did not kill.

They came again every now and then for a month, as long as they could find people to carry away. They used to tie them by the feet, except when they were taking them off, and then they let them loose; but if they offered to run away, they would shoot them. I lost a great many friends and relations at Egie; about a dozen. They sold all they carried away, to be slaves. I know this because I afterwards saw them as slaves on the other side of the sea. They took away brothers, and sisters, and husbands, and wives; they

did not care about this. They were sold for cloth or gunpowder, sometimes for salt or guns; sometimes they got four or five guns for a man: they were English guns, made like my master's that I clean for his shooting. The Adinyes burnt a great many places besides Egie. They burnt all the country wherever they found villages; they used to shoot men, women, and children, if they ran away.

They came to us about eleven o'clock one day, and directly they came they set our house on fire. All of us had run away. We kept together and went into the woods, and stopped there two days. The Adinyes then went away, and we returned home and found every thing burnt. We tried to build a little shed, and were beginning to get comfortable again. We found several of our neighbours lying about wounded; they had been shot. I saw the bodies of four or five little children whom they had killed with blows on the head. They had carried away their fathers and mothers, but the children were too small for slaves, so they killed them. They had killed several others, but these were all that I saw. I saw them lying in the street like dead dogs.

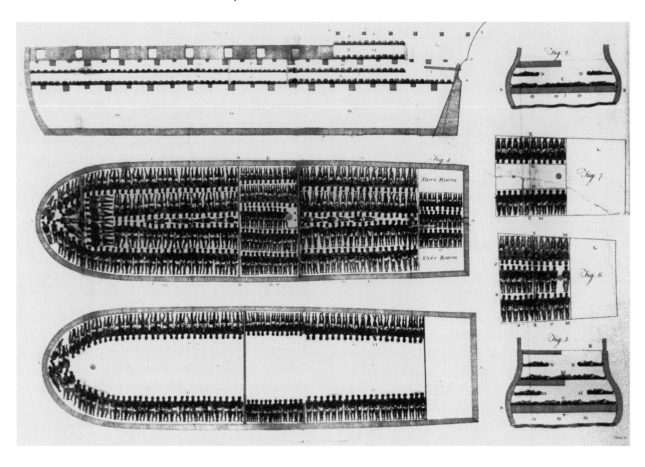

This diagram of a slave ship loaded with its human cargo illustrates the conditions under which Africans were brought to the Americas. Many Africans died during the Middle Passage, of sickness, suffocation, despair, and suicide. Because of the high death rate, and the daily jettisoning overboard of the dead or dying, the slave ships brought sharks in their wake. **THE LIBRARY OF CONGRESS**

In about a week after we got back, the Adinyes returned, and burnt all the sheds and houses they had left standing. We all ran away again; we went to the woods as we had done before.—They followed us the next day. We went farther into the woods, and staid there about four days and nights; we were half starved; we only got a few potatoes. My uncle Otou was with us. At the end of this time, the Adinyes found us. We ran away. They called my uncle to go to them; but he refused, and they shot him immediately: they killed him. The rest of us ran on, and they did not get at us till the next day. I ran up into a tree: they followed me and brought me down. They tied my feet. I do not know if they found my father and mother, and brothers and sisters: they had run faster than me, and were half a mile farther when I got up into the tree: I have never seen them since. —There was a man who ran up into the tree with me: I believe they shot him, for I never saw him again.

They carried away about twenty besides me. They carried us to the sea. They did not beat us: they only killed one man, who was very ill and too weak to carry his load: they made all of us carry chickens and meat for our food; but this poor man could not carry his load,

and they ran him through the body with a sword. —He was a neighbour of ours. When we got to the sea they sold all of us, but not to the same person. They sold us for money; and I was sold six times over, sometimes for money, sometimes for cloth, and sometimes for a gun. I was about thirteen years old. It was about half a year from the time I was taken, before I saw the white people.

We were taken in a boat from place to place, and sold at every place we stopped at. In about six months we got to a ship, in which we first saw white people: they were French. They bought us. We found here a great many other slaves; there were about eighty, including women and children. The Frenchmen sent away all but five of us into another very large ship. We five staid on board till we got to England, which was about five or six months. The slaves we saw on board the ship were chained together by the legs below deck, so close they could not move. They were flogged very cruelly: I saw one of them flogged till he died; we could not tell what for. They gave them enough to eat. The place they were confined in below deck was so hot and nasty I could not bear to be in it. A great many of the slaves were ill, but they were not attended to. They used to flog me very bad on board the ship: the captain cut my head very bad one time.

I am very happy to be in England, as far as I am very well;—but I have no friend belonging to me, but God, who will take care of me as he has done already. I am very glad I have come to England, to know who God is. I should like much to see my friends again, but I do not now wish to go back to them: for if I go back to my own country, I might be taken as a slave again. I would rather stay here, where I am free, than go back to my country to be sold. I shall stay in England as long as (please God) I shall live. I wish the King of England could know all I have told you. I wish it that he may see how cruelly we are used. We had no king in our country, or he would have stop it. I think the king of England might stop it, and this is why I wish him to know it all. I have heard say he is good; and if he is, he will stop it if he can. I am well off myself, for I am well taken care of, and have good bed and good clothes; but I wish my own people to be as comfortable.

Louis Asa-Asa.
London, January 31, 1831.

PRIMARY SOURCE DOCUMENT

"An Agreement to Deliver 17 Negro Slaves"

INTRODUCTION The contract reprinted here, between Leonard Calvert and John Skinner, was executed in 1642, long before slavery became a statutory institution in Virginia. It is a contract of barter, like many of the early colonial contracts, and stipulates an exchange of goods and services between the two men.

Calvert agrees to give Skinner three pieces of property and "to finish the dwelling house at Pinie Neck," in exchange for "fourteen Negro men-slaves and three women slaves, of between 16 and 26 yeare olde able and sound in body and limbs." The contract identifies John Skinner as a "mariner," that is, a seaman or a sailor, and makes clear that he will be importing slaves from abroad. The slaves are further treated as inheritable property, which may be passed down from Leonard Calvert to his "assigns" or heirs.

Leonard Calvert Esq. etc. acknowledged that he hath conveyed and sold unto John Skinner mariner, all those his 3 Mannors of St. Michael, St. Gabriel, and Trinity Mannor, with all the tenements and hereditaments in or upon them or any of them, and all his right title and interest in and to the premises or any part thereof, to have and to hold the same to the said John Skinner his heires and assignes for ever. And that he hath further covenanted to finish the dwelling house at Pinie neck, with a stack of brick chimneyes (conteining 2 chimneys) neare about the middle of the house now standing and to make the partition by the said chimneyes, and doores and windowes, and to underpin the frame of it wth stone or brick. In consideration wherof the said John Skinner covenanted and bargained to deliver unto the said Leonard Calvert, fourteene

Virginia was the colony where captive Africans first set foot, and Massachusetts the colony which gave first legal recognition to slavery. But in 1646, the Dutch colony of New Amsterdam became the first to import and auction off African slaves, as shown in this illustration entitled "Choicest Pieces of Her Cargo Were Sold at Auction."

negro men-slaves, and three women slaves, of betweene 16 and 26 yeare old able and sound in body and limbs, at some time before the first of march come twelve-month, at St. Maries, if he bring so many within the Capes, by himselfe or any assignes betweene this and the said first of march, or afterward within the said yeare, to be delivered as aforesaid to him the said Leonard Calvert or his assignes in the case aforesaid. And in case he shall not so doe, then he willeth and granteth that foure and twenty thousand weight of tobacco, be leavied upon any the lands goods or chattells of him the said John Skinner, to the use of him the said Leonard Calvert and his assignes.

PRIMARY SOURCE DOCUMENT

Virginia Passes the "Casual Slave Killing Act"

INTRODUCTION In 1669 the Virginia Assembly passed an act acquitting masters of "felony murder" for the killing of slaves during the course of punishment. It was called an "Act about the Casual Killing of Slaves," and was part of a flourish of early legislation put in place that gave slavery in the United States its particularly brutal and dehumanizing character.

The legislation is presented here precisely as it was written, including the spellings and diction commonly used at that time.

The Punishment of Refractory Servants

Act I, An Act About the Casuall Killing of Slaves, from Laws of Virginia

Whereas the only law in force for the punishment of refractory servants (a) resisting their master, mistris or overseer cannot be inflicted upon negroes, nor the obstinacy of many of them by other then violent meanes supprest, Be it enacted and declared by this grand assembly, if any slave resist his master (or other by his masters order connecting him) and by the extremity of the correction should chance to die, that his death shall not be accompted ffelony, but the master (or that other person appointed by the master to punish him) be acquit from molestation, since it cannot be presumed that prepensed malice (which alone makes murther ffelony) should induce any man to destroy his owne estate.

PRIMARY SOURCE DOCUMENT

The First Slavery Statute and First Anti-Literacy Act

INTRODUCTION Very early on, the young colonies began to put laws on the books limiting the rights of African Americans, whether they were or were not slaves. In the first decades of the colonies, the color of one's skin was not an automatic indicator of slave status. Many came to the New World in a state of indentured servitude and paid off their transport by working for various landowners, farmers, and merchants. Here are examples of some of the early laws to appear on the books.

This first document, the 91st Article of the Code of Fundamentals, or Body of Liberties of the Massachusetts Colony in New England, guaranteed the freedom of English settlers and also allowed for the enslavement of Indians and Africans. Ironically, many of the egalitarian sentiments of this document turned up later in the Declaration of Independence and the Bill of Rights.

The second piece of legislation is a prime example of the types of laws that were created in order to maintain and strengthen the bonds of slavery. The anti-literacy act called for a ban on the education of slaves, in effect instituting a ban on the education of all peoples of color.

Liberties of Forreiners and Strangers (The First Slavery Statute passed by Massachusetts, 1641)

There shall never be any bond slaverie, villinage or captivitie amongst us unles it be lawfull captives taken in just warres, and such strangers as willingly selle themselves or are sold to us. And these shall have all the liberties and Christian usages which the law of God established in Israell concerning such persons doeth morally require. This exempts none from servitude who shall be Judged thereto by Authoritie.

The South Carolina Anti-Literacy Act of 1740 (The First Anti-Literacy Act)

Whereas, the having slaves taught to write, or suffering them to be employed in writing, may be attended with great inconveniences; Be it enacted, that all and every person and persons whatsoever, who shall hereafter teach or cause any slave or slaves to be taught to write, or shall use or employ any slave as a scribe, in any manner of writing whatsoever, hereafter taught to write, every such person or persons shall, for every such offense, forfeit the sum of one hundred pounds, current money.

PRIMARY SOURCE DOCUMENT

Tracing the Roots of African American Cultural Traditions in Early Slave Narratives

INTRODUCTION The trace elements of an evolved and vibrant African American cultural tradition can be found in the early slave texts produced in the United States. This excerpt from *Incidents in the Life of a Slave Girl* by Harriet Jacobs provides a window into the daily life and psychological concerns of the narrator and presents early examples of a number of traditions that would grow and flourish in African American cultural expression. It is an example of the narrative as a quest for personal identity, an early form of protest literature, and a valuable source of insight into the dynamics of family life for those living in slavery. The ironic, double-edged slave song to be sung to the master when he has not given a sufficient "trifle" synthesizes elements of musical tradition with a form of sarcastic baiting that both pleases and mocks its intended target. Also, Jacobs's description of the "dark hole" with a trap door constructed by her uncle is similar to the "pit" that later evolved in the writings of the novelist Ralph Ellison and the poet Robert Hayden. The entire construction of a controlled "pit"—at once a dark and stifling place and a place that provides a unique vantage point from which to view the activities of those supposedly in control—is a fascinating amalgam of various elements found in African and African American cultural traditions.

XXI

The Loophole of Retreat A small shed had been added to my grandmother's house years ago. Some boards were laid across the joists at the top, and between these boards and the roof was a very small garret, never occupied by any thing but rats and mice. It was a pent roof, covered with nothing but shingles, according to the southern custom for such buildings. The garret was only nine feet long and seven wide. The highest part was three feet high, and sloped down abruptly to the loose board floor. There was no admission for either light or air. My uncle Phillip, who was a carpenter, had very skilfully made a concealed trap-door, which communicated with the storeroom. He had been doing this while I was waiting in the swamp. The storeroom opened upon a piazza. To this

CASH!

All persons that have **SLAVES** to dispose of, will do well by giving me a call, as I will give the

HIGHEST PRICE FOR

Men, Women, &
CHILDREN.

Any person that wishes to sell, will call at Hill's tavern, or at Shannon Hill for me, and any information they want will be promptly attended to.

Thomas Griggs.

Charlestown, May 7, 1835.

PRINTED AT THE FREE PRESS OFFICE, CHARLESTOWN.

Slavetraders circulated advertisements like this one informing slaveholders of their willingness to pay cash for slaves. Once sold to a trader, the slaves were usually removed far from home and family and resold to new owners. When a slaveholder disposed of his human property in this way, he was said to have "put a slave in his pocket." **THE LIBRARY OF CONGRESS**

hole I was conveyed as soon as I entered the house. The air was stifling; the darkness total. A bed had been spread on the floor. I could sleep quite comfortably on one side; but the slope was so sudden that I could not turn on the other without hitting the roof. The rats and mice ran over my bed; but I was weary, and I slept such sleep as the wretched may, when a tempest has passed over them. Morning came. I knew it only by the noises I heard; for in my small den day and night were all the same. I suffered for air even more than for light. But I was not comfortless. I heard the voices of my children. There was joy and there was sadness in the sound. It made my tears flow. How I longed to speak to them! I was eager to look on their faces; but there was no hole, no crack, through which I could peep. This continued darkness was oppressive. It seemed horrible to sit or lie in a cramped position day after day, without one gleam of light. Yet I would have chosen this, rather than my lot as a slave,

though white people considered it an easy one; and it was so compared with the fate of others. I was never cruelly over-worked; I was never lacerated with the whip from head to foot; I was never so beaten and bruised that I could not turn from one side to the other; I never had my heel-strings cut to prevent my running away; I was never chained to a log and forced to drag it about, while I toiled in the fields from morning till night; I was never branded with hot iron, or torn by bloodhounds. On the contrary, I had always been kindly treated, and tenderly cared for, until I came into the hands of Dr. Flint. I had never wished for freedom till then. But though my life in slavery was comparatively devoid of hardships, God pity the woman who is compelled to lead such a life!

My food was passed up to me through the trap-door my uncle had contrived; and my grandmother, my uncle Phillip, and aunt Nancy would seize such opportunities as they could, to mount up there and chat with me at the opening. But of course this was not safe in the daytime. It must all be done in darkness. It was impossible for me to move in an erect position, but I crawled about my den for exercise. One day I hit my head against something, and found it was a gimlet. My uncle had left it sticking there when he made the trap-door. I was as rejoiced as Robinson Crusoe could have been at finding such a treasure. It put a lucky thought into my head. I said to myself, "Now I will have some light. Now I will see my children." I did not dare to begin my work during the daytime, for fear of attracting attention. But I groped round; and having found the side next the street, where I could frequently see my children, I stuck the gimlet in and waited for evening. I bored three rows of holes, one above another; then I bored out the interstices between. I thus succeeded in making one hole about an inch long and an inch broad. I sat by it till late into the night, to enjoy the little whiff of air that floated in. In the morning I watched for my children. The first person I saw in the street was Dr. Flint. I had a shuddering, superstitious feeling that it was a bad omen. Several familiar faces passed by. At last I heard the merry laugh of children, and presently two sweet little faces were looking up at me, as though they knew I was there, and were conscious of the joy they imparted. How I longed to tell them I was there!

My condition was now a little improved. But for weeks I was tormented by hundreds of little red insects, fine as a needle's point, that pierced through my skin, and produced an intolerable burning. The good grandmother gave me herb teas and cooling medicines, and finally I got rid of them. The heat of my den was intense, for nothing but thin shingles protected me from the scorching summer's sun. But I had my consolations. Through my peeping-hole I could watch the children, and when they were near enough, I could hear their talk. Aunt Nancy brought me all the news she could hear at Dr. Flint's. From her I learned that the doctor had written to New York to a colored woman, who had been born and raised in our neighborhood, and had breathed his contaminating atmosphere. He offered her a reward if she could find out any thing about me. I know not what was the nature of her reply; but he soon after started for New York in haste, saying to his family that he had business of importance to transact. I peeped at him as he passed on his way to the steamboat. It was a satisfaction to have miles of land and water between us, even for a little while; and it was a still greater satisfaction to know that he believed me to be in the Free States. My little den seemed less dreary than it had done. He returned, as he did from his former journey to New York, without obtaining any satisfactory information. When he passed our house next morning, Benny was standing at the gate. He had heard them say that he had gone to find me, and he called out, "Dr. Flint, did you bring my mother home? I want to see her." The doctor stamped his foot at him in a rage, and exclaimed, "Get out of the way, you little damned rascal! If you don't, I'll cut off your head."

Benny ran terrified into the house, saying, "You can't put me in jail again. I don't belong to you now." It was well that the wind carried the words away from the doctor's ear. I told my grandmother of it, when we had our next conference at the trap-door; and begged of her not to allow the children to be impertinent to the irascible old man.

Autumn came, with a pleasant abatement of heat. My eyes had become accustomed to the dim light, and by holding my book or work in a certain position near the aperture I contrived to read and sew. That was a great relief to the tedious monotony of my life. But when winter came, the cold penetrated through the thin shingle roof, and I was dreadfully chilled. The winters there are not so long, or so severe, as in northern latitudes; but the houses are not built to shelter from cold, and my little den was peculiarly comfortless. The kind grandmother brought me bed-clothes and warm drinks. Often I was obliged to lie in bed all day to keep comfortable; but with all my precautions, my shoulders and feet were frostbitten. O, those long, gloomy days, with no object for my eye to rest upon, and no thoughts to occupy my mind, except the dreary past and the uncertain future! I was thankful when there came a day sufficiently mild for me to wrap myself up and sit at the loophole to watch the passers by. Southerners have the habit of stopping and talking in the streets, and I heard many conversations not intended to meet my ears. I heard slave-hunters planning how to catch some poor fugitive. Several times I heard allusions to Dr. Flint, myself, and the history of my children, who, perhaps, were playing near the gate. One would say, "I wouldn't move my little finger to catch her, as old Flint's property." Another would say, "I'll catch any nigger for the reward. A man ought to have what belongs to him, if he is a damned brute." The opinion was often expressed that I was in the Free States. Very rarely did any one suggest that I might be in the vicinity. Had the least suspicion rested on my grandmother's house, it would have been burned to the ground. But it was the last place they thought of. Yet there was no place, where slavery existed, that could have afforded me so good a place of concealment.

Dr. Flint and his family repeatedly tried to coax and bribe my children to tell something they had heard said about me. One day the doctor took them into a shop, and offered them some bright little silver pieces and gay handkerchiefs if they would tell where their mother was. Ellen shrank away from him, and would not speak; but Benny spoke up, and said, "Dr. Flint, I don't know where my mother is I guess she's in New York; and when you go there again. I wish you'd ask her to come home, for I want to see her; but if you put her in jail, or tell her you'll cut her head off, I'll tell her to go right back."

Sept. 27, 1856.]   THE ILLUSTRATED LONDON NEWS   315

The Illustrated London News ran this picture of a dignified black woman being sold at an auction. Slaves on the block were exposed to full view, thoroughly examined by prospective buyers. On the right hand side of this picture, a black man has evidently just come off the block. Possibly the husband of the woman, he faces away in despair or disgust. **THE LIBRARY OF CONGRESS**

XXII

Christmas Festivities Christmas was approaching. Grandmother brought me materials, and I busied myself making some new garments and little playthings for my children. Were it not that hiring day is near at hand, and many families are fearfully looking forward to the probability of separation in a few days, Christmas might be a happy season for the poor slaves. Even slave mothers try to gladden the hearts of their little ones on that occasion. Benny and Ellen had their Christmas stockings filled. Their imprisoned mother could not have the privilege of witnessing their surprise and joy. But I had the pleasure of peeping at them as they went into the street with their new suits on. I heard Benny ask a little playmate whether Santa Claus brought him any thing. "Yes," replied the boy; "but Santa Claus ain't a real man. It's the children's mothers that put things into the stockings." "No, that can't be," replied Benny, "for Santa Claus brought Ellen and me these new clothes, and my mother has been gone this long time."

How I longed to tell him that his mother made those garments, and that many a tear fell on them while she worked!

Every child rises early on Christmas morning to see the Johnkannaus. Without them, Christmas would be shorn of its greatest attraction. They consist of companies of slaves from the plantations, generally of the lower class. Two athletic men, in calico wrappers, have a net thrown over them, covered with all manner of bright-colored stripes. Cows' tails are fastened to their backs, and their heads are decorated with horns. A box, covered with sheepskin, is called the gumbo box. A dozen beat on this, while others strike triangles and jawbones, to which bands of dancers keep time. For a month previous they are composing songs, which are sung on this occasion. These companies, of a hundred each, turn out early in the morning, and are allowed to go round till twelve o'clock, begging for contributions. Not a door is left unvisited where there is the least chance of obtaining a penny or a glass of rum. They do not drink while they are out, but carry the rum home in jugs, to have a carousal. These Christmas donations frequently amount to twenty or thirty dollars. It is seldom that any white man or child refuses to give them a trifle. If he does, they regale his ears with the following song:—

Poor massa, so dey say;
Down in de heel, so dey say;
Got no money, so dey say;
Not one shillin, so dey say;
God A'mighty bress you, so dey say.

Christmas is a day of feasting, both with white and colored people. Slaves, who are lucky enough to have a few shillings, are sure to spend them for good eating; and many a turkey and pig is captured, without saying, "By your leave, sir." Those who cannot obtain these, cook a 'possum, or a raccoon, from which savory dishes can be made. My grandmother raised poultry and pigs for sale;

and it was her established custom to have both a turkey and a pig roasted for Christmas dinner.

On this occasion, I was warned to keep extremely quiet, because two guests had been invited. One was the town constable, and the other was a free colored man, who tried to pass himself off for white, and who was always ready to do any mean work for the sake of currying favor with white people. My grandmother had a motive for inviting them. She managed to take them all over the house. All the rooms on the lower floor were thrown open for them to pass in and out; and after dinner, they were invited up stairs to look at a fine mocking bird my uncle had just brought home. There, too, the rooms were all thrown open, that they might look in. When I heard them talking on the piazza, my heart almost stood still. I knew this colored man had spent many nights hunting for me. Every body knew he had the blood of a slave father in his veins; but for the sake of passing himself off for white, he was ready to kiss the slaveholders' feet. How I despised him! As for the constable, he wore no false colors. The duties of his office were despicable, but he was superior to his companion, inasmuch as he did not pretend to be what he was not. Any white man, who could raise money enough to buy a slave, would have considered himself degraded by being a constable; but the office enabled its possessor to exercise authority. If he found any slave out after nine o'clock, he could whip him as much as he liked; and that was a privilege to be coveted. When the guests were ready to depart, my grandmother gave each of them some of her nice pudding, as a present for their wives. Through my peep-hole I saw them go out of the gate, and I was glad when it closed after them. So passed the first Christmas in my den.

XXIII

Still in Prison When spring returned, and I took in the little patch of green the aperture commanded, I asked myself how many more summers and winters I must be condemned to spend thus. I longed to draw in a plentiful draught of fresh air, to stretch my cramped limbs, to have room to stand erect, to feel the earth under my feet again. My relatives were constantly on the lookout for a chance of escape; but none offered that seemed practicable, and even tolerably safe. The hot summer came again, and made the turpentine drop from the thin roof over my head.

During the long nights I was restless for want of air, and I had no room to toss and turn. There was but one compensation; the atmosphere was so stifled that even mosquitos would not condescend to buzz in it. With all my detestation of Dr. Flint, I could hardly wish him a worse punishment, either in this world or that which is to come, than to suffer what I suffered in one single summer. Yet the laws allowed him to be out in the free air, while I, guiltless of crime, was pent up here, as the only means of avoiding the cruelties the laws allowed him to inflict upon me! I don't know what kept life within me. Again and again, I thought I should die before long; but I saw the leaves of another autumn whirl through the air, and felt the touch of another winter. In summer the most terrible thunder storms were acceptable, for the rain came through the roof, and I rolled up my bed that it might cool the hot boards under it. Later in the season, storms sometimes wet my clothes through and through, and that was not comfortable when the air grew chilly. Moderate storms I could keep out by filling the chinks with oakum.

But uncomfortable as my situation was, I had glimpses of things out of doors, which made me thankful for my wretched hiding-place. One day I saw a slave pass our gate, muttering, "It's his own, and he can kill it if he will." My grandmother told me that woman's history. Her mistress had that day seen her baby for the first time, and in the lineaments of its fair face she saw a likeness to her husband. She turned the bondwoman and her child out of doors, and forbade her ever to return. The slave went to her master, and told him what had happened. He promised to talk with her mistress, and make it all right. The next day she and her baby were sold to a Georgia trader.

Another time I saw a woman rush wildly by, pursued by two men. She was a slave, the wet nurse of her mistress's children. For some trifling offence her mistress ordered her to be stripped and whipped. To escape the degradation and the torture, she rushed to the river, jumped in, and ended her wrongs in death.

Senator Brown, of Mississippi, could not be ignorant of many such facts as these, for they are of frequent occurrence in every Southern State. Yet he stood up in the Congress of the United States, and declared that slavery was "a great moral, social, and political blessing; a blessing to the master, and a blessing to the slave!"

I suffered much more during the second winter than I did during the first. My limbs were benumbed by inaction, and the cold filled them with cramp. I had a very painful sensation of coldness in my head; even my face and tongue stiffened, and I lost the power of speech. Of course it was impossible, under the circumstances, to summon any physician. My brother William came and did all he could for me. Uncle Phillip also watched tenderly over me; and poor grandmother crept up and down to inquire whether there were any signs of returning life. I was restored to consciousness by the dashing of cold water in my face, and found myself leaning against my brother's arm, while he bent over me with streaming eyes. He afterwards told me he thought I was dying, for I had been in an unconscious state sixteen hours. I next became delirious, and was in great danger of betraying myself and my friends. To prevent this, they stupefied me with drugs.

I remained in bed six weeks, weary in body and sick at heart. How to get medical advice was the question. William finally went to a Thompsonian doctor, and described himself as having all my pains and aches. He returned with herbs, roots, and ointment. He was especially charged to rub on the ointment by a fire; but how could a fire be made in my little den? Charcoal in a furnace was tried, but there was no outlet for the gas, and it nearly cost me my life. Afterwards coals, already kindled, were brought up in an iron pan, and placed on bricks. I was so weak, and it was so long since I had enjoyed the warmth of a fire, that those few coals actually made me weep. I think the medicines did me some good; but my recovery was very slow. Dark thoughts passed through my mind as I lay there day after day. I tried to be thankful for my little cell, dismal as it was, and even to love it, as part of the price I had paid for the redemption of my children. Sometimes I thought God was a compassionate Father, who would forgive my sins for the sake of my sufferings. At other times, it seemed to me there was no justice or mercy in the divine government. I asked why the curse of slavery was permitted to exist, and why I had been so persecuted and wronged from youth upward. These things took the shape of mystery, which is to this day not so clear to my soul as I trust it will be hereafter.

In the midst of my illness, grandmother broke down under the weight of anxiety and toil. The idea of losing her, who had always been my best friend and a mother to my children, was the sorest trial I had yet had. O, how earnestly I prayed that she might recover! How hard it seemed, that I could not tend upon her, who had so long and so tenderly watched over me!

One day the screams of a child nerved me with strength to crawl to my peeping-hole, and I saw my son covered with blood. A fierce dog, usually kept chained, had seized and bitten him. A doctor was sent for, and I heard the groans and screams of my child while the wounds were being sewed up. O, what torture to a mother's heart, to listen to this and be unable to go to him!

But childhood is like a day in spring, alternately shower and sunshine. Before night Benny was bright and lively, threatening the destruction of the dog; and great was his delight when the doctor told him the next day that the dog had bitten another boy and been shot. Benny recovered from his wounds; but it was long before he could walk.

When my grandmother's illness became known, many ladies, who were her customers, called to bring her some little comforts, and to inquire whether she had every thing she wanted. Aunt Nancy one night asked permission to watch with her sick mother, and Mrs. Flint replied, "I don't see any need of your going. I can't spare you." But when she found other ladies in the neighborhood were so attentive, not wishing to be outdone in

---

The Roots of African American Cultural and Artistic Traditions

The story of African Americans in the United States is about a people kidnapped and forced into slavery who went on to mark every element of American culture, from the highbrow to the low. Black Americans have participated in virtually every field of American cultural endeavor and established the very roots of some great American contributions to the world, such as jazz and rock-and-roll. At its heart that expression, rock-and-roll, is deeply rooted in various traditions of African American culture.

The roots of many trademark elements of African American culture, such as call and response structure and the exchange of humorous insults known as "signifying," can be traced to West African roots. West African cultures are known for their strong sense of irony and fate. In the Yoruba tradition, for example, there is a pantheon of gods, each with a two-sided nature. The god of iron, Ogun, represents both the will to control one's surroundings and the destruction and chaos that may result from this impulse to control. This brand of ironic, allegorical dialectic has had a strong influence on American personality and self-expression.

Christian charity, she also sallied forth, in magnificent condescension, and stood by the bedside of her who had loved her in her infancy, and who had been repaid by such grievous wrongs. She seemed surprised to find her so ill, and scolded uncle Phillip for not sending for Dr. Flint. She herself sent for him immediately, and he came. Secure as I was in my retreat, I should have been terrified if I had known he was so near me. He pronounced my grandmother in a very critical situation, and said if her attending physician wished it, he would visit her. Nobody wished to have him coming to the house at all hours, and we were not disposed to give him a chance to make out a long bill.

As Mrs. Flint went out, Sally told her the reason Benny was lame was, that a dog had bitten him. "I'm glad of it," replied she. "I wish he had killed him. It would be good news to send to his mother. Her day will come. The dogs will grab her yet." With these Christian words she and her husband departed, and, to my great satisfaction, returned no more.

I heard from uncle Phillip, with feelings of unspeakable joy and gratitude, that the crisis was passed and grandmother would live. I could now say from my heart, "God is merciful. He has spared me the anguish of feeling that I caused her death."

XXIV

The Candidate for Congress The summer had nearly ended, when Dr. Flint made a third visit to New York, in search of me. Two candidates were running for Congress, and he returned in season to vote. The father of my children was the Whig candidate. The doctor had hitherto been a stanch Whig; but now he exerted all his energies for the defeat of Mr. Sands. He invited large parties of men to dine in the shade of his trees, and supplied them with plenty of rum and brandy. If any poor fellow drowned his wits in the bowl, and, in the openness of his convivial heart, proclaimed that he did not mean to vote the Democratic ticket, he was shoved into the street without ceremony.

The doctor expended his liquor in vain. Mr. Sands was elected; an event which occasioned me some anxious thoughts. He had not emancipated my children, and if he should die they would be at the mercy of his heirs. Two little voices, that frequently met my ear, seemed to plead with me not to let their father depart without striving to make their freedom secure. Years had passed since I had spoken to him. I had not even seen him since the night I passed him, unrecognized, in my disguise of a sailor. I supposed he would call before he left, to say something to my grandmother concerning the children, and I resolved what course to take.

The day before his departure for Washington I made arrangements, towards evening, to get from my hiding-place into the storeroom below. I found myself so stiff and clumsy that it was with great difficulty I could hitch from one resting place to another. When I reached the storeroom my ankles gave way under me, and I sank exhausted on the floor. It seemed as if I could never use my limbs again. But the purpose I had in view roused all the strength I had. I crawled on my hands and knees to the window, and, screened behind a barrel, I waited for his coming. The clock struck nine, and I knew the steamboat would leave between ten and eleven. My hopes were failing. But presently I heard his voice, saying to some one, "Wait for me a moment. I wish to see aunt Martha." When he came out, as he passed the window, I said, "Stop one moment, and let me speak for my children." He started, hesitated, and then passed on, and went out of the gate. I closed the shutter I had partially opened, and sank down behind the barrel. I had suffered much; but seldom had I experienced a keener pang than I then

felt. Had my children, then, become of so little consequence to him? And had he so little feeling for their wretched mother that he would not listen a moment while she pleaded for them? Painful memories were so busy within me, that I forgot I had not hooked the shutter, till I heard some one opening it. I looked up. He had come back. "Who called me?" said he, in a low tone. "I did," I replied. "Oh, Linda," said he, "I knew your voice; but I was afraid to answer, lest my friend should hear me. Why do you come here? Is it possible you risk yourself in this house? They are mad to allow it. I shall expect to hear that you are all ruined." I did not wish to implicate him, by letting him know my place of concealment; so I merely said, "I thought you would come to bid grandmother good by, and so I came here to speak a few words to you about emancipating my children. Many changes may take place during the six months you are gone to Washington, and it does not seem right for you to expose them to the risk of such changes. I want nothing for myself; all I ask is, that you will free my children, or authorize some friend to do it, before you go."

He promised he would do it, and also expressed a readiness to make any arrangements whereby I could be purchased.

I heard footsteps approaching, and closed the shutter hastily. I wanted to crawl back to my den, without letting the family know what I had done; for I knew they would deem it very imprudent. But he stepped back into the house, to tell my grandmother that he had spoken with me at the storeroom window, and to beg of her not to allow me to remain in the house over night. He said it was the height of madness for me to be there; that we should certainly all be ruined. Luckily, he was in too much of a hurry to wait for a reply, or the dear old woman would surely have told him all.

I tried to go back to my den, but found it more difficult to go up than I had to come down. Now that my mission was fulfilled, the little strength that had supported me through it was gone, and I sank helpless on the floor. My grandmother, alarmed at the risk I had run, came into the storeroom in the dark, and locked the door behind her. "Linda," she whispered, "where are you?"

"I am here by the window," I replied. "I couldn't have him go away without emancipating the children. Who knows what may happen?"

"Come, come, child," said she, "it won't do for you to stay here another minute. You've done wrong; but I can't blame you, poor thing!"

I told her I could not return without assistance, and she must call my uncle. Uncle Phillip came, and pity prevented him from scolding me. He carried me back to my dungeon, laid me tenderly on the bed, gave me some medicine, and asked me if there was any thing more he could do. Then he went away, and I was left with my own thoughts—starless as the midnight darkness around me.

My friends feared I should become a cripple for life; and I was so weary of my long imprisonment that, had it not been for the hope of serving my children, I should have been thankful to die; but, for their sakes, I was willing to bear on.

XXV

Competition in Cunning Dr. Flint had not given me up. Every now and then he would say to my grandmother that I would yet come back, and voluntarily surrender myself; and that when I did, I could be purchased by my relatives, or any one who wished to buy me. I knew his cunning nature too well not to perceive that this was a trap laid for me; and so all my friends understood it. I resolved to match my cunning against his cunning. In order to make him believe that I was in New York, I resolved to write him a letter dated from that place. I sent for my friend Peter, and asked him if he knew any trustworthy seafaring person, who would carry such a letter to New York, and put it in the post office there. He said he knew one that he would trust with his own life to the ends of the world. I reminded him that it was a hazardous thing for him to undertake. He said he knew it, but he was willing to do any thing to help me. I expressed a wish for a New York paper, to ascertain the names of some of the streets. He run his hand into his pocket, and said, "Here is half a one, that was round a cap I bought of a pedler yesterday." I told him the letter would be ready the next evening. He bade me good by, adding, "Keep up your spirits, Linda; brighter days will come by and by."

My uncle Phillip kept watch over the gate until our brief interview was over. Early the next morning, I seated myself near the little aperture to examine the newspaper. It was a piece of the New York Herald; and, for once, the paper that systematically abuses the colored people, was made to render them a service. Having obtained what information I wanted concerning streets and numbers, I wrote two letters, one to my grandmother, the other to Dr. Flint. I reminded him how he, a gray-headed man, had treated a helpless child, who had been placed in his power, and what years of misery he had brought upon her. To my grandmother, I expressed a wish to have my children sent to me at the north, where I could teach them to respect themselves, and set them a virtuous example; which a slave mother was not allowed to do at the south. I asked her to direct her answer to a certain street in Boston, as I did not live in New York, though I went there sometimes. I dated these letters ahead, to allow for the time it would take to carry them, and sent a memorandum of the date to the messenger. When my friend came for the letters, I said, "God bless and reward you, Peter, for this disinterested kindness. Pray be care-

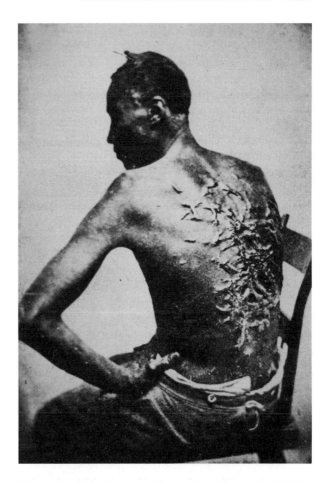

A slave who had been severely beaten many times exposed his scarred back to the camera for this famous photograph, all the while looking off into the distance. Abolitionists used such images effectively to make the case that slavery was brutal and dehumanizing. **NATIONAL ARCHIVES AND RECORDS ADMINISTRATION**

ful. If you are detected, both you and I will have to suffer dreadfully. I have not a relative who would dare to do it for me." He replied, "You may trust to me, Linda. I don't forget that your father was my best friend, and I will be a friend to his children so long as God lets me live."

It was necessary to tell my grandmother what I had done, in order that she might be ready for the letter, and prepared to hear what Dr. Flint might say about my being at the north. She was sadly troubled. She felt sure mischief would come of it. I also told my plan to aunt Nancy, in order that she might report to us what was said at Dr. Flint's house. I whispered it to her through a crack, and she whispered back, "I hope it will succeed. I shan't mind being a slave all my life, if I can only see you and the children free."

I had directed that my letters should be put into the New York post office on the 20th of the month. On the evening of the 24th my aunt came to say that Dr. Flint and his wife had been talking in a low voice about a letter he had received, and that when he went to his office he promised to bring it when he came to tea. So I concluded I should hear my letter read the next morning. I told my grandmother Dr. Flint would be sure to come, and asked her to have him sit near a certain door, and leave it open, that I might hear what he said. The next morning I took my station within sound of that door, and remained motionless as a statue. It was not long before I heard the gate slam, and the well-known footsteps enter the house. He seated himself in the chair that was placed for him, and said, "Well, Martha, I've brought you a letter from Linda. She has sent me a letter, also. I know exactly where to find her; but I don't choose to go to Boston for her. I had rather she would come back of her own accord, in a respectable manner. Her uncle Phillip is the best person to go for her. With him, she would feel perfectly free to act. I am willing to pay his expenses going and returning. She shall be sold to her friends. Her children are free; at least I suppose they are; and when you obtain her freedom, you'll make a happy family. I suppose, Martha, you have no objection to my reading to you the letter Linda has written to you."

He broke the seal, and I heard him read it. The old villain! He had suppressed the letter I wrote to grandmother, and prepared a substitute of his own, the purport of which was as follows:—

"Dear Grandmother: I have long wanted to write to you; but the disgraceful manner in which I left you and my children made me ashamed to do it. If you knew how much I have suffered since I ran away, you would pity and forgive me. I have purchased freedom at a dear rate. If any arrangement could be made for me to return to the south without being a slave, I would gladly come. If not, I beg of you to send my children to the north. I cannot live any longer without them. Let me know in time, and I will meet them in New York or Philadelphia, whichever place best suits my uncle's convenience. Write as soon as possible to your unhappy daughter."

Linda.

"It is very much as I expected it would be," said the old hypocrite, rising to go. "You see the foolish girl has repented of her rashness, and wants to return. We must help her to do it, Martha. Talk with Phillip about it. If he will go for her, she will trust to him, and come back. I should like an answer tomorrow. Good morning, Martha."

As he stepped out on the piazza, he stumbled over my little girl. "Ah, Ellen, is that you?" he said, in his most gracious manner. "I didn't see you. How do you do?"

"Pretty well, sir," she replied. "I heard you tell grandmother that my mother is coming home. I want to see her."

"Yes, Ellen, I am going to bring her home very soon," rejoined he; "and you shall see her as much as you like, you little curly-headed nigger."

This was as good as a comedy to me, who had heard it all; but grandmother was frightened and distressed, because the doctor wanted my uncle to go for me.

The next evening Dr. Flint called to talk the matter over. My uncle told him that from what he had heard of Massachusetts, he judged he should be mobbed if he went there after a runaway slave. "All stuff and nonsense, Phillip!" replied the doctor. "Do you suppose I want you to kick up a row in Boston? The business can all be done quietly. Linda writes that she wants to come back. You are her relative, and she would trust you. The case would be different if I went. She might object to coming with me; and the damned abolitionists, if they knew I was her master, would not believe me, if I told them she had begged to go back. They would get up a row; and I should not like to see Linda dragged through the streets like a common negro. She has been very ungrateful to me for all my kindness; but I forgive her, and want to act the part of a friend towards her. I have no wish to hold her as my slave. Her friends can buy her as soon as she arrives here."

Finding that his arguments failed to convince my uncle, the doctor "let the cat out of the bag," by saying that he had written to the mayor of Boston, to ascertain whether there was a person of my description at the street and number from which my letter was dated. He had omitted this date in the letter he had made up to read to my grandmother. If I had dated from New York, the old man would probably have made another journey to that city. But even in that dark region, where knowledge is so carefully excluded from the slave, I had heard enough about Massachusetts to come to the conclusion that slaveholders did not consider it a comfortable place to go to in search of a runaway. That was before the Fugitive Slave Law was passed; before Massachusetts had consented to become a "nigger hunter" for the south.

My grandmother, who had become skittish by seeing her family always in danger, came to me with a very distressed countenance, and said, "What will you do if the mayor of Boston sends him word that you haven't been there? Then he will suspect the letter was a trick; and maybe he'll find out something about it, and we shall all get into trouble. O Linda, I wish you had never sent the letter."

"Don't worry yourself, grandmother," said I. "The mayor of Boston won't trouble himself to hunt niggers for Dr. Flint. The letters will do good in the end. I shall get out of this dark hole some time or other."

"I hope you will, child," replied the good, patient old friend. "You have been here a long time; almost five years; but whenever you do go, it will break your old grandmother's heart. I should be expecting every day to hear that you were brought back in irons and put in jail. God help you, poor child! Let us be thankful that some time or other we shall go 'where the wicked cease from

THE SEPARATION OF THE MOTHER AND CHILD.

" The old men of the company, partly by persuasion and partly by force, loosed the poor creature's last despairing hold, and, as they led her off to her new master's waggon, strove to comfort her."—Page 104.

This illustration by George Cruikshank depicts the painful separation of a child torn from his mother. The picture appeared in Harriet Beecher Stowe's popular fiction novel *Uncle Tom's Cabin.* **CORBIS-BETTMANN**

troubling, and the weary are at rest.'" My heart responded, Amen.

The fact that Dr. Flint had written to the mayor of Boston convinced me that he believed my letter to be genuine, and of course that he had no suspicion of my being any where in the vicinity. It was a great object to keep up this delusion, for it made me and my friends feel less anxious, and it would be very convenient whenever there was a chance to escape. I resolved, therefore, to continue to write letters from the north from time to time.

Two or three weeks passed, and as no news came from the mayor of Boston, grandmother began to listen to my entreaty to be allowed to leave my cell, sometimes, and exercise my limbs to prevent my becoming a cripple. I was allowed to slip down into the small storeroom, early in the morning, and remain there a little while. The room was all filled up with barrels, except a small open space under my trap-door. This faced the door, the upper part of which was of glass, and purposely left uncurtained, that the curious might look in. The air of this place was close; but it was so much better than the atmosphere of my cell, that I dreaded to return. I came down as soon as it was light, and remained till eight o'clock, when people began to be about, and there was danger that some one might come on the piazza. I had tried various applications to bring warmth and feeling into my limbs, but

without avail. They were so numb and stiff that it was a painful effort to move; and had my enemies come upon me during the first mornings I tried to exercise them a little in the small unoccupied space of the storeroom, it would have been impossible for me to have escaped.

Free African Americans in the United States

ADAPTED FROM ESSAYS BY PATRICK RAEL, BOWDOIN COLLEGE

When we think of how black people lived in the years of the first colonies, the newly formed nation and beyond, we almost always think of slavery. And it is true: only African Americans were ever held as property by other Americans. Yet along with the four million African Americans held in bondage on the eve of the Civil War, almost five hundred thousand were not. Though legally not slaves, these African Americans confronted a host of oppressive measures that kept them from enjoying complete freedom. They lived somewhere between slavery and freedom.

FREE BLACK PEOPLE IN THE COLONIAL PERIOD: 1619–1660

The development of a free black community in what became the United States began with the earliest Africans brought to mainland North America—the "twenty Negars" whom the Virginian John Rolphe reported arriving in the colony in 1619. In these early days of slavery in the colonies, Englishmen had yet to define the legal boundaries of slavery and freedom. They held negative views of Africans, whom they considered heathen and uncivilized, but they had yet to codify in law the principle that all black people should be slaves. As a result, this early era was a time of limited possibilities for Africans in the colonies. Among the black people brought to Virginia in the early 1600s, a few were probably indentured servants rather than slaves. Like English indentured servants, these Africans could be bought and sold, but they gained their freedom after laboring for their masters for a certain number of years. This small group of freed servants helped form the basis of America's first free black population.

Other black people in seventeenth-century North America were fortunate enough to gain their freedom in a variety of ways. Because European women were scarce, Englishmen sometimes intermingled with black women. When sexual relations between English planters and slave women produced offspring, an affectionate master might free, or manumit, the infant. Far more common were the children born of a union between an indentured servant and a slave—most often, a slave woman and an indentured Englishman. In these cases, the law might provide for the limited freedom of the child, or the free parent might successfully petition the government for the freedom of his offspring. With little education and few resources, these freed slaves faced difficult lives.

SEE PRIMARY SOURCE DOCUMENT *The Runaway Slave Act*

FREE BLACK PEOPLE IN THE COLONIAL PERIOD: 1660–1775

The period between 1660 and the American Revolution witnessed the growth and legal codification of black slavery in North America. During that time, the cash crop economies of the colonial South expanded, while the supply of indentured servants from England declined. As a result, colonial planters demanded that more slaves be brought into the colonies to labor. While colonies in the South expanded through agriculture, northern cities like Boston and New York became centers for trade, including the trade in African slaves for the southern market.

The rise in the black population from the slave trade caused great anxiety among whites, who feared a revolt of the enslaved people in their midst. In places like South Carolina, where blacks were actually a majority by 1710, racial tensions ran high. Because whites feared that free blacks would assist slaves in any general uprising, they targeted them in new laws. During the first half of the 1700s, the status of free African Americans—and,

indeed, of black people in general—became increasingly well defined, as law replaced custom and improvisation. Colonies varied in their legal treatment of black people, but in nearly all cases those with any African heritage were defined as different and inferior, even when free. As early as the 1660s, a Virginia statute claimed that free black people "ought not in all respects … be admitted to a full fruition of the exemptions and impunities of the English." In colonies like Virginia and South Carolina, laws at various times prohibited the manumission of bondsmen or required freed slaves to leave the colony. Other laws prevented free black people from testifying against whites, owning land, marrying whites, or in other ways enjoying a life equal to that of European Americans. The racial prejudice of English settlers prevented them from granting equality even to black people who were legally free.

This hardening of racial relations, which took place primarily during the first half of the 1700s, inhibited opportunities for enslaved black people to become free. The flexibility that marked the 1600s disappeared, and the numbers of free blacks decreased. By 1750, not more than 5 percent of all black people in America enjoyed liberty. Despite restrictions, however, a small free black society developed during the colonial era.

COLOR AND STATUS AMONG COLONIAL FREE AFRICAN AMERICANS

Within this small society, distinctions based on skin color were very important. Because free black people tended to be the offspring of interracial relations, colonial America's free African Americans tended to be lighter-skinned than its slave population. This difference in skin color developed into a significant (though hardly inflexible) marker of elevated social status.

Oftentimes, light skin color signaled that a black person had a relationship with a white person, a relationship that might ease the burdens imposed by a society deeply imbued with prejudice against people of color. For instance, a wealthy, benevolent master might free his "mulatto" child born of a union with a female slave and give that child training in a craft or money with which to start a new life. Such manumissions were rare, however, and free black people still faced a host of legal and social prejudices.

THE IMPACT OF THE AMERICAN REVOLUTION

The American Revolution was the single most important event in the development of free African American society. The war itself placed huge demands for troops and laborers on both the British and the colonists. Leaders on both sides followed the example of Lord Dunmore, the royal governor of Virginia, who, in 1775, promised freedom for any slave willing to bear arms for Britain. Dunmore's promise kindled the hopes of slaves everywhere, though many never had the chance to take him up on his offer. In the chaos of the revolution, slaves took every opportunity to gain their freedom. They fled to British lines, and even to colonial lines, where labor-needy officers asked few questions about their origins. SEE PRIMARY SOURCE DOCUMENT *A Witness Tells of Crispus Attucks's Death*

In addition to the practical effects of war, the ideals and philosophy of the American Revolution also contributed to the creation of a free black community. When the colonists began their war against Great Britain, they did so armed with a philosophy of fundamental human equality. Written in 1776 by Thomas Jefferson (1743–1826), a slaveholder, the Declaration of Independence declared "that all Men are created equal, [and] that they are endowed by their Creator with certain unalienable Rights." It was with this idea that Americans demanded equal rights from the mother country. During and after the war, this philosophy of "natural rights" raised an important question for Americans: Were not slaves also people? And if so, were they not also entitled to the freedom all humans were endowed with?

Spurred by this deeply held belief in human liberty, some slaveholders freed their slaves. The rate at which these manumissions took place varied, depending on the region. In the new states of the North, slavery had never been the mainstay of the economy, so it was easier for white Americans there to give up the institution. While there was some opposition to ending slavery in the North, by 1805 all the northern states had either abolished slavery or provided for the eventual abolition of it.

In the states of the upper South (Maryland and Virginia), the story was different. There, slavery was simply too important for ideals to take priority over the profits made possible by tobacco, wheat, and cotton. In the North, many masters had been compensated for the loss of their slaves, but the large numbers of slaves in the upper South made this abolitionist strategy unfeasible. Yet, after the revolution, a decline in tobacco growing and the beginnings of industry in the upper South signaled that a change was under way. Spurred by democratic sentiment and buoyed by these economic changes, some individual slaveholders manumitted their slaves, but the institution itself did not die.

In the lower South (the Carolinas and Georgia), black labor was so crucial to the economy that few masters even contemplated manumission. There, black labor was needed to work profitable crops of rice, indigo, and cotton. And the low proportion of whites to blacks made the specter of freed slaves frightening to white masters. Benevolent masters might still manumit favored slaves, often their children, but they never considered manumission in large numbers.

The Virginia Manumission Law

Despite the humane intentions of some landowners after the Revolutionary War and the creation of the Declaration of Independence, the institution of slavery continued to operate in most of the southern states. In 1782 the state of Virginia put a manumission law on the books, detailing the right of slaveholders in the eyes of state to set their slaves free. Curiously, the law outlined conditions and constraints upon newly freed slaves very similar to those contained in the black codes created after the Civil War.

There were, among other conditions, a series of taxes required, and what was in effect an early vagrancy law, violation of which could be punishable by incarceration. Like most legislation designed to keep African Americans "in their place," the law used an amalgam of racial and class distinctions to create a web of contradictory prohibitions that were almost impossible to abide by. This effectively gave whites, and the figures of law, the ability to control blacks in any way they saw fit, particularly in times of rebellion when fears of slave uprisings rose among plantation owners.

SEE PRIMARY SOURCE DOCUMENT *"Oration on the Abolition of the Slave Trade" by Peter Williams Jr.*

BIBLIOGRAPHY

Berlin, Ira. *Slaves without Masters: The Free Negro in the Antebellum South.* New York: Oxford University Press, 1974.

Breen, T.H., and Stephen Innes. *"Myne Owne Ground": Race and Freedom on Virginia's Eastern Shore, 1640–1676.* New York: Oxford University Press, 1980.

Cohen, David W., and Jack P. Greene, eds. *Neither Slave nor Free: The Freedmen of African Descent in the Slave Societies of the New World.* Baltimore: The Johns Hopkins University Press, 1972.

Curry, Leonard P. *The Free Black in Urban America, 1800–1850: The Shadow of the Dream.* Chicago: University of Chicago Press, 1981.

George, Carol V.R. "Widening the Circle: The Black Church and the Abolitionist Crusade, 1830–1860." In *Antislavery Reconsidered: New Perspectives on the Abolitionists,* ed. Lewis Perry and Michael Fellman. Baton Rouge: Louisiana State University Press, 1979.

Acknowledging Permanent Slavery: the Escape and Capture of the Slave John Punch

Although many were held before 1641 in conditions we would term slavery, it was not until that year, when the Massachusetts Colony promulgated the first slavery statute, that slavery became a formal, legal condition. Prior to that, Africans served under indenture contracts, whereby they were in servitude for a limited number of years, after which they were made free. The twenty Africans who arrived in Jamestown Harbor in 1619 were sold as indentured servants, and many if not all of them went on to become free persons, acquiring land and servants of their own.

This changed in 1640, when an African indentured servant named John Punch ran away with two other servants, both of them white. The three were captured, and as punishment for running away, John Punch alone was made a "slave for life." He is the first recorded slave in the North American colonies, and his punishment marked the beginning of more than two hundred years of racial slavery. A year after John Punch was enslaved, Massachusetts instituted the first formal slavery statute.

Greene, Lorenzo Johnson. *The Negro in Colonial New England.* New York: Columbia University Press, 1942.

Horton, James O. *Free People of Color: Inside the African-American Community.* Washington, D.C.: Smithsonian Institution Press, 1993.

Horton, James O., and Lois E. Horton. *Black Bostonians: Family Life and Community Struggle in the Antebellum North.* New York: Holmes and Meier, 1979.

Johnson, Michael P., and James L. Roark. *Black Masters: A Free Family of Color in the Old South.* New York: W.W. Norton, 1984.

———, eds. *No Chariot Let Down: Charleston's Free People of Color on the Eve of the Civil War.* New York: W.W. Norton, 1984.

Litwack, Leon F. *North of Slavery: The Negro in the Free States, 1790–1860.* Chicago: University of Chicago Press, 1961.

Pierson, William D. *Black Yankees: The Development of an Afro-American Subculture in Eighteenth-Century New England.* Amherst: University of Massachusetts Press, 1988.

Quarles, Benjamin. *Black Abolitionists.* New York: Oxford University Press, 1969.

Zilversmit, Arthur. *The First Emancipation: The Abolition of Slavery in the North.* Chicago: University of Chicago Press, 1967.

PRIMARY SOURCE DOCUMENT

The Runaway Slave Act

INTRODUCTION Reprinted here is Act CII, regarding Runaway Slaves in the state of Virginia.

This act, passed in 1661, marked the early legislative efforts to deny citizenship to Africans in the new colonies. Like much of the legislation regarding slavery that followed over the centuries, the Runaway Slave Act uses language designed to create fear regarding the protection of property and the possibility of "dangerous strangers" in proper society. These techniques appeared in every stage of discriminatory legislative policy enacted during the course of United States history.

Whereas there are diverse loytering runaways in this country who very often absent themselves from their masters service and sometimes in a long time cannot be found, that loss of the time and the charge in the seeking them often exceeding the value of their labor: Bee it therefore enacted that all runaways that shall absent themselves from their said masters service, shalbe lyable to make satisfaction by service after the times by custom or indenture is expired (vizt.) double their times of service soe neglected, and if the time of their running away was in the crop or the charge of recovering them extraordinary the court shall lymitt a longer time of service proportionable to the damage the master shall make appeare he hath susteyned, and because the adjudging the time they should serve is often referred until the time by indenture is expired, when the proofe of what is due is very uncertaine, it is enacted that the master of any runaway that intends to take the benefit of this act, shall as soone as he hath recovered him carry him to the next commissioner and there declare and prove the time of his absence, and the charge he hath bin at in his recovery, which commissioner thereupon shall grant his certificate, and the court on that certificate passe judgment for the time he shall serve for his absence; and in case any English servant shall run away in company of any negroes who are incapable of making satisfaction by addition of a time, it is enacted that the English soe running away in the company with them shall at the time of service to their owne masters expired, serve the masters of the said negroes for their absence soe long as they should have done by this act if they had not beene slaves, every christian in company with them shall by proportion among them, either pay fower thousand five hundred pounds of tobacco and caske or fower yeares service for every negroe soe lost or dead.

PRIMARY SOURCE DOCUMENT

A Witness Tells of Crispus Attucks's Death

INTRODUCTION The first patriot to die in the cause of American independence was Crispus Attucks, an escaped slave of African and Indian heritage. Born in Framingham, Massachusetts, in the early 1720s, Attucks was in Boston on the evening of March 5, 1770, when armed British soldiers began menacing the citizens. Attucks urged his fellow townsmen to stand their ground, and in the ensuing fray he and four other men were shot dead. The event became known as "The Boston Massacre," and was memorialized in a famous engraving by Paul Revere that circulated among the colonists.

In the murder trial that followed, a young slave named Andrew gave the following eyewitness testimony. Andrew could read and write, according to his owner, and he had never been known to lie. On the basis of Andrew's account of the Boston Massacre, the British soldiers were acquitted of murder, although two were found guilty of manslaughter and branded with the letter.

It is commonly believed that Crispus Attucks, a runaway slave from Framingham, Massachusetts, was the first to defy the British in the event that became known as the Boston Massacre. Attucks, who was killed in the massacre, was considered a hero by many. This engraving was made by the patriot artist Paul Revere. **THE LIBRARY OF CONGRESS**

Slave Andrew's Testimony in the Boston Massacre Trial

On the evening of the fifth of March I was at home. I heard the bells ring and went to the gate. I stayed there a little and saw Mr. Lovell coming back with his buckets. I asked him where was the fire. He said it was not fire.

After that, I went into the street and saw one of my acquaintances coming up … holding his arm. I asked him, "What's the matter?"

He said the soldiers were fighting, had got cutlasses, and were killing everybody, and that one of them had struck him on the arm and almost cut it off. He told me I had best not go down.

I said a good club was better than a cutlass, and he had better go down and see if he could not cut some too.

I went to the Town House, saw the sentinels. Numbers of boys on the other side of the way were throwing snowballs at them. The sentinels were enraged and swearing at the boys. The boys called them, "Lobsters, bloody backs," and hollered, "Who buys lobsters!"

One of my acquaintance came and told me that the soldiers had been fighting, and the people had drove them to Murray's barracks. I saw a number of people coming from Murray's barracks who went down by Jackson's corner into King Street.

Presently I heard three cheers given in King Street. I said, "We had better go down and see what's the matter." We went down to the whipping post and stood by Waldo's shop. I saw a number of people 'round the sentinel at the Custom House.

There were also a number of people who stood where I did and were picking up pieces of sea coal that had been thrown out thereabout and snowballs, and throwing them over at the sentinel. While I was standing there, there were two or three boys run out from among the people and cried, "We have got his gun away and now we will have him!"

Presently I heard three cheers given by the people at the Custom House. I said to my acquaintance I would run up and see whether the guard would turn out. I passed round the guard house and went as far as the west door of the Town House.

I saw a file of men, with an officer with a laced hat on before them. Upon that, we all went to go towards him, and when we had got about half way to them, the officer said something to them, and they filed off down the street.

Upon that, I went in the shadow towards the guard house and followed them down as far as Mr. Peck's corner. I saw them pass through the crowd and plant themselves by the Custom House. As soon as they got there, the people gave three cheers.

I went to cross over to where the soldiers were and as soon as I got a glimpse of them, I heard somebody huzza and say, "Here is old Murray with the riot act"— and they began to pelt snowballs.

A man set out and run, and I followed him as far as Philips's corner, and I do not know where he went. I turned back and went through the people until I got to the head of Royal Exchange Lane right against the soldiers. The first word I heard was a grenadier say to a man by me, "Damn you, stand back."

Question. How near was he to him?

Answer. He was so near that the grenadier might have run him through if he had stepped one step forward. While I stopped to look at him, a person came to get through betwixt the grenadier and me, and the soldier had like to have pricked him. He turned about and said, "You damned lobster, bloody back, are you going to stab me?"

The soldier said, "By God, will I!"

Presently somebody took hold of me by the shoulder and told me to go home or I should be hurt. At the same time there were a number of people towards the Town House who said, "Come away and let the guard alone. You have nothing at all to do with them."

I turned about and saw the officer standing before the men, and one or two persons engaged in talk with him. A number were jumping on the backs of those that were talking with the officer, to get as near as they could.

Question. Did you hear what they said?

Answer. No. Upon this, I went to go as close to the officer as I could. One of the persons who was talking with the officer turned about quick to the people and said, "Damn him, he is going to fire!" Upon that, they cried out, "Fire and be damned, who cares! Damn you, you dare not fire," and began to throw snowballs and other things, which then flew pretty thick.

Question. Did they hit any of them?

Answer. Yes, I saw two or three of them hit. One struck a grenadier on the hat. And the people who were right before them had sticks, and as the soldiers were pushing their guns back and forth, they struck their guns, and one hit a grenadier on the fingers.

At this time, the people up at the Town House called again, "Come away! Come away!" A stout man who stood near me and right before the grenadiers as they pushed with their bayonets the length of their arms, kept striking on their guns.

The people seemed to be leaving the soldiers and to turn from them when there came down a number from Jackson's corner huzzaing and crying, "Damn them, they dare not fire!" "We are not afraid of them!"

One of these people, a stout man with a long cordwood stick, threw himself in and made a blow at the officer. I saw the office try to fend off the stroke. Whether he struck him or not, I do not know. The stout man then turned round and struck the grenadier's gun at the Captain's right hand and immediately fell in with his club and knocked his gun away and struck him over the head. The blow came either on the soldier's cheek or hat.

This stout man held the bayonet with his left hand and twitched it and cried, "Kill the dogs! Knock them over!" This was the general cry. The people then crowded in and, upon that, the grenadier gave a twitch back and relieved his gun, and he up with it and began to pay away on the people.

I was then betwixt the officer and this grenadier. I turned to go off. When I had got away about the length of a gun, I turned to look towards the officer, and I heard the word, "Fire!" I thought I heard the report of a gun and, upon hearing the report, I saw the same grenadier swing his gun and immediately he discharged it.

Question. Did the soldiers of that party, or any of them, step or move out of the rank in which they stood to push the people?

Answer. No, and if they had they might have killed me and many others with their bayonets.

Question. Did you, as you passed through the people towards Royal Exchange Lane and the party, see a number of people take up any and everything they could find in the street and throw them at the soldiers?

Answer. Yes, I saw ten or fifteen round me do it.

Question. Did you yourself ….

Answer. Yes, I did.

Question. After the gun fired, where did you go?

Answer. I run as fast as I could into the first door I saw open … I was very much frightened.

PRIMARY SOURCE DOCUMENT

"Oration on the Abolition of the Slave Trade" by Peter Williams Jr.

INTRODUCTION Peter Williams Jr., son of the founder of New York City's African Methodist Episcopal Zion Church, delivered this speech on January 1, 1808, the day mandated by the Constitution as the official end of the nation's slave trade.

It is primarily a speech of thanksgiving, as befits the occasion. While it paints the horrors suffered by those caught up in the slave trade, it stops well short of calling for the abolition of slavery itself, which continued—as did slave trading—long after this date. Rather, Williams reminds his listeners of the progress they have made, of how many now enjoy freedom and the fruits of education, and calls upon them to move forward "by a steady and upright deportment, by a strict obedience and respect to the laws of the land."

Fathers, Brethren, and Fellow Citizens: At this auspicious moment I felicitate you on the abolition of the Slave Trade. This inhuman branch of commerce which, for some centuries past, has been carried on to a considerable extent, is, by the singular interposition of Divine

Providence, this day extinguished. An event so important, so pregnant with happy consequences, must be extremely consonant to every philanthropic heart.

But to us, Africans and descendants of Africans, this period is deeply interesting. We have felt, sensibly felt, the sad effects of this abominable traffic. It has made, if not ourselves, our forefathers and kinsmen its unhappy victims; and pronounced on them, and their posterity, the sentence of perpetual slavery. But benevolent men have voluntarily stepped forward to obviate the consequences of this injustice and barbarity. They have striven, assiduously, to restore our natural rights; to guaranty them from fresh innovations; to furnish us with necessary information; and to stop the source from whence our evils have flowed.

The fruits of these laudable endeavors have long been visible; each moment they appear more conspicuous; and this day has produced an event which shall ever be memorable and glorious in the annals of history. We are now assembled to celebrate this momentous era; to recognize the beneficial influences of humane exertions; and by suitable demonstrations of joy, thanksgiving, and gratitude, to return to our heavenly Father, and to our earthly benefactors, our sincere acknowledgments.

Review, for a moment, my brethren, the history of the Slave Trade. Engendered in the foul recesses of the sordid mind, the unnatural monster inflicted gross evils on the human race. Its baneful footsteps are marked with blood; its infectious breath spreads war and desolation; and its train is composed of the complicated miseries of cruel and unceasing bondage.

Before the enterprising spirit of European genius explored the western coast of Africa, the state of our forefathers was a state of simplicity, innocence, and contentment. Unskilled in the arts of dissimulation, their bosoms were the seats of confidence; and their lips were the organs of truth. Strangers to the refinements of civilized society, they followed with implicit obedience the (simple) dictates of nature. Peculiarly observant of hospitality, they offered a place of refreshment to the weary, and an asylum to the unfortunate. Ardent in their affections, their minds were susceptible of the warmest emotions of love, friendship, and gratitude.

Although unacquainted with the diversified luxuries and amusements of civilized nations, they enjoyed some singular advantages from the bountiful hand of nature and from their own innocent and amiable manners, which rendered them a happy people. But, alas! this delightful picture has long since vanished; the angel of bliss has deserted their dwelling; and the demon of indescribable misery has rioted, uncontrolled, on the fair fields of our ancestors. After the Columbus unfolded to civilized man the vast treasures of this western world, the desire of gain, which had chiefly induced the first colonists of

In 1808, the U.S. Congress passed a law that made it illegal for Americans to participate in the Atlantic slave trade. However, Africans continued to be brought into ports such as Key West on slave ships like the *Wildfire* well into the mid-19th century. This wood engraving, which appeared in *Harper's Weekly* in June 1860, is dated April 30, 1860. **THE LIBRARY OF CONGRESS**

America to cross the waters of the Atlantic, surpassing the bounds of reasonable acquisition, violated the sacred injunctions of the gospel, frustrated the designs of the pious and humane, and, enslaving the harmless aborigines, compelled them to drudge in the mines.

The severities of this employment was so insupportable to men who were unaccustomed to fatigue that, according to Robertson's "History of America," upwards of nine hundred thousand were destroyed in the space of fifteen years on the island of Hispaniola. A consumption so rapid must, in a short period, have deprived them of the instruments of labor, had not the same genius which first produced it found out another method to obtain them. This was no other than the importation of slaves from the coast of Africa.

The Genoese made the first regular importation, in the year 1517, by virtue of a patent granted by Charles of Austria to a Flemish favorite; since which, this commerce has increased to an astonishing and almost incredible degree.

After the manner of ancient piracy, descents were first made on the African coast; the towns bordering on the ocean were surprised, and a number of the inhabitants carried into slavery.

Alarmed at these depredations, the natives fled to the interior, and there united to secure themselves from the common foe. But the subtle invaders were not easily deterred from their purpose. Their experience, corroborated by historical testimony, convinced them that this spirit of unity would baffle every violent attempt; and that the most powerful method to dissolve it would be to diffuse in them the same avaricious disposition which they themselves possessed; and to afford them the means of gratifying it, by ruining each other. Fatal engine: fatal thou hast proved to man in all ages: where the greatest violence has proved ineffectual, their undermining principles have wrought destruction. By thy deadly power, the strong Grecian arm, which bid the world defiance, fell nerveless; by thy potent attacks, the solid pillars of Roman grandeur shook to their base; and, oh! Africans! by this parent of the Slave Trade, this grandsire of misery, the mortal blow was struck which crushed the peace and happiness of our country. Affairs now assumed a different aspect; the appearances of war were changed into the most amicable pretensions; presents apparently inestimable were made; and all the bewitching and alluring wiles of the seducer were practiced. The harmless African, taught to believe a friendly countenance, the sure token of a corresponding heart, soon disbanded his fears and evinced a favorable disposition towards his flattering enemies.

Thus the foe, obtaining an intercourse by a dazzling display of European finery, bewildered their simple understandings and corrupted their morals. Mutual agreements were then made; the Europeans were to supply the Africans with those gaudy trifles which so strongly affected them; and the Africans in return were to grant the Europeans their prisoners of war and convicts as slaves. These stipulations, naturally tending to delude the mind, answered the twofold purpose of enlarging their criminal code and of exciting incessant war at the same time that it furnished a specious pretext for the prosecution of this inhuman traffic. Bad as this may appear, had it prescribed the bounds of injustice, millions of unhappy victims might have still been spared. But, extending widely beyond measure and without control, large additions of slaves were made by kidnaping and the most unpalliated seizures.

Trace the past scenes of Africa and you will manifestly perceive these flagrant violations of human rights. The prince who once delighted in the happiness of his people, who felt himself bound by a sacred contract to defend their persons and property, was turned into their tyrant and scourge: he, who once strove to preserve peace and good understanding with the different nations, who never unsheathed his sword but in the cause of justice, at the signal of a slave ship assembled his warriors and rushed furiously upon his unsuspecting friends. What a scene does that town now present, which a few moments past was the abode of tranquillity. At the approach of the foe, alarm and confusion pervade every part; horror and dismay are depicted on every countenance; the aged chief, starting from his couch, calls forth his men to repulse the hostile invader: all ages obey the summons; feeble youth and decrepit age join the standard; while the foe, to effect his purpose, fires the town.

Now, with unimaginable terror the battle commences: hear now the shrieks of the women, the cries of the children, the shouts of the warriors, and the groans of the dying. See with what desperation the inhabitants fight in defense of their darling joys. But, alas! overpowered by a superior foe, their force is broken; their ablest warriors fall; and the wretched remnant are taken captives.

Where are now those pleasant dwellings, where peace and harmony reigned incessant? where those beautiful fields, whose smiling crops and enchanting verdure enlivened the heart of every beholder? Alas! those tenements are now enveloped in destructive flames; those fair fields are not bedewed with blood and covered with mangled carcasses. Where are now those sounds of mirth and gladness, which loudly rang throughout the village? where those darling youth, those venerable aged, who mutually animated the festive throng? Alas! those exhilarating peals are now changed into the dismal groans of inconceivable distress; the survivors of those happy people are now carried into cruel captivity. Ah! driven from their native soil, they cast their languishing eyes behind, and with aching hearts bid adieu to every prospect of joy and comfort.

A spectacle so truly distressing is sufficient to blow into a blaze the most latent spark of humanity; but, the adamantine heart of avarice, dead to every sensation of pity, regards not the voice of the sufferers, but hastily drives them to market for sale.

Oh, Africa, Africa! to what horrid inhumanities have thy shores been witness; thy shores, which were once the garden of the world, the seal of almost paradisaical joys, have been transformed into regions of woe; thy sons, who were once the happiest of mortals, are reduced to slavery, and bound in weighty shackles, now fill the trader's ship. But, though defeated in the contest for liberty, their magnanimous souls scorn the gross indignity, and choose death in preference to slavery. Painful; ah! painful, must be that existence which the rational mind can deliberately doom to self-destruction. Thus the poor Africans, robbed of every joy, while they see not the saddened hearts, sink into the abyss of consummate misery. Their lives, embittered by reflection, anticipation, and present sorrows, they feel burthensome; and death (whose dreary mansions appal the stoutest hearts) they view as their only shelter.

You, my brethren, beloved Africans, who had passed the days of infancy when you left your country, you best can tell the aggravated sufferings of our unfortunate race;

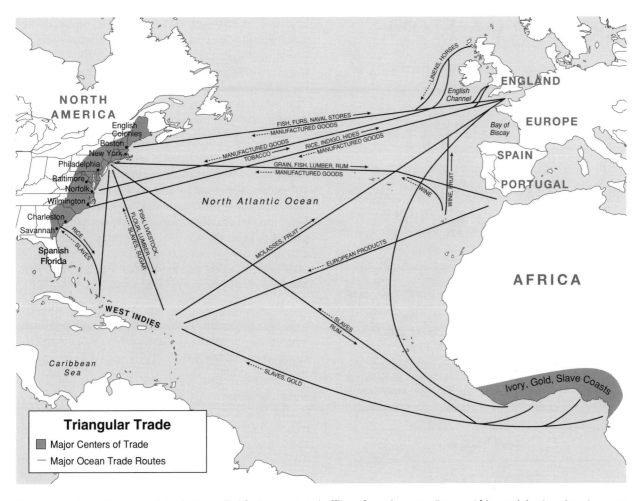

Triangular Trade
- Major Centers of Trade
- Major Ocean Trade Routes

This map illustrates the "triangle trade," so called for its constant shuffling of goods among Europe, Africa, and the Americas. In many ways this was the principal engine that drove the slave trade, and with it the economic development of the New World and the young United States. **THE GALE GROUP**

your memories can bring to view these scenes of bitter grief. What, my brethren, when dragged from your native land on board the slave ship, what was the anguish which you saw, which you felt? what the pain, what the dreadful forebodings which filled your throbbing bosoms?

But you, my brethren, descendants of African forefathers, I call upon you to view a scene of unfathomable distress. Let your imagination carry you back to former days. Behold a vessel, bearing our forefathers and brethen from the place of their nativity to a distant and inhospitable clime; behold their dejected countenances, their streaming eyes, their fettered limbs; hear them, with piercing cries, and pitiful moans, deploring their wretched fate. After their arrival in port, see them separated without regard to the ties of blood or friendship: husband from wife; parent from child; brother from sister; friend from friend. See the parting tear rolling down their fallen cheeks; hear the parting sigh die on their quivering lips.

But let us no longer pursue a theme of boundless affliction. An enchanting sound now demands your attention. Hail! hail! glorious day, whose resplendent ris-

ing disperseth the clouds which have hovered with destruction over the land of Africa, and illumines it by the most brilliant rays of future prosperity. Rejoice, oh! Africans! No longer shall tyranny, war, and injustice, with irresistible sway, desolate your native country; no longer shall torrents of human blood deluge its delightful plains; no longer shall it witness your countrymen wielding among each other than instruments of death; nor the insidious kidnapper, darting from his midnight haunt, on the feeble and unprotected; no longer shall its shores resound with the awful howlings of infatuated warriors, the deathlike groans of vanquished innocents, nor the clanking fetters of woe-doomed captives. Rejoice, oh, ye descendants of Africans! No longer shall the United States of America, nor the extensive colonies of Great Britain, admit the degrading commerce of the human species; no longer shall they swell the tide of African misery by the importation of slaves. Rejoice, my brethren, that the channels are obstructed through which slavery, and its direful concomitants, have been entailed on the African race. But let incessant strains of gratitude be mingled with your expressions of joy.

OBSERVATIONS

On the Inflaving, importing and purchafing of

Negroes;

With fome Advice thereon, extracted from the Epiftle of the Yearly-Meeting of the People called QUAKERS, held at *London* in the Year 1748.

Anthony Benezet

When ye fpread forth your Hands, I will hide mine Eyes from you, yea when ye make many Prayers I will not hear; your Hands are full of Blood. Wafh ye, make you clean, put away the Evil of your Doings from before mine Eyes Ifai. 1, 15.

Is not this the Feaft that I have chofen, to loofe the Bands of Wickednefs, to undo the heavy Burden, to let the Oppreffed go free, and that ye break every Toke, Chap. 58, 7.

Second Edition.

GERMANTOWN:
Printed by CHRISTOPHER SOWER. 1760.

Quakers believed that slavery was wicked and those participating in it would be punished by God. Anthony Benezet's "Observations," published in 1760, admonishes Quakers against slavery. Benezet founded the first free school for African Americans in Philadelphia in 1750 and endowed it from his estate upon his death. **CORBIS-BETTMANN**

Through the infinite mercy of the great Jehovah, this day announces the abolition of the Slave Trade. Let, therefore, the heart that is warmed by the smallest drop of African blood glow in grateful transports, and cause the lofty arches of the sky to reverberate eternal praise to his boundless goodness.

Oh God! we thank Thee, that thou didst condescend to listen to the cries of Africa's wretched sons, and that Thou didst interfere in their behalf. At Thy call humanity sprang forth and espoused the cause of the oppressed; one hand she employed in drawing from their vitals the deadly arrows of injustice; and the other in holding a shield, to defend them from fresh assaults; and at that illustrious moment, when the sons of '76 pronounced these United States free and independent; when the spirit of patriotism erected a temple sacred to liberty; when the inspired voice of Americans first uttered those noble sentiments, "We

hold these truths to be self-evident, that all men are created equal; that they are endowed by their Creator with certain unalienable rights; among which are life, liberty, and the pursuit of happiness"; and when the bleeding African, lifting his fetters, exclaimed, "Am I not a man and a brother"; then, with redoubled efforts, the angel of humanity strove to restore to the African race the inherent rights of man.

To the instruments of divine goodness, those benovolent men who voluntarily obeyed the dictates of humanity, we owe much. Surrounded with innumerable difficulties, their undaunted spirits dared to oppose a powerful host of interested men. Heedless to the voice of fame, their independent souls dared to oppose the strong gales of popular prejudice. Actuated by principles of genuine philanthropy, they dared to despise the emoluments of ill-gotten wealth, and to sacrifice much of their temporal interests at the shrine of benevolence.

As an American, I glory in informing you that Columbia boasts the first men who distinguished themselves eminently in the vindication of our rights and the improvement of our state.

Conscious that slavery was unfavorable to the benign influences of Christianity, the pious Woolman loudly declaimed against it; and, although destitute of fortune, he resolved to spare neither time nor pains to check its progress. With this view he traveled over several parts of North America on foot and exhorted his brethren, of the denomination of Friends, to abjure the iniquitous custom. These, convinced by the cogency of his arguments, denied the privileges of their society to the slaveholder, and zealously engaged in destroying the aggravated evil. Thus, through the beneficial labors of this pattern of piety and brotherly kindness, commenced a work which has since been promoted by the humane of every denomination. His memory ought therefore to be deeply engraven on the tablets of our hearts; and ought ever to inspire us with the most ardent esteem.

Nor less to be prized are the useful exertions of Anthony Benezet. This inestimable person, sensible of the equality of mankind, rose superior to the illiberal opinions of the age; and, disallowing an inferiority in the African genius, established the first school to cultivate our understandings and to better our condition.

Thus, by enlightening the mind and implanting the seeds of virtue, he banished, in a degree, the mists of prejudice, and laid the foundations of our future happiness. Let, therefore, a due sense of his meritorious actions ever create in us a deep reverence of his beloved name. Justice to the occasion, as well as his merits, forbid me to pass in silence over the name of the honorable William Wilberforce. Possessing talents capable of adorning the greatest subjects, his comprehensive mind found none more worthy his constant attention than the abolition of the Slave Trade. For this he soared to the zenith of his towering eloquence, and for this he struggled with perpetual ardor. Thus, anxious in defense of our rights, he pledged himself never to desert the cause; and, by his repeated and strenuous exertions, he finally obtained the desirable end. His extensive services have, therefore, entitled him to a large share of our affections, and to a lasting tribute of our unfeigned thanks.

But think not, my brethren, that I pretend to enumerate the persons who have proved our strenuous advocates, or that I have portrayed the merits of those I have mentioned. No, I have given but a few specimens of a countless number, and no more than the rude outlines of the beneficence of these. Perhaps there never existed a human institution which has displayed more intrinsic merit than the societies for the abolition of slavery.

Reared on the pure basis of philanthropy, they extend to different quarters of the globe, and comprise a considerable number of humane and respectable men. These, greatly impressed with the importance of the work, entered into it with such disinterestedness, engagedness, and prudence, as does honor to their wisdom and virtue. To effect the purposes of these societies no legal means were left untried which afforded the smallest prospects of success. Books were disseminated, and discourses delivered, wherein every argument was employed which the penetrating mind could adduce from religion, justice or reason, to prove the turpitude of slavery, and numerous instances related calculated to awaken sentiments of compassion. To further their charitable intentions, applications were constantly made to different bodies of legislature, and every concession improved to our best possible advantage. Taught by preceding occurrences, that the waves of oppression are ever ready to overwhelm the defenseless, they became the vigilant guardians of all our reinstated joys. Sensible that the inexperienced mind is greatly exposed to the allurements of vice, they cautioned us, by the most salutary precepts and virtuous examples against its fatal encroachments; and the better to establish us in the paths of rectitude they instituted schools to instruct us in the knowledge of letters and the principles of virtue.

By these and similar methods, with divine assistance they assailed the dark dungeon of slavery; shattered its rugged wall, and enlarging thousands of the captives, bestowed on them the blessings of civil society. Yes, my brethren, through their efficiency, numbers of us now enjoy the invaluable gem of liberty; numbers have been secured from a relapse into bondage, and numbers have attained a useful education.

I need not, my brethren, take a further view of our present circumstances, to convince you of the providential benefits which we have derived from our patrons; for if you take a retrospect of the past situation of Africans, and descendants of Africans, in this and other countries, to your observation our advancements must be obvious. From these considerations, added to the happy event which we now celebrate, let us ever entertain the profoundest veneration for our munificent benefactors, and return to them from the altars of our hearts the fragrant incense of incessant gratitude. But let not, my brethren, our demonstrations of gratitude be confined to the mere expressions of our lips.

The active part which the friends of humanity have taken to ameliorate our sufferings has rendered them, in a measure, the pledges of our integrity. You must be well aware that notwithstanding their endeavors, they have yet remaining, from interest and prejudice, a number of opposers. These, carefully watching for every opportunity to injure the cause, will not fail to augment the smallest defects in our lives and conversation; and reproach our benefactors with them as the fruits of their actions.

Let us, therefore, by a steady and upright deportment, by a strict obedience and respect to the laws of the land, form an invulnerable bulwark against the shafts of malice. Thus, evincing to the world that our garments are unpolluted by the stains of ingratitude, we shall reap increasing advantages from the favors conferred; the spirits of our departed ancestors shall smile with complacency on the change of our state; and posterity shall exult in the pleasing remembrance.

May the time speedily commence when Ethiopia shall stretch forth her hands; when the sun of liberty shall beam resplendent on the whole African race; and its genial influences promote the luxuriant growth of knowledge and virtue.

African American Soldiers in the Colonial Period

ADAPTED FROM ESSAYS BY BARBARA SAVAGE,
UNIVERSITY OF PENNSYLVANIA

AFRICAN AMERICAN SOLDIERS IN THE COLONIAL PERIOD

Most colonial militia specifically excluded all African Americans from serving, whether free or slave, in part out of fear of armed slave insurrections. But when the colonies began to prepare for full-scale war against Britain in 1775, freed African Americans were permitted to serve in the army, and evidently some slaves also joined the fighting. At the Battle of Bunker Hill, for example, Peter Salem (1750–1816), a former Massachusetts slave, distinguished himself through his valor.

Despite Salem's bravery and that of other blacks who fought in militia units, the official policy for military service drawn up by General George Washington (1732–1799) specifically excluded the "negro," slave and free, from enlisting in the Continental army. This policy would have prevailed had the British not countered by freely opening their armed ranks to African Americans. When this happened, some free African Americans were permitted to join the army, especially after the number of white volunteers began to decline.

There were five thousand African Americans among the three hundred thousand soldiers in the Revolutionary War. The overwhelming majority of these black soldiers came from northern colonies, but they fought in battles in all regions of the country. Prince Whipple and Oliver Cromwell, both African Americans, were with General Washington when he crossed the Delaware in December 1776. Black sailors, pilots, and boatswains also served in the navy during the war, helping to defend coastal cities and towns from the British.

The war for independence ended victoriously, but not for those African Americans who had hoped that the revolutionary cry for freedom would also end slavery. That change would come only after they had served in yet another war.

FREE BLACK SOCIETY FROM THE REVOLUTION TO THE CIVIL WAR

By the early 1800s, when manumissions inspired by revolutionary ideals had ended, the contours of free black society in the United States were established. Members of this society were not a homogeneous group. They differed markedly, according to a variety of factors: whether they lived in cities or in the countryside; whether they lived in the North, the upper South, or the lower South; whether they were light- or dark-skinned; whether they were skilled or unskilled; and whether they were manumitted through benevolent paternalism or the random impulse of revolutionary ideals. These factors all helped determine the varied experiences of free black life. They also help explain why some free African Americans identified closely with those still in bondage while others considered themselves a separate group, as distinct from enslaved blacks as they were from whites.

In the states of the upper South, many masters had freed their slaves indiscriminately—that is, without regard to parentage or skin color. These freed African Americans were less likely to be light-skinned, for they were less likely to be the products of relations between white masters and black slaves. They were also less likely to possess the skills and resources a benevolent master might bestow on his own mixed-race child. In this region, there were also enough white people to occupy the ranks of skilled labor, so that most free black people were confined to the lowest rungs of the economy. As a result of all these factors, free African Americans in the upper South tended to see themselves as closely related to those who remained enslaved—as mere free counterparts to their brethren in chains.

In the lower South, however, free African Americans were fewer and more likely to be related to white colonial elites. Whites also formed a much smaller percentage of the population in the states of the lower South. In some places, whites were so scarce that slaves and free blacks were taught the artisan skills needed to make plantations and cities work. African Americans swelled the ranks of coopers, blacksmiths, and carpenters. Such skills allowed some free black men to occupy jobs and enjoy a social status unthinkable farther north. Skilled mulattoes—often manumitted by benevolent masters—sometimes were able to join the middle ranks of society. Because of their greater social opportunities, these "freemen" often regarded themselves as distinct from darker-skinned slaves, whose lives they had never shared.

Throughout the South, it also mattered a great deal whether a free black person lived in the city or in the countryside. Most free African Americans lived in rural areas, possessing few of the skills and resources necessary to succeed in cities. They had little choice but to hire themselves out as cheap agricultural labor, working under terms and conditions similar to those faced by slaves. Most lived in hovels on the margin of a plantation; some even lived in slave quarters. Their struggle for survival tempered their freedom severely, rendering it a mere mockery of the freedom enjoyed by whites. Poor and feared by a hostile white society, some of these free blacks traded their dubious freedom for the relative security of slavery. Others lost their free status when they committed any of a number of minor legal infractions, or through the guile of labor-hungry planters and slave traders.

A small number of free black southerners lived in cities; and in places like Charleston and Savannah, where whites were few, free African Americans with skills and resources served as an intermediate class of artisans and merchants. This preferred group often enjoyed a status far higher than that of unskilled free plantation laborers. In addition, urban life offered possibilities for independence denied on plantations. Cities were far from utopias for any black people, but for free African Americans with skills and resources, the complex urban economies offered opportunity and a comfortable anonymity in a hostile world.

SEE PRIMARY SOURCE DOCUMENT *"African Rights and Liberty" by Maria W. Stewart*

Another set of factors shaped life for free black people in the North. They had always formed a much smaller part of the population than in the South. Starting in the 1820s, this imbalance grew worse as European immigrants began to swell the labor ranks. Northern free black people were often the descendants of slaves manumitted indiscriminately in the upper South after the revolution. For this reason, they generally lacked the skills and opportunities necessary to play vital roles in the economy.

While nearly all free black northerners lived in cities, they fared far worse than their skilled counterparts in southern cities. White northerners, motivated by racial prejudice, excluded black laborers from working in the skilled crafts, confining them instead to low-paying, unskilled wage labor. Blacks in the North, though free, became an outcast group and the target of numerous race riots. Finally, in the North, skin color often had little to do with social status. Far removed from the Deep South phenomenon of paternalistic manumission, black northerners made fewer distinctions on the basis of skin color. For this reason, they were more likely to consider all people of African descent as a unified group.

The irony of free black life in antebellum America was that those with the highest status, skills, and wealth tended to be from regions where slavery was most firmly entrenched. In the lower South, where the abolition of slavery had never been seriously contemplated, a small number of free mulattoes enjoyed lives that would have been the envy of free blacks in the upper South and North. And in those regions where white Americans had liberated slaves in accordance with their democratic principles, freed black people suffered from poverty and a lack of skills. Differences in status and skill among free African Americans had important implications for black society. While most free African Americans suffered in poverty, a few skilled craftsmen and merchants experienced a better fate, especially in cities like Charleston and New Orleans. This group of light-skinned, urban, relatively wealthy mulattoes occupied a distinct position in American society. Some actually owned slaves, and elite social groups like the Brown Fellowship Society of Charleston excluded dark-skinned African Americans from joining. The free mulatto elites occupied a space between black slaves and white masters—they considered themselves their own, in-between race. The existence of this group seems especially strange to us today, in an America where people are considered either black or white. Yet mulatto elites actually existed in many New World societies. Brazil, the Caribbean islands, and other parts of Latin America witnessed the formation of multi-tiered racial caste systems in which free mulatto elites played important roles.

THE FREE BLACK POPULATION AND RESISTANCE TO SLAVERY

Given its position between a free white world and the world of black slaves, what role did this anomalous group of free African Americans play in the history of slavery in the United States? Did free blacks undermine or uphold the slave system? Was the very existence of an unenslaved black population a challenge to the idea that African-descended people were fit only for servitude? Or did free black people serve as a buffer between resentful slaves and their repressive masters? White southerners certainly saw free black people as a threat to their way of

The Constitution and the Omission of the Word "Slave" in its Framing

Animated by the spirit of liberty that had triumphed in the American Revolution, many of the members of the Philadelphia Convention, which met in 1787 to draw up a constitution for the new nation, wished to abolish slavery altogether. Even slaveholders like Thomas Jefferson understood that slavery was a mark upon the new nation, an offense to the egalitarian principles of the Revolution and a corrupting influence on slaveholder and slave alike.

But slavery was by then an entrenched economic feature of American life, the source of millions of dollars in human property that would have been wiped off the books had the spirit of liberty held sway. In a compromise that prepared the way for a bloody civil war some seventy years later, the framers of the Constitution refused to incorporate the words "slave," "slaveholder," or "slave trade" in the document they fashioned, but bowed to slaveholding interests in a variety of ways. Article IV, Section 2, allowed slaveholders to recover slaves who escaped to free states. Article V allowed the slave trade to continue until 1808. Article I, Section 2, allowed slaveholding states to count three-fifths of their enslaved population in the apportionment of representatives to Congress, even though that population had no rights and could not vote.

life. As the debate over slavery heated up, slaveholders increasingly saw the very existence of free blacks as a threat to the cherished institution. In the decades before the Civil War, fearful whites instituted a backlash against the freeing of slaves. Laws prohibiting manumission in the southern states increased, and some whites advocated the forced removal of free blacks from the region.

Again, regional differences were important. Free black people in the slave South lived tenuous lives, subject to the whim of local whites. Many sought to protect the little freedom they had gained, rather than risk losing all in supporting slaves' bids for freedom. Still, many took risks, hiring slaves so that they could live away from

The Gradual Abolition of Slavery

In 1780, Pennsylvania became the first state to pass an act providing for the gradual abolition of slavery within its borders. The act stipulated that all persons born after passage of it, "as well Negroes and Mulattoes as others," could not be held in perpetual slavery. However, children born after the act who would have been slaves "in case this Act had not been made"—that is, children born to enslaved mothers—could be held in servitude by their owners until the age of twenty-eight. Hence, "gradual abolition."

masters, helping slaves escape by forging passes for them, and even hiding fugitive slaves. Yet there is little evidence that many free black people took an active role in slave conspiracies. In fact, some wealthy mulattoes, who did not consider themselves black at all, expressed disdain for the "rascally Negroes" who slaved for their masters.

In the North, where nearly all black people were free, the question of supporting slave resistance was much clearer. There, free African Americans played a vital role in the destruction of slavery. African Americans in the antebellum North took part in a broad range of activities designed to achieve both the abolition of slavery in the South and the equality of free black people in the North. This latter effort was necessary, for free black northerners faced a number of obstacles. In many states, like New Jersey and Pennsylvania, black people were denied the right to vote. By 1840, 93 percent of northern black people were denied equal voting rights. So-called black laws such as those in Ohio and Illinois required black people to post a "bond" (put up a sum of money) when they entered the state as a guarantee of their good behavior. Like their counterparts in the South, free African Americans in the North remained far from equal.

SEE PRIMARY SOURCE DOCUMENT *The Pennsylvania Act and the Abolition of Slavery*

In response to these circumstances, black northerners created a variety of institutions designed to achieve equality and abolition. They established separate black churches, such as the Free African Society of Philadelphia, which was founded by Richard Allen (1760–1831) and Absalom Jones (1746–1817) in 1787. They also established newspapers dedicated solely to the needs and interests of black people. Published in New York starting in 1827, *Freedom's Journal* was the first of these. In addition, black leaders began in 1830 to hold a series of state and national conventions. These were designed to forge black solidarity and demonstrate African Americans' fitness for equality. Finally, African Americans developed an array of local vigilance committees, literary societies, and informal meetings to address the needs of black northerners.

Most importantly, black northerners took part in abolitionist activities. African American activists in the North—people like Frederick Douglass (1817–1895), Maria Stewart (1803–1879), Samuel Cornish (1795–1859), Martin R. Delany (1812–1885), and Mary Ann Shadd Cary (1823–1893), to name only a few—forged strong ties with the white abolitionist movement. But such leaders were not merely the black counterparts of white antislavery workers. They espoused a distinct set of ideas, uniquely suited to the interests of black people. Unlike many white abolitionists, they fought for the equality of African Americans in the North, as well as for the abolition of slavery in the South.

SEE PRIMARY SOURCE DOCUMENT *The Vested Interest of the Framers of the Constitution in the Business of Slavery*

Some of these activists were fugitive slaves, free not by birth but because they had made daring escapes to the North. Fugitive slaves like Frederick Douglass, William Wells Brown (1815–1884), and William (1824–1900) and Ellen Craft (c. 1826–1891) became famous by publishing their life stories and by lecturing antislavery audiences on the horrors of the peculiar institution. They demonstrated the affinities between free black people in the North and free and enslaved African Americans in the South. Other black northerners like David Walker (1785–1830) and Henry Highland Garnet (1815–1882) came very close to calling for violent slave uprisings.

Black activists in the North continually pressured the nation to face up to the hypocrisy of holding both slaves and democratic principles. By doing so, they helped push the nation into the war that would finally end slavery and make all African Americans free. In the process, they also helped forge an African American culture that was unique among the countries that fell under the slaver's lash—a culture that fostered political unity among black people both slave and free.

BIBLIOGRAPHY

Nalty, Bernard C. *Strength for the Fight: A History of Black Americans in the Military.* New York: Free Press, 1986.

Quarles, Benjamin. *The Negro in the American Revolution.* Chapel Hill: University of North Carolina Press, 1961.

PRIMARY SOURCE DOCUMENT

"African Rights and Liberty" by Maria W. Stewart

INTRODUCTION Born to free parents in Hartford, Connecticut, in 1803, Maria Stewart was orphaned at a young age and spent most of her childhood bound out as a servant in a clergy-man's household. Her only education came from attending Sabbath schools as a teenager and young woman. Despite her limited training and prevailing attitudes that discouraged women from taking a public role in political matters, Stewart became the first American woman to speak before public audiences, vigorously addressing the cause of women and enslaved African Americans on many occasions.

The following speech was delivered at the African Mason Hall in Boston on February 23, 1833. In it, Stewart calls on other free African Americans to take a more active part in the struggle against slavery.

African rights and liberty is a subject that ought to fire the breast of every free man of color in these United States, and excite in his bosom a lively, deep, decided and heart-felt interest. When I cast my eyes on the long list of illustrious names that are enrolled on the bright annals of fame amongst the whites, I turn my eyes within, and ask my thoughts, "Where are the names of our illustrious ones?" It must certainly have been for the want of energy on the part of the free people of color that they have been long willing to bear the yoke of oppression. It must have been the want of ambition and force that has given the whites occasion to say that our natural abilities are not as good, and our capacities by nature inferior to theirs. They boldly assert that, did we possess a natural independence of soul, and feel a love for liberty within our breasts, some one of our sable race, long before this, would have testified it, notwithstanding the disadvantages under which we labor. We have made ourselves appear altogether unqualified to speak in our own defence, and are therefore looked upon as objects of pity and commiseration. We have been imposed upon, insulted and derided on every side; and now, if we complain, it is considered as the height of impertinence. We have suffered ourselves to be considered as dastards, cowards, mean, faint-hearted wretches; and on this account, (not because of our complexion,) many despise us and would gladly spurn us from their presence.

These things have fired my soul with a holy indignation, and compelled me thus to come forward, and endeavor to turn their attention to knowledge and improvement; for knowledge is power. I would ask, is it blindness of mind, or stupidity of soul, or the want of education, that has caused our men who are 60 to 70 years of age, never to let their voices be heard nor their hands be raised in behalf of their color? Or has it been for the fear of offending the whites? If it has, O ye fearful ones, throw off your fearfulness, and come forth in the name of the Lord, and in the strength of the God of Justice, and make yourselves useful and active members in society; for they admire a noble and patriotic spirit in other—and should they not admire it in us? If you are men, convince them that you possess the spirit of men; and as your day, so shall your strength be. Have the sons of Africa no souls? feel they no ambitious desires? shall

the chains of ignorance forever confine them? shall the insipid appellation of "clever negroes," or "good creatures," any longer content them? Where can we find amongst ourselves the man of science, or a philosopher, or an able statesman, or a counsellor at law? Show me our fearless and brave, our noble and gallant ones. Where are our lecturers on natural history, and our critics in useful knowledge? There may be a few such men amongst us, but they are rare. It is true, our fathers bled and died in the revolutionary war, and others fought bravely under the command of Jackson, in defence of liberty. But where is the man that has distinguished himself in these modern days by acting wholly in the defence of African rights and liberty? There was one—although he sleeps, his memory lives.

I am sensible that there are many highly intelligent gentlemen of color in these United States, in the force of whose arguments, doubtless, I should discover my inferiority; but if they are blest with wit and talent, friends and fortune, why have they not made themselves men of eminence, by striving to take all the reproach that is cast upon the people of color, and in endeavoring to alleviate the woes of their brethren in bondage? Talk, without effort, is nothing; you are abundantly capable, gentlemen, of making yourselves men of distinction; and this gross neglect, on your part, causes my blood to boil within me. Here is the grand cause which hinders the rise and progress of the people of color. It is their want of laudable ambition and requisite courage.

Individuals have been distinguished according to their genius and talents, ever since the first formation of man, and will continue to be whilst the world stands. The different grades rise to honor and respectability as their merits may deserve. History informs us that we sprung from one of the most learned nations of the whole earth—from the seat, if not the parent of science; yes, poor, despised Africa was once the resort of sages and legislators of other nations, was esteemed the school for learning, and the most illustrious men in Greece flocked thither for instruction. But it was our gross sins and abominations that provoked the Almighty to frown thus heavily upon us, and give our glory unto others. Sin and prodigality have caused the downfall of nations, kings and emperors; and were it not that God in wrath remembers mercy, we might indeed despair; but a promise is left us; "Ethiopia shall again stretch forth her hands unto God."

But it is of no use for us to boast that we sprung from this learned and enlightened nation, for this day a thick mist of moral gloom hangs over millions of our race. Our condition as a people has been low for hundreds of years, and it will continue to be so, unless, by the true piety and virtue, we strive to regain that which we have lost. White Americans, by their prudence, economy

In 1672, King Charles II chartered the Royal African Company to trade in slaves. Its traders set up stations along the West African coast, rarely venturing more than a few miles into the interior of the continent, but relying on Africans to capture and deliver other Africans to them. Captives were examined, traded, and held in slave forts or "barracoons" awaiting passage to the Americas. This 19th-century illustration entitled "Inspection and Sale of a Negro" suggests the role Africans played in trading other Africans, at least in the early stages of the slave trade. The captive stands quietly while a white man inspects his head. The group of four men, including a dark-skinned man in a turban and another African, may be arguing over his price. **THE LIBRARY OF CONGRESS**

and exertions, have sprung up and become one of the most flourishing nations in the world, distinguished for their knowledge of the arts and sciences, for their polite literature. Whilst our minds are vacant and starving for want of knowledge, theirs are filled to overflowing. Most of our color have been taught to stand in fear of the white man from their earliest infancy, to work as soon as they could walk, and call "master" before they scarce could lisp the name of mother. Continual fear and laborious servitude have in some degree lessened in us that natural force and energy which belong to man; or else, in defiance of opposition, our men before this would have nobly and boldly contended for their rights. But give the man of color an equal opportunity with the white, from the cradle to manhood, and from manhood to the grave, and you would discover the dignified statesman, the man of science, and the philosopher. But there is no such opportunity for the sons of Africa, and I fear that our powerful ones are fully determined that there never shall be. Forbid, ye Powers on High, that it should any longer

be said that our men possess no force. O ye sons of Africa, when will your voices be heard in our legislative halls, in defiance of your enemies, contending for equal rights and liberty? How can you, when you reflect from what you have fallen, refrain from crying mightily unto God, to turn away from us the fierceness of his anger, and remember our transgressions against us no more forever. But a God of infinite purity will not regard the prayers of those who hold religion in one hand, and prejudice, sin and pollution in the other; he will not regard the prayers of self-righteousness and hypocrisy. Is it possible, I exclaim, that for the want of knowledge, we have labored for thousands of years to support others, and been content to receive what they chose to give us in return? Cast your eyes about—look as far as you can see—all, all is owned by the lordly white, except here and there a lowly dwelling which the man of color, midst deprivations, fraud and opposition, has been scarce able to procure. Like King Solomon, who put neither nail nor hammer to the temple, yet received the praise; so also have the white Americans gained themselves a name, like the names of the great men who are in the earth, whilst in reality we have been their principal foundation and support. We have pursued the shadow, they have obtained the substance; we have performed the labor, they have received the profits; we have planted the vines, they have eaten the fruits of them.

I would implore our men, and especially our rising youth, to flee from the gambling board and the dance hall; for we are poor, and have no money to throw away. I do not consider dancing as criminal in itself, but it is astonishing to me that our young men are so blind to their own interest and the future welfare of their children, as to spend their hard earnings for this frivolous amusement; for it has been carried on among us to such an unbecoming extent that it has become absolutely disgusting. "Faithful are the wounds of a friend, but the kisses of an enemy are deceitful." Had those men amongst us, who have had an opportunity, turned their attention as assiduously to mental and moral improvement as they have to gambling and dancing, I might have remained quietly at home, and they stood contending in my place. These polite accomplishments will never enroll your names on the bright annals of fame, who admire the belle void of intellectual knowledge, or applaud the dandy that talks largely on politics, without striving to assist his fellow in the revolution, when the nerves and muscles of every other man forced him into the field of action. You have a right to rejoice, and to let your hearts cheer you in the days of your youth; yet remember that for all these things God will bring you into judgment. Then, O ye sons of Africa, turn your mind from these perishable objects, and contend for the cause of God and the rights of man. Form yourselves into temperance societies. There are temperate men amongst you; then why will you any longer neglect to strive, by your example, to suppress vice in all its abhorrent forms? You have been told repeatedly of the glorious results arising from temperance, and can you bear to see the whites arising in honor and respectability, without endeavoring to grasp after that honor and respectability also?

But I forbear. Let our money, instead of being thrown away as heretofore, be appropriated for schools and seminaries of learning for our children and youth. We ought to follow the example of the whites in this respect. Nothing would raise our respectability, add to our peace and happiness and reflect so much honor upon us, as to be ourselves the promoters of temperance, and the supporters, as far as we are able, of useful and scientific knowledge. The rays of light and knowledge have been hid from our view; we have been taught to consider ourselves as scarce superior to the brute creation; and have performed the most laborious part of American drudgery. Had we as people received one half the early advantages the whites have received, I would

defy the government of these United States to deprive us any longer of our rights.

I am informed that the agent of the Colonization Society has recently formed an association of young men, for the purpose of influencing those of us to go to Liberia who may feel disposed. The colonizationalists are blind to their own interest, for should the nations of the earth make war with America, they would find their forces much weakened by our absence; or should we remain here, can our "brave soldiers" and "fellow citizens," as they were termed in time of calamity, condescend to defend the rights of the whites, and be again deprived of their own, or sent to Liberia in return? O, if the colonizationists are real friends to Africa, let them expend the money which they collect in erecting a college to educate her injured sons in this land of gospel light and liberty; for it would be most thankfully received on our part, and convince us of the truth of their professions, and save time, expense and anxiety. Let them place before us noble objects, worthy of pursuit, and see if we prove ourselves to be those unambitious Negroes they term us. But ah! methinks their hearts are so frozen towards us, they had rather their money should be sunk in the ocean than to administer it to our relief; and I fear, if they dared, like Pharaoh king of Egypt, they would order every male child amongst us to be drowned. But the most high God is still as able to subdue the lofty pride of these white Americans, as He was the heart of that ancient rebel. They say though we are looked upon as things, yet we sprang from a scientific people. Had our men the requisite force and energy, they would soon convince them, by their efforts both in public and private, that they were men, or things in the shape of men. Well may the colonizationists laugh us to scorn for our negligence; well may they cry, "Shame to the sons of Africa." As the burden of the Israelites was too great for Moses to bear, so also is our burden too great for our noble advocate to bear. You must feel interested, my brethren, in what he undertakes, and hold up his hands by your good words, or in spite of himself his soul will become discouraged, and his heart will die within him; for he has, as it were, the strong bulls of Bashan to contend with.

It is of no use for us to wait any longer for a generation of well educated men to arise. We have slumbered and slept too long already; the day is far spent; the night of death approaches; and you have sound sense and good judgment sufficient to begin with, if you feel disposed to make a right use of it. Let every man of color throughout the United States, who possesses the spirit and principles of a man, sign a petition to Congress to abolish slavery in the District of Columbia, and grant you the rights and privileges of common free citizens; for if you had had faith as a grain of mustard seed, long before this the mountains of prejudice might have been removed. We are all sensible that the Anti-Slavery Society has taken hold of the arm of our whole population, in order to

These women were identified as "darkies" in the original description of this image. They were photographed in 1899, sweeping the yard with bambusa brooms in Belton, South Carolina. This circle of cleared ground, which can still be seen around houses throughout the South, is thought to be a survival from West Africa, where plants that might breed insects and other pests were kept far from people's dwellings. **NATIONAL ARCHIVES AND RECORDS ADMINISTRATION**

raise them out of the mire. Now all we have to do is, by a spirit of virtuous ambition to strive to raise ourselves; and I am happy to have it in my power thus publicly to say that the colored inhabitants of this city, in some respects, are beginning to improve. Had the free people of color in these United States nobly and boldly contended for their rights, and showed a natural genius and talent, although not so brilliant as some; had they up, encouraged and patronized each other; nothing could have hindered us from being a thriving and flourishing people. There has been a fault amongst us. The reason why our distinguished men have not made themselves more influential is, because they fear the strong current of opposition through which they must pass, would cause their downfall and prove their overthrow. And what gives rise to this opposition? Envy. And what has it amounted to? Nothing. And who are the cause of it? Our whited sepulchres who want to be great, and don't know how; who love to be called of men "Rabbi, Rabbi," who put on false sanctity, and humble themselves to their brethren, for the sake of acquiring the highest place in the synagogue, and the uppermost seats at the feast. You,

dearly beloved, who are the genuine followers of our Lord Jesus Christ, the salt of the earth and the light of the world, are not so culpable. As I told you, in the very first of my writing, I tell you again, I am but as one drop in the bucket—as one particle of the small dust of the earth. God will surely raise up those amongst us who will plead the cause of virtue, and the pure principles of morality, more eloquently than I am able to do.

It appears to me that America has become like the great city of Babylon, for she has boasted in her heart,— "I sit a queen, and am no widow, and shall see no sorrow." She is indeed a seller of slaves and the souls of men; she has made the Africans drunk with the wine of her fornication; she has put them completely beneath her feet, and she means to keep them there; her right hand supports the reins of government, and her left hand the wheel of power, and she is determined not to let go her grasp. But many powerful sons and daughters of Africa will shortly arise, who will put down vice and immorality amongst us, and declare by Him that sitteth upon the throne, that they will have their rights; and if refused, I am afraid they will spread horror and devastation around. I believe that the oppression of injured Africa has come up before the majesty of Heaven; and when our cries shall have reached the ears of the Most High, it will be a tremendous day for the people of this land; for strong is the arm of the Lord God Almighty.

Life has almost lost its charms for me; death has lost its sting and the grave its terrors; and at times I have a strong desire to depart and dwell with Christ, which is far better. Let me entreat my white brethren to awake and save our sons from dissipation, and our daughters from ruin. Lend the hand of assistance to feeble merit, and plead the cause of virtue amongst our sable race; so shall our curses upon you be turned into blessings; and though you shall endeavor to drive us from these shores, still we will cling to you the more firmly; nor will we attempt to rise above you; we will presume to be called equals only.

The unfriendly whites first drove the native American from his much loved home. Then they stole our fathers from their peaceful and quiet dwellings, and brought them hither and made bond men and bond women of them and their little ones; they have obliged our brethren to labor, kept them in utter ignorance, nourished them in vice and raised them in degradation; and now that we have enriched their soil, and filled their coffers, they say that we are not capable of becoming like white men, and that we never can rise to respectability in this country. They would drive us to a strange land. But before I go, the bayonet shall pierce me through. African rights and liberty is a subject that ought to fire the breast of every free man of color in these United States, and excite in his bosom a lively, deep, decided and heartfelt interest.

PRIMARY SOURCE DOCUMENT

The Pennsylvania Act and the Abolition of Slavery

INTRODUCTION In the years following the American Revolution, Pennsylvania's act, passed in 1780, became a model for other northern states seeking to end slavery. This was not a view shared by the southern states and differences of opinion regarding the role of slavery in the nation would eventually bring about the conflicts leading to the outbreak of the Civil War.

An Act for the Gradual Abolition of Slavery

When we contemplate our abhorrence of that condition to which the arms and tyranny of Great-Britain were exerted to reduce us; when we look back on the variety of dangers to which we have been exposed, and how miraculously our wants in many instances have been supplied, and our deliverances wrought, when even hope and human fortitude have become unequal to the conflict; we are unavoidably led to a serious and grateful sense of the manifold blessings which we have unde-

servedly received from the hand of that Being from whom every good and perfect gift cometh. Impressed with these ideas, we conceive that it is our duty, and we rejoice that it is in our power, to extend a portion of that freedom to others, which hath been extended to us; and a release from that state of thraldom, to which we ourselves were tyrannically doomed, and from which we have now every prospect of being delivered. It is not for us to inquire, why, in the creation of mankind, the inhabitants of the several parts of the earth were distinguished by a difference in feature or complexion. It is sufficient to know, that all are the work of an Almighty Hand. We find in the distribution of the human species, that the most fertile, as well as the most barren parts of the earth, are inhabited by men of complexions different from ours, and from each other, from whence we may reasonably, as well as religiously infer, that He, who placed them in their various situations, hath extended equally His care and protection to all, and that it becometh not us to counteract His mercies. We esteem it a peculiar blessing granted to us, that we are enabled this day, to add one more step to universal civilization, by removing as much as possible, the sorrows of those who have lived in undeserved bondage, and from which, by the assumed authority of the Kings of Britain, no effectual legal relief, could be obtained. Weaned by a long course of experience, from those narrow prejudices and partialities we had imbibed, we find our hearts enlarged with kindness and benevolence, towards men of all conditions and nations; and we conceive ourselves at this particular period extraordinarily called upon, by the blessings which we have received, to manifest the sincerity of our profession, and to give a substantial proof of our gratitude.

And whereas the condition of those persons who have heretofore been denominated Negroe and Mulatto slaves, has been attended with circumstances, which not only deprived them of the common blessings that they were by nature entitled to, but has cast them into the deepest afflictions, by an unnatural separation and sale of husband and wife from each other, and from their children; an injury the greatness of which, can only be conceived, by supposing, that we were in the same unhappy case. In justice therefore, to persons so unhappily circumstanced, and who, having no prospect before them, whereon they may rest their sorrows and their hopes, have no reasonable inducement, to render that service to society, which they otherwise might; and also, in grateful commemoration of our own happy deliverance, from that state of unconditional submission, to which we were doomed by the tyranny of Britain.

Be it enacted, and it is hereby enacted, by the Representatives of the Freemen of the Commonwealth of Pennsylvania, in General Assembly met, and by the authority of the same, That all persons, as well Negroes and Mulattos as others, who shall be born within this State, from and after the passing of this Act, shall not be deemed and considered as servants for life or slaves; and that all servitude for life, or slavery of children, in consequence of the slavery of their mothers, in the case of all children born within this State, from and after the passing of this Act as aforesaid, shall be, and hereby is utterly taken away, extinguished and for ever abolished.

Provided always, and be it further enacted by the authority aforesaid, That every Negroe and Mulatto child born within this State, after the passing of this Act as aforesaid, who would, in case this Act had not been made, have been born a servant for years, or life or a slave, shall be deemed to be and shall be by virtue of this Act, the servant of such person or his or her assigns, who would in such case have been intitled to the service of such child, until such child shall attain unto the age of twenty eight years, in the manner and on the conditions whereon servants bound by indenture for four years, are or may be retained and holden; and shall be liable to like correction and punishment, and intitled to like relief in case he or she be evily treated by his or her master of mistress, and to like freedom dues and other privileges as servants bound by indenture for four years, are or may be intitled, unless the person to whom the service of any such child shall belong, shall abandon his or her claim to the same, in which case the Overseers of the Poor of the city, township or district respectively, where such child shall be so abandoned, shall by indenture bind out every child so abandoned, as an apprentice for a time not exceeding the age herein before limited, for the service of such children.

The Vested Interest of the Framers of the Constitution in the Business of Slavery

INTRODUCTION It is the kind of contradiction that is apparent throughout American history. The early Constitution was drafted by men of learning and power, men from families with land, some from plantations. So despite high-minded values of liberty and the pursuit of happiness, the Constitution also reflected the interests of men of power and influence. As a result, the language dealing with the issues of slavery and the rights of Africans in the Americas were drafted with a careful vagueness. Article I, Section 2, is reprinted below with its exact language—the famous "3/5ths" designation for slaves—designed to keep certain members of the society separate, unequal, and unrepresented.

Article I, Section 2, of the Constitution of the United States of America

The House of Representatives shall be composed of members chosen every second year by the people of the several States, and the electors in each State shall have the qualifications requisite for electors of the most numerous branch of the State Legislature.

No person shall be a Representative who shall not have attained to the age of twenty-five years, and been seven years a citizen of the United States, and who shall not, when elected, be an inhabitant of that State in which he shall be chosen.

Representatives and direct taxes shall be apportioned among the several States which may be included within this Union, according to their respective numbers, which shall be determined by adding to the whole number of free persons, including those bound to service for a term of years and excluding Indians not taxed, three-fifths of all other persons. The actual enumeration shall be made within three years after the first meeting of the Congress of the United States, and within every subsequent term of ten years, in such manner as they shall by law direct. The number of Representatives shall not exceed one for every thirty thousand, but each State shall have at least one Representative; and until such enumeration shall be made, the State of New Hampshire shall be entitled to choose three, Massachusetts eight, Rhode Island and Providence Plantations one, Connecticut five, New York six, New Jersey four, Pennsylvania eight, Delaware one, Maryland six Virginia ten, North Carolina five, South Carolina five, and Georgia three.

When vacancies happen in the representation from any State, the Executive authority thereof shall issue writs of election to fill such vacancies.

The House of Representatives shall choose their Speaker and other officers; and shall have the sole power of impeachment.

The Debate over Slavery in the United States

ADAPTED FROM ESSAYS BY LAURA MITCHELL, UNIVERSITY OF CALIFORNIA, AND JONATHAN HOLLOWAY, YALE UNIVERSITY

EARLY CONDEMNATIONS OF SLAVERY

The first formal protests against slavery in the colonies of North America were heard in the late seventeenth century, at the same time that the system was taking root along the continent's eastern seaboard. In 1688, a handful of German Quakers in Germantown, Pennsylvania, published a petition condemning the trading and owning of black slaves. They characterized enslavement as unlawful kidnapping and defended the seized Africans' right to armed rebellion. They asserted further that slavery was contrary to the golden rule of treating others as one would wish to be treated. In 1693, another Pennsylvania Quaker named George Keith (1639–1716) published an exhortation to his co-religionists urging them to cleanse themselves of

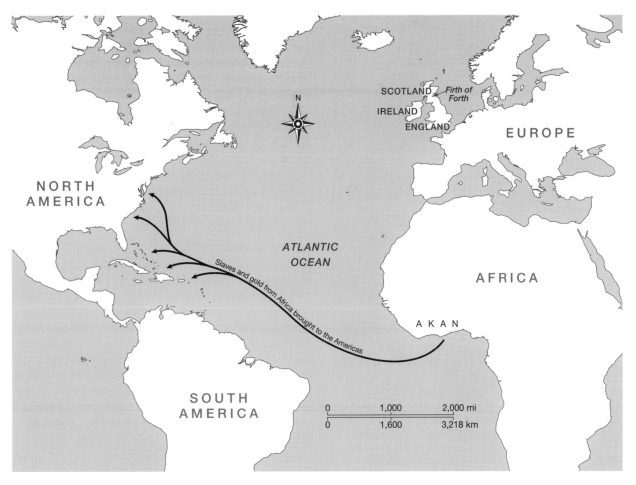

This map depicts the route taken by slave ships bringing African gold and slaves to the New World. (Map created by XNR Productions.)
THE GALE GROUP

the sin of slave holding. In making these arguments, Quakers in Pennsylvania echoed their fellow members of the Society of Friends in England and the Caribbean.

At about the same time, a Massachusetts Puritan also published a tract critical of slavery. In 1700, the eminent colonial jurist Samuel Sewall (1652–1730) published *The Selling of Joseph*. The title referred to the biblical Joseph, whose brothers sold him into slavery in Egypt. Sewall, who had been a member of the court presiding over the Salem witch trials, argued that all humans are equal under God's love. Meshing biblical concepts with natural law, Sewall contended that all men are entitled to life and liberty.

These isolated protests made little impact. Quaker leaders failed to act on the Germantown protest or on Keith's exhortation. According to Samuel Sewall, his thoughts about slavery met only with hostility. A fellow Puritan judge, John Saffin (1632–1710), published a rebuttal to Sewall that argued that the Bible explicitly sanctioned slavery. Saffin argued further that humans exist in a hierarchy that puts some in positions of power over others; slavery is simply the lowest rung on this ladder.

QUAKER REFORM AND THE GROWTH OF ANTISLAVERY SENTIMENT

After a half century in which the public debate among whites waned, Pennsylvania Quakers launched a concerted attack on slavery. Led by John Woolman (1720–1772), Anthony Benezet (1713–1784), and others, the Quakers' protest was the first in the colonies to mobilize a group of individuals against the institution.

Since the formation of the Society of Friends in the seventeenth century, Quakers had owned slaves and participated in the slave trade. In the mid-eighteenth century, members of the Society of Friends in the New World and in England were in the process of reforming their community. An important part of this purification was the abolition of slavery within the society. Decisive action came slowly, but in 1776, amid the fervor of the American Revolution, Quaker leaders decided officially and conclusively that slave trading and slaveholding were incompatible with their religious beliefs. Quakers who persisted in either activity were to be excommunicated.

In the wake of the revolution, Americans were generally optimistic that slavery would die of its own accord. By

Eli Whitney's cotton gin increased the production of cotton a hundredfold, giving slavery a new life. It easily removed the stubborn seeds from the short-staple variety of cotton which was grown in most places. **THE LIBRARY OF CONGRESS**

1808, the year that the slave trade was declared illegal, several northern states either had abolished slavery or had passed laws providing for the gradual emancipation of slaves. In general, Americans assumed that this represented a trend. Although some trafficking in slaves continued, most Americans were confident that slavery was in a state of decline and that little action was needed to hasten that decline.

SEE PRIMARY SOURCE DOCUMENT *Pennsylvania Quakers Protest Slavery*

ATTITUDES TOWARD SLAVERY IN A YOUNG NATION

Despite an antipathy to slavery and a hopeful assumption that slavery would soon fade away, popular attitudes and actions in the young nation implicitly sanctioned slavery. Those in positions of power felt little or no responsibility to improve the well-being of slaves. Furthermore, most in Congress contended that, because of provisions in the federal Constitution, they were legally unable to influence individual states in regard to their "domestic" institutions, such as slavery. Political leaders frequently defended their inaction by blaming the British for introducing slave labor two centuries earlier. This disingenuous excuse for slavery became a mainstay of the defense of the institution up to and during the Civil War.

SEE PRIMARY SOURCE DOCUMENT *An Account of the* Amistad *Revolt*

At the same time, plantation slavery proved increasingly profitable and showed few signs of imminent death. By the late eighteenth century, the United States was beginning to acquire wealth from an international cotton boom brought about in part by the introduction of the cotton gin. Both South and North benefited economically from the expansion of cotton production. Southern planters grew cotton for commercial production, and northern industrialists processed the raw material in factories. Thus both regions profited from and became dependent on slave labor.

As southern planters devoted more and more acreage to cotton, their demand for slave labor and land increased. This push to expand slavery into new territories led to some of the most important political battles in U.S. history. By the second decade of the nineteenth century, the political debate over slavery was becoming increasingly divisive and contentious. Congress heatedly debated whether or not slavery should be extended into the territories. In 1820, it attempted to settle the issue with the Missouri Compromise, which permitted slavery below the 36 degree, 30 minute latitude line and prohibited it above the line with the exception of Missouri. Many within and outside Congress proclaimed the compromise a final settlement of the issue.

SEE PRIMARY SOURCE DOCUMENT *The Louisiana Purchase and the Missouri Compromise*

THE EMERGENCE OF RADICAL ABOLITIONISM

The period in U.S. history from 1820 to 1860 is often referred to as the antebellum period, coming from the Latin words for "before the war." During this time, arguments for and against slavery, which were previously isolated and sporadic, developed into fully articulated belief systems and platforms for action. Historians have long debated which came first, agitation against slavery or proslavery defenses of the institution. What is certain is that both the attack on slavery and the defense of it have long histories and that they grew in tandem, each influencing the other over time.

The antebellum period was characterized by religious revival and a zeal for social reform among the nation's white population, particularly in the North. Men and women formed numerous societies to battle the nation's moral ills, and by 1830, organizations dedicated to goals such as temperance, Bible reading, and educational reform dotted the nation. During this same period, the number of slaves and free blacks also grew rapidly, pushing the issue of slavery to the foreground. Concern for the slaves and worries over the impact of slavery on the nation's moral well-being intensified. Just like the Quakers in the second half of the eighteenth century, a small number of Americans now became convinced that putting an end to slavery was necessary in order to cleanse the nation.

Prior to 1820, most Americans who called for an end to slavery advocated that slaves be emancipated gradually. In the 1820s, however, a small number of men and women began to demand that the slaves be emancipated at once. In 1826, a Quaker named Elizabeth Heyrick published a pamphlet demanding immediate emancipation. Three years later, the black abolitionist David Walker (1785–1830) published his widely read *Appeal to the Colored Citizens of the World.*

A Boston clothes dealer, Walker forcefully and eloquently described the essential injustice of slavery. He condemned the hypocrisy of the established churches that condoned human bondage, and excoriated slaveholders and other whites who implicitly defended the institution. Walker also called on slaves to free themselves, using violence if necessary. Walker's *Appeal* created a tempest in the North, where many whites condemned his call for violence. In the South, slaveholders called for his arrest.

ORGANIZED ABOLITIONISM

In 1831, on the heels of Walker's *Appeal,* a white abolitionist named William Lloyd Garrison (1805–1879) published the first issue of his abolitionist paper, the *Liberator.* Garrison's fiery rhetoric caught the attention of white audiences throughout the nation. Unlike Walker, he did not condone violence. Instead, Garrison advocated a strategy of "moral suasion" by which abolitionists, occupying the moral high ground, would persuade others that slavery ought to be abolished. At the beginning, few whites supported Garrison, and subscriptions to the *Liberator* came primarily from blacks.

Soon after he founded the *Liberator,* Garrison also established the New England Anti-Slavery Society, which was the first of many antislavery societies in the North. These societies, like the other reform organizations of the period, distributed literature, sponsored traveling lecturers, and held mass meetings to build support and to raise money for their cause. In print, from the pulpit, and from the podium, the abolitionists denounced slavery, using the same biblical and natural law arguments of previous centuries. In addition, they drew on the nation's revolutionary heritage to point out the essential contradiction of holding slaves in a nation ostensibly dedicated to freedom. Drawing on the Declaration of Independence and the biblical command to love one's neighbor as oneself, abolitionists contended that in a nation claiming to be both Christian and democratic, slavery was national hypocrisy. It was nothing short of a national sin.

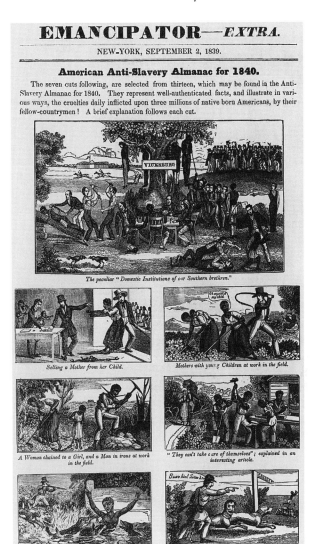

The front page of the antislavery newspaper the *Emancipator.* Established in 1820 in Jonesborough, Tennessee by Elihu Embree, the son of a Quaker minister, it was the first publication devoted to the abolition of slavery. **CORBIS-BETTMANN**

SEE PRIMARY SOURCE DOCUMENT *"A Short Catechism: Adapted to All Parts of the United States" by William Lloyd Garrison*

Antebellum abolitionists also tried to persuade the nation to abolish slavery on the ground that it was cruel and inhumane. In his 1839 tract *Slavery As It Is* the white abolitionist Theodore D. Weld (1803–1895) described in painful detail the misery and humiliation that slaves endured. He focused on slavery's impact on the family, describing horrendous scenes where slave families were torn apart on the auction block. Weld also graphically described how masters and overseers viciously beat and whipped their slaves. Weld's account of the life of slaves was widely circulated in the North and had a strong impact on public opinion. Even more influential, however, were the numerous former slaves who told their per-

African American Intellectuals: Frederick Douglass (1817–1895)

Frederick Douglass was very likely the greatest African American intellectual leader of the nineteenth century and is one of the pivotal personalities of American history.

Born a slave, Douglass escaped bondage and traveled north to freedom, and became deeply involved in the abolitionist movement. There the similarities end, however. In addition to his brilliant talents as an orator, Douglass proved early in his life that he was a skilled writer as well. His first autobiography, *Narrative of the Life of Frederick Douglass* (1845), was a bestseller in its day and remains one of the most compelling slave narratives ever written. Douglass created a name for himself as a newspaperman, editing and publishing such important periodicals as the *North Star, Frederick Douglass's Paper,* and the *New National Era.* More than any American before him, Douglass filled the role of public intellectual. He devoted his considerable capacities to explicitly political ends and, by so doing, paved the way for future generations of African American intellectuals who would do the same.

ABOVE: A photograph of Frederick Douglass, taken in his later years. Following the Civil War, Douglass edited the *New National Era* in Washington and served in several government posts. He died in Washington, D.C., on February 25, 1895, and was buried in Rochester, New York, his long-time home. **THE LIBRARY OF CONGRESS**

SEE PRIMARY SOURCE DOCUMENTS *Letters Between H. C. Wright and Frederick Douglass on the Purchase of Douglass's Freedom* and *"A Fugitive's Necessary Silence"*

sonal stories. Towering figures such as Frederick Douglass (1817–1895) and Sojourner Truth (1797–1883) traveled throughout the North giving eyewitness accounts of their bondage and answering questions from predominantly white audiences. Douglass also traveled to England, where he was warmly received. Douglass, Truth, and others also published their personal histories, and these narratives were widely distributed.

BLACK ABOLITIONISTS

Northern blacks were involved in the movement to end slavery throughout the antebellum period. In 1827, two free blacks, John Russwurm (1799–1851) and Samuel E. Cornish (1795–1859), started the nation's first black newspaper, *Freedom's Journal.* The paper highlighted the evils of slavery and sought to improve the condition of blacks in the North.

In the 1830s, blacks were highly involved in the abolitionist movement and were members of the mostly white antislavery societies. However, the societies' white leaders only rarely allowed blacks to serve in positions of authority. Aware of the profound racism embedded in northern society, white abolitionists often feared that socializing with blacks or giving them authority would alienate potential white supporters. White leaders such as Garrison encouraged black abolitionists to remain in the role of spokespersons, touring the country and educating the population about slavery's ills.

By the late 1830s, black abolitionists who had filled the roles assigned to them became increasingly dissatisfied with their white colleagues' expectations and actions. White abolitionists, although ahead of their white peers, suffered from their own racial prejudices and exerted little effort to improve the lot of free blacks in the North. Black abolitionists, in contrast, had always pursued a single goal: the elevation of blacks in the United States. In the South, that meant emancipation, and in the North, economic opportunity and political equality.

Black abolitionists also grew impatient with white abolitionists' tactics. The Garrisonians believed that they should distance themselves from the political process and seek abolition only through moral suasion. They also favored the disbandment of the Union as a means of cleansing the nation of the sin of slavery and refused to countenance violence for any purpose. As the years wore on and moral suasion failed to convince many Americans of slavery's evil nature, many black abolitionists (and some white abolitionists as well) concluded that these methods were ineffectual and that new strategies were necessary.

To that end, black abolitionists helped to establish two antislavery political parties, the Liberty party, which ran the white abolitionist James G. Birney (1792–1857) for president in 1840, and the Free-Soil party, formed in 1848. Neither party presented a serious challenge to the Democrats or the Whigs, the major parties, but their presence did give abolitionists a political organization.

Among the black abolitionists who slowly drifted away from Garrison was Frederick Douglass. For years Douglass had lectured throughout the United States. An extraordinarily intelligent and eloquent man, Douglass wanted to speak both about slavery and about the plight of black people in the North. White abolitionists, however, wanted him to speak only about his experiences as a slave. They also wanted him to speak in a less sophisticated manner, fearing that his oratorical skills would undermine his credibility.

Frustrated by the attitudes of white abolitionists and by their consistent failure to seek the improvement of blacks' condition in the North, Douglass began to act independently. In 1847, he founded a newspaper called the *North Star*. At an antislavery convention in 1851, Douglass officially separated himself from the Garrisonian position. He announced that he no longer favored the dissolution of the Union because it would abandon the slave, and that he favored political action and resistance as a means of obtaining emancipation.

In the last thirty years of slavery, there was an insatiable taste among the American reading public for tales of slavery and escape, those told by fugitive slaves as well as fictional works, like Harriet Beecher Stowe's *Uncle Tom's Cabin*. The great demand for such tales did not always spring from sympathy for the enslaved. The more horrific stories, especially those containing scenes of violence against women and children, pandered to the public's taste for thrills as well.

Tales of the cruelties of slavery and hairbreadth escapes sold well, but they were not always wisely conceived. In particular, the publication of details having to do with escape—Underground Railroad routes, disguises and other stratagems fugitive slaves practiced, the names of those who assisted them—could seriously compromise the escape plans of other slaves, a point Frederick Douglass made time and again in his public speaking and writing. **SEE PRIMARY SOURCE DOCUMENTS** *Letters Between H.C. Wright and Frederick Douglass on the Purchase of Douglass's Freedom* and *"A Fugitive's Necessary Silence" by Frederick Douglass*

THE COLONIZATIONISTS

To most Americans, north and south, the abolitionists were idealists at best and frightening revolutionaries at worst. Most northerners did not favor emancipation of the slaves, and the few who did wanted a gradual process, not immediate freedom for slaves. This hostility often led to threats of violence against both black and white abolitionists.

A major reason most northerners did not favor emancipation was that they did not want former slaves to settle in the North. The majority of northerners considered people of African origin and descent to be their physical, intellectual, and moral inferiors and refused to accept the idea of a biracial society. In sermons, speeches, newspapers, magazines, and novels, they predicted that terrible consequences would follow an influx of free blacks into northern society.

Senator Henry Clay (1777–1852), who did not favor the extension of slavery, shared these racist fears. Convinced that dark- and light-skinned people could never live together peacefully and prosperously, he concluded with many others that the freed slaves should be returned to Africa. Along with a number of other men, Clay helped to found the American Colonization Society in 1817. The society's goal was to relocate freed slaves in Africa, where the freedmen would bring the blessings of liberty and Christianity to other members of their race. The society raised enough money to establish a colony on the western coast of Africa, naming the new country Liberia and calling the capital Monrovia in honor of President James Monroe (1758–1831).

Colonization had wide appeal among whites who wanted to abolish slavery gradually and avoid integrating free blacks into their communities. However, the American Colonization Society was never able to raise enough money to transport more than a few hundred free blacks out of the United States. It repeatedly petitioned Congress to fund the project, but to no avail. In the end, colonization failed for lack of financial support and because few blacks wished to emigrate.

Black and white abolitionists severely condemned colonization and demanded that slaves be freed and allowed to live and thrive in the country of their birth, the United States of America. They saw colonization as a capitulation to whites' prejudices against blacks. However, some blacks, such as Martin Delany (1812–1885) and Henry Highland Garnet (1815–1882), supported the idea of colonization. While they in no way condoned the North's virulent racism, they believed that only in another country could blacks fulfill their potential. During the Civil War, Delany and Garnet worked to settle blacks in Haiti.

SEE PRIMARY SOURCE DOCUMENT *"Memorial Discourse" by Henry Highland Garnet*

A POSITIVE GOOD

In response to the attack on slavery, southerners and some northerners launched a defense of the South's "peculiar institution." Apologists for slavery argued that it was constitutional, moral, and beneficial to both blacks and whites. The constitutional defense of slavery was predicated on the existence of slavery in the southern

The Solomon Northup Kidnapping and the Rise of the Slave Narrative and Escape Tales as Best-selling Literature

Solomon Northup was born free in Minerva, New York, in 1808, the descendant of African Americans who had been in the Northeast since the beginning of colonial settlement. In addition to being literate, Northup had another valuable skill—from an early age he had played the violin.

In 1829, Northup married Anne Hampton, a free African American woman, and they began to raise a family. They lived and worked in Saratoga Springs, Anne as a cook and Solomon on a variety of jobs, including the repair of the Champlain Canal. He also earned money playing his violin at dances, weddings, and other various gatherings.

In 1841, well-established and with three growing children, Northup attracted the attention of two men who proposed that he accompany them to Washington, D.C., to perform in a circus to which they claimed a connection. The circus turned out to be slavery. First drugged and then chained and sold, Northup soon found himself laboring as a slave on the bayous of Louisiana. For twelve years he remained a slave, hiding the skills he had gained in freedom, resisting brutal treatment whenever he could, and above all, observing what went on around him.

Northup went on to publish an account of his ordeal to great success. The tales of slaves kidnapped, escaping, and surviving as fugitives constituted one of the literary trends of the century. Much like stories of adventure at sea gave rise to the literature of Robert Louis Stevenson and Herman Melville, slave narratives were perhaps one of the greatest influences to turn public opinion against the sordid business of owning people in the decades that preceded the Civil War.

---

states when the Constitution was adopted. The Constitution, slavery's defenders argued, sanctioned slavery and deprived Congress of the power to influence the states' domestic policies. Furthermore, proponents of slavery argued, the South had a constitutional right to share in the nation's expansion. Slavery therefore should be allowed in the territories and in the new states as they joined the Union.

To establish the morality of slavery, proslavery theorists turned to the Bible. They pointed out that the Old Testament patriarchs owned slaves and that Christ and his apostles never uttered a word in condemnation of slavery. Quite on the contrary, they observed, New Testament figures encouraged slaves to be humble and obedient. Proslavery exegetes also repeated the centuries-old argument that the curse of Canaan, recorded in Genesis, condemned the descendants of Ham to slavery. Africans, they reasoned, were those descendants, and so their bondage was prophetically sealed.

Slavery's defenders also argued that it was beneficial to the slaves. When enslaved, Africans were brought from a heathen society into the light of a Christian democracy. Furthermore, the argument continued, Africans were inherently inferior and unable to care for themselves.

Slavery was therefore a blessing to them, because through it they received care and guidance.

Over the course of the antebellum period, the defense of slavery turned into an expression of unqualified approval. Increasingly, southern religious, political, social, and economic apologists characterized slavery not only as acceptable and beneficial, but as a positive good. Armed with the notion that slavery was preferable to free labor, southerners became more and more strident in their demands for the extension of slavery.

SEE PRIMARY SOURCE DOCUMENT Twelve Years a Slave *by Solomon Northup*

THE NATION HEADS TOWARD WAR

In the 1850s, both anti- and proslavery proponents hardened in their positions. The Fugitive Slave Act of 1850, the Kansas-Nebraska Act of 1854, the Dred Scott decision, and John Brown's raid rallied northerners to the abolitionists' cause. The Fugitive Slave Act prompted increasing numbers of abolitionists to advocate forcible resistance to law. The Kansas-Nebraska Act, which overturned the Missouri Compromise of 1820, and the Dred Scott decision, which denied blacks the rights of national citizenship, reinforced their commitment to use any means available to secure the emancipation of slaves.

SEE PRIMARY SOURCE DOCUMENT *The Final Moments of John Brown*

Southerners observed the growth of antislavery sentiment in the North with fear. By the decade's end, they were convinced that the North meant to prevent the expansion of slavery into the territories and to abolish slavery where it existed. Determined to prevent this outcome, southern states began to secede in late 1860, and with their secession, the war that freed the slaves began.

BIBLIOGRAPHY

Barnes, Gilbert H. *The Antislavery Impulse, 1830–1844.* New York: Appleton-Century, 1933.

Davis, David. *The Problem of Slavery in Western Culture.* Ithaca: Cornell University Press, 1966.

———. *The Problem of Slavery in the Age of Revolution, 1770–1823.* Ithaca: Cornell University Press, 1975.

Faust, Drew G., ed. *The Ideology of Slavery: Proslavery Thought in the Antebellum South, 1830–1860.* Baton Rouge: Louisiana State University Press, 1981.

Fredrickson, George. *The Black Image in the White Mind: The Debate on Afro-American Character and Destiny, 1817–1914.* New York: Harper & Row, 1971.

Jenkins, William S. *Pro-Slavery Thought in the Old South.* Chapel Hill: University of North Carolina Press, 1935.

Litwack, Leon. *North of Slavery: The Negro in the Free States 1790–1860.* Chicago: University of Chicago Press, 1961.

Pease, Jane H., and William H. Pease. *They Who Would Be Free: Blacks' Search for Freedom 1830–1861.* New York: Atheneum, 1974.

Quarles, Benjamin. *Black Abolitionists.* New York: Oxford University Press, 1969.

Stewart, James B. *Holy Warriors: The Abolitionists and American Slavery.* New York: Hill and Wang, 1976.

Tise, Larry. *Proslavery.* Athens: University of Georgia Press, 1987.

Walters, Ronald G. *The Antislavery Appeal: American Abolitionism after 1830.* Baltimore: The Johns Hopkins University Press, 1976.

PRIMARY SOURCE DOCUMENT

Pennsylvania Quakers Protest Slavery

INTRODUCTION The following is a pamphlet composed in 1783 by a Quaker farmer named David Cooper. The pamphlet was entitled "A Serious Address to the Rulers of America, on the Inconsistency of Their Conduct Respecting Slavery." The Quakers' various protests constituted an important part of the white abolitionist movement, pointing out the fundamental contradiction in the young nation based on principles of equality and a respect for God condoning the institution of slavery.

"Ye pretended votaries for freedom! ye trifling patriots!" exclaimed the New England Baptist minister John Allen in 1774, "continuing this lawless, cruel, inhuman, and abominable

A Plan for Thwarting Slave Hunters

Congress passed the nation's second fugitive slave law on September 18, 1850. It allowed for the punishment, by fine or imprisonment, of anyone who attempted to help escaping slaves and authorized federal marshals to search houses where they suspected runaways might be hiding. It also denied fugitives the right to a jury trial, as well as the right to testify on their own behalf. Judges were empowered to remand fugitives to slavery and were paid ten dollars for every fugitive they returned but only five for each fugitive they freed. Many northerners who had been indifferent to the antislavery cause saw the law as illegal federal interference with local governments, and they now joined with abolitionists to thwart enforcement of it.

practice of enslaving your fellow creatures." Allen's attack on the gross contradiction between waging a revolution based on inherent human rights while continuing to hold one-fifth of the population in bondage continued through the war years and into the early years of peace after 1783. David Cooper, a New Jersey Quaker, took up the antislavery cudgels and held back nothing in assaulting the hypocrisy of his fellow Americans in committing what he called "treason" against the natural rights of man and in making a mockery of the noble words of the Declaration of Independence. Anthony Benezet, only a year from his death, made sure that every member of the Congress received a copy of Cooper's biting pamphlet, printed here. (The copy of Cooper's pamphlet in the Boston Athenaeum is signed by George Washington, indicating that he had read this antislavery tract.)

A Sound mind in a sound body, is said to be a state of the highest human happiness individually; when these blessings are separate, a sound mind, wise and prudent conduct, tend much to support and preserve an unsound body: On the other hand, where the body is sound, the constitution strong and healthy, if the mind is unsound, the governing principle weak and feeble, the body feels the injuries which ensue, the health and constitution often become enfeebled and sickly, and untimely death closes the scene. This reasoning holds good politically, being sometimes realized in bodies politick, and perhaps never more so than in the conduct lately exhibited to mankind by Great-Britain. Her constitution was sound, strong and firm, in a degree that drew admiration from the whole world; but, for want of a sound mind, her

Slaves being unloaded in America. **THE LIBRARY OF CONGRESS**

directing and governing powers being imprudent and unwise, to such a debilitated and sickly state is this fine constitution reduced, that, without a change of regimen, her decease may not be very remote. America is a child of this parent, who long since, with many severe pangs, struggled into birth, and is now arrived to the state of manhood, and thrown off the restraints of an unwise parent, is become master of his own will, and, like a lovely youth, hath stepped upon the stage of action. State physicians pronounce his constitution strong and sound: the eyes of the world are singularly attentive to his conduct, in order to determine with certainty on the soundness of his mind. It is the general Congress, as the head, that must give the colouring, and stamp wisdom or folly on the counsels of America. May they demonstrate to the world, that these blessings, a sound mind in a sound body, are in America politically united!

It was a claim of freedom unfettered from the arbitrary control of others, so essential to free agents, and equally the gift of our beneficent Creator to all his rational children, which put fleets and armies into motion, covered earth and seas with rapine and carnage, disturbed the repose of Europe, and exhausted the treasure of nations. Now is the time to demonstrate to Europe, to the whole world, that America was in earnest, and meant what she said, when, with peculiar energy, and unan-

swerable reasoning, she plead the cause of human nature, and with undaunted firmness insisted, that all mankind came from the hand of their Creator equally free. Let not the world have an opportunity to charge her conduct with a contradiction to her solemn and often repeated declarations; or to say that her sons are not real friends to freedom; that they have been actuated in this awful contest by no higher motive than selfishness and interest, like the wicked servant in the gospel, who, after his Lord had forgiven his debt which he was utterly unable to pay, shewed the most cruel severity to a fellow servant for a trifling demand, and thereby brought on himself a punishment which his conduct justly merited. Ye rulers of America beware: Let it appear to future ages, from the records of this day, that you not only professed to be advocates for freedom, but really were inspired by the love of mankind, and wished to secure the invaluable blessing to all; that, as you disdained to submit to the unlimited control of others, you equally abhorred the crying crime of holding your fellow men, as much entitled to freedom as yourselves, the subjects of your undisputed will and pleasure.

However habit and custom may have rendered familiar the degrading and ignominious distinctions, which are made between people with a black skin and ourselves, I am not ashamed to declare myself an advocate for the rights of that highly injured and abused people; and were I master of all the resistless persuasion of Tully and Demosthenes, could not employ it better, than in vindicating their rights as men, and forcing a blush on every American slaveholder, who has complained of the treatment we have received from Britain, which is no more to be equalled, with ours to negroes, than a barley corn is to the globe we inhabit. Must not every generous foreigner feel a secret indignation rise in his breast when he hears the language of Americans upon any of their own rights as freemen, being in the least infringed, and reflects that these very people are holding thousands and tens of thousands of their innocent fellow men in the most debasing and abject slavery, deprived of every right of freemen, except light and air? How similar to an atrocious pirate, setting in all the solemn pomp of a judge, passing sentence of death on a petty thief. Let us try the likeness by the standard of facts.

The first settlers of these colonies emigrated from England, under the sanction of royal charters, held all their lands under the crown, and were protected and defended by the parent state, who claimed and exercised a control over their internal police, and at length attempted to levy taxes upon them, and, by statute, declared the colonies to be under their jurisdiction, and that they had, and ought to have, a right to make laws to bind them in all cases whatsoever.

The American Congress in their declaration, July 1775, say,

If it were possible for men who exercise their reason to believe that the divine Author of our existence intended a part of the human race to hold an absolute property in, and an unbounded power over others, marked out by infinite goodness and wisdom, as the objects of a legal denomination never rightly resistible, however severe and oppressive; the inhabitants of these colonies might at least require from the parliament of Great-Britain some evidence, that this dreadful authority over them has been granted to that body. But a reverence for our great Creator, principles of humanity, and the dictates of common sense, must convince all those who reflect upon the subject, that government was instituted to promote the welfare of mankind, and ought to be administered for the attainment of that end.

Again they say,

By this perfidy (Howe's conduct in Boston) wives are separated from their husbands, children from their parents, the aged and sick from their relations and friends, who wish to attend and comfort them. We most solemnly before God and the world declare, that exerting the utmost energy of those

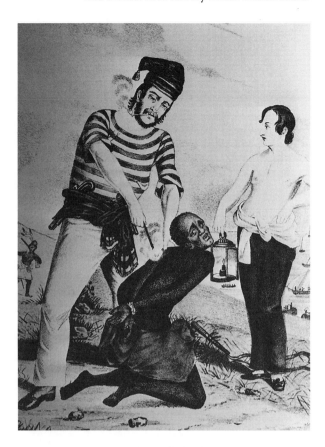

A slave is branded on the coast of Africa before being shipped to the New World. This lithograph captures the violence and horror of the event in the slave's face, while his captors look on with indifference. **CORBIS-BETTMANN**

powers which our beneficent Creator hath graciously bestowed upon us, the arms we have been compelled by our enemies to assume, we will in defiance of every hazard, with unabated firmness and perseverance, employ for the preservation of our liberties, being with one mind resolved to die freemen rather than live slaves.

We exhibit to mankind the remarkable spectacle of a people attacked by unprovoked enemies, without any imputation, or even suspicion, of offence. —They boast of their privileges and civilization, and yet proffer no milder conditions than servitude or death.

In our own native land, in defence of the freedom that is our birthright, and which we ever enjoyed till the late violation of it; for the protection of our property acquired solely by the honest industry of our forefathers and ourselves; against violence actually offered, we have taken up arms.

In a resolve of Congress, October 1774, they say,

That the Inhabitants of the English colonies in North-America, by the immutable laws of nature, are entitled to life, liberty and property; and they have never ceded to any sovereign power whatever a right to dispose of either without their consent.

To the people of Great-Britain.

Know then that we consider ourselves, and do insist, that we are and ought to be, as free as our fellow-subjects in Britain, and that no power on earth has a right to take our property from us without our consent.

Are the proprietors of the soil of America less lords of their property than you are of yours? &c.—Reason looks with indignation on such distinctions, and freemen can never perceive their propriety; and yet, however, chimerical and unjust such discriminations are; the Parliament assert, that they have a right to bind us in all cases without exception, whether we consent or not; that they may take and use our property when and in what manner they please; that we are pensioners on their bounty for all we possess, and can hold it no longer than they vouchsafe to permit.

If neither the voice of justice, the dictates of the law, the principles of the constitution, or the suggestions of humanity, can restrain your hands from shedding human blood in such an impious cause: we must then tell you, that we never will submit to be hewers of wood or drawers of water for any ministry or nation on earth. And in future, let justice and humanity cease to be the boast of your nation.

To the inhabitants of the colonies.

Weigh in the opposite balance, the endless miseries you and your descendants must endure, from an established arbitrary power.

Declaration of independence in Congress, 4th July, 1776.

We hold these truths to be self-evident, that all men are created equal, that they are endowed by their Creator with certain unalienable rights; that among these are life, liberty, and the pursuit of happiness.

Declaration of rights of Pennsylvania, July 15, 1776.

That all men are born equally free and independent, and have certain natural inherent, and unalienable rights, among which are, the enjoying and defending life and liberty, acquiring, possessing and protecting property, and pursuing and obtaining happiness and safety.

Declaration of rights of Massachusetts, Sep. 1, 1779.

All men are born free and equal, and have certain natural essential and unalienable rights; among which may be reckoned the right of enjoying and defending their lives and liberties; that of acquir-

ing, possessing and protecting property; in fine, of seeking and obtaining safety and happiness.

Africa lies many thousand miles distant, its inhabitants as independent of us, as we are of them; we sail there, and foment wars among them in order that we may purchase the prisoner, and encourage the stealing one another to sell them to us; we bring them to America, and consider them and their posterity forever, our slaves, subject to our arbitrary will and pleasure; and if they imitate our example, and offer by force to assert their native freedom, they are condemned as traitors, and a hasty gibbet strikes terror on their survivors, and rivets their chains more secure.

Does not this forcible reasoning apply equally to Africans? Have we a better right to enslave them and their posterity, than Great-Britain had to demand Three-pence per pound for an article of luxury we could do very well without? And Oh! America, will not a reverence for our great Creator, principles of humanity, nor the dictates of common sense, awaken thee to reflect, how far thy government falls short of impartially promoting the welfare of mankind, when its laws suffer, yea justify men in murdering, torturing and abusing their fellow men, in a manner shocking to humanity?

How abundantly more aggravated is our conduct in these respects to Africans, in bringing them from their own country, and separating by sale these near connections, never more to see each other, or afford the least comfort of tender endearment of social life. But they are black, and ought to obey; we are white, and ought to rule. —Can a better reason be given for the distinction, that Howe's conduct is perfidy, and ours innocent and blameless, and justified by our laws?

Thou wicked servant, out of thine own mouth shalt thou be judged. —Is a claim to take thy property without thy consent so galling, that thou wilt defy every hazard rather than submit to it? And at the same time hold untold numbers of thy fellow men in slavery, (which robs them of every thing valuable in life) as firmly riveted by thee, as thou art resolved to use the utmost energy of thy power, to preserve thy own freedom?

Have the Africans offered us the least provocation to make us their enemies? —Have their infants committed, or are they even suspected of any offence? And yet we leave them no alternative but servitude or death.

The unenlightened Africans, in their own native land, enjoyed freedom which was their birthright, until the more savage christians transported them by thousands, and sold them for slaves in the wilds of America, to cultivate it for their lordly oppressors.

With equal justice may negroes say, By the immutable laws of nature, we are equally entitled to life, liberty and property with our lordly masters, and have never ceded to any power whatever, a right to deprive us thereof.

Does this reasoning apply more forcibly in favour of a white skin than a black one? Why ought a negro to be less free than the subjects of Britain, or a white face in America? "Have we not all one father? Hath not one God created us? Why do we deal treacherously every man against his brother?" Mal. ii. 10.

Do Americans reprobate this doctrine when applied to themselves? And at the same time enforce it with ten-fold rigor upon others, who are indeed pensioners on their bounty for all they possess, nor can they hold a single enjoyment of life longer than they vouchsafe to permit?

You who have read a description of the inhuman scenes occasioned by the slave-trade, in obtaining, branding, transporting, selling, and keeping in subjection millions of human creatures; reflect a moment, and then determine which is the most impious cause: and after this, if neither the voice of justice nor suggestions of humanity, can restrain your hands from being contaminated with the practice; cease to boast the christian name from him who commanded his followers "to do unto others as they would others should do unto them."

Who would believe the same persons whose feelings are so exquisitely sensible respecting themselves, could be so callous toward negroes, and the miseries which, by their arbitrary power, they wantonly inflict.

If these solemn truths, uttered at such an awful crisis, are self-evident: unless we can shew that the African race are not men, words can hardly express the amazement which naturally arises on reflecting, that the very people who make these pompous declarations are slave-holders, and, by their legislative conduct, tell us, that these blessings were only meant to be the rights of whitemen not of all men: and would seem to verify the observation of an eminent writer; "When men talk of liberty, they mean their own liberty, and seldom suffer their thoughts on that point to stray to their neighbours."

This was the voice, the language of the supreme council of America, in vindication of their rights as men, against imposition and unjust control: —Yes, it was the voice of all America, through her representatives in solemn Congress uttered. How clear, full and conclusive! "We hold these truths to be self-evident, that all men are created equal, and endowed by their Creator with the unalienable rights of life, liberty and the pursuit of happiness." "By the immutable laws of nature all men are entitled to life and liberty." We need not now turn over the libraries of Europe for authorities to prove that blacks are born equally free with whites; it is declared and recorded as the sense of America: Cease then ye

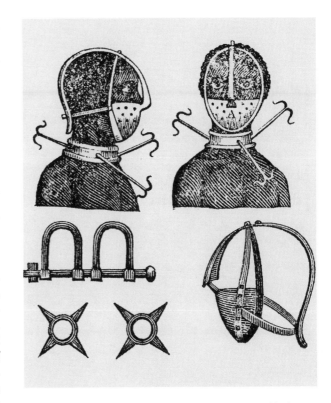

This device, when fastened into place, made it impossible for the wearer to speak, eat, lie down, or move quickly—thus hindering or preventing escape. The illustration, which also shows leg shackles and spurs, appeared in Thomas Branagan's 1807 *The Penitential Tyrant, or, Slave Trader Reformed,* an antislavery poem in four cantos. **THE LIBRARY OF CONGRESS**

cruel taskmasters, ye petty tyrants, from attempting to vindicate your having the same interest in your fellow men as in your cattle, and let blushing and confusion of face strike every American, who henceforth shall behold advertisements offering their brethren to sale, on a footing with brute beasts.

But what shall I say! Forgive it, Oh Heaven, but give ear, Oh earth! while we are execrating our parent state with all the bitterness of invective, for attempting to abridge our freedom, and invade our property; we are holding our brethren in the most servile bondage, cast out from the benefit of our laws, and subjected to the cruel treatment of the most imperious and savage tempers, without redress, without advocate or friend.

Our rulers have appointed days for humiliation, and offering up of prayer to our common Father to deliver us from our oppressors, when sighs and groans are piercing his holy ears from oppressions which we commit a thousand fold more grievous: pouring forth blood and treasure year after year in defence of our own rights; exerting the most assiduous attention and care to secure them by laws and sanctions, while the poor Africans are continued in chains of slavery as creatures unworthy of notice in these high concerns,

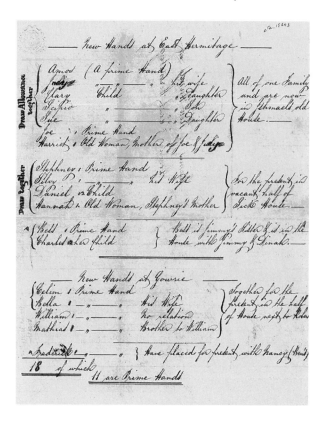

This detailed record from around 1860 shows the names of various slaves, their residences, and their relationships to one another. Records like these were commonly kept and, in the cases of larger plantations with long histories, can provide astonishing records of entire families of African Americans through multiple generations.
SPECIAL COLLECTIONS LIBRARY, DUKE UNIVERSITY

the nether millstone; can sport with the rights of men; wallow and riot in the plunder, which their unhallowed hands have squeezed from others! But only touch their immaculate interests, and what an unceasing outcry invades every ear. A love for my country, a regard for the honour of America, raises an ardent wish, that this picture may never be realized in her rulers.

It may be objected that there are many difficulties to be guarded against in setting of negroes free, and that, were they all to be freed at once, they would be in a worse condition than at present. I admit that there is some weight in these objections; but are not these difficulties of our own creating? And must the innocent continue to suffer because we have involved ourselves in difficulties? Let us do justice as far as circumstances will admit, give such measure as we ask, if we expect Heaven to favour us with the continuance of our hard earned liberty. The work must be begun, or it can never be completed. "It is begun and many negroes are set free." True, it is begun, but not in a manner likely to produce the desired end, the entire abolition of slavery. This is the business of the superintending authority, the main spring which gives motion to the whole political machine; which, were they to undertake in good earnest, I have no doubt but we should soon see a period fixed, when our land should no longer be polluted with slaveholders, nor give forth her increase to feed slaves: And indeed it hath been a matter of wonder to many, that that body, who have been so much employed in the study and defence of the rights of humanity, should suffer so many years to elapse without any effectual movement in this business. Had they, with the declaration of independence, recommended it to the different Legislatures to provide laws, declaring, that no person imported into, or born in America after that date, should be held in slavery; it would have been a step correspondent with our own claims, and in time, have completed the work, nor can I see any impropriety, but what the nature of the case will justify, to have it still take place.

To shew the necessity of this matter taking its rise at the head, if any thing effectual is done, I may instance the Quakers. Some among them, it is said, always bore a testimony against slavery from its first introduction, and the uneasiness increasing, advices were given forth cautioning their members against being concerned in importing slaves, to use those well whom they were possessed of, school their children, &c. but some of the foremost of that society having experienced the profits of their labour, no effectual stop could be put to the practice, tho' many became uneasy, and set their negroes free, until the difficulties attending the late French and Indian war, brought the rights of men into a more close inspection, when a rule was agreed upon, prohibiting their members from being concerned with importing, buying, or selling of slaves; and some years after a fur-

and left subject to laws disgraceful to humanity, and opposite to every precept of christianity. One of these in effect gives Fifteen Pounds for the murder of a slave; that is, after a slave has absconded a certain time, Twenty Pounds is given to any one who shall bring his head, and but Five Pounds if he is brought alive. Another, which empowers certain officers to seize negroes set free, and sell them for the benefit of government: And, even during the present contest, negroes have been seized with the estates of persons who had gone over to the British, and sold by publick auction into perpetual slavery, and the proceeds cast into stock for the defence of American liberty. Of the same complexion is an instance in New-Jersey: A female Quaker, about seven years since, manumitted her negroes; the times having reduced her so as to be unable fully to discharge a debt for which she was only surety, the creditor, a great declaimer in behalf of American freedom, although he was offered his principal money, obtains a judgment, levies on these free negroes, who by the assistance of some real friends of freedom, procured a habeas corpus, and removed their case before the justices of the supreme court. How many such mock patriots hath this day discovered, whose flinty hearts are as impervious to the tender feelings of humanity and commiseration as

ther rule was made, enjoining all those who held slaves to set them free, otherwise to be separated from religious membership. —The work was then soon accomplished, and they now say there are very few members belonging to the yearly meeting of Philadelphia who hold a slave.

When a grievance is general, it is but trifling to apply partial means; it is like attempting to destroy a great tree by nibbling at its branches. It is only the supreme power which pervades the whole that can take it up by the roots. —The disquisitions and reasonings of the present day on the rights of men, have opened the eyes of multitudes who clearly see, that, in advocating the rights of humanity, their slaves are equally included with themselves, and that the arguments which they advance to convict others, rebounds with re-doubled force back on themselves, so that few among us are now hardy enough to justify slavery, and yet will not release their slaves; like hardened sinners, acknowledge their guilt, but discover no inclination to reform. It is true these convictions have occasioned the release of many slaves, and two or three states to make some feeble efforts looking that way; but I fear, after the sunshine of peace takes place, we have little more to expect, unless the sovereign power is exerted to finish this sin, and put an end to this crying transgression.

Let me now address that August body, who are by their brethren clothed with sovereign power, to sit at the helm, and give a direction to the important concerns of the American union. You, gentlemen, have, in behalf of America, declared to Europe, to the world, "That all men are born equal, and, by the immutable laws of nature, are equally entitled to liberty." We expect, mankind expects, you to demonstrate your faith by your works; the sincerity of your words by your actions, in giving the power, with which you are invested, its utmost energy in promoting equal and impartial liberty to all whose lots are cast within the reach of its influence—then will you be revered as the real friends of mankind, and escape the execrations which pursue human tyrants, who shew no remorse at sacrificing the ease and happiness of any number of their fellow-men to the increase and advancement of their own, are wholly regardless of others rights if theirs are but safe and secure. We are encouraged in this expectation by the second article of your nonimportation agreement in behalf of America, October 1774, viz. "That we will neither import nor purchase any slave imported after the first day of December next, after which time we will wholly discontinue the slave-trade, and will neither be concerned in it ourselves, nor will we hire our vessels nor sell our commodities or manufactures to those who are concerned in it." —And much would it have been for the honour of America, had it been added and confirmed by laws in each state (nor will we suffer such a

stigma to remain on our land, as that it can produce slaves, therefore no child, born in any of the United States after this date, shall be held in slavery.) —But the children of slaves are private property, and cannot be taken from their masters without a compensation! What! After it hath so often been echoed from America, "All men are born equally free." "No man or body of men can have a legitimate property in, or control over their fellow-men, but by their own consent expressed or implied." Shall we now disown it in order to hold our slaves? Forbid it all honest men; it is treason against the rights of humanity, against the principles upon which the American revolution stands, and by which the present contest can only be justified; to deny it, is to justify Britain in her claims, and declare ourselves rebels. Wherefore our rulers undoubtedly ought to give these principles, these laws which themselves have declared immutable, a due force and efficacy. This every well-wisher to their country, either in a religious or political sense have a right to ask and expect. But we have laws that will maintain us in the possession of our slaves: "The fundamental law of nature being the good of mankind, no human sanctions can be good, or valid against it, but are of themselves void, and ought to be resisted," Lock[e]. Therefore none can have just cause of complaint, should so desirable an event take place, as that no person brought into, or born within any of the United States after the declaration of independence, shall be held a slave.

When I read the constitutions of the different states, they afford a mournful idea of the partiality and selfishness of man; the extraordinary care, and wise precautions they manifest to guard and secure our own rights and privileges, without the least notice of the injured Africans, or gleam of expectation afforded them, of being sharers of the golden fruitage, except in that of the Delaware state, who, to their lasting honour, while they were hedging in their own, provided against the invasion of the rights of others. By the twenty-sixth article of their constitution they resolve, that "No person hereafter imported into this state from Africa, ought to be held in slavery under any pretence whatever; and no negro, indian or mulatto slave, ought to be brought into this state for sale from any part of the world." Had they went further and made provision by which slavery must at length have terminated within their jurisdiction, it would have been doing something to the purpose; and, as this is the only constitution in which posterity will see any regard paid to that abused people, I hope the same humane considerations which led them so far, will induce them to take the lead in doing their part toward putting an effectual end to this crying evil, which will ever remain a stain to the annals of America.

And you who in the several states are clothed with legislative authority, and have now an opportunity of

This mid-nineteenth century political cartoon shows the "Rise," "Progress," and "End" of abolitionism. **CORBIS-BETTMANN**

displaying your wisdom and virtue by your laws freed from every foreign control, although this people were below notice, and their rights and interest thought unworthy of a sanction in your constitutions; let me beseech you, if you wish your country to escape the reproach and lasting infamy of denying to others what she hath so often, and in the most conclusive language, declared were the rights of all; if you wish to retain the name of christians, of friends to human nature, and of looking up acceptably in prayer to the common father of men to deal with you in the same tenderness and mercy as you deal with others; that you would even now regard the rigorous oppressions of his other children, and your brethren, which they suffer under laws which you only can abrogate. View your negro laws calculated not to protect and defend them, but to augment and heighten their calamitous situation! Cast out and rejected by the regulations formed for the defence and

security of the rights and privileges, and to guard and improve the morals and virtue of the whites: Left open to the gratification of every passion and criminal commerce with one another, as though they were brutes and not men; fornication, adultery, and all the rights of marriage union among blacks, considered beneath the notice of those rules and sanctions formed to humanize and restrain corrupt nature, or the regard of those whose duty it is to enforce them. Yes, blush Americans! Ye have laws, with severe penalties annexed, against these crimes when committed between whites; but, if committed by blacks, or by white men with black women, with the aggravated circumstances of force and violence, they pass as subjects of mirth, not within the cognizance of law or magistrates inquiry, and lose the very name of crimes. Hence children often become familiar with these scenes of corruption and wickedness, before they are capable of distinguishing between the duties of christianity, and the appetites of unrestrained nature. No marvel then if slave-holders are often scourged by the vices of their own offspring, which their untutored slaves have been a means of inflicting—children who, instead of being educated in the nurture and admonition of the Lord, are too often nurtured in pride, idleness, lewdness, and the indulgence of every natural appetite; that, were there no other inducement, this singly is sufficient to cause every real christian to lift a hand against, and exert their utmost influence in, bringing this hydra mischief to a period. But when we consider the accumulated guilt, in other respects, abundantly set forth by other writers on this subject, brought on this land through the introduction of this infernal traffick, at a time when we were denied the privilege of making laws to check the mighty evil; and that near ten years have now elapsed since this restraint hath been removed, and no effectual advance yet made towards loosing the bands of wickedness, and letting the oppressed go free, or even of putting it in a train whereby it may at length come to an end; I say, it is matter of anxious sorrow, and affords a gloomy presage to the true friends of America. Have we reason to expect, or dare we ask of him whose ways are all equal, the continuance of his blessings to us, whilst our ways are so unequal.

I shall now conclude with the words of Congress to the people of England, a little varied to suit the present subject.

If neither the voice of justice, the dictates of humanity, the rights of human nature, and establishment of impartial liberty now in your power, the good of your country, nor the fear of an avenging God, can restrain your hands from this impious practice of holding your fellow-men in slavery; making traffick of, and advertising in your publick prints for sale as common merchandize, your

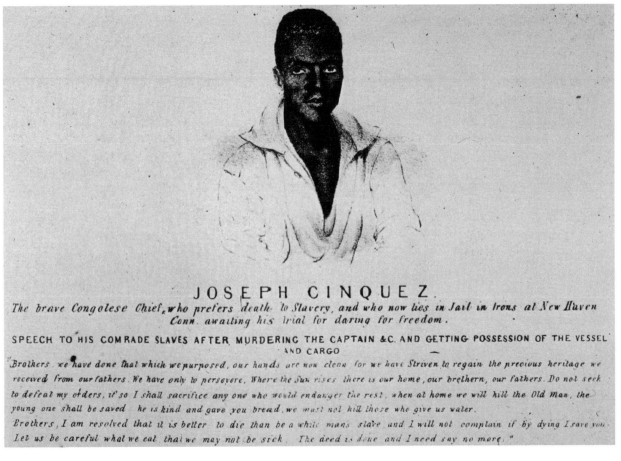

JOSEPH CINQUEZ.

The brave Congolese Chief, who prefers death to Slavery, and who now lies in Jail in Irons at New Haven Conn. awaiting his trial for daring for freedom.

SPEECH TO HIS COMRADE SLAVES AFTER MURDERING THE CAPTAIN &C. AND GETTING POSSESSION OF THE VESSEL AND CARGO

"Brothers, we have done that which we purposed, our hands are now clean for we have Striven to regain the precious heritage we received from our fathers. We have only to persevere. Where the Sun rises there is our home, our brethren, our fathers. Do not seek to defeat my orders, if so I shall sacrifice any one who would endanger the rest, when at home we will kill the Old Man, the young one shall be saved he is kind and gave you bread, we must not kill those who give us water.

Brothers, I am resolved that it is better to die than be a white mans slave and I will not complain if by dying I save you. Let us be careful what we eat that we may not be sick. The deed is done and I need say no more."

Joseph Cinque, a Mende prince, led the rebellion on the slave ship *Amistad* in 1839. While confined in New Haven in the year and a half following the revolt, Cinque learned English and became a convert to Christianity, afterwards returning to West Africa as a missionary. **ARCHIVE PHOTOS, INC.**

brethren possessed of immortal souls equal with yourselves; then let justice, humanity, advocates for liberty, and the sacred name of christians, cease to be the boast of American rulers.

PRIMARY SOURCE DOCUMENT

An Account of the *Amistad* Revolt

INTRODUCTION The American Revolution was already a half century old when the *Amistad* appeared in the waters of Long Island Sound, most of its crew dead and its human cargo at the mercy of those who remained. The slave trade technically had been abolished in 1808, but it still delivered African slaves to out of the way ports in North America, while slavery itself was growing and expanding ever westward along the southern frontier. The following is an excerpt from the *History of the Negro Race in America from 1619 to 1880* by George W. Williams and gives a detailed portrait of the events as reported by various persons involved in the incident.

On the 28th of June, 1839, the "Amistad," a Spanish slaver (schooner), with Captain Ramon Ferrer in command, sailed from Havana, Cuba, for Porto Principe, a place in the island of Cuba, about 100 leagues distant.

The passengers were Don Pedro Montes and Jose Ruiz, with fifty-four Africans just from their native country, Lemboko, as slaves. Among the slaves was one man, called in Spanish, Joseph Cinquez, said to be the son of an African prince. He was possessed of wonderful natural abilities, and was endowed with all the elements of an intelligent and intrepid leader. The treatment these captives received was very cruel. They were chained down between the decks—space not more than four feet—by their wrists and ankles; forced to eat rice, sick or well, and whipped upon the slightest provocation. On the fifth night out, Cinquez chose a few trusty companions of his misfortunes, and made a successful attack upon the officers and crew. The captain and cook struck down, two sailors put ashore, the Negroes were in full possession of the vessel. Montes was compelled, under paid of death, to navigate the vessel to Africa. He steered eastwardly during the daytime, but at night put about hoping to touch the American shore. Thus the vessel wandered until it was cited off of the coast of the United States during the month of August. It was described as a "long, low, black schooner." Notice was sent to all the collectors of the ports along the Atlantic Coast, and a steamer and several revenue cutters were dispatched

Death of Capt. Ferrer, the Captain of the Amistad, July, 1839.

Don Jose Ruiz and Don Pedro Montez, of the Island of Cuba, having purchased fifty-three slaves at Havana, recently imported from Africa, put them on board the Amistad, Capt. Ferrer, in order to transport them to Principe, another port on the Island of Cuba. After being out from Havana about four days, the African captives on board, in order to obtain their freedom, and return to Africa, armed themselves with cane knives, and rose upon the Captain and crew of the vessel. Capt. Ferrer and the cook of the vessel were killed; two of the crew escaped; Ruiz and Montez were made prisoners.

Slaves aboard the Spanish ship *Amistad* take control and kill Capt. Ferrer with hopes of returning to Africa. Don Jose Ruiz and Don Pedro Montez, the men who purchased the slaves, were made prisoners and told to take them back to Africa. Instead, Ruiz and Montez deceived their captors and steered for the United States. **CORBIS-BETTMANN**

after her. Finally, on the 26th of August, 1839, Lieut. Gedney, U. S. Navy, captured the "Amistad," and took her into New London, Connecticut.

The two Spaniards and a Creole cabin boy were examined before Judge Andrew T. Judson, of the United States Court, who, without examining the Negroes, bound them over to be tried as pirates. The poor Africans were cast into the prison at New London. Public curiosity was at a high pitch; and for a long time the "Amistad captives" occupied a large place in public attention. The Africans proved to be natives of the Mendi country, and quite intelligent. The romantic story of their sufferings and meanderings was given to the country through a competent interpreter; and many Christian hearts turned toward them in their lonely captivity in a strange land. The trial was continued several months. During this time the anti-slavery friends provided instruction for the Africans. Their minds were active and receptive. They soon learned to read, write, and do sums in arithmetic. They cultivated a garden of some fifteen acres, and proved themselves an intelligent and industrious people.

The final decision of the court was that the "Amistad captives" were not slaves, but freemen, and, as such, were entitled to their liberty. The good and liberal Lewis Tappan had taken a lively interest in these people from the first, and now that they were released from prison, felt that they should be sent back to their native shores and a mission started amongst their countrymen. Accordingly he took charge of them and appeared before the public in a number of cities of New England. An admission fee of fifty cents was required at the door, and the proceeds were devoted to leasing a vessel to take them home. Large

audiences greeted them everywhere, and the impression they made was of the highest order. Mr. Tappan would state the desire of the people to return to their native land, appeal to the philanthropic to aid them, and then call upon the people to read the Scriptures, sing songs in their own language, and then in the English. Cinquez would then deliver an account of their capture, the horrors of the voyage, how he succeeded in getting his manacles off, how he aided his brethren to loose their fetters, how he invited them to follow him in an attempt to gain their liberty, the attack, and their rescue, etc., etc. He was a man of magnificent physique, commanding presence, graceful manners, and effective oratory. His speeches were delivered in Mendi, and translated into English by an interpreter.

"It is impossible," wrote Mr. Tappan from Boston, "to describe the novel and deeply interesting manner in which he acquitted himself. The subject of his speech was similar to that of his countrymen who had spoken in English; but he related more minutely and graphically the occurrences on board the 'Amistad.' The easy manner of Cinquez, his natural, graceful, and energetic action, the rapidity of his utterance, and the remarkable and various expressions of his countenance, excited admiration and applause. He was pronounced a powerful natural orator, and one born to sway the minds of his fellow-men. Should he be converted and become a preacher of the cross in Africa what delightful results may be anticipated!"

A little fellow called Kali, only eleven years of age, pleased the audience everywhere he went by his ability not only to spell any word in the Gospels, but sentences, without blundering. For example, he would spell out a sentence like the following sentence, naming each letter and syllable, and recapitulating as he went along, until he pronounced the whole sentence: "Blessed are the meek, for they shall inherit the earth."

Of their doings in Philadelphia, Mr. Joseph Sturge wrote:

> On this occasion, a very crowded and miscellaneous assembly collected to see and hear the Mendians, although the admission had been fixed as high as half a dollar, with the view of raising a fund to carry them to their native country. Fifteen of them were present, including one little boy and three girls. Cinque, their chief, spoke with great fluency in his native language; and his action and manner were very animated and graceful. Not much of his speech was translated, yet he greatly interested his audience. The little boy could speak our language with facility; and each of them read, without hesitation, one or two verses in the New Testament. It was impossible for any one to go away with the impression, that in native intellect these people were inferior to the whites. The information which I privately received from their tutor, and others who had full opportunities of appreciating their capacities and attainments, fully confirmed my own very favorable impressions.

But all the while their sad hearts were turning toward their home and the dear ones so far away. One of them eloquently declared: "If Merica men offer me as much gold as fill this cap full up, and give me houses, land, and every ting, so dat I stay in this country, I say: 'No! no! I want to see my father, my mother, my brother, my sister.'" Nothing could have been more tender and expressive. They were willing to endure any hardships short of life that they might once more see their own, their native land. The religious instruction they had enjoyed made a wonderful impression on their minds. One of them said: "We owe every thing to God; he keeps us alive, and makes us free. When we go to home to Mendi we tell our brethren about God, Jesus Christ, and heaven." Another one was asked: "What is faith?" and replied: "Believing in Jesus Christ, and trusting in him." Reverting to the murder of the captain and cook of the "Amistad," one of the Africans said that if it were to be done over again he would pray for rather than kill them. Cinque, hearing this, smiled and shook his head. When asked if he would not pray for them, said: "Yes, I would pray 'em, an' kill 'em too."

These captives were returned to their native country in the fall of 1841, accompanied by five missionaries. Their objective point was Sierra Leone, from which place the British Government assisted them to their homes. Their stay in the United States did the anti-slavery cause great good. Here were poor, naked, savage pagans, unable to speak English, in less than three years able to speak the English language and appreciate the blessings of a Christian civilization.

PRIMARY SOURCE DOCUMENT

The Louisiana Purchase and the Missouri Compromise

INTRODUCTION When the United States purchased the lands that would become known as the Louisiana Purchase from France, the stage was set for a fierce battle as to whether the incoming territories would become slave states or not. On the one side were the powerful lobbies of southern businessmen as well as adventurers and entrepreneurs who wished to develop the new land. On the other side were the abolitionists. Like so many battles regarding the rights of African Americans, the battle concerned more than just the slavery issue. It would set the tone for the growing nation. In the end the compromise effectively divided the nation down racial and political fault lines. The following is the original document as prepared by Henry Clay. Note section 8 in which slavery is prohibited in territories north of the 36 degrees, 30 minutes, line of latitude—with the exception of Missouri. This is the section that was repealed in the Kansas-Nebraska Act of 1854, effectively the final straw, propelling the nation into the Civil War.

Establishing Slave State Boundaries: The Missouri Compromise by Henry Clay, 1819–1821

The Territory of Missouri was part of the Louisiana Purchase; by the terms of this purchase the inhabitants of the Territory were guaranteed in their liberty, property, and religion. When in 1818 Missouri petitioned for admission to the Union as a State, the question arose whether this guaranty covered property in slaves of whom there were some two or three thousand in the Territory. In the course of the discussion of the enabling act, Representative Tallmadge of New York offered an amendment excluding slavery from the State. This amendment passed the House but failed in the Senate. That summer and fall the Missouri question was the chief political issue before the country; Congress was bombarded with petitions from State legislatures and other bodies on the slavery issue. In the new Congress the positions of the House and the Senate are indicated by the passage in the House of the Taylor Amendment, in the Senate of the Thomas Amendment. The application of Maine for admission as a State offered Congress a way out of the difficulty. A conference committee reported bills to admit Maine to Statehood, and to admit Missouri with the Thomas Amendment. An act authorizing Missouri to form a state government was approved March 6, but the constitution which the Missouri Convention drew up contained a clause obnoxious to the anti-slavery element, and probably unconstitutional, and Congress refused to admit the State under this constitution. A conference committee worked out a solution to the problem which was provided in the Resolutions for the admission of Missouri of March 2. The conditions laid down were accepted by the legislature of Missouri in June, and Missouri was admitted to Statehood by proclamation of August 10.

1. The Tallmadge Amendment
February 13, 1819

(Journal of the House of Representatives, 15th Congress, 2nd. Sess. p. 272)
And provided also, That the further introduction of slavery or involuntary servitude be prohibited, except for the punishment of crimes, whereof the party shall be duly convicted; and that all children of slaves, born within the said state, after the admission thereof into the Union, shall be free but may be held to service until the age of twenty-five years.

2. The Taylor Amendment
January 26, 1820

(Annals of the Congress of the United States, 16th Cong. 1st. Sess. Vol. I, p. 947)
The reading of the bill proceeded as far as the fourth section; when

Mr. Taylor, of New York, proposed to amend the bill by incorporating in that section the following provision:

Section 4, line 25, insert the following after the word "State"; "And shall ordain and establish, that there shall be neither slavery nor involuntary servitude in the said State, otherwise than in the punishment of crimes, whereof the party shall have been duly convicted: Provided, always, That any person escaping into the same, from whom labor or service is lawfully claimed in any other State, such fugitive may be lawfully reclaimed, and conveyed to the person claiming his or her labor or service as aforesaid: And provided, also, That the said provision shall not be construed to alter the condition or civil rights of any person now held to service or labor in the said Territory."

3. The Thomas Amendment
February 17, 1820

(Annals of the Congress of the United States, 16th Cong. 1st Sess. Vol. I, p. 427)
And be it further enacted, That, in all that territory ceded by France to the United States, under the name of Louisiana, which lies north of thirty-six degrees and thirty minutes north latitude, excepting only such part thereof as is included within the limits of the State contemplated by this act, slavery and involuntary servitude, otherwise than in the punishment of crimes whereof the party shall have been duly convicted, shall be and is hereby forever prohibited: Provided always, That any person

escaping into the same, from whom labor or service is lawfully claimed in any State or Territory of the United States, such fugitive may be lawfully reclaimed, and conveyed to the person claiming his or her labor or service, as aforesaid.

4. Missouri Enabling Act
March 6, 1820

(U.S. Statutes at Large, Vol. III, p. 545 ff.)
An Act to authorize the people of the Missouri territory to form a constitution and state government, and for the admission of such state into the Union on an equal footing with the original states, and to prohibit slavery in certain territories.

Be it enacted That the inhabitants of that portion of the Missouri territory included within the boundaries hereinafter designated, be, and they are hereby, authorized to form for themselves a constitution and state government, and to assume such name as they shall deem proper; and the said state, when formed, shall be admitted into the Union, upon an equal footing with the original states, in all respects whatsoever.

Sec. 2. That the said state shall consist of all the territory included within the following boundaries, to wit: Beginning in the middle of the Mississippi river, on the parallel of thirty-six degrees of north latitude; thence west, along that parallel of latitude, to the St. Francois river; thence up, and following the course of that river, in the middle of the main channel thereof, to the parallel of latitude of thirty-six degrees and thirty minutes; thence west, along the same, to a point where the said parallel is intersected by a meridian line passing through the middle of the month of the Kansas river, where the same empties into the Missouri river, thence, from the point aforesaid north, along the said meridian line, to the intersection of the parallel of latitude which passes through the rapids of the river Des Moines, making the said line to correspond with the Indian boundary line; thence east, from the point of intersection last aforesaid, along the said parallel of latitude, to the middle of the channel of the main fork of the said river Des Moines; thence down and along the middle of the main channel of the said river Des Moines, to the mouth of the same, where it empties into the Mississippi river; thence, due east, to the middle of the main channel of the Mississippi river; thence down, and following the course of the Mississippi river, in the middle of the main channel thereof, to the place of beginning: ...

Sec. 3. That all free white male citizens of the United States, who shall have arrived at the age of twenty-one years, and have resided in said territory three months previous to the day of election, and all other persons qualified to vote for representatives to the general assembly of the said territory, shall be qualified to be elected, and they are hereby qualified and authorized to vote, and choose representatives to form a convention....

Sec. 8. That in all that territory ceded by France to the United States, under the name of Louisiana, which lies north of thirty-six degrees and thirty minutes north latitude, not included within the limits of the state, contemplated by this act, slavery and involuntary servitude, otherwise than in the punishment of crimes, whereof the parties shall have been duly convicted, shall be, and is hereby, forever prohibited: Provided always, That any person escaping into the same, from whom labour or service is lawfully claimed, in any state or territory of the United States, such fugitive may be lawfully reclaimed and conveyed to the person claiming his or her labour or service as aforesaid.

5. The Constitution of Missouri
July 19, 1820

(Poore, ed., Federal and State Constitutions, Vol. II, p. 1107–8)

Sec. 26. The general assembly shall not have power to pass laws—

1. For the emancipation of slaves without the consent of their owners; or without paying them, before such emancipation, a full equivalent for such slaves so emancipated; and,

2. To prevent bona-fide immigrants to this State, or actual settlers therein, from bringing from any of the United States, or from any of their Territories, such persons as may there be deemed to be slaves, so long as any persons of the same description are allowed to be held as slaves by the laws of this State.

They shall have power to pass laws—

1. To prevent bona-fide immigrants to this State of any slaves who may have committed any high crime in any other State or Territory;

2. To prohibit the introduction of any slave for the purpose of speculation, or as an article of trade or merchandise;

3. To prohibit the introduction of any slave, or the offspring of any slave, who heretofore may have been, or who hereafter may be, imported from any foreign country into the United States, or any Territory thereof, in contravention of any existing statute of the United States; and,

4. To permit the owners of slaves to emancipate them, saving the right of creditors, where the person so emancipating will give security that the slave so emancipated shall not become a public charge.

It shall be their duty, as soon as may be, to pass such laws as may be necessary—

1. To prevent free negroes end [and] mulattoes from coming to and settling in this State, under any pretext whatsoever; and,

2. To oblige the owners of slaves to treat them with humanity, and to abstain from all injuries to them extending to life or limb.

6. Resolution for the Admission of Missouri
March 2, 1821

(U.S. Statutes at Large, Vol. III, p. 645)

Resolution providing for the admission of the State of Missouri into the Union, on a certain condition.

Resolved, That Missouri shall be admitted into this union on an equal footing with the original states, in all respects whatever, upon the fundamental condition, that the fourth clause of the twenty-sixth section of the third article of the constitution submitted on the part of said state to Congress, shall never be construed to authorize the passage of any law, and that no law shall be passed in conformity thereto, by which any citizen, of either of the states in this Union, shall be excluded from the enjoyment of any of the privileges and immunities to which such citizen is entitled under the constitution of the United States: Provided, That the legislature of the said state, by a solemn public act, shall declare the assent of the said state to the said fundamental condition, and shall transmit to the President of the United States, on or before the fourth Monday in November next, an authentic copy of the said act; upon the receipt whereof, the President, by proclamation, shall announce the fact; whereupon, and without any further proceeding on the part of Congress, the admission of the said state into this Union shall be considered as complete.

PRIMARY SOURCE DOCUMENT

"A Short Catechism: Adapted to All Parts of the United States" by William Lloyd Garrison

INTRODUCTION William Lloyd Garrison was one of the angriest, as well as one of the wittiest, of the abolitionist writers and speakers—and absolutely uncompromising in his call for immediate, unconditional, and universal emancipation. His antislavery approach of "moral suasion" was rooted in noncomformist religious belief. It demanded that abolitionists refrain from political activity, including voting, on the ground that such activity supported a manifestly corrupt government. It also demanded that abolitionists be entirely pacifist in their activities, refraining from any coercive physical action to bring down slavery. Moral suasion alone, by appealing to the public's higher faculties of reason and spiritual insight, was to win the day.

As the years wore on and slavery remained as entrenched as ever, many abolitionists departed from the Garrisonian view, calling for vigorous political action or the violent overthrow of slavery, or both. Garrison himself, however, never wavered in his commitment to changing minds and hearts. He understood that while slavery itself was the exercise of sheer power, proslavery arguments rested on a series of spurious rationales, appealing, or seeming to appeal, to human reason. Combining his anger and wit, Garrison often took aim at proslavery reasoning, exposing its logic as absurd, self-serving, or simply racist.

The racism of proslavery arguments is his target in "A Short Catechism," which appeared in the pages of the *Liberator* for November 17, 1837. Here, Garrison reduces every proslavery argument—and what he saw as the related arguments for gradual abolition and colonization—to a single racist formula: "because they are black." As religious catechism forces respondents to recognize church doctrine, so Garrison's catechism forces them to recognize their own racism.

1. Why is American slaveholding in all cases not sinful? Because its victims are black. 2. Why is gradual emancipation right? Because the slaves are black. 3. Why is immediate emancipation wrong and dangerous? Because the slaves are black. 4. Why ought one-sixth portion of the American population to be exiled from their native soil? Because they are black. 5. Why would the slaves if emancipated, cut the throats of their masters? Because they are black. 6. Why are our slaves not fit for freedom? Because they are black. 7. Why are American slaveholders not thieves, tyrants and men-stealers? Because their victims are black. 8. Why does the Bible justify American slavery? Because its victims are black. 9. Why ought not the Priest and the Levite, 'passing by on the other side,' to be sternly rebuked? Because the man who has fallen among thieves, and lies weltering in his blood, is black. 10. Why are abolitionists fanatics, madmen and incendiaries? Because those for whom they plead are black. 11. Why are they wrong in their principles and measures? Because the slaves are black. 12. Why is all the prudence, moderation, judiciousness, philanthropy and piety on the side of their opponents? Because the slaves are black. 13. Why ought not the free discussion of slavery to be tolerated? Because its victims are black. 14. Why is Lynch law, as applied to abolitionists, better than common law? Because the slaves, whom they seek to emancipate, are black. 15. Why are the slaves contented and happy? Because they are black! 16. Why don't they want to be free? Because they are black! 17. Why are they not created in the image of God? Because their skin is black. 18. Why are they not cruelly treated, but enjoy unusual comforts and privileges? Because they are black! 19. Why are they not our brethren and countrymen? Because they are black. 20. Why is it unconstitutional to pity and defend them? Because they are black. 21. Why is it a violation of the national compact to rebuke their masters? Because they are black. 22. Why will they be lazy, improvident, and worthless, if set free? Because their skin is black. 23. Why will the whites wish to amalgamate with them in a state of freedom? Because they are black!! 24. Why must the Union be dissolved, should Congress abolish slavery in the District of Columbia? Because the slaves in that District are black.

PRIMARY SOURCE DOCUMENT

"Memorial Discourse" by Henry Highland Garnet

INTRODUCTION In the year 1865, following the end of the Civil War, Henry Highland Garnet was asked to deliver his *Memorial Discourse* before the House of Representatives. Garnet went on to become president of Avery College and later pastor of New York's Shiloh Baptist Church. In 1881, Garnet was named consul general to the nation of Liberia, and there he died and was buried in 1882.

The discourse highlights the early debate among African American intellectual leaders on the course that should be taken for the advancement of black Americans. While Garnet was respected as a man of reason, his stance was hardly that of the accomodationists, later personified in Booker T. Washington.

A Call to Rebellion: An Address to the Slaves of the United States of America, by Henry Highland Garnet
Preface The following Address was first read at the National Convention held at Buffalo, N. Y., in 1843. Since that time it has been slightly modified, retaining, however, all of its original doctrine. The document elicited more discussion than any other paper that was ever brought before that, or any other deliberative body of colored persons, and their friends. Gentlemen who opposed the Address, based their objections on these grounds. 1. That the document was war-like, and encouraged insurrection; and 2. That if the Convention should adopt it, that those delegates who lived near the borders of the slave states, would not dare to return to their homes. The Address was rejected by a small majority; and now in compliance with the earnest request of many who heard it, and in conformity to the wishes of numerous friends who are anxious to see it, the author now gives it to the public, praying God that this little book may be borne on the four winds of heaven, until the principles it contains shall be understood and adopted by every slave in the Union.

H. H. G.

Troy, N.Y., April 15, 1848.

Address to the Slaves of the U.S.

Brethren and Fellow Citizens:
Your brethren of the north, east, and west have been accustomed to meet together in National Conventions, to sympathize with each other, and to weep over your unhappy condition. In these meetings we have addressed all classes of the free, but we have never until this time, sent a word of consolation and advice to you. We have been contented in sitting still and mourning over your sorrows, earnestly hoping that before this day, your

African American Intellectuals: Henry Highland Garnet (1815–1882)

Born into slavery in Maryland in 1815, Henry Highland Garnet escaped with his family to Pennsylvania when he was ten years old. They eventually moved to New York City, where they settled next to Alexander Crummell's family, and where Henry received an education, first at the Free African School and later at the newly founded Negro High School. In 1835, Garnet and Crummell traveled north together to attend Noyes Academy in Canaan, New Hampshire. When local farmers, infuriated by their presence, attacked the school, Garnet held them at bay with a shotgun.

Garnet was ordained a minister in the Presbyterian church in 1843, and that same year he delivered the address reprinted here. Garnet was a member of the New York school of abolitionists. Unlike the Bostonians, who were led by William Lloyd Garrison, Garnet and his fellow New York abolitionists took a pragmatic approach to the great issues facing African Americans, slave and free. They favored

political action over acts of conscience and promoted all-black newspapers, schools, churches, and the like, wherever and whenever racial prejudice made integrated institutions an unlikely dream. Many, Garnet among them, supported the violent overthrow of slavery as the only course likely to bring about a change. Garnet made this theme public in his 1843 *Address* before a convention of African American men held in Buffalo. By a narrow vote of nineteen to eighteen, the convention refused to endorse Garnet's speech. Among those voting against it was Frederick Douglass, though he would later come to embrace its call to arms.

Like David Walker's *Appeal,* Garnet's *Address* called upon slaves to enter into open, mass rebellion against those who held them in bondage. His *Address* was printed together with Walker's *Appeal* under a single cover in 1848, the cost of the printing paid for, it is said, by John Brown.

---

sacred liberties would have been restored. But, we have hoped in vain. Years have rolled on, and tens of thousands have been borne on streams of blood, and tears, to the shores of eternity. While you have been oppressed, we have also been partakers with you; nor can we be free while you are enslaved. We therefore write to you as being bound with you.

Many of you are bound to us, not only by the ties of a common humanity, but we are connected by the more tender relations of parents, wives, husbands, children, brothers, and sisters, and friends. As such we most affectionately address you.

Slavery has fixed a deep gulf between you and us, and while it shuts out from you the relief and consolation which your friends would willingly render, it afflicts and persecutes you with a fierceness which we might not expect to see in the fiends of hell. But still the Almighty Father of Mercies has left to us a glimmering ray of hope, which shines out like a lone star in a cloudy sky. Mankind are becoming wiser, and better—the oppressor's power is fading, and you, every day, are becoming better informed, and more numerous. Your grievances, brethren, are many. We shall not attempt, in this short address, to present to the world, all the dark catalogue of

this nation's sins, which have been committed upon an innocent people. Nor is it indeed, necessary, for you feel them from day to day, and all the civilized world look upon them with amazement.

Two hundred and twenty-seven years ago, the first of our injured race were brought to the shores of America. They came not with glad spirits to select their homes, in the New World. They came not with their own consent, to find an unmolested enjoyment of the blessings of this fruitful soil. The first dealings which they had with men calling themselves Christians, exhibited to them the worst features of corrupt and sordid hearts; and convinced them that no cruelty is too great, no villainy, and no robbery too abhorrent for even enlightened men to perform, when influenced by avarice, and lust. Neither did they come flying upon the wings of Liberty, to a land of freedom. But, they came with broken hearts, from their beloved native land, and were doomed to unrequited toil, and deep degradation. Nor did the evil of their bondage end at their emancipation by death. Succeeding generations inherited their chains, and millions have come from eternity into time, and have returned again to the world of spirits, cursed, and ruined by American Slavery.

The propagators of the system, or their immediate ancestors very soon discovered its growing evil, and its tremendous wickedness, and secret promises were made to destroy it. The gross inconsistency of a people holding slaves, who had themselves "ferried o'er the wave," for freedom's sake, was too apparent to be entirely overlooked. The voice of Freedom cried, "emancipate your Slaves." Humanity supplicated with tears, for the deliverance of the children of Africa. Wisdom urged her solemn plea. The bleeding captive plead his innocence, and pointed to Christianity who stood weeping at the cross. Jehovah frowned upon the nefarious institution, and thunderbolts, red with vengeance, struggled to leap forth to blast the guilty wretches who maintained it. But all was vain. Slavery had stretched its dark wings of death over the land, the Church stood silently by—the priests prophesied falsely, and the people loved to have it so. Its throne is established, and now it reigns triumphantly.

Nearly three millions of your fellow citizens, are prohibited by law, and public opinion, (which in this country is stronger than law), from reading the Book of Life. Your intellect has been destroyed as much as possible, and every ray of light they have attempted to shut out from your minds. The oppressors themselves have become involved in the ruin. They have become weak, sensual, and rapacious. They have cursed you—they have cursed themselves—they have cursed the earth which they have trod. In the language of a southern statesman, we can truly say, "even the wolf, driven back long since by the approach of man, now returns after the lapse of a hundred years, and howls amid the desolations of slavery."

The colonists threw the blame upon England. They said that the mother country entailed the evil upon them, and that they would rid themselves of it if they could. The world thought they were sincere, and the philanthropic pitied them. But time soon tested their sincerity. In a few years, the colonists grew strong 2nd severed themselves from the British Government. Their Independence was declared, and they took their station among the sovereign powers of the earth. The declaration was a glorious document. Sages admired it, and the patriotic of every nation reverenced the Godlike sentiments which it contained. When the power of Government returned to their hands, did they emancipate the slaves? No; they rather added new links to our chains. Were they ignorant of the principles of Liberty? Certainly they were not. The sentiments of their revolutionary orators fell in burning eloquence upon their hearts, and with one voice they cried, Liberty or Death. O, what a sentence was that! It ran from soul to soul like electric fire, and nerved the arm of thousands to fight in the holy cause of Freedom. Among the diversity of opinions that are entertained in regard to physical resistance, there are but a few found to gainsay that stern declaration. We are among those who do not.

Slavery! How much misery is comprehended in that single word. What mind is there that does not shrink from its direful effects? Unless the image of God is obliterated from the soul, all men cherish the love of Liberty. The nice discerning political economist does not regard the sacred right, more than the untutored African who roams in the wilds of Congo. Nor has the one more right to the full enjoyment of his freedom than the other. In every man's mind the good seeds of liberty are planted, and he who brings his fellow down so low, as to make him contented with a condition of slavery, commits the highest crime against God and man. Brethren, your oppressors aim to do this. They endeavor to make you as much like brutes as possible. When they have blinded the eyes of your mind—when they have embittered the sweet waters of life—when they have shut out the light which shines from the word of God—then, and not till then has American slavery done its perfect work.

To such degradation it is sinful in the extreme for you to make voluntary submission. The divine commandments, you are in duty bound to reverence, and obey. If you do not obey them you will surely meet with the displeasure of the Almighty He requires you to love him supremely, and your neighbor as yourself—to keep the Sabbath day holy—to search the Scriptures—and bring up your children with respect for his laws, and to worship no other God but him. But slavery sets all these at naught and hurls defiance in the face of Jehovah. The forlorn condition in which you are placed does not destroy your moral obligation to God. You are not certain of Heaven, because you suffer yourselves to remain in a state of slavery, where you cannot obey the commandments of the Sovereign of the universe. If the ignorance of slavery is a passport to heaven, then it is a blessing, and no curse, and you should rather desire its perpetuity than its abolition. God will not receive slavery, nor ignorance, nor any other state of mind, for love, and obedience to him. Your condition does not absolve you from your moral obligation. The diabolical injustice by which your liberties are cloven down, neither God, nor angels, or just men, command you to suffer for a single moment. Therefore it is your solemn and imperative duty to use every means, both moral, intellectual, and physical, that promise success. If a band of heathen men should attempt to enslave a race of Christians, and to place their children under the influence of some false religion, surely, heaven would frown upon the men who would not resist such aggression, even to death. If, on the other hand, a band of Christians should attempt to enslave a race of heathen men and to entail slavery upon them, and to keep them in heathenism in the midst of Christianity, the God of heaven would smile upon every effort which the injured might make to disenthral themselves.

Brethren, it is as wrong for your lordly oppressors to keep you in slavery, as it was for the man thief to steal

The 1850 Fugitive Slave Law imperiled free African Americans and fugitives who had settled in the North for many years. The men being chased are dressed fashionably in waistcoats and ties, suggesting that they are prosperous city men. Out of place in this rural scene and stampeded by slave catchers, they are clearly terrified. **THE LIBRARY OF CONGRESS**

our ancestors from the coast of Africa. You should therefore now use the same manner of resistance, as would have been just in our ancestors, when the bloody foot prints of the first remorseless soul thief was placed upon the shores of our fatherland. The humblest peasant is as free in the sight of God, as the proudest monarch that ever swayed a sceptre. Liberty is a spirit sent out from God, and like its great Author, is no respecter of persons.

Brethren, the time has come when you must act for yourselves. It is an old and true saying, that "if hereditary bondmen would be free, they must themselves strike the blow." You can plead your own cause, and do the work of emancipation better than any others. The nations of the old world are moving in the great cause of universal freedom, and some of them at least, will ere long, do you justice. The combined powers of Europe have placed their broad seal of disapprobation upon the African slave trade. But in the slave holding parts of the United States, the trade is as brisk as ever. They buy and sell you as though you were brute beasts. The North has done much—her opinion of slavery in the abstract is known. But in regard to the South, we adopt he opinion of the New York Evangelist—"We have advanced so far, that the cause apparently waits for a more effectual door to be thrown open than has been yet." We are about to point you to that more effectual door. Look around you,

and behold the bosoms of your loving wives, heaving with untold agonies! Hear the cries of your poor children! Remember the stripes your fathers bore. Think of the torture and disgrace of your noble mothers. Think of your wretched sisters, loving virtue and purity, as they are driven into concubinage, and are exposed to the unbridled lusts of incarnate devils. Think of the undying glory that hangs around the ancient name of Africa:—and forget not that you are native-born American citizens, and as such, you are justly entitled to all the rights that are granted to the freest. Think how many tears you have poured out upon the soil which you have cultivated with unrequited toil, and enriched with your blood; and then go to your lordly enslavers, and tell them plainly, that you are determined to be free. Appeal to their sense of justice, and tell them that they have no more right to oppress you, than you have to enslave them. Entreat them to remove the grievous burdens which they have imposed upon you, and to remunerate you for your labor. Promise them renewed diligence in the cultivation of the soil, if they will render to you an equivalent for your services. Point them to the increase of happiness and prosperity in the British West Indies, since the act of Emancipation. Tell them in language which they cannot misunderstand, of the exceeding sinfulness of slavery, and of a future judgment, and of the righteous retributions of an indignant God. Inform

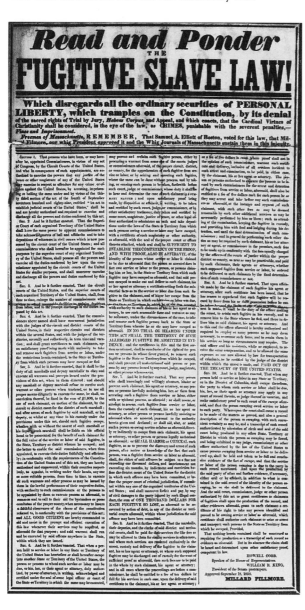

An editorial protesting the Fugitive Slave Law of 1850. The law, which required citizens to aid in the return of escaped slaves and enacted heavy penalties on anyone that helped them escape, infuriated many northerners who felt it trampled on personal liberty. **CORBIS-BETTMANN**

make a grand Exodus from the land of bondage. The Pharaohs are on both sides of the bloodred waters! You cannot remove en masse, to the dominions of the British Queen—nor can you pass through Florida, and overrun Texas, and at last find peace in Mexico. The propagators of American slavery are spending their blood and treasure, that they may plant the black flag in the heart of Mexico, and riot in the halls of the Montezumas. In the language of the Rev. Robert Hall, when addressing the volunteers of Bristol, who were rushing forth to repel the invasion of Napoleon, who threatened to lay waste the fair homes of England, "Religion is too much interested in your behalf, not to shed over you her most gracious influences."

You will not be compelled to spend much time in order to become inured to hardships. From the first moment that you breathed the air of heaven, you have been accustomed to nothing else but hardships. The heroes of the American Revolution were never put upon harder fare, than a peck of corn, and a few herrings per week. You have not become enervated by the luxuries of life. Your sternest energies have been beaten out upon the anvil of severe trial. Slavery has done more this, to make you subservient to its own purposes; but it has done than this, it has prepared you for any emergency. If you receive good treatment, it is what you could hardly expect; if you meet with pain, sorrow, and even death, these are the common lot of the slaves.

Fellow-men! patient sufferers! behold your dearest rights crushed to the earth! See your sons murdered, and your wives, mothers, and sisters, doomed to prostitution! In the name of the merciful God! and by all that life is worth, let it no longer be a debateable question, whether it is better to choose Liberty or Death!

In 1822, Denmark Veazie, of South Carolina, formed a plan for the liberation of his fellow men. In the whole history of human efforts to overthrow slavery, a more complicated and tremendous plan was never formed. He was betrayed by the treachery of his own people, and died a martyr to freedom. Many a brave hero fell, but History, faithful to her high trust, will transcribe his name on the same monument with Moses, Hampden, Tell, Bruce, and Wallace, Touissaint L'Overteur, Lafayette and Washington. That tremendous movement shook the whole empire of slavery. The guilty soul thieves were overwhelmed with fear. It is a matter of fact, that at that time, and in consequence of the threatened revolution, the slave states talked strongly of emancipation. But they blew but one blast of the trumpet of freedom, and then laid it aside As these men became quiet, the slaveholders ceased to talk about emancipation: and now, behold your condition to-day! Angels sigh over it, and humanity has long since exhausted her tears in weeping on your account!

them that all you desire, is Freedom, and that nothing else will suffice. Do this, and for ever after cease to toil for the heartless tyrants, who give you no other reward but stripes and abuse. If they then commence the work of death, they, and not you, will be responsible for the consequences. You had far better all die—die immediately, than live slaves, and entail your wretchedness upon your posterity. If you would be free in this generation, here is your only hope. However much you and all of us may desire it, there is not much hope of Redemption without the shedding of blood. If you must bleed, let it all come at once—rather, die freemen, than live to be slaves. It is impossible, like the children of Israel, to

The patriotic Nathaniel Turner followed Denmark Veazie. He was goaded to desperation by wrong and injustice. By Despotism, his name has been recorded on the list of infamy, but future generations will number him among the noble and brave.

Next arose the immortal Joseph Cinque, the hero of the Amistad. He was a native African, and by the help of God he emancipated a whole ship-load of his fellow men on the high seas. And he now sings of liberty on the sunny hills of Africa, and beneath his native palm trees, where he hears the lion roar, and feels himself as free as that king of the forest. Next arose Madison Washington, that bright star of freedom, and took his station in the constellation of freedom. He was a slave on board the brig Creole, of Richmond, bound to New Orleans, that great slave mart, with a hundred and four others. Nineteen struck for liberty or death. But one life was taken, and the whole were emancipated, and the vessel was carried into Nassau, New Providence. Noble men! Those who have fallen in freedom's conflict, their memories will be cherished by the true hearted, and the God-fearing, in all future generations; those who are living, their names are surrounded by a halo of glory.

We do not advise you to attempt a revolution with the sword, because it would be inexpedient. Your numbers are too small, and moreover the rising spirit of the age, and the spirit of the gospel, are opposed to war and bloodshed. But from this moment cease to labor for tyrants who will not remunerate you. Let every slave throughout the land do this, and the days of slavery are numbered. You cannot be more oppressed than you have been—you cannot suffer greater cruelties than you have already. Rather die freemen, than live to be slaves. Remember that you are Three Millions.

It is in your power so to torment the God-cursed slaveholders, that they will be glad to let you go free. If the scale was turned and black men were the masters, and white men the slaves, every destructive agent and element would be employed to lay the oppressor low. Danger and death would hang over their heads day and night. Yes, the tyrants would meet with plagues more terrible than those of Pharaoh. But you are a patient people. You act as though you were made for the special use of these devils. You act as though your daughters were born to pamper the lusts of your masters and overseers. And worse than all, you tamely submit, while your lords tear your wives from your embraces, and defile them before your eyes. In the name of God we ask, are you men? Where is the blood of your fathers? Has it all run out of your veins? Awake, awake; millions of voices are calling you! Your dead fathers speak to you from their graves. Heaven, as with a voice of thunder, calls on you to arise from the dust.

Let your motto be resistance! resistance! resistance! — No oppressed people have ever secured their liberty without resistance. What kind of resistance you had better make,

you must decide by the circumstances that surround you, and according to the suggestion of expediency. Brethren, adieu. Trust in the living God. Labor for the peace of the human race, and remember that you are three millions.

PRIMARY SOURCE DOCUMENT

Letters Between H. C. Wright and Frederick Douglass on the Purchase of Douglass's Freedom

INTRODUCTION In 1846, while Frederick Douglass was touring the British Isles speaking to antislavery audiences, a group of British abolitionists raised the money to purchase his manumission from the Auld family of Maryland. The price paid for the freedom of this great American was 150 pounds sterling, or 711 dollars.

In December 1846, a fellow abolitionist, H. C. Wright, wrote to Douglass opposing the sale on moral grounds. "I cannot think of the transaction without vexation," Wright told Douglass. "I would see you free—you are free—you always were free, and the man is a villain who claims you as a slave."

Douglass replied a few days later, defending the purchase. He wished to return home, and the price of his return was to "allow Hugh Auld to rob me, or my friends, of 150 pounds. I must have a 'bit of paper, signed and sealed,' or my liberty must be taken from me and I must be torn from my family and friends." At the same time, Douglass assured Wright, "I will hold up those papers before the world, in proof of the plundering character of the American government."

The exchange of letters between Wright and Douglass was published in the January 29, 1847, issue of the *Liberator,* under the heading "The Ransom."

Letter from H. C. Wright
Doncaster, Dec. 12th, 1846.

Dear Frederick:

This is the first letter of advice I ever wrote to you—it is the last. I like to bear the responsibility of my own existence. I like to see others bear theirs. I say what I am about to say, because I think it is my right and duty to say it; at the same time, not wishing to interfere with your right to follow my advice, or not, as you shall see fit. That Certificate of your freedom, that Bill of Sale of your body and soul, from that villain, Auld, who dared to claim you as a chattel, and set a price on you as such, and to demand and take a price for you as such, I wish you would not touch it. I cannot bear to think of you as being a party to such a transaction, even by silence. If others will take that paper, and keep it as an evidence of your freedom, you cannot prevent them; but I wish you would see it to be your duty, publicly to disown the deed, and never to recognize that hateful Bill!—nor to refer to it, as of any authority to establish the fact that you are a Freeman, and not a Slave—a Man, and not a Chattel.

The moment you entered a non-slave State, your position ceased to be Frederick Douglass, versus Thomas

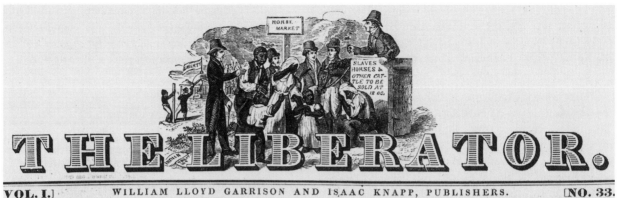

THE LIBERATOR.

VOL. I.] WILLIAM LLOYD GARRISON AND ISAAC KNAPP, PUBLISHERS. **[NO. 33.**

Boston, Massachusetts.] OUR COUNTRY IS THE WORLD—OUR COUNTRYMEN ARE MANKIND. [Saturday, August 13, 1831.

The masthead of the abolitionist newspaper the *Liberator* was intended to make people think about the inhumanity of slavery, how slavery allowed African Americans to be treated as animals. The placards among the slaves and slaveholders read, "Horse Market" and "Slaves, Horses, and other cattle to be sold at …" **THE LIBRARY OF CONGRESS**

Auld, and became Frederick Douglass, versus the United States. From that hour, you became the antagonist of that Republic.

As a nation, that confederacy, professing to be based upon the principle, that God made you free, and gave you an inalienable right to liberty, claims a right of property in your body and soul—to turn you into a chattel, a slave, again, at any moment. That claim you denied; the authority and power of the whole nation you spurned and defied, when, by running away, you spurned that miserable wretch, who held you as a slave. It was no longer a contest between you and that praying, psalm-singing slave-breeder, but a struggle between you and 17,000,000 of liberty-loving Republicans. By their laws and constitution, you are not a freeman, but a slave; you are not a man, but a chattel. You planted your foot upon their laws and constitution, and asserted your freedom and your manhood. You arraigned your antagonist—the slave-breeding Republic—before the tribunal of mankind, and of God. You have stated your case, and pleaded your cause, as none other could state and plead it. Your position, as the slave of that Republic, as the marketable commodity, the dehumanized, outraged man of a powerful nation, whose claim and power over you, you have dared to despise, invests you with influence among all to whom your appeal is made, and gathers around you their deep-felt, absorbing, and efficient sympathy. Your appeal to mankind is not against the grovelling thief, Thomas Auld, but against the more daring, more impudent and potent thief—the Republic of the United States of America. You will lose the advantages of this truly manly, and, to my view, sublime position; you will be shorn of your strength—you will sink in your own estimation, if you accept that detestable certificate of your freedom, that blasphemous forgery, that accursed Bill of Sale of your body and soul; or, even by silence,

acknowledge its validity. So I think. I cannot think of the transaction without vexation. I would see you free—you are free—you always were free, and the man is a villain who claims you as a slave, and should be treated as such; and the nation is a blasphemous hypocrite, that claims power over you as a chattel. I would see your right to freedom, and to a standing on the platform of humanity, openly acknowledged by every human being—not on the testimony of a bit of paper, signed and sealed by an acknowledged thief, but by the declaration of a penitent nation, prostrate at your feet, in tears, suing to you and to God for forgiveness, for the outrages committed against God and man, in your person.

That slave-breeding nation has dared to claim you, and 3,000,000 of your fellow-men, as chattels—slaves—to be bought and sold; and has pledged all its power to crush you down, and to keep you from rising from ignorance to knowledge—from degradation to respectability—from misery to happiness—from slavery to freedom—from a Chattel to a Man. As an advocate for yourself, and your 3,000,000 brethren, you have joined issue with it—and, in the name of God and humanity, you will conquer! The nation must and shall be humbled before its victims,—not by a blasphemous bill of sale, alias Certificate of freedom, for which 150 pounds are paid, but by renouncing its claim, blotting out its slavery-sustaining constitution, acknowledge itself conquered, and seek forgiveness of the victims of its injustice and tyranny. The plea, that this is the same as a ransom paid for a capture of some Algerine pirate, or Bedouin Arab, is naught. You have already, by your own energy, escaped the grasp of the pirate Auld. He has no more power over you. The spell of his influence over you is forever broken. Why go to him? Why ask the sacrilegious villain to set a price upon your body and soul? Why give him his price? The mean, brutal slaveholder—daring to price your freedom, your soul, in dollars and cents, and with cool, consum-

$200 Reward.

RANAWAY from the subscriber, on the night of Thursday, the 30th of Sepember,

FIVE NEGRO SLAVES,

To-wit : one Negro man, his wife, and three children.

The man is a black negro, full height, very erect, his face a little thin. He is about forty years of age, and calls himself *Washington Reed*, and is known by the name of Washington. He is probably well dressed, possibly takes with him an ivory headed cane, and is of good address. Several of his teeth are gone.

Mary, his wife, is about thirty years of age, a bright mulatto woman, and quite stout and strong.

The oldest of the children is a boy, of the name of FIELDING, twelve years of age, a dark mulatto, with heavy eyelids. He probably wore a new cloth cap.

MATILDA, the second child, is a girl, six years of age, rather a dark mulatto, but a bright and smart looking child.

MALCOLM, the youngest, is a boy, four years old, a lighter mulatto than the last, and about equally as bright. He probably also wore a cloth cap. If examined, he will be found to have a swelling at the navel.

Washington and Mary have lived at or near St. Louis, with the subscriber, for about 15 years.

It is supposed that they are making their way to Chicago, and that a white man accompanies them, that they will travel chiefly at night, and most probably in a covered wagon.

A reward of $150 will be paid for their apprehension, so that I can get them, if taken within one hundred miles of St. Louis, and $200 if taken beyond that, and secured so that I can get them, and other reasonable additional charges, if delivered to the subscriber, or to THOMAS ALLEN, Esq., at St. Louis, Mo. The above negroes, for the last few years, have been in possession of Thomas Allen, Esq., of St. Louis.

WM. RUSSELL.

ST. LOUIS, Oct. 1, 1847.

A reward of two hundred dollars was offered by this poster, dated October 1, 1847, to anyone providing information regarding the family of Washington Reed, which had been in the possession of Thomas Allen of St. Louis, Missouri. **THE LIBRARY OF CONGRESS**

mate impudence, and villany unsurpassed, saying "I'll be satisfied with 750 dollars—I'll give up my right of property in your person, and acknowledge you to be a freeman, and not a slave—a man, and not a beast—for £150.' 'Satisfied' forsooth!" You cancelled his villanous claims, when you turned your back upon him, and walked away. But the nation claims you as a slave. It does! Let it dare to assert that claim, and attempt your re-enslavement! It is worth running some risk, for the sake of the conflict, and the certain result.

Your wife and children are there, it is true, and you must return to them; but the greater will be your power to grapple with the monster; the shorter and more glorious will be the conflict; the more sure and complete the victory, if you go as the antagonist of a nation that claims you as a slave, as a chattel, a man turned into an article of merchandise. You would be armed with an irresistible power, when, as a self-emancipated captive, you arraigned that piratical Republic before the world. You would be sheltered and sustained by the sympathies of

millions. The advantages of your present position should not be sacrificed to a desire for greater security.

But I will go no further. You will think that what I have said has more of indignation than of reason in it. It may be so. Feeling is often a safer and a wiser guide than logic. Of all guilty men, the American slaveholder is the most guilty, and the meanest, the most impudent, most despicable, and most inexcusable in his guilt; except, it may be, those, who, in the non-slave States, and in Scotland and England, stand sponsors for his social respectability and personal Christianity, and who thus associate our Redeemer in loving fellowship with men who are the living embodiment of the sum of all villany.

Before concluding, I wish to add, that, in what I have said, I would not arraign the motives of those who have, as they believe, sought to befriend you in this matter. I believe Anna Richardson, and all who have taken part in this transaction, have been actuated by the purest motives of kindness to you and your family, and by a desire, through the purchase of your freedom, to benefit the American slaves. But they have erred in judgment, as it appears to me. Forgive this, if it needs forgiveness. I delight to see you loved and honored by all, and to see you made an instrument, by the God of the oppressed, of humbling in the dust, that gigantic liar and hypocrite, the American Republic, that stands with the Bible and Declaration of Independence in its hands, and its heel planted on the necks of 3,000,000 of slaves.

Thine sincerely,
H. C. Wright.

Frederick Douglass's Reply
22, St. Ann's Square, Manchester, 22d Dec., 1846.

Henry C. Wright:

Dear Friend:—Your letter of the 12th December reached me at this place, yesterday. Please accept my heartfelt thanks for it. I am sorry that you deemed it necessary to assure me, that it would be the last letter of advice you would ever write me. It looked as if you were about to cast me off for ever! I do not, however, think you meant to convey any such meaning; and if you did, I am sure you will see cause to change your mind, and to receive me again into the fold of those, whom it should ever be your pleasure to advise and instruct.

The subject of your letter is one of deep importance, and upon which, I have thought and felt much; and, being the party of all others most deeply concerned, it is natural to suppose I have an opinion, and ought to be able to give it on all fitting occasions. I deem this a fitting occasion, and shall act accordingly.

You have given me your opinion: I am glad you have done so. You have given it to me direct, in your own emphatic way. You never speak insipidly, smoothly, or mincingly; you have strictly adhered to your custom, in the letter before me. I now take great pleasure in giving you my opinion, as plainly and unreservedly as you have given yours, and I trust with equal good feeling and purity of motive. I take it, that nearly all that can be said against my position is contained in your letter; for if any man in the wide world would be likely to find valid objections to such a transaction as the one under consideration, I regard you as that man. I must, however, tell you, that I have read your letter over, and over again, and have sought in vain to find anything like what I can regard a valid reason against the purchase of my body, or against my receiving the manumission papers, if they are ever presented to me.

Let me, in the first place, state the facts and circumstances of the transaction which you so strongly condemn. It is your right to do so, and God forbid that I should ever cherish the slightest desire to restrain you in the exercise of that right. I say to you at once, and in all

the fulness of sincerity, speak out; speak freely; keep nothing back; let me know your whole mind. 'Hew to the line, though the chips fly in my face.' Tell me, and tell me plainly, when you think I am deviating from the strict line of duty and principle; and when I become unwilling to hear, I shall have attained a character which I now despise, and from which I would hope to be preserved. But to the facts.

I am in England, my family are in the United States. My sphere of usefulness is in the United States; my public and domestic duties are there; and there it seems my duty to go. But I am legally the property of Thomas Auld, and if I go to the United States, (no matter to what part, for there is no City of Refuge there, no spot sacred to freedom there,) Thomas Auld, aided by the American Government, can seize, bind and fetter, and drag me from my family, feed his cruel revenge upon me, and doom me to unending slavery. In view of this simple statement of facts, a few friends, desirous of seeing me released from the terrible liability, and to relieve my wife and children from the painful trepidation, consequent upon the liability, and to place me on an equal footing of safety with all other anti-slavery lecturers in the United States, and to enhance my usefulness by enlarging the field of my labors in the United States, have nobly and generously paid Hugh Auld, the agent of Thomas Auld, 150 pounds—in consideration of which, Hugh Auld (acting as his agent) and the Government of the United States agree, that I shall be free from all further liability.

These, dear friend, are the facts of the whole transaction. The principle here acted on by my friends, and that upon which I shall act in receiving the manumission papers, I deem quite defensible.

First, as to those who acted as my friends, and their actions. The actuating motive was, to secure me from a liability full of horrible forebodings to myself and family. With this object, I will do you the justice to say, I believe you fully unite, although some parts of your letters would seem to justify a different belief.

Then, as to the measure adopted to secure this result. Does it violate a fundamental principle, or does it not? This is the question, and to my mind the only question of importance, involved in the discussion. I believe that, on our part, no just or holy principle has been violated.

Before entering upon the argument in support of this view, I will take the liberty (and I know you will pardon it) to say, I think you should have pointed out some principle violated in the transaction, before you proceeded to exhort me to repentance. You have given me any amount of indignation against 'Auld' and the United States, in all which I cordially unite, and felt refreshed by reading; but it has no bearing whatever upon the conduct of myself, or friends, in the matter under consideration. It does not prove that I have done wrong, nor does it demonstrate what is right, or the proper course to be pursued. Now that the matter has reached its present point, before entering upon the argument, let me say one other word; it is this—I do not think you have acted quite consistently with your character for promptness, in delaying your advice till the transaction was completed. You knew of the movement at its conception, and have known it through its progress, and have never, to my knowledge, uttered one syllable against it, in conversation or letter, till now that the deed is done. I regret this, not because I think your earlier advice would have altered the result, but because it would have left me more free than I can now be, since the thing is done. Of course, you will not think hard of my alluding to this circumstance. Now, then, to the main question.

The principle which you appear to regard as violated by the transaction in question, may be stated as follows:—Every man has a natural and inalienable right to himself. The inference from this is, 'that man cannot hold property in man'—and as man cannot hold property in man, neither can Hugh Auld nor the United States have any right of property in me—and having no right of property in me, they have no right to sell me—and, having no right to sell me, no one has a right to buy me. I think I have now stated the principle, and the inference from the principle, distinctly and fairly. Now, the question upon which the whole controversy turns is, simply, this: does the transaction, which you condemn, really violate this principle? I own that, to a superficial observer, it would seem to do so. But I think I am prepared to show, that, so far from being a violation of that principle, it is truly a noble vindication of it. Before going further, let me state here, briefly, what sort of a purchase would have been a violation of this principle, which, in common with yourself, I reverence, and am anxious to preserve inviolate.

PRIMARY SOURCE DOCUMENT

"A Fugitive's Necessary Silence" by Frederick Douglass

INTRODUCTION Called upon in abolitionist gatherings to tell the story of his life in slavery, Frederick Douglass consistently refused to divulge any details of his 1838 escape. In the final chapter of the 1845 *Narrative of the Life of Frederick Douglass, an American Slave,* he took up the subject.

Chapter XI

I now come to that part of my life during which I planned, and finally succeeded in making, my escape from slavery. But before narrating any of the peculiar circumstances, I deem it proper to make known my intention not to state all the facts connected with the transaction. My reasons

for pursuing this course may be understood from the following: First, were I to give a minute statement of all the facts, it is not only possible, but quite probable, that others would thereby be involved in the most embarrassing difficulties. Secondly, such a statement would most undoubtedly induce greater vigilance on the part of slaveholders than has existed heretofore among them; which would, of course, be the means of guarding a door whereby some dear brother bondman might escape his galling chains. I deeply regret the necessity that impels me to suppress any thing of importance connected with my experience in slavery. It would afford me great pleasure indeed, as well as materially add to the interest of my narrative, were I at liberty to gratify a curiosity, which I know exists in the minds of many, by an accurate statement of all the facts pertaining to my most fortunate escape. But I must deprive myself of this pleasure, and the curious of the gratification which such a statement would afford. I would allow myself to suffer under the greatest imputations which evil-minded men might suggest, rather than exculpate myself, and thereby run the hazard of closing the slightest avenue by which a brother slave might clear himself of the chains and fetters of slavery.

I have never approved of the very public manner in which some of our western friends have conducted what they call the underground railroad, but which I think, by their open declarations, has been made most emphatically the upperground railroad. I honor those good men and women for their noble daring, and applaud them for willingly subjecting themselves to bloody persecution, by openly avowing their participation in the escape of slaves. I, however, can see very little good resulting from such a course, either to themselves or the slaves escaping; while, upon the other hand, I see and feel assured that those open declarations are a positive evil to the slaves remaining, who are seeking to escape. They do nothing towards enlightening the slave, whilst they do much towards enlightening the master. They stimulate him to greater watchfulness, and enhance his power to capture his slave. We owe something to the slave south of the line as well as to those north of it; and in aiding the latter on their way to freedom, we should be careful to do nothing which would be likely to hinder the former from escaping from slavery. I would keep the merciless slaveholder profoundly ignorant of the means of flight adopted by the slave. I would leave him to imagine himself surrounded by myriads of invisible tormentors, ever ready to snatch from his infernal grasp his trembling prey. Let him be left to feel his way in the dark; let darkness commensurate with his crime hover over him; and let him feel that at every step he takes, in pursuit of the flying bondman, he is running the frightful risk of having his hot brains dashed out by an invisible agency. Let us render the tyrant no aid; let us not hold the light by which he can trace the footprints of our flying brother. But enough of this. I will now proceed to the statement of

The first man to crate himself for shipment north was Henry "Box" Brown of Richmond, Virginia. Like many escaping slaves, he was assisted by a "conductor" on the Underground Railroad. In 1849 Brown published the details of his escape in a narrative of his ordeal. Frederick Douglass is depicted helping with the box top (left of center). **THE LIBRARY OF CONGRESS**

those facts, connected with my escape, for which I am alone responsible, and for which no one can be made to suffer but myself.

In the early part of the year 1838, I became quite restless. I could see no reason why I should, at the end of each week, pour the reward of my toil into the purse of my master. When I carried to him my weekly wages, he would, after counting the money, look me in the face with a robber-like fierceness, and ask, "Is this all?" He was satisfied with nothing less than the last cent. He would, however, when I made him six dollars, sometimes give me six cents, to encourage me. It had the opposite effect. I regarded it as a sort of admission of my right to the whole. The fact that he gave me any part of my wages was proof, to my mind, that he believed me entitled to the whole of them. I always felt worse for having received any thing; for I feared that the giving me a few cents would ease his conscience, and make him feel himself to be a pretty honorable sort of robber. My discontent grew upon me. I was ever on the look-out for means of escape; and, finding no direct means, I determined to try to hire my time, with a view of getting money with which to make my escape. In the spring of 1838, when Master Thomas came to Baltimore to purchase his spring goods, I got an opportunity, and applied to him to allow me to hire my time. He unhesitatingly refused my request, and

told me this was another stratagem by which to escape. He told me I could go nowhere but that he could get me; and that, in the event of my running away, he should spare no pains in his efforts to catch me. He exhorted me to content myself, and be obedient. He told me, if I would be happy, I must lay out no plans for the future. He said, if I behaved myself properly, he would take care of me. Indeed, he advised me to complete thoughtlessness of the future, and taught me to depend solely upon him for happiness. He seemed to see fully the pressing necessity of setting aside my intellectual nature, in order to contentment in slavery. But in spite of him, and even in spite of myself, I continued to think, and to think about the injustice of my enslavement, and the means of escape.

About two months after this, I applied to Master Hugh for the privilege of hiring my time. He was not acquainted with the fact that I had applied to Master Thomas, and had been refused. He too, at first, seemed disposed to refuse; but, after some reflection, he granted me the privilege, and proposed the following terms: I was to be allowed all my time, make all contracts with those for whom I worked, and find my own employment; and, in return for this liberty, I was to pay him three dollars at the end of each week; find myself in calking tools, and in board and clothing. My board was two dollars and a half per week. This, with the wear and tear of clothing and calking tools, made my regular expenses about six dollars per week. This amount I was compelled to make up, or relinquish the privilege of hiring my time. Rain or shine, work or no work, at the end of each week the money must be forthcoming, or I must give up my privilege. This arrangement, it will be perceived, was decidedly in my master's favor. It relieved him of all need of looking after me. His money was sure. He received all the benefits of slaveholding without its evils; while I endured all the evils of a slave, and suffered all the care and anxiety of a freeman. I found it a hard bargain. But, hard as it was, I thought it better than the old mode of getting along. It was a step towards freedom to be allowed to bear the responsibilities of a freeman, and I was determined to hold on upon it. I bent myself to the work of making money. I was ready to work at night as well as day, and by the most untiring perseverance and industry, I made enough to meet my expenses, and lay up a little money every week. I went on thus from May till August. Master Hugh then refused to allow me to hire my time longer. The ground for his refusal was a failure on my part, one Saturday night, to pay him for my week's time. This failure was occasioned by my attending a camp meeting about ten miles from Baltimore. During the week, I had entered into an engagement with a number of young friends to start from Baltimore to the camp ground early Saturday evening; and being detained by my employer, I was unable to get down to Master Hugh's without disappointing the company. I knew that Master Hugh was in no special need of the money that night. I therefore decided to go to camp meeting, and upon my return pay him the three dollars. I stayed at the camp meeting one day longer than I intended when I left. But as soon as I returned, I called upon him to pay him what he considered his due. I found him very angry; he could scarce restrain his wrath. He said he had a great mind to give me a severe whipping. He wished to know how I dared go out of the city without asking his permission. I told him I hired my time, and while I paid him the price which he asked for it, I did not know that I was bound to ask him when and where I should go. This reply troubled him; and, after reflecting a few moments; he turned to me, and said I should hire my time no longer; that the next thing he should know of, I would be running away. Upon the same plea, he told me to bring my tools and clothing home forthwith. I did so; but instead of seeking work, as I had been accustomed to do previously to hiring my time, I spent the whole week without the performance of a single stroke of work. I did this in retaliation. Saturday night, he called upon me as usual for my week's wages. I told him I had no wages; I had done no work that week. Here we were upon the point of coming to blows. He raved, and swore his determination to get hold of me. I did not allow myself a single word; but was resolved, if he laid the weight of his hand upon me, it should be blow for blow. He did not strike me, but told me that he would

find me in constant employment in future. I thought the matter over during the next day, Sunday, and finally resolved upon the third day of September, as the day upon which I would make a second attempt to secure my freedom. I now had three weeks during which to prepare for my journey. Early on Monday morning, before Master Hugh had time to make any engagement for me, I went out and got employment of Mr. Butler, at his shipyard near the drawbridge, upon what is called the City Block, thus making it unnecessary for him to seek employment for me. At the end of the week, I brought him between and nine dollars. He seemed very well pleased, and asked why I did not do the same the week before. He little knew what my plans were. My object in working steadily was to remove any suspicion he might entertain of my intent to run away; and in this I succeeded admirably. I suppose he thought I was never better satisfied with my condition than at the very time during which I was planning my escape. The second week passed, and again I carried him my full wages; and so well pleased was he, that he gave me twenty-five cents, (quite a large sum for a slaveholder to give a slave,) and bade me to make a good use of it. I told him I would.

Things went on without very smoothly indeed, but within there was trouble. It is impossible for me to describe my feelings as the time of my contemplated start drew near. I had a number of warm-hearted friends in Baltimore,—friends that I loved almost as I did my life,—and the thought of being separated from them forever was painful beyond expression. It is my opinion that thousands would escape from slavery, who now remain, but for the strong cords of affection that bind them to their friends. The thought of leaving my friends was decidedly the most painful thought with which I had to contend. The love of them was my tender point, and shook my decision more than all things else. Besides the pain of separation, the dread and apprehension of a failure exceeded what I had experienced at my first attempt. The appalling defeat I then sustained returned to torment me. I felt assured that, if I failed in this attempt, my case would be a hopeless one—it would seal my fate as a slave forever. I could not hope to get off with any thing less than the severest punishment, and being placed beyond the means of escape. It required no very vivid imagination to depict the most frightful scenes through which I should have to pass, in case I failed. The wretchedness of slavery, and the blessedness of freedom, were perpetually before me. It was life and death with me. But I remained firm, and, accordingly to my resolution, on the third day of September, 1838, I left my chains, and succeeded in reaching New York without the slightest interruption of any kind. How I did so,—what means I adopted,—what direction I travelled, and by what mode of conveyance,—I must leave unexplained, for the reasons before mentioned.

Artist Eastman Johnson depicted a family of fugitive slaves riding on horseback in this Civil War–era painting entitled *A Ride for Liberty* *(c. 1862).* **CORBIS-BETTMANN**

I have been frequently asked how I felt when I found myself in a free State. I have never been able to answer the question with any satisfaction to myself. It was a moment of the highest excitement I ever experienced. I suppose I felt as one may imagine the unarmed mariner to feel when he is rescued by a friendly man-of-war from the pursuit of a pirate. In writing to a dear friend, immediately after my arrival at New York, I said I felt like one who had escaped a den of hungry lions. This state of mind, however, very soon subsided; and I was again seized with a feeling of great insecurity and loneliness. I was yet liable to be taken back, and subjected to all the tortures of slavery. This in itself was enough to damp the ardor of my enthusiasm. But the loneliness overcame me. There I was in the midst of thousands, and yet a perfect stranger; without home and without friends, in the midst of thousands of my own brethren—children of a common Father, and yet I dared not to unfold to any of them my sad condition. I was afraid to speak to any one for fear of speaking to the wrong one, and thereby falling into the hands of money-loving kidnappers, whose business it was to lie in wait for the panting fugitive, as the ferocious beasts of the forest lie in wait for their prey. The motto which I adopted when I started from slavery was this—

"Trust no man!" I saw in every white man an enemy, and in almost every colored man cause for distrust. It was a most painful situation; and, to understand it, one must needs experience it, or imagine himself in similar circumstances. Let him be a fugitive slave in a strange land—a land given up to be the hunting-ground for slaveholders—whose inhabitants are legalized kidnappers—where he is every moment subjected to the terrible liability of being seized upon by his fellowmen, as the hideous crocodile seizes upon his prey! —I say, let him place himself in my situation—without home or friends—without money or credit—wanting shelter, and no one to give it—wanting bread, and no money to buy it,—and at the same time let him feel that he is pursued by merciless men-hunters, and in total darkness as to what to do, where to go, or where to stay,—perfectly helpless both as to the means of defence and means of escape,—in the midst of plenty, yet suffering the terrible gnawings of hunger,—in the midst of houses, yet having no home,—among fellow-men, yet feeling as if in the midst of wild beasts, whose greediness to swallow up the trembling and half-famished fugitive is only equalled by that with which the monsters of the deep swallow up the helpless fish upon which they subsist,—I say, let him be placed in this most trying situation,—the situation in which I was placed,—then, and not till then, will he fully appreciate the hardships of, and know how to sympathize with, the toil-worn and whip-scarred fugitive slave.

Thank Heaven, I remained but a short time in this distressed situation. I was relieved from it by the humane hand of Mr. David Ruggles, whose vigilance, kindness, and perseverance, I shall never forget. I am glad of an opportunity to express, as far as words can, the love and gratitude I bear him. Mr. Ruggles is now afflicted with blindness, and is himself in need of the same kind offices which he was once so forward in the performance of toward others. I had been in New York but a few days, when Mr. Ruggles sought me out, and very kindly took me to his boarding-house at the corner of Church and Lespenard Streets. Mr. Ruggles was then very deeply engaged in the memorable Darg case, as well as attending to a number of other fugitive slaves, devising ways and means for their successful escape; and, though watched and hemmed in on almost every side, he seemed to be more than a match for his enemies.

Very soon after I went to Mr. Ruggles, he wished to know of me where I wanted to go; as he deemed it unsafe for me to remain in New York. I told him I was a calker, and should like to go where I could get work. I thought of going to Canada; but he decided against it, and in favor of my going to New Bedford, thinking I should be able to get work there at my trade. At this time, Anna, my intended wife, came on; for I wrote to her immediately after my arrival at New York, (notwithstanding my homeless, houseless, and helpless condition,) informing her of my successful flight, and wishing her to come on forthwith. In a few days after her arrival, Mr. Ruggles called in the Rev. J. W. C. Pennington, who, in the presence of Mr. Ruggles, Mrs. Michaels, and two or three others, performed the marriage ceremony, and gave us a certificate, of which the following is an exact copy:—

"This may certify, that I joined together in holy matrimony Frederick Johnson and Anna Murray, as man and wife, in the presence of Mr. David Ruggles and Mrs. Michaels."

James W. C. Pennington
New York, Sept. 15, 1838.

Upon receiving this certificate, and a five-dollar bill from Mr. Ruggles, I shouldered one part of our baggage, and Anna took up the other, and we set out forthwith to take passage on board of the steamboat John W. Richmond for Newport, on our way to New Bedford. Mr. Ruggles gave me a letter to a Mr. Shaw in Newport, and told me, in case my money did not serve me to New Bedford, to stop in Newport and obtain further assistance, but upon our arrival at Newport, we were so anxious to get to a place of safety, that, notwithstanding we lacked the nec-

essary money to pay our fare, we decided to take seats in the stage, and promise to pay when we got to New Bedford. We were encouraged to do this by two excellent gentlemen, residents of New Bedford, whose names I afterward ascertained to be Joseph Ricketson and William C. Taber. They seemed at once to understand our circumstances, and gave us such assurance of their friendliness as put us fully at ease in their presence. It was good indeed to meet with such friends, at such a time. Upon reaching New Bedford, we were directed to the house of Mr. Nathan Johnson, by whom we were kindly received, and hospitably provided for. Both Mr. and Mrs. Johnson took a deep and lively interest in our welfare. They proved themselves quite worthy of the name of abolitionists. When the stage-driver found us unable to pay our fare, he held on upon our baggage as security for the debt. I had but to mention the fact to Mr. Johnson, and he forthwith advanced the money.

We now began to feel a degree of safety, and to prepare ourselves for the duties and responsibilities of a life of freedom. On the morning after our arrival at New Bedford, while at the breakfast-table, the question arose as to what name I should be called by. The name given me by my mother was, "Frederick Augustus Washington Bailey." I, however, had dispensed with the two middle names long before I left Maryland so that I was generally known by the name of "Frederick Bailey." I started from Baltimore bearing the name of "Stanley." When I got to New York, I again changed my name to "Frederick Johnson," and thought that would be the last change. But when I got to New Bedford, I found it necessary again to change my name. The reason of this necessity was, that there were so many Johnsons in New Bedford, it was already quite difficult to distinguish between them. I gave Mr. Johnson the privilege of choosing me a name, but told him he must not take from me the name of "Frederick." I must hold on to that, to preserve a sense of my identity. Mr. Johnson had just been reading the "Lady of the Lake," and at once suggested that my name be "Douglass." From that time until now I have been called "Frederick Douglass;" and as I am more widely known by that name than by either of the others, I shall continue to use it as my own.

I was quite disappointed at the general appearance of things in New Bedford. The impression which I had received respecting the character and condition of the people of the north, I found to be singularly erroneous. I had very strangely supposed, while in slavery, that few of the comforts, and scarcely any of the luxuries, of life were enjoyed at the north, compared with what were enjoyed by the slaveholders of the south. I probably came to this conclusion from the fact that northern people owned no slaves. I supposed that they were about upon a level with the non-slaveholding population of the south. I knew they were exceedingly poor, and I had been accustomed to regard their poverty as the necessary consequence of their being non-slaveholders. I had somehow imbibed the opinion that, in the absence of slaves, there could be no wealth, and very little refinement. And upon coming to the north, I expected to meet with a rough, hard-handed, and uncultivated population, living in the most Spartan-like simplicity, knowing nothing of the ease, luxury, pomp, and grandeur of southern slaveholders. Such being my conjectures, any one acquainted with the appearance of New Bedford may very readily infer how palpably I must have seen my mistake.

In the afternoon of the day when I reached New Bedford, I visited the wharves, to take a view of the shipping. Here I found myself surrounded with the strongest proofs of wealth. Lying at the wharves, and riding in the stream, I saw many ships of the finest model, in the best order, and of the largest size. Upon the right and left, I was walled in by granite warehouses of the widest dimensions, stowed to their utmost capacity with the necessaries and comforts of life. Added to this, almost every body seemed to be at work, but noiselessly so, compared with what I had been accustomed to in Baltimore. There were no loud songs heard from those engaged in loading and unloading ships. I heard no deep oaths or horrid curses on the laborer. I saw no whipping of men; but all seemed to go smoothly on. Every man appeared to understand his work, and went at it with a sober, yet cheerful earnestness, which betokened the deep interest which he felt in what he was doing, as well as a sense of his own dignity as a man. To me this looked exceedingly strange. From the wharves I strolled around and over the town, gazing with wonder and admiration at the splendid churches, beautiful dwellings, and finely-cultivated gardens; evincing an amount of wealth, comfort, taste, and refinement, such as I had never seen in any part of slaveholding Maryland.

Every thing looked clean, new, and beautiful. I saw few or no dilapidated houses, with poverty-stricken inmates; no half-naked children and bare-footed women, such as I had been accustomed to see in Hillsborough, Easton, St. Michael's, and Baltimore. The people looked more able, stronger, healthier, and happier, than those of Maryland. I was for once made glad by a view of extreme wealth, without being saddened by seeing extreme poverty. But the most astonishing as well as the most interesting thing to me was the condition of the colored people, a great many of whom, like myself, had escaped thither as a refuge from the hunters of men. I found many, who had not been seven years out of their chains, living in finer houses, and evidently enjoying more of the comforts of life, than the average of slaveholders in Maryland. I will venture to assert, that my friend Mr. Nathan Johnson (of whom I can say with a grateful hear, "I was hungry, and he gave me meat; I was thirsty, and he gave me drink; I was a stranger, and he took me in") lived in a neater house; dined at a better table; took, paid for, and read, more newspapers; better understood the moral, religious, and political character of the nation,—than nine tenths of the slaveholders in Talbot county Maryland. Yet Mr. Johnson was a working man. His hands were hardened by toil, and not his alone, but those also of Mrs. Johnson. I found the colored people much more spirited than I had supposed they would be. I found among them a determination to protect each other from the blood-thirsty kidnapper, at all hazards. Soon after my arrival, I was told of a circumstance which illustrated their spirit. A colored man and a fugitive slave were on unfriendly terms. The former was heard to threaten the latter with informing his master of his whereabouts. Straightway a meeting was called among the colored people, under the stereotyped notice, "Business of importance!" The betrayer was invited to attend. The people came at the appointed hour, and organized the meeting by appointing a very religious old gentleman as president, who, I believe, made a prayer, after which he addressed the meeting as follows: "Friends, we have got him here, and I would recommend that you young men just take him outside the door, and kill him!" With this, a number of them bolted at him; but they were intercepted by some more timid than themselves, and the betrayer escaped their vengeance, and has not been seen in New Bedford since. I believe there have been no more such threats, and should there be hereafter, I doubt not that death would be the consequence.

I found employment, the third day after my arrival, in stowing a sloop with a load of oil. It was new, dirty, and hard work for me; but I went at it with a glad heart and a willing hand. I was now my own master. It was a happy moment, the rapture of which can be understood only by those who have been slaves. It was the first work, the reward of which was to be entirely my own. There was no Master Hugh standing ready, the moment I earned the money, to rob me of it. I worked that day with a pleasure I had never before experienced. I was at work for myself and newly-married wife. It was to me the starting-point of a new existence. When I got through with that job, I went in pursuit of a job of calking; but such was the strength of prejudice against color, among the white calkers, that they refused to work with me, and of course I could get no employment. Finding my trade of no immediate benefit, I threw off my calking habiliments, and prepared myself to do any kind of work I could get to do. Mr. Johnson kindly let me have his woodhorse and saw, and I very soon found myself a plenty of work. There was no work too hard—none too dirty. I was ready to saw wood, shovel coal, carry wood, sweep the chimney, or roll oil casks,—all of which I did for nearly three years in New Bedford, before I became known to the anti-slavery world.

In about four months after I went to New Bedford, there came a young man to me, and inquired if I did not

James H. Birch was a prominent Washington resident who did a lively business in the slave trade. He rarely inquired about the "property" that passed through his hands, as the kidnapped Solomon Northup attested in his autobiography, *Twelve Years a Slave*. This is a photograph of a building where slaves were kept in Alexandria, Virginia, perhaps the very one in which Northup was imprisoned prior to being sold south. **NATIONAL ARCHIVES AND RECORDS ADMINISTRATION**

wish to take the "Liberator." I told him I did; but, just having made my escape from slavery, I remarked that I was unable to pay for it then. I, however, finally became a subscriber to it. The paper came, and I read it from week to week with such feelings as it would be quite idle for me to attempt to describe. The paper became my meat and my drink. My soul was set all on fire. Its sympathy for my brethren in bonds—its scathing denunciations of slaveholders—its faithful exposures of slavery—and its powerful attacks upon the upholders of the institution—sent a thrill of joy through my soul, such as I had never felt before!

I had not long been a reader of the "Liberator," before I got a pretty correct idea of the principles, measures and spirit of the anti-slavery reform. I took right hold of the cause. I could do but little; but what I could, I did with a joyful heart, and never felt happier than when in an anti-slavery meeting. I seldom had much to say at the meetings, because what I wanted to say was said so much better by others. But, while attending an anti-slavery convention at Nantucket, on the 11th of August, 1841, I felt strongly

moved to speak, and was at the same time much urged to do so by Mr. William C. Coffin, a gentleman who had heard me speak in the colored people's meeting at New Bedford. It was a severe cross, and I took it up reluctantly. The truth was, I felt myself a slave, and the idea of speaking to white people weighed me down. I spoke but a few moments, when I felt a degree of freedom, and said what I desired with considerable ease. From that time until now, I have been engaged in pleading the cause of my brethren—with what success, and with what devotion, I leave those acquainted with my labors to decide.

PRIMARY SOURCE DOCUMENT

Twelve Years a Slave by Solomon Northup

INTRODUCTION Solomon Northup, born free but kidnapped into slavery in 1841, was finally rescued in 1853 and returned to his family. He then set about recording everything he had seen and everything that had happened to him. His *Twelve Years a Slave* provides a detailed picture of slavery on the western frontier. Although Northup and his supporters attempted to bring those responsible for his kidnapping to justice, the criminals were acquitted of any wrongdoing. In the chapter reprinted here, Northup recounts his kidnapping and sale.

Chapter II

One morning, towards the latter part of the month of March, 1841, having at that time no particular business to engage my attention, I was walking about the village of Saratoga Springs, thinking to myself where I might obtain some present employment, until the busy season should arrive. Anne, as was her usual custom, had gone over to Sandy Hill, a distance of some twenty miles, to take charge of the culinary department at Sherrill's Coffee House, during the session of the court. Elizabeth, I think, had accompanied her. Margaret and Alonzo were with their aunt at Saratoga.

On the corner of Congress street and Broadway, near the tavern, then, and for aught I know to the contrary, still kept by Mr. Moon, I was met by two gentlemen of respectable appearance, both of whom were entirely unknown to me. I have the impression that they were introduced to me by some one of my acquaintants, but who, I have in vain endeavored to recall, with the remark that I was an expert player on the violin.

At any rate, they immediately entered into conversation on that subject, making numerous inquiries touching my proficiency in that respect. My responses being to all appearances satisfactory, they proposed to engage my services for a short period, stating, at the same time, I was just such a person as their business required. Their names, as they afterwards gave them to me, were Merrill Brown and Abram Hamilton, though whether these were their true appellations, I have strong reasons to doubt. The former was a man apparently forty years of age, somewhat short and thick-set, with a countenance indicating shrewdness and intelligence. He wore a black frock coat and black hat, and said he resided either at Rochester or at Syracuse. The latter was a young man of fair complexion and light eyes, and, I should judge, had not passed the age of twenty-five. He was tall and slender, dressed in a snuff-colored coat, with glossy hat, and vest of elegant pattern. His whole apparel was in the extreme of fashion. His appearance was somewhat effeminate, but prepossessing, and there was about him an easy air, that showed he had mingled with the world. They were connected, as they informed me, with a circus company, then in the city of Washington; that they were on their way thither to rejoin it, having left it for a short time to make an excursion northward, for the purpose of seeing the country, and were paying their expenses by an occasional exhibition. They also remarked that they had found much difficulty in procuring music for their entertainments, and that if I would accompany them as far as New-York, they would give me one dollar for each day's services, and three dol-

lars in addition for every night I played at their performances, besides sufficient to pay the expenses of my return from New-York to Saratoga.

I at once accepted the tempting offer, both for the reward it promised, and from a desire to visit the metropolis. They were anxious to leave immediately. Thinking my absence would be brief, I did not deem it necessary to write to Anne whither I had gone; in fact supposing that my return, perhaps, would be as soon as hers. So taking a change of linen and my violin, I was ready to depart. The carriage was brought round—a covered one, drawn by a pair of noble bays, altogether forming an elegant establishment. Their baggage, consisting of three large trunks, was fastened on the rack, and mounting to the driver's seat, while they took their places in the rear, I drove away from Saratoga on the road to Albany, elated with my new position, and happy as I had ever been, on any day in all my life.

We passed through Ballston, and striking the ridge road, as it is called, if my memory correctly serves me, followed it direct to Albany. We reached that city before dark, and stopped at a hotel southward from the Museum.

This night I had an opportunity of witnessing one of their performances—the only one, during the whole period I was with them. Hamilton was stationed at the door; I formed the orchestra, while Brown provided the entertainment. It consisted in throwing balls, dancing on the rope, frying pancakes in a hat, causing invisible pigs to squeal, and other like feats of ventriloquism and legerdemain. The audience was extraordinarily sparse, and not of the selectest character at that, and Hamilton's report of the proceeds presented but a "beggarly account of empty boxes."

Early next morning we renewed our journey. The burden of their conversation now was the expression of an anxiety to reach the circus without delay. They hurried forward, without again stopping to exhibit, and in due course of time, we reached New-York, taking lodgings at a house on the west side of the city, in a street running from Broadway to the river. I supposed my journey was at an end, and expected in a day or two at least, to return to my friends and family at Saratoga. Brown and Hamilton, however, began to importune me to continue with them to Washington. They alleged that immediately on their arrival, now that the summer season was approaching, the circus would set out for the north. They promised me a situation and high wages if I would accompany them. Largely did they expatiate on the advantages that would result to me, and such were the flattering representations they made, that I finally concluded to accept the offer.

The next morning they suggested that, inasmuch as we were about entering a slave State, it would be well, before leaving New-York, to procure free papers. The

This photograph of the interior of a slave pen was taken sometime during the Civil War. Slave pens like this one were used to hold slaves who had been sold to traders and were about to be taken to markets elsewhere. They were also used to jail slaves who were being punished for one infraction or another. **THE LIBRARY OF CONGRESS**

idea struck me as a prudent one, though I think it would scarcely have occurred to me, had they not proposed it. We proceeded at once to what I understood to be the Custom House. They made oath to certain facts showing I was a free man. A paper was drawn up and handed us, with the direction to take it to the clerk's office. We did so, and the clerk having added something to it, for which he was paid six shillings, we returned again to the Custom House. Some further formalities were gone through with before it was completed, when, paying the officer two dollars, I placed the papers in my pocket, and started with my two friends to our hotel. I thought at the time, I

must confess, that the papers were scarcely worth the cost of obtaining them—the apprehension of danger to my personal safety never having suggested itself to me in the remotest manner. The clerk, to whom we were directed, I remember, made a memorandum in a large book, which, I presume, is in the office yet. A reference to the entries during the latter part of March, or first of April, 1841, I have no doubt will satisfy the incredulous, at least so far as this particular transaction is concerned.

With the evidence of freedom in my profession, the next day after our arrival in New-York, we crossed the ferry to Jersey City, and took the road to Philadelphia. Here we remained one night, continuing our journey towards Baltimore early in the morning. In due time, we arrived in the latter city, and stopped at a hotel near the railroad depot, either kept by a Mr. Rathbone, or known as the Rathbone House. All the way from New-York, their anxiety to reach the circus seemed to grow more and more intense. We left the carriage at Baltimore, and entering the cars, proceeded to Washington, at which place we arrived just at nightfall, the evening previous to the funeral of General Harrison, and stopped at Gadsby's Hotel, on Pennsylvania Avenue.

After supper they called me to their apartments, and paid me forty-three dollars, a sum greater than my wages amounted to, which act of generosity was in consequence, they said, of their not having exhibited as often as they had given me to anticipate, during our trip from Saratoga. They moreover informed me that it had been the intention of the circus company to leave Washington the next morning, but that on account of the funeral, they had concluded to remain another day. They were then, as they had been from the time of our first meeting, extremely kind. No opportunity was omitted of addressing me in the language of approbation; while, on the other hand, I was certainly much prepossessed in their favor. I gave them my confidence without reserve, and would freely have trusted them to almost any extent. Their constant conversation and manner towards me—their foresight in suggesting the idea of free papers, and a hundred other little acts, unnecessary to be repeated—all indicated that they were friends indeed, sincerely solicitous for my welfare. I know not but they were. I know not but they were innocent of the great wickedness of which I now believe them guilty. Whether they were accessory to my misfortunes—subtle and inhuman monsters in the shape of men—designedly luring me away from home and family, and liberty, for the sake of gold—those who read these pages will have the same means of determining as myself. If they were innocent, my sudden disappearance must have been unaccountable indeed; but revolving in my mind all the attending circumstances, I never yet could indulge, towards them, so charitable a supposition.

After receiving the money from them, of which they appeared to have an abundance, they advised me not to go into the streets that night, inasmuch as I was unacquainted with the customs of the city. Promising to remember their advice, I left them together, and soon after was shown by a colored servant to a sleeping room in the back part of the hotel, on the ground floor. I laid down to rest, thinking of home and wife, and children, and the long distance that stretched between us, until I fell asleep. But no good angel of pity came to my bedside, bidding me to fly—no voice of mercy forewarned me in my dreams of the trials that were just at hand.

The next day there was a great pageant in Washington. The roar of cannon and the tolling of bells filled the air, while many houses were shrouded with crape, and the streets were black with people. As the day advanced, the procession made its appearance, coming slowly through the Avenue, carriage after carriage, in long succession, while thousands upon thousands followed on foot—all moving to the sound of melancholy music. They were bearing the dead body of Harrison to the grave.

From early in the morning, I was constantly in the company of Hamilton and Brown. They were the only persons I knew in Washington. We stood together as the funeral pomp passed by. I remember distinctly how the window glass would break and rattle to the ground, after each report of the cannon they were firing in the burial ground. We went to the Capitol, and walked a long time about the grounds. In the afternoon, they strolled towards the President's House, all the time keeping me near to them, and pointing out various places of interest. As yet, I had seen nothing of the circus. In fact, I had thought of it but little, if at all, amidst the excitement of the day.

My friends, several times during the afternoon, entered drinking saloons, and called for liquor. They were by no means in the habit, however, so far as I knew them, of indulging to excess. On these occasions, after serving themselves, they would pour out a glass and hand it to me. I did not become intoxicated, as may be inferred from what subsequently occurred. Towards evening, and soon after partaking of one of these potations, I began to experience most unpleasant sensations. I felt extremely ill. My head commenced aching—a dull, heavy pain, inexpressibly disagreeable. At the supper table, I was without appetite; the sight and flavor of food was nauseous. About dark the same servant conducted me to the room I had occupied the previous night. Brown and Hamilton advised me to retire, commiserating me kindly, and expressing hopes that I would be better in the morning. Divesting myself of coat and boots merely, I threw myself upon the bed. It was impossible to sleep. The pain in my head continued to increase, until it became almost unbearable. In a short time I became thirsty. My lips were parched. I could think of nothing but water—of lakes and flowing rivers, of brooks where I had stopped to drink, and of the dripping bucket, rising with its cool and overflowing nectar, from the bottom of the well. Towards midnight, as near as I could judge, I arose, unable longer to bear such intensity of thirst. I was a stranger in the house, and knew nothing of its apartments. There was no one up, as I could observe. Groping about at random, I knew not where, I found the way at last to a kitchen in the basement. Two or three colored servants were moving through it, one of whom, a woman, gave me two glasses of water. It afforded momentary relief, but by the time I had reached my room again, the same burning desire of drink, the same tormenting thirst, had again returned. It was even more torturing than before, as was also the wild pain in my head, if such a thing could be. I was in sore distress—in most excruciating agony! I seemed to stand on the brink of madness! The memory of that night of horrible suffering will follow me to the grave.

In the course of an hour or more after my return from the kitchen, I was conscious of some one entering my room. There seemed to be several—a mingling of various voices,—but how many, or who they were, I cannot tell. Whether Brown and Hamilton were among them, is a mere matter of conjecture. I only remember, with any degree of distinctness, that I was told it was necessary to go to a physician and procure medicine, and that pulling on my boots, without coat or hat, I followed them through a long passage-way, or alley, into the open street. It ran out at right angles from Pennsylvania Avenue. On the opposite side there was a light burning in a window. My impression is there were then three persons with me, but it is altogether indefinite and vague, and like the memory of a painful dream. Going towards the light, which I imagined proceeded from a physician's office, and which seemed to recede as I advanced, is the last glimmering recollection I can now recall. From that moment I was insensible. How long I remained in that condition—whether only that night, or many days and nights—I do not know; but when consciousness returned, I found myself alone, in utter darkness, and in chains.

The pain in my head had subsided in a measure, but I was very faint and weak. I was sitting upon a low bench, made of rough boards, and without coat or hat. I was hand-cuffed. Around my ankles also were a pair of heavy fetters. One end of a chain was fastened to a large ring in the floor, the other to the fetters on my ankles. I tried in vain to stand upon my feet. Walking from such a painful trance, it was some time before I could collect my thoughts. Where was I? What was the meaning of these chains? Where were Brown and Hamilton? What had I done to deserve imprisonment in such a dungeon? I could not comprehend. There was a blank of some indefinite period, preceding my awakening in that lonely place, the events of which the utmost stretch of memory was unable to recall. I listened intently for some sign or sound of life, but nothing broke the oppressive silence, save the clinking of my chains, whenever I chanced to move. I spoke aloud, but the sound of my voice startled me. I felt of my pockets, so far as the fetters would allow—far enough, indeed, to ascertain that I had not only been robbed of liberty, but that my money and free papers were also gone! Then did the idea begin to break upon my mind, at first dim and confused, that I had been kidnapped. But that I thought was incredible. There must have been some misapprehension—some unfortunate mistake. It could not be that a free citizen of New-York, who had wronged no man, nor violated any law, should

A receipt for the appraisal and sale of a slave during the Civil War. The transaction is itemized much like the sale of any other goods and includes prices for the slave's clothing. CORBIS-BETTMANN

be dealt with thus inhumanly. The more I contemplated my situation, however, the more I became confirmed in my suspicions. It was a desolate thought, indeed. I felt there was no trust or mercy in unfeeling man; and commending myself to the God of the oppressed, bowed my head upon my fettered hands, and wept most bitterly.

PRIMARY SOURCE DOCUMENT

The Final Moments of John Brown

INTRODUCTION Thomas Hamilton devoted the December 1859 issue of the *Anglo-African Magazine* to the events in Virginia, including this account of the final moments of John Brown, who was convicted and sentenced to death for his involvement in slave uprisings earlier in the year.

The Execution of John Brown.

This execution, which took place Dec. 2, at 11.15 A.M., was in the highest degree imposing and solemn, and without disturbance of any kind. Lines of patrols and pickets encircled the field for ten miles around, and over

John Brown's Attack on Harpers Ferry

Born in Torrington, Connecticut, in 1800, John Brown grew up in Ohio, a hotbed of sentiment on both sides of the slavery issue. A fierce foe of American slavery, Brown helped many slaves escape across Ohio and then, in 1855, moved to Kansas, where four of his sons had settled the year before. According to the 1854 Kansas-Nebraska Act, which repealed the 1820 Missouri Compromise, the question of whether the new territories would be slave or free was to be left to popular vote. Free-Soilers easily prevailed in the more northern territory of Nebraska, but the debate turned violent to the south, earning Kansas the epithet of "Bleeding Kansas."

John Brown and his sons took a vigorous role in the events, retaliating for an 1855 attack on the antislavery town of Lawrence by murdering proslavery settlers in their neighborhood of Osawatomie Creek. Voices calling for the violent overthrow of the slavocracy were being raised throughout the abolitionist ranks, and John Brown's actions in Kansas brought him not only national attention but a following among those who felt that the antislavery tactic of moral persuasion, urged by Garrison and others, was no longer effective.

In 1858, John Brown and others met in the free black community of Chatham, Ontario, to devise a plan for mass uprisings among the slaves of northern Virginia. The raid on Harpers Ferry was the first step in their plan, an action intended to establish a base to which Virginia slaves might escape and from which they could operate, in what was conceived as a widening war against slavery from within. On October 16, 1859, John Brown and his men attacked the federal arsenal in Harpers Ferry and took brief possession of it, but were eventually defeated by Robert E. Lee's militia forces. Ten of Brown's men were killed in the attempt, and Brown himself was wounded, captured, found guilty of treason, and sentenced to be hanged.

---

five hundred troops were posted about the gallows. At 7 o'clock in the morning workmen began to erect the scaffold, the timber having been hauled the night previous. At 8 troops began to arrive. Troopers were posted around the field at fifty feet apart, and two lines of sentries further in. The troops did not form hollow around the gallows, but were so disposed as to command every approach. The sun shone brightly, and the picture presented to the eye was really splendid. As each company arrived, it took its allotted position. On the easterly side were the Cadets, with their right wing flanked by a detachment of men with howitzers; on the north-east, the Richmond Grays; on the south, Company F of Richmond; on the north, the Winchester Continentals, and, to preserve order in the crowd, the Alexandria Riflemen and Captain Gibson's Rockingham Company were stationed at the entrance gate, and on the outskirts.

On leaving the jail, John Brown had on his face an expression of calmness and serenity characteristic of the patriot who is about to die with a living consciousness that he is laying down his life for the good of his fellow creatures. His face was even joyous, and a forgiving smile rested upon his lips. His was the lightest heart, among friend or foe, in all Charlestown that day, and not a word was spoken that was not an intuitive appreciation of his manly courage. Firmly and with elastic step he moved forward. No flinching of a coward's heart there. He stood in the midst of that organized mob, from whose despotic hearts petty tyranny seemed for the nonce eliminated by the admiration they had in once beholding a man—for John Brown was there every inch a man.

As he stepped out of the door, a black woman, with her little child in arms, stood near his way. The twain were of the despised race for whose emancipation and elevation to the dignity of the children of God he was about to lay down his life. His thoughts at that moment none can know except as his acts interpret them. He stopped for a moment in his course, stooped over, and with the tenderness of one whose love is as broad as the brotherhood of man, kissed the child affectionately. That mother will be proud of that mark of distinction for her offspring, and some day, when over the ashes of John Brown the temple of Virginia liberty is reared, she may join in the joyful song of praise which on that soil will do justice to his memory.

The vehicle which was to convey Brown to the scaffold was a furniture wagon. On the front seat was the driver, a man named Hawks, said to be a native of Massachusetts, but for many years a resident of Virginia, and by his side was seated Mr. Sadler, the undertaker. In the box was placed the coffin, made of black walnut, inclosed in a poplar box with a flat lid, in which coffin and remains were to be transported from the county. John Brown mounted the wagon, and took his place in the seat with Capt. Avis, the jailor, whose admiration of his prisoner is of the profoundest nature. Mr. Sadler, too, was one of Brown's staunchest friends in his confinement, and pays a noble tribute to his manly qualities.

"What a beautiful country you have," said Capt. Brown to Capt. Avis.

"Yes," was the response.

"It seems the more beautiful to behold because I have been so long shut out from it."

"You are more cheerful than I am, Capt. Brown," said Mr. Sadler.

"Yes," said the Captain, "I ought to be."

He continued, "I see no citizens here—where are they?"

"The citizens are not allowed to be present—none but the soldiers," was the reply.

"That ought not to be," said the old man; "citizens should be allowed to be present as well as others."

The cortege passed half around the gallows to the east side, where it halted. The troops composing the escort took up their assigned position, but the Petersburg Grays, as the immediate body-Guard, remained as before, closely hemming in the prisoner. They finaliy opened ranks to let him pass out, when, with the assistance of two men, he desended from the wagon, bidding good-bye to those within it; and then, with firm step and erect form, he strode past jailor, sheriff, and officers, and was the first person to mount the scaffold steps.

There is no faltering in his step, but firmly and erect he stands amid the almost breathless lines of soldiery that surround him. With a graceful motion of his pinioned right arm, he takes the slouched hat from his head, and carelessly casts it upon the platform by his side. The cap is drawn over his eyes, and the rope adjusted about his neck. John Brown is ready to meet his God.

But what next? The military have yet to go through some senseless evolutions, and near ten minutes elapse before Gen. Taliaferro's chivalrous hosts are in their proper position, during which time John Brown stands with the cap drawn over his head, and the hangman's knot under his ear.

Each moment seems an hour, and some of the people, unable to restrain an expression of their sense of the outrage, murmur "Shame!" "Shame!"

At last Virginia's troops are arranged a la mode.

"Captain Brown, you are not standing on the drop; will you come forward?" said the Sheriff.

"I can't see, gentlemen." was the reply; "you must lead me."

The Sheriff led his prisoner forward to the centre of the drop.

"Shall I give you a hankerchief, and let you drop it as a signal?" inquired the Sheriff.

"No, I am ready at any time; but don't keep me waiting needlessly," was the reply.

A moment after, the Sheriff springs the latch, the drop falls, and the body of John Brown is suspended between heaven and earth. A few convulsive twitches of the arms are observed. These cease after a moment.

After the body had dangled in mid air for twenty minutes, it was examined by the surgeon for signs of life. First the Charlestown physicians went up and made their examination, and after them the military surgeons, the prisoner being executed by the civil power and with military assistance as well. To see them lifting up the arms, now powerless, that once were so strong, and placing their ears on the breast of the corpse, holding it steady by passing an arm around it, was revolting in the extreme.

And so the body dangled and swung by its neck, turning to this side or that when moved by the surgeons, and swinging, pendulem-like, from the force of the south wind that was blowing, until after thirty-eight minutes from the time of swinging off, it was ordered to be cut down, the authorities being quite satisfied that their dreaded enemy was dead. The body was lifted upon the scaffold, and fell into a heap as limp as a rag. It was then put into the black walnut coffin, the body-guard closed in about the wagon, the cavalry led the van, and the mournful procession moved off.

Throughout the whole sad proceedings the utmost order and decorum reigned. I think that when the prisoner was on the gallows, words in ordinary tones might have been heard all over the forty-acre field. In less than fifteen minutes the whole military force had left the field of execution, a dozen sentries alone, perhaps, remaining. The towns-people having been kept at a considerable distance, and none from the country about being allowed to approach nearer than a mile, there were not, I think, counting soldiers and civilians, more than a thousand spectators. A great feeling of exasperation prevails in consequence of this foolish stringency, and it is a wonder that conflicts have not arisen between the citizens and their protectors.

The Civil War

On the eve of the Civil War, the American legacy of slavery and African American disenfranchisement, or as the novelist Ralph Ellison referred to it, the American reality made up of "the word and the contradiction of the word," was already well in place. The New World had been a place of promise and freedom for religiously oppressed and even ethnically oppressed Europeans, and yet for African Americans the opening of the New World marked the beginning of a long history of poverty and second-class citizenship that few Africans could have ever imagined in their native villages. When it came time to draft the young nation's Constitution, a powerful document was created, one that drew on the best of various threads of European intellectual and social thought. Indeed, in that Constitution lay the "word," a curiously idealistic treatise on the "inalienable" rights of mankind. The U.S. Constitution was an optimistic and visionary document more akin to poetry or a philosopher's theorem than to the documents created to inaugurate the beginnings of new nations. In the document's reality, however, lay the convenient and calculated omission of a definition of the "mankind" to whom those rights should apply. As a result, the social reality for Africans in the United States was from the country's inception one of disenfranchisement. The United States was a nation that aspired to the highest ideals, while enforcing a series of feudal and markedly undemocratic laws designed to keep certain persons locked out of the nation's promise. This is precisely what Ellison referred to when he spoke of the "word and the contradiction of the word", the "word" being the Constitution and the "contradiction" being the daily reality of Africans brought to the New World.

When the Revolutionary War broke out, African Americans fought to free the young nation, but at the same time they were indentured and enslaved, and they faced the potential danger of being capriciously murdered at the hands of their owners as a part of legally legitimate "punishment." When it came time for the Civil War, African Americans, rather than being able to participate as soldiers or citizens, were treated more as pawns in the political process and the backroom cigar and whiskey machinations of landholders and presidents. In most ways African Americans were not even afforded the protections

The battle of Fort Hudson in 1863 was one of the first major battles where freed African Americans fought on the side of the Union. The siege lasted from May 21 to July 9, and although the attacks failed, they proved that black soldiers would be valuable in the war. **ARCHIVE PHOTOS, INC.**

given to servants, who might expect the basic level of protection accorded to an employee or to a piece of property having some significant financial value. To the contrary, American slavery, often called the "peculiar institution," was more a nightmare experiment in degradation—a set of perverse psychologies that reflected the most base desires and fears of the slaveholders—and it transferred that contorted relationship onto the lives and psyches of those who suffered within the system of slavery.

Historians today recognize that Abraham Lincoln's freeing of the slaves, despite the heartfelt wish to see justice done and the stunning oratory of his second inaugural address, was more a game of political chess. It is true that the racial atmosphere had changed within the nation. The abolitionist cause had been pursued for many decades and had given birth to various persuasive apologists. In a twist as classically American as any in our history, however, it was the overwhelming success of slave narratives and, more importantly, those fascinating tales of escape printed up in the papers—the best-selling murder mysteries or Hollywood action films of their age—that had brought the plight and astounding conditions of the black person's life to the attention of the nation. As the Southern states seceded in an effort to

protect the way of life they had built over a century, President Lincoln understood that by forcing the issue and declaring the slaves who joined the Union's cause to be free, he would drive a political wedge between the powerful men in the South and the very manpower they had used to build up their plantations and homes, their armies, and their sense of self. The Republican president co-opted for himself and his cause the moral high ground and with it the willingness of the people he served to suffer the casualties and economic hardships that go with any war. Nevertheless, while it is true that without the figure of Lincoln the institution of slavery most likely would not have been dismantled at the time that it was, it is important that one look a little below the surface and see the truer nature of the times and the motivations of the principal characters on that stage.

The Civil War was a bloody, vicious, lengthy war. It was a war between America the ideal and America the reality, and a war between the word and its contradiction, with African Americans once again the invisible force both at the frontlines (Lincoln's realization that he would lose the war without the help of African American soldiers is an even darker truth behind the Emancipation Proclamation) and hovering somewhere between the lines of the nation's collective psyche. In the end, neither the Emancipation Proclamation nor the war that was ostensibly fought around it would change the social and economic realities for African Americans. With the Civil War and the golden age of Reconstruction that followed it, the United States logged another chapter in the continuing drama of the dream and its deferral—a particularly bloody chapter, and one that, despite its promise or name, in many ways marked the beginnings of racism and discriminatory hate going underground in the United States, where they would be able to continue largely unchecked and seldom spoken about for many decades to come. ■

The Final Century of Slavery in the United States

ADAPTED FROM ESSAYS BY ROB FORBES,
GILDER LEHRMAN CENTER

As a legal institution in the Western Hemisphere, slavery survived the American War of Independence by less than a century. If the military operations of the revolution damaged slavery significantly, the revolution's ideals of liberty and equality wounded the institution far more deeply, though the wounds would not prove fatal until the Civil War.

SLAVERY IN THE ERA OF THE REVOLUTION

At the time of the revolution, more than one out of every five Americans was a slave—a higher proportion than at any other time in the country's history. Slavery was legal, and practiced, in all thirteen states.

Throughout New England, the well-to-do employed slaves as badges of wealth and status. Prince, a slave from New Hampshire, served as the body servant of Captain William Whipple (1730–1785), a former slave trader who was a signer of the Declaration of Independence. The slave Frank belonged to the Reverend William Emerson (1769–1811) of Concord, Massachusetts, pastor to the minutemen and grandfather of Ralph Waldo Emerson.

But the North had more than a token investment in slavery. The flourishing valleys of Pennsylvania and New Jersey, the fertile farms of Long Island and Connecticut, and the stock-breeding regions of Rhode Island all supported substantial slave-produced agriculture. The North had fewer slaves than the South, not because of any moral objections to slavery, but because slaves commanded a much higher price in the highly productive southern regions. Profits from their sale were often pocketed by the New Englanders who dominated the American branch of the slave trade.

In the southern colonies, slaves made up 40 percent of the population. As tensions with Britain grew in the 1760s and early 1770s, many southern legislatures grew concerned that the large numbers of recently imported Africans posed a threat to the colonies' security. Parliament routinely vetoed colonial laws to halt or slow the slave trade, leading Thomas Jefferson (1743–1826), in his initial draft of the Declaration of Independence, to denounce George III for "waging cruel war against human nature itself … to keep open a market where *Men* should be bought and sold." The Continental Congress prudently deleted this passage, since it was the Americans who were doing the buying and much of the selling.

Inevitably, slaves played a key strategic role in the revolution. As Jefferson's censored passage from the Declaration of Independence shows, white Americans well understood that they were owed no loyalty by people they had subjugated and exploited. The British understood this too. One of Washington's first acts after taking command of the Continental troops was to bar the recruitment of black soldiers (although those already enrolled were not expelled). Washington reversed himself, however, after Britain's Lord Dunmore issued a proclamation promising freedom to slaves who joined the British cause. Thousands of African Americans streamed across the British lines. One was Thomas Peters (b. circa 1750), an ex-slave from North Carolina, who rose to the rank of sergeant in a British regiment and later led a band of black loyalists to Nova Scotia and then to the African settlement of Sierra Leone. A smaller number lent their services to the patriots, including "Captain" Starlins and Caesar Tarrant, who served with great heroism as pilots in the Virginia navy.

In practice, however, neither side proved willing to take significant steps against slavery, and many brave recruits were sent back into bondage at the end of the war. Although the revolution severely disrupted slavery, natural increase and a postwar slave-buying spree soon raised the number of slaves to above its prewar high.

SLAVERY IN THE EARLY NATIONAL ERA

"Would anyone believe," the patriot leader Patrick Henry (1736–1799) wrote to an acquaintance after the revolution, "that I am master of Slave[s] of my own purchase: I am drawn along by the general inconveniency of living without them, I will not, I cannot justify it." While the material effects of the revolution on slavery were short-lived, the impact of revolutionary ideals ultimately proved decisive.

Most Americans recognized the clear contradiction between their freedom-loving pronouncements and their slave-holding practices. Many masters were willing to suffer the "inconveniency" of living without slaves rather than betray their principles. When Captain Whipple's slave Prince pointedly stated, "Master, *you* are going

This curious image shows George Washington observing his slaves harvest hay under the watchful eye of the overseer. It may have been intended to persuade viewers of the idyllic nature of slavery, or of the paternal benevolence of the "father of the country." **THE LIBRARY OF CONGRESS**

to fight for your *liberty,* but I have none to fight for," the chastened former slave trader freed him on the spot.

Private manumissions reached an all-time high in the decade after the revolution. People in the North, where the cost of emancipation was lowest, took the most substantial steps against slavery. The General Assembly of Vermont wrote a prohibition against slavery into its 1777 constitution, and Pennsylvania lawmakers passed a measure for gradual emancipation in 1780, becoming the first legislative body to end slavery anywhere in the world. Massachusetts abolished slavery by judicial decree in the same year. One by one, the rest of the northern states followed suit, so that by 1804 slavery was on the road to extinction throughout the region. Of even greater importance, the Northwest Ordinance (1787) blocked the expansion of slavery into the territory north of the Ohio River.

Even so, the end of northern slavery came achingly slowly. Sojourner Truth (1797–1883), abolitionist and feminist, received her freedom only in 1827, when New

York's Emancipation Act took effect. Slavery lasted in Connecticut until 1848, and at least a few slaves remained in New Jersey when Abraham Lincoln (1809–1865) became president in 1861. **SEE PRIMARY SOURCE DOCUMENT** *Sojourner Truth's Address Before the Convention on Women's Rights*

Climate and economics affected the outcome of slavery at least as much as laws did. In the eastern border states, for example, slavery seemed likely to die out by itself without much legislative assistance. Maryland's free black population grew at a much higher rate than its slave population throughout the nineteenth century. Delaware, which consistently identified itself as a northern state, had just 1,798 slaves in 1860, only 8.3 percent of its black population. Closely tied to northern commerce and industry, these small states also had no "back country" into which slave agriculture could expand. Hence, slavery increasingly seemed a thing of the past, not the future.

In Virginia, the situation was less clear. Tobacco, the state's chief crop, had declined in importance from colonial times, and its cultivation had depleted the soil. More than half of the nation's approximately five hundred thousand slaves still lived in Virginia, but in many parts of the state planters did not have sufficient work to occupy them, making manumission a wise economic as well as philanthropic decision. Some innovative slaveholders, such as Thomas Jefferson, turned to diversified agriculture and small-scale manufacturing; in addition to cash crops, Monticello's slaves tended orchards, wheat fields, and vegetable gardens and produced barrels, nails, and horseshoes. Jefferson chose not to free his slaves, although he permitted those who were less than one-sixteenth black (and hence white, according to Virginia law) to "run away" without pursuing them.

Conditions for slaves in North Carolina were more complex still. Although slaves outnumbered whites in the wealthy agricultural counties of the tidewater, where they chiefly tended tobacco, the state as a whole—due largely to poor soil and minimal transportation facilities—had a smaller proportion of slaves than any other low-country state. Some western counties in North Carolina had few slaves or no slaves at all. No other state had a greater range in the conditions of slavery, with some slaves earning wages, others actually owning property, and still others seemingly slaves in name alone. Until 1835, free black property owners in North Carolina could—and did—vote.

In South Carolina and Georgia, rice continued to be the principal cash crop, with indigo and tobacco falling behind. Increasingly profitable, however, was cotton. Innovations in Britain in cotton textile technology opened a seemingly limitless demand for the versatile fiber. But the long-staple variety, with its easily removable seeds, could only be grown successfully on the Georgia and South Carolina Sea Islands, while the stubborn seeds of the easy-to-grow short-staple cotton drastically limited its usefulness.

Several southern states offered prizes for the invention of an efficient seed-removing machine, or cotton gin. So it was not completely unexpected when, in 1793, the Connecticut inventor Eli Whitney (1765–1825) developed such a device. Still, the impact of Whitney's cotton gin was astonishing. A trained slave using an early hand gin could sort about five pounds of cotton from seeds a week. With Whitney's earliest machine, the same slave could clean about fifty pounds a day. When a horse was harnessed to it, a modified gin could process as much cotton in one day as a skilled laborer could produce by hand in a year.

Cotton exports skyrocketed (from about 3,000 bales in 1790 to 178,000 bales in 1810), as did the value of slaves. Because cotton was a staple that could be cultivated profitably on a small scale, cotton planting became the ticket to riches for thousands of whites, and slavery became more deeply entrenched than ever in American society.

SLAVERY IN THE ERA OF REBELLIONS

Ironically, the same year that saw the creation of the cotton gin—1793—also witnessed the most successful slave revolt in history. Inflamed by revolutionary events in France, slaves in the Caribbean colony of St. Domingue rose in rebellion.

The independent nation of Haiti, led by Toussaint L'Ouverture (1743–1803), became an inspiration to slaves throughout the Americas, and a terror to slaveholders. Thousands of French planter refugees flooded into southern ports, bringing their slaves, some of whom had connections to the successful revolutionaries. American slaveholders feared that their own slaves would be "contaminated" by contact with Haitian blacks and passed laws banning the importation of new slaves. Such fears proved justified, for now the United States entered a long period of slave revolts, inspired by Haiti's example and in some cases led by former Haitian slaves.

One American who was greatly influenced by Haiti was a tall Virginia slave named Gabriel, known as "a fellow of courage and intellect above his rank in life." In the summer of 1800, he orchestrated what may have been the most extensive slave conspiracy in U.S. history. Gabriel's plot called for an armed force of several hundred slaves to march to Richmond, Virginia, burn the warehouses, capture the armory, and take the governor hostage. Other conspirators would strike at Norfolk and Petersburg. A heavy rainstorm prevented the march, and two frightened plotters revealed the plan to their masters. Gabriel and twenty-six others were hanged, and many more were transported or sold farther south. According to Governor James Monroe (1758–1831), the plot "embraced most of the slaves in this city and neighborhood," and knowledge of it probably "pervaded other parts, if not the whole state." Gabriel's conspiracy clearly demonstrated the revolutionary potential of slave insurrection in the United States.

In 1803, the purchase of the Louisiana Territory from France nearly doubled the size of the United States and stimulated a huge increase in the demand for slaves to cultivate the fertile new lands. In response, South Carolina reopened the legal slave trade. This horrified officials of other states, who opposed the move partly for humanitarian reasons but more pointedly because of the danger of insurrection posed by the newly enslaved Africans.

In 1807, Congress voted to outlaw the Atlantic slave trade, a move that drastically changed the face of U.S. slavery, in contradictory ways. On the one hand, since slaveholders could no longer obtain replacements from Africa, they had an incentive to treat their slaves with greater care. On the other hand, the closing of the Atlantic slave trade signaled the opening of the domestic trade—the large-scale forced migration of slaves from Maryland and Virginia to the expanding cotton lands of

This photograph from 1910 shows African American boys on a sugar plantation in Louisiana. Although the photo was taken after the end of slavery, it shows that into the twentieth century the harvesting of sugar cane was still dependent on black laborers. **ARCHIVE PHOTOS, INC.**

the Southwest, the sugar plantations of Louisiana and Florida, and the rice plantations of South Carolina and Georgia. Slave coffles—lines of men and women chained together—dotted the countryside, and cities such as New Orleans, Charleston, and Richmond became major regional slave markets, as did Washington, D.C., where slave auctions took place within sight of the Capitol.

The 1810s and 1820s witnessed a firestorm of revolts, scares, and small-scale acts of resistance such as arson, sabotage, and poisoning. It is impossible to determine the number and size of slave revolts, since slaveholders suppressed news of them, fearing that publicity would spread rebellion. Little is known, for instance, about an 1811 uprising near New Orleans led by a Haitian slave named Charles, except that it was probably the largest slave revolt on U.S. soil. A contemporary described the incident, involving between 150 and 500 rebels, as a "miniature representation of the horrors of St. Domingo."

Nor do historians have a clear picture of the scope of "maroonage," the establishment of communities of runaway slaves, or "outliers." The most important maroon community was outside the nation's southern border in West Florida, where escaped blacks and Choctaw Indians established a formidable military garrison and launched

raids into Georgia, until their fort was destroyed in 1816 by a shot from an American gunboat.

Few events in U.S. history had greater significance for slavery, both immediate and long-term, than the Missouri statehood debates of 1819–1821. Most Northerners wanted to keep slavery out of new states, while southerners opposed such restrictions. Ultimately, Congress adopted the Missouri Compromise, which allowed Missouri to enter the Union as a slave state but barred slavery from the rest of the Louisiana Territory above the line of 36 degrees 30 minutes north latitude. In practice, this limited the South to just two more slave states, Arkansas and Florida. That meant the United States would have to acquire more land, either peacefully or by conquest, for the slave states to keep up with the North.

A year after the Missouri crisis was resolved, Charleston slaveholders were rocked by the Denmark Vesey (c. 1767–1822) conspiracy. The former slave of a slave trader, Vesey had traveled widely throughout the Atlantic world and knew and detested every facet of the slave system. Although he had purchased his freedom with a lottery jackpot, Vesey, like many free blacks, had family members still in slavery.

Newspaper accounts of the Missouri debates convinced Vesey that the government in Washington would never send troops to suppress a slave insurrection, and he began in earnest to develop his plan. Citing the biblical story of Exodus, the Declaration of Independence, and the Missouri speeches, Vesey sought to persuade his fellows that slavery was wrong. Appealing to their Christian faith, to the power of traditional African religions, and to the example of the Haitian Revolution, he sought to convince them that a revolt against slavery could succeed. When the Charleston authorities took steps in 1821 to suppress the African Church, one of the few institutions blacks controlled, Vesey converted many bitter church members to his cause, including "Gullah Jack" Pritchard, an Angolan-born conjuror; Ned and Rolla Bennett, favored slaves of the governor; and Monday Gell, described by a white official as "firm, resolute, discreet, and intelligent."

Vesey's plan called for his men to sweep into the city at seven separate points after midnight on a Saturday, seize weapons from the armory, burn the town, and call on the region's slaves to rise in mass revolt. Most threatening to white Charlestonians, the rebels also planned to poison the city's water supply. Like Gabriel's revolt, Denmark Vesey's rebellion was betrayed by reluctant slaves who informed their masters. Vesey and at least thirty-five followers met death by hanging, but their story lived on to inspire others.

A still greater turning point in the course of American slavery occurred in Southampton County, Virginia, in the summer of 1831, when a charismatic, religiously

This woodcut of scenes from Nat Turner's Rebellion presents the insurrection in a negative light. The action is described at the bottom of the print as follows: "The Scenes which the above Plate is designed to represent are—Fig. 1. A mother intreating for the lives of her children.—2. Mr. Travis, cruelly murdered by his own Slaves.—3. Mr. Barrow, who bravely defended himself until his wife escaped.—4. A comp. of mounted Dragoons in pursuit of the Blacks." **THE LIBRARY OF CONGRESS**

inspired slave named Nat Turner (1800–1831) led the bloodiest slave uprising of the antebellum era. Guided by visions, dreams, and strange celestial events, Turner became convinced that the day of judgment for slaveholders was near, and that he was to be their executioner.

He first planned his attack for July 4, but postponed it when he became sick. Finally, on the night of August 22, Turner and six followers, armed with a broadsword and an axe, began the work of destruction. Starting with the family of Turner's owners, the rebels systematically slaughtered the white men, women, and children they encountered on their passage to the county seat of Jerusalem. This time, no wary slaves betrayed the plot; indeed, more than sixty others rallied to the rebels' cause. By the next night, fifty-seven whites were dead, and the slave-holding South was plunged into a state of panic from which it never really recovered. Although most of his army was rounded up and captured within days, Turner himself eluded capture until October, while rumors and false reports of new attacks swirled through the state.

The first effect of Nat Turner's revolt was to trigger frenzied assaults by Virginia's whites on slaves in which perhaps hundreds of innocent blacks were killed. Yet it also forced the serious debate over slavery that the South had until then avoided. In meetings throughout Virginia, citizens called for action on slavery, ranging from simply sending free blacks out of the state to immediate and total abolition. Led by a nephew of Thomas Jefferson, antislavery members of the Virginia legislature proposed a gradual emancipation act for the state. For a short time, the act appeared likely to pass, but defenders of slavery, led by Professor Thomas R. Dew (1802–1846), successfully defended the status quo, and the last great chance for the peaceful end of slavery was lost. **SEE PRIMARY SOURCE DOCUMENT** *Nat Turner's Revolt and the Subsequent "Bill Concerning Slaves, Free Negroes and Mulattoes"*

The Virginia emancipation debates of 1831–1832 marked the close of the southern antislavery debate. They appear to have ended the era of rebellions as well, although it is unclear whether the decline in reports of unrest reflected a real decline in incidents or simply a stronger resolve by slaveholders to keep silent about such events in the aftermath of Nat Turner's uprising. In either case, the period of rebellion now gave way to an era of constructive political activity, with the rise of abolitionism in the North, increased antislavery activism on the part of free blacks, and even multiracial coalitions against slavery.

SLAVERY IN THE "OLD" SOUTH, 1831–1861

The years from 1831 to 1861, representing the high point of cotton plantation culture, have been enshrined by history books and Hollywood as the classic era of the "Old South." However, they constituted only a small fraction of the period of slavery in America and can hardly be regarded as typical. In large part, the focus on this period stems from the central and overwhelming importance of the slavery issue in national politics at this time.

It was not until the 1830s that slaveholders fully embraced the defense of slavery as a "positive good." Pressed by growing antislavery sentiment at home and abroad (the British abolished slavery in their colonies in 1833), they began to paint an idealized portrait of plantation life, stressing gentle masters and happy, contented slaves. After the destruction of the Civil War, many Americans viewed the plantation legend with nostalgia, and later generations accepted it largely as fact.

Although atypical, these years were nonetheless critical ones for African Americans. While regional variations in slavery remained important, as they had been in the colonial era, the three decades before the Civil War saw the emergence of a distinct, semiautonomous African American culture, transcending boundaries of geography and even of slave or free status. In part, this cultural cohesion developed as a response to the false racial justifications of slavery. The hardening of racial attitudes during this period tied the destinies of free blacks and slaves together and made black solidarity an urgent necessity.

The overwhelming fact of slave life was work. Most slaves worked every day except Sunday and received a few days off at Christmas. In the Chesapeake Bay region, work took a wide variety of forms. Many slaves still labored in large gangs on plantations producing tobacco or wheat, but others worked in small groups of five or even fewer. Many slaves were hired out to a variety of employers—working in the fields during planting and harvest season and in town during the winter, as their owners shifted them to the most profitable employment at any given time. While in town, the slaves would be paid by their temporary "bosses" in cash, which they would give to their owners, keeping a portion for themselves to pay for food and other expenses.

"Hiring-out" was often a thankless experience for the slave, who might be mistreated or cheated by his employer and then punished by his owner for not ten-

dering the expected fees. Nonetheless, the greater independence and contact with free blacks offered by the hiring-out arrangement helped to loosen the bonds of slavery, and has been described as a "halfway house" to free labor. The increasing urbanization of the upper Chesapeake, together with failing soil fertility throughout the region, put pressure on slaveholders either to emancipate their slaves or to sell them farther south.

Much of this southward migration was directed to the booming cotton lands of the Southwest. Mississippi, with a slave population of only 32,000 in 1820, had more than 436,000 slaves on the eve of the Civil War. The growth of slavery in Arkansas over the same period was even more dramatic, from just 1,617 slaves to 111,115. The kind of work slaves performed in these newer regions changed over time. It began with the backbreaking work of clearing the land of trees and carving out new fields, and progressed to the more manageable labor required to operate a mature cotton plantation.

Because most people know that slaves in the upper South dreaded being sold to plantations in the Deep South, cotton has a reputation as the most oppressive crop to produce. In fact, slaves chiefly feared being sold because of the rupture of family ties, not the harshness of the cotton regime. Cotton growing required huge bursts of labor during the fall harvest, when the bolls had to be picked before the onset of rains, ginned, pressed into bales, and loaded for shipment. But this meant that planters could grow only as much cotton as their slaves could harvest—not as much as their land could produce. To ensure that slaves would not be idle during the growing season, slaveholders often planted food crops (usually corn or wheat) to keep their "hands" busy and to reap extra profit. While this second crop meant increased work for slaves, they were compensated by the improved diet it offered.

By the 1830s, many large planters had adopted the "task system" of management developed on the tidewater rice plantations. Under this system, slaves would be assigned a particular task to complete for the day, and the rest of the time would be their own. Slaves worked in "gangs" under black "drivers," who in turn came under the direction of a white overseer who reported to the master. While slave drivers could be as oppressive as whites—one former slave described his driver as "de meanest devil dat ever lived on de Lord's green earth"—others mediated between the field hands and the overseer, conveying grievances to the owner and tempering harsh punishments. In some instances, the most senior drivers had as much say in particular decisions as the overseer, who could be fired at will. The task system of agriculture with its organization into gangs proved enormously efficient and brought reliable profits for slaveholders. At the same time, it promoted cohesion and a sense of camaraderie among the slaves that, in many cases, persisted after emancipation.

Slaves working in a cotton field pick the cotton and deposit it into large woven baskets. **THE LIBRARY OF CONGRESS**

In contrast to the hard but manageable life on the cotton plantations, work on the sugar plantations of Louisiana, Texas, and Florida was hardly bearable. Cane planting was backbreaking stoop labor. The growing stalk required delicate and almost constant hoeing to keep back weeds. The crop required two harvests—of the seed cane in September, and of the mature stalks in October. Performed with razor-sharp machetes, this task was among the most dangerous, as well as the hardest, of the slave economy. Finally came the boiling of the sugar, a complex, hot, labor-intensive operation requiring all hands and proceeding night and day without pause until nearly Christmas.

The sugar industry was the nation's most voracious consumer of bondsmen, who were supplied by the sprawling New Orleans slave mart. It was said that the planters had computed the ideal working life of a slave, for maximum profit, at seven years. Slaves in the upper South considered being "sold down the river"—that is, sold down the Mississippi to the Louisiana sugar plantations—to be virtually a sentence of death. Yet even in this brutal environment, ties of family and faith gave meaning to slaves' lives.

Nowhere was the "plantation legend" more stridently affirmed than in the antebellum low country of Georgia and the Carolinas. During the 1840s and 1850s, as South Carolina and Georgia slaveholders more and more

vigorously asserted the "natural" fitness of African Americans for slavery, the conditions of slaves in this region actually appear to have improved. In part, this was because planters sought to convince outsiders—and themselves—of the truth of their claims. It also stemmed from increasing concentrations of slaves and a consequent increase in African American autonomy in the most heavily black districts.

Even in regions where they outnumbered whites by five to one or as much as ten to one, however, African Americans found it wiser to seek accommodation with the slave system than to try to overthrow or escape it. Such regions were hundreds or even thousands of miles from the "free" states, where federal laws could still send them back to slavery. Of the thousands of slaves who successfully fled to freedom in the North or in Canada, most came from the upper South.

SEE PRIMARY SOURCE DOCUMENT *Excerpt from* The Fugitive Blacksmith *by James Pennington*

Yet even on the remotest plantations, slaves employed day-to-day resistance in order to carve out a margin of control. Bondsmen used the force of custom and tradition to defend themselves from their masters' efforts to impose new burdens or withdraw privileges. When that failed, planters might discover that a barn had been burned, equipment sabotaged, or a cotton crop picked too slowly

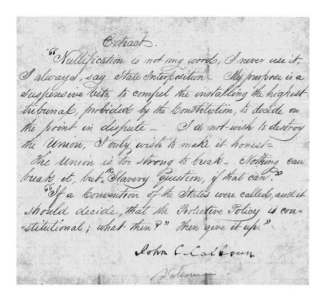

"*Nullification is not my words, I never use it. I always say State Interposition. My purpose is a suspensive veto, to compel the installing the highest tribunal, provided by the Constitution, to decide on the point in dispute. I do not wish to destroy the Union, I only wish to make it honest—*

The Union is too strong to break. Nothing can break it, but the Slavery question, if that can.

If a Convention of the States were called, and it should decide, that the Protective Policy is constitutional; what then?" Then give it up."

John C. Calhoun, a southerner, feared the issue of slavery could eventually dissolve the country. Calhoun, who supported slavery, thought individual states should be able to reject or nullify laws made by Congress, ensuring that northern states could not force the South to give up its institution. **CORBIS-BETTMANN**

to save it from rain. In these ways, masters learned not to make unreasonable demands upon their "hands."

SEE PRIMARY SOURCE DOCUMENT *"Reception and Treatment of Kidnappers"*

THE DREAM OF FREEDOM

It would be a mistake to romanticize slave life, as has sometimes been done both by apologists for slavery and by sympathetic historians. Slavery unquestionably broke the will of many of its victims and left others injured physically as well as psychologically.

Those who, against tremendous odds, survived with their humanity intact were sustained by the conviction that slavery was wrong and that it did not define who they were. Although they worked for long hours, slaves often felt that their true lives did not begin until their laboring day was done. Ignoring fatigue, husbands would often walk miles to visit wives on distant plantations and return to work again at daybreak. The music of banjos or fiddles frequently filled the slave quarters until well after midnight. Funerals, too, took place at night, and they retained more of African practice than almost any other activity of slave culture.

African Americans were sustained as well by the faith that slavery would not last forever. In this faith, they strongly identified with the children of Israel, whom Moses freed from Egyptian bondage. They also believed in the ultimate fulfillment of the revolutionary promise that "all men are created equal"—as witnessed by the slave revolts, including Nat Turner's, planned to begin on the Fourth of July.

Moreover, just as slaveholders had feared, the free black class contributed significantly to the slaves' struggle for freedom. Simply by existing as free people and not slaves, free blacks undermined the racial justification for slavery. But they promoted freedom in active ways as well. In most other slave societies, manumitted slaves have identified closely with their former masters, in order to distance themselves from the slave status they have left behind. In America, where race was used to justify slavery, free blacks could not escape from its stigma, and most recognized that their destinies were directly tied to the destinies of the slaves. This led to an unprecedented sense of community between slaves and former slaves.

It seems almost a contradiction in terms to speak of chattel slaves as having a "culture," since slavery by its nature would seem designed to prevent those in its grasp from ever developing one. Yet African American slaves did indeed develop a culture, one that contributed essential elements to American society—including a deepened understanding of the meaning, and the value, of freedom.

BIBLIOGRAPHY

Berlin, Ira, and Ronald Hoffman. *Slavery and Freedom in the Age of the American Revolution.* Urbana and Chicago: University of Illinois Press, 1983.

Blassingame, John W. *The Slave Community: Plantation Life in the Antebellum South.* Rev. ed. New York: Oxford University Press, 1979.

Boles, John B. *Black Southerners 1619–1869.* Lexington: University Press of Kentucky, 1983.

Campbell, Edward D.C., and Kym S. Rice, eds. *Before Freedom Came: African American Life in the Antebellum South.* Richmond and Charlottesville: Museum of the Confederacy and the University Press of Virginia, 1992.

Davis, David B. *The Problem of Slavery in the Age of Revolution.* Ithaca: Cornell University Press, 1975.

Egerton, Douglas R. *Gabriel's Rebellion: The Virginia Slave Conspiracies of 1800 and 1802.* Chapel Hill: University of North Carolina Press, 1993.

Elkins, Stanley M. *Slavery: A Problem in American Institutional and Intellectual Life.* 3d ed. Chicago: University of Chicago Press, 1976.

Frey, Sylvia. *Water from the Rock: Black Resistance in a Revolutionary Age.* Princeton: Princeton University Press, 1991.

Genovese, Eugene. *Roll, Jordan, Roll: The World the Slaves Made.* New York: Pantheon Books, 1974.

Gutman, Herbert G. *The Black Family in Slavery and Freedom, 1750–1925.* New York: Pantheon Books, 1976.

Huggins, Nathan Irvin. *Black Odyssey: Afro-American Ordeal in Slavery.* New York: Pantheon Books, 1977.

Joyner, Charles W. *Remember Me: Slave Life in Coastal Georgia.* Atlanta: Georgia Humanities Council, 1989.

Kolchin, Peter. *American Slavery, 1619–1877.* New York: Hill and Wang, 1993.

Rawick, George P., ed. *The American Slave: A Composite Autobiography.* 12 vols. Westport: Greenwood Publishing Co., 1977.

Wright, Donald. *African Americans in the Early Republic, 1789–1813.* Arlington Heights: Harlan Davidson, 1993.

Sojourner Truth's Address Before the Convention on Women's Rights

INTRODUCTION Sojourner Truth was an unforgettable orator. A religious mystic, six feet tall and with a mighty voice that commanded her audience's attention, she was the most prominent woman orator in the abolitionist movement, and she devoted most of her life to traveling and speaking in the cause of abolition and women's rights. In 1851, she united those two themes in a powerful address before the Convention on Women's Rights in Akron, Ohio. Frances Gage, the president of the Convention, recorded the event in writing, offering Sojourner Truth's speech in its entirety.

"Sojourner Truth," by Frances D. Gage

The leaders of the movement trembled on seeing a tall, gaunt black woman in a gray dress and white turban, surmounted with an uncouth sun-bonnet, march deliberately into the church, walk with the air of a queen up the aisle, and take her seat upon the pulpit steps. A buzz of disapprobation was heard all over the house, and there fell on the listening ear, "An abolition affair!" "Woman's rights and niggers!" "I told you so!" "Go it, darkey!"

I chanced on that occasion to wear my first laurels in public life as president of the meeting. At my request order was restored, and the business of the Convention went on. Morning, afternoon, and evening exercises came and went. Through all these sessions old Sojourner, quiet and reticent as the "Lybian Statue," sat crouched against the wall on the corner of the pulpit stairs, her sun-bonnet shading her eyes, her elbows on her knees, her chin resting upon her broad, hard palms. At intermission she was busy selling the "Life of Sojourner Truth," a narrative of her own strange and adventurous life. Again and again, timorous and trembling ones came to me and said, with earnestness, "Don't let her speak, Mrs. Gage, it will ruin us. Every newspaper in the land will have our cause mixed up with abolition and niggers, and we shall be utterly denounced." My only answer was, "We shall see when the time comes."

The second day the work waxed warm. Methodist, Baptist, Episcopal, Presbyterian, and Universalist ministers came in to hear and discuss the resolutions presented. One claimed superior rights and privileges for man, on the ground of "superior intellect"; another, because of the "manhood of Christ; if God had desired the equality of woman, He would have given some token of His will through the birth, life, and death of the Saviour." Another gave us a theological view of the "sin of our first mother."

There were very few women in those days who dared to "speak in meeting"; and the august teachers of the people were seemingly getting the better of us, while the boys in the galleries, and the sneerers among the

Sojourner Truth
(1797–1883)

Like many former slaves, Sojourner Truth remained illiterate. She told her life's story to her biographer Olive Gilbert, whose name appeared as writer on later editions of the *Narrative*. Sojourner Truth was born into slavery in 1797 in upstate New York, the daughter of enslaved parents belonging to a wealthy Dutch settler. Christened Isabella, she was sold away from her family at a young age, and during the course of her enslavement she bore five children, three of whom were also sold away.

In 1827, as New York State's statutory emancipation was about to take effect, Isabella escaped with the help of a Quaker family, the van Wageners. She moved to New York City, where, as Isabella van Wagener, she worked as a domestic servant and took vigorous part in the Evangelical movement of her time. Then, in 1843, she renamed herself Sojourner Truth, and commenced her unique life of travel and public speaking.

ABOVE: Born a slave in upstate New York, Sojourner Truth later became a traveling preacher, adding abolition and women's rights to religion to her speaking points. **ARCHIVE PHOTOS, INC.**

pews, were hugely enjoying the discomfiture, as they supposed, of the "strong-minded." Some of the tender-skinned friends were on the point of losing dignity, and the atmosphere betokened a storm. When, slowly from her seat in the corner rose Sojourner Truth, who, till now, had scarcely lifted her head. "Don't let her speak!" gasped half a dozen in my ear. She moved slowly and solemnly to the front, laid her old bonnet at her feet, and turned her great speaking eyes to me. There was a hissing sound of disapprobation above and below. I rose and announced "Sojourner Truth," and begged the audience to keep silence for a few moments.

The tumult subsided at once, and every eye was fixed on this almost Amazon form, which stood nearly six feet high, head erect, and eyes piercing the upper air like one in a dream. At her first word there was a profound hush. She spoke in deep tones, which, though not loud, reached every ear in the house, and away through the throng at the doors and windows.

"Wall, chilern, whar dar is so much racket dar must be somethin' out o' kilter. I tink dat 'twixt de niggers of de Souf and de womin at de Norf, all talkin' 'bout rights, de white men will be in a fix pretty soon. But what's all dis here talkin' 'bout?

"Dat man ober dar say dat womin needs to be helped into carriages, and lifted ober ditches, and to hab de best place everywhar. Nobody eber helps me into carriages, or ober mud-puddles, or gibs me any best place!" And raising herself to her full height, and her voice to a pitch like rolling thunder, she asked, "And a'n't I a woman? Look at me! Look at my arm! (and she bared her right arm to the shoulder, showing her tremendous muscular power). I have ploughed, and planted, and gathered into barns, and no man could head me! And a'n't I a woman! I could work as much and eat as much as a man—when I could get it—and bear de lash as well! And a'n't I a woman? I have borne thirteen chilern, and seen 'em mos' all sold off to slavery, and when I cried out with my mother's grief, none but Jesus heard me! And a'n't I a woman?

"Den dey talks 'bout dis ting in de head; what dis dey call it?" ("Intellect," whispered some one near.) "Dat's it, honey. What's dat got to do wid womin's rights or nigger's rights? If my cup won't hold but a pint, and yourn holds a quart, wouldn't ye be mean not to let me have my little half-measure full?" And she pointed her significant finger, and sent a keen glance at the minister who had made the argument. The cheering was long and loud.

"Den dat little man in black dar, he say women can't have as much rights as men, 'cause Christ wan't a woman! Whar did your Christ come from?" Rolling thunder couldn't have stilled that crowd, as did those deep, wonderful tones, as she stood there with outstretched arms and eyes of fire. Raising her voice still louder, she repeated, "Whar did your Christ come from? From God and a woman! Man had nothin' to do wid Him." Oh, what a rebuke that was to that little man.

Turning again to another objector, she took up the defense of Mother Eve. I can not follow her through it all. It was pointed, and witty, and solemn; eliciting at almost every sentence deafening applause; and she ended by asserting: "If de fust woman God ever made was strong enough to turn de world upside down all alone, dese women togedder (and she glanced her eye over the platform) ought to be able to turn it back, and get it right

side up again! And now dey is asking to do it, de men better let 'em." Long-continued cheering greeted this. "'Bleeged to ye for hearin' on me, and now ole Sojourner han't got nothin' more to say."

Amid roars of applause, she returned to her corner, leaving more than one of us with streaming eyes, and hearts beating with gratitude. She had taken us up in her strong arms and carried us safely over the slough of difficulty turning the whole tide in our favor. I have never in my life seen anything like the magical influence that subdued the mobbish spirit of the day, and turned the sneers and jeers of an excited crowd into notes of respect and admiration. Hundreds rushed up to shake hands with her, and congratulate the glorious old mother, and bid her God-speed on her mission of "testifyin' agin concerning the wickedness of this 'ere people."

PRIMARY SOURCE DOCUMENT

Nat Turner's Revolt and the Subsequent "Bill Concerning Slaves, Free Negroes and Mulattoes"

INTRODUCTION The Nat Turner revolt caused veritable panic among white landowners, lawmakers, and the population at large. This bill drafted by the Virginia House of Delegates in the wake of the insurrection, drastically curtailed the rights of free blacks and mulattoes, reducing them to a status only slightly above slaves and at the same time diminishing the few protections that slaves held as property of tax-paying white citizens.

Perhaps more interesting is the way the law was used not only to prohibit the freedoms of slaves and freed blacks, but also as an instrument to deliver freed blacks back into slavery. In reaction to the perception that Turner's revolt had been inspired by religious fanaticism, the first provision of the bill prohibited all preaching and "exhorting" by slaves and free blacks, prescribing enslavement and transportation as punishment for a second offense by a freeman. Free blacks were also prohibited from traveling without a pass, owning land or firearms, or selling "any thing whatever" without a certificate of ownership signed by two whites.

Aftermath of Turner Revolt: Draft of a Bill Concerning Slaves, Free Negroes and Mulattoes
A Bill To amend an act, entitled "an act reducing into one, the several acts concerning slaves, free negroes and mulattoes," and for other purposes.

1. Be it enacted by the general assembly, That no slave, free negro, or mulatto, whether he shall have been ordained, or licensed, or otherwise, shall hereafter undertake to preach, exhort, or conduct, or hold any assembly, or meeting, for religious or other purposes, either in the day time, or at night; and any slave, free negro, or mulatto, so offending, shall for the first offence be punished with stripes, at the discretion of any justice of the peace, not exceeding lashes; and any person desiring so to do, shall have authority, without any previous

written precept or otherwise, to apprehend any such offender, and carry him before such justice. And any such slave, free negro, or mulatto, so offending a second time, shall be held guilty of felony, and prosecuted as slaves are now tried for felony, and on conviction, shall, if a slave, and if a free person of colour, shall be sold as a slave, and transported beyond the limits of the United States, in the manner prescribed by law for the sale and transportation of slaves under sentence of death.

2. Any slave, free negro, or mulatto, who shall hereafter attend any preaching, meeting, or other assembly, held, or pretended to be held, for religious purposes, or other instruction, in the night time, although conducted by a white minister, ordained or otherwise; and if a slave, although he or she shall have a written permission from his or her owner, shall be punished by stripes at the discretion of any justice of the peace, not exceeding lashes, and may for that purpose be apprehended by any person, as above authorized: Provided, That nothing herein contained shall be so construed as to prevent the masters or owners of slaves, or any white person to whom any free negro or mulatto is bound, or in whose employment, or on whose plantation or lot, such free negro or mulatto lives, from carrying, or permitting any such slave, free negro or mulatto, to go with him, her, or them, or with any part of his, her, or their white family to any place of religious worship, conducted by a white minister, in the night time: And provided also, That nothing in this, or any former law, shall be so construed as to prevent any ordained, or licensed white minister of the gospel, or any layman licensed for that purpose by the denomination to which he may belong, from preaching, or giving religious instruction to slaves, free negroes and mulattoes, in the day time; nor to deprive any masters, or owners of slaves of the right to engage, or employ any free white person whom they may think proper, to give religious instruction to their slaves; nor to prevent the assembling of the slaves of any one owner or master together, at any time for religious devotion.

3. It shall not be lawful hereafter for any free negro or mulatto to go out of the county or corporation in which he or she resides and is registered, without a certificate in writing signed by some justice of the peace of the said county, stating to what other county or corporation, and for what time, the bearer desired to go. Nor shall it be lawful for any free negro or mulatto, who shall have thus gone from the county or corporation in which he had therefore resided, into any other, to remain in the latter more than one month, without having obtained permission to that effect, from the county or corporation court, where he shall have gone, entered on record; which order of permission may at any time be revoked by the court, within one year next after it shall have been granted. And any free negro or mulatto, found out of the county or corporation of his proper residence, otherwise

This wood engraving of Anthony Burns was made from a daguerreotype by Whipple and Black. Burns was a slave who escaped and was recaptured. His story was sensational news in 1855. It quickly captured the imagination of the popular press, and pictures of Burns and the real or imagined scenes of his life were reprinted in newspapers and magazines. **THE LIBRARY OF CONGRESS**

than as aforesaid, shall be punished by stripes, at the discretion of a justice of the peace, not exceeding lashes, and may for that purpose, be apprehended by any person as above authorized, and shall be liable to the same punishment once in every week he or she shall continue to remain in such county or corporation, contrary to law, unless it shall manifestly appear, that he or she had been prevented from removing by sickness or other physical inability. It shall not be lawful for any free negro or mulatto, whether he or she shall have previously emigrated from this state or not, to migrate into this commonwealth, or to come into it, whether with a view to permanent residence, or temporary sojourn, or for any object or purpose whatsoever; and every free negro or mulatto, who shall come into this commonwealth by land or by water, contrary to this act, shall and may be apprehended, and carried by any citizen before some justice of the peace of the county where he shall be taken; which justice is hereby authorized to examine, send and remove, every such free negro or mulatto out of this commonwealth, into that state, or country, or island, from whence it shall appear, he or she last came; and for this purpose, the sheriff or other officer, or any other person or persons, may by such justice be employed within this state, upon the same terms as are by law directed in the removal of criminals from one county to another; and the expenses and charges of such removal, to be audited and paid out of the treasury, as other public charges. And every free negro or mulatto, who shall have come, or been brought into this commonwealth by water, from any country, state, or island, may and shall be exported to the place from whence he or she came or was brought, and the charges attending the same shall be paid by the importer; to be recovered by motion in the name of the commonwealth, upon ten days previous notice thereof, in any court of record; and any such free negro or mulatto, may, by the order of the justice taking cognizance of the case, at his discretion, be punished by stripes in the first instance, if it shall appear to him to have been an intentional and known violation of this act, not exceeding thirty-nine lashes; and every free negro or mulatto, so removed or exported, and thereafter returning into this commonwealth, (unless it be in consequence of shipwreck or other unavoidable necessity,) shall be deemed guilty of felony, and shall be prosecuted therefor, as slaves are now tried for felonies, and on conviction, shall be sold as a slave, and transported beyond the limits of the United States, in the manner prescribed by law, for the sale and transportation of slaves under sentence of death. And so much of the sixty-sixth section of the before recited act, as authorizes masters of vessels to bring into this state, any free negro or mulatto, employed on board, and belonging to such vessel, and who shall therewith depart, shall be and the same is hereby repealed. And it shall not be lawful for any master or owner of any vessel about to sail from any Atlantic port in this commonwealth, to any other port in the United States, north thereof, to employ on board such vessel, any slave, free negro or mulatto; and any master or owner of such vessel, as shall offend herein, shall forfeit and pay one thousand dollars, to be recovered in the same manner and to the same uses as aforesaid.

4. No free negro or mulatto, shall hereafter be capable of purchasing, or otherwise acquiring title to any real estate of any description, in fee, for life, or for a longer term than year: or of purchasing, or hiring, or otherwise acquiring title or ownership, permanent or temporary, to any slave; and all contracts, for any such purchase, hire, or other acquisition, are hereby declared to be null and void.

5. It shall not hereafter be lawful for any free negro, or mulatto, to sell, or transfer otherwise, to any person, any thing whatever, without having procured, and exhibiting at the time of such sale, or transfer, a written certificate of two freeholders of the county or corporation, in which he, or she resides, enumerating the commodities to be sold, and the quantity or number, and stating that the article, if of agricultural production, stock, or

fowls, was in the belief of the certifiers, raised, and then owned by such free negro, or mulatto; and if any other article, their belief that he or she had honestly acquired it. And if any person shall purchase, or receive, of any free negro, or mulatto, any vendible commodity whatever, without the production of such certificate, he shall be held guilty of a misdemeanor, and forfeit and pay the sum of ____ dollars, to be recovered by information, or indictment, in any court of record, one half to the informer, and the other half to the use of the commonwealth.

6. No free negro or mulatto, shall be suffered to keep or carry any firelock of any kind, any military weapon, or any powder or lead; and any free negro or mulatto, who shall so offend, shall, on conviction before a justice of the peace, forfeit all such arms and ammunition, to the use of the informer, and shall, moreover, be punished with stripes, at the discretion of the justice, not exceeding thirty-nine lashes. And the proviso, to the seventh section, of the act entitled "an act reducing into one the several acts concerning slaves, free negroes and mulattoes," passed the second day of March, one thousand eight hundred and nineteen, authorizing justices of the peace, in certain cases, to permit slaves to keep and use guns or other weapons, powder and shot; and so much of the eighth section of the said recited act, as authorizes the county and corporation courts, to grant licenses to free negroes and mulattoes, to keep or carry any firelock of any kind, any military weapon, or any powder or lead, shall be, and the same are hereby repealed.

7. No free negro or mulatto, tradesman or mechanic, shall, after an opportunity has been presented to him, on public means, or means other than his own, of removing from the state of Virginia to Liberia, or any other place without the limits of the United States, at which free persons of colour from Virginia may be colonized, be permitted to work at, or carry on his trade, or handicraft, in this commonwealth, except by special permission of the court of the county or corporation, in which he may reside, entered of record, and which license may be revoked, or again renewed, by the courts at pleasure. And no such free negro, or mulatto tradesman, or mechanic, shall, under any circumstances, be hereafter allowed to take apprentices, or to teach their trade, or art, to any other person, except that coloured barbers may take apprentices. Nor shall any slave, free negro, or mulatto, hereafter be employed, or act, as a musician to any military company in this commonwealth. And any free negro or mulatto, who shall violate any of the provisions of this act, shall pay a fine not exceeding dollars, to be adjudged of by any justice of the peace to whom the information is given, one half to the informer, and the other half to the commonwealth, and moreover shall be punished by stripes, not exceeding thirty-nine lashes, at the discretion of the justice of the peace.

8. No white person, free negro, or mulatto, shall buy, sell, or receive of, to, or from a slave, any commodity whatsoever, without the written consent of the master, owner, or overseer of such slave, specifying what articles and quantity or number the slave is allowed to sell, or what amount of money to expend; and if any person shall presume to deal with any slave without such written consent, he or she so offending, shall forfeit and pay to the master or owner of such slave, four times the value of the thing so bought, sold, or received, to be recovered with costs, by warrant, without regard to the amount, before a justice of the peace, in the same manner as other debts, not exceeding twenty dollars, are recovered; and shall also forfeit and pay the further sum of twenty dollars, recoverable with costs, in like manner, to any person who will warrant for the same, or receive on his or her bare back thirty-nine lashes, well laid on; and shall, nevertheless, be liable to pay the costs of such warrant. And if any white person shall sell any ardent spirit to a slave, without such written permission as aforesaid, specifying also the quantity of spirituous liquor, which the slave is authorized to purchase, he or she so offending, in addition to the penalties above imposed, shall also forfeit the sum of one hundred dollars, to be recovered to the use of the commonwealth, by presentment, information, or indictment, in any court of record.

9. No slave, free negro, or mulatto, shall hereafter be permitted to sell, give, or otherwise dispose of any ardent or spirituous liquor, at, or within one mile of any muster, preaching, or other public assembly, of black or white persons; and any slave, free negro, or mulatto so offending shall be punished by stripes, at the discretion of a justice of the peace, not exceeding thirty-nine; and if the offender be a slave, the master, or owner of such slave, whether consenting to such violation of law or not, shall forfeit and pay the sum of dollars, to be recovered with costs, by any person who will sue for the same, by warrant before a justice of the peace, in the same manner as other debts, not exceeding twenty dollars.

10. If it shall be proved to the satisfaction of any court of record, or justice of the peace, that any person hath been guilty of buying, selling, or receiving, to or from any slave, free negro or mulatto, without such license, permission, or certificate, as is by this act required, and contrary to the true intent and meaning of this act, it shall be lawful for such court or justice, to rule such person to give security for his or her good behaviour, for one year or longer, at the discretion of such court or justice; and on failure of such person to give the security required, he or she shall be committed to jail, there to remain until the security be given, or he or she be otherwise discharged by due course of law.

11. If any slave, free negro, or mulatto, shall hereafter, wilfully and maliciously assault and beat any white person, with intention in so doing to kill such white person; every such slave, free negro, or mulatto, so offending, and being thereof lawfully convicted, shall be adjudged and deemed guilty of felony, and shall suffer death, without benefit of clergy.

12. If any person, shall hereafter write, print, or cause to be written, or printed, any book, pamphlet or other writing, advising, or inciting persons of colour within this state, to make insurrection, or to rebel, or shall knowingly circulate, or cause to be circulated, any book, pamphlet, or other writing, written or printed, advising, or inciting persons of colour in this commonwealth, to commit insurrection or rebellion; such person, if a slave, free negro, or mulatto, shall on conviction before any justice of the peace, be punished for the first offence with stripes, at the discretion of the said justice, not exceeding thirty-nine lashes, and for the second offence shall be deemed guilty of felony, and on due conviction shall be punished with death, without benefit of clergy; and if the person so offending be a white person, he or she shall be punished on conviction

13. Riots, routs, unlawful assemblies, trespasses and seditious speeches, by free negroes, or mulattoes, shall hereafter be punished with stripes, in the same mode, and to the same extent, as slaves are directed to be punished by the twelfth section of the before recited act. If any free negro, or mulatto, shall hereafter commit simple larceny, of any money, bank note, goods, chattels, or other thing, of the value of twenty dollars, or less, he or she for every such offence shall be tried and punished in the same manner as slaves are directed to be tried and punished by the fifth section of the act, entitled "an act concerning the trial and punishment of slaves, free negroes, and mulattoes, in certain cases," passed the twelfth day of February, one thousand eight hundred and twenty-eight.

14. The fourth section of the last recited act, repealing so much of several previous acts as provided that for certain offences, free negroes and mulattoes should be punished with stripes, transportation, and sale, shall be, and the same is hereby repealed, and the said several acts, repealed by the said fourth clause, are hereby revived, and declared valid.

15. All persons, whether white, free negroes, or mulattoes, who shall hereafter receive any stolen goods, knowing the said goods to have been stolen, shall be adjudged guilty of larceny of the said goods, and punished in the same manner, and to the same extent, as if the receiver had actually stolen the said goods; but nothing herein contained shall be so construed as to prevent the prosecution, conviction, and punishment of the person who actually shall have stolen them, as heretofore.

16. Free negroes and mulattoes, shall hereafter be prosecuted, tried, convicted, and punished for any felony, by justices of oyer and terminer, in the same manner as slaves are now prosecuted, tried, convicted and punished, and any court summoned or adjourned for such trial, shall have and exercise all the powers and incidents of a court summoned or adjourned, for the trial of a slave; and the governor shall have the same power and authority to effect the sale and transportation of any free negro or mulatto, who may be under sentence of death, as if the person so convicted, were a slave, and in all cases, the money thus received, shall be accounted for to the commonwealth.

17. Hereafter, no court or other authority shall grant any license to any person whatever, to keep a tavern, or to retail groceries, unless the party applying for such license will make oath before the court, a copy of which is to be entered on record, that he or she had not sold or delivered any spirituous liquor, to any slave, contrary to the provisions of this act, since its passage, and that he or she would not do so during the continuance of the license so applied for.

18. Nothing in this act contained, shall be so construed, as to bar or conclude any prosecution for any offence committed previously to this act going into operation, but the same shall be so conducted, decided and executed, as if this act had never passed.

19. It shall be the duty of the several judges of this commonwealth, and presiding justices of the county and corporation courts, constantly to give this act in charge to the grand juries; and it is moreover made the duty of all attorneys prosecuting for the commonwealth in any court therein, who may know of, or have good reason to suspect any violation of this act, to lodge information thereof before the proper court or grand jury, and to institute forthwith the proper prosecution for his or her conviction.

PRIMARY SOURCE DOCUMENT

Excerpt from *The Fugitive Blacksmith* by James Pennington

INTRODUCTION James W. C. Pennington was born into slavery in Maryland in 1807. There were many children in his family, and they were lucky enough to remain together when James was growing up. But even though they were not separated, the Pennington family had its sufferings. Remembering those years in his 1849 abolitionist narrative *The Fugitive Blacksmith*, Pennington stressed the anguish he felt as a child seeing his parents repeatedly mistreated and humiliated by their owners.

In 1828, Pennington decided he had had enough and fled north, becoming in time an ordained minister and abolitionist leader. In this opening section from *The Fugitive Blacksmith*,

Pennington describes his birth and family and the event that led to his decision.

Chapter 1. My Birth and Parentage—The Treatment of Slaves Generally in Maryland

I was born in the state of Maryland, which is one of the smallest and most northern of the slaveholding states; the products of this state are wheat, rye, Indian corn, tobacco, with some hemp, flax, &c. By looking at the map, it will be seen that Maryland, like Virginia her neighbor, is divided by the Chesapeake Bay into eastern and western shores. My birth-place was on the eastern shore, where there are seven or eight small counties; the farms are small, and tobacco is mostly raised.

At an early period in the history of Maryland, her lands began to be exhausted by the bad cultivation peculiar to slave states; and hence she soon commenced the business of breeding slaves for the more southern states. This has given an enormity to slavery, in Maryland, differing from that which attaches to the system in Louisiana, and equalled by none of the kind, except Virginia and Kentucky, and not by either of these in extent.

My parents did not both belong to the same owner: my father belonged to a man named ___; my mother belonged to a man named ___. This not only made me a slave, but made me the slave of him to whom my mother belonged; as the primary law of slavery is, that the child shall follow the condition of the mother.

When I was about four years of age, my mother, an older brother, and myself were given to a son of my master, who had studied for the medical profession, but who had now married wealthy, and was about to settle as a wheat planter in Washington County, on the western shore. This began the first of our family troubles that I knew anything about, as it occasioned a separation between my mother and the only two children she then had, and my father, to a distance of about two hundred miles. But this separation did not continue long; my father being a valuable slave, my master was glad to purchase him.

About this time, I began to feel another evil of slavery—I mean the want of parental care and attention. My parents were not able to give any attention to their children during the day. I often suffered much from hunger and other similar causes. To estimate the sad state of a slave child, you must look at it as a helpless human being thrown upon the world without the benefit of its natural guardians. It is thrown into the world without a social circle to flee to for hope, shelter, comfort, or instruction. The social circle, with all its heaven-ordained blessings, is of the utmost importance to the tender child; but of this, the slave child, however tender and delicate, is robbed.

There is another source of evil to slave children, which I cannot forbear to mention here, as one which early embittered my life; I mean the tyranny of the master's children. My master had two sons, about the ages and sizes of my older brother and myself. We were not only required to recognize these young sirs as our young masters, but they felt themselves to be such; and, in consequence of this feeling, they sought to treat us with the same air of authority that their father did the older slaves.

Another evil of slavery that I felt severely about this time was the tyranny and abuse of the overseers. These men seem to look with an evil eye upon children. I was once visiting a menagerie, and being struck with the fact, that the lion was comparatively indifferent to everyone around his cage, while he eyed with peculiar keenness a little boy I had; the keeper informed me that such was always the case. Such is true of those human beings in the slave states, called overseers. They seem to take pleasure in torturing the children of slaves, long before they are large enough to be put at the hoe, and consequently under the whip.

We had an overseer named Blackstone; he was an extremely cruel man to the working hands. He always carried a long hickory whip—a kind of pole. He kept three or four of these, in order that he might not at any time be without one.

I once found one of these hickories lying in the yard, and supposing that he had thrown it away, I picked it up, and boy-like, was using it for a horse; he came along from the field, and seeing me with it, fell upon me with the one he then had in his hand, and flogged me most cruelly. From that, I lived in constant dread of that man; and he would show how much he delighted in cruelty by chasing me from my play with threats and imprecations. I have lain for hours in a wood, or behind a fence, to hide from his eye.

At this time my days were extremely dreary. When I was nine years of age, myself and my brother were hired out from home; my brother was placed with a pump-maker, and I was placed with a stonemason. We were both in a town some six miles from home. As the men with whom we lived were not slaveholders, we enjoyed some relief from the peculiar evils of slavery. Each of us lived in a family where there was no other Negro.

The slaveholders in that state often hire the children of their slaves out to non-slaveholders, not only because they save themselves the expense of taking care of them, but in this way they get among their slaves useful trades. They put a bright slave boy with a tradesman, until he gets such a knowledge of the trade as to be able to do his own work, and then he takes him home. I remained with the stonemason until I was eleven years of age; at this time I was taken home. This was another serious period in my childhood; I was separated from my older brother, to whom I was much attached; he continued at his place, and not only learned the trade to great perfection, but

finally became the property of the man with whom he lived, so that our separation was permanent, as we never lived nearer, after, than six miles. My master owned an excellent blacksmith, who had obtained his trade in the way I have mentioned above. When I returned home at the age of eleven, I was set about assisting to do the mason work of a new smith's shop. This being done, I was placed at the business, which I soon learned, so as to be called a "first-rate blacksmith." I continued to work at this business for nine years, or until I was twenty-one, with the exception of the last seven months.

In the spring of 1828, my master sold me to a Methodist man, named _____, for the sum of seven hundred dollars. It soon proved that he had not work enough to keep me employed as a smith, and he offered me for sale again. On hearing of this, my old master repurchased me, and proposed to me to undertake the carpentering business. I had been working at this trade six months with a white workman, who was building a large barn when I left. I will now relate the abuses which occasioned me to fly.

Three or four of our farm hands had their wives and families on other plantations. In such cases, it is the custom in Maryland to allow the men to go on Saturday evening to see their families, stay over the Sabbath, and return on Monday morning, not later than "half-an-hour by sun." To overstay their time is a grave fault, for which, especially at busy seasons, they are punished.

"One Monday morning, two of these men had not been so fortunate as to get home at the required time; one of them was an uncle of mine. Besides these, two young men who had no families, and for whom no such provision of time was made, having gone somewhere to spend the Sabbath, were absent. My master was greatly irritated, and had resolved to have," as he said, "a general whipping-match among them."

Preparatory to this, he had a rope in his pocket, and a cowhide in his hand, walking about the premises, and speaking to everyone he met in a very insolent manner, and finding fault with some without just cause. My father, among other numerous and responsible duties, discharged that of shepherd to a large and valuable flock of Merino sheep. This morning he was engaged in the tenderest of a shepherd's duties: a little lamb, not able to go alone, lost its mother; he was feeding it by hand. He had been keeping it in the house for several days. As he stooped over it in the yard, with a vessel of new milk he had obtained, with which to feed it, my master came along, and without the least provocation, began by asking, "Bazil, have you fed the flock?"

"Yes, sir."

"Were you away yesterday?"

"No, sir."

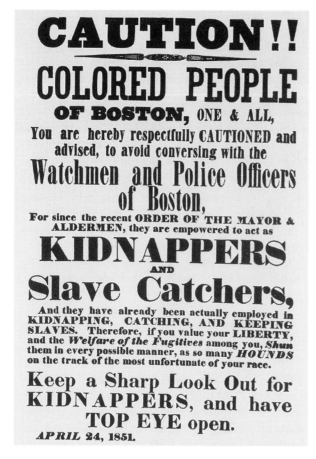

CAUTION!!
COLORED PEOPLE
OF BOSTON, ONE & ALL,
You are hereby respectfully CAUTIONED and advised, to avoid conversing with the
Watchmen and Police Officers of Boston,
For since the recent ORDER OF THE MAYOR & ALDERMEN, they are empowered to act as
KIDNAPPERS
AND
Slave Catchers,
And they have already been actually employed in KIDNAPPING, CATCHING, AND KEEPING SLAVES. Therefore, if you value your LIBERTY, and the *Welfare of the Fugitives* among you, *Shun* them in every possible manner, as so many *HOUNDS* on the track of the most unfortunate of your race.
Keep a Sharp Look Out for KIDNAPPERS, and have TOP EYE open.
APRIL 24, 1851.

This handbill was circulated in Boston to warn the city's African Americans of the danger of being kidnapped following the passage of the 1850 Fugitive Slave Law. Many African Americans who had escaped north years before fled following the enactment of the new law. Many free-born African Americans were also driven away, for they too could be kidnapped and claimed as property. **THE LIBRARY OF CONGRESS**

"Do you know why these boys have not got home this morning yet?"

"No, sir, I have not seen any of them since Saturday night."

"By the Eternal, I'll make them know their hour. The fact is, I have too many of you; my people are getting to be the most careless, lazy, and worthless in the country."

"Master," said my father, "I am always at my post; Monday morning never finds me off the plantation."

"Hush Bazil! I shall have to sell some of you; and then the rest will have enough to do; I have not work enough to keep you all tightly employed; I have too many of you."

All this was said in an angry, threatening, and exceedingly insulting tone. My father was a high-spirited man, and feeling deeply the insult, replied to the last expression, "If I am one too many, sir, give me a chance to get a purchaser, and I am willing to be sold when it may suit you."

"Bazil, I told you to hush!" and suiting the action to the word, he drew forth the cowhide from under his arm, fell upon him with most savage cruelty, and inflicted fifteen or twenty severe stripes with all his strength, over his shoulders and the small of his back. As he raised himself upon his toes, and gave the last stripe, he said, "By the * * * I will make you know that I am master of your tongue as well as of your time!"

Being a tradesman, and just at that time getting my breakfast, I was near enough to hear the insolent words that were spoken to my father, and to hear, see, and even count the savage stripes inflicted upon him.

Let me ask any one of Anglo-Saxon blood and spirit, how would you expect a son to feel at such a sight?

This act created an open rupture with our family—each member felt the deep insult that had been inflicted upon our head; the spirit of the whole family was roused; we talked of it in our nightly gatherings, and showed it in our daily melancholy aspect. The oppressor saw this, and with the heartlessness that was in perfect keeping with the first insult, commenced a series of tauntings, threatenings, and insinuations, with a view to crush the spirit of the whole family.

Although it was some time after this event before I took the decisive step, yet in my mind and spirit, I never was a Slave after it.

PRIMARY SOURCE DOCUMENT

"Reception and Treatment of Kidnappers"

INTRODUCTION In the January 31, 1851, issue of the *Liberator* appeared the following instructions for the "Reception and Treatment of Kidnappers." It cites the famous case of William and Ellen Craft, who escaped from Macon, Georgia, disguised as servant and master, and reminds readers of how the slave hunters sent to capture them were defeated by public attention and harassment. Charles King Whipple, the author of this piece, was a young associate of William Lloyd Garrison from Newburyport, Massachusetts.

"The *Liberator*'s Rules on the Reception and Treatment of Kidnappers," by Charles King Whipple

It will be remembered that the slave-hunters Hughes and Knight, agents of the pretended owner of William and Ellen Crafts, fled from Boston so secretly that for some time the mode of their departure could not be traced. When they were asked, on the morning of that day, by members of the Vigilance Committee, why they had not fulfilled their promise of going in the earliest train, they replied—"Do you think we wanted to be followed all the way to the cars by a crowd of people calling out Slave-hunter, Slave-hunter?"

This speech must not be forgotten. It is most convincing testimony of the efficacy of a plan for the treatment of those kidnappers, which was debated before the Vigilance Committee, but never fully matured, nor thoroughly put in practice. The following brief outline of it is published for the benefit of friends of the slave, in those towns to which such blood-hounds in human shape may hereafter come.

As soon as the arrival of one or more slave-hunters is known, let the Vigilance Committee appoint a sub-committee of the most active and devoted friends of liberty, sufficiently numerous for the thorough accomplishment of the following purposes, namely:

To keep themselves informed, by active, open, personal supervision, of every step the kidnappers take, every act they do, and every person they visit, as long as they remain in the place:

By personal interference, and calling aloud upon the citizens for rescue, to prevent them from seizing any man or woman as a slave:

To point them out to the people, wherever they go, as Slave-hunters: and, finally,

When they leave the town, to go with them and point them out to members of the Vigilance Committee or other friends of freedom in the first place in which they stop, that similar attention may be paid them there.

Every part of this course of action is important; and if all be faithfully put in operation, it will be hardly possible for them to kidnap a resident in any town of New England; not even in Marshfield or Andover.

As soon as the kidnappers arrive in any town, large handbills should be posted in all the public places, containing their names, with a description of their persons and the business on which they come.

An attempt should be made to induce the landlord of any hotel or boarding-house to which they may go, to refuse them entertainment, on the ground of their being persons infamous by profession, like pickpockets, gamblers, or horse-stealers.

If this proves unsuccessful, some of the committee of attendance should take lodgings in the same house with the kidnappers, and take, if possible, sleeping rooms and seats at table directly opposite to them.

The doors of the house should be watched carefully, day and night, and whenever they go out, two resolute, unarmed men should follow each of them wherever he goes, pointing him out from time to time with the word Slave-Hunter. They should follow him into every shop, office, or place of public business into which he may go,

and if he enters a private dwelling, wait outside, watching all the avenues, and ready to renew the attendance when he comes out. If he takes a coach, they should follow in another; if he drives out of town, they should follow; if he takes a seat in a railroad car, they should go with him, and make him known as a Slave-hunter to the passengers in the car, and to the people of the town where he stops. He should have not one moment's relief from the feeling that his object is understood, that he cannot act in secret, that he is surrounded by men who loathe his person and detest his purpose, and who have means always at hand to prevent the possibility of success.

The efficient treatment of the first cases that arise is all-important. Let a few kidnappers be passed through New England in this way, and we are freed from the pestilent brood forever. Even the hardened and brutal wretches who usually perform this office cannot stand before such treatment. Even the moderate degree of it which was practised towards Hughes and Knight so disconcerted and annoyed them, that they not only felt unable to stay in Boston, but dared not go openly. If members of the Vigilance Committee, relieving each other as often as necessary, had kept them constantly in sight, followed their coach to the out-of-town railroad station, taken seats with them in the cars, and pointed them out as Slave-hunters to the passengers there, and the people of every town they stopped at, as far as New York, the example would have been far more thorough and effectual.

Let us do full justice to the next opportunity.

C. K. W.

African Americans and the Civil War

ADAPTED FROM ESSAYS BY LAURA MITCHELL, UNIVERSITY OF CALIFORNIA, AND BARBARA SAVAGE, UNIVERSITY OF PENNSYLVANIA

AFRICAN AMERICANS ON THE EVE OF THE CIVIL WAR

Northern blacks took a keen interest in the campaign and election of 1860. The Republican party's presidential candidate, Abraham Lincoln (1809–1865), enjoyed wide support among the North's small free black population, although many blacks remained dissatisfied with that party's platform because it failed to call for emancipation. Others supported the Radical Abolition party candidate, Gerrit Smith (1791–1874). Although the Republican platform fell short of their wishes, blacks still welcomed the election of Abraham Lincoln as a step in the right direction.

Members of the great Republican Reform party, pictured as stereotypes, approach the 1856 presidential candidate, John C. Fremont, shown at the right. They each represent a special interest group, from left to right: a Yankee reformer opposed to tobacco, animal food, and alcohol; a feminist; a utopian socialist; an advocate of free love; a Roman Catholic priest; and a free man of color. **THE LIBRARY OF CONGRESS**

Soon after Lincoln's election, slave states began to secede. Lincoln lamented their decision and strove to prevent others from following suit. Black leaders, however, tired of watching northern politicians make compromises with southern slaveholders, welcomed secession. Now that the two regions were separate, they reasoned, the North would no longer enforce the abhorrent fugitive slave law, and all slaves who escaped north would be free.

Blacks also welcomed the outbreak of war, seeing it as the first step toward the end of slavery, even though abolition was not a stated war aim. "The American people and the Government at Washington may refuse to recognize it for a time," Frederick Douglass (1817–1895) wrote in May 1861, but nevertheless, he insisted, the "war now being waged in this land is a war for and against slavery."

SEE PRIMARY SOURCE DOCUMENT *Letter from Frederick Douglass to Harriet Tubman*

SLAVERY DURING THE WAR

Southern blacks, largely illiterate and unfamiliar with the activities of northern abolitionists, observed the out-

break of war more cautiously. However, once they understood that the war could hasten their freedom, most grasped every opportunity to aid the Union army. Their reactions to the war's outbreak destroyed the myth of the happy slave. Apologists for the South's peculiar institution had long contended that slaves loved their masters and would not take freedom if it were offered. In fact, slaves fled to freedom when they had the opportunity; during the war, approximately five hundred thousand slaves escaped or came within Union lines.

The coming of war changed slaves' lives in several ways. Many plantations shifted from cash crops such as cotton to staples such as corn and wheat to feed the army and the civilian population. Families lost loved ones as able-bodied male slaves were forced to aid the war effort. Many experienced severe dislocation. As Union armies approached, masters often fled, taking their human property into the hinterland. In some cases, masters fled and left slaves behind. These slaves were emancipated and often continued to farm under the direction of the Union army.

Many slaves were pressed into service in the Confederate army. Although the Confederacy never officially

Slaves that escaped after the Civil War had begun were considered contraband, and were not subject to return to their masters. They frequently attached themselves to the Union Army, both for protection and to join in the fight against slavery. In this drawing, an escaped slave stands before a Union fort and taunts his former master with his new status. **THE LIBRARY OF CONGRESS**

conscripted or armed free blacks and slaves, slaves were forced to build defensive fortifications and to cook, clean, and perform other tasks in army camps. In the war's early stages, some went to battle as their masters' personal slaves. Some blacks, perhaps hoping to earn their freedom or to prove that they were the whites' equals, volunteered to serve in the army, but their numbers were very small. **SEE PRIMARY SOURCE DOCUMENT** *H. C. Chambers's Address Regarding the Use of Slaves in War*

As the war dragged on and the need for more soldiers increased, several Southern generals discussed the possibility of pressing blacks into service. Although Jefferson Davis (1808–1889) concluded in early 1865 that arming blacks was a military necessity, most Confederate leaders were skeptical about the loyalty of free and enslaved blacks, especially as their desertion rate was high. After some deliberation, Confederate leaders decided against the idea.

CONTRABAND

From the war's onset, fugitive slaves were a difficult issue for the Union army. Lincoln had made clear that he believed secession was not legally possible. In his eyes, the Southern states were still a part of the Union and in rebellion against it. All federal laws regarding slavery were therefore still in effect, including the Fugitive Slave Act of 1850. In keeping with this law, Union officers were supposed to return fugitive slaves who had taken refuge behind their lines.

In May 1861, three fugitives escaped to the Union army camped at Fortress Monroe, Virginia. The army's commander, Benjamin Butler (1818–1893), declared them contraband of war, meaning that they were property of the enemy that could be confiscated. Butler harbored the runaways because he recognized that they were of material aid to the Confederates. Despite his commitment to enforce the fugitive slave law, Lincoln approved Butler's decision. The fugitives continued to arrive, and by July 1861, over nine hundred contraband slaves had taken refuge with Butler's troops.

In early August, Congress passed an act providing for the confiscation of all property that aided the rebellion, including slaves. Slaves owned by those who were loyal to the Union or had not contributed to the war effort were to remain slaves. Later that same August, John C. Fremont (1813–1890), Union commander in the Western Department, declared martial law in Missouri. In violation of Congress's confiscation law, he issued a declaration that all slaves owned by rebels were to be freed. Lincoln sharply rebuked Fremont, fearing that this action would alienate the other loyal slave states. He ordered Fremont to comply with the confiscation act; when Fremont refused, Lincoln revoked Fremont's order and soon thereafter relieved him of his command.

The contraband issue became increasingly pressing as the war continued. More and more slaves flooded behind Union lines, often arriving as families, not just as

This 1864 illustration shows freed slaves approaching a Union camp. Virginia's Fortress Monroe, under the command of Benjamin Butler, was the first Union encampment to shelter escaping slaves, whom Butler termed "contraband of war." The phrase, with its official ring, meant that fugitives were now considered enemy property that might be "confiscated." Contrabands were put to work in the Union war effort, building fortifications, cooking and laundering, and performing a variety of other jobs. **THE LIBRARY OF CONGRESS**

able-bodied men who could claim that Confederates had put them to work in the war effort. In March 1862, General David Hunter (1802–1886) followed Fremont's example of the previous summer and declared the slaves of South Carolina, Georgia, and Florida to be free. As he had before, Lincoln overruled the emancipation order. The black press excoriated Lincoln on moral and strategic grounds, denouncing his failure to seize an opportunity to free the slaves and his apparent inability to see the immense value of emancipation for the Union cause.

The growing presence of slaves behind Union lines revealed the inherent link between the contraband and the war. Because of the confiscation act, the southward-moving Union troops were essentially armies of emancipation. In April 1862, Congress passed further laws prohibiting the return of fugitive slaves who had escaped to Union forces, prohibiting slavery in the territories, providing for a real end to the African slave trade, and abolishing slavery in the District of Columbia. In July 1862, Congress followed these legislative efforts with yet another confiscation act further guaranteeing the freedom of slaves held by rebels.

SEE PRIMARY SOURCE DOCUMENT *Excerpt from* **Behind the Scenes** *by Elizabeth Keckley*

AFRICAN AMERICANS AID THE WAR EFFORT

From the beginning of the war, black males throughout the North offered themselves as soldiers in the Union army, but their services were refused. A federal law barred them from serving in state militia, and in 1860, there were no blacks in United States Army.

Despite the army's refusal to enlist them, black men in Boston organized a drill company and repeatedly petitioned the Massachusetts legislature to allow them to fight. Similar companies were formed in other Northern cities. Abolitionists tried to pressure President Lincoln to allow white officers to lead companies of black soldiers, but their suggestion met with resistance. Because of their deep racism, few white soldiers wanted to fight alongside blacks, and few officers believed that blacks would make good soldiers.

In addition, many white politicians and editors insisted that the war was a white man's war for the preservation of the Union, not for the emancipation of the slaves. To allow blacks to fight would be to admit that emancipation was a war goal and perhaps to alienate whites who had no desire to free the slaves. In the early stages of the war, Abraham Lincoln had made this very clear. His attitude prompted some blacks to question whether or not they should continue to offer their services to a government that was hostile to them. Despite these reservations, however, numerous black men continued to organize and train, waiting for an opportunity to fight.

While they waited, black leaders in the North waged a war of words, demanding the abolition of slavery in both rebel and loyal states. Black leaders such as Frederick Douglass argued forcefully that the only way to put an end to the war against slaveholders was to put an end to slavery itself. Slavery was a source of immense military strength, black leaders argued, and emancipation would strike directly at the South's capacity for war.

By the summer of 1862, Lincoln had begun to agree. In the previous spring, he had encouraged Congress to offer compensation to any state that would adopt a policy of gradual emancipation. Although Congress enacted other legislative blows against slavery at this time, the border states vehemently opposed Lincoln's plan and secured its defeat in Congress. While Congress was making some strides toward emancipation, Lincoln began to draft the Emancipation Proclamation. He understood that emancipation had become a military necessity. The Union needed to deprive the South of its slaves and put them in Union uniforms. In July 1862, he presented the idea to his cabinet, which advised him to wait for a military victory before announcing his plan to the nation.

That victory came at Antietam in September 1862, and Lincoln issued a preliminary draft of the proclamation that same month. The proclamation decreed that as of January 1, 1863, all slaves in the rebellious states would be forever free. Blacks rejoiced at Lincoln's decision and celebrated throughout the North. The black press praised Lincoln for taking the step, at the same time noting that the proclamation did not free slaves in the states that remained loyal to the Union. Nevertheless, after the proclamation was issued, the Union army officially became an instrument of emancipation.

The Emancipation Proclamation called on all freed slaves to join the army and fight for the Union. Black men immediately answered the call, forming numerous units, including the heralded Fifty-fourth and Fifty-fifth Massachusetts regiments and the First South Carolina Volunteers. Units of black soldiers fought under the leadership of white men, including the abolitionists Col. Robert Gould Shaw (1837–1863) and Col. Thomas Wentworth Higginson (1823–1911). Black soldiers fought courageously in every theater of the war, but they were paid less than their white counterparts until 1864. **SEE PRIMARY SOURCE DOCUMENT** *The Emancipation Proclamation*

By the war's end, over 186,000 blacks had enlisted in the Union army. They served in all capacities, as soldiers, hospital surgeons, chaplains, and spies. A few attained

The Emancipation Proclamation and President Lincoln's Wartime Politics

Unlike many in the abolitionist movement, Abraham Lincoln was willing to compromise on the issue of slavery. Because the Constitution protected it, President Lincoln was willing to allow it to continue in those states where it existed, though he opposed its extension into new territories. But with the coming of the Civil War, things changed. The Union army lost as many battles as it won in the first two years of the war, owing in large part to the services slaves provided to the Confederacy. The Emancipation Proclamation freed those slaves within the Confederate states, and opened the Union army to African American soldiers. It left untouched, however, the status of slaves in slaveholding border states that remained within the Union, and in various other localities. Their bondage would end only with the passage of the Thirteenth Amendment in 1865.

The practical effect of the Emancipation Proclamation was to make the war truly a war about freedom. Though people were still held in slavery in the Confederacy, every inch of ground the Union army now won became free soil. Throughout the South, wherever they could, enslaved people escaped behind Union lines, many of them taking up arms against their old masters. As a result of Lincoln's proclamation, almost two hundred thousand African Americans took part in the Civil War.

high rank and were decorated for valor. Nearly 40,000 black soldiers died in the war, almost a quarter of all who enlisted, a casualty rate 40 percent higher than that of whites. Blacks' contributions to the war effort proved undeniably that they had won their own victory and their own freedom.

In the South, slaves learned of Lincoln's proclamation by word of mouth and from Southern newspapers. When Union troops occupied an area, army commanders appointed a superintendent of freedmen's affairs to organize the freedmen. These superintendents put the ex-slaves to work on abandoned plantations or as laborers in camps. In theory, the former slaves were to receive wages for their labor, but in some cases, they lived and worked in conditions scarcely different from slavery.

Northerners organized numerous societies to aid the freedmen and sent men and women south to teach and train them. One of the most famous and successful of these programs was in the South Carolina Sea Islands. Among the teachers who went there was Charlotte Forten (1837–1917), granddaughter of the famous abolitionist James Forten. In the Sea Islands and elsewhere, the contraband camps demonstrated that, with assistance, blacks could make the transition from slavery to freedom.

COLONIZATION

The realization that the slaves were acquiring their freedom focused white attention on the blacks' future in the nation. Most whites believed that blacks were innately inferior to whites and loathed the idea of living in a biracial society. This racism gave new energy to the American Colonization Society, founded nearly a half century earlier by a small group of influential white men. The colonizationists had founded Liberia, but they had never successfully settled many free blacks in this West African colony.

Colonizationists assumed that whites and blacks could never live peacefully and prosperously together and that blacks would never be able to rise above white racial prejudice. Abraham Lincoln fully shared this view. When Lincoln met with five blacks at the White House in August 1862, he told his visitors that the differences between the Negro and the Caucasian made it impossible for them to live together as equals. Lincoln did not defend his characterization of the situation; he simply asserted that it was true. Separation, he argued, was the only remedy and would benefit both blacks and whites. He encouraged the visitors to organize families to emigrate to South America, where they could thrive undaunted by racism.

Lincoln's meeting with the small group was widely publicized. The black press harshly criticized the president and reminded him that blacks had the same rights as whites to live in the land of their birth. Fully cognizant of the weight of the white population's racism, they stated that their unequivocal goal was to elevate the black race in the United States.

Other Northern blacks, however, supported the idea of colonization. Although always a small group, they were a high-profile minority that included such famous critics of slavery as Henry Highland Garnet (1815–1882) and Martin Delany (1812–1885). Garnet and Delany participated in a plan to settle blacks in Haiti, and over the course of the war, more than a thousand blacks emigrated to that island nation. In the end, however, colonization failed during the Civil War because few blacks volunteered to emigrate.

THE CIVIL WAR ENDS

As civilians and soldiers, in the North and the South, blacks made significant contributions to the war effort and proved that they were the whites' equals. In a very real way, blacks freed themselves in the Civil War. Freedom did not come easily, despite the Emancipation Proclamation and later the Thirteenth Amendment. White prejudice remained strong after the war and seriously compromised the efforts of Reconstruction. The Civil War had ended, but the struggle for true freedom continued.

BIBLIOGRAPHY

Berry, Mary Frances. *Military Necessity and Civil Rights Policy: Black Citizenship and the Constitution, 1861–1868*. Port Washington: Kennikat Press, 1967.

Cornish, Dudley T. *The Sable Arm: Negro Troops in the Union Army, 1861–1865*. New York: Longmans, Green, 1956.

Emilio, Luis F. *A Brave Black Regiment: The History of the Fifty-fourth Regiment of Massachusetts Volunteer Infantry, 1863–1865*. New York: Da Capo Press, 1995.

Higginson, Thomas W. *Army Life in a Black Regiment*. Boston: Fields, Osgood, and Co., 1870.

McPherson, James M. *The Negro's Civil War: How American Blacks Felt and Acted during the War for the Union*. New York: Pantheon Books, 1965.

Nieman, Donald G., ed. *The Day of the Jubilee: The Civil War Experience of Black Southerners*. New York: Garland, 1994.

Quarles, Benjamin. *The Negro in the Civil War*. Boston: Little, Brown, 1953.

Redkey, Edwin S., ed. *A Grand Army of Black Men: Letters from African-American Soldiers in the Union Army, 1861–1865*. New York: Cambridge University Press, 1992.

Wiley, Bell I. *Southern Negroes, 1861–1865*. Baton Rouge: Louisiana State University Press, 1938.

Williams, George W. *A History of the Negro Troops in the War of the Rebellion, 1861–1865*. New York: Negro Universities Press, 1969.

PRIMARY SOURCE DOCUMENT

Letter from Frederick Douglass to Harriet Tubman

INTRODUCTION Despite all of Harriet Tubman's activity, male fugitive slaves tended to receive more attention in the North. In this letter, Frederick Douglass concedes that his work has garnered him far more public acclaim than Tubman's bravery. She has gone down in history, however, as the greatest conductor of the Underground Railroad.

Rochester, August 29, 1868.

Dear Harriet: I am glad to know that the story of your eventful life has been written by a kind lady, and that the same is soon to be published. You ask for what you do not need when you call upon me for a word of commendation. I need such words from you far more than you can need them from me, especially where your superior labors and devotion to the cause of the lately enslaved of our land are known as I know them. The difference between us is very marked. Most that I have done and suffered in the service of our cause has been in public, and I have received much encouragement at every step of the way. You, on the other hand, have labored in a private way. I have wrought in the day—you in the night. I have had the applause of the crowd and the satisfaction that comes of being approved by the multitude, while the most that you have done has been witnessed by a few trembling, scarred, and foot-sore bondmen and women, whom you have led out of the house of bondage, and whose heartfelt "God bless you" has been your only reward. The midnight sky and the silent stars have been the witnesses of your devotion to freedom and of your heroism. Excepting John Brown—of sacred memory—I know of no one who has willingly encountered more perils and hardships to serve our enslaved people than you have. Much that you have done would seem improbable to those who do not know you as I know you. It is to me a great pleasure and a great privilege to bear testimony to your character and your works, and to say to those to whom you may come, that I regard you in every way truthful and trustworthy.

Your friend,
Frederick Douglass.

PRIMARY SOURCE DOCUMENT

H. C. Chambers's Address Regarding the Use of Slaves in War

INTRODUCTION Late in the year 1864, as the Confederate government began contemplating the use of black troops in its war effort, H. C. Chambers of Mississippi rose in the Confederate House of Representatives to argue against such a policy. The Confederate army, which was losing ground to the Union army on several fronts, had been depleted through losses and desertions, yet Chambers maintained that "victory itself would be robbed of its glory if shared with slaves. God grant that our noble army of martyrs may never have to drink of this cup!"

Chambers's speech is reprinted here in its entirety and is valuable for two reasons: it offers a detailed view of the war from a Confederate point of view, and it displays in full the racial attitudes of the slaveholding planter class which, it may be argued, were a central element to the demise of the Confederate army when confronted by the policies and war machine of the ideologically more malleable Lincoln administration and Union army.

Use of Slaves in Confederate Army Argued Against Policy of Employing Negro Troops, Speech of Hon. H. C. Chambers, Of Mississippi

In the House of Representatives of the Congress of the Confederate States, Thursday, November 10, 1864, on the special order for that day, being the resolution offered by him on the first day of the session, in the following words:

Resolved, That the valour, constancy and endurance of our citizen-soldiers, with the steady co-operation of all classes of population not in the field, will continue a sufficient guaranty of the Rights of the States and the Independence of the Confederate States.

Black Soldiers Proclaimed Criminals by Confederate Army

During the Revolutionary War, Lord Dunmore invited slaves to come to the side of the British. General Washington had proclaimed no blacks would be allowed to fight, but upon seeing the sizable advantage this provided the British, he reversed his order. In times of war, the aid of African Americans has often been the difference between victory and defeat—however, time and time again, many generals disdained the efforts of black Americans.

Historians speculate that the efforts of black soldiers fighting for the Union cause resulted in victory for the North in the Civil War. The Confederates were stubborn in this regard, and after banning blacks from their regiments, they proclaimed that any blacks who put on uniforms were criminals.

Mr. Chambers said:

Mr. Speaker: This resolution which I had the honor to offer the first day of the session, a little in advance of the reception of the President's message, expresses an abiding faith in the continued ability of the citizen-soldiers of the country to defend the Rights of the States and the Independence of the Confederate States, without further assistance or guaranty than may be derived from the steady co-operation of all classes of population not liable to military duty;—without the aid of negro troops; without the aid of a convention to which we have been conditionally invited by a political party in the United States, on their own terms—that is to say, on a basis which excludes the idea of the permanent existence of this Government; and without the alternative of accepting such guaranties as that party, if it accede to power, may offer to secure our return to the old Union—guaranties which, if faithfully adhered to by that party during their four or eight years' possession of power, would certainly be repudiated by the party next succeeding—succeeding, as in all probability they would, on the special ground of their hostility to the bargain made with us. Thus, after a short interval of repose, our country would again have to choose between war and submission, and, choosing war, enter upon a new conflict, not less bloody, but, perchance, less hopeful than the contest in which we are now engaged.

On the introduction of this resolution, candour compelled me to advise the House that it had been drawn in such terms as would suggest important public questions; and requesting this day to be fixed for its consideration, an avowal was thus explicitly made by me that, in my opinion, those questions should be discussed now and here.

From over caution, from an excessive desire not to disturb the people with agitating questions, pending the war, Congress has, perhaps, too long forborne to consider, in public debate, the many profoundly interesting topics which have arisen out of the present struggle. The Representatives of the people have been silent or reserved until their constituencies are beginning to make themselves heard on delicate issues. We, who sit here, and who might have more fully advised them of the relations of all important questions to events as they arose, and so have assisted in forming and preserving a healthy tone of public sentiment, have, perhaps, too often sealed our lips or closed our doors—until the people, ceasing to look to us for instruction or sympathy, at last manifest no doubtful indications of finding conclusions without our assistance.

No man of observation can be unaware of the present anxious and unsettled condition of public sentiment. The popular mind is groping in a labyrinth of perplexity, seeking solutions for great questions, to some of which allusion has been made. How to increase our armies, how to bring about peace and independence, and in some quarters, let it be confessed, whether it might not be prudent to entertain even the project of reconstruction, these; Sir, are some of the enquiries that are arresting the attention of the country. It cannot be denied that at least one proposition of a startling character is forced upon our consideration. I allude to the employment of negro troops. Undoubtedly, as I think, if this question was not raised with evil design, it must have originated with timid or despairing patriots, who, ignorant of the relative numbers of the contending armies and the statistics of their loss and increase, imagine the worst. But, however or by whomsoever brought forward, it presents itself now with imposing sponsors, and must be met. The President in his message has not disdained to notice it, and distinguished gentlemen on this floor have pronounced it worthy of grave consideration. I shall barely allude to distinguished and influential personages currently reported as advocates of the measure, fearful, if I were to name them, of doing injustice to their views, or of smothering myself at once under the weight of their authority.

The proposition to employ negro troops proceeds upon the assumption that our armies, and the usual source from which they have been recruited, are approximating exhaustion. It is remarkable, however, that this question comes upon us near the close of the most successful campaign, vouchsafed to Confederate arms since

Free African Americans began volunteering for service in the Union army in 1862 after Congress passed the Militia Act, at the same time that their courage and worth as soldiers was being publicly debated by white Americans throughout the North. This print of black Civil War soldiers was probably used for recruiting purposes.

the first year of the war—a campaign in which the efforts of the enemy have been unprecedentedly great, and his losses compared to ours unprecedentedly large; in which, if his reinforcements have been greater than ours, his original ranks have steadily diminished in a corresponding ratio: and the belligerents now find themselves approaching the fourth winter of hostilities with armies of nearly the same numerical relation as existed between them at the beginning. It may be safely asserted that, embracing the Trans-Mississippi Department in the account, the contending forces are as nearly equal now as they were a year ago.

And with reference to the territory lost and recovered, what has been the result of the campaign? Let the President tell the story. He says: "At the beginning of the year the State of Texas was partially in possession of the enemy, and large portions of Louisiana and Arkansas lay apparently defenceless. Of the Federals who invaded Texas, none are known to remain except as prisoners of war. In Northwestern Louisiana, a large and well appointed army, aided by a powerful fleet, was repeatedly defeated, and deemed itself fortunate in finally escaping with a loss of one-third of its numbers, a large part of its

military trains, and many transports and gunboats. The enemy's occupation of the State is reduced to the narrow district commanded by the guns of his fleet. Arkansas has been recovered, with the exception of a few fortified posts, while our forces have penetrated into central Missouri, affording to our oppressed brethren in that State an opportunity, of which many have availed themselves, of striking for liberation from the tyranny to which they have been subjected. Nearly the whole of Northern and Western Mississippi, of Northern Alabama, and of Western Tennessee are again in our possession, and all attempts to penetrate from the coast line into the interior of the Atlantic and Gulf States have been baffled. On the entire Ocean and Gulf coast of the Confederacy, the whole successes of the enemy, with the enormous resources at his command, have been limited to the capture of the outer defences of Mobile bay. In Southwestern Virginia, successive armies, which threatened the capture of Lynchburg and Saltville, have been routed and driven out of the country, and a portion of Eastern Tennessee reconquered by our troops. In Northern Virginia, extensive districts formerly occupied by the enemy are now free from their presence. The main army, after a series of defeats, in which its losses have been enormous, is, with the aid of reinforcements, but with, it is hoped, waning prospect of further progress in the design, still engaged in an effort, commenced more than four months ago, to capture the town of Petersburg. The army of Gen. Sherman, although succeeding at the end of summer in obtaining possession of Atlanta, has been unable to secure any ultimate advantage from his success—compelled to withdraw on the line of his advance, without obtaining control of a single mile of territory beyond the narrow track of his march." Such is the account of last year's operations. Strange, indeed, is it that under such encouraging results as these, a proposition should be made to employ negro troops; nor is it easy to avoid the suspicion that it must have originated in some oblique and unavowed design.

At the same time it must be admitted that our armies are not as large as they should be—not nearly so large as they might be with greater efficiency in the execution of the laws designed to increase them.

In 1862 there were 700,000 men between the ages of 18 and 45, in the cotton States, and over half a million more in Virginia, North Carolina and Tennessee. With a large allowance for physical disability, exemptions and details, here were about one million of men liable to field service under the acts of conscription, exclusive of all recruits from Kentucky and Missouri. Allowing one-fifth of the whole to be now within the enemy's lines, there would still remain 800,000 men; and if one half of this number have been lost or disabled in service (which is impossible), there would still remain 400,000 a force more than sufficient to end this war soon and successfully, to say nothing of the Confederate Reserves and the Militia in the several States.

Sir, it is true the men are not all present with the army; but they exist and will continue with more or less rapidity to supply recruits. The President has told us (as I understand) in a recent speech, that one-third of the number liable to service in the field were absent, yet our armies have been able and are now able to cope with the enemy and even win territory from his grasp. Does this look like exhaustion? If it be, then the same exhaustion afflicts the foe; for after all his immense drafts or attempts at drafting, with huge bounties offered to recruits—with continual relays of foreign paupers to fill up his waning lines—still he finds his numerical relation to us little changed: still he finds himself unable to advance.

The history of nations often exhibits the fact, that there is a point of drain to the field beyond which no population can be forced to go and sustain itself in protracted war. There is besides a conservative instinct in every people, which teaches them when this point has been reached, and neither blandishment nor coercion will easily prevail with them to go beyond it. It is said that not more than four per cent. of the whole popula-

tion, or the male adult head of every fifth family, can be spared to war. When he is taken from the number of producers and converted into a soldier, his family of four consumers remain to be supported by the producers of the four nearest families—a burden of one additional consumer to each male adult at home, which, added to the other exactions of war, has been ascertained to be as heavy as any nation can long sustain.

Now, sir, the North, with its population of some twenty millions at the beginning of the war, divided into four million families, might have spared nearly a million to the field; and it is believed that in the course of this unusually bloody and protracted struggle nearly that number of the enemy has been destroyed or disabled; even Foreign immigration does not enable him greatly to increase his aggregate force in the field, and all appearances, and all information received, indicate that the conservative instincts of the Northern people, admonishing them of approximate exhaustion of resources, rebel against the continuance of the war. But sooner or later, it is argued, the South must be exhausted. I might reply, sufficient for the day is the evil thereof. I choose, however, not so to evade the point.

The limit at which the war drain on population must be stopped, has been referred to. That rule applies only to free population—not to slaves. The number of laborers or producers among slaves is three times as great as among free people. With the former there are three in each family who labour a field, with the latter only one; and with the former, those who do not labor can hardly be called consumers. In the beginning the whole South had 4,000,000 slaves, divisible into 800,000 families of five, and including 2,400,000 labourers. The North, on the other hand, had about 20,000,000 whites, of which 12,000,000 would afford only 2,400,000 labourers, and the remaining 8,000,000 of her population were precisely the number of the white population of the South.

I shall not here stop to comment on the greater efficiency of slave labour over free in producing subsistence for armies; nor upon our more fertile soil and more propitious skies. Enough has been said to show that the disparity between the sections was originally much less than was generally supposed, and it may be safely asserted that the South, as a slave country, has the greater capacity to endure long war. True, a slave country, though not easily exhausted, is easily invaded. The slave produces abundantly the supplies for war; but cannot be employed in local defence. He cannot be made a minute man; and those who would employ slave troops in our large armies have not yet had the hardihood to propose a slave militia. Yet, if they can be relied on to fight for the country on the frontier, assuredly they could be relied on to fight for their immediate homes. This bare suggestion, however, gives an air of absurdity to the whole scheme.

This triptych illustrates the theme of salvation, both spiritual and temporal. In the center panel, African Americans kneel and rejoice before the Bible. On the left, Lincoln holds the Emancipation Proclamation; while on the right, a Union soldier delivers the news about emancipation. **THE LIBRARY OF CONGRESS**

Fortunately, we are not yet reduced to extremity. Although our territory is more limited, supplies of food are more abundant than ever; our soldiers suffer from disease much less than formerly; acting chiefly on the defensive and behind works, they must suffer much smaller losses in battle than the enemy, and being in their own country and climate, must suffer also much less from disease; and this day, I repeat, the South is displaying more of original vigor than the North. If exhaustion approaches, its advance is too slow to be alarming: the period of its arrival cannot be calculated; while in the North, potentous signs indicate no distant catastrophe. At least, we are still strong enough to afford to watch and wait, without hazarding experiments on our military, social and political systems, that may precipitate present disaster and entail future woe.

Still our army must be increased. It has already been said that fully one-third of those now liable to military service are absent from the field. This source of supply must be made to yield its proper fruits. Though there have been many, too many, desertions, and this evil will continue more or less to exist, yet it has not been so great in our army as in that of the enemy. The majority of the number improperly out of service have never been brought into it. Congress must assist in applying a reme-

dy. New sanctions must be added to old laws, and new laws must be passed, for filling up the ranks. Above all, let appeals be made to the patriotism of the country—let a corrective be attempted from these halls, of that spirit of contempt for law—that lax obedience to authority—that slow and reluctant compliance with the behests of the legislative power, where those behests do not comport with individual ease or opinion—which, running down the whole official gamut, civil and military, from capital to camp, (with numerous exceptions, of course) accumulating abuses as it descends, paralyzes the fighting power of the country, and renders the law of the land too often a dead letter. Let every man, here or elsewhere, feel under obligation to point the finger of scorn at every one who shirks or skulks from his duty, at home or in the field; and especially at that officer, whoever he may be, who extends an unnecessary furlough to relative or favorite, or permits him to lie around his headquarters, or otherwise by his indulgence avoid the fight. As said in the beginning, much good may be done by free discussion here. Let us throw off the shackles of an over-caution as to criticism of men and measures; and freely confessing abuses, charge home the responsibility for their existence, and invite both Government and people to hear. It is a great mistake to suppose our people cannot bear the whole truth on every and any question, social,

In 1792, following the Colonial victory in the Revolutionary War, the new Congress passed a law banning African Americans from military service. This law was repealed seventy years later in the summer of 1862, during the Civil War, when the Militia Act was passed, allowing for the recruitment of African American men to the Union Army. The Act stipulated the black soldiers were to furnish their own clothing out of their pay of ten dollars per month, while white soldiers were to receive pay plus a clothing allowance. **THE LIBRARY OF CONGRESS**

political, military, and even diplomatic: and from our enemies there is no longer anything to be concealed. The strength of our armies, the number at home still liable to service, the extent of all our resources, the depth of every harbor, the navigable length of every river, the height of every mountain, the width of every plain, and almost the producing capacity of every acre, are already known to them; and it is to be hoped that none of these things are better known to them than to us. The particular mea-

sures of legislation which should be adopted to assist in the great work of bringing men to the field and keeping them there, it would be out of place now to discuss. Already other members have suggested, by bill or resolution, more than one salutary exactment.

But, sir, if all these calculations fail—if, as our despairing friends declare, we have approximated to final exhaustion, and must find some extraordinary source of re-inforcements—will negro troops answer the purpose—will the African save us? There is no moral, no pecuniary objection to employing them, if they can be made to serve the occasion. The question is not whether they have not been known to fight, but whether they can be relied on to fight successfully for us now in the present death grapple with our enemies. In what form of organization is it proposed to use them? It can hardly be designed to intermingle them in the same companies with our citizen soldiers; no one has yet had the audacity to propose that. Would it be safe to confide to negro troops so much of the line of battle as would be occupied by a regiment or a brigade—much less a division or a corps? And an entire lien so composed might by sudden flight or wholesale surrender involve the whole army in confusion and disaster. To surrender to them the duty of defending forts or outposts would be to place the keys of the situation in their hands. Then, but one alternative remains; it is to form them into companies and place these in alternation with white companies in the same regiments. The electric current of mutual confidence and devotion—the triumphant glance, the answering smile, the sympathetic cheer—no longer passes from company to company. The silence of distrust now broods along the line, which hesitates, halts, wavers, breaks, and the black troops fly—perhaps to the embraces of the enemy. Even victory itself would be robbed of its glory if shared with slaves. God grant that our noble army of martyrs may never have to drink of this cup!

That our army will be recruited so as to maintain at least its present strength—and probably with a large increase of its present numbers—cannot be doubted. But even without another recruit, at the present slow rate of decrease of its veteran force, it would long maintain a defence of the country; long enough to wear out the resources of the enemy. Do gentlemen see no signs of exhaustion at the North? Do they derive no hope from the consideration of financial disasters impending there? How long they can carry on an aggressive war under a debt whose annual interest already equals that of the debt of Great Britain, accumulated during centuries marked by expensive wars—a debt still accumulating at the rate of over two millions a day—cannot be precisely calculated; but the end is certain and near. The intelligent Northern mind is already grasping the great fact that the entire property of the South, less the slaves, if confiscated and sold tomorrow, would not pay their pre-

This photograph shows African American troops in front of General Grant and President Johnson as part of the Grand Review, 1865.
NATIONAL ARCHIVES AND RECORDS ADMINISTRATION

sent debt. The property of the thirteen Confederate States, exclusive of slaves, was, in 1860, estimated at about 4,000 millions of dollars, and the Northern debt, already audited, is about 2,500 millions. Allowing for the depreciation of values in the South, which would ensue on abolition and subjugation, it is obvious that our whole property would not discharge it. How long they may be able to put off the day of bankruptcy, when every hour but adds to the amount of Government obligations, which, with every hour, grow more worthless, and which soon must be valueless to hire even foreign mercenaries, cannot with certainty be foretold; but at least this can be said, and in the name of our brave army of citizen-soldiers I say it, that under such circumstances we can defend as long as they can strike.

This argument proceeds upon the presumption that the negro, whether slave or free, cannot be made a good soldier. The law of his race forbids it. Of all others the best adapted to slavery, he is therefore of all others, the least adapted for military service. Of great simplicity of disposition, tractable, prone to obedience, and highly imitative, he is easily drilled; but timid, averse to effort, without ambition, he has none of the higher qualities of the soldier. It is difficult to conceive a being less fit for plucking honor from the cannon's mouth. At the beginning of this war, he fled to the enemy to avoid work; his local attachment was not sufficient to retain him; now he remains to avoid military service in the Yankee army—his aversion to work being greater than his aversion to slavery, and only less than his aversion to war. Such is his character as it appears in history. It is not denied that, under the influence of revenge, of a desire for plunder, or other maddening or special excitement, he has been known to surrender himself to slaughter and to wade deep in blood; so in his native Africa, he surrenders himself a sacrifice to his gods; but history will be searched in vain to prove him a good soldier. In the revolution of 1776, Lord Dunmore proclaimed all the negroes of Virginia free, and invited them to join his standard; but less than three hundred accepted the invitation. They preferred slavery to military service. And in the battle he fought near Norfolk against the Virginia militia, we are informed by the historian (Botta) that his negro troops "behaved very shabbily and saved themselves by flight." In St. Domingo, the English, in 1793, with less than 1,000 men, captured several fortified places from the French authorities, who had over 20,000 troops, chiefly negroes and mulattoes; and finally, with less than 2,000 men, captured Port au Prince, the capital of the island. The

French, in extremity, offered freedom to the slaves, more than 400,000 in number, on condition of military service; but only 6,000 accepted the boon. Yet the hands of these slaves were still bloody with the massacres perpetrated in the memorable insurrection of 1790. Sir, on what motive is he to fight our battles? He is after all a human being, and acts upon motives. Will you offer him his freedom? The enemy will offer him his freedom, and also as a deserter, immunity from military service. Will you offer him the privilege of return home to his family, a freeman, after the war? That you dare not do, remembering it was the free negroes of St. Domingo, who had been trained to arms, that excited the insurrection of the slaves. And the enemy would meet even that offer with the promise of a return free to his southern home and the right of property in it. The amount of it all is, that in despair of achieving our independence with our own right arms, we turn for succor to the slave and implore him to establish our freedom and fix slavery upon himself, or at least upon his family and his race, forever. He, at least, after the expiration of his term of service, is to be banished to Liberia or other inhospitable shore, for the States could never permit an army of negroes to be returned home, either free or slave.

Sir, if the employment of negro troops should be attempted successfully, our army would soon contain only slaves. There are not less than 400,000 adult male slaves still in the Confederacy, physically capable of performing military service, and far less than this number of good troops would ensure our independence. If they will answer, the end is certain: they alone will be employed during the war, and as a standing army after peace. Promised their freedom for a certain term of service, as proposed by the President, they return free to their homes, or are deported; a new purchase or draft takes place to fill up the vacancies so occasioned; a continual drain is set up on the slave population at home to supply who army; the able-bodied are taken; the women and children, and the feeble, whose productive force is diminished one-third by the absence of the usual proportion of the able, are left an expense on the owner's hands; and ultimately the institution fails! Sir, this war is to be fought solely by white soldiers and black laborers, or white laborers and black soldiers: try to intermingle the two when you may, the attempt will fail; the strands will separate; when the negro enters the army the white soldier will leave it. He becomes the laborer—not reposing as a veteran upon his laurels—enjoying the repose of home after his long services: but the natural laborer of the country being absent in the military service, he supplies the place left void in the field; his labor must support himself, his family and the negro soldier. Sir, this scheme, if attempted, will end in rapid emancipation and colonization—colonization in the North by bringing up the slaves by regiments and brigades to the opportunity of escape to the enemy; emancipation and colo-

nization abroad to those who render service to us for a specified period. I argue on the presumption that nothing of the kind will be attempted without the consent of the States, whether as to employing them on the promise of freedom, or as to returning them free and disciplined to their old homes. By means of the power of impressment or purchase, this Government could not safely be permitted, without the consent of the States, to inaugurate a system of emancipation that might end in the abolition of the institution, nor do I suppose that the President designed the contrary. In suggesting freedom as the motive to be offered to the slave, he performed a simple official duty, leaving to Congress if it adopted the suggestion, to provide by law all the conditions it might be proper to impose.

In any aspect of the case, this is a proposition to subvert the labour system, the social system and the political system of our country. Better, far, to employ mercenaries from abroad, if dangerous and impracticable expedients are to be attempted, and preserve that institution which is not only the foundation of our wealth but the palladium of our liberties. Make the experiment, of course, with negro troops as the last means to prevent subjugation; but when we shall be reduced to the extremity of exclaiming to the slave, "help us, or we sink," it will already have become quite immaterial what course we pursue!

But if the experiment must be made, let him be used still as a slave, without promise of special reward. Let him be made to fight as he has been made to work, as a duty exacted under the authority of his owner. So he has been accustomed to live and move and have his being, and so he will continue to render any service with less reluctance and with less inquiry.

The resolution under consideration expresses the fullest faith in the will and the power of the citizen soldiers of the country, not only to make a successful defence against the armies of the North, and to establish our independence, but under all circumstances to protect the Rights of the States whenever and by whomsoever menaced. They rushed to arms to protect those rights before this Confederacy existed, and they will still protect them with their valour, their constancy and their endurance, even should it cease to exist. I know it has been said that already the exigencies of this war have turned this Government into a military despotism, that our independence, if achieved, cannot be permanently secured, except under some other form of Government, better adapted to develop the greatest possible war power of the country. The conscript acts, the impressment acts, the currency and tax laws, and indeed, all the strong measures of the Government, have been denounced as unconstitutional, or at least as an abuse of power. If those who entertain these views had charitably reversed the argument, and given Congress, the Chief Executive and the Courts of the country, who have passed or

In 1866, Congress authorized the formation of four black units, the Ninth and Tenth cavalry regiments and the Twenty-fourth and Twenty-fifth infantry, to be used primarily to protect settlers in the West. **U.S. SIGNAL CORPS**

approved these laws, due credit for ordinary patriotism and intelligence, and ordinary fidelity to their oaths of office, they might have reached the conclusion that, perhaps, these measures were consistent with this form of Government. If they be, then not only these acts themselves but their most happy effects in enabling us to make a glorious resistance to the superior forces and appliances of the invader, prove that we have a form of Government adapted to develop the greatest possible war power of the country. I admit it is a peace establishment in time of peace; but it is, nevertheless, a war establishment in time of war. Its rapid constitutional adaptation to these varying conditions, is one of the chief glories of its founders.

The original war powers possessed by the people of the several States, in their sovereign capacity—powers which embraced all the possible moral and physical forces of the country—have been transferred almost without limitation to the Confederate Government. Under the Constitution, it is authorized to raise and support armies, provide and maintain a navy, lay and collect taxes for the common defence, and to pay debt, regulate commerce, declare war, make rules for the government of the land and naval forces, provide for calling out the militia to suppress insurrection and repel invasion, impress private property for public uses on the payment of just compensation, coin money, suspend the writ of habeas

corpus, and make all laws necessary and proper to carry these powers into execution. But this is not all. At this very moment, when some charge that the Government has not only exhausted but transcended its constitutional war powers, the President recommends the passage of a law, in compliance with the express words of the Constitution, namely, to provide for organizing, arming, disciplining, and governing the militia of the States.

When it is added, that this Government has also the exclusive right to make peace, and no State can enter into any contract or agreement with another State, or with a foreign Power, it is, indeed, difficult to perceive what war power is absent. The people, intelligent, brave, faithful to their institutions, attached to their Government, looking to their own welfare, to their common security against insurrection and invasion, and to guard against the hazards of controversies between the States, have with profound design devolved all the responsibility of their foreign relations, including making war and contracting peace, upon this Government, and invested it with all the powers necessary to execute the delegated trusts. Not the Czar of Russia, not even Peter the Great, who was restrained by no traditions and alarmed by no fears, could have brought into the field so promptly and thoroughly the entire war power of that despotism, as this Government has brought out the war power of the several States in defence of the rights of the States. For this purpose, the

Following the Civil War, Congress approved the formation of all-black regiments to serve during peace time. Shown here are members of Troop H, 10th Cavalry, made up of freed slaves and Civil War veterans. The soldiers served on the frontier supporting the U.S. push westward and were dubbed the Buffalo Soldiers. **THE LIBRARY OF CONGRESS**

first gun fired at Fort Sumter summoned our citizens to arms; and they will be at all times ready to rush to the field in the same sacred cause. When the last man shall have sunk in his tracks—when the last steed shall have fallen beneath his rider—when the last morsel of food shall have vanished from the land—then, and not till then, will the war power of this Government be exhausted.

This Confederacy now exhibits to the world a spectacle instructive for the lovers of liberty in all future times—the spectacle of free institutions displaying the maximum war power possible in the number of its people. History will consider herself sufficiently accurate in asserting they rose as one man in defence of their rights, and shall be privileged to record that they endured till God crowned their efforts with success.

Complaints are made of the exercise of extreme power by the military authorities of the land. Let it be remembered that more than two thousand years ago it was proverbial that, "in the midst of arms the laws are silent." If we are repeating history, in many respects, in this particular at least, we are repeating it with some improvement. The laws are not wholly silent here. The civil authorities of the States still exercise control over persons not in the military service of the Confederate States; life and property are, in the main, secure; schools and churches are open, under exemptions granted by this Government; charitable associations flourish; mobs and riots are unknown, and woman is still every where honoured and protected.

Mr. Speaker, we are furnishing to history only another example of severe trial and heroic endurance for civil and political rights. Let us not delude ourselves with the belief that ours is a peculiar case, or that our heroism is unparalleled. If we endure what other people have been known to suffer in defence of their liberties and independence, our efforts will be crowned with success, as have been the efforts of other nations. Before our time nations have been exhausted far more than we are likely to be, of all their fighting population—of all their material resources—when struggling against superior numbers.

Before our time it was said:

The harvests of Arretium,
This year old men shall reap;
This year, young boys in Umbro
Shall plunge the struggling sheep;
And in the vats of Luna,
This year, the must shall foam
Round the white feet of laughing girls,
Whose sires have marched on Rome.

Let not him complain of our present condition who has heretofore rendered the homage of a glowing admiration to the achievements of those heroic nations who, in times past, have fought for life and liberty in the midst of civil horrors unknown to us: when laws were not only silent, but dead; and liberty and law were at last seen to rise together from the ashes of a people consumed in the fires of war. It will be sufficient for our cause if we equal the great deeds of the past.

Romans, in Rome's quarrel,
Spared neither land nor gold,
Nor son nor wife, nor limb nor life,
In the brave days of old.

PRIMARY SOURCE DOCUMENT

Excerpt from *Behind the Scenes* by Elizabeth Keckley

INTRODUCTION In her 1868 autobiography *Behind the Scenes*, Keckley discusses the activities of the Contraband Relief Association. In addition, she provides a portrait of what metropolitan life was like for a woman of color with powerful friends in the nation's capital on the eve of the Civil War.

Chapter VII

Washington in 1862–3. In the summer of 1862, freedmen began to flock into Washington from Maryland and Virginia. They came with a great hope in their hearts, and with all their worldly goods on their backs. Fresh from the bonds of slavery, fresh from the benighted regions of the plantation, they came to the Capital looking for liberty, and many of them not knowing it when they found it. Many good friends reached forth kind hands, but the North is not warm and impulsive. For one kind work spoken, two harsh ones were uttered; there was something repelling in the atmosphere, and the bright joyous dreams of freedom to the slave faded— were sadly altered, in the presence of that stern, practical mother, reality. Instead of flowery paths, days of perpetual sunshine, and bowers hanging with golden fruit, the road was rugged and full of thorns, the sunshine was eclipsed by shadows, and the mute appeals for help too often were answered by cold neglect. Poor dusky children of slavery, men and women of my own race—the transition from slavery to freedom was too sudden for you! The bright dreams were too rudely dispelled; you were not prepared for the new life that opened before you, and the great masses of the North learned to look upon your helplessness with indifference—learned to speak of you as an idle, dependent race. Reason should have prompted kinder thoughts. Charity is ever kind.

One fair summer evening I was walking the streets of Washington, accompanied by a friend, when a band of music was heard in the distance. We wondered what it could mean, and curiosity prompted us to find out its meaning. We quickened our steps, and discovered that it came from the house of Mrs. Farnham. The yard was bril-

liantly lighted, ladies and gentlemen were moving about, and the band was playing some of its sweetest airs. We approached the sentinel on duty at the gate, and asked what was going on. He told us that it was a festival given for the benefit of the sick and wounded soldiers in the city. This suggested an idea to me. If the white people can give festivals to raise funds for the relief of suffering soldiers, why should not the well-to-do colored people go to work to do something for the benefit of the suffering blacks? I could not rest. The thought was ever present with me, and the next Sunday I made a suggestion in the colored church, that a society of colored people be formed to labor for the benefit of the unfortunate freedmen. The idea proved popular, and in two weeks "the Contraband Relief Association" was organized, with forty working members.

In September of 1862, Mrs. Lincoln left Washington for New York, and requested me to follow her in a few days, and join her at the Metropolitan Hotel. I was glad of the opportunity to do so, for I thought that in New York I would be able to do something in the interests of our society. Armed with credentials, I took the train for New York, and went to the Metropolitan, where Mrs. Lincoln had secured accommodations for me. The next morning I told Mrs. Lincoln of my project; and she immediately headed my list with a subscription of $200. I circulated among the colored people, and got them thoroughly interested in the subject, when I was called to Boston by Mrs. Lincoln, who wished to visit her son Robert, attending college in that city. I met Mr. Wendell Phillips, and other Boston philanthropists, who gave all the assistance in their power. We held a mass meeting at the Colored Baptist Church, Rev. Mr. Grimes, in Boston, raised a sum of money, and organized there a branch society. The society was organized by Mrs. Grimes, wife of the pastor, assisted by Mrs. Martin, wife of Rev. Stella Martin. This branch of the main society, during the war, was able to send us over eighty large boxes of goods, contributed exclusively by the colored people of Boston. Returning to New York, we held a successful meeting at the Shiloh Church, Rev. Henry Highland Garnet, pastor. The Metropolitan Hotel, at that time as now, employed colored help. I suggested the object of my mission to Robert Thompson, Steward of the Hotel, who immediately raised quite a sum of money among the dining-room waiters. Mr. Frederick Douglass contributed $200, besides lecturing for us. Other prominent colored men sent in liberal contributions. From England a large quantity of stores was received. Mrs. Lincoln made frequent contributions, as also did the President. In 1863 I was re-elected President of the Association, which office I continue to hold.

For two years after Willie's death the White House was the scene of no fashionable display. The memory of the dead boy was duly respected. In some things Mrs. Lincoln was an altered woman. Sometimes, when in her room, with no one present but myself, the mere mention

Elizabeth Keckley, Dressmaker to Lincoln's Wife, and the Contraband Relief Association

While stories of hardship and degradation tend to dominate the discussion of African American history in the Civil War years, there were also many figures already integrated into society and leading vibrant lives.

Elizabeth Keckley (1818–1907), a Virginia-born slave, bought her freedom and moved to Washington, D.C. There she opened a dressmaking shop where she employed twenty girls and served the wives of the city's white elite. Introduced to Mary Todd Lincoln the day after the president's inauguration, Keckley became the first lady's dressmaker and close friend.

Early in the Civil War, Keckley began to argue that wealthy African Americans should assist black contrabands in the city. Keckley's story provides a counterpoint to the tales of whippings and escapes on the Underground Railroad. Though not a member of "society," Keckley interacted with a range of people at the highest levels of government, assisting social functions not simply as a servant, but as a trusted confidante and renowned figure.

of Willie's name would excite her emotion, and any trifling memento that recalled him would move her to tears. She could not bear to look upon his picture; and after his death she never crossed the threshold of the Guest's Room in which he died, or the Green Room in which he was embalmed. There was something super-natural in her dread of these things, and something that she could not explain. Tad's nature was the opposite of Willie's, and he was always regarded as his father's favorite child. His black eyes fairly sparkled with mischief.

The war progressed, fair fields had been stained with blood, thousands of brave men had fallen, and thousands of eyes were weeping for the fallen at home. There were desolate hearthstones in the South as well as in the North, and as the people of my race watched the sanguinary struggle, the ebb and flow of the tide of battle, they lifted their faces Zionward, as if they hoped to catch a glimpse of the Promised Land beyond the sulphureous clouds of smoke which shifted now and then but to reveal ghastly rows of new-made graves. Sometimes the very life of the nation seemed to tremble with the fierce shock of arms. In 1863 the Confederates were flushed with victory, and sometimes it looked as if the proud flag of the Union, the glorious old Stars and Stripes, must yield half its nationality to the tree-barred flag that floated grandly over long columns of gray. These were sad, anxious days to Mr. Lincoln, and those who saw the man in privacy only could tell how much he suffered. One day he came into the room where I was fitting a dress on Mrs. Lincoln. His step was slow and heavy, and his face sad. Like a tired child he threw himself upon a sofa, and shaded his eyes with his hands. He was a complete picture of dejection. Mrs. Lincoln, observing his troubled look, asked:

"Where have you been, father?"

"To the War Department," was the brief, almost sullen answer.

"Any news?"

"Yes, plenty of news, but no good news. It is dark, dark everywhere."

He reached forth one of his long arms, and took a small Bible from a stand near the head of the sofa, opened the pages of the holy book, and soon was absorbed in reading them. A quarter of an hour passed, and on glancing at the sofa the face of the President seemed more cheerful. The dejected look was gone, and the countenance was lighted up with new resolution and hope. The change was so marked that I could not but wonder at it, and wonder led to the desire to know what book of the Bible afforded so much comfort to the reader. Making the search for a missing article an excuse, I walked gently around the sofa, and looking into the open book, I discovered that Mr. Lincoln was reading that divine comforter, Job. He read with Christian eagerness, and the courage and hope that he derived from the inspired pages made him a new man. I almost imagined that I could hear the Lord speaking to him from out the whirlwind of battle: "Gird up thy loins now, like a man: I will demand of thee, and declare thou unto me." What a sublime picture was this! A ruler of a mighty nation going to the pages of the Bible with simple Christian earnestness for comfort and courage, and finding both in the darkest hours of a nation's calamity. Ponder it, O ye scoffers at God's Holy Word, and then hang your heads for very shame!

Frequent letters were received warning Mr. Lincoln of assassination, but he never gave a second thought to the mysterious warnings. The letters, however, sorely troubled his wife. She seemed to read impending danger in every rustling leaf, in every whisper of the wind.

"Where are you going now, father?" she would say to him, as she observed him putting on his overshoes and shawl.

"I am going over to the War Department, mother, to try and learn some news."

"But, father, you should not go out alone. You know you are surrounded with danger."

"All imagination. What does any one want to harm me for? Don't worry about me, mother, as if I were a little child, for no one is going to molest me;" and with a confident, unsuspecting air he would close the door behind him, descend the stairs, and pass out to his lonely walk.

For weeks, when trouble was anticipated, friends of the President would sleep in the White House to guard him from danger.

Robert would come home every few months, bringing new joy to the family circle. He was very anxious to quit school and enter the army, but the move was sternly opposed by his mother.

"We have lost one son, and his loss is as much as I can bear, without being called upon to make another sacrifice," she would say, when the subject was under discussion.

"But many a poor mother has given up all her sons," mildly suggested Mr. Lincoln, "and our son is not more dear to us than the sons of other people are to their mothers."

"That may be; but I cannot bear to have Robert exposed to danger. His services are not required in the field, and the sacrifice would be a needless one."

"The services of every man who loves his country are required in this war. You should take a liberal instead of a selfish view of the question, mother."

Argument at last prevailed, and permission was granted Robert to enter the army. With the rank of Captain and A. D. C. he went to the field, and remained in the army till the close of the war.

I well recollect a little incident that gave me a clearer insight into Robert's character. He was at home at the time the Tom Thumb combination was at Washington. The marriage of little Hop-o'-my-thumb—Charles Stratton—to Miss Warren created no little excitement in the world, and the people of Washington participated in the general curiosity. Some of Mrs. Lincoln's friends made her believe that it was the duty of Mrs. Lincoln to show some attention to the remarkable dwarfs. Tom Thumb had been caressed by royalty in the Old World, and why should not the wife of the President of his native country smile upon him also? Verily, duty is one of the greatest bug-bears in life. A hasty reception was arranged, and cards of invitation issued. I had dressed Mrs. Lincoln, and she was ready to go below and receive her guests, when Robert entered his mother's, room.

"You are at leisure this afternoon, are you not, Robert?"

"Yes, mother."

"Of course, then, you will dress and come down-stairs."

"No, mother, I do not propose to assist in entertaining Tom Thumb. My notions of duty, perhaps, are somewhat different from yours."

Robert had a lofty soul, and he could not stoop to all of the follies and absurdities of the ephemeral current of fashionable life.

Mrs. Lincoln's love for her husband sometimes prompted her to act very strangely. She was extremely jealous of him, and if a lady desired to court her displeasure, she could select no surer way to do it than to pay marked attention to the President. These little jealous freaks often were a source of perplexity to Mr. Lincoln. If it was a reception for which they were dressing, he would come into her room to conduct her down-stairs, and while pulling on his gloves ask, with merry twinkle in his eyes:

"Well, mother, who must I talk with to-night —shall it be Mrs. D.?"

"That deceitful woman! No, you shall not listen to her flattery."

"Well, then, what do you say to Miss C.? She is too young and handsome to practise deceit."

"Young and handsome, you call her! You should not judge beauty for me. No, she is in league with Mrs. D., and you shall not talk with her."

"Well, mother, I must talk with some one. Is there any one that you do not object to?" trying to button his glove, with a mock expression of gravity.

"I don't know as it is necessary that you should talk to anybody in particular. You know well enough, Mr. Lincoln, that I do not approve of your flirtations with silly women, just as if you were a beardless boy, fresh from school."

"But, mother, I insist that I must talk with somebody I can't stand around like a simpleton, and say nothing. If you will not tell me who I may talk with, please tell me who I may not talk with."

"There is Mrs. D. and Miss C. in particular. I detest them both. Mrs. B. also will come around you, but you need not listen to her flattery. These are the ones in particular."

This scene shows Abraham Lincoln, with members of his cabinet, reading a draft of the Emancipation Proclamation. Lincoln issued a preliminary draft of the Emancipation Proclamation on September 22 as a warning to the Confederacy. It became law on January 1, 1863. **THE LIBRARY OF CONGRESS**

"Very well, mother; now that we have settled the question to your satisfaction, we will go down-stairs;" and always with stately dignity, he proffered his arm and led the way.

PRIMARY SOURCE DOCUMENT

The Emancipation Proclamation

INTRODUCTION Following the Union victory at Antietam in September 1862, President Abraham Lincoln issued a preliminary draft of the Emancipation Proclamation. The final version was proclaimed and took effect on January 1, 1863. While the document represents a watershed moment in the history of the nation, it is important to note the cautious language used by the president as he took this step—one widely regarded as a political move of a war-time president, rather than as a great announcement of moral intent regarding the fate of Africans in the United States.

January 1, 1863, by the President of the United States of America

A Proclamation Whereas on the 22d day of September, A.D. 1862, a proclamation was issued by the President of the United States, containing, among other things, the following, to wit:

That on the 1st day of January, A.D. 1863, all persons held as slaves within any State or designated part of a State the people whereof shall then, be in rebellion against the United States shall be thenceforward, and forever free; and the executive government of the United States, including the military and naval authority thereof, will recognize and maintain the freedom of such persons and will do no act or acts to repress such persons, or any of them, in any efforts they may make for their actual freedom.

That the executive will on the 1st day of January aforesaid, by proclamation, designate the States and parts of States, if any, in which the people thereof, respectively, shall then be in rebellion against the United States; and the fact that any State or the people thereof shall on that day be in good faith represented in the Congress of the United States by members chosen thereto at elections wherein a majority of the qualified voters of such States shall have participated shall, in the absence of strong countervailing testimony, be deemed conclusive evidence that such State and the people thereof are not then in rebellion against the United States.

Now, therefore, I, Abraham Lincoln, President of the United States, by virtue of the power in me vested as Commander-in-Chief of the Army and Navy of the United

States in time of actual armed rebellion against the authority and government of the United States, and as a fit and necessary war measure for suppressing said rebellion, do, on this 1st day of January, A.D. 1863, and in accordance with my purpose so to do, publicly proclaimed for the full period of one hundred days from the first day above mentioned, order and designate as the States and parts of States wherein the people thereof, respectively, are this day in rebellion against the United States the following, to wit:

Arkansas, Texas, Louisiana (except the parishes of St. Bernard, Plaquemines, Jefferson, St. John, St. Charles, St. James, Ascension, Assumption, Terrebonne, Lafourche, St. Mary, St. Martin, and Orleans, including the city of New Orleans), Mississippi, Alabama, Florida, Georgia, South Carolina, North Carolina, and Virginia (except the forty-eight counties designated as West Virginia, and also the counties of Berkeley, Accomac, Northampton, Elizabeth City, York, Princess Anne, and Norfolk, including the cities of Norfolk and Portsmouth), and which excepted parts are for the present left precisely as if this proclamation were not issued.

And by virtue of the power and for the purpose aforesaid, I do order and declare that all persons held as slaves within said designated States and parts of States are, and henceforward shall be, free; and that the Executive Government of the United States, including the military and naval authorities thereof, will recognize and maintain the freedom of said persons.

And I hereby enjoin upon the people so declared to be free to abstain from all violence, unless in necessary self-defense; and I recommend to them that, in all cases when allowed, they labor faithfully for reasonable wages.

And I further declare and make known that such persons of suitable condition will be received into the armed service of the United States to garrison forts, positions, stations, and other places, and to man vessels of all sorts in said service.

And upon this act, sincerely believed to be an act of justice, warranted by the Constitution upon military necessity, I invoke the considerate judgment of mankind and the gracious favor of Almighty God.

Reconstruction

Reconstruction was to be the period in which the institution of slavery and its effects on African Americans and the nation could begin to be reversed. But the roots that ran below the surface of the slave institution ran deep.

Generations of Africans had been brought to the United States and had been stripped of their names and identities. And what if their names and identities had not been stripped away? Would it have made any difference? The story of the failed Reconstruction and the many difficult decades that followed is essentially the beginnings of the process of integration—an integration between peoples of African cultural origins and peoples from a hodgepodge of European backgrounds. Indeed, as we are just beginning at the start of the twenty-first century to live in a United States where these two cultures have had some extended history side by side, and where some of the difficult processes of integration have begun to be achieved, we are realizing the extent to which this meeting of two cultures is the story of America.

Most of the newly emancipated slaves did not have the wherewithal, the finances, or the skills to simply head out into the young nation. Many felt fortunate to stay on the plantations where they had been born and raised and to continue working there. Others headed north to such cities as New York, Boston, and Chicago. Others set out for the expanding West. In any case, just as African Americans had played a major role in the building of the East and the South over the course of the first century of American life, a new chapter was beginning in which black Americans would again be a part of battles to tame the land, fish the seas, and build up the cities. This has until even recently, however, not necessarily been the version of history told in the United States.

The decades that followed the close of the Civil War saw a fascinating and perversely complex weave of laws, mores, and social codes put in place to assure that African Americans continued to live an existence that

The Origin of Jim Crow

The term Jim Crow came into use prior to the Civil War when minstrel shows began featuring a character of the same name who would dance and sing in an unflattering fashion. The white performers who portrayed Jim Crow in blackface perpetuated stereotypes and unwittingly provided the name Jim Crow to a body of laws designed to discriminate against African Americans.

had far more in common with their recent bondage than with the inalienable rights to freedom and the pursuit of happiness described by the founding fathers. The second half of the nineteenth century would see the black codes and Jim Crow come to be the spoken—or unspoken—norms of African American life. It is a peculiar feature of the post-slavery years of the final decades of the nineteenth century that racism and discriminatory practices rather than diminishing, were taken to a new level. There is a sort of rage and hysteria that marks the phase of black-white relations that developed between 1870 and as late as the 1930s or 1940s. Perhaps it was a feature of the *institutional* nature of the former discrimination that made it, well, better, or at least not possessed with the kind of white-knuckled fear that grew in the post-Reconstruction years. It is no coincidence that the first Ku Klux Klan meetings were held in the decades immediately following emancipation. There was from the 1860s until far into the twentieth century a steadily increasing number of lynchings each year.

In Europe, the grand experiment of the Enlightenment had run into the roadblock of the French Revolution and the guillotine. With the French Revolution, the American fight for independence, and the writing of the U.S. Constitution, the world saw the birth of many of the democratic principles which are still promoted to this day. Thomas Jefferson and other leading intellectuals in the United States closely followed all of these developments. The world was being discovered and plundered; colonization was ever on the rise. Still, as distasteful as the European ideas of the "noble savage" were, in the writings of Jean-Jacques Rousseau there was ardent talk of the nobility of all beings. There were fervent, even sincere words to the effect that the Europeans had much to learn from these peoples of color. But within a few short years that kind of open expansiveness would be a distant memory. It was as if a new sort of hatred was about to be born. The crimes to date had been ones of greed, finan-

cial opportunity, a weakness of Christian character—but the new atmosphere would be one in which all innocence was lost. The sentiment expressed toward people of color—the savages, the blacks, the heretics—was evolving, becoming poisonous and tinged with fear.

Charles Darwin and his theories of natural selection both rocked the European world and put it on edge. Nationalism, colonialism, science—these were the pillars that the modernizing world was to be built upon. Before the close of the nineteenth century, scientist-sociologist-philosophers such as Georges Cuvier had composed treatises on the characteristics of a national identity based on a pseudoscience of skull and genital measurements. Joseph-Arthur de Gobineau published his tripartied system of the races in which he explained for the scholarly and scientific communities the inherent superiority of the white race, followed by the yellow race, and finally the black race at the bottom. Gobineau, as it turned out, was a favorite read for the German composer Richard Wagner, who in turn wrote extensively on the scourge of the "outsider" Jew in European society. The young Adolf Hitler consumed all of the above when formulating his theories for the "final solution" and a "cleansed" society free of blacks, Jews, and homosexuals.

Meanwhile in the United States, the Industrial Revolution and the great immigrant boom that fueled the building of an empire were just about to begin. In the year 1900, more than 90 percent of African Americans were still in eight southern states, the vast majority of those in the Deep South. In the three-and-a-half decades that followed the Civil War, life for black Americans had not changed from the conditions during slavery—rather, it had grown worse. It would take the Great Migrations out of the South to even get the ball rolling. ∎

Reconstruction and the Rise of Jim Crow

ADAPTED FROM ESSAYS BY MARCY SACKS,
ALBION COLLEGE/HAMILTON COLLEGE

On April 9, 1865, the Union general Ulysses S. Grant (1822–1885) accepted the Confederate general Robert E. Lee's (1807–1870) surrender at Appomattox Court House, Virginia. The four years of bloodshed during the United States Civil War marked the deadliest period of fighting in this country's history. By the time the North could claim victory, 620,000 men had been killed, more than that had been wounded, and physical devastation marked portions of the Southern landscape. And while the Northern economy had boomed during the conflict, the South's economic infrastructure was devastated by the war.

While Southern whites mourned their losses, blacks throughout the country rejoiced at the victory, believing that whites would, at long last, recognize them as equal citizens. Former slaves in the South appropriated their freedom in numerous ways, most notably through their physical mobility. "I must go," one newly freed slave explained to his former master, "for if I stay here I'll never know I am free." Others demonstrated their freedom by their refusal to work, by legalizing their marriages, and by shedding the outwardly submissive behavior they had been forced to adopt during the days of slavery. "There was to be no more Marster and Mistress now," a Richmond freedman joyously declared to his former master. "All the land belongs to the Yankees now and they gwine divide it out among de coloured people."

But the process of reconstructing the South was not so simple and proved less rewarding for the former slaves than they had hoped. The nation had no guidelines explaining how to bring the rebel states back into the Union, and almost everyone seemed to have a different opinion about the best way to do so.

In the end, a fundamental belief in the inalienable right to property and a lack of concern for black people led to few essential alterations in the nature of race relations in the South, a situation that was not to change until the Civil Rights movement of the twentieth century.

SEE PRIMARY SOURCE DOCUMENT *Excerpt from* The South *by J. T. Trowbridge*

PRESIDENTIAL RECONSTRUCTION

President Abraham Lincoln (1809–1865) had little opportunity to implement the reconstruction program he had devised during the war. While the fighting still raged, Lincoln outlined his "10 percent plan," which laid out the terms for readmitting the rebel states to the Union. Under this plan, Lincoln offered full pardon and amnesty to all Southerners (except high-ranking Confederate civil and military officers) who reestablished their allegiance to the United States by taking an oath of loyalty and by accepting the abolition of slavery. Confiscated property other than slaves would then be returned to those individuals. When the number of loyal Southerners in any state reached 10 percent of the number of votes cast there in the 1860 election, that minority could create a new state government and send representatives to the United States Congress. Conciliatory in his tone, Lincoln said little regarding the former slaves other than that they could not be returned to bondage.

Lincoln was shot by John Wilkes Booth (1838–1865) on April 14, 1865, only five days after Lee's surrender at Appomattox. Vice President Andrew Johnson (1808–1875), a former Democrat who had joined the Republicans only a year earlier, suddenly became president of a still-divided nation. For nearly eight months,

After the Civil War, the city of Charleston, South Carolina, was left in ruins. Scenes of devastation like this one were repeated throughout the South, which spent many years rebuilding its cities and towns in the years following the Civil War. Much that was destroyed was never reconstructed. **CORBIS-BETTMANN**

Johnson had complete control over reconstruction policy because Congress had already recessed for the summer. During that period, Johnson implemented a plan that initially appeared to strip the South's aristocrats of their wealth and power.

Following the outlines of Lincoln's program, Johnson offered amnesty to those who took an oath of allegiance. However, the new president barred officials of the Confederacy and the very wealthy (Southerners who aided the rebellion and who owned taxable property worth more than twenty thousand dollars) from receiving a pardon without direct application to Johnson himself. Johnson seemed bent on fundamentally altering the structure of Southern society.

But the president quickly changed his reconstruction policy. Under the provisional state governments set up by Johnson, members of the South's old elite reasserted their influence. Many won state and federal elections, returning them to positions of power. Furthermore,

There was a sharp increase in the number of white supremacist groups during the Reconstruction period. Their intent was to intimidate blacks and prevent them from participating fully as free citizens in the government. The tactics they used, however, frequently led to the death of the people they were harassing.

Johnson somewhat inexplicably began pardoning aristocrats and leading rebels, allowing them to take office.

As a result, by December 1865 many former Confederate officials had traveled to Washington to claim their newly acquired seats in Congress. But Radical Republicans in Congress, frustrated with both Lincoln's and Johnson's moderate policies, refused to seat their Southern counterparts or recognize the new state governments. Unlike either Lincoln or Johnson, the Radicals envisioned a new social order in the South emerging from the ruins of the war.

RADICAL RECONSTRUCTION

Even before Lincoln's death, Radical Republicans had pushed for a more complete reconstruction of Southern society. Led by Northerners such as Thaddeus Stevens (1792–1868) in the House of Representatives and Charles Sumner (1811–1874) in the Senate, Congress in early 1865 adopted the Thirteenth Amendment to the Constitution, which would abolish slavery throughout the United States. The states ratified the amendment that December. (The last state to do so, Mississippi, finally ratified the Thirteenth Amendment 130 years later in March of 1995.) In March of 1865, Congress established the Freedmen's Bureau, an agency of the army led by General Oliver O. Howard (1830–1909). Authorized to operate for one year, the bureau helped establish schools, legalize marriages of former slaves, negotiate labor con-

tracts for freed people, and distribute food to millions of people, white and black.

After Johnson's accession to office and the apparent return of the old Southern planter class to power, Radicals pushed even harder in their efforts to transform Southern society. By the time Congress met in December 1865, many Southern states had already established so-called black codes under the belief that the freed people would not work except by force. These laws, while recognizing the abolition of slavery, prohibited blacks from bearing arms, voting, holding public office, or assembling freely. Some states forbade blacks to work in skilled positions in which they would compete with white labor.

But the vagrancy provisions of the black codes proved to be the most offensive. The Georgia law, representative of similar statutes throughout the South, stipulated that any persons caught "wandering or strolling about in idleness, who are able to work and who have no property to support them" could be arrested and forced to labor on chain gangs or contracted out to planters. The black codes helped convince Republicans in Congress that under Johnson's reconstruction policy Southern society would remain much as it had been in the decades before the war.

Reconvening at the end of 1865, Congress took swift action to repudiate Johnson's policies. It began by refusing to seat the Southern representatives. Early the following year, Congress enacted a bill over President Johnson's veto extending the life and expanding the powers of the Freedmen's Bureau. It then quickly passed the first Civil Rights Act, also over the president's veto, which declared blacks to be citizens of the United States and empowered the federal government to intervene in state affairs in order to protect the rights of citizens.

Concerned about the constitutionality of the Civil Rights Act, Congress that summer approved the Fourteenth Amendment, which defined American citizenship for the first time. The first portion of the amendment identified "all persons born or naturalized in the United States" as citizens, and consequently entitled to equal protection under both state and federal laws. With this definition, Congress automatically extended citizenship privileges to American-born blacks. The second section of the amendment, while not granting blacks the vote, did penalize any state for withholding it from any of its adult male citizens. (This was the first time the Constitution had made reference to gender, quite clearly identifying suffrage rights as belonging solely to men.) Finally, the Fourteenth Amendment prohibited all Confederates who had taken an oath before the Civil War to uphold the Constitution from holding a federal or state office unless two-thirds of Congress voted to pardon them. The states finally ratified the Fourteenth Amendment in July 1868, two years after Congress initially approved it.

Blanche K. Bruce and Hiram Revels are pictured on either side of Frederick Douglass. Bruce and Revels, both from Mississippi, were the only two blacks to serve in the U.S. Senate during Reconstruction. The picture also features scenes of African American life and small portraits of other notables, such as Abraham Lincoln and John Brown. **CORBIS-BETTMANN**

Of the many pieces of legislation emerging from the Radical Congress, the First Reconstruction Act had the most dramatic impact on Southern political life. The congressional plan divided the South into five military districts under the direction of a military general. The general had the responsibility of calling a constitutional convention in each state. The delegates were to be elected by universal adult male suffrage, black and white, excluding those deprived of the vote under the proposed Fourteenth Amendment. Once a new state government had been established and had ratified the Fourteenth Amendment, it could petition Congress for readmission to the Union. Congress passed this act in 1867 over President Johnson's veto. By 1870, all of the Confederate states had been reconstructed.

IMPEACHMENT OF PRESIDENT JOHNSON
The Radical Congress and President Johnson continually clashed over their conflicting views of how to restore the Southern states to the Union. Mounting tensions ultimately resulted in an attempt to impeach the president. Despite his attempts to undermine Congress's reconstruc-

tion policies, no evidence existed to indicate that Johnson had ever committed "high crimes and misdemeanors"— the only constitutional grounds for impeachment.

Nonetheless, on February 24, 1868, the House voted for impeachment, 126 to 47. The trial before the Senate lasted for two months. At the end, the Radicals were one vote short of the two-thirds majority needed to remove the president. The impeachment campaign was dead.

THE REALITIES OF RECONSTRUCTION
In the meantime, the Southern states were adjusting to their new political and social realities. The passage of the First Reconstruction Act initiated an unprecedented era of biracial democracy. For the first time in United States history, the state governments in the South had been organized on the basis of universal male suffrage. Blacks and whites confronted the presence of black voters, officeholders, jurors, and police officers. In Alabama, Florida, South Carolina, Louisiana, and Mississippi, blacks were the majority of the state's voters. But only in South Carolina did black legislators outnumber whites. And no state elected a black person to be governor.

The period immediately following the Civil War was extraordinary in that African Americans from various states were elected to Congress. Two African Americans from Mississippi, Blanche K. Bruce and Hiram Rhoades Revels, were elected to the Senate during the nineteenth century. However, whites in government, in particular the conservative Democrats, responded with a determined campaign to win back the seats occupied by African Americans. Not until 1929, with the election of Oscar Stanton DePriest, was another African American elected to these high offices.

During the years following the Civil War, Mississippi led the way in devising legislative and openly discriminatory practices that would effectively disenfranchise black voters and circumvent the Fifteenth Amendment. Its numerous tactics, which included intimidation and violence, became known as "the Mississippi plan," and served as a model for other southern states that were anxious to preserve a governmental structure that excluded African Americans. So while the first decades of Reconstruction offered promise, it was not long before the "Mississippi plan" reversed the trend of political opportunity for African Americans.

Still, between 1869 and 1877, fourteen blacks won southern seats in the United States House of Representatives, and two (Hiram Revels [1827–1901] and Blanche K. Bruce [1841–1898] of Mississippi) in the United States Senate.

The new state governments made dramatic changes in Southern society. Starting essentially from scratch, many new state constitutions expanded democracy for blacks and whites by eliminating all property qualifications for voting and holding office. Blacks could finally sit on juries, and imprisonment for debt was abolished.

Most importantly, many Southern states provided state-funded public education for the first time. Seeking the education that had been legally denied them during slavery, blacks throughout the South clamored for the opportunity to learn. Black children flocked to the new schools; by 1877, more than six hundred thousand black pupils had enrolled. Night schools for adults flourished as well, and several colleges and universities, including Howard, Fisk, Atlanta, and the Hampton Institute, opened during this period.

Even in this new reformist atmosphere, however, Radical governments stopped short of fundamentally altering Southern society. Despite former slaves' demands for "forty acres and a mule," neither state legislatures nor Congress was willing to offer even a token payment to blacks for their years of unpaid labor.

THE END OF RECONSTRUCTION AND THE RISE OF JIM CROW

Even as the federal government was working to protect blacks' rights in the South, white supremacist organizations emerged to reassert whites' dominance and racial superiority. Members of the Ku Klux Klan, the Knights of the White Camellia, and other secret organizations terrorized blacks and their supporters throughout the South.

The so-called Mississippi plan (see sidebar) became a model for the effective overthrow of Republican government. Through the systematic use of violence and repression, Democrats regained control of the state in 1875. President Grant refused to provide assistance to protect Republican voters. Encouraged by the federal government's failure to act, other Southern states quickly followed Mississippi's example. Within ten years after it had begun, Reconstruction and the experiment in biracial democracy had ended.

Although the period of Radical Reconstruction came to a close in 1877 with the election of Rutherford B. Hayes (1822–1893) to the presidency, white southerners did not succeed in disfranchising blacks until the end of the century. Mississippi again led the way with a new state constitution in 1890 that formalized white rule. The other southern states all followed suit. Within twenty years, black voting throughout the South had virtually ceased.

Considering the horrors that were yet to come, with the age of Jim Crow, and the radical rise in lynchings in the South in the last decades of the nineteenth century and the first half of the twentieth century, it is worth asking whether a different course would have produced different results. Should the Federal Reconstruction government have left matters more in the hands of the southern states, or should they have worked harder to enforce the changes of Reconstruction in the years following 1875–1890? Should they have maintained the presence of marshals and federal troops in the South? Should they have resisted the efforts of the Conservative Democrats bent upon a political terrorism designed to retake the various houses of the Southern state legislatures? Even after decades had passed, the Conservative Democrats continued to organize with the same intensity. Well into the twentieth century, the same forces were undiminished in their racial rage. During the same period, Jim Crow laws legalized racial segregation in everything from education to public facilities to religion. In 1896 the United States Supreme Court upheld the "separate but equal" philosophy in *Plessy* v. *Ferguson.*

Most blacks in the South, now politically powerless, remained economically dependent as well. Few owned their own land; with each passing year they grew increasingly indebted to white landlords. And those who managed to achieve a level of economic success faced the daily threat of whites' wrath. In an effort to preserve their superiority and keep blacks "in their place," whites in the South enforced the color line with the use of physical violence. Between 1889 and 1941, an estimated 3,811 blacks were lynched in this country, often with thousands of white spectators cheering the event.

With the end of Reconstruction came the end of an era of tremendous promise. Blacks had envisioned a complete restructuring of southern society, in which they would have the chance to demonstrate their ability to act as respectable and educated citizens of the republic and thereby convince whites to abandon their racism. The restoration of white supremacy came with serious costs for the South: the escalation of tensions between whites and blacks, political and economic backwardness, and rampant illiteracy and poverty.

Nearly a century would pass before the South would again have the opportunity to make fundamental changes in its racial policies.

UNDERSTANDING RECONSTRUCTION–HISTORICAL INTERPRETATIONS

Almost before the period of Reconstruction came to an end, Southerners began interpreting this unprecedented time in American history. The impression that survived this era suggested that Reconstruction had been a "tragic" experience. Unscrupulous Northern white carpetbaggers, popular belief held, flooded the South to join poor white scalawags and ignorant and inferior blacks in a general ravishment of southern society. Nostalgia for the old South with its supposedly docile and happy slaves propelled this interpretation of history. The image of a prostrate South victimized by ineptitude and corruption passed into the nation's consciousness through movies and novels such as *The Birth of a Nation* and *Gone with the Wind.*

Historians quickly offered "proof" that Reconstruction had been a devastating time for the South. William A. Dunning became the most influential early historian to argue this position in his 1907 study *Reconstruction, Political and Economic.* Despite challenges to this interpretation, most notably by the eminent black scholar W. E. B. Du Bois (1868–1963) in *Black Reconstruction* (1935), Dunning's view remained generally accepted by both scholars and the public.

In the 1960s, however, new students of the period thoroughly revised our understanding of Reconstruction. While admitting that corruption did exist in some southern legislatures during the period, these historians pointed to the many reforms undertaken by Reconstruction governments. The efforts to make biracial democracy a success were their most outstanding achievements.

Despite the repression that followed Reconstruction, recent scholarship points to some of the lasting accomplishments of that period. Even in the face of Jim Crow legislation, blacks were no longer slaves. And they continued to assert their freedom and citizenship in countless ways. Historians will continue to explore this turbulent era in United States history as they seek to understand fully the meaning of freedom for black Americans.

SEE PRIMARY SOURCE DOCUMENT *Excerpt from* **The South since the War** *by Sidney Andrews*

BIBLIOGRAPHY

Ayers, Edward L. *The Promise of the New South: Life after Reconstruction.* New York: Oxford University Press, 1992.

Du Bois, W. E. B. *Black Reconstruction in America 1860–1880.* New York: Atheneum, 1935.

Foner, Eric. *Nothing but Freedom: Emancipation and Its Legacy.* Baton Rouge: LSU Press, 1983.

———. *Reconstruction: America's Unfinished Revolution, 1863–1877.* New York: Harper & Row, 1988.

———. *A Short History of Reconstruction.* New York: Harper & Row, 1990.

Holt, Thomas. *Black over White: Negro Political Leadership in South Carolina during Reconstruction.* Urbana: University of Illinois Press, 1977.

Litwack, Leon F. *Been in the Storm So Long: The Aftermath of Slavery.* New York: Knopf, 1979.

McMillen, Neil R. *Dark Journey: Black Mississippians in the Age of Jim Crow.* Urbana: University of Illinois Press, 1990.

Painter, Nell Irvin. *Exodusters: Black Migration to Kansas after Reconstruction.* New York: Knopf, 1976.

Rabinowitz, Howard N. *Race Relations in the Urban South, 1865–1890.* New York: Oxford University Press, 1978.

Rosengarten, Theodore. *All God's Dangers: The Life of Nate Shaw.* New York: Knopf, 1974.

Stampp, Kenneth M. *The Era of Reconstruction, 1865–1877.* New York: Vintage Books, 1965.

Williamson, Joel. *The Crucible of Race: Black-White Relations in the American South since Emancipation.* New York: Oxford University Press, 1984.

Woodward, C. Vann. *Origins of the New South, 1877–1913.* Baton Rouge: LSU Press, 1951.

———. *The Strange Career of Jim Crow.* New York: Oxford University Press, 1974.

PRIMARY SOURCE DOCUMENT

Excerpt from *The South* by J. T. Trowbridge

INTRODUCTION Traveling through the recently defeated South during the summer of 1865, John Trowbridge saw much that was discouraging. White Southerners remained defiant of federal reconstruction and eager to thwart the progress of emancipated slaves. Freed people themselves lived in conditions of poverty and neglect and under the constant threat of violence. The record of Trowbridge's travels, *The South*, published in 1866, did much to push the North toward the firmer policies of Radical Reconstruction.

In his travels, Trowbridge also found scenes of hope. In Hampton, Virginia, he visited a new settlement of freed people working to establish independent lives. In the chapter entitled "About Hampton," Trowbridge described their efforts.

Chapter XXIX.

About Hampton.

As it was my intention to visit some of the freedmen's settlements in the vicinity, the General kindly placed a horse at my disposal, and I took leave of him. A short gallop brought me to the village of Hampton, distant from the Fortress something over two miles.

"The village of Hampton," says a copy of the "Richmond Examiner" for 1861, "is beautifully situated on an arm of the sea setting in from the adjacent roadstead which bears its name. The late census showed that the aggregate white and black population was nearly two thousand." Some of the residences were of brick, erected at a heavy cost, and having large gardens, out-houses, and other valuable improvements. The oldest building, and the second oldest church in the State, was the Episcopal Church, made of imported brick, and surrounded by a cemetery of ancient graves. "Here repose the remains of many a cavalier and gentlemen, whose names are borne by numerous families all over the Southern States."

On the night of August 7th, 1861, the Rebels, under General Magruder, initiated what has been termed the "warfare against women and children and private property," which has marked the war of the Rebellion, by laying this old aristocratic town in ashes. It had been mostly abandoned by the secessionist inhabitants on its occupation by our troops, and only a few white families, with between one and two hundred negroes, remained. Many of the former residents came back with the Rebel troops and set fire to their own and their neighbors' houses. Less than a dozen buildings remained standing; the place being reduced to a wilderness of naked chimneys, burnt-out shells, and heaps of ashes.

I found it a thrifty village, occupied chiefly by freedmen. The former aristocratic residences had been replaced by negro huts. These were very generally built of split boards, called pales, overlapping each other like clapboards or shingles. There was an air of neatness and comfort about them which surprised me, no less than the rapidity with which they were constructed. One man had just completed his house. He told me that it took him a week to make the pales for it and bring them from the woods, and four days more to build it.

A sash-factory and blacksmith's shop, shoemakers' shops and stores, enlivened the streets. The business of the place was carried on chiefly by freedmen, many of whom were becoming wealthy, and paying heavy taxes to the government.

Every house had its wood-pile, poultry and pigs, and little garden devoted to corn and vegetables. Many a one had its stable and cow, and horse and cart. The village was surrounded by freedmen's farms, occupying the abandoned plantations of recent Rebels. The crops looked well, though the soil was said to be poor. Indeed, this was by far the thriftiest portion of Virginia I had seen.

In company with a gentleman who was in search of laborers, I made an extensive tour of these farms, anxious to see with my own eyes what the emancipated blacks were doing for themselves. I found no idleness anywhere. Happiness and industry were the universal rule. I conversed with many of the people, and heard their simple stories. They had but one trouble: the owners of the lands they occupied were coming back with their pardons and demanding the restoration of their estates. Here they had settled on abandoned Rebel lands, under the direction of the government, and with the government's pledge, given through its officers, and secured by act of Congress, that they should be protected in the use and enjoyment of those lands for a term of three years, each freedman occupying no more than forty acres, and paying an annual rent to government not exceeding six per cent. of their value. Here, under the shelter of that promise, they had built their little houses and established their humble homes. What was to become of them? On one estate of six hundred acres there was a thriving community of eight hundred freedmen. The owner had been pardoned unconditionally by the President, who, in his mercy to one class, seemed to forget what justice was due to another.

The terms which some of these returning Rebels proposed to the freedmen they found in possession of their lands, interested me. One man, whose estate was worth sixteen dollars an acre, offered to rent it to the families living on it for eight dollars an acre, provided that the houses, which they had themselves build, should revert to him at the end of the year.

My friend broke a bolt in his buggy, and we stopped at a blacksmith-shop to get another. While the smith, a

After the Civil War, African Americans were left homeless throughout the South. The Freedmen's Bureau was established to assist them to find jobs and also to help house, feed and clothe them. This illustration shows a member of the Freedmen's Bureau standing between armed groups of African Americans and Euro-Americans. **HARPER'S WEEKLY**

negro, was making a new bolt, and fitting it neatly to its place, I questioned him. He had a little lot of half an acre; upon which he had built his own house and shop and shed. He had a family, which he was supporting without any aid from the government. He was doing very well until the owner of the soil appeared, with the President's pardon, and orders to have his property restored to him. The land was worth twenty dollars an acre. He told the blacksmith that he could remain where he was, by paying twenty-four dollars a year rent for his half acre. "I am going to leave," said the poor man, quietly, and without uttering a complaint.

Except on the government farm, where old and infirm persons and orphan children were placed, I did not find anybody who was receiving aid from the government. Said one, "I have a family of seven children. Four are my own, and three are my brother's. I have twenty acres. I get no help from government, and do not want any as long as I can have land." I stopped at another little farm-house, beside which was a large pile of wood, and a still larger heap of unhusked corn, two farm wagons, a market wagon, and a pair of mules. The occupant of this place also had but twenty acres, and he was "getting rich."

"Has government helped you any this year?" I asked a young fellow we met on the road.

"Government helped me?" he retorted proudly. "No; I am helping government."

We stopped at a little cobbler's shop, the proprietor of which was supporting not only his own wife and children, but his aged mother and widowed sister. "Has government helped you any?" we inquired. "Nary lick in the world!" he replied, hammering away at his shoe.

Driving across a farm, we saw an old negro without legs hitching along on his stumps in a cornfield, pulling out grass between the rows, and making it up into bundles to sell. He hailed us, and wished to know if we wanted to buy any hay. He seemed delighted when my companion told him he would take all he had, at his own price. He said he froze his legs one winter when he was a slave, and had to have them taken off in consequence. Formerly he had received rations from the government, but now he was earning his own support, except what little he received from his friends.

It was very common to hear of families that were helping not only their own relatives, but others who had no such claim of kindred upon them. And here I may add that the account which these people gave of themselves was fully corroborated by officers of the government and others who knew them.

My friend did not succeed very well in obtaining laborers for his mills. The height of the freedmen's ambition was to have little homes of their own and to work for themselves. And who could blame this simple, strong instinct, since it was not only pointing them the way of their own prosperity, but serving also the needs of the country?

Notwithstanding the pending difficulty with the land-owners, those who had had their lots assigned them were going on to put up new houses, from which they might be driven at any day,—so great was their faith in the honor of the government which had already done so much for them.

Revisiting Virginia some months later, I learned that the Freedmen's Bureau had interposed to protect these people in their rights, showing that their faith had not been in vain.

PRIMARY SOURCE DOCUMENT

Excerpt from *The South since the War* by Sidney Andrews

INTRODUCTION The journalist Sidney Andrews was born in Massachusetts in 1834 and spent much of his youth in Dixon, Illinois. As a young man, he edited the *Daily Courier* in Alton, Illinois, where Elijah Lovejoy had once tried to set up an abolitionist press. Lovejoy's work ended when an angry mob of slavery advocates shot him. During the Civil War, Andrews moved to Washington, D.C., and began writing journalistic pieces under the pen name of Dixon.

In the fall of 1865, following the Confederate surrender, Andrews spent fourteen weeks traveling in the Carolinas and Georgia. His aim was to report on the progress of Reconstruction policies and on the various state conventions taking place in Southern states, and to provide a general picture of conditions and attitudes in the postwar South. His essays were published as they were written in the Chicago *Tribune* and the Boston *Advertiser,* and collected in the 1866 volume *The South since the War.*

Already in 1865, Andrews could see that President Andrew Johnson's leniency toward Southern rebels was frustrating Northern hopes for a thoroughgoing reconstruction of the region's economy and racial practices. In "The Situation with Respect to the Negro," Andrews detailed his conversations with a number of white Southerners whose racial attitudes boded ill for emancipated African Americans. The end of the essay suggests the coming racial violence that would be used everywhere in the South to keep freed people in submission.

Orangeburg C. H., September 9, 1865.
Recalling how persistently the whites of this State have claimed, for twenty-five years, to be the negro's special friends, and seeing, as the traveller does, how these whites treat this poor black, one cannot help praying that he may be saved from his friends in future. Yet this cannot be. Talk never so plausibly and eloquently as any one may of colonization or deportation, the inexorable fact remains, that the negro is in South Carolina, and must remain here till God pleases to call him away. The problem involved in his future must be met on the soil of which he is native; and any attempt to solve it elsewhere than in the house of these his so-called special friends will be futile.

The work of the North, in respect to South Carolina, is twofold: the white man must be taught what the negro's rights are, and the negro must be taught to wait patiently and wisely for the full recognition of those rights in his own old home. He waited so long in the house of bondage for the birthright of freedom, that waiting is weary work for him now; yet there is nothing else for him and us, — nothing but faith, and labor, and waiting, and, finally, rest in victory.

The city negro and the country negro are as much unlike as two races. So, too, the city white man and the country white man differ much from each other. The latter, however, is just what he chooses to be, while the country negro is just what slavery and his late owners have made him. Tell me what you will derogatory of the country negro, and very likely I shall assent to most of the language you use. He is very often, and perhaps generally, idle, vicious, improvident, negligent, and unfit to care well for his interests. In himself, he is a hard, coarse, unlovely fact, and no amount of idealizing can make him otherwise. Yet, for all that, he is worth quite as much as the average country white.

The negro, one may say, is made by his master. I even doubt if he is, in many cases, morally responsible for his acts. With him there is no theft when he takes small property from the white; there is, of course, crime in the eye of the law, but there is none in the design or consciousness of the negro. Has not every day of his existence taught him that robbery is no crime? So, too, if this uncouth freedman, just from the plantation, falls into a passion and half kills somebody, you will utterly fail in your effort to make him understand that he has committed a grave crime. Has not his whole life been witness of just such right and lawful outrage on humanity? This language may indicate a bad state of affairs; but it points out certain conditions with respect to the negro that must be taken into account by any one undertaking to deal with him as a freedman.

Everybody talks about the negro, at all hours of the day, and under all circumstances. One might in truth say — using the elegant language of opposition orators in Congress — that "the people have got nigger on the brain." Let conversation begin where it will, it ends with Sambo.

Life remained hard for African Americans after the Civil War was over and they had gained their freedom. Northerners devoured magazine stories and images of the defeated South in the years following the war. As time went on, however, many lost interest in the plight of black Southerners. **THE LIBRARY OF CONGRESS**

I scarcely talk with any white man who fails to tell me how anxious many of the negroes are to return to their old homes. In coming up from Charleston I heard of not less than eleven in this condition, and mention has been made to me here in Orangeburg of at least a score. The first curious circumstance is, that none of them are allowed to return; and the second is, that I can't find any of those desirous of returning. I presume I have asked over a hundred negroes here and in Charleston if they wanted to go back and live with their old masters as slaves, or if they knew any negro who did desire to return to that condition, and I have yet to find the first one who hesitates an instant in answering "No."

I spoke of this difficulty I have in finding a single negro who loved slavery better than he does freedom to an intelligent gentleman whom I met here last evening, — a member of the Rhett family. "I am surprised to hear that," said he; "but I suppose it's because you are from the North, and the negro don't dare to tell you his real feel-

ing." I asked if the blacks don't generally consider Northern men their friends. "O yes," he answered, "and that's the very reason why you can't find out what they think."

They deserve better treatment than they get at our hands in Orangeburg, at least; and I am told that what I see here is a forecast of what I shall see in all parts of the State. Theoretically, and in the intent of Congress, the Freedmen's Bureau stands as the next friend of the blacks; practically, and in the custom of the country, it appears to stand too often as their next enemy. That General Saxton is their good friend does not need to be asserted. Very likely the district commissioners under him are wise and humane men, and unquestionably the general regulations for the State are meant to secure justice to the freedmen.

The trouble arises from the fact that it is impossible for the State Commissioner or his chief deputies to personally know all, or even half, their various local agents. Take the case right in hand. Head-quarters for this dis-

Under Reconstruction, many whites, especially those who had been slaveholders, did not believe their former slaves could live without a master's care. In this illustration, a man seated with his family on his porch says to an African American man, "My boy—we've toiled and taken care of you long enough—now you've got to work!" **THE LIBRARY OF CONGRESS**

trict are thirty miles below here; and the ranking officer of the bureau has, probably, agents in at least forty different towns, the majority of whom are doubtless lieutenants from the volunteer forces of the army. They are detailed for this duty by the military commander of the post or the district, — sometimes after consultation with the district commissioner, but quite generally without. As the post garrisons are constantly changing, there may be a new agent of the bureau once a month in each town of the district; and I need not add, that the probabilities are that half the aggregate number on duty at any given time are wholly unfit for the work intrusted to them.

Again, take the case right in hand. The acting agent here at present is a lieutenant from a New York regiment. He is detailed by the colonel commanding, and has been on duty several weeks. Yet he never has seen the district commissioner of the bureau. His duties are to examine, and approve or disapprove, all contracts between the planters and the negroes, and to hear and determine all cases of complaint or grievance arising between the negroes themselves, or between the whites and the negroes. He treats me courteously, but he has no sympathy with the poor and lowly; and his ideas of justice are of the bar-room order, — might makes right. He doesn't really intend to outrage the rights of the negroes, but he has very little idea that they have any rights except such as the planters choose to give them. His position, of course, is a difficult one; and he brings to it a head more or less muddled with liquor, a rough and coarse manner, a dictatorial and impatient temper, a most remarkable ability for cursing, and a hearty contempt for "the whole d—n pack o' niggers." I speak from the observation of a good deal of time spent in and around his office.

I found Charleston full of country negroes. Whites of all classes concur in saying that there is a general impression throughout the back districts that lands are to be given the freed people on the sea-coast; and this, I am told, renders them uneasy and unreliable as plantation hands. Whites of all classes also concur in saying that they will not work.

"I lost sixteen niggers," said a Charleston gentleman; "but I don't mind it, for they were always a nuisance, and you'll find them so in less than a year." I asked, as usual, what they are now doing. Two or three of the men went into the army, one of the women had gone North as a cook, another is chambermaid on a steamer, and he found three of the men at work on one wharf the other day. "But," said I, laughing, "I thought the free negro would n't work." "O well, this is only a temporary state of affairs, and they'll all be idle before winter; and I don't look for nothing else when cold weather comes but to have them all asking me to take them back; but I sha'n't do it. I would n't give ten cents apiece for them."

Many of the private soldiers on duty here tell me that the planters generally overreach the negroes on every possible occasion; and my observation among such as I have seen in town tends to confirm this assertion to a considerable extent.

Coming up in the ears from Charleston I had for seatmate part of the way one of the delegates to the Convention which meets at Columbia next week. He was a very courteous and agreeable gentleman, past middle age, and late the owner of twenty-two negroes. He was good enough to instruct me at some length in respect to the character of the negro. "You Northern people are utterly mistaken in supposing anything can be done with these negroes in a free condition. They can't be governed except with the whip. Now on my plantation there was n't much whipping, say once a fortnight; but the negroes knew they would be whipped if they did n't behave themselves, and the fear of the lash kept them in good order." He went on to explain what a good home they always had; laying stress on the fact that they never were obliged to think for themselves, but were always tenderly cared for, both in health and sickness; "and yet these niggers all left me the day after the Federals got into Charleston!" I asked where they now are; and he replied that he had n't seen anybody but his old cook since they ran away; but he believed they were all at work except two, who had died. Yet I am told constantly that these ungrateful wretches, the negroes, cannot possibly live as free people.

Yesterday morning while I sat in the office of the agent of the Freedmen's Bureau there came in, with a score of other men, a planter living in this district, but some sixteen miles from town. He had a woful tale of an assault upon himself by one of his "niggers," — "a boy who I broughten up, and who's allers had a good home down ter my place." While the boy was coming in from the street the man turned to me and explained, "It never don't do no good to show favor to a nigger, for they's the most ongratefullest creeturs in the world." The dreadful assault consisted in throwing a hatchet at the white man by one of a crowd of negroes who were having a dispute among themselves, and suddenly discovered, in the early evening, somebody sneaking along by the fence. The boy said it was n't a hatchet, but a bit of brick; and added, that the man was so far away that no one could tell whether he was white or black, and that he did n't throw the brick till after he called out and told the man to go away. I followed the negro out after he had received his lecture from the officer, and had some talk with him. "D—n him," said he, referring to his employer, "he never done nufin all his d—n life but beat me and kick me and knock me down; an' I hopes I git eben with him some day."

Riding with an ex-Confederate major, we stopped at a house for water. The owner of the property, which was a very handsome one, was absent; and it was in charge of a dozen negroes, former slaves of the proprietor.

"Now here," said the late officer, "here is a place where the negroes always had the pleasantest sort of a home, — everything to eat and drink and wear, and a most kind master and mistress."

Pompey, aged about twelve, came to bring us the water.

"Pompey," said the Major, "Pompey, how do you like your freedom?"

He hung his head, and answered, "Dun know, mawssa."

"O, well, speak right out; don't be afraid; tell us just how it is now," said he again.

Whereupon Pompey: "Likes to be free man, sah; but we 's all workin' on yer like we did afore."

"That's right, Pompey," said I; "keep on working; don't be a lazy boy."

"It won't do," said the Major; "he'll grow up idle and impudent and worthless, like all the rest."

"No, sah," answered Pompey, "I 's free nigger now, and I 's goin' to work."

There is much talk among the country people about a rising of the blacks. A planter who stopped here last night, and who lives twelve miles to the west, told me that it was believed in his neighborhood that they had guns and pistols hid in the timber, and were organizing to use them. His ideas were not very clear about the matter; but he appeared to think they would make serious trouble after the crops are gathered. Another man, living in Union district, told the company, with evident pleasure, that they 'd been able to keep control of the niggers up to his section till 'bout three weeks ago; he 'lowed thar 'd bin some lickin', but no more 'n was good fur the fellows. Now the Federals had come in, and the negroes were in a state of glad excitement, and everybody feared there would be bloody business right away.

A thing that much shocks me is the prevalent indifference to the negro's fate and life. It is a sad, but solemn fact, that three fourths of the native whites consider him a nuisance, and would gladly be rid of his presence, even at the expense of his existence. And this is face of the fact that all the planters are complaining about the insufficiency of labor. Thus, in Charleston, a merchant told me, with relishing detail, a story to the effect that, soon after the promulgation of the order against wearing Confederate buttons, a negro soldier doing duty in the city halted a young man, informed him of the regulations, and told him that if he was seen on the street again wearing the obnoxious buttons, he would probably be arrested; whereupon the hopeful scion of the Charleston aristocracy whipped out a large knife, seized the negro by the beard, and cut his throat. The soldier died in about a week; but nothing had been done with the man who killed him. So, too, a man who seems to be acting as stage-agent here says "a d—d big black buck nigger" was shot near Lewisville about three weeks ago; and the citizens all shield the man who shot him, and sanction his course. All the talk of men about the hotel indicates that it is held to be an evidence of smartness, rather than otherwise, to kill a freedman; and I have not found a man here who seems to believe that it is a sin against Divine law.

African Americans in Political Office

ADAPTED FROM ESSAYS BY ADAM GREEN, YALE UNIVERSITY

Significant African American participation in electoral politics did not begin until after the Civil War. Inspired by federal emancipation (1863–1865), constitutional reform (1865–1870), and Reconstruction (1863–1877), blacks in the South consolidated newly recognized vot-

Black members of Congress are depicted in this Currier and Ives lithograph. Seated from left to right are Hiram Revels (Mississippi), Benjamin S. Turner (Alabama), Josiah T. Walls (Florida), Joseph H. Rainey (South Carolina), and Robert Brown Elliott (South Carolina). Standing behind them from left to right are Robert De Large (South Carolina) and Jefferson H. Long (Georgia). **THE LIBRARY OF CONGRESS**

ing rights into a strong network of political leaders sponsored by the Republican party. These elements point out a critical rule of black electoral politics, then and now: participation in government depends on the extent to which African Americans' right to vote is respected by others and exercised by blacks themselves.

BLACK POLITICS DURING RECONSTRUCTION

Because most southern white men were disqualified from voting due to their participation in the Confederate rebellion (women could not vote anywhere in the United States prior to 1920) southern black voters worked to elect their share of representatives. The first African American to serve in Congress, Senator Hiram Revels of Mississippi (1870–1871), had been a minister and local alderman before being nominated to serve an abbreviated term in Washington. Revels exerted influence on the Senate floor, speaking out against nullification of black voting rights in Georgia and advocating integrated public education in Washington, D.C. Four years later, his fellow Mississippian Blanche Bruce began a full term in the Senate (1875–1881).

In the House of Representatives, blacks enjoyed greater success: twenty were elected between 1870 and 1901, with South Carolina alone sending seven. Several of these leaders were especially noteworthy. Robert Smalls of South Carolina, a former slave and Union navy hero, represented Beaufort County in Congress from 1875 to 1889. Robert Brown Elliott, also from South Carolina, held the seat (1871–1875) once occupied by the notorious proslavery congressman Preston Brooks. Elliott supported the 1874 civil rights bill with one of the most eloquent speeches of the Reconstruction era, delivered on January 6, 1874. John Lynch of Mississippi went from serving as speaker of the state legislature to joining Congress in 1872—all before his twenty-seventh birthday. After departing Congress in 1882, Lynch chaired the Mississippi Republican party until 1892.

Black congressmen spent most of their time protecting the rights of newly freed slaves and promoting equitable redevelopment in the war-torn South. Ironically, another duty was championing the political rights of ex-Confederates: each congressman sponsored numerous petitions of loyalty to the Union from Southern veterans seeking to regain voting privileges. Unfortunately, the former rebels rarely reciprocated with similar faith in their sponsors: Georgia's Jefferson Long (1871) and South Carolina's Robert DeLarge (1871–1873) were unable to serve out full terms in Congress due to trumped-up misconduct charges brought by white rivals. In Louisiana, J. Willis Menard (1869) and P.B.S. Pinchback (1873) were unable even to take their seats as a result of white opposition.

At state and local levels as well, African Americans made gains during the Reconstruction years. Nearly eight hundred blacks were elected to state and local office between 1869 and 1901. The base from which black politicians drew their strength was the expanded number of black voters and the determination with which those voters exercised their right. Beaufort County, South Carolina, for example, was able to send Robert Smalls to Congress for seven consecutive terms because black voters outnumbered whites by seven to one; even the return of voting rights to former Confederates did not initially challenge Smalls's majority. The Republican party, home to all black politicians, also embraced Thaddeus Stevens, Charles Sumner, and other white architects of Reconstruction policies. This meant that blacks looked to the party to help guarantee franchise rights. Former Confederates, made livid by the new multiracial politics, resolved to strip away the political rights of blacks and regain supremacy.

SEE PRIMARY SOURCE DOCUMENT *Senator Blanche K. Bruce, Senator from Mississippi, and the Fifteenth Amendment*

THE DISENFRANCHISEMENT OF SOUTHERN BLACK VOTERS

Prior to the end of Reconstruction in 1876, blacks saw the fragile supports upon which their voting rights rested beginning to crumble. In 1872, Congress, over vehement objection by black congressmen, passed the Amnesty Act, softening loyalty tests for Confederate veterans and accelerating their reentry into the electorate. Vigilante groups such as the Ku Klux Klan intimidated black voters throughout the South. Massacres of blacks occurred in Grant Parish, Louisiana (1873), Yazoo City, Mississippi (1875), and Hamburg, South Carolina (1876), with countless beatings and murders occurring elsewhere in the South.

After the decision of President Rutherford B. Hayes in 1877 to remove federal troops from the South, African Americans were left to cope with what southern whites called "redemption" alone. Black disenfranchisement was not complete until the turn of the century; occasionally, black politicians won elections and held office. But with the exit of George H. White from Congress in 1901, black representation in the South entered a period of dormancy extending to the 1960s.

DISENFRANCHISEMENT AND THE MIGRATION NORTH

Disenfranchisement was a significant factor encouraging African Americans to migrate to major cities in the North. By the late nineteenth century, while voting rights were being stripped in the South, blacks were being recognized as voters in the North. With the growth of machine politics in the Democratic and Republican parties in cities such as Chicago, New York, Philadelphia, and Cleveland, it fast became apparent that black voters, although not an outright majority as they had been in portions of the South, were still an important constituency to be courted. As the so-called Great Migration (1916–1930) increased the number of blacks in the North, the significance of their votes and the extent of their representation also grew.

A good example of these developments is Chicago, site of the strongest black political network to the present day. Several African Americans served in state and city office during the migration years: Oscar DePriest, elected alderman in 1915, moved up to Congress in 1928, the first African American to do so in over a generation. Like Reconstruction black politicians, DePriest was a Republican, closely allied to the white mayor, William Thompson.

DePriest was unseated by a black Democratic challenger, Arthur Mitchell, in 1934, a development heralding the shift of northern black voters from the Republicans to the Democratic party. In 1942, William L. Dawson, a recent Democratic convert, was elected to replace Mitchell. Dawson served nearly thirty years, becoming the quintessential "insider" in local and national Democratic politics. Illinois's First Congressional District seat has remained in African American hands since Dawson's death—the current officeholder is Bobby Rush, former deputy defense minister in the Illinois Black Panther party—making it the longest-held federal post in black history.

Other northern black enclaves were established in local politics during the migration years: Cleveland voters, for example, had elected three blacks to the city council by 1930. But frustration with the sponsorship and supervision of white urban machines, as well as an inability to duplicate DePriest's election to Congress anywhere else before World War II, inspired blacks to map out a different course from that taken in Chicago.

The line of African American citizens registering to vote stretches outside Antioch Baptist Church, 1948. **THE LIBRARY OF CONGRESS**

Adam Clayton Powell Jr.'s rise in Harlem politics, culminating in his election to Congress in 1944, typified the more independent spirit of black politics. Although Powell ran as a Democrat, throughout his long career he challenged party authority, defining his base not as Democratic voters but instead all citizens of Harlem. Powell's outspokenness (he is often credited with originating the slogan "black power") made him a highly visible target. Despite his status as a House committee chairman, fellow congressmen barred him from his seat in 1967, just as they had barred J. Willis Menard a century earlier. Several other black representatives of this period proved eager to take stands for social justice: Augustus Hawkins, Charles Diggs, and Robert Nix were all strong supporters of job creation and civil rights bills during the 1960s.

SEE PRIMARY SOURCE DOCUMENT *Thurgood Marshall's Speech before the NAACP Wartime Conference*

THE VOTING RIGHTS MOVEMENT
Although the civil rights movement is remembered mainly for overturning Jim Crow segregation, restoration of franchise rights in the South was its primary accomplishment. With passage of the Voting Rights Act of 1965, African Americans in the South matched northern political efforts of the previous decades and renewed the Reconstruction dream of self-determination. Independent political parties were initiated, such as the Mississippi Freedom Democratic party led by Fannie Lou Hamer in 1964 and the Black Panther party in Lowndes County, Alabama, in 1966.

The number of black elected officials grew nationwide from 103 in 1964 to 3,503 in 1975: many of these were county supervisors, mayors, and sheriffs in the South. By 1973, southern black representation in Congress was once again a reality, with Barbara Jordan and Andrew Young elected respectively from Texas and Georgia. It would be another sixteen years before an African American, Douglas Wilder, would serve again as the governor of a southern state—in this case, Virginia.

RECENT TRENDS IN BLACK POLITICS
In recent decades, there have been two notable developments in African American political representation. The first is the growth of the number of African American mayors since the late 1960s. The pioneering elections of Carl Stokes in Cleveland (1967), Coleman Young in Detroit (1973), and Maynard Jackson in Atlanta (1973) have been followed by more triumphs: six of the ten largest American cities have elected black mayors. Perhaps the most notable triumph to date was the successful grassroots campaigns of Chicago's Harold Washington

in 1983 and 1987, seen as a stunning rejection of the "clientage" politics practiced locally by Congressman Dawson and other black officials in the decades before.

The second development is the expansion of the black congressional delegation into a bloc wielding considerable power. More than thirty African Americans have made up the Congressional Black Caucus since the 1992 election, and members of the House such as Maxine Waters, Kwesi Mfume, Carrie Meek, and John Conyers have helped the group exert substantial influence on such recent national concerns as U.S.–Haitian relations, federal crime policy, and the growing affirmative-action debate. There is no similar voting bloc in the Senate; Carol Mosley Braun of Illinois served from 1993 to 1999 as the first African American woman senator, and was the sole black member of the Senate at the time.

In 1993, there were more than 8,000 black elected officials: 571 in state and national offices, 4,825 in city and county positions, 923 in law enforcement, and 1,694 in education. Given uncertainty about renewal of the Voting Rights Act in the current Congress, as well as reduced turnout of black voters in recent years, it is unclear whether this figure will continue to rise at it has in the past three decades since the Voting Rights Act was passed.

BIBLIOGRAPHY

Bush, Rod, ed. *The New Black Vote: Politics and Power in Four American Cities.* San Francisco: Synthesis Publications, 1984.

Chisholm, Shirley. *Unbought and Unbossed.* Boston: Houghton Mifflin, 1970.

Christopher, Maurine. *Black Americans in Congress.* New York: Thomas Y. Crowell, 1976.

Dymally, Mervyn M., ed. *The Black Politician: His Struggle for Power.* Belmont: Duxbury Press, 1971.

Frye, Hardy T. *Black Parties and Political Power: A Case Study.* Boston: G.K. Hall, 1980.

Hamilton, Charles V. *Adam Clayton Powell: The Political Biography of an American Dilemma.* New York: Antheneum, 1991.

Holden, Matthew, Jr. *The Politics of the Black "Nation".* New York: Intext Press, 1973.

Powell, Adam Clayton, Jr. *Adam by Adam.* New York: Dial Press, 1971.

Rivlin, Gary. *Fire on the Prairie: Chicago's Harold Washington and the Politics of Race.* New York: Henry Holt, 1992.

Stokes, Carl B. *Promises of Power: A Political Autobiography.* New York: Simon & Schuster, 1973.

Travis, Dempsey. *An Autobiography of Black Politics.* Chicago: Urban Research Press, 1987.

Walter, John. *The Harlem Fox: J. Raymond Jones and Tammany, 1920–1970.* Albany: SUNY Press, 1989.

Watter, Pat, and Reese Cleghorn, eds. *Climbing Jacob's Ladder: The Arrival of Negroes in Southern Politics.* New York: Harcourt, Brace & World, 1967.

Wilson, James Q. *Negro Politics: The Search for Leadership.* Glencoe: Free Press, 1960.

Senator Blanche K. Bruce, Senator from Mississippi, and the Fifteenth Amendment

INTRODUCTION The election of a black senator from a state in the Deep South fueled the fires that gave birth to the "Mississippi plan." Senator Blanche K. Bruce of Mississippi rose in the U.S. Senate on March 31, 1876, to urge his fellow senators to preserve the Constitutional rights of black citizens in Mississippi, reminding them of the service African Americans had given the nation in its various wars. The original language of the Fifteenth Amendment to the Constitution, adopted in 1870, appears below. Some historians have pointed to the remarkably terse and non-specific language of the document as an indication that perhaps the amendment was more of an invitation for the matter to be pursued in subsequent legislation (note Section 2), than any kind of clearly spelled-out guarantee of voting rights for African Americans.

Amendment XV

[Adopted 1870]

Section 1 The right of citizens of the United States to vote shall not be denied or abridged by the United States or by any State on account of race, color, or previous condition of servitude.

Section 2 The Congress shall have power to enforce this article by appropriate legislation.

Thurgood Marshall's Speech before the NAACP Wartime Conference

INTRODUCTION In the summer of 1944, Thurgood Marshall, at that time director of the NAACP Legal Defense Fund, had just won another battle in the case of *Smith* v. *Allwright* and was in the process of mounting an attack on the restrictive housing covenants, which would lead to the landmark 1948 *Shelley* v. *Kraemer* decision. On July 13, Marshall gave the following address to the NAACP Wartime Conference. His purpose was to describe the legal approach to remedying the "problems facing us today," problems that other speakers at the Conference had already addressed. Marshall began by listing the various protections afforded by the Thirteenth, Fourteenth, and Fifteenth Amendments as well as the Federal Civil Rights statute, along with the criminal penalties stipulated for violation of these laws. Marshall pointed out that prosecutors and judges in the South refused to honor either the letter or the spirit of these laws, designed essentially to make the rights and responsibilities of the two races the same.

Speech on Securing Civil Rights

The Legal Attack to Secure Civil Rights, by Thurgood Marshall

On last night we heard a clear statement of some of the problems facing us today. My job tonight is to point out a part of the general program to secure full citizenship rights.

Thurgood Marshall (1908–1993), Father of African American Legislative Rights

As the United States exited the nineteenth century, no case had a greater effect on the lives and rights of black Americans than the case of *Plessy* v. *Ferguson*. The Supreme Court's infamous ruling of "separate but equal" effectively extended the grasp of Jim Crow, the black codes, and even slavery out into a modern, industrialized America. Put simply, the disabling of this racist legislation can be largely attributed to one man: Thurgood Marshall. The segregation situation did not begin to improve until the 1930s, when labor movement lawyers and the Legal Defense Fund of the National Association for the Advancement of Colored People (NAACP), with Marshall's help, began to act on the offensive against racist Jim Crow laws. Marshall headed up this organization, mounting case after case challenging the legal underpinnings of racial injustice. It is likely no coincidence that the first African American elected to Congress since Reconstruction, Oscar Stanton DePriest, was elected at this same time. Marshall in effect spearheaded the turnaround of Jim Crow segregated America.

This effort would continue throughout Marshall's lifetime and culminate in his appointment to the Supreme Court.

The struggle for full citizenship rights can be speeded by enforcement of existing statutory provisions protecting our civil rights. The attack on discrimination by use of legal machinery has only scratched the surface. An understanding of the existing statutes protecting our civil rights is necessary if we are to work toward enforcement of these statutes.

The titles "civil rights" and "civil liberties" have grown to include large numbers of subjects, some of which are properly included under these titles and others which should not be included. One legal treatise has defined the subject of civil rights as follows: "In its broadest sense, the term civil rights includes those rights which are the outgrowth of civilization, the existence and exercise of which necessarily follow from the rights that repose in the subjects of a country exercising self-government."

The Fourteenth and Fifteenth Amendments to the Constitution are prohibitions against action by the states and state officers violating civil rights. In addition to these provisions of the United States Constitution and a few others, there are several statutes of the United States which also attempt to protect the rights of individual citizens against private persons as well as public officers. Whether these provisions are included under the title of "civil rights" or "civil liberties" or any other subject is more or less unimportant as long as we bear in mind the provisions themselves.

All of the statutes, both federal and state, which protect the individual rights of Americans are important to Negroes as well as other citizens. Many of these provisions, however, are of peculiar significance to Negroes because of the fact that in many instances these statutes are the only protection to which Negroes can look for redress. It should also be pointed out that many officials of both state and federal governments are reluctant to protect the rights of Negroes. It is often difficult to enforce our rights when they are perfectly clear. It is practically impossible to secure enforcement of any of our rights if there is any doubt whatsoever as to whether or not a particular statute applies to the particular state of facts.

As to law enforcement itself, the rule as to most American citizens is that if there is any way possible to prosecute individuals who have willfully interfered with the rights of other individuals such prosecution is attempted. However, when the complaining party is a Negro, the rule is usually to look for any possible grounds for not prosecuting. It is therefore imperative that Negroes be thoroughly familiar with the rights guaranteed them by law in order that they may be in a position to insist that all of their fundamental rights as American citizens be protected.

The Thirteenth Amendment to the Constitution, abolishing slavery, the Fourteenth Amendment, prohibiting any action of state officials denying due process of the equal protection of its laws, and the Fifteenth Amendment, prohibiting discrimination by the states in voting are well-known to all of us. In addition to these provisions of the Constitution, there are the so-called Federal "Civil Rights Statutes" which include several Acts of Congress such as the Civil Rights Act and other statutes which have been amended from time to time and are now grouped together in several sections of the United States Code. The original Civil Rights Act was passed in Congress in 1866, but was vetoed by President Andrew Jackson the same year. It was, however, passed over the veto. It was reintroduced and passed in 1870 because there was some doubt as to its constitutionality, having been passed before the Fourteenth Amendment was ratified. The second bill has been construed several times and has been held constitutional by the United States Supreme Court, which in one case stated that "the plain objects of these statutes, as of the Constitution which authorized them, was to place the colored race, in respect to civil rights, upon a level with the whites. They made the rights and responsibilities, civil and criminal, of the two races exactly the same." (Virginia v. Rives, 100 U.S. 313 [1879])

The Thirteenth and Fourteenth and Fifteenth Amendments, along with the civil rights statutes protect the following rights:

1. Slavery is abolished and peonage is punishable as a federal crime. (13th amendment)

2. All persons born or naturalized in the U.S. are citizens and no state shall make or enforce any law abridging their privileges or immunities, or deny them equal protection of the law. (14th amendment)

3. The right of citizens to vote cannot be abridged by the United States or by any state on account of race or color. (15th amendment)

4. All persons within the jurisdiction of the United States shall have the same right to enforce contracts, or sue, be parties, give evidence, and to the full and equal benefit of all laws and proceedings as is enjoyed by white citizens.

5. All persons shall be subject to like punishment, pains, penalties, taxes, licenses, and extractions of every kind, and to no other.

6. All citizens shall have the same right in every state and territory, as is enjoyed by white citizens to inherit, purchase, lease, sell, hold and convey property.

7. Every person who, under color of statutes, custom or usage, subjects any citizen of the United States or person within the jurisdiction thereof to the deprivation of any rights, privileges, or immunities secured by the Constitution and laws is liable in an action at law, suit in equity, or other proper proceedings for redress.

8. Citizens possessing all other qualifications may not be disqualified from jury service in federal or state courts on account of race or color; any officer charged with the duty of selection or summoning of jurors who shall exclude citizens for reasons of race or color shall be guilty of a misdemeanor.

9. A conspiracy of two or more persons to deprive any person or class of persons of any rights guaranteed by constitution and laws is punishable as a crime and the conspirators are also liable in damages.

Most of these provisions only protect the citizen against wrong doing by public officials, although the peonage statutes and one or two others protect against wrongs by private persons.

Despite the purposes of these Acts which the United States Supreme Court insisted in 1879 "made the rights and responsibilities, civil and criminal, of the two races exactly the same," the experience of all of us points to the fact that this purpose has not as yet been accomplished. There are several reasons for this. In the first place, in certain sections of this country, especially in the deep south, judges, prosecutors and members of grand and petit juries, have simply refused to follow the letter or spirit of these provisions. Very often it happens that although the judge and prosecutor are anxious to enforce the laws, members of the jury are reluctant to protect the rights of Negroes. A third reason is that many Negroes themselves for one reason or another hesitate to avail themselves of the protection afforded by the United States Constitution and statutes.

These statutes protecting our civil rights in several instances provide for both criminal and civil redress. Some are criminal only and others are for civil action only. Criminal prosecution for violation of the federal statutes can be obtained only through the United States Department of Justice.

Up through and including the administration of Attorney General Homer S. Cummings, Negroes were unable to persuade the U.S. Department of Justice to enforce any of the civil rights statutes where Negroes were the complaining parties. The NAACP and its staff made repeated requests and in many instances filed detailed statements and briefs requesting prosecution for lynch mobs, persons guilty of peonage and other apparent violations of the federal statutes. It was not until the administration of Attorney General Frank Murphy that any substantial efforts were made to enforce the civil rights statutes as they apply to Negroes. Attorney General Murphy established a Civil Rights Section in the Department of Justice.

During the present administration of Attorney General Francis Biddle there have been several instances of prosecution of members of lynch mobs for the first time in the history of the United States Department of Justice. There have also been numerous successful prosecutions of persons guilty of peonage and slavery. However, other cases involving the question of the beating and killing of Negro soldiers by local police officers, the case involving the action of Sheriff Tip Hunter, of Brownsville, Tennessee who killed at least one Negro citizen and forced several others to leave town, the several cases of refusal to permit qualified Negroes to vote, as well as other cases, have received the attention of the Department of Justice only to the extent of "investigating." Our civil rights as guaranteed by the federal statutes will never become a reality until the U.S. Department of Justice decides that it represents the entire United States and is not required to fear offending any section of the country which believes that it has the God-given right to be above the laws of the United States and the United States Supreme Court.

One interesting example of the apparent failure to enforce the criminal statutes is that although the statute making it a crime to exclude persons from jury service because of race or color was declared unconstitutional by the U.S. Supreme Court in 1879, and is still on the statute books, there have been no prosecutions by the Department of Justice in recent years for the obvious violations of these statutes. The Department of Justice has most certainly on several occasions been put on notice as to these violations by the many cases carried to the Supreme Court by the NAACP and in which cases the Supreme Court has reversed the convictions on the ground that Negroes were systematically excluded from jury service. One wholehearted prosecution of a judge or other official for excluding Negroes from jury service because of their race would do more to make this particular law a reality than dozens of other cases merely reversing the conviction of individual defendants.

There are, however, certain bright spots in the enforcement of the federal statutes. In addition to the lynching and peonage cases handled by the Washington office of the Department of Justice, there have been a few instances of courageous United States Attorneys in such places as Georgia who have vigorously prosecuted police officers who have used the power of their office as a cloak for beating up Negro citizens.

As a result of the recent decision in the Texas Primary Case, it is possible to use an example of criminal prosecution under the civil rights statutes by taking a typical case of the refusal to permit the Negroes to vote in the Democratic Primary elections. Let us see how a prosecution is started: In Waycross, Georgia, for example, we will suppose a Negro elector on July 4, 1944, went to the polls with his tax receipt and demanded to vote in the Democratic Primary. He should, of course, have witnesses with him. Let us also assume that the election officials refused to let him vote solely because of his race or color.

As a matter of law, the election officials violated a federal criminal law and are subject to fine and imprisonment. But how should the voter or the organized Negro citizens, or the local NAACP Branch go about trying to get the machinery of criminal justice in motion? Of course, the details of what happens must be put in writing and sworn to by the person who tried to vote and also by his witnesses. Then the matter must be placed before the United States Attorney. This is the federal district attorney.

I wonder how many of the delegates here know who is the United States Attorney for their district, or even where his office is. Every Branch should know the United States Attorney for that area, even if a delegation goes in just to get acquainted and let him know that we expect him to enforce the civil rights laws with the same vigor as used in enforcing other criminal statutes.

But back to the voting case. The affidavits must be presented to the United States Attorney with a demand that he investigate and place the evidence before the Federal Grand Jury. At the same time copies of the affidavits and statements in the case should be sent to the National Office. We will see that they get to the Attorney General in Washington. I wish that I could guarantee you that the Attorney General would put pressure on local United States Attorneys who seem reluctant to prosecute. At least we can assure you that we will give the Attorney General no rest unless he gets behind these reluctant United States attorneys throughout the south.

There is no reason why a hundred clear cases of this sort should not be placed before the United States Attorneys and the Attorney General every year until the election officials discover that it is both wiser and safer to follow the United States laws than to violate them. It is up to us to see that these officials of the Department of Justice are called upon to act again and again wherever there are violations of the civil rights statutes. Unfortunately, there are plenty of such cases. It is equally unfortunate that there are not enough individuals and groups presenting these cases and demanding action.

The responsibility for enforcement of the civil provisions of the civil rights statutes rests solely with the individual. In the past we have neglected to make full use of these studies. Although they have been on the books since 1870, there were very few cases under these statutes until recent years. Whereas in the field of general law there are many, many precedents for all other types of action, there are very few precedents for the protection of civil liberties.

The most important of the civil rights provisions is the one which provides that "every person who, under color of any statute, ordinance, regulation, custom or usage of any state or territory subjects or causes to be subjected any citizen of the United States or person within the jurisdiction thereof to the deprivation of any rights, privileges or immunities secured by the Constitution and laws shall be liable to the party injured in an action at law, suit in equity or other proper proceeding for redress." Under this statute any officer of a state, county or municipality who while acting in an official capacity, denies to any citizen or person within the state any of the rights guaranteed by the Constitution or laws is subject to a civil action. This statute has been used to equalize teachers' salaries and to obtain bus transportation for Negro school children. It can be used to attack every form of discrimination against Negroes by public school systems.

Under Jim Crow, blacks and whites had separate waiting rooms at public transportation depots like this one. For many southern migrants, such segregated facilities were their last taste of the Jim Crow South. New forms of segregation—in housing, school, and employment—awaited them in the North. **THE LIBRARY OF CONGRESS**

The statute has also been used to enjoin municipalities from refusing to permit Negroes to take certain civil service examinations and to attack segregation ordinances of municipalities. It can likewise be used to attack all types of discrimination against Negroes by municipalities as well as by states themselves.

This statute, along with other of the civil rights statutes, can be used to enforce the right to register and vote throughout the country. The threats of many of the bigots in the south to disregard the ruling of the Supreme Court of the United States in the recent Texas Primary decision has not intimidated a single person. The United States Supreme Court remains the highest court in this land. Election officials in states affected by this decision will either let Negroes vote in the Democratic Primaries, or they will be subjected to both criminal and civil prosecution under the civil rights statutes. In every state in the deep south Negroes have this year attempted to vote in the primary elections. Affidavits

concerning the refusal to permit them to vote in Alabama, Florida and Georgia have already been sent to the United States Department of Justice. We will insist that these election officials be prosecuted and will also file civil suits against the guilty officials.

It can be seen from these examples that we have just begun to scratch the surface in the fight for full enforcement of these statutes. The NAACP can move no faster than the individuals who have been discriminated against. We only take up cases where we are requested to do so by persons who have been discriminated against.

Another crucial problem is the ever-present problem of segregation. Whereas the principle has been established by cases handled by the NAACP that neither states nor municipalities can pass ordinances segregating residences by race, the growing problem today is the problem of segregation by means of restrictive covenants, whereby private owners band together to prevent Negro occupan-

Thurgood Marshall is best known as the first African American to sit on the Supreme Court. **CORBIS-BETTMANN**

cy of particular neighborhoods. Although this problem is particularly acute in Chicago, it is at same time growing in intensity throughout the country. It has the full support of the real estate boards in the several cities, as well as most of the banks and other leading agencies. The legal attack on this problem has met with spotty success. In several instances restrictive covenants have been declared invalid because the neighborhood has changed, or for other reasons. Other cases have been lost. However, the NAACP is in the process of preparing a detailed memorandum and will establish procedure which will lead to an all-out legal attack on restrictive covenants. Whether or not this attack will be successful cannot be determined at this time.

The National Housing Agency and the Federal Public Housing Authority have established a policy of segregation in federal public housing projects. A test case has been filed in Detroit, Mich., and is still pending in the local federal courts. The Detroit situation is the same as in other sections of the country. Despite the fact that the Housing Authority and other agencies insist that they will maintain separate but equal facilities, it never develops that the separate facilities are equal in all respects. In Detroit separate projects were built and it developed that by the first of this year every single white family in the area eligible for public housing had been accommodated and there were still some 800 "white" units vacant with "no takers." At the same time there were some 45,000 Negroes inadequately housed and with no units open to them. This is the inevitable result of "separate but equal" treatment.

I understand that in Chicago a public housing project to be principally occupied by Negroes is being opposed by other Negroes on the ground that it will depreciate their property. It is almost unbelievable that Negroes would oppose public housing for the same reason used by real estate boards and other interests who are determined to keep Negroes in slum areas so that they may be further exploited. The NAACP is in favor of public housing and works toward that end every day. It will continue to do so despite real estate boards and other selfish interests opposing public housing whether they be white or Negro. The NAACP is, of course, opposed to segregation in public housing and will continue to fight segregation in public housing.

We should also be mindful of the several so-called civil rights statutes in the several states. There are civil rights acts in at least 18 states, all of which are in the north and middle west. These statutes are in California, Colorado, Connecticut, Illinois, Indiana, Iowa, Kansas, Massachusetts, Michigan, Minnesota, Nebraska, New Jersey, New York, Ohio, Pennsylvania, Rhode Island and Washington. California provides only for civil action. Illinois, Kansas, Minnesota, New York and Ohio have both civil and criminal provisions. In New Jersey the only action is a criminal action, or an action for penalty in the name of the state, the amount of the penalty going to the state.

In those states not having civil rights statutes it is necessary that every effort be made to secure passage of one. In states having weak civil rights statutes efforts should be made to have them strengthened. In states with reasonably strong civil rights statutes, like Illinois and New York, it is necessary that every effort be made to enforce them.

The Chicago branch has the record of more successful prosecutions for violation of the local civil rights statute than any other Branch of the NAACP. In New York City resort to the enforcement of the criminal provisions has greatly lessened the number of cases. Outside of New York City there are very few successful cases against the civil rights statutes because of the fact that members of the jury are usually reluctant to enforce the statutes. I understand the same is true for Illinois. The only method of counteracting this vicious practice is by means of educating the general public, from which juries are chosen, to the plight of the Negro.

It should also be pointed out that many of our friends of other races are not as loud and vociferous as the enemies of our race. In northern and mid-western cities it repeatedly happens that a prejudiced southerner on entering a hotel or restaurant, seeing Negroes present makes an immediate and loud protest to the manager. It is very seldom that any of our friends go to the managers of places where Negroes are excluded and complain to them of this fact. Quite a job can be done if our friends of other races will only realize the importance of this problem and get up from their comfortable chairs and actually go to work on the problem.

Thus it seems clear that although it is necessary and vital to all of us that we continue our program for additional legislation to guarantee and enforce certain of our rights, at the same time we must continue with ever-increasing vigor to enforce those few statutes, both federal and state, which are now on the statute books. We must not be delayed by people who say "the time is not ripe," nor should we proceed with caution for fear of destroying the "status quo." Persons who deny to us our civil rights should be brought to justice now. Many people believe the time is always "ripe" to discriminate against Negroes. All right then—the time is always "ripe" to bring them to justice. The responsibility for the enforcement of these statutes rests with every American citizen regardless of race or color. However, the real job has to be done by the Negro population with whatever friends of the other races are willing to join in.

African Americans on the Frontier

ADAPTED FROM ESSAYS BY STACY SHORTER

The history of the United States is in part the story of a continuing series of frontiers. The borders between land already settled and territory still to be explored, conquered, and claimed have constantly shifted. When European explorers first landed on North American shores, the entire continent was a frontier. As exploration and settlement progressed, the frontier's location changed. For many years, Americans considered all land west of the Appalachian Mountains to be frontier territory. Now, when we speak of the frontier, we usually mean the land west of the Mississippi River.

The history of African Americans on the frontier, then, begins with their first appearance in North America. Spanish and Portuguese explorers of the fifteenth and sixteenth centuries included Africans among their crews as they sailed to the Americas. Estevanico, a slave and member of a 1528 Spanish expedition, lived among Native Americans in Mexico and the area of present-day Arizona and New Mexico.

The British also brought Africans to North America, first as indentured servants, later as slaves. When Africans were put to work clearing frontier areas, they often came into contact with Native Americans who had inhabited the continent for thousands of years.

As the black population grew, early African contacts with indigenous peoples in frontier areas were duplicated all over the continent, as in the case of runaway slaves who established maroon colonies among the Seminole people of Spanish Florida. Native American and African American people share a history that has been marked by bonds of blood and culture, as well as violence and prejudice.

TRAPPERS, TRADERS AND EXPLORERS
North American explorers soon recognized the vast wealth the continent held. Much of it was in the form of

Postcards of the wild west were popular at the turn of the century and sometimes featured black cowboys. Some historians conjecture that one out of every five cowboys was African American. One of them, Bill Pickett, went on to fame as a screen actor in early black westerns. **CORBIS-BETTMANN**

animal pelts, and during the eighteenth and nineteenth centuries the fur trade emerged as a primary economic activity along the frontier. Life as a fur trader in the wilderness could be isolating and dangerous, but for many blacks it was preferable to the oppressive life slaves and free blacks faced in more settled areas.

Jean Baptiste Pointe Du Sable (1745?–1818) was one African American who chose the fur trader's life. Born a slave in Haiti and freed by his French father, in 1793 Du Sable established an independent fur trading post at the mouth of the Chicago River. George Bonga, the son of a slave and a Chippewa woman, worked for John Jacob Astor's American Fur Company and became a prominent trader in his own right.

After the colonies won their independence from Great Britain, the newly formed United States government engaged in rapid territorial expansion and westward exploration. In 1804, John Lewis (1774–1809) and Meriwether Clark (1770–1838) were commissioned by Thomas Jefferson (1743–1826) to survey the vast Louisiana Territory, just purchased from France. Begin-

ning at the Missouri River, the expedition traveled across the Rocky Mountains to the Pacific Northwest, reaching the Pacific Ocean and returning home in just over two years. One member of the Lewis and Clark expedition was Clark's slave, a man known only as York. York proved invaluable to the expedition as a negotiator and interpreter between the explorers and the Indian nations they encountered.

James Beckwourth (1798–1866), a black trapper and explorer, became a member of the Crow nation, married a Crow woman, and served as a Crow chief. Beckwourth Pass, a mountain gateway between the Sierras and the Pacific Ocean, bears his name.

SEE PRIMARY SOURCE DOCUMENT *The Autobiography of Nat Love, Cowboy*

EARLY MIGRATION

As the nineteenth century progressed, the United States acquired more territory and extended its boundaries farther westward. The promise of land ownership lured thousands of migrants to frontier areas, where they established homesteads, farms, and communities. Thousands more moved to northern California after gold was discovered there in 1848.

Among the "forty-niners" who flocked to California were free blacks and slaves who traveled over miles of harsh and unfamiliar terrain. The migration, fueled by "gold fever," caused California's population to mushroom, and helps to explain why California had the largest black population in the West during the years before the Civil War.

One of the gold rush migrants was Biddy Mason (1818–1891). Mason and her three daughters walked the nearly two thousand miles from Mississippi to California behind their master's wagon, herding cattle the entire way. When her master decided to return to Mississippi in 1856, Mason sued for and won her family's freedom and their right to remain in California, a free state.

COWBOYS

The frontier state of Texas also had a large black population by western standards. Cattle raising was an important part of the Texas economy, and slaves were among the workers who tended the herds. By the 1860s, cowboys were increasingly in demand to herd cattle along trails to northern railroad depots on their way to market. A substantial number of these cowboys were black. Although they earned wages comparable to their white counterparts, black cowboys generally had the low-status job of horse wrangler and seldom became crew chiefs.

Some black cowboys found a measure of fame as skilled riders and ropers. Bill Pickett (c.1860–1932), a star of the Miller and Lux Wild 101 West Show, is credited with inventing the rodeo event known as bulldogging. Nat Love (1854–1921), also known as "Deadwood Dick," spent years as a cowboy in the Southwest and became a Pullman porter after his retirement. His name lives on through a series of dime novels written by Edward L. Wheeler and through his own autobiography, which chronicles his life as a cowboy in sometimes unbelievable terms.

THE BUFFALO SOLDIERS

Cowboys were not the only blacks to ride the range. Members of the Ninth and Tenth cavalries and Twenty-fourth and Twenty-fifth infantries, better known as the "buffalo soldiers," maintained a constant presence on the western frontier. They performed such essential tasks as fire fighting, building and maintaining military posts and telegraph lines, and protecting stagecoaches and mail routes.

They also served as a police presence in areas where there was a lack of adequate law enforcement. In many frontier areas, the soldiers were the most reliable source of law and order available. Their work included everything from settling civil disputes among settlers to capturing cattle thieves and murderers. Their most important duty, however, was to protect settlers and their land from encroachments by Native Americans. The buffalo soldiers were involved in battles with the Comanche, Kiowa, southern Cheyenne, and Arapaho Indian nations, to name a few.

The buffalo soldiers battled more than Indians. In some cases, their worst enemies were the very civilians whose lives they were sworn to protect. In 1892, soldiers from the Ninth Cavalry were dispatched to Johnson County, Wyoming, to maintain order between stock growers and cattle rustlers during the Johnson County War. There they found themselves the targets of some white citizens in Suggs, Wyoming, who violently objected to the soldiers' presence. Tensions between white settlers and the black soldiers led to a shootout that left one soldier dead.

At other times, though, black soldiers were treated with respect by the white settlers. Their treatment was dependent upon a number of factors, most notably the threat from Native Americans.

EXODUSTERS AND BLACK TOWNS

Black settlers throughout the West experienced the same uncertain treatment as the buffalo soldiers. Generally, the abundance of cheap land and the pioneers' reliance on each other made for fairly peaceful relations between black and white settlers. But as frontier areas became more populous, settled, and "civilized," old patterns of prejudice began to emerge.

Nevertheless, thousands of African American migrants swarmed into Kansas beginning in 1879, when conditions in the South after Reconstruction had

John Ware, a former slave from South Carolina, came to Alberta in 1882. Ware was probably the first black homesteader in western Canada. "Big John" is seen here with his wife, Mildred, daughter, Nettie, and son, Robert. **GLENBOW ARCHIVES, NA-263-1**

become unbearable. The lack of economic and political opportunity, as well as state-sanctioned racial violence, drove them from their homes. The hope for a better life and the promises of land speculators, both black and white, drove them on. More than twenty thousand blacks migrated to Kansas and other parts of the West between 1879 and 1880.

This migration, called the "Exoduster" movement, was led by Benjamin "Pap" Singleton (1809–1892), a seventy-year-old man who was motivated by religious faith to help deliver his people to the promised land of Kansas. Families gathered themselves and all the belongings they could carry and boarded river boats traveling up the Mississippi River. Migrants then traveled on foot or by horse or wagon to reach a place where their lives and their rights might be respected.

The migration caused a national outcry. White landowners in the South feared the loss of their cheap labor force. The Exodusters encountered many hardships upon their arrival. In 1880, Congress formed a special committee to investigate the causes of the migration.

From the Exoduster movement emerged a host of black towns in Kansas and neighboring Oklahoma. Towns such as Nicodemus, Kansas, and Langston, Oklahoma, were founded in the 1880s by blacks, primarily as agricultural communities. Farther west, black towns such as Blackdom, New Mexico; Allensworth, California; and Deerfield, Colorado; were founded as places where African American settlers might attain economic and political self-sufficiency. For a variety of reasons, most of these towns failed, and their residents moved away. Nicodemus is one of the few still in existence today. **SEE PRIMARY SOURCE DOCUMENT** *John Mercer Langston Speaks on the Mass Exodus of African Americans from the South*

COMMUNITY

As a result of the Exoduster movement and increased migration westward after the Civil War, the black population in the west grew rapidly. Even with the increase, however, it remained very small, and in most western states this is still the case. For instance, the largest number of African Americans living in Nevada in the nineteenth century was 396, in 1880. Moreover, the majority of black frontier settlers were men. In turn-of-the-century Los Angeles, black females were so scarce that black men "inspected" incoming trains, looking for possible mates.

Those black women who did travel west were usually older and better educated than black women in general. Any woman traveling alone faced dangers specific to her sex, and for black women the dangers were compounded by their race. Despite the risks, black women did migrate west. One such woman was Clara Brown (1800–1885), who at the age of fifty-five traveled from St. Louis to Denver in a covered wagon.

Once migrants settled in their new homes, the isolation and separation from friends and family could be frightening. One migrant to Seattle described the experience: "There were few of our people in Seattle when we came in 1889 and at times I got very lonely." Despite their small numbers, African Americans throughout the West attempted to duplicate familiar community structures such as the church, lodges, and benevolent societies.

Women were especially active as community builders. Lucy Phillips, who moved to Cheyenne, Wyoming, with her family in 1868, donated land for the Allen A.M.E. Church and held meetings in her home in the years before the chapel was built. In Central City, Colorado, Clara Brown became active in church and charitable causes and used some of her earnings as a laundress to help over thirty members of her family relocate to Colorado.

Family and community ties have always been an important feature of the African American experience, and western migrants developed a number of ways to maintain theirs. Pullman porters on the transcontinental railroad served as an informal but critical link between eastern and western black communities. Often they encouraged migration by carrying messages between family members and serving as examples of opportunities the West had to offer.

The West also had a thriving black press. California was home to several black newspapers, including the *Western Appeal,* the *Mirror of the Times,* and the *San Francisco Elevator.* The columns of these papers were filled with letters from African American correspondents writing from all over the west.

OCCUPATIONS

In much of the West, the land was not suitable for farming, and African Americans engaged in other occupations in order to survive. Many operated hotels and boardinghouses. Barney Ford had a spectacular career as a hotelier in both Denver and Cheyenne. After migrating to California from Boston, Mary Ellen Pleasant (1812–1904) became a successful boardinghouse operator and used the money she made to invest in mining stock and real estate. Mary Fields (1832–1914), of Cascade, Montana, worked as a freight hauler, restaurant owner, laundress, and mail coach driver. She was also known for her expertise with a six-shooter, having participated in at least one shootout.

Blacks also participated in the political life of the West. William Hardin was elected to the Wyoming Territorial Legislature in 1879 and 1882, in part because of the black community's support. William Leidesdorff (1810–1848), who moved to California when it was still owned by Mexico, served as American consul after the United States took over the territory.

CHANGING IDEAS OF THE FRONTIER

Today, the frontier lives on as one of the most enduring American symbols, a land of cowboys, shootouts, and wide-open spaces. But many of our perceptions about the West come from television, movies, and books that have romanticized the frontier experience and ignored some of its realities. The precise meanings of "the West" and "the Frontier" are still being debated today.

As the debate rages on, historians attempt to make history more inclusive, gathering information about people like African Americans whose experience is often ignored in popular myths of the frontier. Such work gives us a truer and more interesting account of how all Westerners—not just cowboys—led their lives on the frontier.

BIBLIOGRAPHY

Berwanger, Eugene H. *The Frontier against Slavery: Western Anti-Negro Prejudice and the Slavery Extension Controversy.* Urbana: University of Illinois Press, 1967.

Bontemps, Arna, and Jack Conroy. *Anyplace but Here.* New York: Hill and Wang, 1966.

Carroll, John M., ed. *The Black Military Experience in the American West.* New York: Liveright, 1971.

Daniels, Douglas Henry. *Pioneer Urbanites: A Social and Cultural History of Black San Francisco.* Berkeley: University of California Press, 1990.

Durham, Philip, and Edward Jones. *The Negro Cowboys.* New York: Dodd, Mead, 1965.

Katz, William Loren. *The Black West, A Pictorial History.* 3rd ed. Seattle: Open Hand Publishing, 1987.

Lapp, Rudolph M. *Blacks in Gold Rush California.* New Haven: Yale University Press, 1977.

Painter, Nell Irvin. *Exodusters: Black Migration to Kansas after Reconstruction* New York: W.W. Norton, 1976.

Porter, Kenneth Wiggins. *The Negro on the American Frontier.* New York: Arno Press, 1971.

Rusco, Elmer. *"Good Time Coming?" Black Nevadans in the Nineteenth Century.* Westport: Greenwood Press, 1975.

Savage, W. Sherman. *Blacks in the West.* Westport: Greenwood Press, 1976.

Slatta, Richard W. *Cowboys of the Americas.* New Haven: Yale University Press, 1990.

White, Richard. *"It's Your Misfortune and None of My Own": A New History of the American West.* Norman: University of Oklahoma Press, 1991.

PRIMARY SOURCE DOCUMENT

The Autobiography of Nat Love, Cowboy

INTRODUCTION Of the thousands of black cowboys who herded cattle along the Chisholm Trail in the years following the Civil War, Nat Love (alias Deadwood Dick) is perhaps the best known, thanks in large part to his 1907 autobiography, *The Life and Adventures of Nat Love.*

Excerpt from *The Life and Adventures of Deadwood Dick,* by Nat Love

Chapter VI.

The World is Before me. I Join the Texas Cowboys. Red River Dick. My First Outfit. My First Indian Fight. I Learn to use my Gun. It was on the tenth day of February, 1869, that I left the old home, near Nashville, Tennessee. I was at that time about fifteen years old, and though while young in years the hard work and farm life had made me strong and hearty, much beyond my years, and I had full confidence in myself as being able to take care of myself and making my way.

I at once struck out for Kansas of which I had heard something. And believing it was a good place in which to seek employment. It was in the west, and it was the great west I wanted to see, and so by walking and occasional lifts from farmers going my way and taking advantage of every thing that promised to assist me on my way, I eventually brought up at Dodge City, Kansas, which at that time was a typical frontier city, with a great many saloons, dance halls, and gambling houses, and very little of anything else. When I arrived the town was full of cow boys from the surrounding ranches, and from Texas and other parts of the west. As Kansas was a great cattle cen-

Nat Love, cowboy and later a Pullman porter, included this photograph of himself, "In My Fighting Clothes," in his 1907 autobiography, *The Life and Adventures of Nat Love.* **DENVER PUBLIC LIBRARY**

ter and market, the wild cow boy, prancing horses of which I was very fond, and the wild life generally, all had their attractions for me, and I decided to try for a place with them. Although its seemed to me I had met with a bad outfit, at least some of them, going around among them I watched my chances to get to speak with them, as I wanted to find some one whom I thought would give me a civil answer to the questions I wanted to ask, but they all seemed too wild around town, so the next day I went out where they were in camp.

Approaching a party who were eating their breakfast, I got to speak with them. They asked me to have some breakfast with them, which invitation I gladly accepted. During the meal I got a chance to ask them many questions. They proved to be a Texas outfit, who had just come up with a herd of cattle and having delivered them they were preparing to return. There were several colored cow boys among them, and good ones too. After breakfast I asked the camp boss for a job as cow boy. He asked me if I could ride a wild horse. I said "yes sir." He said if you can I will give you a job. So he spoke

Nat Love (1854–1921), Cowboy

Born into slavery in Tennessee in 1854, Nat Love showed an early love of adventure and became an expert horseman at a young age. With freedom, he began to look around for something other than farming, and at the age of fifteen he headed west for Dodge City, Kansas. There he met a group of cowboys and signed on with them to herd cattle between Texas and points north on the Chisholm Trail.

For the next twenty years, Nat Love worked the range as a cowboy, driving cattle, fighting off Indians and outlaws, becoming an expert sharpshooter, and going from one almost unbelievable scrape to another. His triumphs at the 1876 Deadwood City Rodeo earned him the nickname of "Deadwood Dick." In 1890, as the railroads began to replace the cattle drive, Love signed off as a cowboy and became a Pullman porter.

to one of the colored cow boys called Bronco Jim, and told him to go out and rope old Good Eye, saddle him and put me on his back. Bronco Jim gave me a few pointers and told me to look out for the horse was especially bad on pitching. I told Jim I was a good rider and not afraid of him I thought I had rode pitching horses before, but from the time I mounted old Good Eye I knew I had not learned what pitching was. This proved the worst horse to ride I had ever mounted in my life, but I stayed with him and the cow boys were the most surprised outfit you ever saw, as they had taken me for a tenderfoot, pure and simple. After the horse got tired and I dismounted the boss said he would give me a job and pay me $30.00 per month and more later on. He asked what my name was and I answered Nat Love he said to the boys we will call him Red River Dick. I went by this name for a long time.

The boss took me to the city and got my outfit, which consisted of a new saddle, bridle and spurs, chaps, a pair of blankets and a fine 45 Colt revolver. Now that the business which brought them to Dodge City was concluded, preparations were made to start out for the Pan Handle country in Texas to the home ranch. The outfit of which I was now a member was called the Duval outfit, and their brand was known as the Pig Pen brand. I worked with this outfit for over three years. On this strip there were only about fifteen of us riders, all excepting myself were hardy, experienced

men, always ready for anything that might turn up, but they were as jolly a set of fellows as on could find in a long journey. There now being nothing to keep us longer in Dodge City, we prepared for the return journey, and left the next day over the old Dodge and Sun City lonesome trail, on a journey which was to prove the most eventful of my life up to now.

A few miles out we encountered some of the hardest hail storms I ever saw, causing discomfort to man and beast, but I had no notion of getting discouraged but I resolved to be always ready for any call that might be made on me, of whatever nature it might be, and those with whom I have lived and worked will tell you I have kept that resolve. Not far from Dodge City on our way home we encountered a band of the old Victoria tribe of Indians and had a sharp fight.

These Indians were nearly always harrassing travelers and traders and the stock men of that part of the country, and were very troublesome. In this band we encountered there were about a hundred painted bucks all well mounted. When we saw the Indians they were coming after us yelling like demons. As we were not expecting Indians at this particular time, we were taken somewhat by surprise.

We only had fifteen men in our outfit, but nothing daunted we stood our ground and fought the Indians to a stand. One of the boys was shot off his horse and killed near me. The Indians got his horse, bridle and saddle. During this fight we lost all but six of our horses, our entire packing outfit and our extra saddle horses, which the Indians stampeded, then rounded them up after the fight and drove them off. And as we only had six horses left us, we were unable to follow them, although we had the satisfaction of knowing we had made several good Indians out of bad ones.

This was my first Indian fight and likewise the first Indians I had ever seen. When I saw them coming after us and heard their blood curdling yell, I lost all courage and thought my time had come to die. I was too badly scared to run, some of the boys told me to use my gun and shoot for all I was worth. Now I had just got my outfit and had never shot off a gun in my life, but their words brought me back to earth and seeing they were all using their guns in a way that showed they were used to it, I unlimbered my artillery and after the first shot I lost all fear and fought like a veteran.

We soon routed the Indians and they left, taking with them nearly all we had, and we were powerless to pursue them. We were compelled to finish our journey home almost on foot, as there were only six horses left to fourteen of us. Our friend and companion who was shot in the fight, we buried on the plains, wrapped in his blanket with stones piled over his grave. After this engagement with the Indians I seemed to lose all sense as to what fear was and thereafter during my whole life on the range I never experienced the least feeling of fear, no matter how trying the ordeal or how desperate my position.

The home ranch was located on the Palo Duro river in the western part of the Pan Handle, Texas, which we reached in the latter part of May, if taking us considerably over a month to make the return journey home from Dodge City. I remained in the employ of the Duval outfit for three years, making regular trips to Dodge City every season and to many other places in the surrounding states with herds of horses and cattle for market and to be delivered to other ranch owners all over Texas, Wyoming and the Dakotas. By strict attention to business, born of a genuine love of the free and wild life of the range, and absolute fearlessness, I became known throughout the country as a good all around cow boy and a splendid hand in a stampede.

After returning from one of our trips north with a bunch of cattle in the fall of 1872, I received and accepted a better position with the Pete Gallinger company, whose immense range was located on the Gila River in southern Arizona. So after drawing the balance of my pay from the Duval company and bidding good bye to the true and tried companions of the past three years, who had learned me the business and been with me in many a trying situation, it was with genuine regret that I left them for my new position, one that meant more to me in pay and experience. I stayed with Pete Gallinger company for several years and soon became one of their most trusted men, taking an important part in all the big round-ups and cuttings throughout western Texas, Arizona and other states where the company had interests to be looked after, sometimes riding eighty miles a day for days at a time over the trails of Texas and the surrounding country and naturally I soon became well known among the cowboys rangers, scouts and guides it was my pleasure to meet in my wanderings over the country, in the wake of immense herds of the long horned Texas cattle and large bands of range horses. Many of these men who were my companions on the trail and in camp, have since become famous in story and history, and a braver, truer set of men never lived than these wild sons of the plains whose home was in the saddle and their couch, mother earth, with the sky for a covering. They were always ready to share their blanket and their last ration with a less fortunate fellow companion and always assisted each other in the many trying situations that were continually coming up in a cowboy's life.

When we were not on the trail taking large herds of cattle or horses to market or to be delivered to other ranches we were engaged in range riding, moving large numbers of cattle from one grazing range to another, keeping them together, and hunting up strays which,

despite the most earnest efforts of the range riders would get away from the main herd and wander for miles over the plains before they could be found, overtaken and returned to the main herd.

Then the Indians and the white outlaws who infested the country gave us no end of trouble, as they lost no opportunity to cut out and run off the choicest part of a herd of long horns, or the best of a band of horses, causing the cowboys a ride of many a long mile over the dusty plains in pursuit, and many are the fierce engagements we had, when after a long chase of perhaps hundreds of miles over the ranges we overtook the thieves. It then became a case of "to the victor belongs the spoils," as there was no law respected in this wild country, except the law of might and the persuasive qualities of the 45 Colt pistol.

Accordingly it became absolutely necessary for a cowboy to understand his gun and know how to place its contents where it would do the most good, therefore I in common with my other companions never lost an opportunity to practice with my 45 Colts and the opportunities were not lacking by any means and so in time I became fairly proficient and able in most cases to hit a barn door providing the door was not too far away, and was steadily improving in this as I was in experience and knowledge of the other branches of the business which I had chosen as my life's work and which I had begun to like so well, because while the life was hard and in some ways exacting, yet it was free and wild and contained the elements of danger which my nature craved and which began to manifest itself when I was a pugnacious youngster on the old plantation in our rock battles and the breaking of the wild horses. I gloried in the danger, and the wild and free life of the plains, the new country I was continually traversing, and the many new scenes and incidents continually arising in the life of a rough rider.

PRIMARY SOURCE DOCUMENT

John Mercer Langston Speaks on the Mass Exodus of African Americans from the South

INTRODUCTION In 1879 John Mercer Langston was asked to comment on the mass exodus of African American southerners, or Exodusters, to Kansas and the other plains states. On October 7, he delivered the following speech at Lincoln Hall in Washington, declaring that the "exodus of colored Americans is intimately connected with and inseparable from the continued existence of the old order of things in the South."

The Causes Which Led the Colored People of the South to Leave Their Homes—The Lesson of the Exodus

Seventeen years ago, on the 22d day of September, Abraham Lincoln published his preliminary Proclamation of

Emancipation, and one hundred days thereafter, on the 1st day of January, 1863, he issued the proclamation in which he designated the States and parts of States in which the abolition of slavery, as a war measure, was declared. The abolition of slavery in the border States soon followed; and those persons who, prior to this action, had been held and designated as things, chattels personal, sustaining in the eye of the law only the status of four-footed beasts and creeping things, were given emancipation, and, as supposed, all those dignities which are implied in self-ownership and manhood.

The measure of emancipation, however, was not granted as the consequence of a healthy, moral, public sentiment pervading the country; not upon political considerations advanced, elucidated, and enforced by our leading statesmen; not in answer to appeals of abolition reformers and philanthropists, but as a military necessity at the time felt by the Government and the loyal North engaged in a struggle with and against the slave oligarchy of the South. Had emancipation rested upon moral and political bases, as the result of agitation and debate, the condition of the emancipated class might have been considerably changed. Some distinct governmental provision might have been taken for its due settlement, even upon lands appropriated specially for this purpose; and some system of education provided whereby it might have, in an earlier and more thorough manner, mastered lump.

And more fully appreciated the lessons taught and impressed in freedom and by civil responsibility. But emancipation as a war measure, was instant and speedy; and its consummation, characterized by no prior consideration and debate as to the subsequent situation of the freedman, left him in simple ownership of his person—other destitute in the extreme.

Hence the Negro, yesterday a slave, finds himself to-day, as emancipated, in the enjoyment of the simplest and merest self-ownership. Without property on the one side, and destitute of educational and moral appliances for his elevation on the other, he can look only to the philanthropic, the Christian, the benevolent public even for food, clothing, and those simpler elementary matters of instruction which tend to confirm him in the consciousness of the self-ownership which had just been conferred. All honor to the philanthropic, the Christian and benevolent public of this and other lands for the liberal and generous manner in which responses were made to the wants of the emancipated colored American. Many noble families of the North gave their best son and their best daughter to educate and to elevate, as far as practicable, the newly-made freedman; others their money by thousands to advance his material and educational interests. It was a sight worthy of the civilized, Christian country in which we live to witness how the noble sons and daughters of such heroic, devoted families attempted this work; with what earnestness, vigor, and matchless moral heroism. And the little good we find to-day already accomplished among the freed people of the South is more largely due to the efforts and offerings here referred to than to any Government assistance, State or national, which has been given.

With regard to the emancipation of the American slave, there have existed from the foundation of our Government two opinions, the one favoring and the other opposing it; and as slavery itself grew hoary-headed, the institution becoming more and more deep-seated, hedged about and defended by State action and national recognition, public sentiment against its abolition became more general and fixed. So much was this the case that we have not to travel far back in the history of our country to find when the two great political parties, the Whig and Democratic, pledged themselves to its maintenance and support as a positive, moral, legal, and political finality. Every one of us recollects with the most vivid distinctness the action had by these parties with regard to the compromise measures of 1850; and the American Church, in several of its important branches, as if it would not be outdone by the great political organizations of the day, was not slow in making solemn and positive utterances founded, as was claimed, upon the philosophy and logic, the theology and teachings of the Old and New Testaments, favoring this institution, which made and sustained property in the bodies and souls of men created in the image of our Heavenly Father. It is also within our memory, that memory running back not beyond a quarter of a century of our past, that the leading doctors of divinity, the conspicuous pulpit orators of our country argued, with an ardor befitting a better cause, with an eloquence frequently to the common mind irresistible and overwhelming, that slavery was a divine institution, sanctioned and sanctified by the teachings of Moses and Paul.

It was out of this state of things, a state of things implied in the declarations which I have just made in regard to the national parties and the church, that the great Republican party, organized in 1854, avowing its purpose to stay the extension of slavery, had its origin, and entered upon that glorious national career which is so distinguished by its triumphs in favor of freedom, equal rights, the support of free institutions, the maintenance of the Government, and the perpetuation of the Union of the States. It was upon the vote of this party finally that Abraham Lincoln was made President of the United States; it was the triumph of this party that gave occasion to the slave oligarchy to move in the establishment of a southern Confederacy, and the severance from the union of those States in which this new government was to take control. And as the old Democratic party passed out of power, James Buchanan retiring to the eternal shades of night, forever disgraced by the action which he had taken, or failed to take, (for his sin is at once one of commission and omission,) the great slave-power received that death-blow, under which, staggering, it fell, dying in the midst of the thunders of the great guns, whose echoes, lasting through the ages, are a warning to those who would break our Union and sunder our Government; while they are glad music, the perpetual song of joy to those who, accepting the sentiments of our Declaration and the doctrines of our Constitution, hold life, property and sacred honor in pledge to the maintenance of all those institutions which protect, defend and eternize American freedom with its sacred blessings.

But in the discussions had with regard to the non-extension of slavery, the distinctive principles of the Republican party and its purposes should it come into power, nothing had been said really, with reference to the immediate abolition of slavery in the several States where it existed, and no well-defined position had been taken, no measures suggested for ameliorating the condition of the slave in such States, should he be emancipated. Indeed, the one great purpose, the sole object which the most advanced leader of the Republican party advocated and expected to realize, was the prevention of the spread of slavery into territory then free. But it was discovered in the midst of our war against the rebellion, that the abolition of slavery, as just indicated, was a fitting and necessary war measure; and the brave and true Lincoln, with one mighty stroke of his pen, decreed the emancipation of the Negro, who went out from his prison-house of enslavement, but in the poverty bequeathed by centuries of hard and cruel oppression. He was landless; he was homeless. Destitute mainly of those things which distinguish the humblest life, he has been battling for the past seventeen years of his freedom, in a material sense, for the merest, simplest necessaries of a lowly condition. In fact, the merest emancipation of person and body has been practically the only thing, up to this hour, which has been guaranteed him. In this connection it is our duty to discriminate between simple emancipation, accompanied by a destitution characteristic of slave existence, and practical freedom, in which such destitution does not ordinarily exist; for if provision is not made for the newly emancipated by State or national regulation, opportunity, with fair wages, ought to be given for regular and remunerative labor, with intelligent investment of its proceeds in those things which are indispensable to well-ordered and prosperous life.

This brings me directly to the consideration of the condition of the American ex-slave as we find him to-day, struggling for life, with its common, usual rewards, in the South. This condition ought to be considered in its several relations of protection, industry, and politics. In dwelling on this branch of the subject we are not to forget that our national Constitution has been amended so as to guarantee freedom, civil rights, and the ballot to the freedom; that Congress has legislated in support of any

rights, immunities, and privileges claimed by this class of our citizens; and that it is true that generally in the States of the South laws have been enacted the purpose and object of which seem to be the protection and conservation of the rights, civil and other, which belong to the same class. In a word, as far as mere legislation is concerned, the condition of the freedman seems to be altogether tolerable—indeed good. In a material and industrial point of view, however, as well as political, the difficulty in his case seems to be even more deep-rooted and hard of management. His real condition is described and duly appreciated only when we recollect that although emancipated and legislation has been had in this case, as stated, still he has not been given practical independence of the old slave-holding class, constituting the land-proprietors and employers in the section where he lives and labors for daily support. And besides this, he is left to seek existence in the midst of those classes who of all others are most interested in demonstrating that emancipation is a failure; that the freedman is incapable of cultivating those things that pertain to dignified, honorable life; and that slavery is his natural and normal condition. Not only holding the lands, the old slave-holding class control the wealth and intelligence, as well as the social and governmental appliances of that section. They are masters in the church, masters in the courts, masters in the schools, masters in politics, masters at the polls, and masters of the legislatures, as well as the plantations, directing and controlling according to their caprices, their interests, their prejudices, and their predilections. The non-landholding white of the South must do their bidding; and the non-landholding Negro, also, occupies a subservient position to them. Depending, then, for labor, food, clothing and shelter upon his former master—the property holder—who is his abusive, tyrannical employer, making even harder exactions than he was wont to make of him when a slave, the condition of the freedman is certainly sad.

If what is here stated with regard to the condition of the freedman be true, reasoning a priori, to say the least, one might naturally conclude that the measure of protection accorded him would be limited and inadequate; that his industrial situation and prospects would be anything other than prosperous and promising; and that his exercise of political powers would be circumscribed and obstructed—as far as possible entirely hindered.

Mere philosophying, however, finds no place in this connection. The facts that bear upon this point are clear, positive, and undeniable. The freedman is without protection. His condition as a laborer, whether he work for wages, as a share-farmer, or renter, is not favorable; indeed, it is lamentable; while as a voter, it is well known that he cannot safely cast a free ballot according to the dictates of a wise and patriotic judgment. The "bull-dozing" record of the South is well understood, and the

---

John Mercer Langston (1829–1897)

John Mercer Langston was born into slavery in Virginia in 1829, the son of Ralph Quarles and Lucy Langston. Despite the fact that they were different races, Quarles and Langston lived together as man and wife. Quarles arranged in his will for his family to be sent to Ohio. There, John Mercer grew up under the guardianship of his father's friend, Captain William Gooch. When Gooch sought to relocate to Missouri, a slave state, Langston remained in Ohio where he graduated from Oberlin College in 1849.

Langston rose to achieve considerable fame and position. He was elected to the Brownhelm (Ohio) City Council in 1855, the first known African American to win elective office. In 1868 he became inspector general of the Freedmen's Bureau, and in the same year he founded the Law School at Howard University, serving as its dean from 1870 to 1873.

---

knowledge of the bloody deeds of its instigators and supporters is widespread and fully appreciated by the people of our country. Nor do his appeals to the courts of justice for redress of wrong meet with any success. If he make an appeal on law and fact to a jury of his fellow-citizens, who should, even from their own interest, if from no other and higher consideration, do him justice, what is the result? Even if the facts be plain and the law clear in support of his claim, the jury disagree ordinarily, and the judicial remedy which would naturally work him justice is defeated in its operation. This is true in civil as well as criminal proceedings, especially where the interests of the landed class as against the freedman are involved. In this regard the black man seems to have no rights which the white man is bound to respect.

After seventeen years of emancipation, in a condition of life even worse than that of serfage, in struggles against want and hardship, taxing his utmost endurance, the freedman has at last discovered his real situation and necessities, and has resolved, if possible, to relieve himself by escaping thence. What more natural than his effort in this regard, what more manly, what more worthy of him? What effort is better calculated to relieve him of his servile dependence? This movement is a declaration of the purpose of the freedman to assert and maintain that independence in his own behalf, without which

no individual and no people can rise to the level of dignified and honorable manhood. His exodus, if justified on no other ground, is justified thoroughly and entirely by the fact that it is, on his part, an effort to relieve himself of his present condition of utter dependence upon the old slave-holding class which he has served so faithfully in the past, and thus secure to himself the fact as well as the consciousness of real freedom.

The history of the emancipated classes of the world, whether they have been serfs or slaves, abundantly sustains the assertion that in most cases in which emancipation has occurred, and the emancipated class has been left under the control of the former master class, in the midst of the old associations of its slavery, upon the plantations or estates where it was wont to labor, such class thus situated and thus controlled does not and cannot rise until it has by some means freed itself from the dependence connected with such condition. It remains, in fact, in a servile position, without self-control, self-reliance, or independent character; without the purpose to make earnest, courageous effort to accomplish those things which are worthy of manhood.

It is not astonishing that centuries of enslavement embed in the very soul of the enslaved the spirit of servility and dependence; nor is it astonishing that this feeling once mastering the soul of man, holds it enchained to those things which work degradation and ruin to freedom. The soul of man is only relieved of this feeling as it becomes conscious of its own power in the assertion and maintenance of its own purposes in the struggles and achievements of life. And until the soul is emancipated from this feeling, man does not enjoy real, substantial freedom. While one man leans against another, or in his soul fears him, he is subservient; and in his subserviency loses his freedom as he does the real dignity of his manhood. And this is especially true of a class once enslaved.

To really comprehend the condition of the freed class, it is necessary to understand and appreciate that on the part of the ex-master class there still exists the feeling of superiority; the feeling of the right to rule, direct, and, in fact, to own, if not the body and soul, certainly the services of its former slaves; while on the part of the dependent and serving class, there exists, from long habit connected with its slave condition, the sense of inferiority, of subserviency—a disposition to go and come as commanded. Either the relations of the two classes must be changed entirely, and the change thoroughly recognized and admitted by both, or the former masters will attempt the continuance of their old conduct and ways of mastership; while the other class, not conscious of its freedom, will continue to serve as formerly from fear and force of habit, their freedom being only recognized as something ideal, without the practical benefits which it should bring.

If there be any doubts in the mind of any intelligent person in regard to this matter, he has only to read carefully the history of the emancipation of the serf of Russia and consider his present condition; the history of the West India bondman and consider his situation, to be entirely convinced that the statement is true. Wallace, in dwelling upon the emancipation of the serfs in Russia and in considering the question as to how their condition may be improved, states, in addition to other considerations offered, that "it would be well to organize an extensive system of emigration by which a portion of the peasantry would be transferred from the barren soil of the North and West to the rich fertile lands of the Eastern provinces."

It may be claimed that in this case the only reason why emigration is recommended is that the emancipation law did not confer upon the peasants of Russia as much land as they required, and consequently the peasant, who has merely his legal portion, has neither enough work nor enough revenue. But to one who considers the case of the Russian serf dispassionately and with care, it will be apparent that the real difficulty in his case is that although provision has been made for him, as far as land is concerned, he has been left practically in a state of dependence, if not upon the land proprietors, upon the Commune; and up to this time has not been able—discovering his real condition—to assert his independence of surroundings which tend to hold him in servile position. It will be remembered that the three fundamental principles of the law of emancipation in Russia were, as stated by Wallace, first, that the serf should at once receive the civil rights of the free rural class and that the authority of the proprietor should be replaced by Communal self-government; second, that the rural Communes should, as far as possible, retain the land they actually held, and should in return pay to the proprietor certain yearly dues in money and labor; third, that the government should, by means of credit, assist the Communes to redeem these dues, or, in other words, to purchase the lands ceded to them in usufruct. These conditions constitute the substantial features of the emancipation law of Russia. Upon close examination of these provisions, it will be discovered that although the emancipated serf is given, through the Commune, an interest in the soil, he is not relieved of a dependence which, in fact, keeps him in a servile condition; and until he has that freedom, which is indispensable to the cultivation of the highest possibilities of honorable manhood, he will be restless and his condition unsatisfactory, as it is unfortunate and unhappy. Let him but change his condition, emigrating from the old places so familiar to him, where his oppression and his real condition can never be forgotten, and settling in our own new and free country, where the blessings of liberty are guaranteed to every son and daughter of any and all nationalities, without money and without price, without stint, and without limit other than legal, and he enters upon new life, with new prosperity and new joy. It is emigration with its new conditions that gives to him and his posterity, the blessings of real freedom, which are more precious than rubies, more to be desired than any other human possession.

But that we may understand this subject from the slaveholding standpoint rather than that of serfage, and as connected with our own rather than the Eastern continent, it may be well to consider for a moment the condition of the emancipated bondman of the West India Islands. Here reference need only be made to the Islands of Barbados and Trinidad. In an excellent little work, entitled "The Ordeal of Free Labor in the West Indies," written by William G. Sewell, it is stated, in speaking of the condition of the laborers in the former island, that: "Under the new practice, still in force, a laborer has a house and land-allotment on an estate for which he pays a stipulated rent; but he is under an engagement besides, as a condition of renting, to give to the estate a certain number of days' labor at certain stipulated wages, varying from one-sixth to one-third less than the market price. The rate of wages in Barbados is about twenty-four cents per day; but the laborer, fettered by the system of tenancy-at-will, is compelled to work for his landlord at twenty cents per day. He is, therefore, virtually a slave; for if he resists the condition of his bond he is ejected by summary process, and loses the profit he hoped to reap upon his little stock. This remnant of coercion must be abolished wherever it exists—and it prevails, with some exceptions, in all the West India colonies—before it can be said that emancipation has been thoroughly tested." After making this statement the author gives account of the organization of an association in Barbados for the improvement of the social and moral condition of the laboring population, stating that in the preamble to the resolutions adopted at the first meeting thereof, it was declared that "one of the main barriers to social progress" in the island "arose from a want of confidence between the employer and the employed." He regrets the fact that the proprietor-body set their faces at once against this movement, and he says: "The planters, tenacious of their privileges and like aristocracies all the world over, anxious to retain their power over the masses, met to counteract the new movement, denounced the society for attempting to arouse unjust suspicions in the minds of the ignorant touching their rights, viewing with alarm and as a political movement the demand for a more liberal tenure, and as an effort to jeopardize the successful system of plantation management" as adopted. They maintained that the best of feeling existed between them and their tenants; and, finally, they declared their inherent right to adopt such measures as they might think fit for the good government, safety, and well-doing of their properties. Here is the master class asserting its right to be masters, and in effect believing it to be the duty of the laborer, even when emancipated, to consent to remain in a servile and slavish attitude.

If we turn from Barbados to Trinidad, it will be found that the people in the latter island, having left the estates upon which they were slaves, and thus exchanged a condition of servitude for one of independence, "as a natural consequence are more enlightened, better educated, and more wealthy than their brethren in Barbados." Herein, claims Mr. Sewell, we discover the distinction that should be made between the Negroes in Trinidad and in the other islands where they have been able to leave the estates and work for themselves, and those in Barbados, where, by force of circumstances, they have been compelled to remain on the estates and work for others.

While it is true that in Barbados the ex-slave has shown himself a valuable and persistent laborer, to such a degree and extent that that island is said to be in its culture a beautiful garden, unnatural, unjust distinctions, on account of color, exist to this day, against the black and mulatto classes, and it may be said that the real condition of such classes is that of the free Negro where his social and civil rights are not recognized and respected.

Under the title of "Social Distinctions in Barbados," the author to whom I refer states that "the distinctions of caste are more strikingly observed in Barbados than in any other British West India colony. No person, male or female, with the slightest taint of African blood is admitted to white society. No matter what the standing of a father, his influence cannot secure for his colored offspring the social status that he himself occupies; and the rule is more rigidly carried out among women than it is among the men."

Dwelling still on this subject, Mr. Sewell says: "But when he (the Barbadian planter) and all the other white inhabitants of the island make a difference of color their only line of distinction, and parade their reasons in an offensive and obnoxious way—when white planters refuse to associate with colored planters, white merchants with colored merchants, and white mechanics with colored mechanics—simply because they are colored, the question ceases to be a purely social one and assumes a dangerous political complexion. As long as the colored people were slaves, their heart-burnings and jealousies might be disregarded with impunity or contemptuously ignored. But freedom has opened to them the way to progress and power, and if their present progress and present power have proved, as they have proved, that color is no insuperable barrier to social, intellectual development and refinement, it is but wise to make it no longer an insuperable barrier to social advancement."

But such social discrimination are apt to continue, fostered always and everywhere by the master class against the laborer, especially if the latter has been a slave, and, on his being emancipated, is left thereafter in the conditions and under the control which were connected with his enslavement. Such distinctions will last until, by some manly utterance or courageous deed, he demonstrates his independence of the old servile condition, and his capacity to dare and achieve upon his self-reliance, as a fearless, independent man. It is in recognition of the principle here elaborated that Cassagnac, in his "History of the Working and Burgher Classes," in speaking of the mode of emancipation in France and the allotments of land allowed upon leases made with regard thereto, especially the contracts made for long terms, removing thereby the emancipated far from the influence and control of the former master class, says: "This kind of contract had this advantage, that when they were for a long term, as, for example, for three generations, a century passed, during which the action of the master upon the slave was restrained and weakened; while the slave, almost free in fact, acquired the manners and customs of the father of a family, became industrious, economical, settled, prudent, accumulated small profits and left them to his children. At the end of a century, when three generations had passed away, the master was much less a master, the slave was much less a slave. Both had forgotten whence they came by only seeing where they stood."

The inference to be drawn from the facts adduced is this: In proportion as the emancipated class is relieved of the presence and control of the class formerly owners and masters, from the conditions of its former enslavement, the spirit of servility is removed and that of self-assertion, self-reliance, and independence is cultivated, while steady, solid progress is made in the accumulation of the valuable fruits of industry.

The feeling too generally entertained by the old master toward his former slave, and by the latter toward the former, after emancipation, is strikingly illustrated in the story told by Herodotus with respect to the Scythian, who advised his comrades as to the manner in which they should meet and resist the army of their slaves, who, having taken possession of their households, their wives, and the management of public affairs, resisted them on their return from a protacted military expedition. He counselled his comrades to throw away their weapons, their arrows and their darts, and meet their opponents without any means of defence save the whips which they used upon their horses. Said he: "Whilst they see us with arms, they think themselves our equals in birth and importance; but as soon as they shall see us with whips in our hands, they will be impressed with a sense of their servile condition, and resist no longer." The historian reports that the plan suggested was adopted, and proved to be entirely successful.

How shall the American ex-slave, who has served for two hundred and forty-five years under the influence of which I speak, be relieved of the presence and control of a class heretofore his masters? The history of the world offers but one solution of this question, and that solution is found in his exodus. Let him go forth; and where sympathy and the recognition of liberty and equal rights are accorded him; where labor is to be performed; where struggle is to be made; where the stern realities of life are to be met, there let him demonstrate his courage, his self-reliance, his manly independence. Under such new conditions his capacities, his powers and his efforts will win the crown which befits the brow of noble manhood.

The exodus of the colored American is intimately connected with and inseparable from the continued existence of the old order of things in the South. Up to this time there seems to have been in this regard practically little, if any, change. It is very true that a few plantations, comparatively speaking, have changed hands; a few even of the former slave class have here and there possessed themselves of small homes, have bought small pieces of land, and erected thereon small houses; but "the great house" has not disappeared, nor has the Negro quarter; and in some of the Southern States the old whipping-post, with its proverbial thirty-nine lashes, is still recognized as a judicial institution. Nor have the modes of industry, or the crops grown in that section, been materially changed. Cotton and sugar are the chief products of the South to-day, as they were a half century ago. Nor has there been any change, certainly no general and fundamental change, in the feelings and purposes of the old slave-holding class as to their right to work, drive, and scourge the Negro laborer. Having been his master once, their conduct would indicate that they believe, even in spite of the action of the General Government and the results of our great war, that their mastership is to continue forever. Nor has the feeling of the non-slaveholding class of the South undergone any material change with respect to the freedman. Indeed, it seems to be true that this class hates the colored man more now than when was a slave; and stands ready at the command of the aristocratic class to do its bidding, even to the shedding of his blood. As showing that this condition of affairs is true and that little advancement has been made, one has only to pronounce in your hearing certain terrible words coined in connection with the barbarous, cruel treatment that has been meted out to the emancipated class of Mississippi, Louisiana, and other States formerly slaveholding. What is the meaning of the frightful words, "Ku-Klux," "Bull-dozers;" and the terrible expression, "the shot-gun or Mississippi policy?" The meaning is clear. It is that neither the old slaveholding spirit, nor the old slaveholding purpose or control is dead in the South; that plantocracy, with its fearful power and influences, has not passed away; that the colored American under it is in a condition of practical enslavement, trodden down and outraged by those who exercise control over him. Such things will continue so long as the spirit of slavery exists in the South; so long as the old master class is in power; so long as the freedman consents to remain in a condition more terrible than any serfage of which history gives account. How can this condition of things be broken up? How can the planter-rule be changed? How can the master class be made to realize that it is no longer slaveholding, and that the slave has been set free? And how can the freedman be made to feel and realize that having been emancipated, practical liberty is within his reach, and that it is his duty to accept and enjoy it in its richest fruits; fearing neither the responsibilities of enfranchised manhood, nor trembling as a coward in the presence of trials and dangers?

To the intelligent and sagacious inquirer, who, without feeling, without passion, but philosophically and in a states-man-like manner considers this matter, there can be, as it seems to me, but a single answer. It is this: Let the freedman of the South, as far as practicable, take from the old plantocracy, by his exodus, the strong arms, broad shoulders, stalwart bodies, which, by compulsion, have been made to prop and sustain such system too long already in this day of freedom. Let him stand from beneath and the fabric will fall, and a new necessary reconstruction will follow.

But is it possible to transfer all the freedmen from the Southern part of the country? Perhaps not. It is, however, possible and practicable to so reduce the colored laborers of the South by emigration to the various States of the North and West, as to compel the landholders—the planters—to make and to observe reasonable contracts with those who remain; to compel all white classes there to act in good faith; and address themselves to the necessary labor upon the plantation, as well as elsewhere; obeying the law and respecting the rights of their neighbors.

Thus the old order of things would be speedily changed, and the industrial interests of that section greatly advanced; while the civil and political rights of all would be, through necessity, respected and sustained. Even the exodus movement just commenced, small as it is, insignificant as it appears to be, has produced in this regard a state of feeling in the South which justifies entirely the opinion here expressed.

It is well to recollect that in the South we find a barren, effete civilization—a civilization the natural product of slavery and slave-holding institutions. The school, the college, the institution of learning, publicly or privately established by the State or in connection with the church, has not taken deep root there, bearing fruit in natural abundance. The masses of the freed people are illiterate. How could it be otherwise? But a large portion of the whites are also illiterate. The existence of slavery accounts for the condition of both these classes in this respect. All those things which appertain to an advancing civilization—healthful, vigorous and manly—seem to be wanting in the Southern section of our country.

KEEP THE NEGRO ACROSS THE LINE

THE WINNIPEG BOARD OF TRADE TAKES DECIDED ACTION

Not Good Settlers or Agreeable Neighbors Either

Winnipeg, Man., April 19.—The Winnipeg board of trade this evening passed a strongly worded resolution, which will be forwarded to Ottawa, condemning the admission of negroes into Canada as settlers.

It is set forth in the resolution that these new-comers are not successful farmers nor agreeable neighbors for white settlers. The board also passed a resolution similar to that of the Manufacturers' association on the proposal to amend the railway act to enable the railway commission to suspend railway tariffs or charges on appeals from patrons of the railways against which grievances are held.

After the Civil War, the United States was not the only place where African Americans had a hard time finding a place where they were welcomed. This 1910 Canadian article reports on a resolution passed by the Winnipeg Board of Trade condemning admission of African Americans into Canada. The resolution stated that blacks were poor farmers and unsuitable neighbors.
GLENBOW ARCHIVES, NA-3556-1

Let the freedman come to the North, let him go to the West, and his contact with new men, new things, a new order of life, new moral and educational influences will advance him in the scale of being in an incomparably short time, even beyond the expectations of the most sanguine. In his new home he will cultivate personal independence and free thought, acquiring in the meantime experience, knowledge and wisdom, which will enlarge his mind, ennoble his soul, and fit him for those higher walks of life, as merchant, mechanic, lawyer, doctor, minister, scientist or scholar. In other words still, the same benefits, the same blessings enjoyed by the newcomer from Ireland, England, and other foreign countries, tending so largely to elevate the thought, the purposes of such person, will be given to the ex-slave, and operate with equal power in the improvement of his mind and condition.

But as things are at present constituted in the South, the old methods of slavery and slave labor still prevailing, there is a large excess of laborers in that section. It is to be remembered that in slavery seven men, at least, were required to do the work of a single man in freedom. The exodus works at once the salvation of such surplus laborers by furnishing them a field for their muscle and labor in the unimproved acres of the West and North, thus not only benefiting them, but aiding in the development of the sections where they may locate. This consideration the people of the West and North appreciate, and their invitation to the poor freedman comes from them cordially and heartily. Cassagnac, in his work heretofore referred to—"The History of the Working and Burgher Classes"—in dwelling upon the Proletariat, says that it embraces: First, working men; second, mendicants; third, thieves; and fourth, women of the town. In explaining what he means by these several designations, he states that a working man is a proletary who works and gains wages for a living; a mendicant is a proletary who will not or cannot work, and who begs for a living; a thief is a proletary who will neither work nor beg, and who steals for a living; a woman of the town is a proletary who will neither work nor beg nor steal, and who prostitutes herself for a living. As the friend of the freedman, as one who would see him other and better than either of the classes here named composing the Proletariat of Cassagnac; who would see him more than the ordinary working man in the sense explained; who would see him a landholder and owner; who would see him master, as he is father, of his own household, rearing his family and his children in the fear and the admonition of his Heavenly Father; growing sons, indeed, to the State, with shoulders broad and Atlantean, fit to bear the responsibilities of earnest, dignified, manly life, I do not fear but approve and advocate his emigration.

Where shall he go? It has already been indicated that the North and the West furnish the localities open for the freedman, and to which he should go. It certainly would not be wise for him in large numbers to settle in any one State of the Union; but even in thousands he would be received and welcomed to kind, hospitable homes in the various States of the sections named, where labor, educational advantages, and the opportunity to rise as a man, a citizen and a voter would be furnished him.

But to his emigration there are objections:

First. It is claimed that the Negro should remain in the South, and demand of the Government protection from the wrongs which are perpetrated against him, it being asserted that for him to emigrate at this time therefrom is to surrender the fundamental principle of protection which is guaranteed him, as well as every other citizen of the Republic, by the Constitution of the United States. Here it must be remembered that in emigrating from the South to the North the freedman is simply moving from one section of our common country to another, simply exercising his individual right to go when and where it suits his convenience and his advantage. In the next place, it is the exercise of such constitutional right that he leaves a section of the country where slavery has created a barbarous and oppressive public sentiment, the source of all the abuses which he suffers, and which it is impossible, certainly impracticable, to reach and eradicate by any legislative enactment had by the General Government, or by any legal fiat; and which, in fact, can only be changed and improved by educational and moral appliances brought to bear upon the masses of the people of the South for an indefinite period. This objection is urged, too, in disregard both of the considerations just now suggested, in reply thereto, and in disregard of the fact that the freedman emigrating to the North or West puts himself in far better condition than he is in the South, in every sense; while he makes himself useful upon a larger and better scale to the country generally.

But it may be claimed, and doubtless is, that if the freedman leaves the South under the oppressions which are heaped upon him, he yields to an unconstitutional proceeding on the part of the dominant classes, and thus weakness, if he does not surrender, the right to demand protection generally. In answer to this opinion it may be justly replied, that the freedman has a right to protection, and it ought to be granted to him at once, if possible; but it can hardly be required of the freedman who desires to leave the South to remain in his present condition and sacrifice himself, make himself a martyr in such manner.

Secondly. It is claimed that the freedman cannot endure a northern and western climate. It is said that the winters of these sections are too severe for him; that in their chilling winds, their biting frosts, their deep, freezing snows, he will find himself sickening and speadily dying. Upon what facts and data this opinion is presented and sustained it is difficult to imagine. It is true, as justified by observation, and as facts and figures would show, could they be secured, that the colored man as he goes north into colder regions adapths himself with ease to the climate. While it is true that in no part of our country does the colored man show more robust health, finer physical development and endurance, and consequent longevity, than in the northern and western portions of our country. In fact so much is this the case that latterly it has become a thing of general observation and remark. It is where the zymotic and malarial disorders prevail that the Negro sickens and dies; and this is abundantly shown in the fearful death rate that is given by sanitarians as connected with the warm and tropical regions of our own and other countries.

In the third place it is objected that if there is any considerable emigration from the South the freedmen who are left behind will be forgotten—their case ignored. But if the views already presented be correct, if emigration will work the results which are claimed, then this objection is fully and completely met. The old plantocracy is abolished; the slave system is entirely overthrown and the industrial systems of the South reconstructed; all oppressions and abuses are removed; protection and fair wages with the prospect of general agricul-

tural improvement and the enjoyment of all civil and political rights are guaranteed; and thus the vexatious Southern problem is solved.

Again it is urged that the freedman is too poor to emigrate. Those who urge this objection ought to remember that it is the poor and oppressed in all ages and in all countries who have emigrated. One never emigrates only as he seeks to improve his condition, to relieve himself and family of want, to escape oppression and abuse, to gain such position as that, while he enjoys his freedom and rights, it is possible for him to cultivate as to himself and his children those circumstances of property, wealth, and intellectual, and moral, and religious culture, which distinguish desirable, wise, human existence.

Is it wise for the poor, starving, oppressed Irishman to quit the country of his nativity to seek a new home in our goodly land, where opportunities of culture, the accumulation of wealth, advancement and success await his endeavors? From whom comes the negative response? Then let no man either despise or oppose the exodus of the freedman, who now, realizing his real condition, emigrates from the old plantation and Negro quarter, from the scenes of his former enslavement, from the hateful and oppressive control of a stupid and tyrannical landed aristocracy, from poverty, from ignorance, from degradation to a home among those who value freedom, free institutions, educational and material, moral and Christian worth, individual effort and achievement—to a home among those who, loyal to God and man, never fail to give sympathy, succor and hospitable welcome to the needy son of Ireland, or the yet more needy son of Mississippi, who comes seeking not only liberty, but the opportunity to labor, to live, and achieve in their midst.

Our own national experience furnishes a valuable lesson upon the subject under consideration; and pondering such lesson wisely, the freedman and his family will do well to act in its light. This lesson is presented in the two-fold character of individual and family emigration, and the success and prosperity gained in connection therewith.

The family of a New England farmer is numerous. His sons are not needed at home; and there is no remunerative labor, manual or other, to be had in the community where this family lives. What is done? What has always been done in such families under such circumstances? Let the well-ordered and worthy household, the beautiful, fertile and productive farm, the substantial and enduring success, the political, the official, or the professional distinction which have been gained, and which now belong to the eldest son of such family, who, leaving home, settled fifty years ago in one of our nearer or more remote Western States, give the answer. But the community is overcrowded. Whole families are without work and pinching want seems to be near the door. What has been, and what is done in such cases? We know full well; for the populous, rich, prosperous, growing, vigorous, matchless West, with its thousands of free, Christian homes, noble sons, intelligent, heroic daughters, makes the answer in full, clear, positive, eloquent manner.

Then, too, in Ohio, Michigan, Indiana, not to mention other States in connection with which the same thing is true, the colored American has moved heretofore from the South, and establishing settlements in the States named, has proved by his complete success the benefit and advantages of emigration. His rich and prosperous settlements in Pike county, Ohio, and in Cass county, Michigan, deserve in this connection special mention. But why dwell on these facts? For the colored man is seen now in all parts of the North; and wherever he is, earnest, sober, and industrious, he makes reasonable advancement, commendable progress, in the honest ways of life.

In view, then of the considerations presented; to secure the highest good of all the parties concerned by the overthrow of the plantocracy of the South and the reconstruction of the industrial system of that section, on the basis of free labor, justice, and fair dealing; to relieve the ex-slave from his dependent and practical slavery, and while giving him the fact and consciousness of his freedom and independence, furnish him the opportunity to cultivate, not only ordinary labor, but to build up his present interests, industrial, material, educational, and moral, with reference to that future of which his past conduct, his capabilities and powers, his loyal and Christian devotion, give such reasonable promise, I do most reverently and heartily accept the lesson contained in the words—

> I have surely seen the affliction of my people which are in Egypt, and have heard their cry by reason of their task-masters; for I know their sorrows; and I am come down to deliver them out of the hand of the Egyptians and to bring them up out of that land into a good land, and large, a land flowing with milk and honey.

SOURCE: Copyright © 1926 by John Mercer Langston, not renewed.

African American Newspapers and Periodicals

ADAPTED FROM ESSAYS BY ADAM GREEN, YALE UNIVERSITY, AND JONATHAN HOLLOWAY, YALE UNIVERSITY

The black press has been both chronicler of and catalyst for change in the African American community. It has developed and adapted in response to every major upheaval in African American history: abolitionism and emancipation, migration and urbanization, the rise of the modern middle class, the civil rights and black power movements. Key leaders and agendas have grown out of the mastheads and columns of black publications. Today, despite larger audiences looking to television, radio, and other mainstream media, the black press continues to influence African American opinions and the opinions of Americans generally.

THE EARLY BLACK PRESS AND THE SLAVERY ISSUE

Early black newspapers were particularly concerned with slavery. The first black paper, *Freedom's Journal,* was an abolitionist weekly started by Samuel Cornish (1795–1889) and John Russwurm (1799–1851) in New York in 1827. It was followed by other publications challenging the slave system: *Freeman's Advocate,* the *Elevator, Aliened American,* and the *North Star,* started in 1847 by the ex-slave and abolitionist Frederick Douglass (1817–1895).

Black-run newspapers were also concerned with amending the poor coverage of African Americans in the northern white press. Although it was supposedly free soil, much of the antebellum North was plagued by racial animus. When Willis A. Hodges (1815–1890) wrote to the New York *Sun* in 1846 defending African American suffrage, he was forced to purchase advertising space to present his views; as the editor put it, "the *Sun* shines for all white men and not for colored men." Hodges's response was to start his own paper, *Ram's Horn,* that same year.

Black periodicals, like black newspapers, also championed abolitionism. The first significant black magazine was *Mirror of Liberty,* started by David Ruggles (1833–1904) in 1837. It was followed by the *Anglo-African Magazine,* the most ambitious black press venture prior to the Civil War. Printed in New York beginning in 1859, its contributors were a who's who of black antislavery leaders: Frances Ellen Watkins Harper (1825–1911), Charles Remond (1810–1873), William Wells Brown (1815–1884), Douglass, and the early nationalist Martin Delany (1812–1885).

The fact that most of these publications originated in northern communities says more about the obstacles to pursuing such projects in the South, where antiliteracy laws prevented many blacks from learning to read and write, than it does about the level of tolerance in the North.

EMANCIPATION AND THE GROWTH OF A NATIONWIDE BLACK PRESS

With legal emancipation at the end of the Civil War, the black press enjoyed a period of significant growth. Increased literacy among African Americans during Reconstruction (1865–1876) meant a growing audience for news relevant to the racial community. The number of black-edited newspapers increased from 12 in 1866 to 31 in 1880. By 1890, there were 575 black newspapers nationwide, with many in former slave states like Virginia, Alabama, and Georgia.

While white abolitionist papers, slave narratives, and escape stories did much to change the national climate regarding the institution of slavery, in the years preceding and following the Civil War, papers like the *Liberator*, the *Defender*, *Voice of the Fugitive*, the New York *Age*, the Washington *Bee*, and the California *Eagle* served a central role in giving African Americans a sense of self and pride. Many of the newspapers also expanded the format of postbellum black newspapers to include general news coverage, society pages, arts and church reporting, and editorial commentary. Particularly during the period directly following manumission, black Americans suddenly found themselves with freedom and a list of supposed rights, but living in a hostile country where every element of organized society was arrayed against their very existence.

While framing national debates on the issues of racial justice, these papers served a critical role as the first public sign that such issues did in fact exist for the freedmen and the first public avenue where their voices might be heard. In addition, these papers had very specific weight and meaning to African Americans. They were symbols of literacy, education, and the hope for an eventual entrance into a situation of economic opportunity. Over the next few decades, hundreds of thousands of African Americans began the Great Migration out of the South to the modern cities of Chicago and New York, where life was often as difficult or even more difficult than it had been in the South. The *Liberator*, the *Defender*, and *Voice of the Fugitive* served as surrogate guides to help recent migrants decipher the unwritten urban rules they were expected to follow.

THE BLACK PRESS AT THE TURN OF THE CENTURY

The black press played a key role in one of most important episodes in African American history: the controversy at the turn of the century surrounding the leadership of Booker T. Washington (1856–1915). Younger black leaders were not only frustrated by Washington's accomodationist position; they also objected to how the "Tuskegee machine" stifled communal debate.

Newspapers and magazines became tools of controversy for both Washington and his critics. Washington sought to control the black press, bringing under his wing two influential publications, the New York *Age* and the *Colored American Magazine*. Among Washington's opponents were Ida B. Wells-Barnett, William Monroe Trotter (1872–1934), publisher of the Boston *Guardian*, and W. E. B. Du Bois (1868–1963), who became editor of the *Crisis* magazine in 1910. The work of these three helped inspire the formation of the National Association for the Advancement of Colored People (NAACP), the parent organization of the *Crisis*. With Washington's death in 1915, the views of columnists like Wells-Barnett and Du Bois increasingly shaped mainstream attitudes in the African American community.

Front page of *The North Star*, the newspaper founded by Frederick Douglass. Published out of Rochester, New York, Douglass named it after the North Star that escaping slaves used as a guide to direct them to freedom. **THE LIBRARY OF CONGRESS**

JOURNALIST, ACTIVIST, AND CRUSADER: IDA B. WELLS-BARNETT

In the aftermath of the Civil War, the crusade against slavery gave way to the crusade against racial violence, a struggle in which the rising black press and in particular the journalist and activist Ida B. Wells-Barnett (1862–1931) played a significant public role. Like many other African American thinkers and leaders, Wells-Barnett was a driven person. After her parents and two of her seven siblings succumbed to a yellow-fever epidemic, Wells-Barnett took charge of her family and began teaching at a rural school at the age of fourteen. In 1882, she moved from Mississippi to Memphis, Tennessee, and taught classes in Shelby County and then at one of the black schools in Memphis.

In 1884, Wells-Barnett faced discrimination firsthand on a train trip to Nashville, Tennessee. En route to Fisk University, Wells-Barnett was told to give up the first-class seat that she had purchased and move to the smoking car. When she refused, the conductor tried to remove her, and Wells-Barnett bit him. She was then escorted off of the train. She later filed suit against the railroad company and won $500, but a higher court

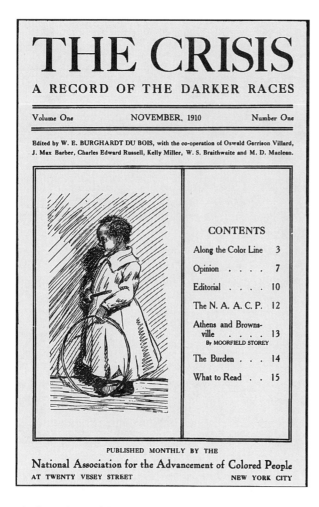

THE CRISIS
A RECORD OF THE DARKER RACES

Volume One   NOVEMBER, 1910   Number One

Edited by W. E. BURGHARDT DU BOIS, with the co-operation of Oswald Garrison Villard, J. Max Barber, Charles Edward Russell, Kelly Miller, W. S. Braithwaite and M. D. Maclean.

CONTENTS

Along the Color Line   3

Opinion   7

Editorial   10

The N. A. A. C. P.   12

Athens and Browns-
ville   13
By MOORFIELD STOREY

The Burden . . .   14

What to Read . .   15

PUBLISHED MONTHLY BY THE
National Association for the Advancement of Colored People
AT TWENTY VESEY STREET   NEW YORK CITY

The first volume of the *Crisis,* edited by W. E. B. Du Bois, the official magazine of the NAACP, which Du Bois helped to found. As editor, he featured many black writers, poets, and artists in the magazine.

reversed the decision believing that Wells-Barnett had intended to disrupt the service provided by the railway.

Wells-Barnett's stance against discrimination played a part in her changing her career. In the mid-1880s she began contributing articles promoting civil rights under the pseudonym "Iola" to prominent African American newspapers. In 1889, she was named editor and became part-owner of the Memphis *Free Speech and Headlight.* A year later, she was elected secretary of the Afro-American Press League, the first woman to hold the post. Her shift away from teaching altogether occurred in 1891 when the Memphis school board fired her for publicly challenging Tennessee's discrimination laws in the press. She then devoted herself fully to a career as a newspaper publisher, journalist, lecturer, and civil rights activist. In 1892, she experienced a bitter loss: Her friend Thomas Moss was lynched in Memphis by a white mob, one instance in a pattern of expanding repression, as Jim Crow segregation was established throughout the South. When she wrote a scathing editorial denouncing the

crime, her newspaper's offices were sacked and her own life threatened. Over the next two years, she investigated racially motivated attacks in the South, writing articles for her own *Free Speech and Headlight* and the New York *Age* that led to the book *On Lynching* (1894), still one of the best analyses of racial violence.

Wells-Barnett became an intellectual tactician, forging strategies of protest that would carry her overseas to seek support for her domestic activities. In 1894, for example, she traveled to England to win allies for her antilynching crusade. She returned to the United States a celebrity—vilified by some, lauded by others, but known by all. She continued her work as a writer and activist until her death in 1931, pushing African American leadership and public opinion to more militant positions. **SEE PRIMARY SOURCE DOCUMENT** *"The Case Stated" and "Lynch Law Statistics" by Ida B. Wells-Barnett*

ROBERT BAGNALL'S REPORT ON THE SOUTH

The 1929 report of the then-field secretary of the NAACP, Robert Bagnall, was an influential piece of journalism that appeared in the *Crisis* in the early twentieth century. Bagnall had been touring the South in the late 1920s, covering flood conditions along the Mississippi.

In addition to providing an account of the damage caused by the flood, he turned his attention to describing relations between blacks and whites in the South. Although he did find instances of white racial violence against black southerners, his account was not altogether pessimistic. He also found causes for hope: changing attitudes among some white southerners and a growing realization among black southerners of both the importance of voting and the very real impediments that had been arrayed against the efforts of African Americans to organize and register voters.

Bagnall concluded his report with a discussion of the beginnings of a realignment in political thinking among black southerners. Traditionally Republican, some had begun to urge black participation in the Democratic party, especially in primary elections, as a way of gaining political power. The Republican party in the South had historically been linked to the abolitionist cause and Radical Reconstruction, while the Democrats, or the Dixiecrats as they were often called, stood for "white man's government." But as one friend told Bagnall, "No one can be elected here except a Democrat.... We mean to support the most friendly Democrat, and if he fails us, we will do our best to put him out."

THE RISE OF BLACK MILITANCY AND THE HARLEM RENAISSANCE

Racial militancy grew during the 1910s and 1920s, spurred on by an invigorated black press. Du Bois continued to take courageous stands in the columns of the *Cri-*

sis, but he found himself challenged, often personally, by a pair of more radical publications. The *Messenger,* published by the black socialists A. Philip Randolph (1889–1979) and Chandler Owen (1889–1967), regularly cast doubt on prospects for racial justice under the American system; for a couple of years following World War I, it was banned by the U.S. Post Office as seditious. *Negro World* was published by Marcus and Amy Jacques Garvey, Jamaican immigrants and champions of the "Back to Africa" movement. Through its reports on blacks in the United States, the Caribbean, and Africa and its advocacy of racial unification under a Pan-African state, *Negro World* anticipated not only the black power movement of the late 1960s but also the idea of "Afrocentricity" today. **SEE PRIMARY SOURCE DOCUMENT** *Marcus Garvey and the "Africa for Africans" Movement*

The growth of black magazines during these years also intertwined with the cultural movement known as the Harlem Renaissance. During the 1920s, Du Bois tried to capitalize on the public's increasing interest in cultural matters, hiring the talented writer Jessie Fauset (1882–1961) to organize the cultural sections of the *Crisis.* Once again, though, Du Bois found his efforts eclipsed. The magazine *Opportunity* printed literary works and sponsored artistic award dinners; its editor, Charles Johnson, was acclaimed as a key "parent" of the renaissance. George Schuyler (1895–1977) and Theophilus Lewis, who both went on to long careers as newspaper columnists, also increased the *Messenger's* coverage of the arts, creating another forum for new artists.

More sensational efforts in cultural journalism came from the artists themselves: in 1926, Wallace Thurman (1902–1934) put out a new magazine, *Fire,* which sought to overturn traditionalism in the black community. Among the editors were many leading figures of the Harlem Renaissance: Zora Neale Hurston (1901–1960), Langston Hughes (1902–1967), Aaron Douglas (1899–1979), and Thurman himself.

THE BLACK PRESS RESPONDS TO THE GREAT MIGRATION

While black magazines stimulated cultural ferment, black newspapers were involved with another historic transformation: the massive waves of black migration and urbanization. Between 1915 and 1930, over a million African Americans left the South and moved to northern cities, and close to four million made the journey between 1940 and 1960. For many migrants, it was papers like the Chicago *Defender* and the Pittsburgh *Courier,* with their flashy coverage of better jobs and nightlife "up north," that helped inspire the journey. In 1917, the *Defender,* published by Robert Abbott (1868–1940) in a tabloid style reminiscent of William Randolph Hearst's papers, went so far as to run a front-

African American teacher and poet Langston Hughes played a major role in the Harlem Renaissance, which promoted arts among the African American community. **AP/WIDE WORLD PHOTOS**

page campaign called the "Great Northern Drive," explicitly encouraging southern blacks to migrate.

As with Reconstruction, migration and urbanization resulted in better education, growing literacy, and, ultimately, larger audiences for black papers. During the 1920s, the *Defender* reached a circulation of 230,000, many of them southern readers. By the 1940s, the *Courier* had nearly 300,000 readers.

CHANGE IN THE POST–WORLD WAR II ERA

After World War II, the emergence of the Johnson Publishing Company marked a new phase in black journalism. Run by an Arkansas migrant named John H. Johnson (b. 1918), the company started several publications: *Negro Digest, Ebony,* and *Jet.* Each of these journals mirrored mainstream American publications—*Negro Digest* followed the example of *Reader's Digest, Ebony* followed *Life,* and so on—and also helped encourage black consumerism through increased advertising copy. Johnson is a multimillionaire today, but in 1942 he had to mortgage his mother's furniture to raise the five hundred dollars he needed to start the *Negro Digest.*

This period also saw political pioneers grow out of the black press. Adam Clayton Powell Jr. (1908–1972), elected the first black congressman from New York City

Founded in 1966 by Huey Newton and Bobby Seale, the Black Panther Party espoused a revolutionary philosophy that brought it into conflict with white society. Here four members raise clenched fists, demonstrating the "black power" salute.
AP/WIDE WORLD PHOTOS

in 1944, established his candidacy from the pages of the weekly *People's Voice,* which he edited for several years prior to his election. Charlotta Bass (1880–1969), the radical publisher of the California *Eagle* in Los Angeles, became the first black woman to be nominated for vice president when she ran on the Progressive party ticket in 1952.

REPORTING ON THE CIVIL RIGHTS MOVEMENT

The black press was also crucial to the growth of the civil rights movement. News of campaigns in Montgomery and Little Rock was featured in major black newspapers and magazines like *Jet.* "Eyewitness" reporting, a staple of news coverage today, was perfected by black journalists during the civil rights years. Beat reporters and photographers such as James Hicks and Moneta Sleet achieved the fame previously reserved for editors and star columnists.

With the growing militancy of the 1960s, new publications expressed ideas associated with the black power movement. The Nation of Islam's newspaper, *Muhammad Speaks* (since renamed the *Final Call*) attracted six

hundred thousand readers with controversial discussions of the history and future of American race relations. The Black Panther party's paper, the *Black Panther,* was also confrontational, criticizing police-community relations in Oakland and Los Angeles.

Still other publications renewed the cultural radicalism of the 1920s. Shirley Graham Du Bois (1906–1977), widow of the famed *Crisis* editor, published *Freedomways,* a Harlem journal that included James Baldwin (1924–1987), Lorraine Hansberry (1930–1965), and John Henrik Clarke (1915–1998) as regular contributors. *Negro Digest* was remade in 1971 into *Black World,* with its editor, Hoyt Fuller (1923–1981), presenting hard-hitting analyses of African American politics and culture.

TODAY'S BLACK PRESS

In the last twenty years, the black press has reversed its traditional pattern of development. Magazines, which up until the 1950s were often limited by small readerships, have become the healthiest arm of the black press. Publications such as *Ebony, Jet, Essence, Black Enterprise,* and *Vibe* now enjoy circulations at or approaching one million, influencing public opinion within and beyond the African American community. Black newspapers, on the other hand, have seen circulation shrink under increasing competition from mainstream newspapers and the radio and television media.

Still, black newspapers continue to have an impact. The historic Chicago mayoral campaign of Harold Washington (1922–1987) in 1983 received critical support from black journalists. In the wake of incidents in Howard Beach and Bensonhurst, increased racial militancy in New York City was fostered by coverage in local black papers like the *Amsterdam News* and the *City Sun.*

BIBLIOGRAPHY

Bullock, Penelope L. *The Afro-American Periodical Press, 1838–1909.* Baton Rouge: Louisiana State University Press, 1981.

Buni, Andrew. *Robert L. Vann of the Pittsburgh Courier.* Pittsburgh: University of Pittsburgh Press, 1974.

Duster, Alfreda, ed. *Crusade for Justice: The Autobiography of Ida B. Wells.* Chicago: University of Chicago Press, 1970.

Hogan, Lawrence D. *A Black National News Service: The Associated Negro Press and Claude Barnett, 1919–1945.* Cranbury: Associated Universities Press, 1984.

Hutton, Frankie. *The Early Black Press in America, 1827–1860.* Westport: Greenwood Press, 1993.

Johnson, Abby, and Ronald Johnson. *Propaganda and Aesthetics: The Literary Politics of Afro-American Magazines in the Twentieth Century.* Amherst: University of Massachusetts Press, 1979.

Ottley, Roi. *The Lonely Warrior: The Life and Times of Robert S. Abbott.* Chicago: Henry Regnery, 1955.

Penn, I. Garland. *The Afro-American Press and Its Editors.* Springfield: Wiley, 1891. Reprint. New York: Arno Press, 1969.

Vincent, Theodore G., ed. *Voices of a Black Nation: Political Journalism in the Harlem Renaissance.* San Francisco: Ramparts Press, 1973.

Wells-Barnett, Ida B. *Selected Works of Ida B. Wells-Barnett.* New York: Oxford University Press, 1991.

Wolselley, Roland E. *The Black Press, U.S.A..* Ames: Iowa State University Press, 1971.

PRIMARY SOURCE DOCUMENT

"The Case Stated" and "Lynch Law Statistics" by Ida B. Wells-Barnett

INTRODUCTION With the 1892 destruction of her Memphis press and the lynching of three of her colleagues, the newspaperwoman Ida B. Wells-Barnett embarked on what was to be the great mission of her life: a tireless crusade against lynching and racial violence. Unafraid, Wells-Barnett rebuilt her paper, the Memphis *Free Speech,* with funds raised by Sarah Thompson Garnet (an educator and the widow of Henry Highland Garnet), among others. For the next forty years, until Wells-Barnett's death in 1931, hers was the principal voice raised against the barbarous practices that claimed thousands of black lives in the century following Emancipation.

In 1895, Wells-Barnett published *A Red Record,* exposing and attacking the national practice of lynching. Reprinted here are the first two chapters. "The Case Stated" offers a brief history of the post–Civil War South, along with a trenchant analysis of the psychological and political motivations behind lynching. "Lynch Law Statistics" lists the names of 159 victims of lynching during 1893 and their supposed "crimes," which include "Race Prejudice" and "Self Defense." Wells-Barnett also offers a brief statistical review of 1892, when 241 people were lynched, the greatest number in a single year.

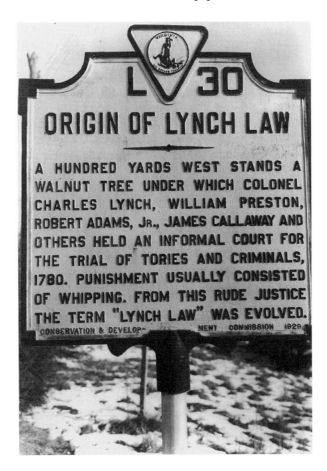

This sign in Virginia explains the origin of Lynch Law. Colonel Charles Lynch, along with his compatriots, held an informal court for Tories and criminals. The sentence usually consisted of whipping. From this sense of justice, the term "Lynch Law" evolved. **THE LIBRARY OF CONGRESS**

Chapter I

The Case Stated

The student of American sociology will find the year 1894 marked by a pronounced awakening of the public conscience to a system of anarchy and outlawry which had grown during a series of ten years to be so common, that scenes of unusual brutality failed to have any visible effect upon the humane sentiments of the people of our land.

Beginning with the emancipation of the Negro, the inevitable result of unbridled power exercised for two and a half centuries, by the white man over the Negro, began to show itself in acts of conscienceless outlawry. During the slave regime, the Southern white man owned the Negro body and soul. It was to his interest to dwarf the soul and preserve the body. Vested with unlimited power over his slave, to subject him to any and all kinds of physical punishment, the white man was still restrained from such punishment as tended to injure the slave by abating his physical powers and thereby reducing his financial worth. While slaves were scourged mercilessly, and in countless cases inhumanly treated in other respects, still the white owner rarely permitted his anger to go so far as to take a life, which would entail upon him a loss of several hundred dollars. The slave was rarely killed, he was too valuable; it was easier and quite as effective, for discipline or revenge, to sell him "Down South."

But Emancipation came and the vested interests of the white man in the Negro's body were lost. The white man had no right to scourge the emancipated Negro, still less has he a right to kill him. But the Southern white people had been educated so long in that school of practice, in which might makes right, that they disdained to draw strict lines of action in dealing with the Negro. In slave times the Negro was kept subservient and submissive by the frequency and severity of the scourging, but, with freedom, a new system of intimidation came into vogue; the Negro was not only whipped and scourged; he was killed.

Not all nor nearly all of the murders done by white men, during the past thirty years in the South, have come to light, but the statistics as gathered and preserved by white men, and which have not been questioned, show that during these years more than ten thousand Negroes have been killed in cold blood, without the formality of judicial trial and legal execution. And yet, as evidence of the absolute impunity with which the white man dares to kill a Negro, the same record shows that during all these years, and for all these murders only three white men have been tried, convicted, and executed. As no white man has been lynched for the murder of colored people, these three executions are the only instances of the death penalty being visited upon white men for murdering Negroes.

Naturally enough the commission of these crimes began to tell upon the public conscience, and the Southern white man, as a tribute to the nineteenth century civilization, was in a manner compelled to give excuses for his barbarism. His excuses have adapted themselves to the emergency, and are aptly outlined by that greatest of all Negroes, Frederick Douglass, in an article of recent date, in which he shows that there have been three distinct eras of Southern barbarism, to account for which three distinct excuses have been made.

The first excuse given to the civilized world for the murder of unoffending Negroes was the necessity of the white man to repress and stamp out alleged "race riots." For years immediately succeeding the war there was an appalling slaughter of colored people, and the wires usually conveyed to northern people and the world the intelligence, first, that an insurrection was being planned by Negroes, which, a few hours later, would prove to have been vigorously resisted by white men, and controlled with a resulting loss of several killed and wounded. It was always a remarkable feature in these insurrections and riots that only Negroes were killed during the rioting, and that all white men escaped unharmed.

From 1865 to 1872, hundreds of colored men and women were mercilessly murdered and the almost invariable reason assigned was that they met their death by being alleged participants in an insurrection or riot. But this story at last wore itself out. No insurrection ever materialized; no Negro rioter was ever apprehended and proven guilty, and no dynamite ever recorded the black man's protest against oppression and wrong. It was too much to ask thoughtful people to believe this transparent story, and the southern white people at last made up their minds that some other excuse must be had.

Then came the second excuse, which had its birth during the turbulent times of reconstruction. By an amendment to the Constitution the Negro was given the right of franchise, and, theoretically at least, his ballot became his invaluable emblem of citizenship. In a government "of the people, for the people, and by the people," the Negro's vote became an important factor in all matters of state and national politics. But this did not last long. The southern white man would not consider that the Negro had any right which a white man was bound to respect, and the idea of a republican form of government in the southern states grew into general con-

tempt. It was maintained that "This is a white man's government," and regardless of numbers the white man should rule. "No Negro domination" became the new legend on the sanguinary banner of the sunny South, and under it rode the Ku Klux Klan, the Regulators, and the lawless mobs, which for any cause chose to murder one man or a dozen as suited their purpose best. It was a long, gory campaign; the blood chills and the heart almost loses faith in Christianity when one thinks of Yazoo, Hamburg, Edgefield, Copiah, and the countless massacres of defenseless Negroes, whose only crime was the attempt to exercise their right to vote.

But it was a bootless strife for colored people. The government which had made the Negro a citizen found itself unable to protect him. It gave him the right to vote, but denied him the protection which should have maintained that right. Scourged from his home; hunted through the swamps; hung by midnight raiders, and openly murdered in the light of day, the Negro clung to his right of franchise with a heroism which would have wrung admiration from the hearts of savages. He believed that in that small white ballot there was a subtle something which stood for manhood as well as citizenship, and thousands of brave black men went to their graves, exemplifying the one by dying for the other.

The white man's victory soon became complete by fraud, violence, intimidation and murder. The franchise vouchsafed to the Negro grew to be a "barren ideality," and regardless of numbers, the colored people found themselves voiceless in the councils of those whose duty it was to rule. With no longer the fear of "Negro Domination" before their eyes, the white man's second excuse became valueless. With the Southern governments all subverted and the Negro actually eliminated from all participation in state and national elections, there could be no longer an excuse for killing Negroes to prevent "Negro Domination."

Brutality still continued; Negroes were whipped, scourged, exiled, shot and hung whenever and wherever it pleased the white man so to treat them, and as the civilized world with increasing persistency held the white people of the South to account for its outlawry, the murderers invented the third excuse—that Negroes had to be killed to avenge their assaults upon women. There could be framed no possible excuse more harmful to the Negro and more unanswerable if true in its sufficiency for the white man.

Humanity abhors the assailant of womanhood, and this charge upon the Negro at once placed him beyond the pale of human sympathy. With such unanimity, earnestness and apparent candor was this charge made and reiterated that the world has accepted the story that the Negro is a monster which the Southern white man has painted him. And to-day, the Christian world feels, that while lynching is a crime, and lawlessness and anarchy the certain precursors of a nation's fall, it can not by word or deed, extend sympathy or help to a race of outlaws, who might mistake their plea for justice and deem it an excuse for their continued wrongs.

The Negro has suffered much and is willing to suffer more. He recognizes that the wrongs of two centuries can not be righted in a day, and he tries to bear his burden with patience for to-day and be hopeful for to-morrow. But there comes a time when the veriest worm will turn, and the Negro feels to-day that after all the work he has done, all the sacrifices he has made, and all the suffering he has endured, if he did not, now, defend his name and manhood from this vile accusation, he would be unworthy even of the contempt of mankind. It is to this charge he now feels he must make answer.

If the Southern people in defense of their lawlessness, would tell the truth and admit that colored men and women are lynched for almost any offense, from murder to a misdemeanor, there would not now be the necessity for this defense. But when they intentionally, maliciously and constantly belie the record and bolster up these falsehoods by the words of legislators, preachers, governors and bishops, then the Negro must give to the world his side of the awful story.

A word as to the charge itself. In considering the third reason assigned by the Southern white people for the butchery of blacks, the question must be asked, what the white man means when he charges the black man with rape. Does he mean the crime which the statutes of the civilized states describe as such? Not by any means. With the Southern white man, any mesalliance existing between a white woman and a colored man is a sufficient foundation for the charge of rape. The Southern white man says that it is impossible for a voluntary alliance to exist between a white woman and a colored man, and therefore, the fact of an alliance is a proof of force. In numerous instances where colored men have been lynched on the charge of rape, it was positively known at the time of lynching, and indisputably proved after the victim's death, that the relationship sustained between the man and woman was voluntary and clandestine, and that in no court of law could even the charge of assault have been successfully maintained.

It was for the assertion of this fact, in the defense of her own race, that the writer hereof became an exile; her property destroyed and her return to her home forbidden under penalty of death, for writing the following editorial which was printed in her paper, the Free Speech, in Memphis, Tenn., May 21, 1892:

Eight Negroes lynched since last issue of the "Free Speech" one at Little Rock, Ark., last Saturday morning where the citizens broke (?) into the penitentiary and got their man; three near Anniston,

---

The Ku Klux Klan Holds Its First National Meeting

After the Civil War, many white southerners were astonished and enraged that former slaves should have the same rights under law that they enjoyed. The atmosphere of white indignation and aggression in the South began to manifest itself in the formation of racist organizations. In April of 1867, the Ku Klux Klan held its first national meeting. In May of the same year, a group of white supremacists organized the Knights of the White Camellia. During the next three decades the organization would go from being an angry discussion held at lunch counters to a loosely organized but effective group of white southerners, often those in power, such as members of law enforcement, foremen, and business owners.

Many of the Klan's rituals served both to publicize and glorify the grassroots terrorism of its members. The infamous cross burnings and white hoods were forms of social terrorism, designed to keep blacks in silence, disorganized and scared. Particularly horrifying were the public lynchings. There are hundreds of reports from the years 1870 to 1920 of public gatherings, complete with home cooking and dancing, where young black men would be hanged while the people in attendance looked on and cheered.

Ala., one near New Orleans; and three at Clarksville, Ga., the last three for killing a white man, and five on the same old racket—the new alarm about raping white women. The same programme of hanging, then shooting bullets into the lifeless bodies was carried out to the letter. Nobody in this section of the country believes the old threadbare lie that Negro men rape white women. If Southern white men are not careful, they will over-reach themselves and public sentiment will have a reaction; a conclusion will then be reached which will be very damaging to the moral reputation of their women.

But threats cannot suppress the truth, and while the Negro suffers the soul deformity, resultant from two and a half centuries of slavery, he is no more guilty of this vilest of all vile charges than the white man who would blacken his name.

During all the years of slavery, no such charge was ever made, not even during the dark days of the rebellion, when the white man, following the fortunes of war went to do battle for the maintenance of slavery. While the master was away fighting to forge the fetters upon the slave, he left his wife and children with no protectors save the Negroes themselves. And yet during those years of trust and peril, no Negro proved recreant to his trust and no white man returned to a home that had been dispoiled.

Likewise during the period of alleged "insurrection," and alarming "race riots," it never occurred to the white man, that his wife and children were in danger of assault. Nor in the Reconstruction era, when the hue and cry was against "Negro Domination," was there ever a thought that the domination would ever contaminate a fireside or strike to death the virtue of womanhood. It must appear strange indeed, to every thoughtful and candid man, that more than a quarter of a century elapsed before the Negro began to show signs of such infamous degeneration.

In his remarkable apology for lynching, Bishop Haygood, of Georgia, says: "No race, not the most savage, tolerates the rape of woman, but it may be said without reflection upon any other people that the Southern people are now and always have been most sensitive concerning the honor of their women—their mothers, wives, sisters and daughters." It is not the purpose of this defense to say one word against the white women of the South. Such need not be said, but it is their misfortune that the chivalrous white men of that section, in order to escape the deserved execration of the civilized world, should shield themselves by their cowardly and infamously false excuse, and call into question that very honor about which their distinguished priestly apologist claims they are most sensitive. To justify their own barbarism they assume a chivalry which they do not possess. True chivalry respects all womanhood, and no one who reads the record, as it is written in the faces of the million mulattoes in the South, will for a minute conceive that the southern white man had a very chivalrous regard for the honor due the women of his own race or respect for the womanhood which circumstances placed in his power. That chivalry which is "most sensitive concerning the honor of women" can hope for but little respect from the civilized world, when it confines itself entirely to the women who happen to be white. Virtue knows no color line, and the chivalry which depends upon complexion of skin and texture of hair can command no honest respect.

When emancipation came to the Negroes, there arose in the northern part of the United States an almost divine sentiment among the noblest, purest and best white women of the North, who felt called to a mission to educate and Christianize the millions of southern ex-slaves. From every nook and corner of the North, brave young white women answered that call and left their cultured homes, their happy associations and their lives of ease, and with heroic determination went to the South to carry light and truth to the benighted blacks. It was a heroism no less than that which calls for volunteers for India, Africa and the Isles of the sea. To educate their unfortunate charges; to teach them the Christian virtues and to inspire in them the moral sentiments manifest in their own lives, these young women braved dangers whose record reads more like fiction than fact. They became social outlaws in the South. The peculiar sensitiveness of the southern white men for women, never shed its protecting influence about them. No friendly word from their own race cheered them in their work; no hospitable doors gave them the companionship like that from which they had come. No chivalrous white man doffed his hat in honor or respect. They were "Nigger teachers"—unpardonable offenders in the social ethics of the South, and were insulted; persecuted and ostracised, not by Negroes, but by the white manhood which boasts of its chivalry toward women.

And yet these northern women worked on, year after year, unselfishly, with a heroism which amounted almost to martyrdom. Threading their way through dense forests, working in schoolhouse, in the cabin and in the church, thrown at all times and in all places among the unfortunate and lowly Negroes, whom they had come to find and to serve, these northern women, thousands of them, have spent more than a quarter of a century in giving to the colored people their splendid lessons for home and heart and soul. Without protection, save that which innocence gives to every good woman, they went about their work, fearing no assault and suffering none. Their chivalrous protectors were hundreds of miles away in their northern homes, and yet they never feared any "great dark faced mobs," they dared night or day to "go beyond their own roof trees." They never complained of assaults, and no mob was ever called into existence to avenge crimes against them. Before the world adjudges the Negro a moral monster, a vicious assailant of womanhood and a menace to the sacred precincts of home, the colored people ask the consideration of the silent record of gratitude, respect, protection and devotion of the millions of the race in the South, to the thousands of northern white women who have served as teachers and missionaries since the war.

The Negro may not have known what chivalry was, but he knew enough to preserve inviolate the womanhood of the South which was entrusted to his hands during the war. The finer sensibilities of his soul may have been crushed out by years of slavery, but his heart was full of gratitude to the white women of the North, who blessed his home and inspired his soul in all these years of freedom. Faithful to his trust in both of these instances, he should now have the impartial ear of the civilized world, when he dares to speak for himself as against the infamy wherewith he stands charged.

It is his regret, that, in his own defense, he must disclose to the world that degree of dehumanizing brutality which fixes upon America the blot of a national crime. Whatever faults and failings other nations may have in their dealings with their own subjects or with other people, no other civilized nation stands condemned before the world with a series of crimes so peculiarly national. It becomes a painful duty of the Negro to reproduce a record which shows that a large portion of the American people avow anarchy, condone murder and defy the contempt of civilization.

These pages are written in no spirit of vindictiveness, for all who give the subject consideration must concede that far too serious is the condition of that civilized government in which the spirit of unrestrained outlawry constantly increases in violence, and casts its blight over a continually growing area of territory. We plead not for the colored people alone, but for all victims of the terrible injustice which puts men and women to death without form of law. During the year 1894, there were 132 persons executed in the United States by due form of law, while in the same year, 197 persons were put to death by mobs who gave the victims no opportunity to make a lawful defense. No comment need be made upon a condition of public sentiment responsible for such alarming results.

The purpose of the pages which follow shall be to give the record which has been made, not by colored men, but that which is the result of compilations made by white men, of reports sent over the civilized world by white men in the South. Out of their own mouths shall the murderers be condemned. For a number of years the *Chicago Tribune,* admittedly one of the leading journals of America, has made a specialty of the compilation of statistics touching upon lynching. The data compiled by that journal and published to the world January 1st, 1894, up to the present time has not been disputed. In order to be safe from the charge of exaggeration, the incidents hereinafter reported have been confined to those vouched for by the *Tribune.*

Chapter II

Lynch Law Statistics

From the record published in the *Chicago Tribune,* January 1, 1894, the following computation of lynching statistics is made referring only to the colored victims of Lynch Law during the year 1893:

Arson: Sept. 15, Paul Hill, Carrollton, Ala.; Sept. 15, Paul Archer, Carrollton, Ala.; Sept. 15, William Archer, Carrollton, Ala.; Sept. 15, Emma Fair, Carrollton, Ala.

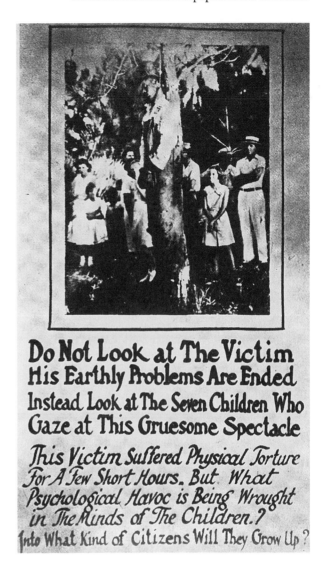

An antilynching poster produced by the NAACP. Not only does the photo draw attention to the lynching of an African American, but also to the psychological damage done to children growing up in such a frightening atmosphere. **ARCHIVE PHOTOS, INC.**

Suspected Robbery: Dec. 23, unknown Negro, Fannin, Miss.

Assault: Dec. 25, Calvin Thomas, near Brainbridge, Ga.

Attempted Assault: Dec. 28, Tillman Green, Columbia, La.

Incendiarism: Jan. 26, Patrick Wells, Quincy, Fla.; Feb. 9, Frank Harrell, Dickery, Miss.; Feb. 9, William Filder, Dickery, Miss.

Attempted Rape: Feb. 21, Richard Mays, Springville, Mo.; Aug. 14, Dug Hazleton, Carrollton, Ga.; Sept. 1, Judge McNeil, Cadiz, Ky.; Sept. 11, Frank Smith, Newton, Miss.; Sept. 16, William Jackson, Nevada, Mo.; Sept. 19, Riley Gulley, Pine Apple, Ala.; Oct. 9, John Davis, Shorterville, Ala.; Nov. 8, Robert Kennedy, Spartansburg, S. C.

Burglary: Feb. 16, Richard Forman, Granada, Miss.

Wife Beating: Oct. 14, David Jackson, Covington, La.

Attempted Murder: Sept. 21, Thomas Smith, Roanoke, Va.

Attempted Robbery: Dec. 12, four unknown negroes, near Selma, Ala.

Race Prejudice: Jan. 30, Thomas Carr, Kosciusko, Miss.; Feb. 7, William Butler, Hickory Creek, Texas; Aug. 27, Charles Tart, Lyons Station, Miss.; Dec. 7, Robert Greenwood, Cross county, Ark,; July 14, Allen Butler, Lawrenceville, Ill.

Thieves: Oct. 24, two unknown negroes, Knox Point, La.

Alleged Barn Burning: Nov. 4, Edward Wagner, Lynchburg, Va.; Nov. 4, William Wagner, Lynchburg, Va.; Nov. 4, Samuel Motlow, Lynchburg, Va.; Nov. 4, Eliza Motlow, Lynchburg, Va.

Alleged Murder: Jan. 21, Robert Landry, St. James Parish, La.; Jan. 21, Chicken George, St. James Parish, La.; Jan. 21, Richard Davis, St. James Parish, La.; Dec. 8, Benjamin Menter, Berlin, Ala.; Dec. 8, Robert Wilkins, Berlin, Ala.; Dec. 8, Joseph Gevhens, Berlin, Ala.

Alleged Complicity In Murder: Sept. 16, Valsin Julian, Jefferson Parish, La.; Sept. 16, Basil Julian, Jefferson Parish, La.; Sept. 16, Paul Julian, Jefferson Parish, La.; Sept. 16, John Willis, Jefferson Parish, La.

Murder: June 29, Samuel Thorp, Savannah, Ga.; June 29, George S. Riechen, Waynesboro, Ga.; June 30, Joseph Bird, Wilberton, I. T.; July 1, James Lamar, Darlen Ga.; July 28, Henry Miller, Dallas, Texas; July 28, Ada Hiers, Walterboro, S. C.; July 28, Alexander Brown, Bastrop, Texas; July 30, W. G. Jamison, Quincy, Ill.; Sept. 1, John Ferguson, Lawrens, S. C.; Sept. 1, Oscar Johnston, Berkeley, S. C.; Sept. 1, Henry Ewing, Berkeley, S. C.; Sept. 8, William Smith, Camden, Ark.; Sept. 15, Staples Green, Livingston, Ala.; Sept. 29, Hiram Jacobs, Mount Vernon, Ga.; Sept. 29, Lucien Mannet, Mount Vernon, Ga.; Sept. 29, Hire Bevington, Mount Vernon, Ga.; Sept. 29, Weldon Gordon, Mount Vernon, Ga.; Sept. 29, Parse Strickland, Mount Vernon, Ga.; Oct. 20, William Dalton, Cartersville, Ga.; Oct. 27, M. B. Taylor, Wise Court House, Va.; Oct. 27, Isaac Williams, Madison, Ga.; Nov. 10, Miller Davis, Center Point, Ark.; Nov. 14, John Johnston, Auburn, N. Y.; Sept. 27, Calvin Stewart, Langley, S. C.; Sept. 29, Henry Coleman, Benton, La.; Oct. 18, William Richards, Summerfield, Ga.; Oct. 18, James Dickson, Summerfield, Ga.; Oct. 27, Edward Jenkins, Clayton county, Ga.; Nov. 9, Henry Boggs, Fort White, Fla.; Nov. 14, three unknown negroes, Lake City Junction, Fla.; Nov. 14, D. T. Nelson, Varney,

Ark.; Nov. 29, Newton Jones, Baxley, Ga.; Dec. 2, Lucius Holt, Concord, Ga.; Dec. 10, two unknown negroes, Richmond, Ala.; July 12, Henry Fleming, Columbus, Miss.; July 17, unknown negro, Briar Field, Ala.; July 18, Meredith Lewis, Roseland, La.; July 29, Edward Bill, Dresden, Tenn.; Aug. 1, Henry Reynolds, Montgomery, Tenn.; Aug. 9, unknown negro, McCreery, Ark.; Aug. 12, unknown negro, Brantford, Fla.; Aug. 18, Charles Walton, Morganfield, Ky.; Aug. 21, Charles Tait, near Memphis, Tenn.; Aug. 28, Leonard Taylor, New Castle, Ky.; Sept. 8, Benjamin Jackson, Quincy, Miss.; Sept. 14, John Williams, Jackson, Tenn.

Self Defense: July 30, unknown negro, Wingo, Ky.

Poisoning Wells: Aug. 18, two unknown negroes, Franklin Parish, La.

Alleged Well Poisoning: Sept. 15, Benjamin Jackson, Jackson, Miss.; Sept. 15, Mahala Jackson, Jackson, Miss.; Sept. 15, Louisa Carter, Jackson, Miss.; Sept. 15, W. A. Haley, Jackson, Miss.; Sept. 15, Rufus Bigley, Jackson, Miss.

Insulting Whites: Feb. 18, John Hughes, Moberly, Mo.; June 2, Isaac Lincoln, Fort Madison, S. C.

Murderous Assault: April 20, Daniel Adams, Selina, Kan.

No Offense: July 21, Charles Martin, Shelby Co., Tenn.; July 30, William Steen, Paris, Miss.; August 31, unknown negro, Yarborough, Tex.; Sept. 30, unknown negro, Houston, Tex.; Dec. 28, Mack Segars, Brantley, Ala.

Alleged Rape: July 7, Charles T. Miller, Bardwell, Ky.; Aug. 10, Daniel Lewis, Waycross, Ga.; Aug. 10, James Taylor, Waycross, Ga.; Aug. 10, John Chambers, Waycross, Ga.

Alleged Stock Poisoning: Dec. 16, Henry G. Givens, Nebro, Ky.

Suspected Murder: Dec. 23, Sloan Allen, West Mississippi.

Suspicion Of Rape: Feb. 14, Andy Blount, Chattanooga, Tenn.

Turning State's Evidence: Dec. 19, William Ferguson, Adele, Ga.

Rape: Jan. 19, James Williams, Pickens Co., Ala.; Feb. 11, unknown negro, Forest Hill, Tenn.; Feb. 26, Joseph Hayne, or Paine, Jellico, Tenn.; Nov. 1, Abner Anthony, Hot Springs, Va.; Nov. 1, Thomas Hill, Spring Place, Ga.; April 24, John Peterson, Denmark, S. C.; May 6, Samuel Gaillard, ____, S. C.; May 10, Haywood Banks, or Marksdale, Columbia, S. C.; May 12, Israel Halliway,

Napoleonville, La.; May 12, unknown negro, Wytheville, Va.; May 31, John Wallace, Jefferson Springs, Ark.; June 3, Samuel Bush, Decatur, Ill.; June 8, L. C. Dumas, Gleason, Tenn.; June 13, William Shorter, Winchester, Va.; June 14, George Williams, near Waco, Tex.; June 24, Daniel Edwards, Selina or Selma, Ala.; June 27, Ernest Murphy, Daleville, Ala.; July 6, unknown negro, Poplar Head, La.; July 6, unknown negro, Poplar Head, La.; July 12, Robert Larkin, Oscola, Tex.; July 17, Warren Dean, Stone Creek, Ga.; July 21, unknown negro, Brantford, Fla.; July 17, John Cotton, Connersville, Ark.; July 22, Lee Walker, New Albany, Miss.; July 26, ____ Handy, Suansea, S. C.; July 30, William Thompson, Columbia, S. C.; July 28, Isaac Harper, Calera, Ala.; July 30, Thomas Preston, Columbia, S. C.; July 30, Handy Kaigler, Columbia, S. C.; Aug. 13, Monroe Smith, Springfield, Ala.; Aug. 19, negro tramp, near Paducah, Ky.; Aug. 21, John Nilson, near Leavenworth, Kan.; Aug. 23, Jacob Davis, Green Wood, S. C.; Sept. 2, William Arkinson, McKenney, Ky.; Sept. 16, unknown negro, Centerville, Ala.; Sept. 16, Jessie Mitchell, Amelia C. H., Va.; Sept. 25, Perry Bratcher, New Boston, Tex.; Oct. 9, William Lacey, Jasper, Ala.; Oct. 22, John Gamble, Pikesville, Tenn.

Offenses Charged Are As Follows: Rape, 39; attempted rape, 8; alleged rape, 4; suspicion of rape, 1; murder 44; alleged murder, 6; alleged complicity in murder, 4; murderous assault, 1; attempted murder, 1; attempted robbery, 4; arson, 4; incendiarism, 3; alleged stock poisoning, 1; poisoning wells, 2; alleged poisoning wells, 5; burglary, 1; wife beating, 1; self defense, 1; suspected robbery, 1; assault and battery, 1; insulting whites, 2; malpractice, 1; alleged barn burning, 4; stealing, 2; unknown offense, 4; no offense, 1; race prejudice, 4; total, 159.

Lynchings By States: Alabama, 25; Arkansas, 7; Florida, 7; Georgia, 24; Indian Territory, 1; Illinois, 3; Kansas, 2; Kentucky, 8; Louisiana, 18; Mississippi, 17; Missouri, 3; New York, 1; South Carolina, 15; Tennessee, 10; Texas, 8; Virginia, 10.

Record For The Year 1892

While is it intended that the record here presented shall include specially the lynchings of 1893, it will not be amiss to give the record for the year preceding. The facts contended for will always appear manifest—that not one-third of the victims lynched were charged with rape, and further that the charges made embraced a range of offenses from murders to misdemeanors.

In 1892 there were 241 persons lynched. The entire number is divided among the following states:

Alabama, 22; Arkansas, 25; California, 3; Florida, 11; Georgia, 17; Idaho, 8; Illinois, 1; Kansas, 3; Kentucky, 9; Louisiana, 29; Maryland, 1; Mississippi, 16; Missouri, 6; Montana, 4; New York, 1; North Carolina, 5; North Dakota, 1; Ohio, 3; South Carolina, 5; Tennessee, 28; Texas, 15; Virginia, 7; West Virginia, 5; Wyoming, 9; Arizona Territory, 3; Oklahoma, 2.

Of this number 160 were of Negro descent. Four of them were lynched in New York, Ohio and Kansas; the remainder were murdered in the South. Five of this number were females. The charges for which they were lynched cover a wide range. They are as follows: Rape, 46; murder, 58; rioting, 3; race prejudice, 6; no cause given, 4; incendiarism, 6; robbery, 6; assault and battery, 1; attempted rape, 11; suspected robbery, 4; larceny, 1; self defense, 1; insulting women, 2; desperadoes, 6; fraud, 1; attempted murder, 2; no offense stated, boy and girl, 2.

In the case of the boy and girl above referred to, their father, named Hastings, was accused of the murder of white man; his fourteen-year-old daughter and sixteen-year-old son were hanged and their bodies filled with bullets, then the father was also lynched. This was in November, 1892, at Jonesville, Louisiana.

PRIMARY SOURCE DOCUMENT

Marcus Garvey and the "Africa for Africans" Movement

INTRODUCTION "Africa for the Africans," written in 1919, is one of Marcus Garvey's most compelling statements of his hopes for the future of Africa and African Americans. It shares many of the tenets of earlier colonization movements, including a belief in the necessity of racial separation. As always in his writings, Garvey emphasized the central role the Universal Negro Improvement Association was to play in uniting black people of the world.

"Africa for the Africans" is one of the principal documents of not only the colonization movement but also of the evolving diaspora of Africans in the Americas. (Marcus Garvey was of West Indian descent.) It also speaks to their efforts to find some solution to the problems of identity and economic and political opportunity experienced by those living in the New World.

Marcus Garvey's Vision of a Redeemed Africa

For five years the Universal Negro Improvement Association has been advocating the cause of Africa for the Africans—that is, that the Negro peoples of the world should concentrate upon the object of building up for themselves a great nation in Africa.

When we started our propaganda toward this end several of the so-called intellectual Negroes who have been bamboozling the race for over half a century said that we were crazy, that the Negro peoples of the western world were not interested in Africa and could not live in Africa.

Marcus Garvey (1887–1940) and the "Africa for Africans" Movement

Marcus Garvey was prosecuted, imprisoned, and then deported to the Caribbean. Garvey's message was infuriating to those in power: on the one hand he emphasized a return to Africa, but on the other his message clearly called for African Americans to unite and to see the power they had in numbers. Garvey's message was a necessary precursor to the work of Martin Luther King Jr. and to Malcolm X many decades later. For many, Garvey's imprisonment and deportation were an obvious attempt to silence one of the few leaders of the African American people to take the national and international stage during the first quarter of the twentieth century.

One editor and leader went so far as to say at his so-called Pan-African Congress that American Negroes could not live in Africa, because the climate was too hot. All kinds of arguments have been adduced by these Negro intellectuals against the colonization of Africa by the black race. Some said that the black man would ultimately work out his existence alongside of the white man in countries founded and established by the latter. Therefore, it was not necessary for Negroes to seek an independent nationality of their own. The old time stories of "African fever," "African bad climate," "African mosquitos," "African savages," have been repeated by these "brainless intellectuals" of ours as a scare against our people in America and the West Indies taking a kindly interest in the new program of building a racial empire of our own in our Motherland. Now that years have rolled by and the Universal Negro Improvement Association has made the circuit of the world with its propaganda, we find eminent statesmen and leaders of the white race coming out boldly advocating the cause of colonizing Africa with the Negroes of the western world. A year ago Senator MacCullum of the Mississippi Legislature introduced a resolution in the House for the purpose of petitioning the Congress of the United States of America and the President to use their good influence in securing from the Allies sufficient territory in Africa in liquidation of the war debt, which territory should be used for the establishing of an independent nation for American Negroes. About the same time Senator France of Maryland gave expression to a similar desire in the Senate of the United States. During a speech on the "Soldiers' Bonus." He said: "We owe a big debt to Africa and one which we have too long ignored. I need not enlarge upon our peculiar interest in the obligation to the people of Africa. Thousands of Americans have for years been contributing to the missionary work which has been carried out by the noble men and women who have been sent out in that field by the churches of America."

This reveals a real change on the part of prominent statesmen in their attitude on the African question. Then comes another suggestion from Germany, for which Dr. Heinrich Schnee, a former Governor of German East Africa, is author. This German statesman suggests in an interview given out in Berlin, and published in New York, that America takes over the mandatories of Great Britain and France in Africa for the colonization of American Negroes. Speaking on the matter, he says, "As regards the attempt to colonize Africa with the surplus American colored population, this would in a long way settle the vexed problem, and under the plan such as Senator France has outlined, might enable France and Great Britain to discharge their duties to the United States, and simultaneously ease the burden of German reparations which is paralyzing economic life."

With expressions as above quoted from prominent world statesmen, and from the demands made by such men as Senators France and McCullum, it is clear that the question of African nationality is not a far-fetched one, but is as reasonable and feasible as was the idea of an American nationality.

A "Program" at Last

I trust that the Negro peoples of the world are now convinced that the work of the Universal Negro Improvement Association is not a visionary one, but very practical, and that it is not so far fetched, but can be realized in a short while if the entire race will only cooperate and work toward the desired end. Now that the work of our organization has started to bear fruit we find that some of these "doubting Thomases" of three and four years ago are endeavoring to mix themselves up with the popular idea of rehabilitating Africa in the interest of the Negro. They are now advancing spurious "programs" and in a short while will endeavor to force themselves upon the public as advocates and leaders of the African idea.

It is felt that those who have followed the career of the Universal Negro Improvement Association will not allow themselves to be deceived by these Negro opportunities who have always sought to live off the ideas of other people.

The Dream of a Negro Empire

It is only a question of a few more years when Africa will be completely colonized by Negroes, as Europe is by the white race. What we want is an independent African nationality, and if America is to help the Negro peoples of the world establish such a nationality, then we welcome the assistance.

It is hoped that when the time comes for American and West Indian Negroes to settle in Africa, they will realize their responsibility and their duty. It will not be to go to Africa for the purpose of exercising an over-lordship over the natives, but it shall be the purpose of the Universal Negro Improvement Association to have established in Africa that brotherly co-operation which will make the interests of the African native and the American and West Indian Negro one and the same, that is to say, we shall enter into a common partnership to build up Africa in the interests of our race.

Oneness of Interests

Everybody knows that there is absolutely no difference between the native African and the American and West Indian Negroes, in that we are descendants from one common family stock. It is only a matter of accident that we have been divided and kept apart for over three hundred years, but it is felt that when the time has come for us to get back together, we shall do so in the spirit of brotherly love, and any Negro who expects that he will be assisted here, there or anywhere by the Universal Improvement Association to exercise a haughty superiority over the fellows of his own race, makes a tremendous mistake. Such men had better remain where they are and not attempt to become in any way interested in the higher development of Africa.

The Negro has had enough of the vaunted practiced of race superiority as inflicted upon him by others, therefore he is not prepared to tolerate a similar assumption on the part of his own people. In America and the West Indies, we have Negroes who believe themselves so much above their fellows as to cause them to think that any readjustment in the affairs of the race should be placed in their hands for them to exercise a kind of an autocratic and despotic control as others have done to us for centuries. Again I say, it would be advisable for such Negroes to take their hands and minds off the now popular idea of colonizing Africa in the interest of the Negro race, because their being identified with this new program will not in any way help us because of the existing feeling among Negroes everywhere not to tolerate the infliction of race or class superiority upon them, as is the desire of the self-appointed and self-created race leadership that we have been having for the last fifty years.

The Basis of an African Aristocracy

The masses of Negroes in America, the West Indies, South and Central America are in sympathetic accord with the aspirations of the native Africans. We desire to help them build up Africa as a Negro Empire, where every black man, whether he was born in Africa or in the Western world, will have the opportunity to develop on his own lines under the protection of the most favorable democratic institutions.

It will be useless, as before stated, for bombastic Negroes to leave America and the West Indies to go to Africa, thinking that they will have privileged positions to inflict upon the race that bastard aristocracy that they have tried to maintain in this Western world at the expense of the masses. Africa shall develop an aristocracy of its own, but it shall be based upon service and loyalty to race. Let all Negroes work toward that end. I feel that it is only a question of a few more years before our program will be accepted not only by the few statesmen of America who are now interested in it, but by the strong statesmen of the world, as the only solution to the great race problem. There is no other way to avoid the threatening war of the races that is bound to engulf all mankind, which has been prophesied by the world's greatest thinkers; there is no better method than by apportioning every race to its own habitat.

The time has really come for the Asiatics to govern themselves in Asia, as the Europeans are in Europe and the Western world, so also is it wise for the Africans to govern themselves at home, and thereby bring peace and satisfaction to the entire human family.

The Future as I See It

It comes to the individual, the race, the nation, once in a life-time to decide upon the course to be pursued as a career. The hour has now struck for the individual Negro as well as the entire race to decide the course that will be pursued in the interest of our own liberty.

We who make up the Universal Negro Improvement Association have decided that we shall go forward, upward and onward toward the great goal of human liberty. We have determined among ourselves that all barriers placed in the way of our progress must be removed, must be cleared away for we desire to see the light of a brighter day.

The Negro Is Ready

The Universal Negro Improvement Association for five years has been proclaiming to the world the readiness of the Negro to carve out a pathway for himself in the course of life. Men of other races and nations have become alarmed at this attitude of the Negro in his desire to do things for himself and by himself. This alarm has become so universal that organizations have been brought into being here, there and everywhere for the purpose of deterring and obstructing this forward move of our race. Propaganda has been waged here, there and everywhere for the purpose of misinterpreting the intention of this organization; some have said that this organization seeks to create discord and discontent among the races; some say we are organized for the purpose of hating other people. Every sensible, sane and honest-minded person knows that the Universal Negro Improvement Association has no such intention. We are organized for the absolute purpose of bettering our condition, industrially, commercially, socially, religiously and politically. We are organized not to hate other men, but to lift ourselves, and to demand respect of all humanity. We have a program that we believe to be righteous; we believe it to be just, and we have made up our minds to lay down ourselves on the altar of sacrifice for the realization of this great hope of ours, based upon the foundation of righteousness. We declare to the world that Africa must be free, that the entire Negro race must be emancipated from industrial bondage, peonage and serfdom; we make no compromise, we make no apology in this our declaration. We do not desire to create offense on the part of other races, but we are determined that we shall be heard, that we shall be given the rights to which we are entitled.

The Propaganda of Our Enemies

For the purpose of creating doubts about the work of the Universal Negro Improvement Association, many attempts have been made to cast shadow and gloom over our work. They have even written the most uncharitable things about our organization; they have spoken so unkindly of our effort, but what do we care? They spoke unkindly and uncharitably about all the reform movements that have helped in the betterment of humanity. They maligned the great movement of the Christian religion; they maligned the great liberation movements of America, of France, of England, of Russia; can we expect, then, to escape being maligned in this, our desire for the liberation of Africa and the freedom of four hundred million Negroes of the world?

We have unscrupulous men and organizations working in opposition to us. Some trying to capitalize the new spirit that has come to the Negro to make profit out of it to their own selfish benefit; some are trying to set back the Negro from seeing the hope of his own liberty, and thereby poisoning our people's mind against the motives of our organization; but every sensible far-seeing Negro in this enlightened age knows what propaganda means. It is the medium of discrediting that which you are opposed to, so that the propaganda of our enemies will be of little avail as soon as we are rendered able to carry to our peoples scattered throughout the world the true message of our great organization.

"Crocodiles" as Friends

Men of the Negro race, let me say to you that a greater future is in store for us; we have no cause to lose hope, to become fainthearted. We must realize that upon ourselves depend our destiny, our future; we must carve out that future, that destiny, and we who make up the Universal Negro Improvement Association have pledged ourselves that nothing in the world shall stand in our way, nothing in the world shall discourage us, but opposition shall make us work harder, shall bring us closer together so that as one man the millions of us will march on toward that goal that we have set for ourselves. The new Negro shall not be deceived. The new Negro refuses to take advice from anyone who has not felt with him, and suffered with him. We have suffered for three hundred years, therefore we feel that the time has come when only those who have suffered with us can interpret our feelings and our spirit. It takes the slave to interpret the feelings of the slave; it takes the unfortunate man to interpret the spirit of his unfortunate brother; and so it takes the suffering Negro to interpret the spirit of his comrade. It is strange that so many people are interested in the Negro now, willing to advise him how to act, and what organizations he should join, yet nobody was interested in the Negro to the extent of not making him a slave for two hundred and fifty years, reducing him to industrial peonage and serfdom after he was freed; it is strange that the same people can be so interested in the Negro now, as to tell him what organization he should follow and what leader he should support.

Whilst we are bordering on a future of brighter things, we are also at our danger period, when we must either accept the right philosophy, or go down by following deceptive propaganda which has hemmed us in for many centuries.

Deceiving the People

There is many a leader of our race who tells us that everything is well, and that all things will work out themselves and that a better day is coming. Yes, all of us know that a better day is coming; we all know that one day we will go home to Paradise, but whilst we are hoping by our Christian virtues to have an entry into Paradise we also realize that we are living on earth, and that the things that are practiced in Paradise are not practiced here. You have to treat this world as the world treats you; we are living in a temporal, material age, an age of activity, an age of racial, national selfishness. What else can you expect but to give back to the world what the world gives to you, and we are calling upon the four hundred million Negroes of the world to take a decided stand, a determined stand, that we shall occupy a firm position; that position shall be an emancipated race and a free nation of our own. We are determined that we shall have a free country; we are determined that we shall have a flag; we are determined that we shall have a government second to none in the world.

An Eye for an Eye

Men may spurn the idea, they may scoff at it; the metropolitan press of this country may deride us; yes, white men may laugh at the idea of Negroes talking about government; but let me tell you there is going to be a government, and let me say to you also that whatsoever you give, in like measure it shall be returned to you. The world is sinful, and therefore man believes in the doctrine of an eye for an eye, a tooth for a tooth. Everybody believes that revenge is God's, but at the same time we are men, and revenge sometimes springs up, even in the most Christian heart.

Why should man write down a history that will react against him? Why should man perpetrate deeds of wickedness upon his brother which will return to him in like measure? Yes, the Germans maltreated the French in the Franco-Prussian war of 1870, but the French got even with the Germans in 1918. It is history, and history will repeat itself. Beat the Negro, brutalize the Negro, kill the Negro, burn the Negro, imprison the Negro, scoff at the Negro, deride the Negro, it may come back to you one of these fine days, because the supreme destiny of man is in the hands of God. God is no respecter of persons, whether that person be white, yellow or black. Today the one race is up, tomorrow it has fallen; today the Negro seems to be the footstool of the other races and nations of the world; tomorrow the Negro may occupy the highest rung of the great human ladder.

But, when we come to consider the history of man, was not the Negro a power, was he not great one? Yes, honest students of history can recall the day when Egypt, Ethiopia and Timbuctoo towered in their civilizations, towered above Europe, towered above Asia. When Europe was inhabited by a race of cannibals, a race of savages, naked men, heathens and pagans, Africa was peopled with a race of cultured black men, who were masters in art, science and literature; men who were cultured and refined; men who, it was said, were like the gods. Even the great poets of old sang in beautiful sonnets of the delight it afforded the gods to be in companionship with the Ethiopians. Why, then, should we lose hope? Black men, you were once great; you shall be great

again. Lose not courage, lose not faith, go forward. The thing to do is to get organized; keep separated and you will be exploited, you will be robbed, you will be killed. Get organized, and you will compel the world to respect you. If the world fails to give you consideration, because you are black men, because you are Negroes, four hundred millions of you shall, through organization, shake the pillars of the universe and bring down creation, even as Samson brought down the temple upon his head and upon the heads of the Philistines.

An Inspiring Vision

So Negroes, I say, through the Universal Negro Improvement Association, that there is much to live for. I have a vision of the future, and I see before me a picture of a redeemed Africa, with her dotted cities, with her beautiful civilization, with her millions of happy children, going to and fro. Why should I lose hope, why should I give up and take a back place in this age of progress? Remember that you are men, that God created you Lords of this creation. Lift up yourselves, men, take yourselves out of the mire and hitch your hopes to the stars; yes, rise as high as the very stars themselves. Let no man pull you down, let no man destroy your ambition, because man is but your companion, your equal; man is your brother; he is not your lord; he is not your sovereign master.

We of the Universal Negro Improvement Association feel happy; we are cheerful. Let them connive to destroy us; let them organize to destroy us; we shall fight the more. Ask me personally the cause of my success, and I say opposition; oppose me, and I fight the more, and if you want to find out the sterling worth of the Negro, oppose him, and under the leadership of the Universal Negro Improvement Association he shall fight his way to victory, and in the days to come, and I believe not far distant, Africa shall reflect a splendid demonstration of the worth of the Negro, of the determination of the Negro, to set himself free and to establish a government of his own.

The Long Journey
Toward Integration

The beginning of the twentieth century was a particularly harsh period in the history of African Americans in the United States. Between "black codes" and Jim Crow in the South and the absence of legitimate financial opportunity in the northern cities, African Americans were caught in a vise of poverty and illiteracy. To a great extent the first quarter of the twentieth century was the most pronounced and infamous period for public whippings and lynchings, and a sizable portion of the enduring stereotypes and racist imagery that Americans spent the better part of the twentieth century dealing with had their origins in this period.

As the nation moved into the post–Civil War era, the debate over racial equality and discrimination moved into the court of law. If we seek to paint the legal story in broad strokes, there are essentially two cases that formed the legal and by extension the social attitudes toward race at the beginning of the twentieth century. In the decade preceding the Civil War, the courts ruled on the Dred Scott case, stating explicitly that blacks were never intended to be citizens of the United States and that they in effect had no rights that whites were bound to respect; perhaps even more to the point, the courts ruled that persons of African descent might be kept in slavery for their own benefit. While this ruling was undone by the Emancipation Proclamation and the Thirteenth, Fourteenth, and Fifteenth Constitutional Amendments following the Civil War, the remainder of the century played out under the specter of the black codes and Jim Crow. The next legal blow, however, was even more sweeping in its implications. Homer Plessy, a biracial African American who could pass for white, brought a suit, argued that segregation violated the Fourteenth Amendment and that it treated him as an inferior following ejection from the "whites only" section of a train car and his subsequent arrest. In 1896, in the infamous case of *Plessy* v. *Ferguson,* the U.S. Supreme Court ruled that the amendment was designed to create "equality" but not to "abolish distinctions based on color." It was this ruling that perpetuated the norms of racial inequality and gave legal support to local governments—primarily in the South, but in the North as well—as they went about instituting the segregated society that would become the direct target of the peaceful demonstrations of the Civil Rights movement of the late 1950s and 1960s.

Dred Scott and *Plessy* v. *Ferguson,* however, indicate more than just the increasing legal machinations of the local and federal establishments in regard to the rights of African Americans. The nation was entering new territory. During the process of modernization and the Industrial Revolution, Americans of European descent were being thrown into contact—and asked to interact—with peoples they had previously expected only to control. The early 1900s were marked with a sort of desperation and fear exhibited by the vicious enforcement of laws and social contructs designed to keep African Americans in positions of educational, social, financial, and even religious inferiority. All these circumstances helped "white America" to maintain a superior self-image that was subsequently challenged by every advance made by African American communities as they worked toward becoming fully involved in American society. ∎

African Americans and the Law

ADAPTED FROM ESSAYS BY KIMBERLY GOFF-CREWS

While laws do not tell us everything about people's behavior, they do tell us what kinds of behavior a given society values, what it permits and even encourages, and what it prohibits. This fact has been particularly important in the history of African Americans.

During the era of slavery, their lives, families, and property were governed (though rarely protected) by laws they did not write, laws intended to permit, encourage, or prohibit the behavior of others toward them. Since Emancipation, and particularly in the twentieth century, African Americans have taken an active role in reshaping the nation's laws to better protect all citizens. Their struggle for equal justice under the law has been at the heart of a reinterpretation and broadening of constitutional protections for all Americans.

IN THE BEGINNING

From the early 1600s until the passage of the Thirteenth Amendment to the Constitution, African Americans' lives were governed by a series of laws and police regulations known as slave codes, originally passed by British colonial territories. These codes restricted the rights and privileges of African American slaves and freedmen and to some

degree controlled how whites could or could not relate to them. The codes regulated a wide range of activities, including access to education, travel, and marriage. They undergirded the institution of slavery, protecting whites from possible violence against them by slaves while enforcing their absolute right to control all aspects of the lives of Africans and their descendants on this continent.

In 1787, the original thirteen colonies ratified the Constitution, which, in concert with the Bill of Rights (the first ten amendments to the Constitution), set forth the rights and privileges afforded to all citizens of the newly formed nation. The original language of the Constitution made it evident that the term "citizen" did not include Africans and their descendants, whether slave or free. For example, paragraph 3 of Article I, Section 2, referred to people of African descent as "three fifths of all other Persons"—thus the term "three-fifths of a man." Furthermore, paragraph 3 of Article IV, Section 2, required that runaway slaves be returned to their masters and effectively denied them the right to be free of servitude should they escape to a state that prohibited slavery.

SEE PRIMARY SOURCE DOCUMENT *Excerpt from the Denmark Vesey Trial Record*

THE CASE OF DRED SCOTT

The Supreme Court underscored the fact that people of African descent were not citizens in the case of *Dred Scott* v. *Sandford.* In that case, Dred Scott (1809–1858) and his wife, both slaves owned by an army physician, moved with their master from a military post in a slave state to one in a free state. While there, the couple gave birth to two children. Upon returning to the slave state, Scott sued his owner for his and his family's freedom on the ground that they had lived in the free state. The trial court ruled in his favor, but the Missouri Supreme Court reversed the ruling.

While the case was being appealed, Dred Scott and his family were bequeathed to another owner. Scott later sued the second owner, a New York native, in federal court, pursuant to laws allowing citizens from different states involved in a single legal action to petition the federal government for redress. The Supreme Court was thus confronted by the issue of whether African Americans were U.S. citizens and thus entitled to sue in federal court. Its decision was based on the constitutional framers' understanding of the term "citizen."

Reviewing the slave codes, the Declaration of Independence, the Constitution, other laws, and the pervasiveness of black servitude, the Court concluded that persons of African descent were not and were never intended to be citizens of the United States. Indeed, the Court stated that blacks "had no rights which the white man was bound to respect; and that the negro might justly and lawfully be reduced to slavery for his benefit."

Under President Andrew Johnson's reconstruction government, black codes were used in an attempt to preserve some remnant of the status quo. "Vagrancy" laws targeted at former slaves forced them, like the man pictured here, into chain gangs and involuntary labor. **THE LIBRARY OF CONGRESS**

SEE PRIMARY SOURCE DOCUMENT *Chief Justice Roger Taney's Majority Decision in* Dred Scott *v.* Sandford

FROM SLAVE CODES TO BLACK CODES
The North's defeat of the South in the Civil War and the passage of the Thirteenth Amendment banning slavery signaled an end to the slave codes. However, during the Reconstruction era, reconstituted Southern state governments passed "black codes" that curtailed the rights of the newly freed slaves. Similar to the former slave codes in tone and intent, the black codes restricted African Americans' rights to own land, carry weapons, or marry anyone outside their race.

SEE PRIMARY SOURCE DOCUMENT *The Thirteenth Amendment*

Over the objections of southern politicians, Radical Republicans passed the Fourteenth and Fifteenth Amendments in 1868 and 1870 respectively in order to address the growing southern backlash, as demonstrated by the codes and antiblack riots. The Fourteenth Amendment states that all persons born or naturalized in this country are citizens, while the Fifteenth Amendment guarantees all male citizens the right to vote.

(Women received the right to vote when the Nineteenth Amendment was ratified in 1920.) **SEE PRIMARY SOURCE DOCUMENT** *The Fourteenth Amendment*

To circumvent the Fifteenth Amendment, southern states passed "Jim Crow" laws designed to deny African Americans the right to vote. The laws created procedures and tests that essentially disqualified African Americans from voting. Such measures ranged from literacy tests, property requirements, and poll taxes to the infamous Louisiana "grandfather" clause whereby only those persons whose ancestors had voted before the ratification of the two amendments were eligible to vote. The Jim Crow laws were not neutralized until the passage of the Voting Rights Act of 1965.

THE FOURTEENTH AMENDMENT AND *PLESSY* v. *FERGUSON*
The Fourteenth Amendment guarantees to all citizens many of the fundamental rights of citizenship explicitly or implicitly outlined in the Bill of Rights. Section 1 of the amendment specifically provides that "all persons born or naturalized in the United States and subject to the jurisdiction thereof, are citizens of the United States

and of the State wherein they reside. No State shall make or enforce any law which shall abridge the privileges or immunities of citizens of the United States; nor shall any State deprive any person of life, liberty, or property, without due process of law; *nor deny to any person within its jurisdiction the equal protection of the laws."*

Note that the Fourteenth Amendment prohibits unlawful interference with citizens' rights on the part of a state government, as opposed to the federal government or private individuals. Thus, in order for the Fourteenth Amendment to be applicable in a case, there must be some showing that state action is involved. This requirement is met when the suing party establishes that a governmental entity, a government official, or a private individual or entity performing a government function is responsible for the offensive activity.

In addition, the amendment's prohibitions are invoked when private individuals discriminate against fellow citizens with the encouragement of laws enacted by the government. Examples of this include regulations mandating segregated public accommodations and enforcement of contractual agreements between private individuals that prevent the sale of land to black persons.

Some of the pivotal cases concerning this amendment interpret the equal protection clause with respect to racial classifications. The clause specifically prohibits the denial of equal treatment. In *Plessy* v. *Ferguson* (1896), the Supreme Court struggled to determine what constitutes equal protection. The immediate question was whether Louisiana could establish and enforce separate but equal railway facilities for black and white patrons without violating the equal protection clause of the Fourteenth Amendment. Homer Plessy, a biracial African American who could pass as a white person, had been ejected from the white section of a train and taken to a local jail. Plessy argued that segregation not only violated the amendment but also "stamps the colored race with a badge of inferiority." The Court disagreed, stating that the amendment was designed to create equality before the law but not to "abolish distinctions based upon color, or to enforce social, as distinguished from political equality, or a commingling of the two races upon terms unsatisfactory to either."

SEE PRIMARY SOURCE DOCUMENT *The Ruling in* Plessy v. Ferguson *and Justice John Marshall Harlan's Dissent*

THE FIGHT FOR EQUAL RIGHTS UNDER THE FOURTEENTH AMENDMENT

Despite *Plessy* v. *Ferguson* and the setbacks of the post–Civil War years, the Fourteenth and Fifteenth Amendments gave those fighting for the rights of African Americans a constitutional basis upon which to launch what would be a series of long legal battles for equality and justice. The individual plaintiffs who coura-

geously fought these battles were supported by their families and communities and were often represented by attorneys working for the Legal Defense Fund (LDF) of the National Association for the Advancement of Colored People. Since its inception in 1939, the LDF has served as the legal arm of the civil rights movement.

From 1896 to 1954, "separate but equal" was the law of the land, with segregated restaurants, transportation services, and other public facilities a part of the canvas of American life. Prodded by cases developed by the LDF, the courts eventually turned their attention to the definition of "equal" under this judicial doctrine.

According to *Plessy* v. *Ferguson*, "equal" meant that facilities were "substantially similar" to each other. This question was explored in a series of education cases in which, to determine whether the "substantially similar" test was met, courts typically compared facilities, staff, and books and supplies. In *Sweatt* v. *Painter* (1950), the Supreme Court also analyzed intangible qualities, such as a school's reputation, the quality of its faculty, and the potential influence of its alumni, to determine whether the "substantially similar" test had been met.

In 1954, the Supreme Court reversed the "separate but equal" doctrine in the landmark decision of *Brown* v. *Board of Education* (sometimes called *Brown I*). A stellar group of LDF attorneys litigated the case, including Thurgood Marshall (1908–1993), who eventually became the first African American to serve on the Court. In consolidated cases from four states, the parents of African American schoolchildren requested admission to all-white secondary schools in their communities.

The cases were carefully selected to challenge the "separate but equal" doctrine at its core. In the school districts in question, there were "substantially similar" schools for black children, but the students contended that segregated schools were unconstitutional per se, a violation of the equal protection clause of the Fourteenth Amendment. Having reviewed numerous sociological and psychological studies showing the negative effects of segregation on black schoolchildren's self-esteem and educational potential, the Court concluded that "separate educational facilities are inherently unequal" and firmly rejected the "separate but equal" doctrine. In *Bolling* v. *Sharpe* (1954), the Court extended this ruling to public school systems in the District of Columbia using the equal protection clause of the Fifth Amendment, since the Fourteenth Amendment applies only to state actions.

As a result of *Brown I*, legal barriers to equal treatment in other aspects of African American life were also removed. The most visible change occurred when a series of court cases found segregated public facilities unconstitutional. In *Mayor and City Council of Baltimore* v. *Dawson* (1955), segregated public beaches and bathhouses were outlawed; in *Gayle* v. *Browder* (1956), segre-

This photograph was taken during the trial of one of the Scottsboro Boys, nine African Americans accused of raping two white women in Alabama. Heywood Patterson, the first of the nine to be tried, is in the center of the photograph, holding a horseshoe and a rabbit's foot for good luck. On either side of him are the defense lawyers: to his left is Daniel C. Liebowitz of New York, and to his right, Roscoe Chamblee of Chattanooga, Tennessee. **NATIONAL ARCHIVES AND RECORDS ADMINISTRATION**

gated municipal buses were outlawed; *New Orleans Park Development Association* v. *Detiege* (1958) prohibited segregated public parks and golf courses; and *Turner* v. *City of Memphis* (1962) outlawed segregated restaurants in municipal airports. Access for all citizens was further secured by the passage of the Civil Rights Act of 1964, which prohibited discrimination in any private business or facility that serves the public.

Ultimately, the Fourteenth Amendment and the painstaking but persistent challenges to the status quo raised by African American plaintiffs have assured all citizens of many basic rights. For example, in the landmark case of *Powell* v. *Alabama* (1932), the Supreme Court held that, pursuant to the Sixth Amendment as applied to the states by the Fourteenth Amendment, the young African American male defendants in the notorious Scottsboro trial had an automatic right to counsel. The case established a fundamental right to legal services where defendants are found to be incapable of protecting themselves against the full weight of the law.

In 1967, the Court reversed vestiges of the slave and black codes when it held in *Loving* v. *Virginia* that laws prohibiting interracial marriage violated the Fourteenth Amendment. And in *Shelley* v. *Kraemer* (1948), the Court prohibited the enforcement of racial covenants or contractual agreements between whites to prevent the sale of property to African Americans and other "non-Caucasians."

THE REVOLUTION IN EDUCATION

Perhaps no decisions have had a more profound impact on African Americans than the *Brown* decisions. As described above, the Supreme Court abolished de jure or legal segregation in *Brown I*. In *Brown II* (1955), the Court ruled that the methods used to desegregate schools should be developed by local school authorities "with all deliberate speed," while the district courts would monitor progress toward that end.

Since then, school districts and legislative bodies across the country have struggled with various methods of desegregating schools and promoting diversity. Some local authorities have actively resisted certain methods, such as busing students to schools outside their neighborhoods, while others have questioned what constitutes a desegregated school system. Progress was excruciatingly slow during the first fifteen years after the decisions were handed down, and the Court ultimately moved from sanctioning desegregation efforts made at "deliberate speed" to demanding that some progress be made "at once" in the case of *Alexander* v. *Holmes County Board of Education* (1969).

The Rodney King incident was captured by a bystander with a video camera and caused an immediate furor across the nation. Officers beat King with clubs after a traffic stop and were acquitted of charges in 1992. In the following year two of the policemen were convicted in federal court of violating King's civil rights. **AP/WIDE WORLD PHOTOS**

In *Swann* v. *Charlotte-Mecklenburg Board of Education* (1971), the Court discussed certain key issues related to desegregation of schools. It determined that racial quotas could be used as a starting point in determining what degree of racial balance needs to be achieved. However, racial quotas were not to be an end unto themselves. The Court also declared that actionable de jure segregation did not exist where there was a small number of one-race or racially segregated schools, provided authorities could prove that the racial composition was not a result of discriminatory state action. Students in such schools should be allowed to transfer to other schools where they would be in the minority.

The Court also approved the creation of school districts of varying sizes and populations (gerrymandering) to provide racially diverse school-age populations, as well as the use of busing plans to achieve proper results. With respect to busing, the Court noted that plans were not permissible where the time and distance traveled would be physically or mentally unhealthy for students.

Finally, in *Regents of the University of California* v. *Bakke* (1978), the Court reviewed the validity of preferential treatment based on race in the college admissions process. In that case, Allan Bakke, a white male applicant to the University of California at Davis Medical School, alleged that he had been denied admission despite superior grades because of a special admissions program that set aside a certain number of places for disadvantaged students. After reviewing the facts, the Court determined that Bakke was indeed denied admission on the basis of race, in violation of the equal protection clause of the Fourteenth Amendment and Title VI of the 1964 Civil Rights Act. It noted that race could be one of the factors used to determine admission but could not be the sole basis for admission.

CONGRESSIONAL ACTION AND CIVIL RIGHTS PROGRESS IN OTHER AREAS

Demonstrations, sit-ins, student protests, and lengthy court battles engaged in by African Americans and citizen groups assured that Congress would be an active partner with the courts in the drive to make the constitutional promise of equal justice a reality for all Americans. Not only has congressional action further institutionalized the Court's interpretation of constitutional rights (and vice versa), but in many cases it has regulated private discriminatory acts that could not be enforced under the Fourteenth Amendment without proof of state action. Examples include the Civil Rights Act of 1968, which made discriminatory practices in the sale and rental of housing units illegal, and the Voting Rights Act of 1965, which outlawed many state attempts to undermine African American voting rights through literacy tests, reapportionment of districts, and burdensome voter qualifications.

Job discrimination was tackled in Title VII of the Civil Rights Act of 1964, which outlaws discrimination by employers, employment agencies, and labor unions on the basis of race, color, religion, or national origin. Employees are specifically protected from intentional discrimination in these categories, from hostile work environments, and from segregation in the workplace. In addition, according to *Griggs* v. *Duke Power Co.* (1971), Title VII also bans unintentional discrimination: "practices that are fair in form, but discriminatory in operation." However, where the discriminatory impact was not intended, the particular practice is permissible if it constitutes a "business necessity." Thus, in *Griggs,* a requirement that applicants have a high school diploma and pass an IQ test was impermissible, even though not discriminatorily applied, because it was not relevant to the job performance needed and unduly affected the minority applicant pool.

CONCLUSION

Despite considerable progress, the nation's struggles with issues of race continue to be played out against the backdrop of legal history. African Americans still encounter discrimination from private individuals and businesses, and they continue to challenge it, as in the case of those who sued Denny's Corp. for systematically refusing to serve minority customers, requiring them to prepay for their meals, and seating them in specific sections of restaurants. "White flight" to the suburbs has once again created single-race school districts, hampering the ability of school authorities to develop the diverse student populations envisioned by the Court in *Brown* v. *Board of Education.* This too is being challenged, as in the case of *Sheff* v. *O'Neill* in the Connecticut courts in 2002.

Challenges to the gains of the past are also ongoing. New attempts to deny rights to illegal and legal aliens, bilingual students, and others threaten to revive old battles fought by the civil rights movement. The canvas of legal history continues to be painted as courageous politicians, civil rights leaders, attorneys, and average citizens—people who believe in the underlying principles of the Declaration of Independence and the Constitution and its amendments—fight to make true equality a reality for all citizens.

BIBLIOGRAPHY

Eastland, Terry. *Counting by Race: Equality from the Founding Fathers to Bakke and Weber.* New York: Basic Books, 1979.

Fede, Andrew. *People without Rights: An Interpretation of the Fundamentals of the Law of Slavery in the U.S. South.* New York: Garland, 1992.

Fehrenbacher, Don E. *The Dred Scott Case: Its Significance in American Law and Politics.* New York: Oxford University Press, 1978.

Finkelman, Paul. *Slavery in the Courtroom: An Annotated Bibliography of American Cases.* Washington, D.C.: Library of Congress, 1985.

———, ed. *Emancipation and Reconstruction.* New York: Garland, 1992.

———, ed. *The Era of Integration and Civil Rights.* New York: Garland, 1992.

Flanigan, Daniel J. *The Criminal Law of Slavery and Freedom: 1800–1868.* New York: Garland, 1987.

Greenberg, Jack. *Crusaders in the Courts: How a Dedicated Band of Lawyers Fought for the Civil Rights Revolution.* New York: Basic Books, 1994.

Higginbotham, A. Leon. *In the Matter of Color: The Colonial Period.* New York: Oxford University Press, 1980.

Kull, Andrew. *The Color-Blind Constitution.* Cambridge: Harvard University Press, 1992.

Lofgren, Charles A. *The Plessy Case: A Legal-Historical Interpretation.* New York: Oxford University Press, 1987.

Wilkinson, J. Harvie, III. *From Brown to Bakke: The Supreme Court and School Integration: 1954–1978.* New York: Oxford University Press, 1979.

PRIMARY SOURCE DOCUMENT

Excerpt from the Denmark Vesey Trial Record

INTRODUCTION In the year 1822, a ship's carpenter named Peter Poyas was Denmark Vesey's second-in-command in a planned rebellion in Charleston, South Carolina. Entirely committed to the rebellion and of unquestioned loyalty, Poyas was given the assignment of capturing Charleston's main guardhouse. The thousands marshaled under Vesey's banner were then to attack and occupy the city itself. As Poyas had feared, their plans were betrayed by fellow servants, and the rebellion never went beyond the planning stages. One such servant offered testimony against Poyas in the trial that followed their arrest, resulting in the execution of both Vesey and Poyas, along with some thirty others. Reprinted here is a portion of the testimony given in the Denmark Vesey trial, namely the testimony given against Peter, "a Negro man, the property of Mr. James Poyas," with Robert Bentham, Esq., acting as his counsel.

Witness No. 5. A Negro man gave the following evidence: I know Peter, he belongs to Mr. James Poyas. In May last Peter and myself met in Legare Street, at the corner of Lambol Street, when the following conversation took place. He asked me the news—I replied none that I know of. He said by George we can't live so—I replied how will we do. He said we can do very well; if you can find anyone to assist us will you join. I asked him how do you mean— he said, why to break the yoke. I replied I don't know. He asked me suppose you were to hear that the whites were going to kill you would you defend yourself—I replied I'd try to escape. He asked have you lately seen Denmark Vesey, and has he spoken to you particularly—I said no. Well then said he that's all now, but call at the shop tomorrow after knocking off work and I will tell you more—we then parted. I met him the next day according to appointment, when he said to me, we intend to see if we can't do something for ourselves, we can't live so, I asked him where he would get men—he said we'll fined them fast enough, we have got enough—we expect men from country and town. But how said I will you manage it—why we will give them notice said he, and they will march down and camp round the city. But what said I

From Armed Uprising to Courtroom Uprising

Throughout the history of slavery many bloody revolts occurred. To avoid such uprisings, masters would try various techniques of physical torture and psychological manipulation to control populations larger than their own, such as a slave population that was determined to gain its freedom. This dynamic between masters and slaves has become etched in the historical memory of the United States.

Many elements of the slaveowner-slave relationship continued to surface during the paranoid and brutal enforcement of the black codes in the years following the Civil War. Although the Civil Rights movement has since changed the dynamic between the races in the United States, it is not difficult to see that earlier paradigm repeated in subtle ways through the years. The history of African Americans, enmeshed with the institutions of slavery and economic disenfranchisement, has produced many who would rebel against those conditions. As the nation has slowly moved toward integration, African American rebellions have morphed from armed uprisings to courtroom challenges and even to politically and socially charged expressions of black culture in the fields of arts and entertainment.

will they do for arms—he answered they will find arms enough, they will bring down their hoes, axes, &c. I said that won't do to fight with here—he said stop, let us get candidates from town with arms, and we will then take the Guard House and Arsenal in town, the Arsenal on the Neck and the upper Guard House, and supply the country people with arms. How said I will you approach these Arsenals for they are guarded—yes said he, I know that, but what are those guards, one man here and one man there, we won't let a man pass before us. Well said I but how will the black people from the country and those from the Islands know when you are to begin; or how will you get the town people together—why said he we will have prayer meetings at night and there notify them when to start and as the clock strikes 12 all must move— But said I, the whites in the back country, Virginia, when they hear the news will turn to and kill you all, and besides you may be betrayed. Well said he what if that, if

one gets hanged we will rise at that minute. We then left his shop and walked towards Broad Street, when he said I want you to take notice of all the shops and stores in town with arms in them, take down the numbers and give them to me. I said I will see to it and then we parted. About the 1st June I saw in the public papers a statement that the white people were going to build Missionary Houses for the blacks, which I carried and showed to Peter and said to him, you see the good they are going to do for us—when he said, what of that, have you not heard that on the 4th July the whites are going to create a false alarm of fire, and every black that comes out will be killed in order to thin them. Do you think that they would be so barbarous said I. Yes said he I do; I fear they have knowledge of an army from Santo Domingo, and they would be right to do it, to prevent us from joining that army if it should march towards this land. I was then very much alarmed—we then parted and I saw no more of him until (the Guards were very strict) about a fortnight ago. At that time I saw Peter and Ned Bennett standing and talking together at the corner of Lambol and Legare Streets— they crossed over and met me by Mrs. Myles, and Ned Bennett said to me, did you hear what those boys were taken up for the other day. I replied No, but some say 'twas for stealing. Ned asked me if I was sure I had never said anything to the whites about what Peter Poyas had spoken to me about—I replied No—says Peter you never did—No I answered—says Ned to me how do you stand—at which, I struck the tree box with my knuckles and said, as firm as this box, I'll never say one word against you. Ned then smiled and nodded his head and said, that will do, when we all separated. Last Tuesday or Wednesday week Peter said to me you see my lad how the white people have got to windward of us—you won't said I be able to do anything. O yes said he we will, by George, we are obliged to—he said all down this way ought to meet and have a collection to purchase powder. What said I is the use of powder, the whites can fire three times to our once—he said but 'twill be such a dead time of night they won't know what is the matter, and our Horse Companies will go about the streets and prevent the whites from assembling. I asked him where will you get horses— why said he there are many butcher boys with horses, and there are the public Livery Stables, where we have several candidates and the waiting men belonging to the white people of the Horse Companies will be told to take away their master's horses. He asked me if my master was not a horseman—I said yes. Has he not got arms in his house—I answered yes. Can't they be got at—I said yes— then said he 'tis good to have them. I asked him what was the plan—why said he after we have taken the Arsenal and Guard Houses, then we will set the town on fire in different places, and as the whites come out we will slay them; if we were to set fire to the town first, the main in the steeple would give the alarm too soon—I am the Captain said he, to take the lower Guard House and Arsenal.

But, I replied, when you are coming up the sentinel will give the alarm—he said he would advance a little distance ahead, and if he could only get a grip at his throat he was a gone man, for his sword was very sharp; he had sharpened it and had made it so sharp it had cut his finger, which he showed me. As to the Arsenal on the Neck he said that is gone as sure as fate, Ned Bennett would manage that with the people from the country, and the people between Hibben's Ferry and Santee would land and take the upper Guard House. I then said, then this thing seems true. My man, said he, God has a hand in it, we have been meeting for four years and are not yet betrayed. I told him I was afraid after all of the white people from the back country and Virginia. He said that the blacks would collect so numerous from the country we need not fear the whites from other parts, for when we have once got the city we can keep them all out. He asked if I had told my boys—I said no—then he said you should do it, for Ned Bennett has his people pretty well ranged; but said he take care and don't mention it to those waiting men who receive presents of old coats from their masters or they'll betray us; I will speak to them. We then parted and I have not conversed with him. He said the rising was to take place last Sunday night (16th June)—that any of the colored people who said a word about this matter would be killed by the others—the little man who can't be killed, shot, or taken is named Jack, a Gullah Negro. Peter said there was a French company in town of 300 men fully armed—that he was to see Monday Gell about expediting the rising. I know that Mingo went often to Mr. Paul's to see Edwin, but don't know if he spoke with William. Peter said he had a sword and I ought to get one—he said he had a letter from the country, I think from St. Thomas', from a Negro man who belonged to the Captain of a Militia Company, who said he could easily get the key of the house where the Company's arms were put after muster, and take them all out and help in that way. This business originates altogether with the African Congregation in which Peter is a leader. When Bennett's Ned asked about those take up, he alluded particularly to Mr. Paul's William, and asked me if I had said anything to him about it.

The owner of Witness No. 5, testified as follows: My servant bears a good character. His general conduct is good. He was raised up in my family, and I would place my life in his hands.

PRIMARY SOURCE DOCUMENT

Chief Justice Roger Taney's Majority Decision in *Dred Scott* v. *Sandford*

INTRODUCTION Reprinted here is an account of the Court proceedings of the *Dred Scott* v. *Sandford* case. Note the infamous Majority Opinion, written by Chief Justice Taney, an invaluable

document because (1) it provides insight into the convoluted reasoning of those in the highest circles of power who would see African Americans stripped of their rights of citizenship and (2) because the Dred Scott case, along with *Plessy* v. *Ferguson,* represent the two landmark decisions which guided more than a century's worth of legislation hampering the efforts of African Americans to gain equal footing under the law.

By way of ruling against Scott, Taney offers a seriously distorted review of early colonial law, ignoring the differing status of free and enslaved African Americans, as well as the rights accorded the latter under colonial law prior to the adoption of the Constitution. Despite the fact that the case would be undone by the Fourteenth Amendment in the following decade, Dred Scott provides a disturbing insight into the malleability of the law in the hands of pro-slavery judges and justices, as well as the ways in which legislation and legal manipulations would come to be used to retard the efforts of African Americans during the history of the nation, both preceding and following the Civil War.

Opinion: Mr. Chief Justice Taney delivered the opinion of the court.

This case has been twice argued. After the argument at the last term, differences of opinion were found to exist among the members of the court; and as the questions in controversy are of the highest importance, and the court was at that time much pressed by the ordinary business of the term, it was deemed advisable to continue the case, and direct a re-argument on some of the points, in order that we might have an opportunity of giving to the whole subject a more deliberate consideration. It has accordingly been again argued by counsel, and considered by the court; and I now proceed to deliver its opinion.

There are two leading questions presented by the record:

1. Had the Circuit Court of the United States jurisdiction to hear and determine the case between these parties? And

2. If it had jurisdiction, is the judgment it has given erroneous or not?

The plaintiff in error, who was also the plaintiff in the court below, was, with his wife and children, held as slaves by the defendant, in the State of Missouri; and he brought this action in the Circuit Court of the United States for that district, to assert the title of himself and his family to freedom.

The declaration is in the form usually adopted in that State to try questions of this description, and contains the averment necessary to give the court jurisdiction; that he and the defendant are citizens of different States; that is, that he is a citizen of Missouri, and the defendant & citizen of New York.

The defendant pleaded in abatement to the jurisdiction of the court, that the plaintiff was not a citizen of

The Dred Scott Case

During the final decades of slavery, the case of Dred Scott garnered national attention and provided a glimpse of the way many battles regarding the rights of African Americans would be handled in the years following manumission. Rather than stage his uprising in the dead of night, Scott turned to the courts in order to confirm his right to freedom as written in the laws of the time. Scott, a native of Virginia, was brought to St. Louis in 1830 when his owners Peter and Elizabeth Blow migrated west with their children and slaves. Following their early deaths, he became the property of an army doctor named John Emerson, with whom he traveled throughout the trans-Mississippi territories in the years that followed.

In 1836, Emerson was assigned to Fort Snelling, near the present-day city of St. Paul, Minnesota, and Scott accompanied him. There Scott met and married his wife, Harriet. According to the Missouri Compromise of 1820, Fort Snelling was in free territory and the state law of Missouri provided that any slave who had been taken into free territory was thereby emancipated.

Armed with these facts, the Scotts filed suit for their own and their two daughters' freedom. In the following years the *Scott* v. *Emerson* cases bounced back and forth between the Missouri Circuit Court and the Missouri Supreme Court, with rulings both for and against Dred and Harriet Scott. But in 1852, with the debate over slavery in the territories heating up, the Missouri Supreme Court gave a final ruling deciding in favor of the slaveholders and denying the Scott family freedom. Here, the matter might have ended, and in some ways it is something of a mystery that it continued at all. The *Scott* v. *Emerson*

the State of Missouri, as alleged in his declaration, being a negro of African descent, whose ancestors were of pure African blood, and who were brought into this country and sold as slaves.

To this plea the plaintiff demurred, and the defendant joined in demurrer. The court overruled the plea, and gave judgment that the defendant should answer over. And he thereupon put in sundry pleas in bar, upon which issues were joined; and at the trial the verdict and judgment were in his favor. Whereupon the plaintiff brought this writ of error.

Before we speak of the pleas in bar, it will be proper to dispose of the questions which have arisen on the plea in abatement.

That plea denies the right of the plaintiff to sue in a court of the United States, for the reasons therein stated.

If the question raised by it is legally before us, and the court should be of opinion that the facts stated in it disqualify the plaintiff from becoming a citizen, in the sense in which that word is used in the Constitution of the United States, then the judgment of the Circuit Court is erroneous, and must be reversed.

…When a plaintiff sues in a court of the United States, it is necessary that he should show, in his pleading, that the suit he brings is within the jurisdiction of the court, and that he is entitled to sue there. And if he omits to do this, and should, by any oversight of the Circuit Court, obtain a judgment in his favor, the judgment would be reversed in the appellate court for want of jurisdiction in the court below. The jurisdiction would not be presumed, as in the case of a common-law English or State court, unless the contrary appeared. But the record, when it comes before the appellate court, must show, affirmatively, that the inferior court had authority, under the Constitution, to hear and determine the case. And if the plaintiff claims a right to sue in a Circuit Court of the United States, under that provision of the Constitution which gives jurisdiction in controversies between citizens of different States, he must distinctly aver in his pleading that they are citizens of different States; and he cannot maintain his suit without showing that fact in the pleadings.

…The question to be decided is, whether the facts stated in the plea are sufficient to show that the plaintiff is not entitled to sue as citizen in a court of the United States.

We think they are before us. The plea in abatement and the judgment of the court upon it, are a part of the judicial proceedings in the Circuit Court, and are there recorded as such; and a writ of error always brings up to the superior court the whole record of the proceedings in the court below. And in the case of the United States v. Smith, (11 Wheat., 172,) this court said, that the case being brought up by writ of error, the whole record was

rulings were never appealed to the United States Supreme Court, which would have been the legal next step. Instead, Scott filed a new suit against John Sanford (whose name was misspelled in the Court record due to a clerical error), Mrs. Emerson's brother and a New York state resident who represented himself as the Scott family's new owner. It was this case, much broader in its implications, that reached the high court four years later as *Dred Scott v. Sandford.*

Some legal historians have suggested that abolitionists had a hand in keeping the suit alive. Others have suggested that pro-slavery forces redefined it to produce a new ruling on the constitutionality of the Missouri Compromise and, hence, slavery in the territories. Regardless, the Supreme Court had to decide two questions in *Dred Scott* v. *Sandford* which the earlier cases had never raised: Was Dred Scott a citizen of Missouri, and thus entitled to bring suit in

federal court against a citizen of another state? And did the Scott family become free at Fort Snelling as a result of the 1820 Missouri Compromise, which placed it in free territory?

In perhaps the most infamous ruling in the history of the Supreme Court, six of the eight justices answered no to both questions. Chief Justice Roger Taney wrote the majority opinion, and he wrote it in broad strokes: Not only was Scott not a citizen, he said, no Negro was according to the Constitution. Not only were the Scotts not emancipated by their residence at Fort Snelling, the court ruled that the Missouri Compromise, in excluding slavery north of the 36 degree 30 minutes line, was itself unconstitutional. The decision was a short-lived victory for pro-slavery forces. Less than five years later, the Civil War would erupt, bringing with it amendments to the Constitution abolishing slavery and establishing beyond doubt the rights of citizenship for African Americans.

under the consideration of this court. And this being the case in the present instance, the plea in abatement is necessarily under the consideration; and it becomes, therefore, our duty to decide whether the facts stated in the plea are or are not sufficient to show that the plaintiff is not entitled to sue as a citizen in a court of the United States.

This is certainly a very serious question, and one that now for the first time has been brought for decision before this court. But it is brought here by those who have a right to bring it, and it is our duty to meet it and decide it.

The question is simply this: Can a negro, whose ancestors were imported into this country, and sold as slaves, become a member of the political community formed and brought into existence by the Constitution of the United States, and as such become entitled to all the rights, and privileges, and immunities, guaranteed by that instrument to the citizen? One of which rights is the privilege of suing in a court of the United States in the cases specified in the Constitution.

It will be observed, that the plea applies to that class of persons only whose ancestors were negroes of the African race, and imported into this country, and sold and held as slaves. The only matter in issue before the court, therefore, is, whether the descendants of such slaves, when they shall be emancipated, or who are born of parents who had become free before their birth, are

citizens of a State, in the sense in which the word citizen is used in the Constitution of the United States. And this being the only matter in dispute on the pleadings, the court must be understood as speaking in this opinion of that class only, that is, of those persons who are the descendants of Africans who were imported into this country, and sold as slaves.

…We proceed to examine the case as presented by the pleadings.

The words "people of the United States" and "citizens" are synonymous terms, and mean the same thing. They both describe the political body who, according to our republican institutions, form the sovereignty, and who hold the power and conduct the Government through their representatives. They are what we familiarly call the "sovereign people," and every citizen is one of this people, and a constituent member of this sovereignty. The question before us is, whether the class of persons described in the plea in abatement compose a portion of this people, and are constituent members of this sovereignty? We think they are not, and that they are not included, and were not intended to be included, under the word "citizens" in the Constitution, and can therefore claim none of the rights and privileges which that instrument provides for and secures to citizens of the United States. On the contrary, they were at that time considered as a subordinate and inferior class of beings, who had been subjugated by the dominant race, and, whether emancipated or not, yet remained subject to their authority, and had no rights or privileges but such as those who held the power and the Government might choose to grant them.

It is not the province of the court to decide upon the justice or injustice, the policy or impolicy, of these laws. The decision of that question belonged to the political or law-making power; to those who formed the sovereignty and framed the Constitution. The duty of the court is, to interpret the instrument they have framed, with the best lights we can obtain on the subject, and to administer it as we find it, according to its true intent and meaning when it was adopted.

In discussing this question, we must not confound the rights of citizenship which a State may confer within its own limits, and the rights of citizenship as a member of the Union. It does not by any means follow, because he has all the rights and privileges of a citizen of a State, that he must be a citizen of the United States. He may have all of the rights and privileges of the citizen of a State, and yet not be entitled to the rights and privileges of a citizen in any other State. For, previous to the adoption of the Constitution of the United States, every State had the undoubted right to confer on whomsoever it pleased the character of citizen, and to endow him with all its rights. But this character of course was confined to the boundaries of the State, and gave him no rights or privileges in other States beyond those secured to him by the laws of nations and the comity of States. Nor have the several States surrendered the power of conferring these rights and privileges by adopting the Constitution of the United States. Each State may still confer them upon an alien, or any one it thinks proper, or upon any class or description of persons; yet he would not be a citizen in the sense in which that word is used in the Constitution of the United States, nor entitled to sue as such in one of its courts, nor to the privileges and immunities of a citizen in the other States. The rights which he would acquire would be restricted to the State which gave them. The Constitution has conferred on Congress the right to establish an uniform rule of naturalization, and this right is evidently exclusive, and has always been held by this court to be so. Consequently, no State, since the adoption of the Constitution, can be naturalizing an alien invest him with the rights and privileges secured to a citizen of a State under the Federal Government, although, so far as the State alone was concerned, he would undoubtedly be entitled to the rights of a citizen, and clothed with all the rights and immunities which the Constitution and laws of the State attached to that character.

It is very clear, therefore, that no State can, by any act or law of its own, passed since the adoption of the Constitution, introduce a new member into the political community created by the Constitution of the United States. It cannot make him a member of this community by making him a member of its own. And for the same reason it cannot introduce any person, or description of persons, who were not intended to be embraced in this new political family, which the Constitution brought into existence, but were intended to be excluded from it.

The question then arises, whether the provisions of the Constitution, in relation to the personal rights and privileges to which the citizen of a State should be entitled, embraced the negro African race, at that time in this country, or who might afterwards be imported, who had then or should afterwards be made free in any State; and to put it in the power of a single State to make him a citizen of the United States, and endue him with the full rights of citizenship in every other State without their consent? Does the Constitution of the United States act upon him whenever he shall be made free under the laws of a State, and raised there to the rank of a citizen, and immediately cloth him with all the privileges of a citizen in every other State, and in its own courts?

The court think the affirmative of these propositions cannot be maintained. And if it cannot, the plaintiff in error could not be a citizen of the State of Missouri, within the meaning of the Constitution of the United States, and, consequently, was not entitled to sue in its courts.

…In the opinion of the court, the legislation and histories of the times, and the language used in the Declaration of Independence, show, that neither the class of persons who had been imported as slaves, nor their descendants, whether they had become free or not, were then acknowledged as a part of the people, nor intended to be included in the general words used in that memorable instrument.

…They had for more than a century before been regarded as beings of an inferior order, and altogether unfit to associate with the white race, either in social or political relations; and so far inferior, that they had no rights which the white man was bound to respect; and that the negro might justly and lawfully be reduced to slavery for his benefit. He was bought and sold, and treated as an ordinary article of merchandise and traffic, whenever a profit could be made by it. This opinion was at that time fixed and universal in the civilized portion of the white race. It was regarded as an axiom in morals as well as in politics, which no one thought of disputing, or supposed to be open to dispute; and men in every grade and position in society daily and habitually acted upon it in their private pursuits, as well as in matters of public concern, without doubting for a moment the correctness of this opinion.

And in no nation was this opinion more firmly fixed or more uniformly acted upon than by the English Government and English people.

…The opinion thus entertained and acted upon in England was naturally impressed upon the colonies they founded on this side of the Atlantic. And, accordingly, a negro of the African race was regarded by them as an article of property, and held, and bought and sold as such, in every one of the thirteen colonies which united in the Declaration of Independence, and afterwards formed the Constitution of the United States. The slaves were more or less numerous in the different colonies, as slave labor was found more or less profitable. But no one seems to have doubted the correctness of the prevailing opinion of the time.

The legislation of the different colonies furnishes positive and indisputable proof of this fact.

…A perpetual and impassable barrier was intended to be erected between the white race and the one which they had reduced to slavery, and governed as subjects with absolute and despotic power, and which they then looked upon as so far below them in the scale of created beings, that intermarriages between white persons and negroes or mulattoes were regarded as unnatural and immoral, and punished as crimes, not only in the parties, but in the person who joined them in marriage. And no distinction in this respect was made between the free negro or mulatto and the slave, but this stigma, of the deepest degradation, was fixed upon the whole race.

We refer to these historical facts for the purpose of showing the fixed opinions concerning that race, upon which the statesmen of that day spoke and acted. It is necessary to do this, in order to determine whether the general terms used in the Constitution of the United States, as to the rights of man and the rights of the people, was intended to include them, or to give to them or their posterity the benefit of any of its provisions.

The language of the Declaration of Independence is equally Conclusive:

It begins by declaring that, "when in the course of human events it becomes necessary for one people to dissolve the political bands which have connected them with another, and to assume among the powers of the earth the separate and equal station to which the laws of nature and nature's God entitle them, a decent respect for the opinions of mankind requires that they should declare the causes which impel them to the separation."

It then proceeds to say: "We hold these truths to be self-evident: that all men are created equal; that they are endowed by their Creator with certain unalienable rights; that among them is life, liberty, and the pursuit of happiness; that to secure these rights, Governments are instituted, deriving their just powers from the consent of the governed."

The general words above quoted would seem to embrace the whole human family, and if they were used

Chief Justice of the Supreme Court Roger Taney, author of the majority opinion in the Dred Scott case. Taney, a slave owner, ruled that slaves or descendents of slaves could not be U.S. citizens and therefore had no right to sue in federal court. The decision affected both enslaved and free African Americans and was a considerable setback to progress for civil rights. **THE LIBRARY OF CONGRESS**

in a similar instrument at this day would be so understood. But it is too clear for dispute, that the enslaved African race were not intended to be included, and formed no part of the people who framed and adopted this declaration; for if the language, as understood in that day, would embrace them, the conduct of the distinguished men who framed the Declaration of Independence would have been utterly and flagrantly inconsistent with the principles they asserted; and instead of the sympathy of mankind, to which they so confidently appeared, they would have deserved and received universal rebuke and reprobation.

…This state of public opinion had undergone no change when the Constitution was adopted, as is equally evident from its provisions and language.

…There are two clauses in the Constitution which point directly and specifically to the negro race as a separate class of persons, and show clearly that they were not regarded as a portion of the people or citizens of the Government then formed.

One of these clauses reserves to each of the thirteen States the right to import slaves until the year 1808, if it thinks proper. And the importation which it thus sanctions was unquestionably of persons of the race of which we are speaking, as the traffic in slaves in the United States had always been confined to them. And by the other provision the States pledge themselves to each other to maintain the right of property of the master, by delivering up to him any slave who may have escaped from his service, and be found within their respective territories. By the first above-mentioned clause, therefore, the right to purchase and hold this property is directly sanctioned and authorized for twenty years by the people who framed the Constitution. And by the second, they pledge themselves to maintain and uphold the right of the master in the manner specified, as long as the Government they then formed should endure. And these two provisions show, conclusively, that neither the description of persons therein referred to, not their descendants, were embraced in any of the other provisions of the Constitution; for certainly these two clauses were not intended to confer on them or their posterity the blessings of liberty, or any of the personal rights so carefully provided for the citizen.

…We need not refer, on this point, particularly to the laws of the present slaveholding States. Their statute books are full of provisions in relation to this class, in the same spirit with the Maryland law which we have before quoted. They have continued to treat them as an inferior class, and to subject them to strict police regulations, drawing a broad line of distinction between the citizen and the slave races, and legislating in relation to them upon the same principle which prevailed at the time of the Declaration of Independence. As related to these States, it is too plain for argument, that they have never been regarded as a part of the people or citizens of the State, nor supposed to possess any political rights which the dominant race might not withhold or grant at their pleasure. And as long ago as 1822, the Court of Appeals of Kentucky decided that free negroes and mulattoes were not citizens within the meaning of the Constitution of the United States; and the connectness of this decision is recognized, and the same doctrine affirmed, in 1 Meigs's Tenn. Reports, 331.

And if we turn to the legislation of the States where slavery had worn out, or measures taken for its speedy abolition, we shall find the same opinions and principles equally fixed and equally acted upon.

…The legislation of the States therefore shows, in a manner not to be mistaken, the inferior and subject condition of that race at the time the Constitution was adopted, and long afterwards, throughout the thirteen States by which that instrument was framed, and it is hardly consistent with the respect due to these States, to suppose that they regarded at that time, as fellow-citizens and members of the sovereignty, a class of beings whom they had thus stigmatized; whom, as we are bound, out of respect to the State sovereignties, to assume they had deemed it just and necessary thus to stigmatize, and upon whom they had impressed such deep and enduring marks of inferiority and degradation; or, that when they met in convention to form the Constitution, they looked upon them as a portion of their constituents, or designed to include them in the provisions so carefully inserted for the security and protection of the liberties and rights of their citizens. It cannot be supposed that they intended to secure to them rights, and privileges, and rank, in the new political body throughout the Union, which every one of them denied within the limits of its own dominion. More especially, it cannot be believed that the large slaveholding States regarded them as included in the word citizens, or would have consented to a Constitution which might compel them to receive them in that character from another State. For if they were so received, and entitled to the privileges and immunities of citizens, it would exempt them from the operation of the special laws and from the police regulations which they considered to be necessary for their own safety. It would give to persons of the negro race, who were recognized as citizens in any one State of the Union, the right to enter every other State whenever they pleased, singly or in companies, without pass or passport, and without obstruction, to sojourn there as long as they pleased, to go where they pleased at every hour of the day or night without molestation, unless they committed some violation of law for which a white man would be punished; and it would give them the full liberty of speech in public and in private upon all subjects upon which its own citizens might speak; to hold public meetings upon political affairs, and to keep and carry arms wherever they went. And all of this would be done in the face of the subject race of the same color, both free and slaves, and inevitably producing discontent and insubordination among them, and endangering the peace and safety of the State.

It is impossible, it would seem, to believe that the great men of the slaveholding States, who took so large a share in framing the Constitution of the United States, and exercised so much influence in procuring its adoption, could have been so forgetful or regardless of their own safety and the safety of those who trusted and confided in them.

Besides, this want of foresight and care would have been utterly inconsistent with the caution displayed in providing for the admission of new members into this political family. For, when they gave to the citizens of each State the privileges and immunities of citizens in the several States, they at the same time took from the several States the power of naturalization, and confined that power exclusively to the Federal Government. No State was willing to permit another State to determine who should or should not be admitted as one of its citizens,

A PUBLIC MEETING

WILL BE HELD ON

THURSDAY EVENING, 2D INSTANT,

at 7½ o'clock, in ISRAEL CHURCH, to consider the atrocious decision of the Supreme Court in the

DRED SCOTT CASE,

and other outrages to which the colored people are subject under the Constitution of the United States.

C. L. REMOND,
ROBERT PURVIS,

and others will be speakers on the occasion. Mrs. MOTT, Mr. M'KIM and B. S. JONES of Ohio, have also accepted invitations to be present. All persons are invited to attend. Admittance free.

The U.S. Supreme Court's *Dred Scott* decision outraged abolitionists and brought the nation one step closer to civil war. This poster advertises a meeting to protest the decision, at which the abolitionists Charles Lenox Remond and Robert Purvis were scheduled to speak.

and entitled to demand equal rights and privileges with their own people, within their own territories. The right of naturalization was therefore, with one accord, surrendered by the States, and confided to the Federal Government. And this power granted to Congress to establish an uniform rule of naturalization is, by the well-understood meaning of the word, confined to persons born in a foreign country, under a foreign Government. It is not a power to raise to the rank of a citizen any one born in the United States, who, from birth or parentage, by the laws of the country, belongs to an inferior and subordinate class. And when we find the States guarding themselves from the indiscreet or improper admission by other States of emigrants from other countries, by giving the power exclusively to Congress, we cannot fail to see that they could never have left with the States a much more important power—that is, the power of transforming into citizens a numerous class of persons, who in that character would be much more dangerous to the peace and safety of a large portion of the Union, than the few foreigners one of the States might improperly naturalize. The Constitution upon its adoption obviously took from the States all power by any subsequent legislation to

introduce as a citizen into the political family of the United States any one, no matter where he was born, or what might be his character or condition; and it gave to Congress the power to confer this character upon those only who were born outside of the dominions of the United States. And no law of a State, therefore, passed since the Constitution was adopted, can give any right of citizenship outside of its own territory.

A clause similar to the one in the Constitution, in relation to the rights and immunities of citizens of one State in the other States, was contained in the Articles of Confederation. But there is a difference of language, which is worthy of note. The provision in the Articles of Confederation was, "that the free inhabitants of each of the States, paupers, vagabonds, and fugitives from justice, excepted, should be entitled to all the privileges and immunities of free citizens in the several States."

It will be observed, that under this Confederation, each State had the right to decide for itself, and in its own tribunals, whom it would acknowledge as a free inhabitant of another State. The term free inhabitant, in the generality of its terms, would certainly include one of the African race who had been manumitted. But no example, we think, can be found of his admission to all the privileges of citizenship in any State of the Union after these Articles were formed, and while they continued in force. And, notwithstanding the generality of the words "free inhabitants," it is very clear that, according to their accepted meaning in that day, they did not include the African race, whether free or not: for the fifth section of the ninth article provides that Congress should have the power "to agree upon the number of land forces to be raised, and to make requisitions from each State for its quota in proportion to the number of white inhabitants in such State, which requisition should be binding."

Words could hardly have been used which more strongly mark the line of distinction between the citizen and the subject; the free and the subjugated races. The latter were not even counted when the inhabitants of a State were to be embodied in proportion to its numbers for the general defence. And it cannot for moment be supposed, that a class of persons thus separated and rejected from those who formed the sovereignty of the States, were yet intended to be included under the words "free inhabitants," in the preceding article, to whom privileges and immunities were so carefully secured in every State.

But although this clause of the Articles of Confederation is the same in principle with that inserted in the Constitution, yet the comprehensive word inhabitant, which might be construed to include an emancipated slave, is omitted; and the privilege is confined to citizens of the State. And this alteration in words would hardly have been made, unless a different meaning was intended to be conveyed, or a possible doubt removed. The just and fair inference is, that as this privilege was about to be placed under the protection of the General Government, and the words expounded by its tribunals, and all power in relation to it taken from the State and its courts, it was deemed prudent to describe with precision and caution the persons to whom this high privilege was given—and the word citizen was on that account substituted for the words free inhabitant. The word citizen excluded, and no doubt intended to exclude, foreigners who had not become citizens of some one of the States when the Constitution was adopted; and also every description of persons who were not fully recognized as citizens in the several States. This, upon any fair construction of the instruments to which we have referred, was evidently the object and purpose of this change of words.

To all this mass of proof we have still to add, that Congress has repeatedly legislated upon the same construction of the Constitution that we have given. Three laws, two of which were passed almost immediately after the Government went into operation, will be abundantly sufficient to show this. The two first are particularly worthy of notice, because many of the men who assisted in framing the Constitution, and took an active part in procuring its adoption, were then in the halls of legislation, and certainly understood what they meant when they used the words "people of the United States" and "citizen" in that well-considered instrument.

The first of these acts is the naturalization law, which was passed at the second session of the first Congress, March 26, 1790, and confines the right of becoming citizens "to aliens being free white persons."

Now, the Constitution does not limit the power of Congress in this respect to white persons. And they may, if they think proper, authorize the naturalization of any one, of any color, who was born under allegiance to another Government. But the language of the law above quoted, shows that citizenship at that time was perfectly understood to be confined to the white race; and that they alone constituted the sovereignty in the Government.

…But it is said that a person may be a citizen, and entitled to that character, although he does not possess all the rights which may belong to other citizens; as, for example, the right to vote, or to hold particular offices; and that yet, when he goes into another State, he is entitled to be recognized there as a citizen, although the State may measure his rights by the rights which it allows to persons of a like character or class resident in the State, and refuse to him the full rights of citizenship.

This argument overlooks the language of the provision in the Constitution of which we are speaking.

Undoubtedly, a person may be a citizen, that is, a member of the community who form the sovereignty, although he exercises no share of the political power, and is incapacitated from holding particular offices. Women and minors, who form a part of the political family, cannot vote; and when a property qualification is required to vote or hold a particular office, those who have not the necessary qualification cannot vote or hold the office, yet they are citizens.

So, too, a person may be entitled to vote by the law of the State, who is not a citizen even of the State itself. And in some of the States of the Union foreigners not naturalized are allowed to vote. And the State may give the right to free negroes and mulattoes, but that does not make them citizens of the State, and still less of the United States. And the provision in the Constitution giving privileges and immunities in other States, does not apply to them.

Neither does it apply to a person who, being the citizen of a State, migrates to another State. For then he becomes subject to the laws of the State in which he lives, and he is no longer a citizen of the State from which he removed. And the State in which he resides may then, unquestionably, determine his status or condition, and place him among the class of persons who are not recog-

Dred and Harriet Scott were photographed in the days following the Supreme Court's decision in *Dred Scott v. Sandford*. Engravings of the photographs appeared on the front page of the June 27, 1857, issue of *Frank Leslie's Illustrated Newspaper*. Though the decision went against them, the Scotts were freed by their new owner, Taylor Blow, on May 26, 1857. **THE LIBRARY OF CONGRESS**

nized as citizens, but belong to an inferior and subject race; and may deny him the privileges and immunities enjoyed by its citizens.

But so far as mere rights of person are concerned, the provision in question is confined to citizens of a State who are temporarily in another State without taking up their residence there. It gives them no political rights in the State, as to voting or holding office, or in any other respect. For a citizen of one State has no right to participate in the government of another. But if he ranks as a citizen in the State to which he belongs, within the meaning of the Constitution of the United States, then, whenever he goes into another State, the Constitution clothes him, as to the rights of person, with all the privileges and immunities which belong to citizens of the State. And if persons of the African race are citizens of a State, and of the United States, they would be entitled to all of these privileges and immunities in every State, and the State could not restrict them; for they would hold these privileges and immunities under the paramount authority of the Federal Government, and its courts would be bound to maintain and enforce them, the Constitution and laws of the State to the contrary notwithstanding. And if the States could limit or restrict them, or place the party in an inferior grade, this clause of the Constitution would be unmeaning, and could have no operation; and would give no rights to the citizen when in another State. He would

have none but what the State itself chose to allow him. This is evidently not the construction or meaning of the clause in question. It guaranties rights to the citizen, and the State cannot withhold them. And these rights are of a character and would lead to consequences which make it absolutely certain that the African race were not included under the name of citizens of a State, and were not in the contemplation of the framers of the Constitution when these privileges and immunities were provided for the protection of the citizen in other States.

...The only two provisions which point to them and include them, treat them as property, and make it the duty of the Government to protect it; no other power, in relation to this race, is to be found in the Constitution; and as it is a Government of special, delegated, powers, no authority beyond these two provisions can be constitutionally exercised. The Government of the United States had no right to interfere for any other purpose but that of protecting the rights of the owner, leaving it altogether with the several States to deal with this race, whether emancipated or not, as each State may think justice, humanity, and the interests and safety of society, require. The States evidently intended to reserve this power exclusively to themselves.

No one, we presume, supposes that any change in public opinion or feeling, in relation to this unfortunate race, in the civilized nations of Europe or in this country, should induce the court to give to the words of the Constitution a more liberal construction in their favor than they were intended to bear when the instrument was framed and adopted. Such an argument would be altogether inadmissible in any tribunal called on to interpret it. If any of its provisions are deemed unjust, there is a mode prescribed in the instrument itself by which it may be amended; but while it remains unaltered, it must be construed now as it was understood at the time of its adoption. It is not only the same in words, but the same in meaning, and delegates the same powers to the Government, and reserves and secures the same rights and privileges to the citizen; and as long as it continues to exist in its present form, it speaks not only in the same words, but with the same meaning and intent with which it spoke when it came from the hands of its framers, and was voted on and adopted by the people of the United States. Any other rule of construction would abrogate the judicial character of this court, and make it the mere reflex of the popular opinion or passion of the day. This court was not created by the Constitution for such purposes. Higher and graver trusts have been confided to it, and it must not falter in the path of duty.

What the construction was at that time, we think can hardly admit of doubt. We have the language of the Declaration of Independence and of the Articles of confederation, in addition to the plain words of the Constitution itself; we have the legislation of the different States, before, about the time, and since, the Constitution was adopted; we have the legislation of Congress, from the time of its adoption to a recent period; and we have the constant and uniform action of the Executive Department, all concurring together, and leading to the same result. And if anything in relation to the construction of the Constitution can be regarded as settled, it is that which we now give to the word "citizen" and the word "people."

And upon a full and careful consideration of the subject, the court is of opinion, that, upon the facts stated in the plea in abatement, Dred Scott was not a citizen of Missouri within the meaning of the Constitution of the United States, and not entitled as such to sue in its courts; and, consequently, that the Circuit Court had no jurisdiction of the case, and that the judgment on the plea in abatement is erroneous.

PRIMARY SOURCE DOCUMENT

The Thirteenth Amendment

INTRODUCTION An amendment to the Constitution was required to free those people still in bondage and to ensure that slavery would never again be made legal anywhere in the United States. The Thirteenth Amendment to the Constitution,

adopted in 1865 following the Union victory over the Confederate army, did just that.

Amendment XIII

[Adopted 1865]

Section 1. Neither slavery nor involuntary servitude, except as a punishment for crime whereof the party shall have been duly convicted, shall exist within the United States, or any place subject to their jurisdiction.

Section 2. Congress shall have power to enforce this article by appropriate legislation.

PRIMARY SOURCE DOCUMENT

The Fourteenth Amendment

INTRODUCTION The Fourteenth Amendment has been one of the most frequently debated items in the Constitution. In 1896, in the case of *Plessy* v. *Ferguson*, the Supreme Court, arguing that the Fourteenth Amendment did not guarantee African Americans equal access to public services, established the doctrine of "separate but equal." In 1954, the Court, under Chief Justice Earl Warren, overturned this doctrine and ordered that American public schools be desegregated with "all deliberate speed." The basis of the Court's decision in 1954 was the Fourteenth Amendment, whose equal protection clause, it argued, was violated by segregation in public schooling.

Amendment XIV

[Adopted 1868]

Section 1. All persons born or naturalized in the United States, and subject to the jurisdiction thereof, are citizens of the United States and of the State wherein they reside. No State shall make or enforce any law which shall abridge the privileges or immunities of citizens of the United States; nor shall any State deprive any person of life, liberty, or property, without due process of law; nor deny to any person within its jurisdiction the equal protection of the laws.

Section 2. Representatives shall be apportioned among the several States according to their respective numbers, counting the whole number of persons in each State, excluding Indians not taxed. But when the right to vote at any election for the choice of Electors for President and Vice-President of the United States, Representatives in Congress, the executive and judicial officers of a State, or the members of the legislature thereof, is denied to any of the male inhabitants of such State, being twenty-one years of age and citizens of the United States, or in any way abridged, except for participation in rebellion, or other crime, the basis of representation therein shall be reduced in the proportion which the number of such male citizens shall bear to the whole number of male citizens twenty-one years of age in such State.

The Reconstruction Amendments

The Constitution adopted in 1787 had rigorously avoided mentioning slavery, though it had acknowledged the fact of slavery in the "three-fifths" clause of Article 1, Section 2, and in its postponement of the abolition of the slave trade until 1808. Lincoln's Emancipation Proclamation had liberated the slaves residing in only those states still in rebellion on January 1, 1863, thus leaving in bondage thousands of people in Maryland, Delaware, Kentucky, Missouri, and various counties and parishes of Virginia and New Orleans.

Despite the passage of the Thirteenth Amendment, Southern states quickly set about trying to reduce freed men and women once again to a condition of slavery, passing black codes that stringently controlled their labor. Such codes stipulated that freed people could rent land only in rural districts, required them to sign year-long work contracts, denied them any pay for their labor if they quit in the middle of a contract, and made them subject to arrest, fines, forced labor, and physical punishment

for being unemployed. Such codes often forbade African Americans from doing any work other than field labor.

Outraged by such laws, Northern interests in Congress passed the 1866 Civil Rights Act over President Johnson's veto. Two years later, Congress drafted the Fourteenth Amendment, intended to give African Americans equal protection under the law.

In 1870 Congress passed the Fifteenth Amendment, which extended the right to vote to African American men. But southern states had any number of ways of getting around the Fifteenth Amendment's extension of suffrage to African American men. One of the more complicated was the "grandfather clause." Louisiana, for example, instituted a literacy test as a requirement for voting, and then, in order to insure that illiterate whites would not be prevented from voting, the state instituted a grandfather clause that exempted anyone from meeting the requirement who had voted, or whose ancestors had voted, prior to January 1, 1866.

Section 3. No person shall be a Senator or Representative in Congress, or Elector of President and Vice-President, or hold any office, civil or military, under the United States, or under any State, who, having previously taken an oath, as a member of Congress, or as an officer of the United States, or as a member of any State legislature, or as an executive or judicial officer of any State, to support the Constitution of the United States, shall have engaged in insurrection or rebellion against the same, or given aid or comfort to the enemies thereof. Congress may, by a vote of two-thirds of each house, remove such disability.

Section 4. The validity of the public debt of the United States, authorized by law, including debts incurred for payment of pensions and bounties for services in suppressing insurrection or rebellion, shall not be questioned. But neither the United States nor any State shall assume or pay any debt or obligation incurred in aid of insurrection or rebellion against the United States, or any claim for the loss of emancipation of any slave; but all such debts, obligations, and claims shall be held illegal and void.

Section 5. The Congress shall have power to enforce, by appropriate legislation, the provisions of this article.

PRIMARY SOURCE DOCUMENT

The Ruling in *Plessy* v. *Ferguson* and Justice John Marshall Harlan's Dissent

INTRODUCTION In 1896, the U.S. Supreme Court ruled on a case involving the constitutionality of a Louisiana law that provided for segregation on passenger railway cars. The Court maintained that segregation was enforceable because such a situation allowed for "separate but equal" treatment of the races.

The lone dissenter in *Plessy* v. *Ferguson* was Justice John Marshall Harlan, a former Kentucky slaveholder who understood that the purpose of the 1890 Louisiana law was not only to separate, but to degrade. Looking ahead to what the future might hold with such laws in place, he wrote that the "present decision ... will not only stimulate aggressions, more or less brutal and irritating, upon the admitted rights of colored citizens, but will encourage the belief that it is possible, by means of state enactments, to defeat the beneficent purposes which the people of the United States had in view when they adopted the recent amendments of the Constitution.... The destinies of the two races, in this country, are indissolubly linked together, and the interests of both require that the common government of all shall not permit the seeds of race hate to be planted under the sanction of law."

Justice Harlan has earned high praise for both the high-mindedness and the accuracy of his prediction. *Plessy* v. *Ferguson* did

NEGRO EXPULSION FROM RAILWAY CAR, PHILADELPHIA.

Though segregation in public transportation is often associated with the South, it was known elsewhere. In this 1868 image, a well-dressed black passenger is being harassed by a white man while the latter's wife and child look on. The title, "Negro Expulsion from Railway Car, Philadelphia," suggests that the man is being forced to give up his place in the car so that the white family may sit down. **THE LIBRARY OF CONGRESS**

indeed plant "the seeds of race hate … under the sanction of law." In its wake, the number of incidents of racial violence soared throughout the country, and a system of discriminatory racial segregation developed from which the nation has yet to recover.

On many occasions during the years following the Civil War, the nation had a chance to reassess its racial practices and move ahead. Though there were a few legal victories, there were more failures, and those failures were summed up in the ruling and dissenting opinions of *Plessy* v. *Ferguson*, excerpts of which are provided below.

Opinion: Mr. Justice Brown, after stating the case, delivered the opinion of the court.

This case turns upon the constitutionality of an act of the General Assembly of the State of Louisiana, passed in 1890, providing for separate railway carriages for the white and colored races. Acts 1890, No. 111, p. 152.

The first section of the statute enacts "that all railway companies carrying passengers in their coaches in this State, shall provide equal but separate accommodations for the white, and colored races, by providing two or more passenger coaches for each passenger train, or by dividing the passenger coaches by a partition so as to secure separate accommodations: Provided, That this section shall not be construed to apply to street railroads.

No person or persons, shall be admitted to occupy seats in coaches, other than, the ones, assigned, to them on account of the race they belong to."

By the second section it was enacted "that the officers of such passenger trains shall have power and are hereby required to assign each passenger to the coach or compartment used for the race to which such passenger belongs; any passenger insisting on going into a coach or compartment to which by race he does not belong, shall be liable to a fine of twenty-five dollars, or in lieu thereof to imprisonment for a period of not more than twenty days in the parish prison, and any officer of any railroad insisting on assigning a passenger to a coach or compartment other than the one set aside for the race to which said passenger belongs, shall be liable to a fine of twenty-five dollars, or in lieu thereof to imprisonment for a period of not more than twenty days in the parish prison; and should any passenger refuse to occupy the coach or compartment to which he or she is assigned by the officer of such railway, said officer shall have power to refuse to carry such passenger on his train, and for such refusal neither he nor the railway company which he represents shall be liable for damages in any of the courts of this State."

The third section provides penalties for the refusal or neglect of the officers, directors, conductors and employes of railway companies to comply with the act, with a proviso that "nothing in this act shall be construed as applying to nurses attending children of the other race." The fourth section is immaterial.

The information filed in the criminal District Court charged in substance that Plessy, being a passenger between two stations within the State of Louisiana, was assigned by officers of the company to the coach used for the race to which he belonged, but he insisted upon going into a coach used by the race to which he did not belong. Neither in the information nor plea was his particular race or color averred.

The petition for the writ of prohibition averred that petitioner was seven eighths Caucasian and one eighth African blood; that the mixture of colored blood was not discernible in him, and that he was entitled to every right, privilege and immunity secured to citizens of the United States of the white race; and that, upon such theory, he took possession of a vacant seat in a coach where passengers of the white race were accommodated, and was ordered by the conductor to vacate said coach and take a seat in another assigned to persons of the colored race, and having refused to comply with such demand he was forcibly ejected with the aid of a police officer, and imprisoned in the parish jail to answer a charge of having violated the above act.

The constitutionality of this act is attacked upon the ground that it conflicts both with the Thirteenth

The Case of *Plessy* v. *Ferguson* and the Doctrine of "Separate but Equal"

In 1890, in an early piece of Jim Crow legislation, Louisiana adopted a law providing for "equal but separate accommodations for the white and colored races" on passenger railroads operating within the state. Black Louisianans immediately set about challenging the constitutionality of the law, and two years later they had a case that could be taken before the U.S. Supreme Court.

On June 7, 1892, Homer Plessy purchased a ticket on the East Louisiana Railway from New Orleans to Covington and refused to take a seat in the car for blacks. He was arrested and arraigned before Judge John Ferguson in New Orleans Criminal Court on a charge of having violated the 1890 law. Before his case could come to trial, Plessy filed a "writ of error" with the Supreme Court, challenging the law under which he was being held on the ground that it violated both the Thirteenth and Fourteenth Amendments to the Constitution.

On April 13, 1896, the Supreme Court handed down its decision in *Plessy* v. *Ferguson*. By a vote of seven to one, the justices ruled against Plessy, dismissing with little comment the argument relating to the Thirteenth Amendment and concentrating instead on the question of whether the Fourteenth Amendment's guarantee of citizenship and equal protection had been violated. Writing for the majority, Justice Henry Billings Brown wrote that, while the purpose of the Fourteenth Amendment was "undoubtedly to enforce the absolute equality of the two races before the law," the laws that permit or even require racial separation "do not necessarily imply the inferiority of either race to the other." "Separate," in other words, could still be "equal." It was, as one legal historian has put it, "bad logic, bad history, bad sociology, and bad constitutional law."

With the exception of *Dred Scott* v. *Sandford,* no case in the Supreme Court's history has been as widely condemned as *Plessy* v. *Ferguson.* Unlike the *Dred Scott* decision, however, *Plessy* v. *Ferguson* remained in force for almost sixty years. Under the cover of its argument, there were few if any activities that might not be legally segregated by state governments. With the Supreme Court's blessing, state legislatures rushed to pen dozens of Jim Crow laws, transforming what had been informal, de facto segregation into a de jure wall separating black and white in housing, transportation, and, most importantly, schooling. Not until *Brown* v. *Board of Education* in 1954 would that wall come down, replaced once again, many would argue, by de facto segregation.

Amendment of the Constitution, abolishing slavery, and the Fourteenth Amendment, which prohibits certain restrictive legislation on the part of the States.

1. That it does not conflict with the Thirteenth Amendment, which abolished slavery and involuntary servitude, except as a punishment for crime, is too clear for argument. Slavery implies involuntary servitude—a state of bondage; the ownership of mankind as a chattel, or at least the control of the labor and services of one man for the benefit of another, and the absence of a legal right to the disposal of his own person, property and services.… This amendment was regarded by the statesmen of that day as insufficient to protect the colored race from certain laws which had been enacted in the Southern States, imposing upon the colored race onerous disabilities and burdens, and curtailing their rights in the pursuit of life, liberty and property to such an extent that their freedom was of little value; and that the Fourteenth Amendment was devised to meet this exigency.

So too, in the Civil Rights cases, 109 U.S. 3, 24, it was said that the act of a mere individual, the owner of an inn, a public conveyance or place of amusement, refusing accommodations to colored people, cannot be justly regarded as imposing any badge of slavery or servitude upon the applicant, but only as involving an ordinary civil injury, properly cognizable by the laws of the State, and presumably subject to redress by those laws until the contrary appears.

…A statute which implies merely a legal distinction between the white and colored races—a distinction which is founded in the color of the two races, and which

At the time of the *Plessy* v. *Ferguson* decision, interaction between African Americans and whites on passenger trains was primarily limited to exchanges between white passengers and African American workers. This 1900 advertisement for Pullman Trains spotlights the service provided in the dining cars. ARCHIVE PHOTOS, INC.

must always exist so long as white men are distinguished from the other race by color—has no tendency to destroy the legal equality of the two races, or reestablish a state of involuntary servitude. Indeed, we do not understand that the Thirteenth Amendment is strenuously relied upon by the plaintiff in error in this connection.

2. By the Fourteenth Amendment, all persons born or naturalized in the United States, and subject to the jurisdiction thereof, are made citizens of the United States and of the State wherein they reside; and the States are forbidden from making or enforcing any law which shall abridge the privileges or immunities of citizens of the United States, or shall deprive any person of life, liberty or property without due process of law, or deny to any person within their jurisdiction the equal protection of the laws.

…It was said generally that its main purpose was to establish the citizenship of the negro; to give definitions of citizenship of the United States and of the States, and to protect from the hostile legislation of the States the privileges and immunities of citizens of the United States, as distinguished from those of citizens of the States.

The object of the amendment was undoubtedly to enforce the absolute equality of the two races before the law, but in the nature of things it could not have been intended to abolish distinctions based upon color, or to enforce social, as distinguished from political equality, or a commingling of the two races upon terms unsatisfactory to either. Laws permitting, and even requiring, their separation in places where they are liable to be brought into contact do not necessarily imply the inferiority of either race to the other, and have been generally, if not universally, recognized as within the competency of the state legislatures in the exercise of their police power. The most common instance of this is connected with the establishment of separate schools for white and colored children, which has been held to be a valid exercise of the legislative power even by courts of States where the political rights of the colored race have been longest and most earnestly enforced.

One of the earliest of these cases is that of Roberts v. City of Boston, 5 Cush. 198, in which the Supreme Judicial Court of Massachusetts held that the general school committee of Boston had power to make provision for the instruction of colored children in separate schools established exclusively for them, and to prohibit their attendance upon the other schools.… It was held that the powers of the committee extended to the establishment of separate schools for children of different ages, sexes and colors, and that they might also establish special schools for poor and neglected children, who have become too old to attend the primary school, and yet have not acquired the rudiments of learning, to enable them to enter the ordinary schools.

…The distinction between laws interfering with the political equality of the negro and those requiring the separation of the two races in schools, theatres and railway carriages has been frequently drawn by this court. Thus in Strauder v. West Virginia, 100 U.S. 303, it was held that a law of West Virginia limiting to white male persons, 21 years of age and citizens of the State, the right to sit upon juries, was a discrimination which implied a legal inferiority in civil society, which lessened the security of the right of the colored race, and was a step toward reducing them to a condition of servility. Indeed, the right of a colored man that, in the selection of jurors to pass upon his life, liberty and property, there shall be no exclusion of his race, and no discrimination against them because of color, has been asserted in a number of cases.… So, where the laws of a particular locality or the charter of a particular railway corporation has provided that no person shall be excluded from the cars on account of color, we have held that this meant that persons of color should travel in the same car as white ones, and that the enactment was not satisfied by the company's providing cars assigned exclusively to people of color, though they were as good as those which they assigned exclusively to white persons. Railroad Company v. Brown, 17 Wall. 445.

Upon the other hand, where a statute of Louisiana required those engaged in the transportation of passengers among the States to give to all persons travelling within that State, upon vessels employed in that business, equal rights and privileges in all parts of the vessel, without distinction on account of race or color, and subjected to an action for damages the owner of such a vessel, who excluded colored passengers on account of their color from the cabin set aside by him for the use of whites, it was held to be so far as it applied to interstate commerce, unconstitutional and void. Hall v. De Cuir, 95 U.S. 485. The court in this case, however, expressly disclaimed that it had anything whatever to do with the statute as a regulation of internal commerce, or affecting anything else than commerce among the States.

In the Civil Rights case, 109 U.S. 3, it was held that an act of Congress, entitling all persons within the jurisdiction of the United States to the full and equal enjoyment of the accommodations, advantages, facilities and privileges of inns, public conveyances, on land or water, theatres and other places of public amusement, and made applicable to citizens of every race and color, regardless of any previous condition of servitude, was unconstitutional and void, upon the ground that the Fourteenth Amendment was prohibitory upon the States only, and the legislation authorized to be adopted by Congress for enforcing it was not direct legislation on matters respecting which the States were prohibited from making or enforcing certain laws, or doing certain acts, but was corrective legislation, such as might be necessary or proper for counteracting and redressing the effect of such laws or acts. In delivering the opinion of the court Mr. Justice Bradley observed that the Fourteenth Amendment "does not invest Congress with power to legislate upon subjects that are within the domain of state legislation; but to provide modes of relief against state legislation, or state action, of the kind referred to. It does not authorize Congress to create a code of municipal law for the regulation of private rights; but to provide modes of redress against the operation of state laws, and the action of state officers, executive or judicial, when these are subversive of the fundamental rights specified in the amendment. Positive rights and privileges are undoubtedly secured by the Fourteenth Amendment; but they are secured by way of prohibition against state laws and state proceedings affecting those rights and privileges, and by power given to Congress to legislate for

the purpose of carrying such prohibition into effect; and such legislation must necessarily be predicated upon such supposed state laws or state proceedings, and be directed to the correction of their operation and effect."

Much nearer, and, indeed, almost directly in point, is the case of the Louisville, New Orleans &c. Railway v. Mississippi, 133 U.S. 587, wherein the railway company was indicted for a violation of a statute of Mississippi, enacting that all railroads carrying passengers should provide equal, but separate, accommodations for the white and colored races, by providing two or more passenger cars for each passenger train, or by dividing the passenger cars by a partition, so as. to secure separate accommodations. The case was presented in a different aspect from the one under consideration, inasmuch as it was an indictment against the railway company for failing to provide the separate accommodations, but the question considered was the constitutionality of the law. In that case, the Supreme Court of Mississippi, 66 Mississippi, 662, had held that the statute applied solely to commerce within the State, and, that being the construction of the state statute by its highest court, was accepted as conclusive. "If it be a matter," said the court, p. 591, "respecting commerce wholly within a State, and not interfering with commerce. between the States, then, obviously, there is no violation of the commerce clause of the Federal Constitution.... No question arises under this section, as to the power of the State to separate in different compartments interstate passengers, or affect, in any manner, the privileges and rights of such passengers. All that we can consider is, whether the State has the power to require that railroad trains within her limits shall have separate accommodations for the two races; that affecting only commerce within the State is no invasion of the power given to Congress by the commerce clause."

A like course of reasoning applies to the case under consideration, since the Supreme Court of Louisiana in the case of the State ex rel. Abbott v. Hicks, Judge, et al., 44 La. Ann. 770, held that the statute in question did not apply to interstate passengers, but was confined in its application to passengers travelling exclusively within the borders of the State. The case was decided largely upon the authority of Railway Co. v. State, 66 Mississippi, 662, and affirmed by this court in 133 U.S. 587. In the present case no question of interference with interstate commerce can possibly arise, since the East Louisiana Railway appears to have been purely a local line, with both its termini within the State of Louisiana....

While we think the enforced separation of the races, as applied to the internal commerce of the State, neither abridges the privileges or immunities of the colored man, deprives him of his property without due process of law, nor denies him the equal protection of the laws, within the meaning of the Fourteenth Amendment, we are not prepared to say that the conductor, in assigning

At this Louisville, Kentucky, bus station, the bathrooms and dining rooms are segregated. This photograph illustrates the inherent injustice of the South's "separate but equal" policies and legislation. Many of the region's resources and much of its energy were devoted to keeping the races apart and black southerners "in their place." © ESTHER BUBLEY/CORBIS-BETTMANN

passengers to the coaches according to their race, does not act at his peril, or that the provision of the second section of the act, that denies to the passenger compensation in damages for a refusal to receive him into the coach in which he properly belongs, is a valid exercise of the legislative power.

...It is claimed by the plaintiff in error that, in any mixed community, the reputation of belonging to the dominant race, in this instance the white race, is property, in the same sense that a right of action, or of inheritance, is property. Conceding this to be so, for the purposes of this case, we are unable to see how this statute deprives him of, or in any way affects his right to, such property. If he be a white man and assigned to a colored coach, he may have his action for damages against the company for being deprived of his so called property. Upon the other hand, if he be a colored man and be so assigned, he has been deprived of no property, since he is not lawfully entitled to the reputation of being a white man.

In this connection, it is also suggested by the learned counsel for the plaintiff in error that the same argument that will justify the state legislature in requiring railways to provide separate accommodations for the two races will also authorize them to require separate cars to be provided for people whose hair is of a certain color, or who are aliens, or who belong to certain nationalities, or to enact laws requiring colored people to walk upon one side of the street, and white people upon the other, or requiring white men's houses to be painted white, and colored men's black, or their vehicles or business signs to

be of different colors, upon the theory that one side of the street is as good as the other, or that a house or vehicle of one color is as good as one of another color. The reply to all this is that every exercise of the police power must be reasonable, and extend only to such laws as are enacted in good faith for the promotion for the public good, and not for the annoyance or oppression of a particular class.

...So far, then, as a conflict with the Fourteenth Amendment is concerned, the case reduces itself to the question whether the statute of Louisiana is a reasonable regulation, and with respect to this there must necessarily be a large discretion on the part of the legislature. In determining the question of reasonableness it is at liberty to act with reference to the established usages, customs and traditions of the people, and with a view to the promotion of their comfort, and the preservation of the public peace and good order. Gauged by this standard, we cannot say that a law which authorizes or even requires the separation of the two races in public conveyances is unreasonable, or more obnoxious to the Fourteenth Amendment than the acts of Congress requiring separate schools for colored children in the District of Columbia, the constitutionality of which does not seem to have been questioned, or the corresponding acts of state legislatures.

We consider the underlying fallacy of the plaintiff's argument to consist in the assumption that the enforced separation of the two races stamps the colored race with a badge of inferiority. If this be so, it is not by reason of anything found in the act, but solely because the colored race chooses to put that construction upon it. The argument necessarily assumes that if, as has been more than once the case, and is not unlikely to be so again, the colored race should become the dominant power in the state legislature, and should enact a law in precisely similar terms, it would thereby relegate the white race to an inferior position. We imagine that the white race, at least, would not acquiesce in this assumption. The argument also assumes that social prejudices may be overcome by legislation, and that equal rights cannot be secured to the negro except by an enforced commingling of the two races. We cannot accept this proposition. If the two races are to meet upon terms of social equality, it must be the result of natural affinities, a mutual appreciation of each other's merits and a voluntary consent of individuals.... Legislation is powerless to eradicate racial instincts or to abolish distinctions based upon physical differences, and the attempt to do so can only result in accentuating the difficulties of the present situation. If the civil and political rights of both races be equal one cannot be inferior to the other civilly or politically. If one race be inferior to the other socially, the Constitution of the United States cannot put them upon the same plane.

It is true that the question of the proportion of colored blood necessary to constitute a colored person, as distinguished from a white person, is one upon which there is a difference of opinion in the different States, some holding that any visible admixture of black blood stamps the person as belonging to the colored race, (State v. Chavers, 5 Jones, [N.C.] 1, p. 11); others that it depends upon the preponderance of blood, (Gray v. State, 4 Ohio, 354; Monroe v. Collins, 17 Ohio St. 665); and still others that the predominance of white blood must only be in the proportion of three fourths. (People v. Dean, 14 Michigan, 406; Jones v. Commonwealth, 80 Virginia, 538.) But these are question to be determined under the laws of each State and are not properly put in issue in this case. Under the allegations of his petition it may undoubtedly become a question of importance whether, under the laws of Louisiana, the petitioner belongs to the white or colored race.

The judgment of the court below is, therefore, Affirmed.

Dissent by: Harlan

Dissent: Mr. Justice Harlan dissenting.

By the Louisiana statute, the validity of which is here involved, all railway companies (other than street railroad companies) carrying passengers in that State are required to have separate but equal accommodations for white and colored persons, "by providing two or more passenger coaches for each passenger train, or by dividing the passenger coaches by a partition so as to secure separate accommodations." Under this statute, no colored person is permitted to occupy a seat in a coach assigned to white persons; nor any white person, to occupy a seat in a coach assigned to colored persons. The managers of the railroad are not allowed to exercise any discretion in the premises, but are required to assign each passenger to some coach or compartment set apart for the exclusive use of his race. If a passenger insists upon going into a coach or compartment not set apart for persons of his race, he is subject to be fined, or to be imprisoned in the parish jail. Penalties are prescribed for the refusal or neglect of the officers, directors, conductors and employes of railroad companies to comply with the provisions of the act.

Only "nurses attending children of the other race" are excepted from the operation of the statute. No exception is made of colored attendants travelling with adults. A white man is not permitted to have his colored servant with him in the same coach, even if his condition of health requires the constant, personal assistance of such servant. If a colored maid insists upon riding in the same coach with a white woman whom she has been employed to serve, and who may need her personal attention while travelling, she is subject to be fined or imprisoned for such an exhibition of zeal in the discharge of duty.

While there may be in Louisiana persons of different races who are not citizens of the United States, the words

in the act, "white and colored races," necessarily include all citizens of the United States of both races residing in that State. So that we have before us a state enactment that compels, under penalties, the separation of the two races in railroad passenger coaches, and makes it a crime for a citizen of either race to enter a coach that has been assigned to citizens of the other race.

Thus the State regulates the use of a public highway by citizens of the United States solely upon the basis of race.

However apparent the injustice of such legislation may be, we have only to consider whether it is consistent with the Constitution of the United States.

That a railroad is a public highway, and that the corporation which owns or operates it is in the exercise of public functions, is not, at this day, to be disputed. Mr. Justice Nelson, speaking for this court in New Jersey Steam Navigation Co. v. Merchants' Bank, 6 How. 344, 382, said that a common carrier was in the exercise "of a sort of public office, and has public duties to perform, from which he should not be permitted to exonerate himself without the assent of the parties concerned." Mr. Justice Strong, delivering the judgment of this court in Olcott v. The Supervisors, 16 Wall. 678, 694, said: "That railroads, though constructed by private corporations and owned by them, are public highways, has been the doctrine of nearly all the courts ever since such conveniences for passage and transportation have had any existence.…"

In respect of civil rights, common to all citizens, the Constitution of the United States does not, I think, permit any public authority to know the race of those entitled to be protected in the enjoyment of such rights. Every true man has pride of race, and under appropriate circumstances when the rights of others, his equals before the law, are not to be affected, it is his privilege to express such pride and to take such action based upon it as to him seems proper. But I deny that any legislative body or judicial tribunal may have regard to the race of citizens when the civil rights of those citizens are involved. Indeed, such legislation, as that here in question, is inconsistent not only with that equality of rights which pertains to citizenship, National and State, but with the personal liberty enjoyed by every one within the United States.

The Thirteenth Amendment does not permit the withholding or the deprivation of any right necessarily inhering in freedom. It not only struck down the institution of slavery as previously existing in the United States, but it prevents the imposition of any burdens or disabilities that constitute badges of slavery or servitude. It decreed universal civil freedom in this country. This court has so adjudged. But that amendment having been found inadequate to the protection of the rights of those who had been in slavery, it was followed by the Four-

These demonstrators from six Texas schools march to the state capitol in Austin to protest school segregation in 1949. **THE LIBRARY OF CONGRESS**

teenth Amendment, which added greatly to the dignity and glory of American citizenship, and to the security of personal liberty, by declaring that "all persons born or naturalized in the United States, and subject to the jurisdiction thereof, are citizens of the United States and of the State wherein they reside," and that "no State shall make or enforce any law which shall abridge the privileges or immunities of citizens of the United States; nor shall any State deprive any person of life, liberty or property without due process of law, nor deny to any person within its jurisdiction the equal protection of the laws." These two amendments, if enforced according to their true intent and meaning, will protect all the civil rights that pertain to freedom and citizenship. Finally, and to the end that no citizen should be denied, on account of his race, the privilege of participating in the political control of his country, it was declared by the Fifteenth Amendment that "the right of citizens of the United States to vote shall not be denied or abridged by the United States or by any State on account of race, color or previous condition of servitude."

These notable additions to the fundamental law were welcomed by the friends of liberty throughout the world. They removed the race line from our governmental systems. They had, as this court has said, a common purpose, namely, to secure "to a race recently emancipated, a race that through many generations have been held in slavery, all the civil rights that the superior race enjoy." They declared, in legal effect, this court has further said, "that the law in the States shall be the same for the black as for the white; that all persons, whether colored or white, shall stand equal before the laws of the States, and, in regard to the colored race, for whose protection the amendment was primarily designed, that no discrimination shall be made against them by law because of their color." We also said: "The words of the amendment, it is true, are prohibitory, but they contain a necessary implication of a positive immunity, or right, most valuable to the colored race—the right to exemption from unfriendly legislation against them distinctively as colored—exemption from legal discriminations, implying inferiority in civil society, lessening the security of their enjoyment of the rights which others enjoy, and discriminations which are steps towards reducing them to the condition of a subject race." It was, consequently, adjudged that a state law that excluded citizens of the colored race from juries, because of their race and however well qualified in other respects to discharge the duties of jurymen, was repugnant to the Fourteenth Amendment.... At the present term, referring to the previous adjudications, this court declared that "underlying all of those decisions is the principle that the Constitution of the United States, in its present form, forbids, so far as civil and political rights are concerned, discrimination by the General Government or the States against any citizen because of his race. All citizens are equal before the law." Gibson v. Mississippi, 162 U.S. 565.

The decisions referred to show the scope of the recent amendments of the Constitution. They also show that it is not within the power of a State to prohibit colored citizens, because of their race, from participating as jurors in the administration of justice.

It was said in argument that the statute of Louisiana does not discriminate against either race, but prescribes a rule applicable alike to white and colored citizens. But this argument does not meet the difficulty. Every one knows that the statute in question had its origin in the purpose, not so much to exclude white persons from railroad cars occupied by blacks, as to exclude colored people from coaches occupied by or assigned to white persons. Railroad corporations of Louisiana did not make discrimination among whites in the matter of accommodation for travelers. The thing to accomplish was, under the guise of giving equal accommodation for whites and blacks, to compel the latter to keep to themselves while travelling in railroad passenger coaches. No one would be so wanting in candor as to assert the contrary. The fundamental objection, therefore, to the statute is that it interferes with the personal freedom of citizens. "Personal liberty," it has been well said, "consists in the power of locomotion, of changing situation, or removing one's person to whatsoever places one's own inclination may direct, without imprisonment or restraint, unless by due course of law." 1 Bl. Com. *134. If a white man and a black man choose to occupy the same public conveyance on a public highway, it is their right to do so, and no government, proceeding alone on grounds of race, can prevent it without infringing the personal liberty of each.

It is one thing for railroad carriers to furnish, or to be required by law to furnish, equal accommodations for all whom they are under a legal duty to carry. It is quite another thing for government to forbid citizens of the white and black races from travelling in the same public conveyance, and to punish officers of railroad companies for permitting parsons of the two races to occupy the same passenger coach. If a State can prescribe, as a rule

of civil conduct, that whites and blacks shall not travel as passengers in the same railroad coach, why may it not so regulate the use of the streets of its cities and towns as to compel white citizens to keep on one side of a street and black citizens to keep on the other? Why may it not, upon like grounds, punish whites and blacks who ride together in street cars or in open vehicles on a public road of street? Why may it not require sheriffs to assign whites to one side of a court-room and blacks to the other? And why may it not also prohibit the commingling of the two races in the galleries of legislative halls or in public assemblages convened for the considerations of the political questions of the day? Further, if this statute of Louisiana is consistent with the personal liberty of citizens, why may not the State require the separation in railroad coaches of native and naturalized citizens of the United States, or of Protestants and Roman Catholics?

The answer given at the argument to these questions was that regulations of the kind they suggest would be unreasonable, and could not, therefore, stand before the law. Is it meant that the determination of questions of legislative power depends upon the inquiry whether the statute whose validity is questioned is, in the judgment of the courts, a reasonable one, taking all the circumstances into consideration? A statute may be unreasonable merely because a sound public policy forbade its enactment. But I do not understand that the courts have anything to do with the policy or expediency of legislation. A statute may be valid, and yet, upon grounds of public policy, may well be characterized as unreasonable. Mr. Sedgwick correctly states the rule when he says that the legislative intention being clearly ascertained, "the courts have no other duty to perform than to execute the legislative will, without any regard to their views as to the wisdom or justice of the particular enactment." Stat. & Const. Constr. 324. There is a dangerous tendency in these latter days to enlarge the functions of the courts, by means of judicial interference with the will of the people as expressed by the legislature. Our institutions have the distinguishing characteristic that the three departments of government are coordinate and separate. Each must keep within the limits defined by the Constitution. And the courts best discharge their duty by executing the will of the law-making power, constitutionally expressed, leaving the results of legislation to be dealt with by the people through their representatives. Statutes must always have a reasonable construction. Sometimes they are to be construed strictly; sometimes, liberally, in order to carry out the legislative will. But however construed, the intent of the legislature is to be respected, if the particular statute in question is valid, although the courts, looking at the public interests, may conceive the statute to be both unreasonable and impolitic. If the power exists to enact a statute, that ends the matter so far as the courts are concerned. The adjudged cases in which statutes have been held to be void, because unreasonable,

Reversing *Plessy* v. *Ferguson*: The Decision to Desegregate Schools

The infamous history set in motion by the *Plessy* v. *Ferguson* decision was finally undone on May 17, 1954. On that date *Brown* v. *Board of Education* and the companion decision *Bolling* v. *Sharpe* were issued by the Supreme Court. A separate decision was required in the case of Washington, D.C., which, as a federal district, was not covered by the Fourteenth Amendment. The justices, ruling again unanimously, found segregation in district schools to be in violation of the Fifth Amendment's guarantee of due process. Referring to their *Brown* v. *Board of Education* ruling, they added that "in view of our decision that the Constitution prohibits the states from maintaining racially segregated public schools, it would be unthinkable that the same Constitution would impose a lesser duty on the Federal Government."

are those in which the means employed by the legislature were not at all germane to the end to which the legislature was competent.

The white race deems itself to be the dominant race in this country. And so it is, in prestige, in achievements, in education, in wealth and in power. So, I doubt not, it will continue to be for all time, if it remains true to its great heritage and holds fast to the principles of constitutional liberty. But in view of the Constitution, in the eye of the law, there is in this country no superior, dominant, ruling class of citizens. There is no caste here. Our Constitution is color-blind, and neither knows nor tolerates classes among citizens. In respect of civil rights, all citizens are equal before the law. The humblest is the peer of the most powerful. The law regards man as man, and takes no account of his surroundings or of his color when his civil rights as guaranteed by the supreme law of the land are involved. It is, therefore, to be regretted that this high tribunal, the final expositor of the fundamental law of the land, has reached the conclusion that it is competent for a State to regulate the enjoyment by citizens of their civil rights solely upon the basis of race.

In my opinion, the judgment this day rendered will, in time, prove to be quite as pernicious as the decision made by this tribunal in the Dred Scott case. It was

adjudged in that case that the descendants of Africans who were imported into this country and sold as slaves were not included nor intended to be included under the word "citizens" in the Constitution, and could not claim any of the rights and privileges which that instrument provided for and secured to citizens of the United States; that at the time of the adoption of the Constitution they were "considered as a subordinate and inferior class of beings, who had been subjugated by the dominant race, and, whether emancipated or not, yet remained subject to their authority, and had no rights or privileges but such as those who held the power and the government might choose to grant them." 19 How. 393, 404. The recent amendments of the Constitution, it was supposed, had eradicated these principles from our institutions. But it seems that we have yet, in some of the States, a dominant race—a superior class of citizens, which assumes to regulate the enjoyment of civil rights, common to all citizens, upon the basis of race. The present decision, it may well be apprehended, will not only stimulate aggressions, more or less brutal and irritating, upon the admitted rights of colored citizens, but will encourage the belief that it is possible, by means of state enactments, to defeat the beneficent purposes which the people of the United States had in view when they adopted the recent amendments of the Constitution, by one of which the blacks of this country were made citizens of the United States and of the States in which they respectively reside, and whose privileges and immunities, as citizens, the States are forbidden to abridge. Sixty millions of whites are in no danger from the presence here of eight millions of blacks. The destinies of the two races, in this country, are indissolubly linked together, and the interests of both require that the common government of all shall not permit the seeds of race hate to be planted under the sanction of law. What can more certainly arouse race hate, what more certainly create and perpetuate a feeling of distrust between these races, than state enactments, which, in fact, proceed on the ground that colored citizens are so inferior and degraded that they cannot be allowed to sit in public coaches occupied by white citizens? That, as all will admit, is the real meaning of such legislation as was enacted in Louisiana.

The sure guarantee of the peace and security of each race is the clear, distinct, unconditional recognition by our governments, National and State, of every right that inheres in civil freedom, and of the equality before the law of all citizens of the United States without regard to race. State enactments, regulating the enjoyment of civil rights, upon the basis of race, and cunningly devised to defeat legitimate results of the war, under the pretence of recognizing equality of rights, can have no other result than to render permanent peace impossible, and to keep alive a conflict of races, the continuance of which must do harm to all concerned. This question is not met by the suggestion that social equality cannot exist between the white and black races in this country. That argument, if it can be properly regarded as one, is scarcely worthy of consideration; for social equality no more exists between two races when travelling in a passenger coach or a public highway than when members of the same races sit by each other in a street car or in the jury box, or stand or sit with each other in a political assembly, or when they use in common the streets of a city or town, or when they are in the same room for the purpose of having their names placed on the registry of voters, or when they approach the ballot-box in order to exercise the high privilege of voting.

There is a race so different from our own that we do not permit those belonging to it to become citizens of the United States. Persons belonging to it are, with few exceptions, absolutely excluded from our country. I allude to the Chinese race. But by the statute in question, a Chinaman can ride in the same passenger coach with white citizens of the United States, while citizens of the black race in Louisiana, many of whom, perhaps, risked their lives for the preservation of the Union, who are entitled, by law, to participate in the political control of the State and nation, who are not excluded, by law or by reason of their race, from public stations of any kind, and who have all the legal rights that belong to white citizens, are yet declared to be criminals, liable to imprisonment, if they ride in a public coach occupied by citizens of the white race. It is scarcely just to say that a colored citizen should not object to occupying a public coach assigned to his own race. He does not object, nor, perhaps, would he object to separate coaches for his race, if his rights under the law were recognized. But he objects, and ought never to cease objecting to the proposition, that citizens of the white and black races can be adjudged criminals because they sit, or claim the right to sit, in the same public coach on a public highway.

The arbitrary separation of citizens, on the basis of race, while they are on a public highway, is a badge of servitude wholly inconsistent with the civil freedom and the equality before the law established by the Constitution. It cannot be justified upon any legal grounds.

If evils will result from the commingling of the two races upon public highways established for the benefit of all, they will be infinitely less than those that will surely come from state legislation regulating the enjoyment of civil rights upon the basis of race. We boast of the freedom enjoyed by our people above all other peoples. But it is difficult to reconcile that boast with a state of the law which, practically, puts the brand of servitude and degradation upon a large class of our fellow-citizens, our equals before the law. The thin disguise of "equal" accommodations for passengers in railroad coaches will not mislead any one, nor atone for the wrong this day done.

The result of the whole matter is, that while this court has frequently adjudged, and at the present term

has recognized the doctrine, that a State cannot, consistently with the Constitution of the United States, prevent white and black citizens, having the required qualifications for jury service, from sitting in the same jury box, it is now solemnly held that a State may prohibit white and black citizens from sitting in the same passenger coach on a public highway, or may require that they be separated by a "partition," when in the same passenger coach. May it not now be reasonably expected that astute men of the dominant race, who affect to be disturbed at the possibility that the integrity of the white race may be corrupted, or that its supremacy will be imperilled, by contact on public highways with black people, will endeavor to procure statutes requiring white and black jurors to be separated in the jury box by a "partition," and that, upon retiring from the court room to consult as to their verdict, such partition, if it be a moveable one, shall be taken to their consultation room, and set up in such way as to prevent black jurors from coming too close to their brother jurors of the white race. If the "partition" used in the court room happens to be stationary, provision could be made for screens with openings through which jurors of the two races could confer as to their verdict without coming into personal contact with each other. I cannot see but that, according to the principles this day announced, such state legislation, although conceived in hostility to, and enacted for the purpose of humiliating citizens of the United States of a particular race, would be held to be consistent with the Constitution.

I do not deem it necessary to review the decisions of state courts to which reference was made in argument. Some, and the most important, of them are wholly inapplicable, because rendered prior to the adoption of the last amendments of the Constitution, when colored people had very few rights which the dominant race felt obliged to respect. Others were made at a time when public opinion, in many localities, was dominated by the institution of slavery; when it would not have been safe to do justice to the black man; and when, so far as the rights of blacks were concerned, race prejudice was, practically, the supreme law of the land. Those decisions cannot be guides in the era introduced by the recent amendments of the supreme law, which established universal civil freedom, gave citizenship to all born or naturalized in the United States and residing her, obliterated the race line from our systems of governments, National and State, and placed our free institutions upon the broad and sure foundation of the equality of all men before the law.

I am of opinion that the statute of Louisiana is inconsistent with the personal liberty of citizens, white and black, in that State, and hostile to both the spirit and letter of the Constitution of the United States. If laws of like character should be enacted in the several States of the Union, the effect would be in the highest degree mischievous. Slavery, as an institution tolerated by law would, it is true, have disappeared from our country, but there would remain a power in the States, by sinister legislation, to interfere with the full enjoyment of the blessings of freedom; to regulate civil rights, common to all citizens, upon the basis of race; and to place in a condition of legal inferiority a large body of American citizens, now constituting a part of the political community called the People of the United States, for whom, and by whom through representatives, our government is administered. Such a system is inconsistent with the guarantee given by the Constitution to each State of a republican form of government, and may be stricken down by Congressional action, or by the courts in the discharge of their solemn duty to maintain the supreme law of the land, anything in the constitution or laws of any State to the contrary notwithstanding.

For the reasons stated, I am constrained to withhold my assent from the opinion and judgment of the majority.

Mr. Justice Brewer did not hear the argument or participate in the decision of this case.

The Education of African Americans

ADAPTED FROM ESSAYS BY ALLISON EPSTEIN

Even before the Declaration of Independence declared that all men are created equal, African Americans were working to achieve equality in American society. This long and difficult struggle has been especially hard fought in the realm of education. At one end of the spectrum were the solitary efforts of slaves and ex-slaves to learn to read and write in the world that was not only hostile to their education, but had made it outright illegal. At the other end are the current-day struggles of African Americans to educate their children in underfinanced and politically invisible school systems in areas of rural poverty and ghettoized urban centers. Throughout this story, conflicts have arisen between blacks and whites and among black Americans themselves concerning the desirability of desegregation and the best approach to achieving educational opportunity and equality. Education has probably been the single most important tool in the struggle for African Americans to better the circumstances of their lives and the lives of their children.

EARLY EDUCATIONAL OPPORTUNITIES FOR AFRICAN AMERICANS

Christian churches were the first organizations in America to offer education to Africans and African Americans. While their main goal was religious instruction and conversion to Christianity, churches also offered general education. From the French Catholics in Louisiana in the early 1600s to the Pennsylvania Quakers in the early 1700s, religious groups worked to improve the lives of black Americans. Their aims were often intertwined with the fight to end slavery. Thus, African free schools in New York, Philadelphia, and Boston upheld antislavery principles at the same time that they offered general and religious instruction.

While religious organizations worked to provide education for African American children, most state governments in antebellum America did not share this goal. As a rule, free public education was understood to exclude black children. As long as slavery continued to exist and dominate American political debate, the majority of states refused to grant equal privileges to their black inhabitants, whether free or enslaved.

In a new constitution enacted in 1820, the state of Maine extended school privileges to all children regardless of skin color. Rhode Island's legislature similarly afforded all citizens equal educational privileges in the state's 1843 constitution. But the majority of states either forbade black education outright or neglected to provide for it in their education laws.

In 1832, Alabama passed an act establishing fines for anyone who attempted to teach free persons of color to read, write, or spell. The state legislature of Georgia ruled in 1829 that anyone who worked for the education of blacks would be punished with a fine, whipping, and/or imprisonment. An 1847 Missouri law forbade the existence of any school that instructed African Americans.

Other states, while not expressly forbidding the education of blacks, adopted education laws that applied only to white students. For example, in Illinois there was no prohibition against the public education of blacks, but the word "white" was used in all state education acts. Similarly, Indiana made no provision for African American education but also did not expressly prohibit it.

Although many government officials did not support efforts to educate African Americans, there were a number of educators dedicated to schooling members of the black community. With the assistance of the Philadelphia Quakers, Anthony Benezet (1713–1784) opened the first free school for blacks in 1750. The Manumission Society opened New York City's first free school for blacks in 1787, and by 1834 the city had seven African free schools, which later became part of the public school system. In 1829, the Saint Francis Academy of Baltimore became the first boarding school for black girls.

COMMUNITY RESISTANCE TO INTEGRATION

A notable example of the resistance to African American education prior to the Civil War occurred in Canterbury, Connecticut, when Prudence Crandall (1803–1890)

This photograph by the great Civil War photographer Mathew Brady shows students at a contraband school somewhere in the South during the Civil War. The Union set up a handful of such schools to educate African American men, women, and children who escaped over Union lines. **NATIONAL ARCHIVES AND RECORDS ADMINISTRATION**

attempted to instruct African American young ladies at her school. Crandall, a well-educated white woman, opened a school for young ladies in 1832. When she accepted a seventeen-year-old black girl who wanted to become a teacher and instruct other African Americans, many of the parents of the other pupils complained.

Crandall ignored their complaints and continued to admit African American girls, not only from Connecticut, but also from Philadelphia, Boston, Providence, and New York City. In reaction to her inclusion of blacks, Crandall was threatened by mobs of outraged citizens, who attacked her house and attempted to set it on fire. Crandall continued to operate her school, but when the state passed a black law forbidding the formal education of African Americans who did not reside in Connecticut, she was imprisoned and brought to trial. Found guilty of violating the new law, Crandall was forced to shut down her school. Connecticut's black law was repealed in 1838.

The Prudence Crandall case is notable because it occurred in the North prior to the Civil War, at a time when most Northerners were denouncing the treatment of blacks in the South. The inability of members of Crandall's community to accept integrated education, even while they opposed slavery, clearly shows that white interest in the African American cause was mostly limit-

ed to abolition. **SEE PRIMARY SOURCE DOCUMENT** *Miss Prudence Crandall and the Canterbury School*

After the end of the Civil War, hundreds of thousands of blacks were left homeless and penniless, dependent on federal assistance for survival. In 1865, Congress created the Freedmen's Bureau to provide food, clothing, shelter, and education to blacks in need. With southern freedmen excluded from segregated schools in their communities, the bureau established more than twenty-five hundred freedmen's schools, and by 1870, it had educated more than 150,000 students.

THE DESEGREGATION OF AMERICAN PUBLIC SCHOOLS

Desegregation was not simply a debate about whether blacks and whites should be educated under the same roof. It was a fundamental dispute over housing segregation, job discrimination, racial stereotypes, and equal protection. Schools influenced where a family decided to live, what types of jobs were available after graduation, and how each individual defined his or her conception of community.

The incorporation of African Americans within American schools has been made even more confusing by the fact that black parents often vacillate between segregated and desegregated schooling for their children. While children attending exclusively black schools are shielded from prejudice and discrimination, these schools tend to be viewed as inferior facilities. Many parents assume that the schools will improve if white children are also in attendance, but in integrated schools, black children have been treated poorly, subjected to racial discrimination and hatred—and have not necessarily received a better education.

The case of *Roberts* v. *City of Boston* (1849) illustrates clearly the dilemma of black parents. Although Boston had no specific law that forbade blacks from attending public schools, racial hatred generally deterred black parents from sending their children. As an alternative, the black community opened the Smith School in 1798. This school was attended by over fifty African American students on a regular basis and was supported through community and private donations. In 1815, the Boston School Committee assumed funding of the school.

Attendance and academic progress remained low at the school, however, for a number of reasons. Many parents could not afford to lose the income their child would have earned if not in school. Moreover, education still afforded blacks few opportunities for political, social, or economic advancement. Finally, travel to and from the school was inconvenient for those who lived at a distance.

The Boston School Committee attributed the students' low attendance and limited academic progress to a lack of interest on the part of the black community. Black parents petitioned the school board numerous times to desegregate Boston public schools, citing poor conditions at the Smith School, but the School Committee continued to insist that the separate school provided adequate instruction for black children and that it was the black parents who insisted on segregated schooling in the first place.

While the decision in the *Roberts* case upheld the Boston School Committee's position, in 1855 the Massachusetts State Legislature passed a law desegregating all public schools. Accommodations for Boston's black children were made within existing all-white schools, but within ten years of the new legislation, Boston schools were again racially identifiable—that is, segregated.

FEDERAL COURT CHALLENGES TO SEGREGATION

The rationale of the court in *Roberts* was later adopted by the Supreme Court in its 1896 *Plessy* v. *Ferguson* decision, which established the doctrine of "separate but equal." While this case argued the constitutionality of maintaining racially segregated train cars, the precedent applied to all public institutions, including schools.

It was not until the Supreme Court's 1954 ruling in *Brown* v. *Board of Education* that "separate" was declared to be "inherently unequal." The Court mandated that all states rectify their school policies to incorporate this ruling and to provide equal opportunities for black and white students. Fearing a backlash of public opinion, however, the Court tempered its position somewhat. Rather than ordering the immediate desegregation of American schools, it asked that the new policy be instituted "with all deliberate speed." This additional proviso allowed many school systems to make relatively superficial changes in their practices, maintaining at least some form of school segregation. **SEE PRIMARY SOURCE DOCUMENT** *Excerpts from* **Brown** v. **Board of Education** *and* **Bolling** v. **Sharpe**

The *Brown* v. *Board of Education* decision and subsequent legislation and court rulings led to the busing of children out of their neighborhoods in order to achieve racial balance in the schools. This was done at the expense and inconvenience of children whose only offense was the color of their skin. Desegregation thus challenged each white and black individual to consider how race related to the community and how much should be sacrificed for the sake of racial equality.

Since the *Brown* decision, American public schools and colleges have taken significant steps down the road to integration. In 1957, Little Rock Central High School enrolled nine black students. In 1962, under court order, the University of Mississippi accepted James Meredith as its first African American student. In 1973, a federal judge ordered Boston to implement a comprehensive desegregation plan.

During the 1960s, the civil rights movement also achieved some success in the desegregation of public education. The Civil Rights Act of 1964 and the Voting Rights Act of 1965 insisted that there could be no laws that upheld political discrimination against blacks. The Fair Housing Act of 1968 also assisted desegregation by enabling black Americans to move to better neighborhoods, which in turn had better schools. The Supreme Court continued to uphold school desegregation laws, and by 1971, almost all schools in the South used a combination of racial balancing and busing to achieve integration.

Although most school systems have now met their desegregation requirements, meeting the needs of African American students remains a pressing and controversial issue. Many inner-city schools are creating alternative facilities and programs to incorporate African American culture and history into the standard curriculum. In response to the inadequate resources of many urban schools, communities are now examining the possibility of integrating inner-city and suburban school districts in order to equalize opportunity for all students.

Despite favorable court decisions, the struggle to desegregate American public schools continues.

TECHNICAL EDUCATION VS. HIGHER EDUCATION

While the desegregation battle raged in public education, in the realm of higher education a different controversy arose between Booker T. Washington (1856–1915) and W. E. B. Du Bois (1868–1963). The most influential black leader of his day, Washington advocated practical, vocational instruction in black colleges. Washington was convinced that for black Americans, the achievement of economic stability must precede the granting of full political and civil rights. He founded the Tuskegee Normal and Industrial Institute in 1881 to teach African Americans trades such as farming, mechanics, and carpentry.

Du Bois, on the other hand, maintained that African Americans would better their place in American society only by actively campaigning against inequality. To further his crusade against racial oppression, Du Bois founded the Niagara Movement in 1905, demanding that whites take responsibility for racial problems, and the National Association for the Advancement of Colored People (NAACP) in 1909. Du Bois also was the first black leader to articulate the importance of Pan-Africanism, the philosophy that all people of African descent must join together to address common problems. Du Bois felt that Washington's emphasis on technical training at the expense of higher education simply confirmed white views of black inferiority.

The conflicting approaches of these two popular, outspoken black leaders reflected the quandary of African Americans in the late nineteenth and early twentieth centuries: Should blacks demand equality? Or did they first need to prove that they were entitled to it?

AFRICAN AMERICAN COLLEGES AND UNIVERSITIES

Most colleges and universities did not begin to admit black students in any significant numbers until the mid-twentieth century. Before then, blacks seeking higher education attended all-black institutions. From 1865 to 1871, a handful of black colleges were founded, including Fisk University and Lincoln Institute (now Lincoln University) in 1866, Augusta Institute (now Morehouse College) in 1867, and Alcorn College (now Alcorn State University) in 1871.

In the early years, the lack of financial support and resources made such black schools poor substitutes for exclusively white institutions. To help support all-black universities, the Morrill Acts of 1862 and 1890 awarded federal assistance through land grants. This legislation provided much-needed aid to the historically black institu-

A tireless researcher and editor of early African American texts, Arna Bontemps also authored many works of fiction, poetry, and drama, including the 1936 novel *Black Thunder,* about Gabriel's Revolt. **AP/WIDE WORLD PHOTOS**

tions, but their dependence on state aid, which was often controlled by whites, impeded their academic freedom.

In addition, unwillingness on the part of most state governments to uphold the "separate but equal" principle by allocating comparable resources to black colleges made these institutions financially unstable. Many black colleges had to rely heavily on private donations and missionary teachers who worked for substandard wages. Nevertheless, by 1900, black colleges had conferred degrees on more than two thousand students.

Black colleges are more popular than ever at the beginning of the twenty-first century, enrolling more than two hundred thousand students each year. At the same time, many formerly all-white colleges have created African American studies programs, curricula, and departments.

CONCLUSION

Over the past several centuries, African American advancement toward equality in education has come in waves. In 1907, Alain Leroy Locke (1886–1954) was named the first black Rhodes scholar, yet it took more than fifty years, until 1960, before a second African American was named. In 1946, the University of Chicago appointed Allison Davis (1902–1983) as its first black professor, but Harvard Business School did not appoint a

Booker T. Washington (1856–1915): "A Slave among Slaves"

Born a slave in Virginia in 1856, Booker T. Washington grew up to become one of the most influential African Americans of the post–Civil War era. In 1881, when he was not yet thirty years old, he founded the Tuskegee Institute in Alabama, modeling its curriculum on the vocational training he had received at Hampton Institute in Virginia. Washington believed that the vocational training of African Americans would eventually lead to their economic independence, and that such independence must precede their full participation in the nation's political and social life. Because he was willing to tolerate Jim Crow segregation and black disenfranchisement, Washington was labeled an "accommodationist." His policies were condemned by many other black intellectuals and leaders.

In 1901, Washington published his autobiography, *Up from Slavery.* As the title indicates, it is a rags-to-riches story, a popular autobiographical form among America's "self-made" achievers. *Up from Slavery* is the tale of Washington's meteoric rise to power and an advertisement for him and the Tuskegee Institute. The first chapter, "A Slave among Slaves," offers Washington's earliest recollections of plantation life. It provides a striking contrast to the portrait of slavery found in pre–Civil War slave narratives. Whereas abolitionist slave narratives had soundly condemned the institution of slavery as degrading and brutalizing, Washington carefully avoids blaming white southerners for the conditions and the ignorance into which he was born, insisting again and again that the freed slaves were not bitter.

Washington's version of slavery contrasts in particular with that of Frederick Douglass in his 1845 *Narrative.* Where Douglass fumes at his lack of any knowledge of his birth date and paternity, Washington says simply, "I suspect I must have been born somewhere and at some time." Where Douglass writes of slave children called "like so many pigs" to the trough, Washington says that his family never ate together "in a civilized manner." Most importantly, in Washington's account Douglass's "hell of slavery" is transformed into "the school of American slavery," designed by "Providence" to prepare African Americans for citizenship.

The figure of Booker T. Washington is controversial, to say the least. While he was undoubtedly a part of the advancement of black Americans he is also a frightening figure to many African Americans. In Ralph Ellison's *Invisible Man,* Washington was lampooned as the "great educator" and "founder" of the school to which the protagonist wins a scholarship after being thrown into a fixed boxing match by the white elders of his town. The great founder Dr. Bledsoe (as in "bled so") sends him off to the big city after he makes a mess of taking one of the school's white benefactors for a drive. The invisible man only later discovers that the "letters of introduction" he carries with him to the city ask of their recipients that they "keep this nigger boy running." This was, in short, Ellison's vision of what Booker T. Washington stood for. The "founder" is something of a confidence man, a man of color who essentially sells out his own people, assuaging white guilt with a version of black male identity that is easily palatable, all the while growing strong and rich on his own sort of southern plantation—one that produces educated men of color that know "their place."

black tenured professor until 1985. The Massachusetts State Legislature mandated the desegregation of all public schools in 1855, but until 1970, when a federal judge forced Boston to adhere to the *Brown* v. *Board of Education* ruling, the city maintained one of the most highly segregated school systems in the nation.

Today, the debate between Booker T. Washington and W. E. B. Du Bois remains unresolved. Must African Americans prove themselves first, before they can enjoy equality, including equal educational opportunities? Or must they confront racial inequalities head on, before all else? In the struggle to obliterate educational inequality once and for all, which approach is most helpful? Whatever parents, educators, and communities decide, whatever legislation is passed, whatever new schools are created, the struggle will go on.

BIBLIOGRAPHY

Abernathy, George L., ed. *The Idea of Equality*. Richmond: John Knox Press, 1959.

Andersen, Margaret L., and Patricia Hill Collins, eds. *Race, Class, and Gender*. Belmont: Wadsworth Publishing Company, 1992.

Bullard, Pamela, and Judith Stoia. *The Hardest Lesson: Personal Accounts of a School Desegregation Crisis*. Boston: Little, Brown, 1980.

Chafe, William H. *The Unfinished Journey*. New York: Oxford University Press, 1991.

Estell, Kenneth, ed. *Reference Library of Black America*, vol. 2. Afro-American Press, 1994.

Furnas, J. C. *Goodbye to Uncle Tom*. New York: H. Wolff, 1956.

Gonzales, Juan L., Jr. *Racial and Ethnic Groups in America*. Dubuque: Kendall-Hunt, 1990.

Huckaby, Elizabeth. *Crisis at Central High: Little Rock 1957–1958*. Baton Rouge: Louisiana State University Press, 1980.

Hughes, Langston, and Milton Metzer. *A Pictorial History of the Negro in America*. New York: Crown Publishers, 1956.

Jaynes, Gerald David, and Robin M. Williams, eds. *A Common Destiny: Blacks and American Society*. Washington: National Academy Press, 1989.

Meredith, James. *Three Years in Mississippi*. Bloomington: Indiana University Press, 1966.

Mergan, Peter M. *The Chronological History of the Negro in America*. New York: Harper & Row, 1969.

Wesley, Charles H. *The Quest for Equality: From Civil War to Civil Rights*. New York: Publishers Company, 1968.

Westin, Alan F., ed. *Freedom Now!* New York: Basic Books, 1964.

PRIMARY SOURCE DOCUMENT

Miss Prudence Crandall and the Canterbury School

INTRODUCTION This is an excerpt from *Some Recollections of Our Anti-Slavery Conflict*, published in 1869 a piece by abolitionist Samuel May published in 1869 regarding the celebrated case of Prudence Crandall and her attempts to open a school for African American children.

Often, during the last thirty, and more often during the last ten years, you must have seen in the newspapers, or heard from speakers in Antislavery and Republican meetings, high commendations of the County of Windham in Connecticut, as bearing the banner of equal human and political rights far above all the rest of that State. In the great election of the year 1866 the people of that county gave a large majority of votes in favor of negro suffrage.

This moral and political elevation of the public sentiment there is undoubtedly owing to the distinct presentation and thorough discussion, throughout that region, of the most vital antislavery questions in 1833 and 1834, called out by the shameful, cruel persecution of Miss Prudence Crandall for attempting to establish in Canterbury a boarding-school for "colored young ladies and little misses."

I was then living in Brooklyn, the shire town of the county, six miles from the immediate scene of the violent conflict, and so was fully drawn into it. I regret that, in the following account of it, allusions to myself and my acts must so often appear. But as Aeneas said to Queen Dido, in telling his story of the Trojan War, so may I say, respecting the contest about the Canterbury school, "All of which I saw, and part of which I was."

In the summer or fall of 1832 I heard that Miss Prudence Crandall, an excellent, well-educated Quaker young lady, who had gained considerable reputation as a teacher in the neighboring town of Plainfield, had been induced by a number of ladies and gentlemen of Canterbury to purchase a commodious, large house in their pretty village, and establish her boarding and day school there, that their daughters might receive instruction in several higher branches of education not taught in the public district schools, without being obliged to live far away from their homes.

For a while the school answered the expectations of its patrons, and enjoyed their favor; but early in the following year a trouble arose. It was in this wise. Not far from the village of Canterbury there lived a worthy colored man named Harris. He was the owner of a good farm, and was otherwise in comfortable circumstances. He had a daughter, Sarah, a bright girl about seventeen years of age. She had passed, with good repute as a scholar, through the school of the district in which she lived, and was hungering and thirsting for more education. This she desired not only for her own sake, but that she might go forth qualified to be a teacher of the colored people of our country, to whose wrongs and oppression she had become very sensitive. Her father encouraged her, and gladly offered to defray the expense of the advantages she might be able to obtain. Sarah applied for admission into this new Canterbury school. Miss Crandall confessed to me that at first she hesitated and almost refused, lest admitting her might offend the parents of her pupils, several of whom were Colonizationists, and none of them Abolitionists. But Sarah urged her request with no little force of argument and depth of feeling. Then she was a young lady of pleasing appearance and manners, well known to many of Miss Crandall's pupils, having been their class-mate in the district school. Moreover, she was accounted a virtuous, pious girl, and had been for some time a member of the church of Canterbury. There could not, therefore, have been a more unexceptionable case. No objection could be made to her admission into the school, excepting only her dark (and not very dark) complexion. Miss Crandall soon saw that

Prudence Crandall (1803–1890) and the School for Black Girls

In 1831, Prudence Crandall, a Quaker schoolteacher, established a boarding school for girls in Canterbury, Connecticut. One year later, however, she lost the majority of her pupils when she chose to admit a black student. Failing her attempt at integration, Crandall then considered opening a school exclusively for African American girls. Around this time she wrote a letter to the white abolitionist William Lloyd Garrison.

On March 2, 1833, Garrison joyfully announced in his newspaper, the *Liberator*, the establishment of "a High School for young colored ladies and misses." Despite widespread approval among white and black abolitionists, the citizens of Canterbury condemned Crandall's actions and tried to get her to close the school down. When persuasion failed, the community adopted a new form of opposition—harassment. Finally, on May 24, the Connecticut legislature, responsible to an all-white electorate, formally prohibited the establishment of any educational institution that would serve black residents of other states. This law successfully shut down Prudence Crandall's school for black girls.

she was unexpectedly called to take some part (how important she could not foresee) in the great contest for impartial liberty that was then beginning to agitate violently our nation. She was called to act either in accordance with, or in opposition to, the unreasonable, cruel, wicked prejudice against the color of their victims, by which the oppressors of millions in our land were everywhere extenuating, if not justifying, their tremendous system of iniquity. She bowed to the claim of humanity, and admitted Sarah Harris to her school.

Her pupils, I believe, made no objection. But in a few days the parents of some of them called and remonstrated. Miss Crandall pressed upon their consideration Sarah's eager desire for more knowledge and culture, the good use she intended to make of her acquirements, her excellent character and lady-like deportment, and, more than all, that she was an accept-

ed member of the same Christian church to which many of them belonged. Her arguments, her entreaties, however, were of no avail. Prejudice blinds the eyes, closes the ears, hardens the heart. "Sarah belonged to the proscribed, despised class, and therefore must not be admitted into a private school with their daughters." This was the gist of all they had to say. Reasons were thrown away, appeals to their sense of right, to their compassion for injured fellow-beings, made no impression. "They would not have it said that their daughters went to school with a nigger girl." Miss Crandall was assured that, if she did not dismiss Sarah Harris, her white pupils would be withdrawn from her.

She could not make up her mind to comply with such a demand, even to save the institution she had so recently established with such fond hopes, and in which she had invested all her property, and a debt of several hundred dollars more. It was, indeed, a severe trial, but she was strengthened to bear it. She determined to act right, and leave the event with God. Accordingly, she gave notice to her neighbors, and, on the 2d day of March, advertised in the *Liberator*, that at the commencement of her next term, on the first Monday of April, her school would be opened for "young ladies and little misses of color."

Only a few days before, on the 27th of February, I was informed of her generous, disinterested determination, and heard that, in consequence, the whole town was in a flame of indignation, kindled and fanned by the influence of the prominent people of the village, her immediate neighbors and her late patrons. Without delay, therefore, although a stranger, I addressed a letter to her, assuring her of my sympathy, and of my readiness to help her all in my power. On the 4th of March her reply came, begging me to come to her so soon as my engagements would permit. Accompanied by my friend, Mr. George W. Benson, I went to Canterbury on the afternoon of that day. On entering the village we were warned that we should be in personal danger if we appeared there as Miss Crandall's friends; and when arrived at her house we learnt that the excitement against her had become furious. She had been grossly insulted, and threatened with various kinds of violence, if she persisted in her purpose, and the most egregious falsehoods had been put in circulation respecting her intentions, the characters of her expected pupils, and of the future supporters of her school. Moreover, we were informed that a town-meeting was to be held on the 9th instant, to devise and adopt such measures as "would effectually avert the nuisance, or speedily abate it, if it should be brought into the village."

Though beat upon by such a storm, we found Miss Crandall resolved and tranquil. The effect of her Quaker discipline appeared in every word she spoke, and in every expression of her countenance. But, as she said, it

Former slaves were anxious to take advantage of education for their children, but also for themselves. Adult education classes and night schools proliferated during the Reconstruction period. **THE LIBRARY OF CONGRESS**

would not do for her to go into the town-meeting; and there was not a man in Canterbury who would dare, if he were disposed, to appear there in her behalf. "Will not you, Friend May, be my attorney?" "Certainly," I replied, "come what will." We then agreed that I should explain to the people how unexpectedly she had been led to take the step which had given so much offence, and show them how she could not have consented to the demand made by her former patrons without wounding deeply the feelings of an excellent girl, known to most of them, and adding to the mountain load of injuries and insults already heaped upon the colored people of our country. With this arrangement, we left her, to await the coming of the ominous meeting of the town.

On the 9th of March I repaired again to Miss Crandall's house, accompanied by my faithful friend, Mr. Benson. There, to our surprise and joy, we found Friend Arnold Buffum, a most worthy man, an able speaker, and then the principal lecturing agent of the New England Antislavery Society. Miss Crandall gave to each of us a respectful letter of introduction to the Moderator of the meeting, in which she requested that we might be heard as her attorneys, and promised to be bound by any

agreement we might see fit to make with the citizens of Canterbury. Miss Crandall concurred with us in the opinion that, as her house was one of the most conspicuous in the village, and not wholly paid for, if her opponents would take it off her hands, repaying what she had given for it, cease from molesting her, and allow her time to procure another house for her school, it would be better that she should move to some more retired part of the town or neighborhood.

Thus commissioned and instructed, Friend Buffum and I proceeded to the town-meeting. It was held in the "Meeting-House," one of the old New England pattern, — galleries on three sides, with room below and above for a thousand persons, sitting and standing. We found it nearly filled to its utmost capacity; and, not without difficulty, we passed up the side aisle into the wall-pew next to the deacon's seat, in which sat the Moderator. Very soon the business commenced. After the "Warning" had been read a series of Resolutions were laid before the meeting, in which were set forth the disgrace and damage that would be brought upon the town if a school for colored girls should be set up there, protesting emphatically against the impending evil, and appointing the civil authority and selectmen a committee to wait upon "the person contemplating the establishment of said school, … point out to her the injurious effects, the incalculable evils, resulting from such an establishment within this town, and persuade her, if possible, to abandon the project." The mover of the resolutions, Rufus Adams, Esq., labored to enforce them by a speech, in which he grossly misrepresented what Miss Crandall had done, her sentiments and purposes, and threw out several mean and low insinuations against the motives of those who were encouraging her enterprise.

As soon as he sat down the Hon. Andrew T. Judson rose. This gentleman was undoubtedly the chief of Miss Crandall's persecutors. He was the great man of the town, a leading politicians in the State, much talked of by the Democrats as soon to be governor, and a few years afterwards was appointed Judge of the United States District Court. His house on Canterbury Green stood next to Miss Crandall's. The idea of having "a school of nigger girls so near him was insupportable." He vented himself in a strain of reckless hostility to his neighbor, her benevolent, self-sacrificing undertaking, and its patrons, and declared his determination to thwart the enterprise. He twanged every chord that could stir the coarser passions of the human heart, and with such sad success that his hearers seemed to be filled with the apprehension that a dire calamity was impending over them, that Miss Crandall was the author or instrument of it, that there were powerful conspirators engaged with her in the plot, and that the people of Canterbury should be roused, by every consideration of self-preservation, as well as self-respect, to prevent the accomplishment of the design, defying the wealth and influence of all who were abetting it.

When he had ended his philippic Mr. Buffum and I silently presented to the Moderator Miss Crandall's letters, requesting that we might be heard on her behalf. He handed them over to Mr. Judson, who instantly broke forth with greater violence than before; accused us of insulting the town by coming there to interfere with its local concerns. Other gentlemen sprang to their feet in hot displeasure; poured out their tirades upon Miss Crandall and her accomplices, and, with fists doubled in our faces, roughly admonished us that, if we opened our lips there, they would inflict upon us the utmost penalty of the law, if not a more immediate vengeance.

Thus forbidden to speak, we of course sat in silence, and let the waves of invective and abuse dash over us. But we sat thus only until we heard from the Moderator the words, "This meeting is adjourned!" Knowing that now we should violate no law by speaking, I sprang to the seat on which I had been sitting, and cried out, "Men of Canterbury, I have a word for you! Hear me!" More than half the crowd turned to listen. I went rapidly over my replies to the misstatements that had been made as to the purposes of Miss Crandall and her friends, the characters of

her expected pupils, and the spirit in which the enterprise had been conceived and would be carried on. As soon as possible I gave place to Friend Buffum. But he had spoken in his impressive manner hardly five minutes, before the trustees of the church to which the house belonged came in and ordered all out, that the doors might be shut. Here again the hand of the law constrained us. So we obeyed with the rest, and having lingered awhile upon the Green to answer questions and explain to those who were willing "to understand the matter," we departed to our homes, musing in our own hearts "what would come of this day's uproar."

Before my espousal of Miss Crandall's cause I had had a pleasant acquaintance with Hon. Andrew T. Judson, which had led almost to a personal friendship. Unwilling, perhaps, to break our connection so abruptly, and conscious, no doubt, that he had treated me rudely, not to say abusively, at the town-meeting on the 9th, he called to see me two days afterwards. He assured me that he had not become unfriendly to me personally, and regretted that he had used some expressions and applied certain epithets to me, in the warmth of his feelings and the excitement of the public indignation of his neighbors and fellow-townsmen, roused as they were to the utmost in opposition to Miss Crandall's project, which he thought I was inconsiderately and unjustly promoting. He went on enlarging upon the disastrous effects the establishment of "a school for nigger girls" in the centre of their village would have upon its desirableness as a place of residence, the value of real estate there, and the general prosperity of the town.

I replied: "If, sir, you had permitted Mr. Buffum and myself to speak at your town-meeting, you would have found that we had come there, not in a contentious spirit, but that we were ready, with Miss Crandall's consent, to settle the difficulty with you and your neighbors peaceably. We should have agreed, if you would repay to Miss Crandall what you had advised her to give for her house, and allow her time quietly to find and purchase a suitable house for her school in some more retired part of the town or vicinity, that she should remove to that place." The honorable gentleman hardly gave me time to finish my sentences ere he said, with great emphasis:—

"Mr. May, we are not merely opposed to the establishment of that school in Canterbury; we mean there shall not be such a school set up anywhere in our State. The colored people never can rise from their menial condition in our country; they ought not to be permitted to rise here. They are an inferior race of beings, and never can or ought to be recognized as the equals of the whites. Africa is the place for them. I am in favor of the Colonization scheme. Let the niggers and their descendants be sent back to their fatherland; and there improve themselves as much as they may, and civilize and Christianize the natives, if they can. I am a Colonizationist. You and your friend Garrison have

The "Tuskegee Mission" promoted the training of teachers who would in turn train poor black southerners to help themselves. With the coming of motorized transportation, the Tuskegee Institute was able to send its students out in the field to help farmers in remote areas. **NATIONAL ARCHIVES AND RECORDS ADMINISTRATION**

undertaken what you cannot accomplish. The condition of the colored population of our country can never be essentially improved on this continent. You are fanatical about them. You are violating the Constitution of our Republic, which settled forever the status of the black men in this land. They belong to Africa. Let them be sent back there, or kept as they are here. The sooner you Abolitionists abandon your project the better for our country, for the niggers, and yourselves."

I replied: "Mr. Judson, there never will be fewer colored people in this country than there are now. Of the vast majority of them this is the native land, as much as it is ours. It will be unjust, inhuman, in us to drive them out, or to make them willing to go by our cruel treatment of them. And, if they should all become willing to depart, it would not be practicable to transport across the Atlantic Ocean and settle properly on the shores of Africa, from year to year, half so many of them as would be born here in the same time, according to the known rate of their natural increase. No, sir, there will never be fewer colored people in our country than there are this day; and the only question is, whether we will recognize the rights which God gave them as men, and encourage and assist them to become all he has made them capable of being, or whether

we will continue wickedly to deny them the privileges we enjoy, condemn them to degradation, enslave and imbrute them; and so bring upon ourselves the condemnation of the Almighty Impartial Father of all men, and the terrible visitation of the God of the oppressed. I trust, sir, you will erelong come to see that we must accord to these men their rights, or incur justly the loss of our own. Education is one of the primal, fundamental rights of all the children of men. Connecticut is the last place where this should be denied. But as, in the providence of God, that right has been denied in a place so near me, I feel that I am summoned to its defence. If you and your neighbors in Canterbury had quietly consented that Sarah Harris, whom you knew to be a bright, good girl, should enjoy the privilege she so eagerly sought, this momentous conflict would not have arisen in your village. But as it has arisen there, we may as well meet it there as elsewhere."

"That nigger school," he rejoined with great warmth, "shall never be allowed in Canterbury, nor in any town of this State."

"How can you prevent it legally?" I inquired; "how but by Lynch law, by violence, which you surely will not countenance?"

"We can expel her pupils from abroad," he replied, "under the provisions of our old pauper and vagrant laws."

"But we will guard against them," I said, "by giving your town ample bonds."

"Then," said he, "we will get a law passed by our Legislature, now in session, forbidding the institution of such a school as Miss Crandall proposes, in any part of Connecticut."

"It would be an unconstitutional law, and I will contend against it as such to the last," I rejoined. "If you, sir, pursue the course you have now indicated, I will dispute every step you take, from the lowest court in Canterbury up to the highest court of the United States."

"You talk big," he cried; "it will cost more than you are aware of to do all that you threaten. Where will you get the means to carry on such a contest at law?"

This defiant question inspired me to say, "Mr. Judson, I had not foreseen all that this conversation has opened to my view. True, I do not possess the pecuniary ability to do what you have made me promise. I have not consulted any one. But I am sure the lovers of impartial liberty, the friends of humanity in our land, the enemies of slavery, will so justly appreciate the importance of sustaining Miss Crandall in her benevolent, pious undertaking, that I shall receive from one quarter and another all the funds I may need to withstand your attempt to crush, by legal means, the Canterbury school." The sequel of my story will show that I did not misjudge the significance of my case, nor put my confidence in those who were not worthy of it. Mr. Judson left me in high displeasure, and I never met him afterwards but as an opponent.

Undismayed by the opposition of her neighbors and the violence of their threats, Miss Crandall received early in April fifteen or twenty colored young ladies and misses from Philadelphia, New York, Providence, and Boston. At once her persecutors commenced operations. All accommodations at the stores in Canterbury were denied her; so that she was obliged to send to neighboring villages for her needful supplies. She and her pupils were insulted whenever they appeared in the streets. The doors and door-steps of her house were besmeared, and her well was filled with filth. Had it not been for the assistance of her father and another Quaker friend who lived in the town, she might have been compelled to abandon "her castle" for the want of water and food. But she was enabled to "hold out," and Miss Crandall and her little band behaved somewhat like the besieged in the immortal Fort Sumter. The spirit that is in the children of men is usually roused by persecution. I visited them repeatedly, and always found teacher and pupils calm and resolute. They evidently felt that it was given them to maintain one of the fundamental, inalienable rights of man.

Before the close of the month, an attempt was made to frighten and drive away these innocent girls, by a process under the obsolete vagrant law, which provided that the selectmen of any town might warn any person, not an inhabitant of the State, to depart forthwith from said town; demand of him or her one dollar and sixty-seven cents for every week he or she remained in said town after having received such warning, and in case such fine should not be paid, and the person so warned should not have departed before the expiration of ten days after being sentenced, then he or she should be whipped on the naked body not exceeding ten stripes.

A warrant to this effect was actually served upon Eliza Ann Hammond, a fine girl from Providence, aged seventeen years. Although I had protected Miss Crandall's pupils against the operation of this old law, by giving to the treasurer of Canterbury a bond in the sum of $10,000, signed by responsible gentlemen of Brooklyn, to save the town from the vagrancy of any of these pupils, I feared they would be intimidated by the actual appearance of the constable, and the imposition of a writ. So, on hearing of the above transaction, I went down to Canterbury to explain the matter if necessary; to assure Miss Hammond that the persecutors would hardly dare proceed to such an extremity, and strengthen her to bear meekly the punishment, if they should in their madness inflict it; knowing that every blow they should strike her would resound throughout the land, if not over the whole civilized world, and call out an expression of indignation before which Mr. Judson and his associates would quail. But I found her ready for the emergency, animated by the spirit of a martyr.

Of course this process was abandoned. But another was resorted to, most disgraceful to the State as well as the town. That shall be the subject of my next.

The Black Law of Connecticut

Foiled in their attempts to frighten away Miss Crandall's pupils by their proceedings under the provisions of the obsolete "Pauper and Vagrant Law," Mr. Judson and his fellow-persecutors urgently pressed upon the Legislature of Connecticut, then in session, a demand for the enactment of a law, by which they should be enabled to effect their purpose. To the lasting shame of the State, be it said, they succeeded. On the 24th of May, 1833, the Black Law was enacted as follows:—

Section 1. Be it enacted by the Senate and House of Representatives, in General Assembly convened, that no person shall set up or establish in this State any school, academy, or literary institution for the instruction or education of colored persons who are not inhabitants of this State; nor instruct or teach in any school, or other literary institution whatsoever, in this State; nor harbor or board, of the purpose of attending or being taught or instructed in any such school, academy, or literary institution, any colored person who is not an inhabitant of any town in this State, without the consent in writing, first obtained, of a majority of the civil authority, and also of the Selectmen of the town, in which such school, academy, or literary institution is situated, &c.

I need not copy any more of this infamous Act. The penalties denounced against the violation of it, you may be sure, were severe enough. That the persecutors of Miss Crandall were determined to visit them upon her, if they might, the sequel of my story will show.

On the receipt of the tidings that the Legislature had passed the law, joy and exultation ran wild in Canterbury. The bells were rung and a cannon fired, until all the inhabitants for miles around were informed of the triumph. So soon as was practicable, on the 27th of June, Miss Crandall was arrested by the sheriff of the county, or the constable of the town, and arraigned before Justices Adams and Bacon, two of the leaders of the conspiracy against her and her humane enterprise. The trial of course was a brief one; the result was predetermined. Before noon of that day a messenger came to let me know that Miss Crandall had been "committed" by the above-named justices, to take her trial at the next session of the Superior Court at Brooklyn in August; that she was in the hands of the sheriff and would be put into jail, unless I or some of her friends would come and "give bonds" for her in the sum of $ 300 or $ 500, I forget which. I calmly told the messenger that there were gentlemen enough in Canterbury whose bond for that amount would be as good or better than mine; and I should leave it for them to do Miss Crandall that favor. "But," said the young man, "are you not her friend?" "Certainly," I replied, "too sincerely her friend to give relief to her enemies in their present embarrassment; and I trust you will not find any one of her friends, or the patrons of her school, who will step forward to help them any more than myself." "But, sir," he cried, "do you mean to allow her to be put into jail?" "Most certainly," was my answer, "if her persecutors are unwise enough to let such an outraged be committed." He turned from me in blank surprise, and hurried back to tell Mr. Judson and the justices of his ill success.

A few days before, when I first heard of the passage of the law, I had visited Miss Crandall with my friend Mr. George W. Benson, and advised with her as to the course she and her friends ought to pursue, when she should be brought to trial. She appreciated at once and fully the importance of leaving her persecutors to show to the world how base they were, and how atrocious was the law they had induced the Legislature to enact, — a law, by the force of which a woman might be fined and

imprisoned as a felon, in the State of Connecticut, for giving instruction to colored girls. She agreed that it would be best for us to leave her in the hands of those with whom the law originated, hoping that, in their madness, they would show forth all its hideous features.

Mr. Benson and I therefore went diligently around to all whom we knew were friendly to Miss Crandall and her school, and counselled them by no means to give bonds to keep her from imprisonment, because nothing would expose so fully to the public the egregious wickedness of the law, and the virulence of her persecutors, as the fact that they had thrust her into jail.

When I found that her resolution was equal to the trial which seemed to be impending, that she was ready to brave and to bear meekly the worst treatment that her enemies would venture to subject her to, I made all the arrangements for her comfort that were practicable in our prison. It fortunately so happened that the most suitable room, not occupied, was the one in which a man named Watkins had recently been confined for the murder of his wife, and out of which he had been taken and executed. This circumstance, we foresaw, would add not a little to the public detestation of the Black Law.

The jailer, at my request, readily put the room in as nice order as was possible, and permitted me to substitute, for the bedstead and mattress on which the murderer had slept, fresh and clean ones from my own house and Mr. Benson's.

About two o'clock P.M. another messenger came to inform me that the sheriff was on the way from Canterbury to the jail with Miss Crandall, and would imprison her, unless her friends would give him the required bail. Although in sympathy with Miss Crandall's persecutors he clearly saw the disgrace that was about to be brought upon the State, and begged me and Mr. Benson to avert it. Of course we refused. I went to the jailer's house and met Miss Crandall on her arrival. We stepped aside. I said:—

"If now you hesitate, if you dread the gloomy place so much as to wish to be saved from it, I will give bonds for you even now."

"O no," she promptly replied; "I am only afraid they will not put me into jail. Their evident hesitation and embarrassment show plainly how much they deprecate the effect of this part of their folly; and therefore I am the more anxious that they should be exposed, if not caught in their own wicked devices."

We therefore returned with her to the sheriff and the company that surrounded him to await his final act. He was ashamed to do it. He knew it would cover the persecutors of Miss Crandall and the State of Connecticut with disgrace. He conferred with several about him, and

African American intellectuals such as Booker T. Washington were educated at the Hampton Institute. Such schools developed to afford blacks educational opportunities that were not readily available, particularly in the South. Here, a group of young students get a math lesson at the Institute around 1935. **ARCHIVE PHOTOS, INC.**

delayed yet longer. Two gentlemen came and remonstrated with me in not very seemly terms:—

"It would be a —— shame, an eternal disgrace to the State, to have her put into jail, — into the very room that Watkins had last occupied.

"Certainly, gentlemen," I replied, "and you may prevent this if you please.

"O," they cried, "we are not her friends; we are not in favor of her school; we don't want any more —— niggers coming among us. It is your place to stand by Miss Crandall and help her now. You and your —— abolition brethren have encouraged her to bring this nuisance into Canterbury, and it is —— mean in you to desert her now."

I rejoined: "She knows we have not deserted her, and do not intend to desert her. The law which her persecutors have persuaded our legislators to enact is an infamous one, worthy of the Dark Ages. It would be just as bad as it is, whether we should give bonds for her or not. But the people generally will not so soon realize how bad, how wicked, how cruel a law it is, unless we suffer her persecutors to inflict upon her all the penalties it prescribes. She is willing to bear them for the sake of the cause she has so nobly espoused. And it is easy to foresee

that Miss Crandall will be glorified, as much as her persecutors and our State will be disgraced, by the transactions of this day and this hour. If you see fit to keep her from imprisonment in the cell of a murderer for having proffered the blessing of a good education to those who, in our country, need it most, you may do so; we shall not."

They turned from us in great wrath, words falling from their lips which I shall not repeat.

The sun had descended nearly to the horizon; the shadows of night were beginning to fall around us. The sheriff could defer the dark deed no longer. With no little emotion, and with words of earnest deprecation, he gave that excellent, heroic, Christian young lady into the hands of the jailer, and she was led into the cell of Watkins. So soon as I had heard the bolts of her prison door turned in the lock, and saw the key taken out, I bowed and said, "The deed is done, completely done. It cannot be recalled. It has passed into the history of our nation and our age." I went away with my steadfast friend, George W. Benson, assured that the legislators of the State had been guilty of a most unrighteous act; and that Miss Crandall's persecutors had also committed a great blunder; that they all would have much more reason to be ashamed of her imprisonment than she or her friends could ever have.

The next day we gave the required bonds. Miss Crandall was released from the cell of the murderer, returned home, and quietly resumed the duties of her school, until she should be summoned as a culprit into court, there to be tried by the infamous "Black Law of Connecticut." And, as we expected, so soon as the evil tidings could be carried in that day, before Professor Morse had given to Rumor her telegraphic wings, it was known all over the country and the civilized world that an excellent young lady had been imprisoned as a criminal,—yes, put into a murderer's cell, — in the State of Connecticut, for opening a school for the instruction of colored girls. The comments that were made upon the deed in almost all the newspapers were far from grateful to the feelings of her persecutors. Even many who, under the same circumstances, would probably have acted as badly as Messrs. A. T. Judson and Company, denounced their procedure as unchristian, inhuman, anti-democratic, base, mean.

Arthur Tappan

The words and manner of Mr. Judson in the interview I had with him on the 11th of March, of which I have given a pretty full report, convinced me that he would do all that could be done by legal and political devices, to abolish Miss Crandall's school. His success in obtaining from the Legislature the enactment of the infamous "Black Law" showed too plainly that the majority of the people of the State were on the side of the oppressor. But I felt sure that God and good men would be our helpers in the contest to which we were committed. Assurances of approval and of sympathy came from many; and ere-long a proffer of all the pecuniary assistance we could need was made by one who was then himself a host. At that time Mr. Arthur Tappan was one of the wealthiest merchants in the country, and was wont to give to religious and philanthropic objects as much, in proportion to his means, as any benefactor who has lived in the land before or since his day. I was not then personally acquainted with him, but he had become deeply interested in the cause of the poor, despised, enslaved millions in our country, and alive to whatever affected them.

Much to my surprise, and much more to my joy, a few weeks after the commencement of the contest, and just after the enactment of the Black Law and the imprisonment of Miss Crandall, I received from Mr. Tappan a most cordial letter. He expressed his entire approbation of the position I had taken in defence of Miss Crandall's benevolent enterprise, and his high appreciation of the importance of maintaining, in Connecticut especially, the right of colored people, not less than of white, to any amount of education they might wish to obtain, and the respect and encouragement due to any teacher who would devote himself or herself to their instruction. He added: "This contest, in which you have been providentially called to engage, will be a serious, perhaps a violent one. It may be prolonged and very expensive. Nevertheless, it ought to be persisted in to the last. I venture to presume, sir, that you cannot well afford what it may cost. You ought not to be left, even if you are willing, to bear alone the pecuniary burden. I shall be most happy to give you all the help of this sort that you may need. Consider me your banker. Spare no necessary expense. Command the services of the ablest lawyers. See to it that this great case shall be thoroughly tried, cost what it may. I will cheerfully honor your drafts to enable you to defray that cost." Thus upheld, you will not wonder that I was somewhat elated. At Mr. Tappan's suggestion I immediately "retained" the Hon. William W. Ellsworth, the Hon. Calvin Goddard, and the Hon. Henry Strong, the three most distinguished members of the Connecticut bar. They all confirmed me in the opinion that the "Black Law" was unconstitutional, and would probably be so pronounced, if we should carry it up to the United States Court. They moreover instructed me that, as the act for which Miss Crandall was to be tried was denounced as criminal, it would be within the province of the jury of our State court to decide upon the character of the law, as well as the conduct of the accused; and that therefore it would be allowable and proper for them to urge the wickedness of the law, in bar of Miss Crandall's condemnation under it. But, before we get to the trials of Miss Crandall under Mr. Judson's law, I have more to tell about Mr. Arthur Tappan.

He requested me to keep him fully informed of the doings of Miss Crandall's persecutors. And I assure you I had too many evil things to report of them. They insulted and annoyed her and her pupils in every way their malice could devise. The storekeepers, the butchers, the milk-pedlers of the town, all refused to supply their wants; and whenever her father, brother, or other relatives, who happily lived but a few miles off, were seen coming to bring her and her pupils the necessaries of life, they were insulted and threatened. Her well was defiled with the most offensive filth, and her neighbors refused her and the thirsty ones about her even a cup of cold water, leaving them to depend for that essential element upon the scanty supplies that could be brought from her father's farm. Nor was this all; the physician of the village refused to minister to any who were sick in Miss Crandall's family, and the trustees of the church forbade her to come, with any of her pupils, into the House of the Lord.

In addition to the insults and annoyances mentioned above, the newspapers of the county and other parts of the State frequently gave currency to the most egregious misrepresentations of the conduct of Miss Crandall and her pupils, and the basest insinuations against her friends and patrons. Yet our corrections and replies were persistently refused a place in their columns. The publisher of one of the county papers, who was personally friendly to me, and whom I had assisted to establish in business, confessed to me that he dared not admit into his paper an article in defence of the Canterbury school. It would be, he said, the destruction of his establishment. Thus situated, we were continually made to feel the great disadvantage at which we were contending with the hosts of our enemies.

In one of my letters to Mr. Tappan, when thus sorely pressed, I let fall from my pen, "O that I could only leave home long enough to visit you! For I could tell you in an hour more things, that I wish you to know, than I can write in a week."

A day or two afterwards, about as quickly as he could then get to me after the receipt of my letter, the door of my study was opened, and in walked Arthur Tappan. I sprang to my feet, and gave him a pressure of the hand which told him more emphatically than words could have done how overjoyed I was to see him. In his usual quiet manner and undertone he said, "Your last letter implied that you were in so much trouble I thought it best to come and see, and consider with you what it will be advisable for us to do." I soon spread before him the circumstances of the case, — the peculiar difficulties by which we were beset, the increased and increasing malignity of Miss Crandall's persecutors, provoked, and almost justified in the public opinion, by the false reports that were diligently circulated, and which we had no means of correcting. "Let me go," said he, "and see for myself Miss Crandall and her school, and learn more of the particulars of the sore trials to which her benevolence and her fortitude seem to be subjected." As soon as possible the horse and chaise were brought to the door, and the good man went to Canterbury. In a few hours he returned. He had been delighted, nay, deeply affected, by the calm determination which Miss Crandall evinced, and the quiet courage with which she had inspired her pupils. He had learned that the treatment to which they were subjected by their neighbors was in some respects worse even than I had represented it to him; and he said in a low, firm tone of voice, which showed how thoroughly in earnest he was, she must be protected and sustained. "The cause of the whole oppressed, despised colored population of our country is to be much affected by the decision of this question."

After some further consultation he rose to his feet and said, "You are almost helpless without the press. You must issue a paper, publish it largely, send it to all the persons whom you know in the county and State, and to all the principal newspapers throughout the country. Many will subscribe for it and contribute otherwise to its support, and I will pay whatever more it may cost." No sooner said than done. We went without delay to the village, where fortunately there was a pretty-well-furnished printing-office that had been lately shut up for want of patronage. We found the proprietor, examined the premises, satisfied ourselves that there were materials enough to begin with, and Mr. Tappan engaged for my use for a year the office, press, types, and whatever else was necessary to commence at once the publication of a newspaper, to be devoted to the advocacy of all human rights in general, and to the defence of the Canterbury school, and its heroic teacher in particular.

We walked back to my house communing together about the great conflict for liberty to which we were committed, the spirit in which it ought to be conducted on our part, and especially the course to be pursued in the further defence of Miss Crandall. Soon after the stage-coach came along. Mr. Tappan, after renewed assurances of support, gave me a hearty farewell and stepped on board to return to New York. He left me the proprietor of a printing-office, and with ample means to maintain, as far as might be necessary, the defence of the Canterbury school against the unrighteous and unconstitutional law of the State of Connecticut. I need now only add that the trials at law were protracted until August, 1834, and that they, together with the conduct of the newspaper, cost me more than six hundred dollars, all of which amount was most promptly and kindly paid by that true philanthropist,—Arthur Tappan.

Charles C. Burleigh

The excitement caused by Mr. Tappan's unexpected visit, the hearty encouragement he had given me, and the great addition he had made to my means of defence, altogether were so grateful to me that I did not at first fully realize how much I had undertaken to do. But a night's rest brought me to my senses, and I clearly saw that I must have some other help than even Mr. Tappan's pecuniary generosity could give me. I was at that time publishing a religious paper,—*The Christian Monitor,*—which, together with my pulpit and parochial duties, filled quite full the measure of my ability. Unfortunately the prospectus of *The Monitor,* issued a year before the beginning of the Canterbury difficulty, precluded from its columns all articles relating to personal or neighborhood quarrels. Therefore, though the editor of a paper, I could not, in that paper, repel the most injurious attacks that were made upon my character. Had it been otherwise, there would have been no need of starting another paper. But, as Mr. Tappan promptly allowed, another paper must be issued, and to edit two papers at the same time was wholly beyond my power. What should I do?

Soon after the enactment of the "Black Law" an admirable article, faithfully criticising it, had appeared in *The Genius of Temperance,* and been copied into *The Emancipator.* It was attributed to Mr. Charles C. Burleigh, living in the adjoining town of Plainfield. I had heard him commended as a young man of great promise, and had once listened to an able speech from him at a Colonization meeting. To him, therefore, in the need of help, my thoughts soon turned. And the morning after Mr. Tappan's visit I drove over to Plainfield. Mr. Burleigh was living with his parents, and helping them carry on their farm, while pursuing as he could his studies preparatory to the profession of a lawyer. It was Friday of the week, in the midst of haying time. I was told at the house that he was in the field as busy as he could be. Nevertheless, I insisted that my business with him was more important than haying. So he was sent for, and in due time appeared. Like other sensible men, at the hard, hot work of haying, he was not attired in his Sunday clothes, but in his shirt-sleeves, with pants the worse for wear; and, although he then believed in shaving, no razor had touched his beard since the first day of the week. Nevertheless, I do not believe that Samuel of old saw, in the ruddy son of Jesse, as he came up from the sheepfold, the man whom the Lord would have him anoint, more clearly than I saw in C. C. Burleigh the man whom I should choose to be my assistant in that emergency. So soon as I had told him what I wanted of him his eye kindled as if eager for the conflict. We made an arrangement to supply his place on his father's farm, and he engaged to come to me early the following week. On Monday, the 14th of July, 1833, according to promise, he came to Brooklyn. He then put on the harness of a soldier in the good fight for equal, impartial liberty, and he has not yet laid it aside, nor are there many, if indeed any, of the antislavery warriors who have done more or better service than Mr. Burleigh.

On the 25th of July, 1833, appeared the first number of our paper, called The Unionist. After the first two or three numbers most of the articles were written or selected by Mr. Burleigh, and it was soon acknowledged by the public that the young editor wielded a powerful weapon. The paper was continued, if I remember correctly, about two years, and it helped us mightily in our controversy with the persecutors of Miss Crandall. After a few months C. C. Burleigh associated with him, in the management of The Unionist, his brother, Mr. William H. Burleigh, who also, at the same time, assisted Miss Crandall in the instruction of her school; and for so doing suffered not a little obloquy, insult, and abuse.

It was still the cherished intention of C. C. Burleigh to devote himself to the law, and without neglecting his duties to The Unionist he so diligently and successfully pursued his preparatory studies, that in January, 1835, he was examined and admitted to the bar. The committee of examination were surprised at his proficiency. He was pronounced the best prepared candidate that had been admitted to the Windham County Bar within the memory of those who were then practising there; and confident predictions were uttered by the most knowing ones of his rapid rise to eminence in the profession. Scarcely did Wendell Phillips awaken higher expectations of success as a lawyer in Boston, than C. C. Burleigh had awakened in Brooklyn. But just at the time of his admission I received a letter from Dr. Farnsworth, of Groton, Massachusetts, then President of the Middlesex Antislavery Society, inquiring urgently for some able lecturer, whose services could be obtained as the general agent of that Society. I knew of no one so able as C. C. Burleigh. So I called upon him, told him of the many high compliments I had heard bestowed upon his appearance on the examination, and then said, "Now I have already a most important case, in which to engage your services," and showed him Dr. Farnsworth's letter. For a few minutes he hesitated, and his countenance fell. The bright prospect of professional eminence was suddenly overcast. He more than suspected that, if he accepted the invitation, he should get so engaged in the antislavery cause as to be unable to leave the field until after its triumph. He would have to renounce all hope of wealth or political preferment, and lead a life of continual conflict with ungenerous opponents; be poorly requited for his labors, and suffer contumely, hatred, persecution. I saw what was passing in his mind, and that the struggle was severe. But it lasted only a little while,—less than an hour. A bright and beautiful expression illuminated his countenance when he replied, "This is not what I expected or intended, but it is what I ought to do. I will accept the invitation." He did so. Before the close of the week he departed for his field of labor. And I believe he ceased not a day to be the agent of one antislavery society or another, until after the lamented President Lincoln had proclaimed emancipation to all who were in bondage in our land.

When, in April, 1835, I became the General Agent of the Massachusetts Antislavery Society, I was brought into more intimate relations with Mr. Burleigh. We were indeed fellow-laborers. Repeatedly did we go forth together on lecturing excursions, and never was I better sustained. With him as my companion I felt sure our course would be successful. I always insisted upon speaking first; for, if I failed to do my best, he would make ample amends, covering the whole ground, exhausting the subject, leaving nothing essential unsaid. And if I did better than ever, Mr. Burleigh would come after me, and fill twelve baskets full of precious fragments. He is a single-minded, pure-hearted, conscientious, self-sacrificing man. He is not blessed with a fine voice nor a graceful manner. And the peculiar dress of his hair and beard has given offence to many, and may have lessened his usefulness. But he has a great command of language. He has a singularly acute and logical intellect. His reasoning, argumentative powers are remarkable. And he often has delighted and astonished his hearers by the brilliancy of his rhetoric, and the surpassing beauty of his imagery, and aptness of his illustrations. The millions of the emancipated in our country are indebted to the labors of few more than to those of Charles C. Burleigh. But to return.

Miss Crandall's Trial

On the 23d of August, 1833, the first trial of Prudence Crandall for the crime of keeping a boarding-school for colored girls in the State of Connecticut, and endeavoring to give them a good education,—the first trial for this crime,—was had in Brooklyn, the seat of the county of Windham, within a stone's throw of the house where lived and died General Israel Putnam, who, with his compatriots of 1776, perilled his life in defence of the self-evident truth that "all men were created equal, and endowed by their Creator with the inalienable right to life, liberty, and the pursuit of happiness." It was had at the County Court, Hon. Joseph Eaton presiding.

The prosecution was conducted by Hon. A. T. Judson, Jonathan A. Welch, Esq., and I. Bulkley, Esq. Miss Crandall's counsel were Hon. Calvin Goddard, Hon. W. W. Ellsworth, and Henry Strong, Esq.

The indictment of Miss Crandall consisted of two counts, which amounted to the same thing. The first set forth, in the technical terms of the law, that "with force and arms" she had received into her school; and the second, that, "with force and arms," she had instructed certain colored girls, who were not inhabitants of the State, without having first obtained, in writing, permission to do so from the majority of the civil authority and selectmen of the town of Canterbury, as required by the law under which she was prosecuted.

Mr. Judson opened the case. He, of course, endeavored to keep out of sight the most odious features of the law which had been disobeyed by Miss Crandall. He insisted that it was only a wise precaution to keep out of the State an injurious kind of population. He urged that the public provisions for the education of all the children of the inhabitants of Connecticut were ample, generous, and that colored children belonging to the State, not less than others, might enjoy the advantages of the common schools, which were under the supervision and control of proper officials in every town. He argued that it was not fair nor safe to allow any person, without the permission of such officials, to come into the State and open a school for any class of pupils she might please to invite from other States. He alleged that other States of the Union, Northern as well as Southern, regarded colored persons as a kind of population respecting which there should be some special legislation. If it were not for such protection as the law in question had provided, the Southerners might free all their slaves, and send them to Connecticut instead of Liberia, which would be overwhelming. Mr. Judson denied that colored persons were citizens in those States, where they were not enfranchised. He claimed that the privilege of being a freeman was higher than the right of being educated, and asked this remarkable question: "Why should a man be educated who could not be a freeman?" He denied, however, that he was opposed to the improvement of any class of the inhabitants of the land, if their improvement could be effected without violating any of the provisions of our Constitution, or endangering the union of the States. His associates labored to maintain the same positions.

These positions were vigorously assailed by Mr. Ellsworth and Mr. Strong, and shown to be untenable by a great array of facts adduced from the history of our own country, of the opinions of some of the most illustrious lawyers and civilians of England and America, and of arguments, the force of which was palpable.

Nevertheless, the Judge saw fit, though somewhat timidly, in his charge to the Jury, to give it as his opinion that "the law was constitutional and obligatory on the people of the State."

The Jury, after an absence of several hours, returned into court, not having agreed upon a verdict. They were instructed on some points, and sent out a second, and again a third time, but with no better success. They stated to the Court that there was no probability they should ever agree. Seven of them were for conviction, and five for acquittal. So they were discharged.

Supposing that this result operated as a continuance of the case to the next term of the County Court, to be held the following December, a few days after the trial I went with my family to spend several weeks with my friends in Boston and the neighborhood. But much to my surprise and discomfort, the last week in September, just as I was starting off to deliver an antislavery lecture, at a distance from Boston, I received the information that the persecutors of Miss Crandall, too impatient to wait until December for the regular course of law, had got up a new prosecution of her, to be tried on the 3d of October, before Judge Daggett of the Supreme Court, who was known to be hostile to the colored people, and a strenuous advocate of the Black Law. It was impossible for me so to dispose of my engagements that I could get back to Brooklyn in time to attend the trial. I could only write and instruct the counsel of Miss Crandall, in case a verdict should be obtained against her, to carry the cause up to the Court of Errors.

The second trial was had on the 3d of October; the same defence as before was set up, and ably maintained. But Chief Justice Daggett's influence with the Jury was overpowering. He delivered an elaborate and able charge, insisting upon the constitutionality of the law; and, without much hesitation, the verdict was given against Miss Crandall. Her counsel at once filed a bill of exceptions, and an appeal to the Court of Errors, which was granted. Before that—the highest legal tribunal in the State—the cause was argued on the 22d of July, 1834. The Hon. W. W. Ellsworth and the Hon. Calvin Goddard argued against the constitutionality of the Black Law, with very great ability and eloquence. The Hon. A. T. Judson and the Hon. C. F. Cleaveland said all that perhaps could be said to prove such a law to be consistent with the Magna Charta of our Republic. All who attended the trial seemed to be deeply interested, and were made to acknowledge the vital importance of the question at issue. Most persons, I believe, were persuaded that the Court ought to and would decide against the law. But they reserved the decision until some future time. And that decision, I am sorry to say, was never given. The Court evaded it the next week by finding that the defects in the information prepared by the State's Attorney were such that it ought to be quashed; thus rendering it "unnecessary for the Court to come to any decision upon the question as to the constitutionality of the law."

Whether her persecutors were or were not in despair of breaking down Miss Crandall's school by legal process, I am unable to say, but they soon resorted to other means, which were effectual.

House Set on Fire

Soon after their failure to get a decision from the Court of Errors, an attempt was made to set her house on fire. Fortunately the match was applied to combustibles tucked under a corner where the sills were somewhat decayed. They burnt like a slow match. Some time before daylight the inmates perceived the smell of fire, but not until nearly nine o'clock did any blaze appear. It was quickly quenched; and I was sent for to advise whether, if her enemies were so malignant as this attempt showed them to be, it was safe and right for her to expose her pupils' and her own life any longer to their wicked devices. It was concluded that she should hold on and bear yet a little longer. Perhaps the atrocity of this attempt to fire her house, and at the same time endanger the dwellings of her neighbors would frighten the leaders and instigators of the persecution to put more restraint upon "the baser sort." But a few nights afterwards it was made only too plain that the enemies of the school were bent upon its destruction. About twelve o'clock, on the night of the 9th of September, Miss Crandall's house was assaulted by a number of persons with heavy clubs and iron bars; five window-sashes were demolished and ninety panes of glass dashed to pieces.

I was summoned next morning to the scene of destruction and the terror-stricken family. Never before had Miss Crandall seemed to quail, and her pupils had become afraid to remain another night under her roof. The front rooms of the house were hardly tenantable; and it seemed foolish to repair them only to be destroyed again. After due consideration, therefore, it was determined that the school should be abandoned. The pupils were called together, and I was requested to announce to them our decision. Never before had I felt so deeply sensible of the cruelty of the persecution which had been carried on for eighteen months, in that New England village against a family of defenceless females. Twenty harmless, well-behaved girls, whose only offence against the peace of the community was that they had come together there to obtain useful knowledge and moral culture, were to be told that they had better go away, because, forsooth, the house in which they dwelt would not be protected by the guardians of the town, the conservators of the peace, the officers of justice, the men of influence in the village where it was situated. The words almost blistered my lips. My bosom glowed with indignation. I felt ashamed of Canterbury, ashamed of Connecticut, ashamed of my country, ashamed of my color. Thus ended the generous, disinterested, philanthropic, Christian enterprise of Prudence Crandall.

This was the second attempt made in Connecticut to establish a school for the education of colored youth. The other was in New Haven, two years before. So prevalent and malignant was our national prejudice against the most injured of our fellow-men!

PRIMARY SOURCE DOCUMENT

Excerpts from *Brown* v. *Board of Education* and *Bolling* v. *Sharpe*

INTRODUCTION In *Brown* v. *Board of Education,* the Supreme Court ruled that segregation in public schools deprived African American children of "equal protection of the law." Segregation was, therefore, a violation of one of the guarantees in the Fourteenth Amendment: "No state shall deny to any person within its jurisdiction the equal protection of the laws." Some sixty years earlier in *Plessy* v. *Ferguson* (1896), the Court had allowed states to provide "separate but equal" facilities for different races. The Court declared in *Brown* that segregation was inherently unequal—effectively reversing the *Plessy* decision.

In *Bolling* v. *Sharpe,* issued the same day as the *Brown* decision, the Court applied the same reasoning to schools in the District of Columbia. The following excerpts provide insight into the landmark decisions that altered the landscape of education in the United States.

Brown v. Board of Education

These cases were decided on May 17, 1954. The opinions of that date, declaring the fundamental principle that racial discrimination in public education is unconstitutional, are incorporated herein by reference. All provisions of federal, state, or local law requiring or permitting such discrimination must yield to this principle. There remains for consideration the manner in which relief is to be accorded.

Because these cases arose under different local conditions and their dispositions will involve a variety of local problems, we requested further argument on the question of relief. In view of the nationwide importance of the decision, we invited the Attorney General of the United States and the Attorneys General of all states requiring or permitting racial discrimination in public education to present their views on that question. The parties, the United States, and the States of Florida, North Carolina, Arkansas, Oklahoma, Maryland, and Texas filed briefs and participated in the oral argument.

These presentations were informative and helpful to the Court in its consideration of the complexities arising from the transition to a system of public education freed of racial discrimination. The presentations also demonstrated that substantial steps to eliminate racial discrimination in public schools have already been taken, not only in some of the communities in which these cases arose, but in some of the states appearing as amici curiae, and in other states as well. Substantial progress has been made in the District of Columbia and in the communities in Kansas and Delaware involved in this litigation. The defendants in the cases coming to us from South Carolina and Virginia are awaiting the decision of this Court concerning relief.

Full implementation of these constitutional principles may require solution of varied local school problems. School authorities have the primary responsibility for elucidating, assessing, and solving these problems; courts will have to consider whether the action of school authorities constitutes good faith implementation of the governing constitutional principles. Because of their proximity to local conditions and the possible need for further hearings, the courts which originally heard these cases can best perform this judicial appraisal. Accordingly, we believe it appropriate to remand the cases to those courts.

In fashioning and effectuating the decrees, the courts will be guided by equitable principles. Traditionally, equity has been characterized by a practical flexibili-

Integration and the National Guard

During the long history of discrimination in the United States frequent efforts have been made to increase the access of African Americans to opportunity. After the legal challenges of the NAACP and the landmark decision of the Supreme Court guaranteeing African Americans legal access to schools across the nation, the battle for equality saw its most charged encounters when black Americans sought to actually exercise those rights by enrolling in universities and other schools. In essence, all the "talk" of equal rights had been fine, but when it came to blacks sitting side-by-side with their white peers in the North as well as the South, fierce emotions were revealed. Looking back from the end of the twentieth century, it becomes apparent that access to education has been a key factor for black Americans during the process of assimilation.

In 1957 the "Little Rock Nine" enrolled in Central High School in Little Rock, Arkansas, sparking a national debate and violent protest from the all-white school and community. For the first time, the federal government stepped in to enforce the Supreme Court decisions, taking on the duties it had previously left (often to be ignored) to the individual states. Across the South legislators and governors—often claiming to be carrying out the will of their constituencies—sought to block access to African Americans, much as they had in decades and centuries past. Finally, President Kennedy called out the National Guard in order to protect African Americans attending previously segregated public schools. This action forced far less liberal presidents who were to come after to enforce the rights of minorities' access to education. These educational battles were followed by challenges from the NAACP and other groups in all realms of public and federal institutions. Access to education at all levels, public and private, to housing, and to the range of government-supported services would come with similar legislative advances during the next twenty years.

ty in shaping its remedies and by a facility for adjusting and reconciling public and private needs. These cases call for the exercise of these traditional attributes of equity power. At stake is the personal interest of the plaintiffs in admission to public schools as soon as practicable on a nondiscriminatory basis. To effectuate this interest may call for elimination of a variety of obstacles in making the transition to school systems operated in accordance with the constitutional principles set forth in our May 17, 1954, decision. Courts of equity may properly take into account the public interest in the elimination of such obstacles in a systematic and effective manner. But it should go without saying that the vitality of these constitutional principles cannot be allowed to yield simply because of disagreement with them.

While giving weight to these public and private considerations, the courts will require that the defendants make a prompt and reasonable start toward full compliance with our May 17, 1954, ruling. Once such a start has been made, the courts may find that additional time is necessary to carry out the ruling in an effective manner. The burden rests upon the defendants to establish that such time is necessary in the public interest and is consistent with good faith compliance at the earliest practi-

cable date. To that end, the courts may consider problems related to administration, arising from the physical condition of the school plant, the school transportation system, personnel, revision of school districts and attendance areas into compact units to achieve a system of determining admission to public schools on a nonracial basis, and revision of local laws and regulations which may be necessary in solving the foregoing problems. They will also consider the adequacy of any plans the defendants may propose to meet these problems and to effectuate a transition to a racially nondiscriminatory school system. During this period of transition, the courts will retain jurisdiction of these cases.

The judgments below, except that in the Delaware case, are accordingly reversed and the cases are remanded to the District Courts to take such proceedings and enter such orders and decrees consistent with this opinion as are necessary and proper to admit to public schools on a racial nondiscriminatory basis with all deliberate speed the parties to these cases. The judgment in the Delaware case—ordering the immediate admission of the plaintiffs to schools previously attended only by white children—is affirmed on the basis of the principles stated in our May 17, 1954, opinion, but the case is

Members of the National Guard assist a student with his bicycle at Central High School in Little Rock, Arkansas, after desegregation.
ARCHIVE PHOTOS, INC.

remanded to the Supreme Court of Delaware for such further proceedings as that Court may deem necessary in light of this opinion.

It is so ordered.

Bolling v. Sharpe

This case challenges the validity of segregation in the public schools of the District of Columbia. The petitioners, minors of the Negro race, allege that such segregation deprives them of due process of law under the Fifth Amendment. They were refused admission to a public school attended by white children solely because of their race. They sought the aid of the District Court for the District of Columbia in obtaining admission. That court dismissed their complaint. The Court granted a writ of certiorari before judgment in the Court of Appeals because of the importance of the constitutional question presented. 344 U.S. 873.

We have this day held that the Equal Protection Clause of the Fourteenth Amendment prohibits the states from maintaining racially segregated public schools. The legal problem in the District of Columbia is somewhat different, however. The Fifth Amendment, which is applicable in the District of Columbia, does not contain an equal protection clause as does the Fourteenth Amendment which applies only to the states. But the concepts of equal protection and due process, both stemming from our equal American ideal of fairness, are not mutually exclusive. The "equal protection of the laws" is a more explicit safeguard of prohibited unfairness than "due process of law," and, therefore, we do not imply that the two are always interchangeable phrases. But, as this Court has recognized, discrimination may be so unjustifiable as to be violative of due process.

Classifications based solely upon race must be scrutinized with particular care, since they are contrary to our traditions and hence constitutionally suspect. As long ago as 1896, this Court declared the principle "that the Constitution of the United States, in its present form, forbids, so far as civil and political rights are concerned, discrimination by the General Government, or by the States, against any citizen because of his race." And in Buchanan v. Warley, 245 U.S. 60, the Court held that a statute which limited the right of a property owner to convey his property to a person of another race was, as an unreasonable discrimination, a denial of due process of law.

Although the Court has not assumed to define "liberty" with any great precision, that term is not confined to mere freedom from bodily restraint. Liberty under law extends to the full range of conduct which the individual is free to pursue, and it cannot be restricted except for a proper governmental objective. Segregation in public education is not reasonably related to any proper governmental objective, and thus it imposes on Negro children of the District of Columbia a burden that constitutes an arbitrary deprivation of their liberty in violation of the Due Process Clause.

In view of our decision that the Constitution prohibits the states from maintaining racially segregated public schools, it would be unthinkable that the same Constitution would impose a lesser duty on the Federal Government. We hold that racial segregation in the public schools of the District of Columbia is a denial of the due process of law guaranteed by the Fifth Amendment to the Constitution.

For the reasons set out in Brown v. Board of Education, this case will be restored to the docket for reargument on Questions 4 and 5 previously propounded by the Court. 345 U.S. 972.

It is so ordered.

The Ongoing Effort for Inclusion in the Military

ADAPTED FROM ESSAYS BY BARBARA SAVAGE, UNIVERSITY OF PENNSYLVANIA

African Americans have served in literally every war fought by the United States, yet in most of those wars their participation was severely limited by policies that enforced racial exclusion, restrictions, and segregation in the military. Such policies were eased and gradually eliminated after the conclusion of World War II, but only as the result of a persistent campaign of protest by African Americans. The experience of African Americans in the military reflects gradual shifts over time in the political and legal status of African Americans generally and in the federal government's role in racial relations.

In each war the nation has fought, a recurring pattern of conflict and debate has emerged over the military's racial policies. Most African Americans believed that military service provided them with opportunities to perform tasks and display qualities denied them in civilian life. They also believed that the opportunity to serve, and to serve well, would bolster their claims for the full rights of citizenship and democracy that the white majority continued to withhold from them. Many white Americans, because of their prejudiced belief in black inferiority and persistent fears of black rebellion, supported policies that severely limited the numbers of African Americans permitted to serve and that relegated them to tasks far removed from combat.

Only in the crisis of war were some of these racially restrictive policies lifted, but only to the extent necessary to win, and only for the duration of the war. Once the emergency passed, the importance of the military service African Americans had rendered was disparaged and denied and the original racial restrictions were re-imposed. Although the circumstances differed with each war, this conflict over how to employ African Americans in the military was repeated from colonial times through the Civil War, the Spanish-American War, World War I, and World War II. In response, African Americans conducted a long campaign for equal opportunity in the military. Their efforts culminated, in 1948, in President Harry S. Truman's (1884–1972) executive order eliminating racial segregation and discrimination in the armed services. This opened the way for the first time to a racially integrated national defense and full opportunities for African Americans in the armed forces.

THE CIVIL WAR

African Americans were made a permanent feature of the U.S. military during the Civil War. Initially, President Abraham Lincoln (1809–1865) was as reluctant as George Washington to enlist African Americans as soldiers. But by 1863, faced with the prospect of losing the war, Lincoln authorized the employment of African American soldiers in the Union army.

African Americans responded eagerly to this opportunity, and soon black soldiers made up between 9 and 10 percent of the Union army's total numbers. By war's end, over 186,000 African Americans had enlisted in the Union army, about half of them from the slave states that had seceded and the remainder from border and free states. These troops were divided into segregated regiments commanded by white officers and, in some rare cases, by black commissioned officers. Initially black soldiers were paid far less than their white counterparts, but after blacks repeatedly objected, the federal government in 1864 authorized equal pay for blacks and whites of equal rank.

African American troops participated in virtually every battle and in every theater of operations, winning many awards for valor along the way. Nearly forty thou-

The 369th Infantry—the New York Colored Fifteenth Infantry—returns home from France and docks in Hoboken, New Jersey. The 369th was the only regiment in World War I that never lost a foot of ground, gave up a trench, or had a man captured by the enemy.
NATIONAL ARCHIVES AND RECORDS ADMINISTRATION

sand African American soldiers died in the Civil War, losing their lives in a proportion far exceeding their numbers in the army. The outcome of the Civil War, which brought freedom to enslaved African Americans, was significantly influenced by the sacrifice and service of African American troops.

AFRICAN AMERICANS IN THE CAVALRY

In recognition of the exemplary service of African American soldiers during the Civil War, Congress in 1866 authorized for the first time four black units in the standing army—the Ninth and Tenth U.S. cavalry regiments and the Twenty-fourth and Twenty-fifth infantry regiments. These outfits were used extensively to protect white settlers in the Southwest and the plains states, often fighting against Native Americans in that region. They were stationed at various times at forts and outposts in Texas, New Mexico, Kansas, Wyoming, Utah, and Montana.

When the Spanish-American War broke out in 1898, these units of African American soldiers joined the campaign, as did several other newly formed black outfits from various states. During this war, the military continued to resist commissioning black officers to head these

all-black units, which with few exceptions remained under the direction of white officers. Soldiers from the original four black units fought in Cuba and the Philippines. Black soldiers in the Ninth and Tenth cavalries were credited with salvaging the battle for San Juan Hill when Theodore Roosevelt's (1858–1919) Rough Riders, the First Volunteer Cavalry, faltered.

WORLD WAR I

Just before the outbreak of World War I, there were 750,000 men in the regular army and National Guard, but only 20,000 of them were African Americans. Policies of racial exclusion prevented great numbers of black men from serving in those units in peacetime. When the military buildup for war began in 1917 with the imposition of a mandatory enlistment policy, African American men responded enthusiastically, and over 367,000 of them were called to serve. Now, in a change of military policy, more than 600 black men were commissioned as officers.

Again, as in previous wars, African Americans who wanted to serve were met with racial restrictions and conditions that limited their assignments and the duties they were allowed to perform. The Marine Corps refused

African American soldiers' clubs were formed to help care for and entertain black soldiers. During World War I, 370,000 black men served in segregated units of the armed services, about half of them in Europe. Soldiers who returned from the "war to save democracy" hoping for a new day at home were sorely disappointed, however. Returning black soldiers, seasoned by war and proud of their service, were expected to fall into old postures of submission. When they did not, they often became the targets of racial violence and lynching. **NATIONAL ARCHIVES AND RECORDS ADMINISTRATION**

them entry altogether, and the navy restricted them to menial jobs. Black women nurses repeatedly petitioned to be permitted to serve overseas, but the military refused them that opportunity until after the fighting had ended. Nearly 90 percent of all black servicemen were in the army, and, apart from the men assigned to newly created black combat units, they belonged primarily to service or labor units. Such units were extremely important to the war effort, however. Black men unloaded tons of supplies and equipment from military ships, built roads, drove trucks, and helped build and maintain the physical infrastructure necessary for war.

During the war, new black combat units were created in the Ninety-second and Ninety-third divisions. The infantry regiments of the Ninety-third were attached to the French army. One of those units, the 369th Infantry, fought alongside the French against German troops, setting a record for service by staying in the trenches for 191 days. The 369th never yielded, nor were any of its members ever captured. The French military exalted these African American soldiers for their bravery and service, awarding the entire 369th the Croix de Guerre and singling out nearly

two hundred of the men for individual awards, including the Legion of Honor for exceptional courage in battle. At a time when the U.S. military refused to use African Americans fully as combat troops, when their sacrifices and service were denied and denigrated, the French government's recognition of the gallantry and loyalty of African American soldiers stood out in sharp contrast.

WORLD WAR II

Although the U.S. military continued to maintain policies of racial discrimination and segregation during World War II, African Americans had greater and wider opportunities to serve than in any previous war. During the course of the war, the Marine Corps and the navy, which had traditionally excluded blacks or assigned them limited roles, gradually opened their ranks. The Women's Auxiliary Corps was also formed, and by the war's end more than four thousand African American women had joined. The famous Tuskegee Airmen were members of the Ninety-ninth Pursuit Squadron, an all-black fighter unit that trained nearly six hundred pilots. Officer candidate training schools were opened to blacks

Men of the first all-black U.S. Army Air Force outfit included Lt. Robert Leon C. Roberts, Lt. Herbert V. Clark, Lt. Willie Fuller, Lt. William Campbell, Lt. Herbert E. Carter, and Lt. Erwin B. Lawrence (The last man is unidentified.) The group was part of the 99th Fighter Squadron. **AP/WIDE WORLD PHOTOS**

during the war, expanding the pool of African American commissioned officers.

These changes in military policy were the result of several factors. African Americans continued to protest aggressively against being asked to serve the cause of democracy in a military that sanctioned racial segregation and discrimination. In the light of Adolph Hitler's racist, white supremacist, and anti-Semitic claims, the United States found its own racial policies—in civilian life and in the armed services—under increasing scrutiny from the international community. African Americans were being asked to share the burdens of war against Hitlerism and fascism, while they themselves were still denied freedom and equal opportunity at home.

That contradiction in turn fueled the demands of many African Americans for fair play, beginning with the military itself. At a time when a unified home front was essential to the success of the war, federal officials, including those in the military, felt pressured to make

changes in the racial policies affecting African Americans in the armed services. Segregation and discriminatory treatment remained in place for the duration of the war, but significant steps toward eliminating disparate treatment were put in place. In 1940, for example, Benjamin O. Davis (1877–1970) became the first African American to be promoted to the rank of brigadier general.

During World War II, approximately one million African American men and women served in the armed services, half of them overseas. Again, as in World War I, black men in significant numbers provided the labor needed for conducting the war. They made up almost half of the transportation corps and truck companies and played a large role in helping to rebuild Europe. There were twenty-two black combat units that fought, among other places, at the Battle of the Bulge and in six European countries.

DESEGREGATION OF THE MILITARY

When World War II ended, some of the racially discriminatory policies that had been eased during the war were

This photograph shows General Colin Powell, the first African American to hold the nation's top military position as chairman of the Joint Chiefs of Staff. General Powell served as chairman from 1989 to 1994. He later was named secretary of state under President George W. Bush. **AP/WIDE WORLD PHOTOS**

reimposed, including a limitation on the number of blacks that would be allowed to reenlist. Throughout the war, African Americans had vehemently protested the continuation of segregated fighting and service units. Although there had been some shift in thinking about race relations as a result of the protests, the war ended with the policies still in place.

The campaign to desegregate the military continued after the war's end. When a new law was passed instituting a peacetime draft, the African American leader A. Philip Randolph (1889–1979) threatened to urge young black men to boycott the draft unless segregation was ended. In response, President Truman signed Executive Order 9981 in 1948, establishing a committee to prepare and plan for the end of the segregated military. **SEE PRIMARY SOURCE DOCUMENTS** *Executive Order 8802* and *Desegregation and the Peace-time Draft*

By 1950, a quota limiting black enlistments had been lifted, and military personnel began to be assigned without regard to race. When the Korean War began in June 1950, these policy changes allowed for the gradual

integration of the armed forces. By the end of the war, almost all the army's units had been racially integrated.

AFRICAN AMERICANS IN THE VIETNAM WAR

The Vietnam War was the first American war fought with fully integrated armed forces. African Americans were able to serve in all branches without regard to race. Blacks served in a proportion slightly greater than their share of the general population, with most serving in the army, which sustained the greatest casualties of war. In 1967, African Americans made up 11 percent of all enlisted personnel in Vietnam, but they were nearly 15 percent of the army. African American soldiers accounted for 22.4 percent of army deaths in 1966. Of the total of 58,174 Americans killed in the war, 7,264, or about 12.5 percent, were African Americans.

The Vietnam War was the subject of much dissension among the American people. Though blacks participated in fighting the war, for African American leaders like Martin Luther King Jr. (1929–1968), the conflict represented a diversion of financial resources needed to alleviate the poverty and joblessness that plagued many Americans, especially blacks. Some other black leaders were solidly supportive of the war effort and sought to keep it separate from the issues of economic and racial justice. **SEE PRIMARY SOURCE DOCUMENT** *Dwight Johnson: "From Dakto to Detroit: Death of a Troubled Hero" by Jon Nordheimer*

But the issue of American involvement in the war overshadowed the Civil Rights movement and President Lyndon Johnson's (1908–1973) War on Poverty. When Julian Bond (b. 1940), a member of the Student Nonviolent Coordinating Committee, was elected to the Georgia legislature in 1966, they refused to seat him because of his antiwar stance. Only under a Supreme Court order was he allowed to assume the seat to which he had been elected.

The gradual desegregation of the U.S. military had begun in 1948, although complaints of racial discrimination within the military did not die. By the time of the Vietnam War, however, desegregation had brought about wider opportunities for African Americans to assume leadership roles within the military. By the 1960s, a large cadre of black officers was in place in the military, including General Colin Powell (b. 1937), who would later become national security adviser to President Ronald Reagan (b. 1911) and chairman of the Joint Chiefs of Staff under Presidents George Bush (b. 1924) and Bill Clinton (b. 1946). As chairman of the Joint Chiefs, Powell was in charge of all the branches of the military service and served as the top military adviser to the commander in chief, a position that earned him great visibility and stature during the 1991 Gulf War. Powell's career stands as an example of the expanded opportunities for African Americans in the armed services.

RECENT EVENTS

While the situation of African Americans in the military has changed, and in some respects improved, in the decades following the Vietnam War, it is difficult to determine whether the overall change has been positive or negative. What is certain is that many without opportunities elsewhere find stable and respectable careers in the military. As such, the U.S. military is greatly composed of African Americans, many of whom have reached positions of great authority. Despite these advancements, however, one need only look to the Persian Gulf War and the numbers of black Americans who returned with biological and chemical warfare poisoning to understand that African Americans were, as they always have been, the first to hit the ground and the group with the greatest numbers of casualties.

BIBLIOGRAPHY

Barbeau, Arthur E., and Florette Henri. *The Unknown Soldiers: Black American Troops in World War I.* Philadelphia: Temple University Press, 1971.

Buchanan, A. Russell. *Black Americans in World War II.* Santa Barbara: Clio Books, 1977.

Dalfiume, Richard M. *Desegregation of the U.S. Armed Forces: Fighting on Two Fronts, 1939–1953.* Columbia: University of Missouri Press, 1969.

Earley, Charity Adams. *One Woman's Army: A Black Officer Remembers the WAC.* College Station: Texas A&M University Press, 1989.

Hine, Darlene Clark. *Black Women in White: Racial Conflict and Cooperation in the Nursing Profession, 1890–1950.* Bloomington: Indiana University Press, 1989.

Hunton, Addie W., and Katherine M. Johnson. *Two Colored Women with the American Expeditionary Forces.* New York: Brooklyn Eagle, 1920.

Leckie, William H. *The Buffalo Soldiers: A Narrative of the Negro Calvary in the West.* Norman: University of Oklahoma Press, 1967.

Lee, Ulysses. *The United States Army in World War II. Special Studies: The Employment of Negro Troops.* Washington: Government Printing Office, 1966.

McPherson, James M. *The Negro's Civil War: How American Negroes Felt and Acted during the War for the Union.* New York: Pantheon Books, 1965.

McQuire, Philip. *He, Too, Spoke for Democracy: Judge Hastie, World War II, and the Black Soldier.* New York: Greenwood Press, 1988.

Morden, Bettie J. *The Women's Army Corps, 1945–1978.* Washington: Center for Military History, United States Army, 1990.

Nalty, Bernard C. *Strength for the Fight: A History of Black Americans in the Military.* New York: Free Press, 1986.

Quarles, Benjamin. *The Negro in the American Revolution.* Chapel Hill: University of North Carolina Press, 1961.

———. *The Negro in the Civil War.* Boston: Little, Brown, 1969.

Scott, Lawrence P. *Double V: The Civil Rights Struggle of the Tuskegee Airmen.* Lansing: Michigan State University Press, 1994.

Terry, Wallace. *Bloods: An Oral History of the Vietnam War by Black Veterans.* New York: Random House, 1984.

Wynn, Neil. *The Afro-American and the Second World War.* London: Elek, 1979.

PRIMARY SOURCE DOCUMENT

Executive Order 8802

INTRODUCTION On June 28, 1941, President Franklin Delano Roosevelt issued Executive Order 8802, desegregating the nation's defense industries and establishing the Fair Employment Practices Commission. The order was issued in response to the call by the labor leader A. Philip Randolph for a march on Washington to protest discrimination in defense work.

Whereas it is the policy of the United States to encourage full participation in the national defense program by all citizens of the United States, regardless of race, creed, color, or national origin, in the firm belief that the democratic way of life within the Nation can be defended successfully only with the help and support of all groups within its borders; and

Whereas there is evidence that available and needed workers have been barred from employment in industries engaged in defense production solely because of considerations of race, creed, color, or national origin, to the detriment of workers' morale and of national unity:

Now, Therefore, by virtue of the authority vested in me by the Constitution and the statutes, and as a prerequisite to the successful conduct of our national defense production effort, I do hereby reaffirm the policy of the United States that there shall be no discrimination in the employment of workers in defense industries or government because of race, creed, color, or national origin, and I do hereby declare that it is the duty of employers and of labor organizations, in furtherance of said policy and of this order, to provide for the full and equitable participation of all workers in defense industries, without discrimination because of race, creed, color, or national origin;

And it is hereby ordered as follows:

1. All departments and agencies of the Government of the United States concerned with vocational and training programs for defense production shall take special measures appropriate to assure that such programs are administered without discrimination because of race, creed, color, or national origin;

2. All contracting agencies of the Government of the United States shall include in all defense contracts hereafter negotiated by them a provision obligating

This World War II poster, featuring a black man and a white man working together, reflected the new integration of the nation's defense industries accomplished by the labor leader A. Philip Randolph. In 1941, following his call for a march on Washington to protect discrimination in defense employment, President Franklin Roosevelt ordered the desegregation of all defense industries.
NATIONAL ARCHIVES AND RECORDS ADMINISTRATION

the contractor not to discriminate against any worker because of race, creed, color, or national origin;

3. There is established in the Office of Production Management a Committee on Fair Employment Practice, which shall consist of a chairman and four other members to be appointed by the President. The Chairman and members of the Committee shall serve as such without compensation, but shall be entitled to actual and necessary transportation, subsistence, and other expenses incidental to performance of their duties. The Committee shall receive and investigate complaints of discrimination in violation of the provisions of this order and shall take appropriate steps to redress grievances which it finds to be valid. The Committee shall also recommend to the several departments and agencies of the Government of the United States and to the President all measures which may be deemed by it necessary or proper to effectuate the provisions of this order.

White House, June 25, 1941

Desegregation and the Peace-time Draft

INTRODUCTION As the nation settled into the cold war following World War II, Congress held hearings on what was to be the first peacetime draft in American history. The armed forces remained segregated, and there was little thought of changing that until A. Philip Randolph made the following statement before the Senate Armed Services Committee.

A staunch and proven foe of segregation in the nation's defenses, Randolph told the committee that, as long as the armed forces remained segregated, he would urge young African Americans to commit civil disobedience by resisting the proposed draft.

Randolph's listeners took him seriously, as they had in 1941 when he proposed a massive march on Washington to protest discrimination in defense-industry employment. Randolph testified on March 31, and on June 26 he organized the League for Non-Violent Civil Disobedience against Military Segregation. On July 26, President Harry Truman issued Executive Order 9981 declaring that "there shall be equality of treatment and opportunity for all persons in the armed services without regard to race, color, religion or national origin."

Testimony before the Senate Armed Services Committee, by A. Philip Randolph
Mr. Chairman:

Mr. Grant Reynolds, national chairman of the Committee Against Jimcrow in Military Service and Training, has prepared for you in his testimony today a summary of wartime injustices to Negro soldiers—injustices by the military authorities and injustices by bigoted segments of the police and civilian population. The fund of material on this issue is endless, and yet, three years after the end of the war, as another crisis approaches, large numbers of white Americans are blissfully unaware of the extent of physical and psychological aggression against and oppression of the Negro soldier.

Without taking time for a thorough probe into these relevant data—a probe which could enlighten the nation—Congress may now heed Mr. Truman's call for Universal Military Training and Selective Service, and in the weeks ahead enact a jimcrow conscription law and appropriate billions for the greatest segregation system of all time. In a campaign year, when both major parties are playing cynical politics with the issue of civil rights, Negroes are about to lose the fight against jimcrowism on a national level. Our hard-won local gains in education, fair employment, hospitalization, housing are in danger of being nullified—being swept aside, Mr. Chairman, after decades of work—by a federally enforced pattern of segregation. I am not beguiled by the Army's use of the word "temporary." Whatever may pass in the way of conscription legislation will become permanent, since the world trend is toward militarism. The Army knows this well. In such an eventuality, how could any permanent Fair Employment Practices Commission dare to criticize job discrimination in private industry if the federal government itself were simultaneously discriminating against Negro youth in military installations all over the world?

There can be no doubt of my facts. Quite bluntly, Chairman Walter G. Andrews of the House Armed Services Committee told a delegation from this organization that the War Department plans segregated white and Negro battalions if Congress passes a draft law. The *Newark Evening News* of March 26, 1948, confirmed this in a Washington dispatch based on official memoranda sent from Secretary Forrestal's office to the House Armed Services Committee. Nine days ago when we called this to the attention of the Commander-in-Chief in a White House conference, he indicated that he was aware of these plans for jimcrow battalions. This despite his Civil Rights message to Congress.

We have released all of this damaging information to the daily press, to leaders of both parties in Congress, and to supposedly liberal organizations. But with a relative handful of exceptions, we have found our white "friends" silent, indifferent, even hostile. Justice Roberts, who provided you last week with vigorous testimony in behalf of the President's draft recommendations, is a trustee of Lincoln University in Pennsylvania, a prominent Negro institution. Yet for nearly four months, Mr. Roberts has not shown us the courtesy to reply to letters asking his support for anti-segregation and civil rights safeguards in any draft law. Three days after the Newark Sunday News embarrassed Congressman Harry L. Towe in his home district by exposing his similar failure to acknowledge our correspondence, Mr. Towe, author of the UMT bill in the House, suddenly found time to answer letters which had been on his desk since December.

This situation—this conspiracy of silence, shall I say?—has naturally commanded wide publicity in the Negro press. I submit for the record a composite of newspaper clippings. In my travels around the country I have sounded out Negro public opinion and confirmed for myself the popular resentment as reflected by the Negro press. I can assure members of the Senate that Negroes do put civil rights above the high cost of living and above every other major issue of the day, as recently reported by the *Fortune Opinion Poll,* I believe. Even more significant is the bitter, angry mood of the Negro in his present determination to win those civil rights in a country that subjects him daily to so many insults and indignities.

With this background, gentlemen, I reported last week to President Truman that Negroes are in no mood to shoulder a gun for democracy abroad so long as they are denied democracy here at home. In particular, they resent the idea of fighting or being drafted into another jimcrow Army. I passed this information on to Mr. Tru-

African Americans had waited for many years for the chance to fly as fighter pilots. When it came in 1941, with the establishment of training for the Tuskegee Airmen, they showed their pride and support in countless ways. This World War II poster featuring a black fighter pilot made a direct appeal to them to purchase war bonds: "Keep Us Flying." **NATIONAL ARCHIVES AND RECORDS ADMINISTRATION**

man not as threat, but rather as a frank, factual survey of Negro opinion.

Today I should like to make clear to the Senate Armed Services Committee and through you, to Congress and the American people that passage now of a jimcrow draft may only result in a mass civil disobedience movement along the lines of the magnificent struggles of the people of India against British imperialism. I must emphasize that the current agitation for civil rights is no longer a mere expression of hope on the part of Negroes. On the one hand, it is a positive, resolute outreaching for full manhood. On the other hand, it is an equally determined will to stop acquiescing in anything less. Negroes demand full, unqualified first-class citizenship.

In resorting to the principles of direct-action techniques of Gandhi, whose death was publicly mourned by many members of Congress and President Truman, Negroes will be serving a higher law than any passed by a national legislature in an era when racism spells our doom. They will be serving a law higher than any decree of the

Lieutenant Harriet Ida Pickens and Ensign Frances Wills were the first African American women commissioned by the U.S. Navy. They graduated from the Naval Reserve Midshipmen's School, Northampton, Massachusetts, in 1944. **NATIONAL ARCHIVES AND RECORDS ADMINISTRATION**

Supreme Court which in the famous Winfred Lynn case evaded ruling on the flagrantly illegal segregation practiced under the wartime Selective Service Act. In refusing to accept compulsory military segregation, Negro youth will be serving their fellow men throughout the world.

I feel qualified to make this claim because of a recent survey of American psychologists, sociologists and anthropologists. The survey revealed an overwhelming belief among these experts that enforced segregation on racial or religious lines has serious and detrimental psychological effects both on the segregated groups and on those enforcing segregation. Experts from the South, I should like to point out, gentlemen, were as positive as those from other sections of the country as to the harmful effects of segregation. The views of these social scientists were based on scientific research and on their own professional experience.

So long as the Armed Services propose to enforce such universally harmful segregation not only here at home but also overseas, Negro youth have a moral obligation not to lend themselves as world-wide carriers of an evil and hellish doctrine. Secretary of the Army Kenneth C. Royall clearly indicated in the New Jersey National Guard situation that the Armed Services do have every

intention of prolonging their anthropologically hoary and untenable policies.

For 25 years now the myth has been carefully cultivated that Soviet Russia has ended all discrimination and intolerance, while here at home the American Communists have skillfully posed as champions of minority groups. To the rank-and-file Negro in World War II, Hitler's racism posed a sufficient threat for him to submit to the jimcrow Army abuses. But this factor of minority group prosecution in Russia is not present, as a popular issue, in the power struggle between Stalin and the United States. I can only repeat that this time Negroes will not take a jimcrow draft lying down. The conscience of the world will be shaken as by nothing else when thousands and thousands of us second-class Americans choose imprisonment in preference to permanent military slavery.

While I cannot with absolute certainty claim results at this hour, I personally will advise Negroes to refuse to fight as slaves for a democracy they cannot possess and cannot enjoy. Let me add that I am speaking only for myself, not even for the Committee Against Jimcrow in Military Service and Training, since I am not sure that all its members would follow my position. But Negro leaders in close touch with GI grievances would feel derelict in their duty if they did not support such a justified civil disobedience movement—especially those of us whose age would protect us from being drafted. Any other course would be a betrayal of those who place their trust in us. I personally pledge myself to openly counsel, aid and abet youth, both white and Negro, to quarantine any jimcrow conscription system, whether it bear the label of UMT or Selective Service.

I shall tell youth of all races not to be tricked by any euphonious election-year registration for a draft. This evasion, which the newspapers increasingly discuss as a convenient way out for Congress, would merely presage a synthetic "crisis" immediately after November 2nd when all talk of equality and civil rights would be branded unpatriotic while the induction machinery would move into high gear. On previous occasions I have seen the "national emergency" psychology mow down legitimate Negro demands.

From coast to coast in my travels I shall call upon all Negro veterans to join this civil disobedience movement and to recruit their younger brothers in an organized refusal to register and be drafted. Many veterans, bitter over Army jimcrow, have indicated that they will act spontaneously in this fashion, regardless of any organized movement. "Never again," they say with finality.

I shall appeal to the thousands of white youth in schools and colleges who are today vigorously shedding the prejudices of their parents and professors. I shall urge then to demonstrate their solidarity with Negro youth by

In 1945, enlisted men on board the U.S.S. *Ticonderoga* celebrated the news of Japan's surrender with music and laughter. This was the end of World War II, in which one million African American servicemen and servicewomen were engaged at home and overseas.
NATIONAL ARCHIVES AND RECORDS ADMINISTRATION

ignoring the entire registration and induction machinery. And finally I shall appeal to Negro parents to lend their moral support to their sons—to stand behind them as they march with heads high to federal prisons as a telling demonstration to the world that Negroes have reached the limit of human endurance—that is, in the words of the spiritual, we'll be buried in our graves before we will be slaves.

May I, in conclusion, Mr. Chairman, point out that political maneuvers have made this drastic program our last resort. Your party, the party of Lincoln, solemnly pledged in its 1994 platform a full-fledged Congressional investigation of injustices to Negro soldiers. Instead of that long overdue probe, the Senate Armed Services Committee on this very day is finally hearing testimony from two or three Negro veterans for a period of 20 min-

utes each. The House Armed Services Committee and Chairman Andrews went one step further and arrogantly refused to hear any at all! Since we cannot obtain an adequate Congressional forum for our grievances, we have no other recourse but to tell our story to the peoples of the world by organized direct action. I don't believe that even a wartime censorship wall could be high enough to conceal news of a civil disobedience program. If we cannot win your support for your own Party commitments, if we cannot ring a bell in you by appealing to human decency, we shall command your respect and the respect of the world by our united refusal to cooperate with tyrannical injustice.

Since the military, with their Southern biases, intend to take over America and institute total encampment of the populace along jimcrow lines, Negroes will resist with the

Black and white soldiers served together in integrated units for the first time during the Korean War. Sergeant Major Cleveland, an African American, instructs his troops in this 1950 photograph. **U.S. ARMY**

power of non-violence, with the weapons of moral principles, with the good-will weapons of the spirit, yes with the weapons that brought freedom to India. I feel morally obligated to disturb and keep disturbed the conscience of jimcrow America. In resisting the insult of jimcrowism to the soul of black America, we are helping to save the soul of America. And let me add that I am opposed to Russian totalitarian communism and all its works. I consider it a menace to freedom. I stand by democracy as expressing the Judean-Christian ethic. But democracy and Christianity must be boldly and courageously applied for all men regardless of race, color, creed or country.

We shall wage a relentless warfare against jimcrow without hate or revenge for the moral and spiritual progress and safety of our country, world peace and freedom.

Finally let me say that Negroes are just sick and tired of being pushed around and we just don't propose to take it, and we do not care what happens.

PRIMARY SOURCE DOCUMENT

Dwight Johnson: "From Dakto to Detroit: Death of a Troubled Hero" by Jon Nordheimer

INTRODUCTION Sergeant Dwight Johnson won the Congressional Medal of Honor for conspicuous bravery in the Vietnam War. As with many African American war heroes before him, Johnson's extraordinary courage under fire left a lasting impression on those who witnessed it. But when he returned home to Detroit, he found that he was a "feather in the cap of a lot of people," including the military brass, who hoped to use Johnson to recruit other black soldiers. Burdened by debts and by excruciating flashbacks of combat in Vietnam and troubled by what he regarded as the army's exploitation of him, Johnson found his life rapidly deteriorating.

A Vietnam War Hero Returns Home

A few tenants living in the E.J. Jefferies Homes, a dreary public housing project in Corktown, an old Detroit neighborhood, can still remember Dwight Johnson as a little boy who lived in one of the rust-brown buildings with his mother and baby brother. They think it strange, after all that has happened to Dwight, to remember him as a gentle boy who hated to fight.

Dwight Johnson died one week from his 24th birthday, shot and killed as he tried to rob a grocery store a mile from his home. The store manager later told the police that a tall Negro had walked in shortly before midnight, drawn a revolver out of his topcoat and demanded money from the cash register.

The manager pulled his own pistol from under the counter and the two men struggled. Seven shots were fired.

Four and one-half hours later, on an operating table at Detroit General Hospital, Dwight (Skip) Johnson died from five gunshot wounds.

Ordinarily, the case would have been closed right there, a routine crime in a city where there were 13,583 armed robberies last year.

But when the detectives went through the dead man's wallet for identification, they found a small white card with its edges rubbed thin from wear. "Congressional Medal of Honor Society—United States of America," it said. "This certifies that Dwight H. Johnson is a member of this society."

The news of the death of Sgt. Dwight Johnson shocked the black community of Detroit. Born out of wedlock when his mother was a teenager and raised on public welfare, he had been the good boy on his block in the dreary housing project, an altar boy and Explorer Scout, one of the few among the thousands of poor black youngsters in Detroit who had struggled against the grinding life of the ghetto and broken free, coming home from Vietnam tall and strong and a hero.

The story of Dwight Johnson and his drift from hero in Dakto, Vietnam, to villain in Detroit is a difficult one to trace. The moments of revelation are rare. There were, of course, those two brief episodes that fixed public attention on him: 30 minutes of "uncommon valor" one cold morning in combat that earned him the nation's highest military decoration, and the 30-second confrontation in the Detroit grocery that ended his life.

Oddly, they are moments of extreme violence, and everyone who knew Dwight Johnson—or thought he did—knew he was not a violent man.

Now that the funeral is over and the out-of-town relatives have gone home and the family conferences that sought clues to explain Dwight's odd behavior have ended in bitter confusion, his mother can sit back and talk wistfully about the days when Skip was a skinny kid who was chased home after school by the Corktown bullies.

"Mama," he would ask, "what do I do if they catch me?" His mother would place an arm around his thin shoulders and draw him close. "Skip," she would say, "don't you fight, honey, and don't let them catch you." The boy would look downcast and worried. "Yes, Mama," he'd say.

"Dwight was a fabulous, all-around guy, bright and with a great sense of humor," reflected Barry Davis, an auburn-haired Californian who flew with his wife to Detroit when he heard on a news report that Dwight had been killed. Three others who had served with him in Vietnam, all of them white, also came, not understanding what aberration had led to his death.

"I can remember our first day at Fort Knox and Dwight was the only colored guy in our platoon," Barry

Davis recalled. "So we're in formation and this wise guy from New Jersey says to Dwight, 'Hey, what's the initials N.A.A.C.P. stand for?'

"And Dwight says, 'The National Association for the Advancement of Colored People.'

"And this wise guy from New Jersey says, 'Naw, that ain't it. It stands for Niggers Acting As Colored People.'

"And I said to myself, 'Wow, those are fighting words,' but Dwight just laughed. From then on he was just one of the guys. As it turned out, Dwight liked this wise guy from New Jersey in the end as much as he liked anybody."

Most of the men who served with Sergeant Dwight Johnson remembered him that way—easy-going, hard to rattle, impossible to anger.

But Stan Enders remembers him another way. Stan was the gunner in Skip's tank that morning in Vietnam three years ago, during the fighting at Dakto.

"No one who was there could ever forget the sight of this guy taking on a whole battalion of North Vietnamese soldiers," Stan said as he stood in the sunshine outside Faith Memorial Church in Corktown three weeks ago, waiting for Skip's funeral service to begin.

Their platoon of four M-48 tanks was racing down a road toward Dakto, in the Central Highlands near the Cambodian border and the Ho Chi Minh Trail, when it was ambushed. Communist rockets knocked out two of the tanks immediately, and waves of foot soldiers sprang out of the nearby woods to attack the two tanks still in commission.

Skip hoisted himself out of the turret hatch and manned the mounted .50-caliber machine gun. He had been assigned to this tank only the night before. His old tank, and the crew he had spent 11 months and 22 days with in Vietnam and had never seen action before, was 60 feet away, burning.

"He was really close to those guys in that tank," Stan said. "He just couldn't sit still and watch it burn with them inside."

Skip ran through heavy crossfire to the tank and opened its hatch. He pulled out the first man he came across in the turret, burned but still alive, and got him to the ground just as the tank's artillery shells exploded, killing everyone left inside.

"When the tank blew up and Dwight saw the bodies all burned and black, well, he just sort of cracked up," said Stan.

For 30 minutes, armed first with a .45-caliber pistol and then with a submachine gun, Skip hunted the Vietnamese on the ground, killing from five to 20 enemy sol-

Joe Louis (1914–1981) and Muhammad Ali (b. 1942) in Wartime

Born to Alabama sharecroppers in 1914, Joe Louis became one of the great folk heroes of modern black America, winning the world heavyweight championship from James Braddock in 1937 and maintaining the title for twelve years. Louis joined the U.S. Army during World War II at the rank of sergeant, for which he was also adored as a symbol of American might in the fight against the Axis powers. In addition, Louis's defeat of German Max Schmeling in 1938 helped the American propaganda cause.

In contrast, heavyweight boxer Muhammad Ali reviled the war in Vietnam, making public statements against both the war and what Ali viewed as the racist policies of a nation which "had not fought for him." Because of his refusal to enter the U.S. Army in 1967, Ali was stripped of his heavyweight title and spent time in jail. Although Ali's decision not to contribute to the war effort was looked upon with disfavor by many at the time, growing antiwar sentiment helped restore Ali's reputation as an American hero over time.

---

diers, nobody knows for sure. When he ran out of ammunition, he killed one with the stock of the machine gun.

At one point he came face to face with a Communist soldier who squeezed the trigger on his weapon aimed point-blank at him. The gun misfired and Skip killed him. But the soldier would come back to haunt him late at night in Detroit, in those dreams in which that anonymous soldier stood in front of him, and barrel of his AK-47 as big as a railroad tunnel, his finger on the trigger, slowly pressing it.

"When it was all over," Stan said, walking up the church steps as the funeral service got under way, "it took three men and three shots of morphine to hold Dwight down. He was raving. He tried to kill the prisoners we had rounded up. They took him away to a hospital in Pleiku in a straightjacket."

Stan saw Skip the next day. He had been released from the hospital, and came by to pick up his personal gear. His Vietnam tour was over and he was going home.

No one there would know anything about Dakto until 10 months later, at the White House Medal of Honor ceremony.

Sergeant Johnson returned home in early 1968, outwardly only little changed from the quiet boy named Skip who had grown up in Detroit and been drafted. Even when he and the other black veterans came home and could not find a job, he seemed to take it in stride.

He had been discharged with $600 in his pocket, and it was enough to buy cigarettes and go out at night with his cousin, Tommy Tillman, and with Eddie Wright, a friend from the Jefferies Homes, and make the rounds to the Shadowbox or the Little Egypt, to drink a little beer and have a few dates.

And at home no one knew about the bad dreams he was having. They would have to learn about that later from an Army psychiatrist.

If anyone asked him about Vietnam he would just shake his head, or laugh and say, "Aw, man, nothing happened," and he would change the subject and talk about the girls in Kuala Lumpur where he went for R & R, or the three-day pass he spent in Louisville, Ky., drinking too much whisky for the first time in his life and ending up in jail.

He returned home just as the Communist Tet offensive erupted in Vietnam, and everyone talked about how lucky he had been to get out before things got hot. They teased him then about his lackluster military career.

"When he came home from Vietnam he was different, sure. I noticed it, all jumpy and nervous and he had to be doing something all the time, it seems," said Eddie Wright. "But mostly he was the same fun-time guy."

Carmen Berry, a close friend of Katrina May, the girl Skip started dating after his discharge, thought she detected nuances of change she attributed to the same mental letdown she had seen in other Vietnam veterans.

"They get quiet," she said. "It's like they don't have too much to say about what it was like over there. Maybe it's because they've killed people and they don't really know why they killed them.

"The only thing that bugged me about Skip then," reflected his cousin Tommy, "and the one thing I thought was kind of strange and unlike him, was the pictures he brought back. He had a stack of pictures of dead people, you know, dead Vietnamese. Color slides."

In the fall he started looking for a job, along with Tommy Tillman.

"We'd go down to the state employment agency every day and take a look at what was listed," his cousin recalled. "Skip was funny; he wouldn't try for any of the hard jobs. If we wrote down the name of a company that had a job that he didn't feel qualified for, he wouldn't even go into the place to ask about it. He'd just sit in the car while I went in.

"Or if he did go in some place, he'd just sit and mumble a few words when they'd ask him questions. It was like he felt inferior. He'd give a terrible impression. But once we got back in the car, it was the same old Skip, laughing and joking."

One day in October two military policemen came to his house. His mother saw the uniforms and before opening the door whispered urgently, "What did you do?"

"I didn't do nothing, honest, Ma," he answered.

The M.P.s asked Skip a few questions. They wanted to know what he was doing and if he had been arrested since his discharge. Fifteen minutes after they left, the telephone rang. It was a colonel, calling from the Department of Defense in Washington. Sergeant Johnson was being awarded the Medal of Honor, he said. Could he and his family be in Washington on Nov. 19 so President Johnson could personally present the award?

One week later, on Nov. 19, 1968, they were all there in the White House, Skip tall and handsome in his dress-blue uniform, his mother, Katrina and Tommy Tillman. The President gave a little speech. The national election was over, the Democrats had lost, but there were signs of movement at the Paris peace talks.

"Our hearts and our hopes are turned to peace as we assemble here in the East Room this morning," the President said. "All our efforts are being bent in its pursuit. But in this company we hear again, in our minds, the sound of distant battles."

Five men received the Medal of Honor that morning. And when Sergeant Johnson stepped stiffly forward and the President looped the pale blue ribbon and sunburst medal around his neck, a citation was read that described his valor.

Later, in the receiving line, when his mother reached Skip she saw tears streaming down his face.

"Honey," she whispered, "what are you crying about? You've made it back."

After he officially became a hero, it seemed that everyone in Detroit wanted to hire Dwight Johnson, the only living Medal of Honor winner in Michigan. Companies that had not been interested in a diffident ex-G.I. named Johnson suddenly found openings for Medal of Honor Winner Johnson.

Among those who wanted him was the United States Army.

"The brass wanted him in the Detroit recruiting office because—let's face it—here was a black Medal of Honor winner, and blacks are our biggest manpower pool in Detroit," said an Army employe who had worked with Skip after he rejoined the service a month after winning the medal. "Personally, I think a lot of promises were made to the guy that couldn't be kept. You got to remember that getting this guy back into the Army was a feather in the cap of a lot of people."

Events began moving quickly then for Skip. He married Katrina in January (the Pontchartrain Hotel gave the couple its bridal suite for their wedding night), and the newlyweds went to Washington in January as guests at the Nixon inaugural. Sergeant Johnson began a long series of personal appearances across Michigan in a public relations campaign mapped by the Army.

In February, 1,500 persons paid $10 a plate to attend a testimonial dinner for the hero in Detroit's Cobo Hall, co-sponsored by the Ford Motor Company and the Chamber of Commerce. A special guest was Gen. William C. Westmoreland, Army Chief of Staff and former commander of United States forces in Vietnam.

"Dwight was a hot property back in those days," recalled Charles Bielak, a civilian information officer for the Army's recruiting operations in Detroit. "I was getting calls for him all over the state. Of course, all this clamor didn't last. It reached a saturation point somewhere along the way and tapered off."

But while it lasted, Skip's life was frenetic. Lions Clubs … Rotary … American Legion. Detroit had a new hero. Tiger Stadium and meet the players. Sit at the dais with the white politicians. Be hailed by the black businessmen who would not have bothered to shake his hand before. Learn which fork to use for the salad. Say something intelligent to the reporters. Pick up the check for dinner for friends. Live like a man who had it made.

But Leroy May, the hero's father-in-law, could still see the child behind the man.

"Dwight and Katrina were a perfect match—they both had a lot of growing up to do," he said. "They didn't know how to handle all the attention they got in those early days. They'd go out to supper so much Katrina complained she couldn't eat any more steak. I had to take them out and buy them hot dogs and soda pop. They were just like a couple of kids."

Bills started piling up. "They were in over their heads as soon as they were married," Mr. May said.

Everyone extended credit to the Medal of Honor winner. Even when he bought the wedding ring, the jeweler would not take a down payment. Take money from a hero? Not then. Later, the Johnsons discovered credit cards.

At first they lived in an $85-a-month apartment. But Katrina wanted a house. Skip signed a mortgage on a

$16,000 house on the west side of Detroit. Monthly payments were $160.

In the spring of 1970, he wrote a bad check for $41.77 at a local market. The check was made good by a black leader in Detroit who was aghast that the Medal of Honor winner had gotten himself into a financial hole.

"I went to see him and told him he couldn't go on like this," said the man, a lawyer who asked to remain anonymous. "I said he was young and black and had the Medal of Honor. He could do anything he wanted. I tried to get him to think about college and law school. The black businessmen would pick up the tab. He wouldn't have any part of it."

Looking back on this meeting, the lawyer said he suspected Skip was burdened by a "ghetto mentality" that limited his horizons. His world had been a public housing project and schools a few blocks away. Now, suddenly, events had thrust him outside the security of his boyhood neighborhood into a world dominated by whites.

He was paralyzed, the lawyer speculated, by an inability to formulate a plan of action in this alien culture that he had been transported to by something that happened on the other side of the globe.

"What does he do when he's introduced to Bunkie Knudsen, the president of Ford?" asked the lawyer. "Does he come across strong and dynamic because he knows there is a $75,000-a-year job waiting for him if he makes a good impression? And what happens to him when he just stands there and fumbles and doesn't know if he should shake hands or just nod his head? He was forced to play a role he was never trained for and never anticipated."

Tommy Tillman remembers how Skip would take several friends downtown to the Pontchartrain Hotel for an expensive meal and sit fumbling with the silverware, watching the others to see what fork to use first. "I'd say to him, 'Shoot, man, what do you care? Go ahead and use anything you want.'

"I wondered how he must feel when he's the guest of honor at one of those fancy meetings he was all the time going to."

It was about this time that the stomach pains started.

"It was all that rich food he was eating," said his father-in-law. His mother recalled that "Skip always did have a nervous stomach."

He began staying away from his job as a recruiter, missed appointments and speaking engagements. "It got so I had to pick him up myself and deliver him to a public appearance," said Mr. Bielak. "I had to handcuff myself to the guy to get him someplace. It was embarrassing. I couldn't understand his attitude."

Last summer it was decided that Sergeant Johnson should report to Selfridge Air Force Base, not far from Detroit, for diagnosis of stomach complaints.

From Selfridge he was sent in September to Valley Forge Army Hospital in Pennsylvania. An Army psychiatrist later mulled over his notes on the patient and talked about them:

Maalox and bland diet prescribed. G.I. series conducted. Results negative. Subject given 30-day convalescent leave to 16 October 1970. Absent without leave until 21 January 1971 when subject returned to Army hospital on own volition. Subsequent hearing recommended dismissal of A.W.O.L. charge and back pay reinstated. Subject agreed to undergo psychiatric evaluation. In cognizance of subject's outstanding record in Vietnam, the division's chief psychiatrist placed in charge of the case. Preliminary analysis: Depression caused by post-Vietnam adjustment problem.

In February, Eddie Wright bumped into Skip on a Detroit street.

"Hey, man, where've you been?"

"I just got out of Valley Forge on a pass."

"How things going there?"

"They got me in the psycho ward."

"Huh, you got to be kidding."

"No, man, they think I'm crazy."

During the convalescent leave, Sergeant Johnson borrowed $4,992 from a Detroit credit union. In his wallet he had a cashier's check for $1,500, the back pay the Army had awarded him. Most of his time he spent at home on the pass but when he went out he would drive to the Jefferies Homes and play basketball with the teenagers after school.

"He was a big man down there with the kids," recalled his cousin. "We had all lived in the project and had been on welfare, just like those kids there today, and we were like heroes because we had broken out of there. We had made it to the outside world, and to them we were big successes. We had made it.

"Skip was something special. He had that medal, and they were proud of him. He'd be down there five minutes and the kids would come around and say, 'Hey man, ain't you Dwight Johnson?'"

His old high school crowd was concerned about some of his new friends, though. "They were strung out on drugs, and they just seemed to be hanging around Skip for his money," said his mother. "I asked him one night if he was taking anything, and he rolled up his sleeves and showed me there were no tracks [needle marks]. 'Ma,' he said, 'I'm not taking a thing.'"

On his return to the hospital, he began analysis with the chief attending psychiatrist.

Subject is bright. His Army G.T. rating is equivalent of 120 I.Q. In first interviews he does not volunteer information. He related he grew up in a Detroit ghetto and never knew his natural father. He sort of laughed when he said he was a "good boy" and did what was expected of him. The only time he can remember losing his temper as a youth was when neighborhood bullies picked on his younger brother. He was so incensed grownups had to drag him off the other boys. In general, there is evidence the subject learned to live up to the expectations of others while there was a build-up of anger he continually suppressed.

The Army hospital is actually in Phoenixville, Pa., several miles from Valley Forge. It is the principal treatment center for psychiatric and orthopedic patients in the Northeast, with 1,200 beds now occupied.

Because of the large number of amputees and wheel-chair patients, the hospital has only two floors and is spread over several acres. Long oak-floored corridors run in all directions, connected by covered walkways and arcades. Someone once measured the hospital and found there were seven miles of corridors in a maze-like jumble. To prevent patients from losing their way, wards are painted different colors.

Dressed in hospital blue denims, the warrior-hero walked the labyrinth late at night, wrestling with the problems that tormented his mind and drained his spirit.

"The first day Dwight arrived here, the hospital's sergeant major brought him to us," said Spec. 6 Herman Avery, a tall Negro with a flat face and close-set eyes, who was master of the ward Dwight was first assigned to at the hospital. "It was the first time the sergeant major ever did that. We got the message. This guy was something special.

"Well, practically the first night he's here they dress him up and take him over to the Freedoms Foundations in Valley Forge to shake hands. When he got back he told me that if they ever did that again he would go A.W.O.L."

There was further psychiatric evaluation.

Subject expressed doubts over his decision to re-enter the Army as a recruiter. He felt the Army didn't honor its commitment to him. The public affairs were satisfactory to him at first, but he started to feel inadequate. People he would meet would pump his hand and slap his back and say, "Johnson, if you ever think about getting out of the Army, come look me up." On several occasions he contacted these individuals and they didn't

remember him. It always took several minutes to remind them who he was.

Back in Detroit on leave on one occasion, his mother asked him to drive her to a doctor's appointment. In the office, an off-duty black Detroit policeman, Ronald Turner, recognized the Medal of Honor winner. When he asked for an account of his experience in Vietnam, Skip replied: "Don't ask me anything about the medal. I don't even know how I won it."

Later, the policeman reported Skip complained that he had been exploited by the Army. He told him that ever since he won the medal he had been set on a hero's path as an inspiration to black kids.

Others recalled how upset he had become when his recruiting talks at some black high schools in Detroit had been picketed by militants who called him an "electronic nigger," a robot the Army was using to recruit blacks for a war in Asia.

With his psychiatrist, he began to discuss his deeper anxieties.

Since coming home from Vietnam the subject has had bad dreams. He didn't confide in his mother or wife, but entertained a lot of moral judgment as to what had happened at Dakto. Why had he been ordered to switch tanks the night before? Why was he spared and not the others? He experienced guilt about his survival. He wondered if he was sane. It made him sad and depressed.

Skip signed out of the hospital on March 28 on a three-day pass to Philadelphia. The next day the newspapers and television were filled with reports of the conviction of First Lieut. William L. Calley Jr. on charges of murdering Vietnamese civilians. Skip turned up in Detroit a few days later and never returned to the Army hospital.

He settled in at home once again and dodged the telephone calls from the Army.

"How can you take punitive action against a Medal of Honor holder?" asked a major at the hospital who tried to convince him to return.

The Army did contact the Ford Motor Company, however, which had been letting Skip use a Thunderbird for the past two years. Ford picked up the car on the theory that without it he might be inconvenienced enough to return to the hospital. Instead, he cashed the cashier's check for $1,500, his Army back pay, and bought a 1967 Mercury for $850. He changed his unlisted phone number to avoid the Army callers and a growing number of bill collectors.

By April, his house mortgage had not been paid for the previous nine months, and foreclosing proceedings had been started. He owed payments on his credit union loan.

The car had to go into a garage for brake repairs on Wednesday, April 28, and Skip was told it would cost $78.50 to get it out. The same day, Katrina entered a hospital for removal of an infected cyst, and he told the admitting office clerk he would pay the $25 deposit the next day.

Lonely and depressed at home, Skip telephoned his cousin. "Let's go out and grab some beers," he said. But his cousin was busy.

He made another phone call that night and spoke to a friend in the Army. "I have a story I'm writing and I want you to peddle it for me," he said. "It starts out like this:

"Sgt. Dwight Johnson is dead and his home has been wiped out.…"

On April 30, Skip visited Katrina at the hospital. She said they were asking about the hospital deposit. He left at 5:30, promising to return later that evening with her hair curlers and bathrobe.

"He was just the same old Dwight, just kidding and teasing," his wife recalled. "When he was going, he said, 'Ain't you going to give me a little kiss good-by?' He said it like a little boy with his thumb in his mouth. So I kissed him and he went."

When Eddie Wright got home from work that night about 9 o'clock, he got a call from Skip. He said he needed a ride to pick up some money someone owed him and wanted to know if Eddie could get his stepfather to drive him. He said he would pay $15 for the ride.

Around 11 o'clock, Eddie, his mother and his stepfather picked up Skip at his home. At his direction they drove west for about a mile to the corner of Orangelawn and Prest.

"Stop here," Skip told him, getting out of the car. "This guy lives down the street and I don't want him to see me coming."

The family waited in the car for 30 minutes. They became nervous, parked in a white neighborhood, and as Eddie explained later to the police, it may have looked odd for a car filled with blacks to be parked on a dark street. "So we pulled the car out under a streetlight so everybody could see us," he said.

At about 11:45 a police car pulled up sharply and two officers with drawn pistols got out. "What are you doing here?" they asked.

"We're waiting for a friend."

"What's his name?"

"Dwight Johnson."

"Dwight Johnson's on the floor of a grocery store around the corner," the officers said. "He's been shot.

"I first hit him with two bullets," the manager, Charles Landeghem, said later. "But he just stood there, with the gun in his hand, and said, 'I'm going to kill you.…'

"I kept pulling the trigger until my gun was empty."

Skip's psychiatrist recalled one of the interviews with him.

The subject remembered coming face to face with a Vietnamese with a gun. He can remember the soldier squeezing the trigger. The gun jammed. The subject has since engaged in some magical thinking about this episode. He also suffers guilt over surviving it, and later winning a high honor for the one time in his life when he lost complete control of himself. He asked: "What would happen if I lost control of myself in Detroit and behaved like I did in Vietnam?" The prospect of such an event apparently was deeply disturbing to him.

The burial at Arlington National Cemetery took place on a muggy and overcast day. The grave, on a grassy slope about 200 yards east of the Kennedy Memorial, overlooks the Potomac and the Pentagon, gray and silent, to the south.

The Army honor guard, in dress blues, carried out its assignment with precision, the sixth burial of the day for the eight-man unit, while tourists took photographs at a discreet distance from the grieving family.

For a few days after the burial, the family weighed the possibility that Skip had been taking narcotics in the last few months of his life and the demands of drugs had sent him into the grocery store with a gun. But the autopsy turned up no trace of narcotics.

Eddie Wright and his family were released by homicide detectives after questioning, even after Eddie could not produce any plausible reason why his best friend had carried out a bizarre crime and implicated him at the same time.

The dead man's mother was the only one who uttered the words that no one else dared to speak.

"Sometimes I wonder if Skip tired of this life and needed someone else to pull the trigger," she said late one night in the living room of her home, her eyes fixed on a large color photograph of her son, handsome in his uniform, with the pale blue ribbon of his country's highest military honor around his neck.

Epilogue

It is both ironic and tragic that a growing number of blacks are refusing service in the armed forces. It is ironic because, after seeking the privilege of serving for two hundred years, many blacks have decided it is not such a privilege after all. Instead, military duty at the front has taken on the aura of still another rejection. That is to say, at this time, when the war itself is in such a disfavor, it appears to some that by sending a disproportionate number of blacks into combat zones the army prefers to spare white lives at the expense of black. The tragedy is that many black youths do not feel that America is worth fighting for to begin with.

Some blacks feel strongly enough about discrimination at home to refuse induction altogether, whatever the consequences. A few find the issue a convenient excuse to dodge the draft, but others are truly committed to the pursuit of civil liberty. An example of this attitude is a man by the name of John Otis Sumrall. Sumrall was one of the first blacks to challenge the legality of segregated draft boards. He asked the court to forbid induction or classification of Negroes until the number of Negroes on draft boards was proportional to the local population. His suit also maintained that the Mississippi State Director of Selective Service had personally intervened to have three criminal charges against him dismissed, and that he was called out of turn for induction so as to terminate

his civil rights activities. In August, 1967, he was sentenced to five years in prison and a $2,500 fine for refusing induction. Sumrall asked the question that an increasing number of young blacks are asking today: "If I am not looked upon as an equal citizen in everyday life, why am I looked upon as an equal citizen when it comes time for me to report for induction?" This is a fair question and one which must be answered satisfactorily if further black alienation is to be prevented.

On the other side of the coin, the armed forces, reflecting American society in general, have traditionally been a source of upward mobility, at least for the white population. It is possible, therefore, that the recent top promotions of black men in both the army and navy indicates a belated recognition of the importance of mobility and equality of opportunity within the services—and possibly, just possibly, a reflection of greater opportunity without.

SOURCE: *New York Times,* May 25, 1971. Reproduced by permission.

African Americans
in the Modern Era

From the year 1900 forward, African Americans began to make slow and steady progress toward the goal of becoming full-fledged members of American society. At many times the progress did not seem to consist of many appreciable advances. Given the legacies of slavery and the Deep South, however, African Americans had an extraordinary journey to undertake. If one considers that nine out of ten black Americans still lived in the South at the beginning of the twentieth century, one realizes both how short the relative history of African American social advance has been and just how far African Americans have come in one hundred years.

By the early twentieth century, the age of the explorers of the American West had already largely passed. The buffalo had been cleared from the Great Plains, and the American Indians had been chased from many of the lands where they had settled after having been pushed westward decades before. The early westward migration had begun—not the Hollywood journey of the covered wagons, but the beginnings of the journey that would find

Many black southerners began the Great Migration north on foot. Scenes like these, multiplied by the thousands, emptied the South of agricultural workers in the years before World War II. **FRANKLIN DELANO ROOSEVELT LIBRARY**

its end in the dust bowls and the silent films that would put Los Angeles on the map for the rest of the world.

In Africa and India the age of colonial domination and pillage, along with missionary efforts to convert the indigenous "godless" populations, was still flourishing. In the United States a different sort of colonization—a colonization from within—was emerging out of the poor and miserable circumstances of necessity and migration. African Americans began to leave the South in droves, the bulk departing during two distinct waves, one occurring approximately between 1915 and 1930 and the second in the post–World War II era between 1945 and 1965. Many left for western Texas, Kansas City, the Southwest, and California. Many more traveled north to Chicago, St. Louis, Philadelphia, New York, and Boston. This segment of American history is recorded in the migratory tracks of the spirituals coming out of the southern plantation societies; the evolution of blues, ragtime, and swing into jazz music; and a secondary progression of all these sources into the roots of rock and roll, soul, and—in the last quarter of the twentieth century—rap and hip-hop. While music is by no means the only, or even the principal contribution of African Americans during the twentieth century, it does provide an excellent example of the weave of black American cultural influences within the development of modern American culture.

And this fact is not without its own very particular and powerful significance. The weaving of African and European traditions—the extraordinary confrontation between these two bodies of cultural information—coincides exactly with the rise of the American empire.

If one asks a young child today on the other side of the globe what the word *America* means, the immediate response is likely to be embodied in two names: Michael Jackson and Michael Jordan. While in the writing of serious history, it may be considered glib to try to convey the significance of any period by invoking the name of a popular music entertainer or professional athlete, this reality has special import as far as the story of America and African Americans in the twentieth century is concerned. The migration of African Americans north, and specifically into the great northern American cities, is the story of the rise in the collective fortunes of the United States. Put another way, much as Paris was the great capital city of the world during the nineteenth century, or Rome was considered such two thousand years ago, the eyes of the world turned to New York during the twentieth century. Principal among the reasons for the world's collective fascination with New York were those elements of American culture that were invented by black Americans during a century in which they struggled to gain full membership in the larger American society. ∎

Migration, Industrialization, and the City

ADAPTED FROM ESSAYS BY CARLO ROTELLA, BOSTON COLLEGE

THE INDUSTRIAL CITY

The black migrations from the rural South to the city were part of a larger series of migrations that shaped American urban life. In the late nineteenth century and early twentieth century—the period of most rapid urban industrialization—streams of migrants flowed into American cities from rural and small-town homes all over the nation and from Europe, Asia, and Latin America. These migrants provided both the labor and the demand for more goods and services, thus driving the growth of urban economies, cultures, and governments.

Especially in the North, cities grew to unprecedented size. More and more, they organized their economies around technologically sophisticated factories that used a combination of machines and plentiful labor to mass-produce goods for sale. Cities organized their space around rail lines that carried raw materials, goods, and people to and from factories, commercial districts, and densely crowded residential neighborhoods.

By 1900, northern industrial cities were some of the world's most important centers of manufacturing and trade. Chicago became famous for its railroads and stockyards, Pittsburgh for its steel mills, and New Haven and Hartford for the production of firearms. New York and Philadelphia were known for thousands of small manufacturing concerns, crammed into loft buildings and producing everything from women's clothing to musical instruments. Supplied with labor by European immigrants, the cities of the North industrialized earlier and more quickly than did the cities of the South, where agrarian slavery and the Civil War had slowed industrialization.

Southern blacks did go to southern cities, however, hoping to improve their economic opportunities and social situation. Until about 1920, more southern blacks moved to southern cities than to northern cities. Some

African American women sometimes worked in factories. These black women, photographed in 1919, are weighing giant coils of wire while their white co-worker records the information. Such industrial work first became available to black women during the industrial boom of World War I. It offered higher pay and better working conditions than the domestic labor to which they were often confined. **NATIONAL ARCHIVES AND RECORDS ADMINISTRATION**

stayed on, while others used southern cities as temporary staging areas for the move north.

THE FIRST GREAT MIGRATION: 1916–1929

Following the Civil War, sharecropping arrangements kept black southerners poor and bound to the land, while the rise of Jim Crow made for strict separation of the races and denied blacks access to a citizen's basic protections and privileges—voting, education, a fair wage, and legal recourse. But racial prejudice was not confined to the South. Northern cities were also segregated, and employers in Chicago or New York City would not hire blacks and pay them well as long as there were whites to do the work.

During World War I, however, war in Europe and new immigration laws stopped the flow of European immigrants to the United States just as a wartime boom in manufacturing made it necessary for factories to hire new workers. A wave of black migrants left the South and headed north to find work. They also came hoping to participate more fully in American democracy.

The Regal Theater was located on Chicago's South Side, on South Parkway—now Martin Luther King Drive. This is the theater where Bigger, the hero of Richard Wright's *Native Son,* went to see *The Gay Woman* and *Trader Horn.* Chicago's Savoy Ballroom is down the street. **THE LIBRARY OF CONGRESS**

These interregional migrations followed three broad paths. Residents of the South Atlantic states—especially the Carolinas and Georgia—tended to move up the Atlantic coast into the string of urban centers that runs north from Washington, D.C., through Baltimore, Philadelphia, New York City, Bridgeport, New Haven, Hartford, and Boston. Migrants from Mississippi, Alabama, and the rest of the Deep South followed rail lines north to Chicago, as well as to Detroit, Cleveland, St. Louis, and the other cities of the Midwest. Finally, blacks from Louisiana, Texas, Arkansas, and Oklahoma went west to the growing cities of California, especially Los Angeles. (This third path became more important during the migrations of the 1940s.)

SEE PRIMARY SOURCE DOCUMENT *Last Affair: Bessie's Blues Song by Michael Harper*

CULTURAL CAPITALS: CHICAGO AND NEW YORK

The First Great Migration led to the expansion of black districts in cities across the nation. Between one and two million blacks moved north between 1916 and 1929. During this period, the South Side in Chicago and New York's Harlem became the cultural capitals of black America. Not only did large numbers of migrants gather in these places, creating an urban popular culture of their own; the most celebrated black artists, political and religious leaders, athletes, and intellectuals also gathered in Chicago and New York, producing a renaissance in black music, literature, painting, scholarship, and political thought.

Chicago was the great industrial metropolis of the Midwest, as well as the nation's great railroad hub. Chicago's leading black newspaper, the *Defender*, circulated widely in the South, and the paper's editors urged southern blacks to come work in Chicago's meat-packing plants and railroad yards. Between 1916 and 1919 alone, about sixty thousand southern blacks moved to Chicago, and many more passed through on their way to other destinations.

New York was not only a great industrial center; it was also the main center for the nation's cultural industries—publishing, radio, film, theater, and fine arts. As the formerly Jewish, Irish, and Italian district of Harlem became a black preserve, it also became a symbol of black cultural achievement. Here, W. E. B. Du Bois (1868–1963), James Weldon Johnson (1871–1938), and Marcus Garvey (1887–1940) created new ideas for an urbanizing people. Black and white connoisseurs looked to Harlem as a place of black cultural influence, where they might find innovation in jazz, poetry, sculpture, and dance.

THE SECOND GREAT MIGRATION: 1940–1965

Black migration slowed during the Great Depression of the 1930s, in part because work was no longer plentiful up north. With the outbreak of World War II, however, and the end of the Depression in the early 1940s, there developed another migratory wave much greater than the first. As the nation's industries geared up for wartime production, there was again good work to be found in the North. Reports of race riots and segregation suggested that the North was as racially divided as the South. Even so, southern blacks still looked to the North to deliver on the promise of a better life.

At the same time, industrialization was finally transforming the rural South. The agrarian way of life had always required a plentiful supply of black labor. Now, the mechanical cotton picker and similar devices were drastically reducing the need for farm workers. Mechanized agriculture did not require a large pool of labor. The decline of southern agriculture helped drive blacks to the cities in search of work.

As before, many southern blacks found their way to the growing southern cities, but more than four million of them went north. This Second Great Migration, from the 1940s through the mid-1960s, finally made black Americans a predominantly urban people.

The second migration also led to drastic changes in the geography of urban life. In Chicago, for instance, blacks pushed beyond the old South Side ghetto and settled on the West Side, which had long been divided into Eastern European, Irish, and Italian ethnic neighborhoods. In New York, Harlem could not hold the influx of migrants, and large new black colonies began to transform the old Jewish and Italian neighborhoods of Brooklyn. Similar expansions of the black inner city—and contractions of the old European immigrant districts—occurred throughout the urban North.

City governments sought to control these changes with the construction of public housing. In the 1950s and early 1960s, federal funds and local politics combined to produce massive high-rise housing projects like Chicago's Robert Taylor Homes and St. Louis's Pruitt-Igoe towers (since demolished), to name two notorious examples. These projects and others came to represent the worst aspects of ghetto life—the concentration of poverty, misery, crime, blocked opportunity, and inept government that became synonymous with the word "ghetto" in the 1960s. Ghetto had once meant any immigrant ethnic district. By 1965, it meant the crisis at the intersection of black history and urban history.

SEE PRIMARY SOURCE DOCUMENT *Excerpt from* Manchild in the Promised Land *by Claude Brown*

BLACKS IN A SUBURBANIZING NATION

The black ghetto of the 1950s and 1960s occupied the inner core of a changing urban world. The Second Great Migration made blacks an urban industrial people, but at the very moment when American cities were becoming less industrial and more suburban.

After World War II ended in 1945, America began to reorganize itself as a suburbanized nation. As new waves of southern blacks arrived in the inner cities, piling into the cramped ghettos, government and private enterprise began to invest more and more of their resources in the expanding suburbs. Federal investment in various forms—loans to homeowners, tax breaks for businesses, the construction of highways—helped make it cheaper to move to the suburbs. Even as America's northern cities underwent dramatic suburbanization, they continued to attract millions of black migrants.

In the late 1940s and 1950s, then, there began another migration—this time of jobs, capital, and overwhelmingly white homeowners and taxpayers to the suburbs. Millions of American city dwellers realized a dream of owning property and leaving the industrial city when they moved to the suburbs. Americans now began to think of the suburbs as the place of upward class mobility and prosperity. They also began to think of inner cities as "declining": crowded, dangerous, dirty, fallen from past greatness.

Black city dwellers found it difficult to follow jobs and capital out of the inner cities. Recent migrants from the South had risked everything to get to the city. They had no reserves to finance another move, let alone to buy property. Those who could afford to move—the comparatively small black middle class of teachers, professionals, and highly skilled workers—encountered an array of legal and illegal barriers designed to keep them where they were.

By the 1960s, it was apparent that the inner city could no longer deliver on the promise of plentiful work and social advancement. The movement of manufacturing to other areas—a process known as deindustrialization—had drained away the factory jobs that initially attracted blacks to northern cities. Urban economies gradually changed over from manufacturing to service work. At the higher end of the pay scale, service work involves the processing of information, the kind of work done by lawyers and other professionals, real estate and finance companies, banks, and universities. At the lower end, it involves low-paying nonfactory labor like serving food and cleaning.

Historically, black Americans had always had the least access to the educational training required for high-end service work. Now, with little prospect of reaching the suburbs, they found themselves isolated in disproportionate numbers in inner-city ghettos, in jobs at the low end of the service economy.

THE URBAN CRISIS OF THE 1960s AND AFTER

The stage was set for the urban crisis of the 1960s, when rioting in black ghettos provided a clear sign that blacks had not found what they sought in the American city. That crisis changed the way Americans thought about their cities and their country. Crime and racial conflict became the leading urban issues. In national politics, the Democrats, who had always relied on urban power bases, lost control of the presidency. Race and racism were now no longer a "southern" problem, but an urban one.

Since the 1960s, the South-to-North and country-to-city migrations of blacks have slowed and in some places even reversed. Urban blacks have begun to make significant moves to suburbia. The industrial city has given way to the service city. The urbanizing nation of 1900 has given way to the suburbanized nation at the end of the century. The Great Migrations of southern blacks to the American inner city have subsided, leaving behind a series of artifacts as varied in their meaning as the persistent ghetto, the urban black middle class, and a popular music that rests in large part on the blues.

BIBLIOGRAPHY

Adero, Malaika. *Up South: Stories, Studies, and Letters of This Century's Black Migrations.* New York: New Press, 1993.

Anderson, Jervis. *This Was Harlem: A Cultural Portrait, 1900–1950.* New York: Farrar, Straus & Giroux, 1982.

Barlow, William. *"Looking Up at Down": The Emergence of Blues Culture.* Philadelphia: Temple University Press, 1989.

Brown, Claude. *Manchild in the Promised Land.* New York: Macmillan, 1965.

Brownell, Blaine A., and David R. Goldfield, eds. *The City in Southern History: The Growth of Urban Civilization in the South.* Port Washington: Kennikat, 1977.

Collins, Keith E. *Black Los Angeles: The Maturing of the Ghetto, 1940–1950.* Saratoga: Century Twenty-One Pub., 1980.

Drake, St. Clair, and Horace Cayton. *Black Metropolis: A Study of Negro Life in a Northern City.* New York: Harcourt, Brace, 1945.

Du Bois, W. E. B. *The Philadelphia Negro: A Social Study.* New York: B. Blom, 1967 [1899].

Grant, Robert B. *The Black Man Comes to the City: A Documentary Account from the Great Migration to the Great Depression, 1915–1930.* Chicago: Nelson-Hall, 1972.

Grossman, James R. *Land of Hope: Chicago, Black Southerners, and the Great Migration.* Chicago: University of Chicago Press, 1989.

Harrison, Alferdteen, ed. *Black Exodus: The Great Migration from the American South.* Jackson: University Press of Mississippi, 1991.

Hirsch, Arnold R. *Making the Second Ghetto: Race and Housing in Chicago, 1940–1960.* New York: Cambridge University Press, 1983.

Kiser, Clyde Vernon. *Sea Island to City: A Study of St. Helena Islanders in Harlem and Other Urban Centers.* New York: AMS Press, 1967.

Kusmer, Kenneth. *A Ghetto Takes Shape: Black Cleveland, 1870–1930.* Urbana: University of Illinois Press, 1976.

Lemann, Nicholas. *The Promised Land: The Great Black Migration and How It Changed America.* New York: Knopf, 1991.

Moon, Elaine Lanzman. *Untold Tales, Unsung Heroes: An Oral History of Detroit's African American Community, 1918–1967.* Detroit: Wayne State University Press, 1994.

Osofsky, Gilbert. *Harlem: The Making of a Ghetto.* New York: Harper, 1966.

Palmer, Robert. *Deep Blues.* New York: Viking, 1981.

Rowe, Mike. *Chicago Breakdown.* New York: Da Capo, 1979.

Spear, Allan H. *Black Chicago: The Making of a Negro Ghetto, 1890–1920.* Chicago: University of Chicago Press, 1967.

Trotter, Joe William, Jr. *The Great Migration in Historical Perspective: New Dimensions of Race, Class, and Gender.* Bloomington: Indiana University Press, 1991.

Wright, Richard. *Black Boy.* New York: Harper, 1945.

PRIMARY SOURCE DOCUMENT

Last Affair: Bessie's Blues Song by Michael Harper

INTRODUCTION The poet Michael Harper's tribute to the great blues singer Bessie Smith uses lyrics from a song, "This Is My Last Affair," made famous by another great singer, Billie Holiday. Bessie Smith died in 1937 at the age of forty-three, bleeding to death on a southern road when, after an automobile accident, the ambulance driver refused to take her to the hospital because she was black.

Harper's poem alternates between the scene of Bessie Smith's death and the song lyrics, drawing them together in a single meaning he calls "the same stacked deck": Bessie's death in the Jim Crow South is reflective of the appropriation and transformation of her genius by the segregated music industry of her day. She bleeds to death metaphorically as well as actually, her song becoming "her blood in all-white big bands." The line *"I'm not the same as I used to be"* provides an echoing commentary on the fate of Bessie Smith in particular and of black musical genius in general.

Disarticulated
arm torn out,
large veins cross
her shoulder intact,
her tourniquet
her blood in all-white big bands:
Can't you see
what love and heartache's done to me
I'm not the same as I used to be
this is my last affair

Mail truck or parked car
in the fast lane,
afloat at forty-three
on a Mississippi road,

This picture of a woman and child was taken in a run-down apartment in Washington, D.C., in 1937. Long a focus of black urban migration, Washington continued to attract newcomers from Virginia, the Carolinas, and Georgia during the Depression years. **THE LIBRARY OF CONGRESS**

Two-hundred-pound muscle on her ham bone,
'nother nigger dead 'fore noon:

Can't you see
what love and heartache's done to me
I'm not the same as I used to be
this is my last affair

Fifty-dollar record
cut the vein in her neck,
fool about her money
toll her black train wreck,
white press missed her fun'ral
in the same stacked deck:

Can't you see
what love and heartache's done to me
I'm not the same as I used to be
this is my last affair

Loved a little blackbird
heard she could sing,
Martha in her vineyard
pestle in her spring,

Bessie had a bad mouth
made my chimes ring:

Can't you see
what love and heartache's done to me
I'm not the same as I used to be
this is my last affair

SOURCE: Harper, Michael S. "Last Affair: Bessie's Blues Song," in *Images of Kin: New and Selected Poems.* University of Illinois Press, 1977. Copyright © 1977 by Michael S. Harper. All rights reserved. Reproduced by permission.

PRIMARY SOURCE DOCUMENT

Excerpt from *Manchild in the Promised Land* by Claude Brown

INTRODUCTION Born in Harlem in the late 1930s, Claude Brown, a self-described child of disillusioned urban pioneers, was part of the last great wave of urban migration. He described himself and his people as "sons and daughters of former southern sharecroppers … the poorest people of the South, who poured into New York City during the decade following the Great Depression." There they found the same poverty, violence, and unbearable crowding that had always faced black southerners moving north in search of something better. Growing up in such conditions, Claude Brown at first seemed likely to be just another victim: by the age of nine, he had joined a gang, and by eleven he was lodged in a school for "emotionally disturbed and deprived" boys. Most of his teenage years were spent in a reformatory. Somehow Brown managed to survive and go on to fulfill the promise of his own life.

While a student at Howard University, Claude Brown wrote *Manchild in the Promised Land*. An unflinching portrayal of ghetto conditions, *Manchild* was and continues to be acclaimed as one of the central texts of the Great Migration. Reprinted here are Brown's foreword and the book's opening scene.

A Child of Disillusioned Colored Pioneers

Foreword

I want to talk about the first Northern urban generation of Negroes. I want to talk about the experiences of a misplaced generation, of a misplaced people in an extremely complex, confused society. This is a story of their searching, their dreams, their sorrows, their small and futile rebellions, and their endless battle to establish their own place in America's greatest metropolis—and in America itself.

The characters are sons and daughters of former Southern share-croppers. These were the poorest people of the South, who poured into New York City during the decade following the Great Depression. These migrants were told that unlimited opportunities for prosperity existed in New York and that there was no "color problem" there. They were told that Negroes lived in houses with bathrooms, electricity, running water, and indoor toilets. To them, this was the "promised land" that Mammy had been singing about in the cotton fields for many years.

Going to New York was good-bye to the cotton fields, good-bye to "Massa Charlie," good-bye to the chain gang, and, most of all, good-bye to those sunup-to-sundown working hours. One no longer had to wait to get to heaven to lay his burden down; burdens could be laid down in New York.

So, they came, from all parts of the South, like all the black chillun o' God following the sound of Gabriel's horn on that long-overdue Judgment Day. The Georgians came as soon as they were able to pick train fare off the peach trees. They came from South Carolina where the cotton stalks were bare. The North Carolinians came with tobacco tar beneath their fingernails.

They felt as the Pilgrims must have felt when they were coming to America. But these descendants of Ham must have been twice as happy as the Pilgrims, because they had been catching twice the hell. Even while planning the trip, they sang spirituals as "Jesus Take My Hand" and "I'm On My Way" and chanted, "Hallelujah, I'm on my way to the promised land!"

It seems that Cousin Willie, in his lying haste, had neglected to tell the folks down home about one of the most important aspects of the promised land: it was a slum ghetto. There was a tremendous difference in the way life was lived up North. There were too many people full of hate and bitterness crowded into a dirty, stinky, uncared-for closet-size section of a great city.

Before the soreness of the cotton fields had left Mama's back, her knees were getting sore from scrubbing "Goldberg's" floor. Nevertheless, she was better off; she had gone from the fire into the frying pan.

The children of these disillusioned colored pioneers inherited the total lot of their parents—the disappointments, the anger. To add to their misery, they had little hope of deliverance. For where does one run to when he's already in the promised land?

Opening Scene

"Run!"

Where?

Oh, hell! Let's get out of here!

"Turk! Turk! I'm shot!"

I could hear Turk's voice calling from a far distance, telling me not to go into the fish-and-chips joint. I heard, but I didn't understand. The only thing I knew was that I was going to die.

I ran. There was a bullet in me trying to take my life, all thirteen years of it.

I climbed up on the bar yelling, "Walsh, I'm shot. I'm shot." I could feel the blood running down my leg. Walsh, the fellow who operated the fish-and-chips joint, pushed me off the bar and onto the floor. I couldn't move now, but I was still completely conscious.

Walsh was saying, "Git outta here, kid. I ain't got no time to play."

A woman was screaming, mumbling something about the Lord, and saying, "Somebody done shot that poor child."

Mama ran in. She jumped up and down, screaming like a crazy woman. I began to think about dying. The worst part of dying was thinking about the things and the people that I'd never see again. As I lay there trying to imagine what being dead was like, the policeman who had been trying to control Mama gave up and bent over me. He asked who had shot me. Before I could answer, he was asking me if I could hear him. I told him that I didn't know who had shot me and would he please tell Mama to stop jumping up and down. Every time Mama came down on that shabby floor, the bullet lodged in my stomach felt like a hot poker.

Five South Side Chicago boys, dressed in their Easter suits, posed for this famous photograph in 1941, one of many taken by Farm Security Administration photographer Russell Lee. As the Works Progress Administration provided work for artists and workers during the Depression, so the FSA project kept photojournalists employed recording the lives of ordinary Americans. **THE LIBRARY OF CONGRESS**

Another policeman had come in and was struggling to keep the crowd outside. I could see Turk in the front of the crowd. Before the cops came, he asked me if I was going to tell them that he was with me. I never answered. I looked at him and wondered if he saw who shot me. Then his question began to ring in my head: "Sonny, you gonna tell 'em I was with you?" I was bleeding on a dirty floor in a fish-and-chips joint, and Turk was standing there in the doorway hoping that I would die before I could tell the cops that he was with me. Not once did Turk ask me how I felt.

Hell, yeah, I thought, I'm gonna tell 'em.

It seemed like hours had passed before the ambulance finally arrived. Mama wanted to go to the hospital with me, but the ambulance attendant said she was too excited. On the way to Harlem Hospital, the cop who was riding with us asked Dad what he had to say. His answer was typical: I told him about hanging out with those "bad-ass boys." The cop was a little surprised. This must be a rookie, I thought.

The next day, Mama was at my bedside telling me that she had prayed and the Lord had told her that I was going to live. Mama said that many of my friends wanted to donate some blood for me, but the hospital would not accept it from narcotics users.

This was one of the worst situations I had ever been in. There was a tube in my nose that went all the way to the pit of my stomach. I was being fed intravenously, and there was a drain in my side. Everybody came to visit me, mainly out of curiosity. The girls were all anxious to know where I had gotten shot. They had heard all kinds of tales about where the bullet struck. The bolder ones wouldn't even bother to ask: they just snatched the cover off me and looked for themselves. In a few days, the word got around that I was in one piece.

On my fourth day in the hospital, I was awakened by a male nurse at about 3 a.m. When he said hello in a very ladyish voice, I thought that he had come to the wrong bed by mistake. After identifying himself, he told me that he had helped Dr. Freeman save my life. The next thing he said, which I didn't understand, had something to do with the hours he had put in working that day. He went on mumbling something about how tired he was and ended up asking me to rub his back. I had already told him that I was grateful to him for helping the doctor save my life. While I rubbed his back above the beltline, he

Leaflet from the Chicago Urban League: "Which for Me?"

In concert with articles printed in papers like the *Chicago Defender,* the largely middle-class Chicago Urban League began passing out leaflets as the Great Migration picked up speed during World War I. *Which for Me?* requested that southern migrants adopt behaviors and wardrobes that would bring them in line with people in the North. It also offered the following credo: "I AM AN AMERICAN CITIZEN. I AM PROUD of our boys 'over there' who have contributed soldier service. I DESIRE to render CITIZEN SERVICE. I REALIZE that our soldiers have learned NEW HABITS of SELF-RESPECT AND CLEANLINESS. I DESIRE to help bring about a NEW ORDER OF LIVING in this community. I WILL ATTEND to the neatness of my personal appearance on the street or when sitting in front doorways. I WILL REFRAIN from wearing dust caps, bungalow aprons, house clothing and bedroom shoes out of doors. I WILL ARRANGE MY TOILET within doors and not on the front porch. I WILL INSIST upon the use of rear entrances for coal-dealers, hucksters, etc. I WILL DO MY BEST to prevent defacement of property either by children or adults."

was visiting her son. Her son had been stabbed in the chest with an ice pick by his wife. She said that his left lung had been punctured, but he was doing fine now, and that Jesus was so-o-o good.

Her name was Mrs. Ganey, and she lived on 145th Street. She said my getting shot when I did "was the work of the Lord." My gang had been stealing sheets and bedspreads off clotheslines for months before I had gotten shot. I asked this godly woman why she thought it was the work of the Lord or Jesus or whoever. She began in a sermonlike tone, saying, "Son, people was gitting tired-a y'all stealing all dey sheets and spreads." She said that on the night that I had gotten shot, she baited her clothesline with two brand-new bedspreads, turned out all the lights in the apartment, and sat at the kitchen window waiting for us to show.

She waited with a double-barreled shotgun.

The godly woman said that most of our victims thought that we were winos or dope fiends and that most of them had vowed to kill us. At the end of the sermon, the godly woman said, "Thank the Lord I didn't shoot nobody's child." When the godly woman had finally departed, I thought, Thank the Lord for taking her away from my bed.

SOURCE: Brown, Claude, foreword to *Manchild in the Promised Land.* The Macmillan Company, 1965. Copyright © 1965 by Claude Brown. All rights reserved. Reproduced by permission.

The History of African American Music

ADAPTED FROM ESSAYS BY LORI BROOKS, BEREA COLLEGE, AND CYNTHIA YOUNG

kept pushing my hand down and saying, "Lower, like you are really grateful to me." I told him that I was sleepy from the needle a nurse had given me. He asked me to pat his behind. After I had done this, he left.

The next day when the fellows came to visit me, I told them about my early-morning visitor. Dunny said he would like to meet him. Tito joked about being able to get a dose of clap in the hospital. The guy with the tired back never showed up again, so the fellows never got a chance to meet him. Some of them were disappointed.

After I had been in the hospital for about a week, I was visited by another character. I had noticed a woman visiting one of the patients on the far side of the ward. She was around fifty-five years old, short and fat, and she was wearing old-lady shoes. While I wondered who this woman was, she started across the room in my direction. After she had introduced herself, she told me that she

From the lyrical cries of black street vendors in eighteenth-century Philadelphia to the infectious dance rhythms of the Motown sound, African American music has been heard at all times and in every corner of America. African American involvement in the nation's music making has influenced every genre of American music, helping to create a sound now recognized as distinctly American. Reflecting both the hardships and triumphs black Americans have experienced in the United States, their music has also served to shape the national identity, profoundly influencing the lives of all Americans.

A MUSIC ROOTED IN AFRICA
The first Africans transported to this country came from a variety of ethnic groups with a long history of distinct and cultivated musical traditions. Some were able to bring musical instruments with them or build new ones in this country. The "banja" or "banshaw," now known as

This illustration, which appeared in *Harper's Weekly* in 1861, is somewhat marred by stereotypical representations in its black figures. However, it does indicate the role music and dancing played in the cultural life of enslaved people. Note the banjo, originally an African instrument. **THE LIBRARY OF CONGRESS**

the banjo, was one of the African instruments that continued to be built and played in America. Africans in America also fashioned numerous types of drums and percussion instruments from whatever materials they could gather. Slaveholders, however, eventually discovered that African slaves were using drums to communicate among themselves and by the 1700s, drums had been banned on many plantations.

African American slaves on southern plantations cultivated their own musical styles, which later evolved into gospel, blues, and what is now known as bluegrass and country music. Slave fiddlers often provided dance music for the southern white gentry, and the sound we recognize today as country fiddling is partially the product of the slave fiddler. Most slaves were not allowed to own instruments or could not afford to purchase them. However, using makeshift instruments and their own bodies, they created unique musical ensembles. One of the most pervasive holdovers from African music was an emphasis on rhythm and the use of complex polyrhythms still found in African music.

Over time, many distinct practices and traditions of African music were either forgotten or blended with other musical traditions. Nevertheless, African music continued to flow into the New World as a result of the slave trade, which continued illegally well into the nineteenth century despite its official abolition in 1808.

THE NEGRO SPIRITUAL

One of the most widespread of early musical forms among southern blacks was the spiritual. Neither black versions of white hymns nor transformations of songs from Africa, spirituals were a distinctly African American response to American conditions. They expressed the longing of slaves for spiritual and bodily freedom, for safety from harm and evil, and for relief from the hardships of slavery.

Many of the songs offered coded messages. Some, like "Follow the Drinking Gourd," "Steal Away," and "Wade in the Water," contained coded instructions for escape to the North. Others, like "(Sometimes I Feel like) A Motherless Child" and "I'm Troubled in Mind," conveyed the feelings of despair that black slaves felt. The spirituals also served as critiques of slavery, using biblical metaphors to protest the enslavement of black people. Such protest can be found in the lyrics of "Go Down, Moses":

Go down, Moses
Way down to Egypt land
Tell ol' Pharaoh
Let my people go.

The spirituals also provided African Americans with a means of transcending their enslaved condition, of imagining a life of freedom, as in the lyric, "Ride on, King Jesus, ride on, / No man can hinder thee."

The musician and composer Scott Joplin is widely recognized as the first practitioner of ragtime. He gained national recognition with his "Maple Leaf Rag." **ARCHIVE PHOTOS, INC.**

With the rise of jubilee singers in the 1870s, the spirituals began to be seen as music that revealed the beauty and depth of African American culture. Beginning in 1871, the Fisk Jubilee Singers toured the United States and Europe performing Negro spirituals for white audiences. Until they brought these songs to national and international attention, Negro spirituals were widely considered crude and embarrassing holdovers from slavery. The success of the Fisk Jubilee Singers spawned a number of similar black jubilee singing groups and contributed a sense of pride to many newly emancipated blacks.

In the early part of the 1900s, as a result of the work of black composers, the performance of Negro spirituals became a tradition among black singers, particularly singers of classical music. Composers like Harry T. Burleigh (1866–1949), Margaret Bonds (1913–1972), and Hall Johnson (1888–1970) set the spirituals to piano accompaniment as a means of preserving and perpetuating the beauty of this traditional black music. In the early 2000s, black concert singers such as Jessye Norman and Kathleen Battle continue to perform the composers' arrangements.

THE RISE OF RAGTIME

Ragtime became the first nationally popular form of American music in 1899, when Scott Joplin's (1868–1917) "Maple Leaf Rag" enjoyed unprecedented success, selling over a million sheet-music copies. But ragtime was not new in 1899. Documents reveal that it was being played as early as the 1870s. Black musicians spoke of "ragging a tune" when describing the use of syncopated rhythms, whether in classical compositions, popular songs, or genteel dance tunes. While black musicians could rag tunes on any instrument, the music we call ragtime developed when the piano replaced the violin as the favorite instrument for dance accompaniment.

The standard ragtime piece consists of several different musical ideas, or strains, held together by a main opening theme. The strains, which are often sixteen bars in length, are highly syncopated and alternate with the main theme throughout the piece. The standard left-hand technique of piano rag evolved from the martial rhythms of marching bands, and later, during the early 1900s, it became the basis for the jazz piano style called "stride." Although the rags we hear in the twenty-first century are played at very fast tempos, the traditional ragtime performances were more stately and unrushed.

Ragtime also evolved out of two other musical styles: the "coon song" and the "cakewalk." Coon song was a racist term used to describe the music of white minstrels performing in blackface, in acts that were supposed to be humorous imitations of black slaves. Blackface minstrelsy, a popular entertainment throughout most of the nineteenth century, was at first performed only by whites, though blacks eventually formed their own minstrel troupes. The great blues singer Gertrude "Ma" Rainey (1886–1939) began her career in a black minstrel troupe known as the Rabbit Foot Minstrels, where she was later joined by Bessie Smith (1898–1937). An early form of popular American music, coon songs were written by both black and white composers.

The cakewalk was a stately ring dance performed by blacks during and after slavery. It was accompanied by music that was similar to ragtime and composed by such African Americans as Ernest Hogan (d. 1990), Will Marion Cook (1869–1944), and the musical team of Bob Cole (1868–1911) and Billy Johnson. These artists popularized this style of music and brought it to the Broadway and off-Broadway stages in the late 1800s.

THE BLUES

The blues is perhaps the simplest American musical form and yet also the most versatile. Along with jazz, blues takes its shape and style in the process of performance, and for this reason it possesses a high degree of flexibility. Although certain musical and lyrical elements of the blues can be traced back to West Africa, the blues, like the spiritual, is a product of slavery. When and where did the blues originate? No one can say for sure. We know only that it began in the South during slavery and, in the years following slavery, spread throughout the region as early bluesmen wandered from place to place. One of them, Bunk Johnson (1879–1949), claimed to have played nothing but blues as a child during the 1880s.

As the nation moved into the twentieth century, the blues evolved, borrowing elements from such other musical genres as gospel and ragtime. A "country" style, in which a solo singer accompanied himself on an acoustic guitar, also developed. It was played on the farms of sharecroppers and in honky-tonk gin joints. People brought the music with them into the cities at the dawn of the industrial age. Early blues was an acoustic musical tradition and was invented and performed by literally a handful of itinerant musicians in search of day labor. Much has been made of the pared down qualities of the music. Early practitioners such as Robert Johnson (1911–1938), widely regarded as the father of what we know as "classical blues" today, relied on the immediacy of a powerful vocal performance with a striking rhythmic counterpoint created as much by the body as by the strings of the guitar, to captivate his audiences. The music has powerful alliances with African rhythmic and vocal traditions.

The blues chronicles the migration of African Americans northward; with the move, the music turned from acoustic to electric. Within the stylistic and cultural traditions of the blues the African American experience of alienation, peril, and outright tragedy within American society have come to light. It is an American art form in the end, one that borrows from various threads of artistic expression, be they African, European, immigrant, slave, rural or urban, country or industrial. The music deals with the great themes of western expression: loves that tend toward the unrequited, fates that lean toward the darkly predetermined, spiritual and sexual energies that drive individuals through the business of living, but, most often, without any obvious or particular personal redemption at hand.

The musical structure of the blues is very simple, built upon three main chords. In the standard blues, called the twelve-bar blues, a certain idea is expressed twice in a repeated lyric and then responded to or completed in a third line. As a way of putting his or her own "signature" on a song, a blues singer will at certain points use vocal scoops, swoops, and slurs, imitate sounds of the accompanying instrument (usually a guitar), or add percussive elements to the rendition.

The songwriter W. C. Handy (1873–1958) popularized the blues when he published his "Memphis Blues" in 1912 and the "St. Louis Blues" in 1914. These two songs created an unprecedented vogue for the blues, and their popularity, and the success of those who sang them, carried the blues all over the world. The 1920s are considered the era of classic blues, a style popularized by black women like Ma Rainey, Bessie Smith, Alberta

McKinley Morganfield, a.k.a. Muddy Waters, was a part of the Great Migration north from his native Mississippi to Chicago. He did not begin to record until the late 1940s and, although generally recognized as one of the originators and innovators of the modern blues tradition, did not always receive the fame or financial compensation achieved by his white contemporaries. **ARCHIVE PHOTOS, INC.**

Hunter (1895–1984), and Ethel Waters (1900–1979). The soulful sophistication and haunting beauty of their blues performances were altogether new to American audiences. Bessie Smith, perhaps the most famous of the classic blues singers, epitomized the form's emotional power, while Ma Rainey's singing captured its racy, theatrical side.

During the 1920s, interest shifted from classic blues sung by women to country blues performed most often by men. This "down-home" blues was sometimes performed with banjo, string, or jug band accompaniment, although the favored accompaniment was the guitar. In country blues, the vocal quality was gritty, strained, and nasal, and the voice was "played" in a variety of ways. Singers used falsetto, hummed, and achieved percussive effects using both voice and instrument. Among the best-known country blues singers were Charlie Jackson, Blind Lemon Jefferson, Robert Johnson (?–1938), Blind Boy Fuller (1908–1941), Gus Cannon, and Huddie Ledbetter ("Leadbelly") (1885–1949), who also performed a variety of nonblues folk music.

W. C. Handy (left), often referred to as the "Father of the Blues," popularized the musical genre with his songs "Memphis Blues" and "St. Louis Blues." Handy is shown here shaking hands with bandleader and composer Duke Ellington in 1945. **ARCHIVE PHOTOS, INC.**

"CHICAGO BLUES"

Migration not only changes social order, it also breeds new forms of culture. The history of the blues in the twentieth century provides one example of the link between black migration and cultural change.

Industrialization brought about technological advances in recording, the growth of radio, a black "race record" industry, and the development of large urban black communities with money to spend on music. In response to such changes, blues traditions spread and came into contact with one another. By the 1940s, a rich and thriving national blues culture embraced both rural and urban blacks.

The Second Great Migration from the Mississippi Delta to Chicago in the 1940s produced a new blues form, known as Chicago blues, native to the industrial city. Muddy Waters (1915–1983) became the leading innovator of the new style after he reached Chicago in 1943.

Muddy Waters and his contemporaries—among them Big Bill Broonzy (1893–1958), Howlin' Wolf (1910–1975), Jimmy Rogers, B. B. King (b. 1925), Bobby Blue Bland (b. 1930), John Lee Hooker (1917–2001), J.B. Lenoir, and Willie Dixon (1915–1992)—had been trained in the country style of acoustic guitars and solo performance. Now they built a new urban style around electric instruments and amplification. Electric guitar, harmonica, drums, bass, guitar, and piano were featured in many performances. Chicago blues offered a tight,

"industrial" sound, a hard-edged and hard-driving ensemble sound especially suited to telling musical stories of a country people's adjustment to the industrial city. Chicago blues was part of the distinctive culture—country-rooted but flowering in the city—made possible by the black migration.

In the 1950s and 1960s, Chicago blues became part of the foundation on which contemporary American popular music was built. A generation of younger Chicago bluesmen, led by the guitar players Otis Rush (b. 1934), Buddy Guy (b. 1936), and Magic Sam (1937–1969), provided important musical inspiration for guitar-based rock 'n' roll.

In a curious migration of musical style, a parallel generation of British musicians absorbed Chicago blues from recordings, sometimes note for note. Members of the Yardbirds, the Rolling Stones, Led Zeppelin, Fleetwood Mac, and the Beatles all credited Chicago bluesmen as their musical "fathers." As leaders of the so-called British invasion of the 1960s, they had a profound effect on American popular music.

Chicago blues also contributed to the development of other musical forms. Bluesmen like Magic Sam, Eddie Floyd, and Ike Turner (later to be eclipsed in fame and musical influence by his ex-wife Tina Turner) helped to create styles that in the 1960s became Motown, rhythm and blues, soul, and funk. At the same time, a revival of folk music in the 1960s identified the Chicago blues of Muddy Waters and Howlin' Wolf, and the country blues tradition from which it developed, as important examples of American songwriting and musicianship.

The historical irony of this should be apparent: just as Chicago blues was gaining attention in the 1950s and 1960s, Americans were turning their attention away from the neighborhoods of the inner cities. As American culture made new and important investments in cultural traditions bred by black migration, American government and private enterprise cut back on the attention and resources devoted to the very places where so many black Americans lived.

The ghetto riots of the 1960s came as a surprise to many Americans who had grown up on blues-influenced rock 'n' roll, rhythm and blues, and the blues itself. Their surprise tells us much: in a suburbanizing age, the cities had become invisible, even as the black presence in those cities was exerting a profound influence on every aspect of American life.

JAZZ

Jazz, which has been called "America's classical music," is perhaps the most creative and complex music the nation has produced. Although no one can say for sure where the origins of jazz lie, it combines the musical traditions

Singer Jimmy Rushing and Count Basie performing in 1946. The Count Basie Orchestra, with its strong foundation in blues, was a popular and influential band during the swing era. **ARCHIVE PHOTOS, INC.**

of black New Orleans with the creative flexibility of the blues. By 1918, the term "jazz" was already in wide use. Early jazz performers included the cornetist Sydney Bechet (1897–1959), the pianists "Jelly Roll" Morton (1885–1941) and Eubie Blake (1883–1983), and the bandleader James Reese Europe (1881–1919). Among the earliest ensembles were the Original Dixieland Jazz Band and King Oliver's Creole Jazz Band.

The trumpeter and singer Louis Armstrong (1900–1971) became the first jazz musician to achieve national and international recognition with the success of his "West End Blues" in the 1920s. Armstrong achieved stardom as a cornetist in King Oliver's Creole Jazz Band and went on to form his own ensembles, the Hot Fives and the Hot Sevens, in the 1920s. Armstrong's lyricism and his technical and improvisational finesse pointed the way for many future jazz artists.

In the 1930s and 1940s, the most popular form of jazz was the big-band sound. Ensembles such as Count Basie's

Big Band set the standard for what was known as "swing," a hard-driving, fast-paced sound in which instruments played in close harmony. The Duke Ellington Band, which spanned over half a century, was among the most innovative of the big bands. Its unique sound was characterized by collective improvisation, innovative harmonies, exceptional arrangements, and wide expressive timbres.

The most revolutionary of jazz styles, bebop, was performed by an ensemble significantly smaller than the big band: a rhythm section consisting of piano, string bass, drums, and sometimes guitar, which backed up soloists on trumpet or alto or tenor saxophone. Bebop evolved in the 1940s out of jam sessions held at Harlem clubs such as Minton's Playhouse. Among those who jammed at Minton's were the trumpeter Dizzy Gillespie (1917–1993), the tenor saxophonist Charlie Parker (1920–1955), the pianist Thelonious Monk (1917–1982), the guitarist Charlie Christian (1916–1942), and the drummer Kenny Clarke (1914–1985). Other bebop

John Coltrane apprenticed in the bands of Miles Davis and others. Though his recordings with Davis are considered some of the greatest jazz music ever recorded, Coltrane would continue to seek out new variations of the jazz sound. **AP/WIDE WORLD PHOTOS**

musicians included the bass player Jimmy Blanton, the pianist Bud Powell (1924–1966), the tenor saxophonist Lester Young (1909–1959), and the drummer Max Roach (b. 1925). These performers and others contributed their own characteristic techniques and styles to the sound of bebop. While bebop took up many of the swing standards of the big-band era, its emphasis on improvisation, as well as its new harmonies, changed both the character and color of the old songs.

Bebop set the standard for every style that followed: cool jazz with its modal sound—developed by Lester Young and popularized by the trumpeter Miles Davis (1926–1991), also a bebop musician—as well as the experimental and introspective transformations of the alto saxophonist John Coltrane (1926–1967). In "hard bop," certain bebop trademarks were combined with other musical styles, such as gospel, blues, and rhythm and blues, to produce a "funkier" and more danceable sound. Hardboppers included Max Roach, the pianist Horace Silver (b. 1928), the saxophonists Dexter Gordon (b. 1923), Julian "Cannonball" Adderly (1928–1975), Jackie McLean (b. 1932), Hank Mobley (b. 1930), and Sonny Rollins (b. 1939), and the trumpeters Fats Navarro (1923–1950), Nat Adderley (b. 1931), Clifford Brown

(1930–1956), Donald Byrd (b. 1932), Lee Morgan (b. 1938), and Jimmy Smith (b. 1928).

During the 1960s and 1970s, jazz artists began to experiment with standard chord and scale structures and the rhythms of traditional jazz. The result, often called "free jazz," was an attempt to expand upon the improvisational and experimental aspects of bebop. Among free-jazz artists were Sun-Ra (1914–1993) and his Arkestra, the saxophonists Ornette Coleman (b. 1930), Albert Ayler (1936–1970), and John Coltrane, the bassist Charlie Mingus (1922–1979), and the bass clarinetist and flutist Eric Dolphy (1928–1964).

THE BLUES AND JAZZ

The blues and jazz are unique forms of African American traditional expression that defy the popular belief that in the field of music there are no truly original ideas, only the rehashing of existing traditions. Both musical genres reveal that, within the African American artistic community, there is a drive to create a wonderful "new story."

The unique histories of musical expression on the European and the African continents play a part in this distinction. While the European musical tradition emphasizes performing patterned music written by others, the African musical tradition incorporates improvisation, the nuanced and explosive language of immediate "call" and "response," or "participation," as a basis for great modes of human expression.

Another aspect of African American music that has been celebrated is "happenstance." The novelist Ralph Ellison wrote about his admiration for Louis Armstrong, who had taken the trumpet, what was essentially a military instrument, and then played it in a different way. Armstrong bent the throat of the instrument upward, creating a new sound, then used that as a point of departure for an entirely new mode of expression.

In looking at the blues and its history, a similar pattern of using mistakes and artistic limitations to create something with a unique and new sound can be found. This stands in direct contrast to the western European classical training mode of "correcting" one's mistakes through practice and artistic penance. A whole musical tradition has grown up around this art of happenstance: the slide guitar method came about from some individual who sat drinking and playing, and one night picked up the glass bottle and played the bottleneck on the strings of the guitar. B. B. King speaks of his early formative days, describing his love of the "bottleneck sound." However, when he tried to play it, he found he was unable, and so he evolved his own "trilling" method of creating and sustaining vibrato, which in turn became a part of his signature sound and a part of the blues tradition. Albert King spoke of his inability to master the scales up and down the neck of the guitar as the reason for developing his signature method of bending the strings.

Happenstance enriched the jazz tradition as well. In the first half of the twentieth century, Charlie Parker and Dizzy Gillespie experimented with a complete and exhaustive reworking of the scales—until they found new classical patterns with a new logic. The decades that followed saw hybrids of jazz and numerous other musical traditions, as well as further investigations into the nature of "classical jazz."

CLASSICAL PERFORMERS AND COMPOSERS

While a number of black female concert singers have achieved great popularity during the last fifty years, their success is not altogether new. Their way was paved by earlier classical singers like Elizabeth Taylor Greenfield (1809–1876). The first of the widely known black vocalists, Greenfield made her debut in 1853 in Philadelphia in a recital that was well reviewed in the white press. Other early African American singers, all sopranos, were Nellie Mitchell Brown, Marie Selika Williams, Rachel Walker, and Flora Batson Bergen. Like Taylor, these women were praised for their wide vocal range and the brilliance of their singing.

Their careers were brief, however, and when the vogue for black sopranos ended in the 1890s, most retired from the concert stage. Black concert singers continued to perform before black audiences into the twentieth century, and a few gained wider popularity, among them the contralto Marian Anderson (1902–1993), the soprano Dorothy Maynor (1910–1996), the tenor Roland Hayes (1887–1977), and the baritones Jules Bledsoe (1848–1943) and Paul Robeson (1889–1976).

These performers broke racial barriers for African Americans, perhaps none so powerfully as Marian Anderson, who was described by the Italian conductor Arturo Toscanini as possessing "a voice which one hears once in a hundred years." In 1955, although a white group tried to prevent her from performing, Anderson became the first African American to sing at the Metropolitan Opera. After the 1950s, many other African American classical musicians came to the concert stage: the singers Robert McFerrin (b. 1921) and Leontyne Price (b. 1927), the pianist Andre Watts (b. 1946), and the conductor Michael Morgan.

African Americans have also had a tradition as composers of classical music. The best known black composers from the early part of the twentieth century are Florence Price (1888–1953), R. Nathaniel Dett (1882–1943), Harry T. Burleigh (1866–1949), Margaret Bonds (1913–1972), and William Grant Still (1895–1978) (who has been called the dean of Afro-American composers). The number of African Americans writing classical music has continued to grow with composers like Ulysses Kay (1917–1995), George Walker (b. 1922), Hale Smith (b. 1925), and Olly

Duke Ellington (1899–1974) and the Evolution of American Classical Music

Perhaps no jazz musician so eloquently makes the argument for jazz as American "classical" music as Duke Ellington. Ellington started out as a bandleader, making his name in the culture of the big band nightclubs that had come out of the Roaring Twenties and continued through the 1940s. Like Cab Calloway and Count Basie, he was a bandleader and an entertainer, and he bore not only the economic hardships of a life of musicianship, but also the troubling reality of the white culture that consumed the music he played and the stereotypes they imposed on that music However, as his career progressed it became clear that Ellington was becoming a living repository of both jazz and American popular culture.

Not only did he compose such jazz standards as "Take the A Train," but, like George Gershwin and Irving Berlin, he composed countless show tunes, scores, and—in later years—orchestral numbers and symphonies. Perhaps no individual had a greater range of musical influences at his fingertips, from the roots of jazz in ragtime, swing, and blues, to the history of jazz and jazz-related popular music. Ellington composed startling, nuanced pieces woven out of American music, exhibiting complete command of a palette of sources from Europe, Africa, and the Americas.

Wilson (b. 1937). Many have incorporated jazz and black folk music, such as spirituals, in their compositions.

GOSPEL MUSIC

The sound of today's gospel music also has a long history in African American music, having been influenced by everything from the ensemble performances of the jubilee singers during the late 1800s and early 1900s to the predominantly male gospel quartets and choirs of the 1930s and 1940s.

By the 1930s, Roberta Martin (1912–1969), Sallie Martin, and Thomas Dorsey (a former bluesman who went by the name "Georgia Tom" Dorsey) (1899–1993) had established a religious music whose sound became known as gospel. In the late 1920s, Dorsey began writing religious songs that combined the sustained lyrical quality of the spirituals with the more modern sound of the blues. His signature song, "Precious Lord," set the standard of early gospel music, known for its slow, expressive, almost unmeasured pace. "Precious Lord" was popularized by the singer Mahalia Jackson (1911–1972), the best known of the early gospel singers, famed for her expressiveness and musical interpretation.

Out of the early jubilee ensembles grew the gospel quartets and choirs of the 1930s and 1940s, groups such as the Dixie Hummingbirds and the Clara Ward Singers. Their close harmonies and a cappella singing gave black church music a unique, soulful sound.

Later gospel singers like Shirley Caesar (b. 1938) and James Cleveland (c. 1931–1991) won fame among gospel enthusiasts for their inspirational and creative solos before choirs. Both Caesar and Cleveland excelled in a technique attributed to Willie Mae Ford Smith (1904–1986) called "sermonizing." Sermonizing involved the soloist's spoken narration of a story (usually of spiritual redemption) either before or during the choir's singing. The soloist joined the choir in singing a refrain either during or after the spoken narration, and the song ended climactically with the soloist and choir singing together.

Although gospel music in the early 2000s often sounds similar to other forms of popular music, it still retains its earlier emphasis on vocal embellishment, dramatic power, and a lengthening of the song for the purposes of creating musical tension. In fact, gospel has had a greater historical influence on popular black music than the reverse. Many soul and rhythm-and-blues singers, like Sam Cooke (1935–1964), Aretha Franklin (b. 1942), and Whitney Houston (b. 1963), began singing in black churches and in gospel choirs.

RAP

Rap is the most complex and influential form of hip-hop culture, combining elements of the African American musical tradition (blues, jazz, and soul) with Caribbean calypso, dub, and dance-hall reggae. Two of its earliest innovators were West Indians, DJ Kool Herc and Grandmaster Flash (b. 1958).

The Jamaican DJ Kool Herc was known for using massive speaker systems and multiple turntables to loop "break beats" into an endless groove of dance beats. Like all of the early hip-hop disc jockeys, Kool Herc used beats from all types of music from rock to soul, thus breaking down the artificial barriers between different musical categories. Sometimes he would recite or talk over the beats. This was one of the earliest forms of rapping. To sound-system technology and break beats, the Barbadian

Grandmaster Flash added "scratching," a technique of spinning records back and forth quickly to create new rhythms and unusual sounds.

The addition of "sampling" to Kool Herc's and Grandmaster Flash's original innovations catapulted rap into musical prominence. Samplers are computers that can digitally duplicate sounds in any key, pitch, or sequence. With samplers, rap producers like Hank Schocklee can reproduce and rearrange anything from a television sitcom theme to a Beethoven symphony. The resulting "samples" can then be woven into rap music to create a multilayered background for rap lyrics.

Rapping is related to the African American tradition of "toasting," a boastful form of storytelling that is usually political in content and aggressive in style. Early rappers worked with disc jockeys to heighten an audience's excitement. They often competed against one another, using their verbal skill and poetic dexterity to "battle" each other.

Rap's subject matter varies. Many rappers tell tragic tales of decaying neighborhoods, vicious murders, and police brutality. Others celebrate black history, black families, and black communities, or they brag of their successes in the bedroom, on the streets, and in the record studio. Women rappers like Queen Latifah (b. 1970) and Yo-Yo complicate these subjects by celebrating female empowerment. In telling their ghetto-centric tales, male and female rappers make use of both American and black popular culture, drawing on characters from blaxploitation films like *Superfly,* gangster films like *Scarface,* and television series like "The Cosby Show." Above all, rap lyrics consistently attack economic and political inequalities, waging a full-scale assault on the institutions that keep most African Americans in poverty. The combination of gritty urban storytelling and beat-driven, technologically sophisticated music keeps hip-hop on the cutting edge of musical innovation.

Since rap exploded into the mainstream in the mid-1980s, it has generated many different schools and styles. Local crews have become regional posses: the West Coast rap style of Ice T, Ice Cube, and Snoop Doggy Dog has battled for ascendancy over the original East Coast style of Run D.M.C., KRS-One, and Gang Starr.

The political content of rap music took a leap forward when the rap group Public Enemy burst onto the music scene in the late 1980s, forging lyrics and performances that made staged high-art entertainment out of the alienation of African Americans and the history of militancy. With a wild, uncanny sense for theatrics and tight, powerful beats, the group produced albums with titles like "It Takes a Nation of Millions to Hold Us Back" and "Fear of a Black Planet."

The rap group Public Enemy, made up of Chuck D., Flavor Flav, and Professor Griff (left to right between men in camoflauge), entertained while preaching a strong message of pride in African American culture and resistance to oppression. (Photograph by Edie Baskin.) © NORMAN NG FOR EDIE BASKIN/OUTLINE PRESS SYNDICATE, INC./CORBIS-BETTMANN

The concerts and videos the group produced for the 24-hour music stations featured them working in syncopation with squads of dancers performing in various military-type uniforms. The imagery recalled the Nation of Islam's clean-cut black suits and ties of the Malcolm X period and gave voice to the latent rage of African Americans. At the same time, Public Enemy sold millions of records to the teenagers and angry middle-class white suburban youths that they were, in a sense, working against. In the early 2000s, Public Enemy, the original "prophets of rage," has been upstaged by "gangsta rap-

pers," whose violent tales of gang murders and the gun trade are set against a backdrop of inner-city decay.

More than ever before, women rappers are challenging male rappers' sexist lyrics and using rap lyrics to define an independent black female identity. For example, Queen Latifah, Salt 'N' Pepa, MC Lyte and Eve criticize men who abuse and manipulate women. At the same time, they redefine the terms on which black women establish relationships with black men. Music video stations like Music Television (MTV) and Black Entertain-

The End of the Age of Exploitation

Perhaps no one is more indicative of the explosion of African American entertainers in the last quarter of the twentieth century than Michael Jackson (b. 1958). While, of course, Motown and other trends created a range of artists who were successful pop entertainers in the 1950s, 1960s, and 1970s (including, of course, the Jackson 5), the so-called "King of Pop" for many represented a new kind of African American pop music star. Like Elvis, the "King" before him, Michael Jackson's music appealed to all segments of society, selling millions and millions of records worldwide. While earlier artists were notoriously undercompensated for their work, Jackson became one of the richest entertainers in the history of music entertainment. At the same time, Jackson's career has been pursued by an endless stream of controversy. Given the undying curiosity and controversy that follows the star, like no other perhaps, the King of Pop personified both the opportunities and the fracturing psychological demands of being a superstar of color in the United States in the late twentieth century.

ABOVE: One of the most popular and most controversial musical artists of the twentieth century, Michael Jackson sold millions of records and led an occasionally bizarre personal life that was the subject of much speculation. **AP/WIDE WORLD PHOTOS**

been involved in America's popular music. The first known American musical group to travel abroad was a Philadelphia band led by a black man, Francis "Frank" Johnson (1792–1844). From the early to the mid-1800s, the Frank Johnson band performed military and dance music for white and black Philadelphians and toured the United States and England as well. In the early twentieth century, blues and jazz musicians provided entertainment and dance music for much of America.

Each innovation in African American popular music has been influenced by what came before. The rise of rhythm and blues in the 1950s was directly influenced by early gospel music and urban blues, particularly a style of music popularized by Louis Jordan (1908–1979) called "jump blues." The singers Chuck Berry (b. 1926) and Little Richard (b. 1932) transformed urban blues and into what became known as rock 'n' roll, perhaps the most popular musical style ever invented. In the 1950s and 1960s, record companies like Motown and Stax recorded numerous groups and soloists whose work left a lasting mark on American musical taste. Rooted in the Motown sound, artists such as Stevie Wonder (b. 1951) and Marvin Gaye (1940–1984) transformed it into a music called "soul."

Even those black artists whose music has been experimental and innovative have their roots in traditional black music. The rock guitarist, singer, and songwriter Jimi Hendrix (1942–1970) began his career in a rhythm and blues band, transforming the blues with a "psychedelic," highly amplified, and improvisational guitar sound. Despite its emphasis on improvisation and experimentation, however, Hendrix's music retained a blues sound.

Tracy Chapman's (b. 1964) folk sound reminds its listeners of Nina Simone's (b. 1933) rich tones and smoky vocals. Bobby McFerrin's (b. 1950) unique instrumental use of his voice harkens back to the a cappella gospel quartets, to jazz instrumentalists and vocalists like Louis Armstrong (1900–1971) and Billie Holiday (1915–1959), and to scat vocalists like Ella Fitzgerald (1918–1996), and it draws as well upon West African and Caribbean rhythms.

Thus, while black musicians always seem to be creating something new, their work remains firmly rooted in the long tradition of African American music.

BIBLIOGRAPHY

Bayles, Martha. *Hole in Our Soul: The Loss of Beauty and Meaning in American Popular Music.* New York: Free Press, 1994.

Berlin, Edward A. *Ragtime: A Musical and Cultural History.* Berkeley.: University of California Press, 1980.

Courlander, Harold. *Negro Folk Music, U.S.A.* New York: Columbia University Press, 1969.

ment Television (BET) have also helped propel female rappers into the spotlight, bringing their less aggressive style to a mainstream audience interested in tales of love rather than terror.

AN EVOLVING TRADITION OF POPULAR MUSIC

From the early slave fiddlers to the black minstrel troupes and beyond, African Americans have always

Dent, Gina ed. *Black Popular Culture: A Project by Michele Wallace.* Bay Press: Seattle, 1992.

Feather, Leonard G. *The Jazz Years: Earwitness to an Era.* New York: Da Capo Press, 1987.

Fordham, John. *The Sound of Jazz.* New York: Gallery Books, 1989.

Friedwald, Will. *Jazz Singing: America's Great Voices from Bessie Smith to Bebop and Beyond.* New York: Charles Scribner's Sons, 1990.

Gammond, Peter. *Scott Joplin and the Ragtime Era.* New York: St. Martin's Press, 1976.

Haralambos, Michael. *Right On: From Blues to Soul in Black America.* New York: Da Capo Press, 1979.

Johnson, James Weldon Johnson and J. Rosamond. *The Books of American Negro Spirituals.* New York: Viking Press, 1942.

Jones, Leroi (Imamu Amiri Baraka). *Blues People: Negro Music in White America.* New York: William Morrow, 1963.

———. *Black Music.* New York: William Morrow, 1967.

Keil, Charles. *Urban Blues.* Chicago: University of Chicago Press, 1966.

Lovell, John. *Black Song, The Forge and the Flame: The Story of How the Afro-American Spiritual Was Hammered Out.* New York: MacMillan, 1972.

Morse, David. *Motown and the Arrival of Black Music.* New York: MacMillan, 1971.

Oliver, Paul. *Conversation with the Blues.* New York: Horizon Press, 1965.

Palmer, Robert. *Deep Blues.* New York: Viking Press, 1981.

Rose, Tricia. *Black Noise: Rap Music and Black Culture in Contemporary America.* Wesleyan University Press: Hanover, 1994.

Rublowsky, John. *Black Music in America.* New York: Basic Books, 1971.

Southern, Eileen. *The Music of Black Americans: A History.* New York: W. W. Norton, 1971.

Stanley, Lawrence A. ed. *Rap: The Lyrics to Rap's Greatest Hits.* Penguin Books: New York, 1992.

African American Folklore and Folkways

ADAPTED FROM ESSAYS BY EDWARD PAVLIC, UNIVERSITY OF WISCONSIN

The African American folk tradition, like any folk tradition, is by nature communal, the creation and expression of a group rather than an individual. Through their folk traditions, communities maintain connections with the past as they change over time, in this way making ancestral wisdom and practices available in the present.

In its concepts, materials, and performance styles, the African American folk tradition conserves West African philosophical and artistic traditions at the same time that it adapts those traditions to the changing circumstances of North American life. Through mass media and marketing, both at home and abroad, it also has a tremendous cultural impact in mainstream America and beyond.

WHAT'S AFRICAN ABOUT AMERICAN?

Because African American culture is the product of adaptation and combination, there is no single African heritage to be found in African American folkways. As early as 1619, with the arrival of the first Africans in Jamestown, West African folk traditions began to combine with one other in North America—Hausa with Yoruba, Wolof with Igbo, Akan with Bakongo.

In this process of combination, general principles have become fundamental African American cultural precepts: for example, Yoruba *itutu,* a state of personal coolness facilitating productive conversation and cooperation, has evolved into the African American imperative "Keep your cool." In their performance names, the contemporary rappers Ice-Cube, Ice-T, Just-ice, Kool G Rap, Kool DJ Red Alert, Kool Mo Dee, LL Cool J, Chill Will, Doug E. Fresh, and Chuck Chillout, among others, pay honor to this Yoruba principle. Miles Davis's (1926–1991) 1949 jazz initiative "Birth of the Cool," along with his signature sunglasses, or "shades," honors the Yoruba conception of "shade" as a cool place where one builds communal relationships.

African words as well as concepts have taken their place in the tradition. The multipurpose African American term "funky" derives directly from the Bakongo term *lu fuki,* which denotes the smell of a worker who has contributed to the common good through labor. The original definition has been expanded to include any behavior that undergirds the distinctive folk identity of African American people. The Yoruba phrase for the act of talking back and forth between people, *ise sise* (pronounced "ee-say-she-shay"), sounds too much like the phrase "he say she say" to be a coincidence. The African American expression "dig it" has its origins in the Wolof term *dega,* meaning "to understand."

Both the Wolof dega and the Yoruba itutu are featured in Langston Hughes's short poem "Motto":

I play it cool
And dig all jive.
That's the reason
I stay alive.

My motto,
As I live and learn,
is: *Dig And Be Dug
In Return.*

(Poem: Langston Hughes, from "Motto," in *Montage of a Dream Deferred,* 1951. Copyright © 1951. All rights reserved. Renewed copyright © 1979 by Langston Hughes. Reproduced by permission.)

Miles Davis (1926–1991), Jazz Innovator

In a genre that includes such legends as Charlie Parker, Dizzy Gillespie, Thelonious Monk, and John Coltrane, Miles Davis is regarded by many as history's greatest practitioner of jazz music. He had the rare ability to identify, perfect, and enhance the best of what performers throughout the years had to offer. In addition, in spite of an ongoing problem with drugs, Davis proved to be a brilliant businessman and bandleader, anticipating—or rather instigating—each new trend in the musical scene.

For many blacks in the late 1940s and the 1950s, Davis's image loomed even larger than his music. Early photos of Davis with his polished, "cool" demeanor and his back to the audience had a very specific meaning for African Americans living in the United States, where "colored only" water fountains were the norm in the South and where black culture was mainly fetishized in the North. At a time in history when economic and cultural realities for blacks were abysmal, Davis, in addition to achieving stardom and respect, presaged black power and the turmoil of the years to come. As he made his music, he did not hesitate to express with words and actions what he really felt about those who were consuming it.

ABOVE: Miles Davis was famous for his aloof posture before the press and the white public that adored his music. **AP/WIDE WORLD PHOTOS**

The connections are fascinating and unending, and combinations are still being forged. In addition to such terms and concepts, many other West African folkways persist in African American culture, again in combined forms, in cooking, burials, weddings, hair styles, and adornment.

AFRO-CHRISTIANITY

In Haiti, Cuba, Brazil, and other places in the Americas where Africans outnumbered Europeans, many West African religious systems remained nearly intact. But in North America, apart from fairly remote communities in the Georgia and South Carolina Sea Islands, the ratio of Africans to Europeans was reversed. For this reason, West African religions soon combined with Christian, mainly Protestant, forms of worship, producing distinctly African American versions of Christianity.

This process is known as syncretism. It occurs when traditions are combined, or mapped onto each other, allowing for the adjustment and adaptation to new communal experiences—for example, the experience of chattel slavery. By the process of syncretism, African communities in North America began to link their experiences to biblical narrative, adapting stories from the Bible to reflect their own bondage and longing for freedom.

The Afro-Christian spiritual "Go Down Moses" clearly maps slave experience onto biblical narrative in the thinly masked folk expression: "Go down Moses, down to Egypt land, and tell old Pharaoh to let my people go." The traditional spiritual "Mary" offers similar counsel: "Mary don't you weep, tell Martha not to moan, 'cause Pharaoh's army drowned in the Red Sea." Other spirituals that combine biblical narrative with slave experience include "Daniel and the Lion's Den" and "Joshua Fit the Battle of Jericho" ("and the walls come tumblin' down"). Deeply influenced by what has been called the "kinetic orality" of West African spirituality, these "syncretic moments" attest to the collective spiritual vision generated by African American folklore.

African American religious syncretism was not limited to eighteenth- and nineteenth-century plantation life or to rural southern or Christian settings. In the mid-1930s, in response to racist conditions in the urban North, Elijah Muhammad (1897–1975) would begin to forge a similarly syncretic hybrid of Islam and black nationalist politics, offering in the Nation of Islam an uncompromising separatist invocation of Islamic belief that attracted many followers. The power of this syncretic faith produced one of the most compelling and well known "folk intellectuals" in the history of the African diaspora, Malcolm X, or El-Hajj Malik El-Shabazz (1925–1965).

The Nation of Islam's call to reevaluate Christianity's relevance to African American life was not new, however. It is heard in many of the early folk tales in which heaven is satirized as a "white" place where the practices of segregated racist America will continue in deified form. The African American folk tradition has always kept a flexible attitude toward—and a critical eye on—the combinations and conversions whereby new African identities have been formed in America.

Romare Bearden (1914–1988) and African American Collage

Romare Bearden is often referred to as a consummate craftsman and color theorist who takes his roots from the lessons of the cubists. In the 1960s, Bearden, anticipating the collage aesthetic of the 1970s and 1980s, created a wholly unique and transforming visual language. He is credited with bringing Realism into the realm of the Cubistic, rendering images out of cut pieces of newspaper, magazine, and hand-painted bits of cloth and paper that made complex jumps in their visual language between various sources, sizes, and color schemes. Essentially, Bearden created an art that captured the dizzying experience of the modern urban life, and specifically that of African Americans thrust into a world of symbols contradicted by hard, flat realities.

While Bearden sought to express universal truths, referencing the mythologies of the Western tradition and playing with the accepted norms of an art world that looked toward Europe even as it tried to find its own way, his collages refer to other tradi-tions as well. The artist's jumbles of figures, arms, legs, and heads dance within the African rhythmic traditions of call and response. His reworking of Western themes in a language wholly apart, vivid, and undeniably attractive and disturbing brings to mind the ferocity with which jazz and swing appro-priated all stylistic devices and norms that lay in their path—all the while singing in a mode that could not be mistaken for its source. His sudden monochromatic square expanses (as in the painting *Black Manhattan*) place the viewer in a discomfort-ing extreme of negative space that immediately recalls the poverty, hardship, and nagging discon-tent that are a continual presence for the poor in the urban ghettos of the North.

For many, Bearden is also credited as one of the first African American artists to gain significant recognition within the mainstream white and Euro-pean art world. His work is in private collections and museums around the world.

TRICKSTERS ALL: FROM JOHN TO TUPAC

West-African trickster motifs play an important role in sto-rytelling traditions in African American culture. The Akan trickster figure, Anansi, appears in diaspora tales under a variety of names, from Hanansi in Jamaica, to Miss Nancy in South Carolina, to Boy Nasty in the Bahamas.

These and other African American tricksters, including Brer Rabbit, are direct descendants of the tricksters in West African lore, but with a twist. One of the primary threats to well-being in West African com-munal societies was fragile or hostile relationships among their members. The role of the West African trickster—Akan Anansi, the Yoruba Esu-Elegbara, and others—was to test the honesty of communal relation-ships and their ability to resolve conflict. By instigating trouble among community members (often represented by a variety of animals—lion, tiger, monkey, and so forth), the trickster brought the community together, for only by establishing communication with each other are they able to discover the source of their predicament. Although the trickster figure was typically punished for his deeds at the story's end, his "trick" served to test and solidify community relationships.

This sequence changed as African communities in America faced new circumstances. When the tales were mapped onto the racist power dynamics of plantation slavery, the trickster's skills in language—his quick, improvised speech—became more of an asset to the community, and his role evolved into that of defending the community against an outside threat. The trickster adversary of West African lore—problematic but neces-sary to communal survival—now became the trickster as kinsman. The ambivalent attitude in African American culture toward outlaws, now present most visibly in "gangsta rap" music, is derived in part from this shift in the West-African worldview and folktale tradition from trickster as adversary to trickster as kinsman.

Brer Rabbit is a version of the trickster as kins-man, working his magic against physically more pow-erful animals such as bear, fox, and wolf, who obvious-ly represent the master in plantation life. The classic African American folk hero John the slave takes up Brer Rabbit's role in postbellum plantation folktales. Shedding the animal disguise, John matches his wits against the power of Master, or "Marse," in ostensibly good-natured duels.

The folk hero Stagolee carries the tradition into the twentieth century, as does the urban practice of "toasts," long narrative poems in rhymed couplets that frequently enact the same exploits as those of John or Brer Rabbit, but in the phrasings of contemporary urban America. As the mask continues to change, the critique of the "master's" power becomes more open: the exploits of Tupac Shakur, Chuck D and Public Enemy, KRS-1, and other socially "conscious rappers" bring the problematic trickster as kinsman role into contemporary African American folklore.

BAD, MEANING GOOD

To conclude where we began, in language itself, the terms that describe the most profoundly "black" moments of African American culture all bridge the boundary between "good" and "evil," the same boundary that the trickster straddles. Like West African trickster lore, African American folkways assume that good things can be produced by bad or evil-seeming actions. The simple division of the world into good and bad, white and black, male and female—what Ralph Ellison called "the basic dualism of the white folk mind"—never describes the complex forms of African American folk culture, which typically combine categories that are commonly understood as separate. For this reason, African American folk products are often stigmatized as "crude," "vile," "lewd," or "vulgar," and its folk heroes must live with one foot on each side of the boundary. But the tradition accepts, even prizes, this seeming affliction, making it a part of itself.

With one foot in each dimension, spiritual and physical, earth and beyond, good and evil, African American folk heroes walk with the trickster's limp, the signature of the Yoruba's Esu-Elegbara himself. In contemporary African American urban folklore, they move with the gangsta's limp: one foot in the world of the trickster as kinsman, with each step enacting their rebellion against white norms of behavior and style, one foot in the world of the West African trickster adversary, challenging the community, especially the women, on whom they occasionally prey.

The audience is involved as well, describing such figures in terms marked with cautious envy and respect. African American folk heroes are not just "good" or "special." They are "bad," "fierce," "vicious," "dope," "stupid," and, in the name of Anansi himself, "nasty"—all terms of honor that express the complex mix of envy and caution associated with many powerful African American folk figures.

Mainstream American media are often condemned for constructing dangerous and demonized images of African Americans. This is true from a certain point of view. But complexity is a necessary vehicle for carrying on West African folk traditions in America, and from this point of view, the mainstream media appear to simplify African American reality, creating safe heroes and role models out of the would-be trickster as kinsman.

The African American folk tradition resists such simplification, however, constantly creating new styles and performances that mainstream American vocabulary cannot fully explain, express, or contain. In its unapologetic, radical combinations of American reality and West African–based sensibilities, it continues to assert the full complexity of African American identity, at the same time exerting a powerful influence on all American identities.

BIBLIOGRAPHY

Abrahams, Roger D. *Deep Down in the Jungle: Negro Narrative Folklore from the Streets of Philadelphia.* Chicago: Aldine Publishing, 1970 .

Courlander, Harold. *A Treasury of Afro-American Folklore.* New York: Crown Publishers, 1976.

Dundes, Alan, ed. *Mother Wit from the Laughing Barrel: Readings in the Interpretation of Afro-American Folklore.* Englewood Cliffs: Prentice-Hall, 1973.

Goss, Linda, and Marian E. Barnes, eds. *Talk That Talk: An Anthology of African-American Storytelling.* New York: Touchstone, 1989.

Hughes, Langston, and Arna Bontemps, eds. *Book of Negro Folklore.* New York: Dodd, Mead, 1958.

Hurston, Zora Neale. *Mules and Men.* Philadelphia: J. B. Lippincott, 1935.

Jackson, Bruce. *"Get Your Ass in the Water and Swim Like Me": Narrative Poetry from the Black Oral Tradition.* Cambridge: Harvard University Press, 1974.

Levine, Lawrence W. *Black Culture and Black Consciousness: Afro-American Folk Thought from Slavery to Freedom.* New York: Oxford University Press, 1977.

Pelton, Robert D. *The Trickster in West Africa: A Study of Mythic Irony and Sacred Delight.* Los Angeles: University of California Press, 1980 .

Spalding, Henry D., ed. *Encyclopedia of Black Folklore and Humor.* New York: Jonathan David Publishers, 1978.

Thompson, Robert Farris. *Flash of the Spirit: African and Afro-American Art and Philosophy.* New York: Vintage, 1983.

The African American Literary Experience

ADAPTED FROM ESSAYS BY EMILY BERNARD, SMITH COLLEGE

In 1746, a sixteen-year-old girl wrote "Bars Fight," a poem about a recent Massachusetts Indian raid. Little did she know that her poem would start a tradition that would continue to the present day.

What is most unusual about this anecdote is not the gender or age of the protagonist, but her race. Lucy Terry (1733–1821) was an African American and a servant, who lived during a period in which it was against the law in many places for blacks to read and write. Although the poem itself is unfamiliar to us today, the incident speaks to the larger meaning of African American literary history. Lucy Terry was the first in a long tradition of African Americans who would create a voice where there was none, taking what was denied them by law and making it their own.

AFRICAN AMERICANS WRITING IN THE 1700s

The eighteenth century was the time for most of the "firsts" in African American literary history. Jupiter Hammon's (ca. 1711–1800) poem "An Evening Thought: Salvation by Christ with Penitential Cries" was published in 1760. Phillis Wheatley (1753–1784) published almost fifty poems before she died at the age of thirty in 1784. In 1773, she published the first volume of poetry by an African American, *Poems on Various Subjects, Religious and Moral.* **SEE PRIMARY SOURCE DOCUMENTS** *A Poem for a General, by Phillis Wheatley, and His Response* and *"An Address to the Negroes of the State of New York" by Jupiter Hammon*

The tradition of African American autobiographical narrative began in the eighteenth century with the works of writers like Venture Smith, John Marrant, Olaudah Equiano and Briton Hammon (no relation to Jupiter Hammon), whose 1760 *Narrative* is considered the first slave narrative. Its full title indicates an attitude toward slavery common among eighteenth-century black writers: *A Narrative of the Uncommon Sufferings, and Surprizing Deliverance of Briton Hammon, a Negro Man … How He Was Cast Away in the Capes of Florida; the Horrid Cruelty and Inhuman Barbarity of the Indians in Murdering the Whole Ship's Crew; and the Manner of His Being Confined Four Years and Seven Months in a Close Dungeon; and the Remarkable Manner in Which He Met with His Good Old Master in London, and Returned to New-England, a Passenger in the Same Ship.*

Critics have complained that Wheatley's poetry does not denounce the institution of slavery or even her own situation as a servant. They claim that she had no unique creative voice and was capable only of imitating the popular white poets of the period. While these criticisms have merit, it is important that we not judge these early black writers by the standards of the early twenty-first century. If you look at them through the lens of their own time, what you see is the remarkable fact that they learned to read and write at all in a society that used every means to keep them ignorant.

A CENTURY OF STRUGGLE REFLECTED IN LITERATURE

In the nineteenth century, black writers began to use their creative powers to respond to the brewing political and racial tensions around them in poetry, novels, and autobiographies. Ideas about the innate inferiority of the darker races began to creep into everyday thought and forced black writers to take a stand. African American writers now had a dual purpose: to tell their stories and to convince a hostile white audience that they deserved human rights.

Producing a written literature was difficult, mainly because of the laws that made literacy among African Americans illegal. Despite this impediment, African American literature developed during this period at an incredible rate, much of it by fugitive slaves who learned to read and write only after their escape from slavery. William Wells Brown was one such writer. In 1853, he published the first African American novel, *Clotel, or The President's Daughter,* a frankly abolitionist reworking of the legend of Thomas Jefferson's slave children.

The most important literary genre produced in the nineteenth century was the slave narrative. Autobiographical portraits of slave life, these works were produced for two reasons. First, they meant to educate primarily white audiences about the horrors of slavery. Second, by their very existence, they challenged the stereotype that African Americans were inhuman, and thereby worthy of enslavement. The challenges these narratives took on were not abstract: at the time of publication of these documents, African Americans were seen as only three-fifths human in the eyes of the law.

The two best known and perhaps most important nineteenth-century slave narratives are Frederick Douglass's (1817–1895) *Narrative of the Life of Frederick Douglass, an American Slave* (1845) and Harriet Jacobs's (1813–1897) *Incidents in the Life of a Slave Girl, Written by Herself* (1861). The similarities between these works are clear to anyone who reads them.

Both narratives are powerful, written by remarkably gifted storytellers. Both detail the horrors experienced by the writers during their lives in slavery. In each narrative, the writer is focused on a single goal, the achievement of freedom, and both Douglass and Jacobs manage complicated but ultimately successful escapes. Their stories are full of the atrocities of slavery—physical, mental, and emotional abuse—and both comment on the hypocrisy of the slave system in the Christian South, and the destruction of the African American family. Both narratives are careful to point out that slavery degrades not only the enslaved, but the enslaver as well. They instruct their readers that, as long as the system remains intact, no one will escape injustice.

Perhaps most importantly, Douglass and Jacobs labored under an identical pressure that would affect African American writers throughout the nineteenth and twentieth centuries: to tell at the same time both the story of one and the story of the group. While the strug-

The Poet Paul Laurence Dunbar (1872–1906)

Paul Laurence Dunbar was born in Ohio, the son of a fugitive slave. He died in 1906 after suffering for seven years with an incurable illness. Though he lived a mere thirty-three years, Dunbar was a prolific writer and poet. His published works include four novels, six volumes of poetry, and a number of collections of short stories, but he is best known for his poetry.

Dunbar is considered by many to be one of the greatest African American poets of the early twentieth century. His poetry exhibits a gift for creating verses that feel true, simple and beautiful. Dunbar was the father of African American "vernacular" poetry, creating verses that celebrate who and what African American peoples are in their own language.

ABOVE: This photograph shows poet Paul Laurence Dunbar as a young man. Born in 1872, the child of a free father and a woman who had once been enslaved, Dunbar earned early fame with his slavery-based poems in black "dialect," though he often expressed annoyance with a public that ignored his verse written in standard English. **THE LIBRARY OF CONGRESS**

gles of African Americans have changed since the days of slavery, what remains is the black writer's struggle with the question of how to represent the race to what is still a majority white reading audience.

Despite their similarities, there are significant differences between Douglass's and Jacobs's narratives having to do with the different genders of the writers, which affected the way they experienced slavery and the way they later wrote about it. For instance, Douglass sees slavery as both physical and mental bondage. He writes with the same vibrancy about his physical escape from slavery and his efforts to learn to read. To Frederick Dou-

glass, physical freedom means nothing without an accompanying liberation from the bonds of ignorance and illiteracy.

Harriet Jacobs also learned to read and write, but in contrast to Douglass, this experience is not the focus of her narrative. Her primary quest has to do with motherhood and her determination to provide for her children. In fact, at the end of her narrative, Jacobs reminds her reader that she does not consider herself totally free because she does not yet have a home for her children. Men and women had significantly different responses, therefore, even to the homogenizing experience of slavery.

CREATING A MODERN AFRICAN AMERICAN LITERATURE

As the twentieth century approached, African American literature took another turn. Between 1890 and 1920, more African American writers than ever before were born free. This period, which followed on the heels of Reconstruction, was also a time when blacks suffered an alarming amount of racial violence and many legal setbacks.

Still, black writing somehow flourished and produced three important writers: Paul Laurence Dunbar (1872–1906), Charles Chesnutt (1858–1932), and Frances E. W. Harper (1825–1911). All three were exceptionally gifted, yet they could not have used more different techniques.

Dunbar and Chesnutt used the vernacular styles that were popular during that time. The works for which they are best known are written in black "dialect." Both writers were interested in exploring other forms, but found that their white audience demanded stories and poems from them that were comforting and not threatening. Critics have found fault with these two writers for choosing to placate their white audiences. The fact remains that their choices were severely limited, if, indeed, a choice existed for them at all as African Americans writing at a time when African American literature was still more of a dream than a reality. **SEE PRIMARY SOURCE DOCUMENT** *"We Wear the Mask" by Paul Laurence Dunbar*

Any discussion about nineteenth century–black writing would be incomplete without mention of the life and work of Frances E. W. Harper (1825–1911). Unlike most African Americans during this time, Harper was born free and even had the benefit of an education. Aside from this, Harper's life is a prime example of the black writer during the nineteenth century. She saw her work as essentially political. She wrote to move people and published her poetry for a mass audience. Harper traveled widely and gave speeches on topics like temperance and women's rights.

Until recently, it was believed that Harper was the first black American woman to write a novel: *Iola Leroy, or Shadows Uplifted,* which was written in 1892. In 1983, however, *Our Nig, or Sketches from the Life of a Free Black,* a novel written by Harriet E. Wilson (c. 1808–1870) in 1859, was discovered.

TWENTIETH CENTURY AFRICAN AMERICAN LETTERS

The birth of twentieth-century African American literature came with the publication of the fictional *Autobiography of An Ex-Coloured Man* (1912), an anonymously published story presented as a true autobiography. By the time the identity of its author, James Weldon Johnson (1871–1938), was made known by the reissuing of the book in 1927, Johnson was already well known for his political and cultural work. In fact, Johnson was serving as U.S. consul to Nicaragua during the time when he wrote the *Autobiography.* Aside from the *Autobiography,* Johnson is best known for his poetry, particularly the poem "Lift Every Voice and Sing," which is known as the black national anthem.

No figure had more impact on twentieth-century African American literature than W. E. B. Du Bois (1868–1963). He was himself no great creative writer; the novels that he wrote were mediocre at best. Du Bois's great passion was nonfiction. His autobiographical writings, editorials, and books bear the mark of his strong political vision. His book *The Souls of Black Folk* puts forth his famous argument that "the problem of the twentieth century is the problem of the color line."

Du Bois may not have produced much creative work in his lifetime, but his opinions on it were definite. He believed that art should serve a political and social purpose for black people. Because of the economic, political, and social disadvantages that African Americans faced, he did not feel that the time was appropriate for blacks to produce art for art's sake. According to him, art should contribute to "racial uplift."

Writers of the 1920s debated, praised, and lambasted Du Bois's ideas about the purpose of black art. Everyone who had an opinion shared it in print and public forums. Some, like Langston Hughes (1902–1967), resisted Du Bois's ideas and believed that art was to be appreciated on aesthetic and not political grounds. Others fell in step with Du Bois and admonished black writers to present the black community in a positive light. Single-handedly, Du Bois started an argument that continues to rage in black literary circles in the early twenty-first century.

Some historians write that the Great Depression devastated Harlem and the entire outpouring of creative expression, but the truth is that there has never been a period when black artists did not make their mark. Still, the stock market crash of 1929 and the ensuing Depres-sion did have a negative effect on black art. Neither black nor white patrons had the money to buy art, hear musicians, or see plays as they had during the affluent Roaring Twenties. As a group, black people were hit hard by the Great Depression.

The hope that inspired the Great Migration was shaken by the economic hard times of the 1930s, and much of the literature that African Americans produced during this period reflected that shift. Many of the successful Harlem Renaissance writers nonetheless continued to produce work during the 1930s. James Weldon Johnson and Countee Cullen (1903–1946), for example, both published books of poetry. It was also the decade in which Zora Neale Hurston (1891–1960) would produce most of her work. She published the remarkable *Their Eyes Were Watching God* in 1937.

The transitional period of the 1930s gave way to the birth of social realism in African American fiction in the 1940s, also known as protest literature. While the fiction of earlier decades was often backward-looking, either romanticizing or denouncing a southern rural past, the fiction of the 1940s faced the problems of the present.

At this moment in history, large numbers of black people had migrated to urban areas, where they struggled with the harshness of the new American cities and the ghettos. Richard Wright (1908–1960) signed his name on the literary movement of social realism with the publication in 1940 of *Native Son,* which describes the degradation experienced by one person in this new urban environment. Implicitly, Wright took his stand in the war of ideas first waged during the Harlem Renaissance by creating a protagonist who has no interest in "racial uplift."

Wright and Ann Petry (1911–1997), author of the 1946 novel *The Street,* used fiction to explore the effects of the urban environment on the individual, showing how the depravity of the slums works to destroy a person's moral fiber. An important African American writer of the period who does not fit this profile is Dorothy West (1909–1998), whose novel *The Living is Easy,* published in 1948, describes the lives of black Boston aristocrats. Her work resembles that of writers of earlier times, like Charles Chesnutt (1858–1932), as well as the Harlem Renaissance novelists Nella Larsen (1891–1964) and Jessie Fauset (1882–1961).

Protest literature novelists realistically portrayed the migration north to cities, horrific lynchings, and the economic hardship that many African Americans endured during the period. But while Petry, Wright, and Chester Himes (1909–1984) were documenting harsh urban realities in stark, often ungraceful prose, some of their peers chose a completely different venue: the medium of poetry.

African American Women Writers: Zora Neale Hurston (1891–1960), Gwendolyn Brooks (1917–2000), and Rita Dove (b. 1952)

The works of Zora Neale Hurston, Gwendolyn Brooks, and Rita Dove have taken African American letters into the upper echelons of world literature, often by tapping into the core of the African American experience in the United States.

In many ways the legacy of twentieth-century African American women writers begins with Hurston and her landmark novel *Their Eyes Were Watching God.* A writer of the Harlem Renaissance period and a contemporary of figures like Richard Wright, Hurston established the path that would guide the work of black women writers throughout the century. Brooks, born in Topeka, Kansas, in 1917, was the first African American to win the Pulitzer Prize in poetry. Her remarkable collections

Writers like Gwendolyn Brooks (1917–2000), Robert Hayden (1913–1980), and Margaret Walker (1915–1998) virtually created African American poetry during this period; their work was both racially conscious and structurally complex. Gwendolyn Brooks won the Pulitzer Prize in 1949 for her collection of poetry *Annie Allen,* becoming the first African American to do so.

The 1950s witnessed the emergence of even more memorable writers and, through them, new genres. This period is famous for producing the one novel of the late Ralph Ellison (1914–1994). *Invisible Man,* published in 1952, is a richly woven and deeply allegorical tale about one man's disillusionment with American culture. To many, *Invisible Man* is *the* story of the American experience, with its descriptions of alienation and yearnings for selfhood that characterize not only African American literature, but American literature as a whole. *Invisible Man* won the National Book Award in 1952. **SEE PRIMARY SOURCE DOCUMENT** *Excerpt from* Invisible Man *by Ralph Ellison*

This period also witnessed some of the most important essays and drama produced by African Americans in the work of James Baldwin (1924–1987) and Lorraine Hansberry (1930–1965). James Baldwin was a gifted novelist, but he is best known for bringing the genre of

the essay to American society in the 1950s. Essayists had made their mark in American society before Baldwin, but not since the days of Du Bois had anyone written so eloquently, and with so much passion, power, and knowledge, about the state of American race relations. At a volatile time in American history, Baldwin spoke for African Americans, explaining to the surrounding world their anger, aspirations, and disappointments with American society. Baldwin's novels and plays were equally powerful, and opened the eyes of all who came into contact with them.

In 1959, American theatergoers wept while viewing Lorraine Hansberry's play *A Raisin in the Sun,* whose title derived from a poem by Langston Hughes (1902–1967). Hansberry's drama told the remarkable story of an ordinary African American family whose different generations try to make sense of each other in politically turbulent and emotionally wrenching times. The play won the New York Drama Critics' Circle Award. More importantly, it expressed the experience of an African American woman where it had rarely been seen before: on the American stage.

The increased racial strife of the late 1950s and 1960s brought a response from the black literary world. Lorraine Hansberry, James Baldwin, and Gwendolyn

of verse exemplify the maturation of the African American poetic tradition. Put simply, Brooks was not only a master of diverse traditional forms—ballads, sonnets, and a range of free verse styles—but also an innovator of those forms. She managed to bring the black American experience, in all of its dialectic and colloquial nuance, to her work, creating poems that came out of America and African America, yet feel immediately "classical" in their scope and balanced impact.

The poet Rita Dove also works in the traditions of verse. Dove exemplifies the best of the African American poetic tradition, while moving forcefully into new poetic landscapes—both in terms of her subject matter and her style. Her work demonstrates an exquisite sensibility, each line seemingly possessed with a silent, mournful grandeur that at once invites the reader in and keeps them at bay, treating them as strangers, rife with the potential for danger. The poet laureate's 1986 book *Thomas and Beulah* is

loosely based on the lives of her grandparents, black southerners who migrated north during the first years of the twentieth century. Although Beulah was just an infant when her family moved, her future husband, Thomas, was already a young man when he came north on a Mississippi riverboat. Haunted by memories of his southern upbringing, Thomas experiences northern life as a kind of exile from a land that was for him both bitter and sweet.

In the worlds Dove creates everyday events, the words of relatives and ancestors, narrations of history, and even the private interchanges between the poet and her daughter make for ethereal metaphors, compound collages of image and word that evoke the mad flurry of information, racial and otherwise, that constitutes life in the late twentieth century.

LEFT: Gwendolyn Brooks is the author of numerous books of poetry, including the Pulitzer Prize–winning *Annie Allen,* published in 1950. She was named Poetry Consultant to the Library of Congress in 1985. **THE LIBRARY OF CONGRESS**

Brooks, among others, felt the need to take a strong political stand in American society. Hansberry and Baldwin served as spokespersons for the cause of civil rights; Brooks chose to support the more radical Black Power Movement.

SEE PRIMARY SOURCE DOCUMENT *"Bitter Fruit of the Tree" by Sterling Brown*

The Black Arts Movement, the cultural wing of the Black Power Movement, dominated this period in African American literary history. In many ways, this movement closely resembled the Harlem Renaissance forty years earlier. In both, a new breed of writers sought to establish their identities in contrast to an earlier generation that had produced what they called "false" art, enslaved to the opinions of a mostly white reading public.

The Black Arts Movement went farther than the Harlem Renaissance in attempting to distance itself from American society. These writers broke literary conventions in both prose and poetry and sometimes even used their own versions of the English language. To ensure that their work would not be manipulated by whites, Black Arts leaders established their own publishing houses, bookstores, and magazines to showcase their art.

Writers in this period believed that black art suffered when it was influenced by white society.

Influential writers of this period include Ishmael Reed (b. 1938), author of several novels and collections of poetry; Amiri Baraka (b. 1934), also known as LeRoi Jones, a playwright, poet, and essayist; Ntozake Shange (b. 1948), a playwright, poet, and novelist; and Nikki Giovanni (b. 1943), a poet and essayist.

Baraka organized the Black Arts Theatre in Harlem in 1964, which was devoted to presenting the best of the creative work being produced by movement writers. He won an Obie award for the best off-Broadway play of 1964 for *The Dutchman.* Baraka, like James Baldwin and W. E. B. Du Bois, had strong convictions about what black writers should be doing for black people, and he shared those ideas through his essays and his creative work. Like many of his peers, Baraka believed that art was intimately linked to politics. Indeed, he believed that art could lead or at least aid in the liberation of black people from both external and internalized subjugation.

African American women writers of this period were just as concerned with politics as their male counterparts. They knew, however, that the oppression they experienced had as much to do with gender as it did with

LeRoi Jones (Amiri Baraka) founded the Black Arts Repertory Theater in 1964, ushering in the black arts movement. Baraka is also known for his poetry, which is complex, thoughtful, searing, and beautiful. He has published numerous volumes of verse and drama, including the award-winning play *The Dutchman,* which takes its title from the 1619 arrival of captive Africans in Jamestown, Virginia. **CORBIS-BETTMANN**

race. Representative women writers of this period were Nikki Giovanni, Alice Walker (b. 1944), and Ntozake Shange. Shange's *for colored girls who have considered suicide, when the rainbow is enuf* was at once praised for its emotional power and literary merit and condemned for its depiction of black men. If the late 1970s and early 1980s were the era when black women told the stories of their oppression, then it also marked the first great rift between black male and female writers. The powerful work of these women came under fire from their black male peers, who felt that their representations of black men were unfair and cruel. Alice Walker's *The Color Purple,* for instance, was lambasted and mocked by writers like Ishmael Reed, who believed that black women writers were gaining unfair attention because their portraits of black men fit society's stereotypes.

If African American literature of the late-twentieth century is sardonic about the present, perhaps this is because it is haunted by the past. It is still trying to explain the brutal and unforgivable history of black people in this country, a history that is warped by continuous oppression.

Important themes do not die, and neither do certain genres. For instance, the autobiography, once a means for African Americans to testify to their status as human beings, is still a vehicle through which many African American writers choose to express themselves. Perhaps the most significant contemporary autobiographer, Maya Angelou (b. 1928), has gone back into her past to produce a four-volume biography, which begins with *I Know Why the Caged Bird Sings* (1969). In the tradition of all great African American autobiographers beginning with the authors of slave narratives, Angelou tells the story of the group through the individual, creating a sense of community and kinship in her narratives.

Into the twenty-first century, African American writers have claimed most of the prizes awarded for literature in this country. However, that hardly means that African American literature has done all it can do. African American literature grows and changes, just like the experiences of the people who make it. One thing that remains constant, however, is that the primary aim of this literature is to make sense of a shared history among African Americans in this country.

African American literature has come a long way since it took its first steps in 1746 through the medium of Lucy Terry's poetry. But no matter how it changes, it will always be asked to be true to the experiences, in all of their complexity, of black Americans, as they continue to create and understand themselves through their literature.

CONTEMPORARY AFRICAN AMERICAN LETTERS

The last quarter of the twentieth century produced a range and breadth of talented black writers unlike any time before. In addition to the African American literary traditions of the personal narrative and the protest novel, African American authors mined black humor, satire, historical memoir, and a very particular and powerful brand of North American "magical-realism," a response to the dark realities of African American disenfranchisement that drew upon South and Central American literary counterparts such as Gabriel Garcia Marquez (b. 1928) and Julio Cortazar (1914–1984).

One particularly encouraging element defined black writing at the close of the twentieth century. As opposed to being in any way limited to a single narrative thread or tradition, African American writers began to draw on anything and everything that might give voice to the nuances of their personal experience and artistic vision. For example, the novelist John Edgar Wideman (b. 1941) has worked in a range of modes, melding the protest tradition with family history and social commentaries; his novels include *Brothers and Keepers, Philadelphia Fire,* and *Fever,* and he has won many of

African American Novelist Toni Morrison (b. 1931)

The author Toni Morrison has taken the African American and American experiences and culled from them what are now regarded as some of the greatest novels of the twentieth century. Morrison worked for years as an editor in a New York publishing house before coming out with her first novel. Among the titles to her name are *Song of Solomon, Sula, The Bluest Eye, Beloved* (winner of the 1988 Pulitzer Prize), *Jazz,* and *Paradise.* In 1999 Toni

Morrison was awarded the Nobel Prize for literature, joining the most elite ranks of novelists and poets in the world.

On the surface, her subject matter is that of black women, the struggle for identity and the human bonds that make the shape of our daily realities. However, her novels have used these as vehicles to get at even larger concerns. As an author in the New World, Morrison is driven by the ghosts of history and the crimes and the motivations of the people who inhabit that land. At its best, Morrison's writing manages to give a voice and a tangible reality to the twisted legacy of slavery in the United States, the impact of the "peculiar institution" and its various permutations on the psychological landscape of Americans throughout the centuries. This is coupled with an ongoing study of the drive and will of African Americans, and the private implications of that daily battle for identity.

ABOVE: Toni Morrison has become one of the most lauded authors of the late twentieth-century, winning virtually all the major national literary awards, including the Nobel Prize for literature in 1999. **AP/WIDE WORLD PHOTOS**

the most prominent national and international awards for writing. The work of Charles Johnson (b. 1948) seeks to rewrite history, examining slave life, an imaginary journey in the Middle Passage, and the life of Martin Luther King Jr. However, Johnson tells his stories in a fantastic light, far from the traditional realism of the protest novel and social critique. They feature phantasmal and literally "inhuman" slave catchers and an omnipotent, multifaced African God boxed up in the hold of a ship on the dreaded Middle Passage. This magical realism vein also appears in the works of Toni Morrison, though it is in a stylized language belonging entirely to the author and giving a particular identity to the African American psycho-historical experience very different from the "magical-realism" works of South and Central American writers. In novels like *Sula, Song of Solomon, Beloved,* and *Paradise,* Morrison turns the slights of history, the troubled ghosts of the American slave past, and the efforts of her lead characters to invent themselves in a world that has made no room for their

identities into the very real flesh and blood protagonists of the worlds they inhabit, side by side with a living past. It is perhaps this vision of American life, of a nation forever working to forget its most shameful acts and forever being forced to confront them within the uneasy specters of personal loss, family life, murder, death, and remembrance, that earned Toni Morrison the Nobel Prize for literature at the close of the twentieth century. The poet Derek Walcott also earned the Nobel Prize for literature in the last decade of the twentieth century. His poetry contains a sweeping, balladic expression of the New World, at once intimate with the material, daily existences and private languages of people living in New World landscapes and aware of the implications and histories that they carry quietly with them.

Perhaps one of the most important turns in the history of African American letters came about in the last two decades of the twentieth century. Whereas black writers had before been limited to the tradi-

Henry Louis Gates Jr. comes out of the traditions of the earliest black intellectuals. A scholar, educator, and public figure who has held positions at Yale, Cornell, Duke, and Harvard Universities, Gates has earned recognition for his contributions to African American studies. His celebrated published works, many of which spotlight the impact of African American writing on American culture, include *Black Literature and Literary Theory,* which he edited, and *Loose Canons: Notes on the Culture Wars* and *Thirteen Ways of Looking at a Black Man,* both of which he wrote. (Photograph by Jerry Bauer.) **©JERRY BAUER**

tions of protest and social satire, for the first time the publishing industry came to recognize the market for a more popular novelistic tradition, giving voice to a handful of authors whose sales are on a par with their more mainstream counterparts. That said, this contemporary African American literature still bears the mark of the satirical work of the 1960s and 1970s. Writers like Reginald McKnight (*I Get On the Bus,* 1990), Trey Ellis (*Platitudes,* 1988), and Darius James (*Negrophobia,* 1992), choose to tell the story of African American history with sharp and pointed wit. Their works use humor to point out the absurdities and hypocrisies in American culture, to make readers aware of the inanities that cause discrimination and racism. On the other side of the gender line, the 1980s and 1990s saw a slew of satirical, "self-empowerment" novels from authors like Terry McMillan (b. 1951), who turned their sights on the troubled lives of black women who spend the twentieth century raising children, holding down jobs, and loving men who appeared to be caught in a form of

ongoing adolescence. Selling millions of copies, these novels went on to be made into feature films. All of this points in the direction of a changing literary tradition, as well as to elements of black culture—warts and all—that are continually entering the mainstream of American life.

BIBLIOGRAPHY

Andrews, William L., ed. *Six Women's Slave Narratives.* New York: Oxford University Press, 1988.

———, ed. *Classic Fiction of the Harlem Renaissance.* New York:Oxford University Press, 1994.

Angelou, Maya. *I Know Why the Caged Bird Sings.* New York: Random House,1969.

Baldwin, James. *Go Tell It on the Mountain.* New York: Dell, 1981.

———. *The Price of the Ticket: Collected Non-Fiction, 1948–1985.* New York: St. Martin's/Marek, 1985.

Baraka, Imamu Amiri (LeRoi Jones). *Dutchman and the Slave: Two Plays.* New York: William Morrow, 1964.

Baraka, Imamu Amiri (LeRoi Jones), and Larry Neal. *Black Fire: An Anthology of Afro-American Writing.* New York: William Morrow, 1968.

Bontemps, Arna, ed. *Great Slave Narratives.* Boston: Beacon Press, 1969.

Chesnutt, Charles W. *The Conjure Woman and Other Conjure Tales.* Durham: Duke University Press, 1993.

Douglass, Frederick. *Narrative of the Life of Frederick Douglass, an American Slave, Written by Himself.* New York: New American Library, 1968.

Du Bois, W. E. B. *The Souls of Black Folk.* New York: New American Library, 1969.

———. *The Seventh Son: The Thought and Writings of W.E.B. Du Bois.* New York: Random House, 1971.

Dunbar, Paul Laurence. *The Collected Poetry of Paul Laurence Dunbar.* Charlottesville: University of Virginia Press, 1993.

Ellis, Trey. *Platitudes.* New York: Vintage, 1988.

Ellison, Ralph. *Invisible Man.* New York: Random House, 1952.

———. *Shadow and Act.* New York: Random House, 1964.

Hansberry, Lorraine. *A Raisin in the Sun.* New York: Signet, 1988.

Harper, Frances E. W. *Iola Leroy, or Shadows Uplifted.* New York: Oxford University Press, 1988.

Harper, Michael, and Anthony Walton. *Every Shut Eye Ain't Asleep: An Anthology of Poetry by African Americans since 1945.* Boston: Little, Brown, 1994.

Hayden, Robert. *Collected Poems.* New York: Liveright, 1985.

Hughes, Langston. *The Langston Hughes Reader.* New York: G. Braziller, 1958.

———. *The Collected Poems of Langston Hughes.* New York: Alfred A. Knopf, 1994.

Hurston, Zora Neale. *Mules and Men.* Bloomington: Indiana University Press, 1978.

———. *Their Eyes Were Watching God.* New York: Perennial Library, 1990.

Jacobs, Harriet. *Incidents in the Life of a Slave Girl, Written by Herself.* Cambridge: Harvard University Press, 1987.

James, Darius. *Negrophobia: An Urban Parable.* New York: Carol Publishing Group, 1992.

Johnson, Charles. *Oxherding Tale.* Bloomington: Indiana University Press, 1982.

Twentieth Century African American Poets: Jay Wright (b. 1935), Michael Harper (b. 1938), Rita Dove (b. 1952), and Derek Walcott (b. 1930)

Derek Walcott, Jay Wright, Michael Harper, and Rita Dove have not only worked within poetic traditions, mastering and redefining them like their forbears, but they are also innovators, creating some of the most powerful and original work in American letters today.

In the work of Jay Wright, for example, it is sometimes hard to find any sort of overt reference to what the readership might recognize as "African American literary concerns." Wright's poems are concerned with investigations of the entire psychohistorical terrain of the New World. His works find the invention—or uncovering—of identity in corners of experience ranging from day-to-day American life to Spain to South and Central American. They are all a part of the "weave" of experience that informs the poet. The poetry of Michael Harper ranges from explosive "stream of consciousness" explorations of the psyche and personal wounds that are contained in the experience of living as a black man in the United States, to a kind of new poetics of African American vernacular. These passages at once refresh the work of past poets, such as Paul Laurence Dunbar, and explode the model, taking the "heartsick" experience of black America and elevating it to the realm of the great literary expositions. In his later work, the poet turned to long-form verses that are in one sense "free verse," and in another sense, minutely controlled by underlying rhythmic and vocalic concerns. The poems in *Healing Song for the Inner Ear* and *Honorable Amendments* read almost as elegies for a private African American existence.

Although she is the youngest of the poets here, Rita Dove's place in the canon of the African American poetic tradition seems assured. Her work possesses that same subtle concern for the qualities of the words, a rhyming far beyond simple concerns of the phonetic. While she works out of the African American tradition, her palette is the world and all of history.

This "diasporic" rendition of history, identity, and personal experience is also at the heart of the work by Derek Walcott. Winner of the Nobel Prize for literature in the late 1990s, Walcott has himself not so much reinvented the forms as exploded them. His roaming, balladic investigations, as in *The Star-Apple Kingdom* and *Omeros,* seek to write through the entirety of literary and world history, collapsing them into the idiosyncrasies of the poet's tongue, with the masterpieces of the original bards, Homer and Shakespeare as his models.

————. *Middle Passage.* New York: Atheneum, 1990.

Johnson, James Weldon. *The Autobiography of an Ex-Coloured Man.* New York: Vintage, 1989.

Lewis, David L., ed. *The Portable Harlem Renaissance Reader.* New York: Viking, 1994.

Morrison, Toni. *Song of Solomon.* New York: Alfred A. Knopf, 1977.

————. *Beloved.* New York: Alfred A. Knopf, 1987.

Mullane, Deirdre. *Crossing the Danger Water: Three Hundred Years of African-American Writing.* New York: Doubleday, 1993.

Osofsky, Gilbert, ed. *Puttin' on Ole Massa: The Slave Narratives of Henry Bibb, William Wells Brown, and Solomon Northup.* New York: Harper & Row, 1969.

Petry, Ann. *The Street.* Boston: Beacon Press, 1985.

Reed, Ishmael. *Flight to Canada.* New York: Random House, 1976.

————. *Poems: New and Collected.* New York: Atheneum, 1988.

Shange, Ntozake. *for colored girls who have considered suicide, when the rainbow is enuf: a choreopoem.* New York: Collier Books, 1989.

Shockley, Ann Allen. *Afro-American Women Writers, 1746–1933.* New York: Meridian, 1988.

Walker, Alice. *The Color Purple.* New York: Harcourt Brace Jovanovich, 1982.

————. *In Search of Our Mothers' Gardens: Womanist Prose.* San Diego: Harcourt Brace Jovanovich, 1984.

Walker, Margaret. *This Is My Century: New and Collected Poems.* Athens: University of Georgia Press, 1989.

West, Dorothy. *The Living Is Easy.* London: Virago Modern Classics, 1987.

Wheatley, Phillis. *The Collected Works of Phillis Wheatley.* New York: Oxford University Press, 1988.

Wilson, Harriet E. *Our Nig, or Sketches from the Life of a Free Black.* New York: Random House, 1983.

Wright, Richard. *Uncle Tom's Children.* New York: Harper & Row, 1965.

———. *Black Boy: A Record of Childhood and Youth.* New York: Perennial Library, 1966.

———. *Native Son.* New York: Perennial Library, 1987.

PRIMARY SOURCE DOCUMENT

A Poem for a General, by Phillis Wheatley, and His Response

INTRODUCTION On October 18, 1775, as the colonies prepared to go to war with England, the Continental Congress adopted a resolution banning African Americans from the Revolutionary army. A week after this decision was made, the enslaved poet Phillis Wheatley sent this poem to George Washington, along with a modest letter introducing herself and reminding him of his commanding position as "Generalissimo of the Armies of North America."

Although the poem made no reference to her race or enslaved condition, it did contain language suggesting that Wheatley knew of the Continental Congress's recent decision. The words, "we demand the grace and glory of thy martial band," seem to deplore the exclusion of African American soldiers from the Revolutionary army, and twice in the poem Wheatley reminds Washington of the "virtue" that should be on his side.

On December 30, 1775, possibly in response to Wheatley's poem, Washington issued orders that army recruiters were to accept any "Free Negroes … desirous of enlisting." Four months after sending the poem to General Washington, he sent her the following courteous reply, apologizing for the delay, thanking her for the poem and inviting her to visit him at his Cambridge headquarters.

To His Excellency General Washington, by Phillis Wheatley

Celestial choir! enthron'd in realms of light,
Columbia's scenes of glorious toils I write.
While freedom's cause her anxious breast alarms,
She flashes dreadful in refulgent arms.
See mother earth her offspring's fate bemoan,
And nations gaze at scenes before unknown!
See the bright beams of heaven's revolving light
Involved in sorrows and the veil of night!

The goddess comes, she moves divinely fair,
Olive and laurel bind her golden hair:
Wherever shines this native of the skies,
Unnumber'd charms and recent graces rise.

Muse! bow propitious while my pen relates
How pour her armies through a thousand gates,
As when Eolus heaven's fair face deforms,
Enwrapp'd in tempest and a night of storms;
Astonish'd ocean feels the wild uproar,
The refluent surges beat the sounding shore;
Or thick as leaves in Autumn's golden reign,

Such, and so many, moves the warrior's train.
In bright array they seek the work of war,
Where high unfurl'd the ensign waves in air.
Shall I to Washington their praise recite?
Enough thou know'st them in the fields of fight.
Thee, first in place and honours,—we demand
The grace and glory of thy martial band.
Fam'd for thy valour, for thy virtues more,
Hear every tongue thy guardian aid implore!

One century scarce perform'd its destined round,
When Gallic powers Columbia's fury found;
And so may you, whoever dares disgrace
The land of freedom's heaven-defended race!
Fix'd are the eyes of nations on the scales,
For in their hopes Columbia's arm prevails.
Anon Britannia droops the pensive head,
While round increase the rising hills of dead.
Ah! cruel blindness to Columbia's state!
Lament thy thirst of boundless power too late.

Proceed, great chief, with virtue on thy side,
Thy ev'ry action let the Goddess guide.
A crown, a mansion, and a throne that shine,
With gold unfading, Washington! be thine.

Letter from George Washington to Phillis Wheatley

Miss Phillis, Your favor of the 26th of October did not reach my hands till the middle of December. Time enough—you will say, to have given answer ere this. Granted. But a variety of important occurrences, continually interposing to distract the mind and withdraw the attention, I hope will apologize for the delay, and plead my excuse for the seeming, but not real neglect. I thank you most sincerely for your polite notice of me in the elegant lines you enclosed; and however undeserving I may be of such encomium and panegyric, the style and manner exhibit a striking proof of your poetical talents; in honor of which, and as a tribute justly due you, I would have published the poem, had I not been apprehensive that, while I only meant to give the world this new instance of your genius, I might have incurred the imputation of vanity. This, and nothing else, determined me not to give it a place in the public prints.

If you should ever come to Cambridge, or near head-quarters, I shall be happy to see a person so favored by the Muses, and to whom nature has been so beneficent in her dispensations. I am with great respect, your obedient and humble servant.

PRIMARY SOURCE DOCUMENT

"An Address to the Negroes of the State of New York" by Jupiter Hammon

INTRODUCTION Jupiter Hammon, the first published American black poet, was born a slave of the Lloyd family on Long Island, New York, in 1711. A favored bondsman, Hammon received an education on his master's premises. His first known publication, an eighty-eight-line poem entitled "An Evening Thought. Salvation by Christ, with Penetential Cries: Composed by Jupiter Hammon, a Negro Belonging to Mr. Lloyd of Queen's Village, on Long Island," appeared in 1761. During the American Revolution, Hammon fled with his master to Hartford, Connecticut where he remained until 1782.

Hammon wrote this address for the members of the African Society in New York. In it, he encouraged other slaves to obey their masters and above all to be good Christians. Hammon died soon after, and the address was published posthumously.

Gentlemen,

I take the liberty to dedicate an Address to my poor brethren to you. If you think it is likely to do good among them, I do not doubt but you will take it under your care. You have discovered so much kindness and good will to those you thought were oppressed, and had no helper, that I am sure you will not despise what I have wrote, if you judge it will be of any service to them. I have nothing to add, but only to wish that "the blessing of many ready to perish, may come upon you."

I am Gentlemen, Your Servant, Jupiter Hammon.

Queen's Village, 24th Sept. 1786.

When I am writing to you with a design to say something to you for your good, and with a view to promote your happiness, I can with truth and sincerity join with the apostle Paul, when speaking of his own nation the Jews, and say: "That I have great heaviness and continual sorrow in my heart for my brethren, my kinsmen according to the flesh." Yes my dear brethren, when I think of you, which is very often, and of the poor, despised and miserable state you are in, as to the things of this world, and when I think of your ignorance and stupidity, and the great wickedness of the most of you, I am pained to the heart. It is at times, almost too much for human nature to bear, and I am obliged to turn my thoughts from the subject or endeavour to still my mind, by considering that it is permitted thus to be, by that God who governs all things, who setteth up one and pulleth down another. While I have been thinking on this subject, I have frequently had great struggles in my own mind, and have been at a loss to know what to do. I have wanted exceedingly to say something to you, to call upon you with the tenderness of a father and friend, and to give you the last, and I may say dying advice, of an old man, who wishes your best good in this world, and in the world to come. But while I have had such desires, a sense of my own ignorance, and unfitness to teach others, has frequently discouraged me from attempting to say any thing to you; yet when I thought of your situation, I could not rest easy.

When I was at Hartford in Connecticut, where I lived during the war, I published several pieces which were well received, not only by those of my own colour, but by a number of the white people, who thought they might do good among their servants. This is one consideration, among others, that emboldens me now to publish what I have written to you. Another is, I think you will be more likely to listen to what is said, when you know it comes from a negro, one of your own nation and colour, and therefore can have no interest in deceiving you, or in saying any thing to you, but what he really thinks is your interest, and duty to comply with. My age, I think, gives me some right to speak to you, and reason to expect you will hearken to my advice. I am now upwards of seventy years old, and cannot expect, though I am well, and able to do almost any kind of business, to live much longer. I have passed the common bounds set for man, and must soon go the way of all the earth. I have had more experience in the world than the most of you, and I have seen a great deal of the vanity and wickedness of it, I have great reason to be thankful that my lot has been so much better than most slaves have had. I suppose I have had more advantages and privileges than most of you, who are slaves, have ever known, and I believe more than many white people have enjoyed, for which I desire to bless God, and pray that he may bless those who have given them to me. I do not, my dear friends, say these things about myself, to make you think that I am wiser or better than others; but that you might hearken, without prejudice, to what I have to say to you on the following particulars.

1st. Respecting obedience to masters. —Now whether it is right, and lawful, in the sight of God, for them to make slaves of us or not, I am certain that while we are slaves, it is our duty to obey our masters, in all their lawful commands, and mind them unless we are bid to do that which we know to be sin, or forbidden in God's word. The apostle Paul says: "Servants be obedient to them that are your masters according to the flesh, with fear and trembling in singleness in your heart as unto Christ: Not with eye service, as men pleasers, but as the servants of Christ doing the will of God from the heart: With good will doing service to the Lord, and not to men: Knowing that whatever thing a man doeth the same shall he receive of the Lord, whether he be bond or free." —Here is a plain command of God for us to obey our masters. It may seem hard for us, if we think our masters wrong in holding us slaves, to obey in all things, but who of us dare dispute with God! He has commanded us to obey, and we ought to do it cheerfully, and freely. This should be done by us, not only because God commands, but because our own peace and comfort depend upon it. As we depend upon our masters, for what we eat and drink and wear, and for all our comfortable things in this world, we cannot be happy, unless we please them. This we cannot do without obeying them freely, without muttering or finding fault. If a servant strives to please his master and studies and takes pains to do it, I believe there are but few masters who would use such a servant cruelly. Good servants frequently make good masters. If your master is really hard, unreasonable and cruel, there is no way so likely for you to convince him of it, as always to obey his commands, and try to serve him, and take care of his interest, and try to promote it all in your power. If you are proud and stubborn and always finding fault, your master will think the fault lies wholly on your side; but if you are humble, and meek, and bear all things patiently, your master may think he is wrong; if he does not, his neighbours will be apt to see it, and will befriend you, and try to alter his conduct. If this does not do, you must cry to him, who has the hearts of all men in his hands, and turneth them as the rivers of waters are turned.

2d. The particular I would mention, is honesty and faithfulness.

You must suffer me now to deal plainly with you, my dear brethren, for I do not mean to flatter, or omit speaking the truth, whether it is for you, or against you. How many of you are there who allow yourselves in stealing from your masters. It is very wicked for you not to take care of your masters goods, but how much worse is it to pilfer and steal from them, whenever you think you shall not be found out. This you must know is very wicked and provoking to God. There are none of you so ignorant, but that you must know that this is wrong. Though you may try to excuse yourselves, by saying that your masters are unjust to you, and though you may try to quiet your consciences in this way, yet if you are honest in owning the truth, you must think it is as wicked, and on some accounts more wicked, to steal from your masters, than from others.

We cannot certainly, have any excuse either for taking any thing that belongs to our masters, without their leave, or for being unfaithful in their business. It is our duty to be faithful, not with eye service as men pleasers. We have no right to stay when we are sent on errands, any longer than to do the business we were sent upon. All the time spent idly, is spent wickedly, and is unfaithfulness to our masters. In these things I must say, that I think many of you are guilty. I know that many of you endeavour to excuse yourselves, and say, that you have nothing that you can call your own, and that you are under great temptations to be unfaithful and take from your masters. But this will not do, God will certainly punish you for stealing and for being unfaithful. All that we have to mind is our own duty. If God has put us in bad circumstances, that is not our fault, and he will not punish us for it. If any are wicked in keeping us so, we cannot help it, they must answer to God for it. Nothing will serve as an excuse to us for not doing our duty. The same God will judge both them and us. Pray then my

dear friends, fear to offend in this way, but be faithful to God, to your masters, and to your own souls.

The next thing I would mention, and warn you against, is profaneness. This you know is forbidden by God. Christ tells us: "swear not at all," and again it is said, "thou shalt not take the name of the Lord thy God in vain, for the Lord will not hold him guiltless, that taketh his name in vain." Now, though the great God has forbidden it, yet how dreadfully profane are many, and I don't know but I may say the most of you? How common is it to hear you take the terrible and awful name of the great God in vain?—To swear by it, and by Jesus Christ, his Son—How common is it to hear you wish damnation to your companions, and to your own souls—and to sport with the name of Heaven and Hell, as if there were no such places for you to hope for, or to fear. Oh my friends, be warned to forsake this dreadful sin of profaneness. Pray my dear friends, believe and realize, that there is a God—that he is great and terrible beyond what you can think—that he keeps you in life every moment—and that he can send you to that awful Hell, that you laugh at, in an instant, and confine you there forever, and that he will certainly do it, if you do not repent. You certainly do not believe, that there is a God, or that there is a Heaven or Hell, or you would never trifle with them. It would make you shudder, if you heard others do it, if you believe them as much, as you believe any thing you see with your bodily eyes.

I have heard some learned and good men say, that the heathen, and all that worshipped false Gods, never spoke lightly or irreverently of their Gods, they never took their names in vain, or jested with those things which they held sacred. Now why should the true God, who made all things, be treated worse in this respect, than those false Gods, that were made of wood and stone. I believe it is because Satan tempts men to do it. He tried to make them love their false Gods, and to speak well of them, but he wishes to have men think lightly of the true God, to take his holy name in vain, and to scoff at, and make a jest of all things that are really good. You may think that Satan has not power to do so much, and have so great influence on the minds of men: But the scripture says: "he goeth about like a roaring Lion, seeking whom he may devour—That he is the prince of the power of the air—and that he rules in the hearts of the children of disobedience,—and that wicked men are led captive by him, to do his will." All those of you who are profane, are serving the Devil. You are doing what he tempts and desires you to do. If you could see him with your bodily eyes, would you like to make an agreement with him, to serve him, and do as he bid you. I believe most of you would be shocked at this; but you may be certain that all of you who allow yourselves in this sin, are as really serving him, and to just as good purpose, as if you met him, and promised to dishonour God, and serve him with all your might. Do you believe this? It is true whether you believe it or not. Some of you excuse yourselves, may plead the example of others, and say that you hear a great many white people, who know more, than such poor ignorant negroes, as you are, and some who are rich and great gentlemen, swear, and talk profanely, and some of you may say this of your masters, and say no more than is true. But all this is not a sufficient excuse for you. You know that murder is wicked. If you saw your master kill a man, do you suppose this would be any excuse for you, if you should commit the same crime? You must know it would not; nor will your hearing him curse and swear, and take the name of God in vain, or any other man, be he ever so great or rich, excuse you. God is greater than all other beings, and him we are bound to obey. To him we must give an account for every idle word that we speak. He will bring us all, rich and poor, white and black, to his judgment seat. If we are found among those who feared his name and trembled at his word, we shall be called good and faithful servants. Our slavery will be at an end, and though ever so mean, low, and despised in this world, we shall sit with God in his kingdom as Kings and Priests, and rejoice forever, and ever. Do not then my dear friends, take God's holy name in vain, or speak profanely in any way. Let not the example of others lead you into the sin, but reverence and fear that great and fearful name, the Lord our God.

I might now caution you against other sins to which you are exposed, but as I meant only to mention those you were exposed to, more than others, by your being slaves, I will concluded what I have to say to you, by advising you to become religious, and to make religion the great business of your lives.

Now I acknowledge that liberty is a great thing, and worth seeking for, if we can get it honestly, and by our good conduct prevail on our masters to set us free. Though for my own part I do not wish to be free: yet I should be glad, if others, especially the young negroes were to be free, for many of us who are grown up slaves, and have always had masters to take care of us, should hardly know how to take care of ourselves; and it may be more for our own comfort to remain as we are. That liberty is a great thing we may know from our own feelings, and we may likewise judge so from the conduct of the white people, in the late war. How much money has been spent, and how many lives have been lost, to defend their liberty. I must say that I have hoped that God would open their eyes, when they were so much engaged for liberty, to think of the state of the poor blacks, and to pity us. He has done it in some measure, and has raised us up many friends, for which we have reason to be thankful, and to hope in his mercy. What may be done further, he only knows, for known unto God are all his ways from

the beginning. But this my dear brethren is by no means, the greatest thing we have to be concerned about. Getting our liberty in this world, is nothing to having the liberty of the children of God. Now the Bible tells us that we are all by nature, sinners, that we are slaves to sin and satan, and that unless we are converted, or born again, we must be miserable forever. Christ says, except a man be born again, he cannot see the kingdom of God, and all that do not see the kingdom of God, must be in the kingdom of darkness. There are but two places where all go after death, white and black, rich and poor; those places are heaven and hell.—Heaven is a place made for those, who are born again, and who love God, and it is a place where they will be happy forever. Hell is a place made for those who hate God, and are his enemies, and where they will be miserable to all eternity. Now you may think you are not enemies of God, and do not hate him: But if your hearts have not been changed, and you have not become true christians, you certainly are enemies to God, and have been opposed to him ever since you were born. Many of you, I suppose, never think of this, and are almost as ignorant as the beasts that perish. Those of you who can read, I must beg you to read the Bible, and whenever you can get time, study the Bible, and if you can get no other time, spare some of your time from sleep, and learn what the mind and will of God is. But what shall I say to them who cannot read? This lay with great weight on my mind, when I thought of writing to my poor brethren, but I hope that those who can read, will take pity on them, and read what I have to say to them. In hopes of this, I will beg of you to spare no pains in trying to learn to read. If you are once engaged, you may learn. Let all the time you can get, be spent in trying to learn to read. Get those who can read, to learn you, but remember that what you learn for, is to read the bible. It tells you what you must do to please God; it tells you how you may escape misery, and be happy forever. If you see most people neglect the bible, and many that can read, never look into it; let it not harden you and make you think lightly of it, and that it is a book of no worth. All those who are really good, love the bible, and meditate on it day and night. In the bible God has told us every thing it is necessary we should know, in order to be happy here and hereafter. The bible is a revelation of the mind and will of God to men. Therein we may learn what God is. That he made all things by the power of his word; and that he made all things for his own glory, and not for our glory. That he is over all, and above all his creatures, and more them than we can think or conceive—that they can do nothing without him—that he upholds them all, and will over-rule all things for his own glory. In the bible likewise we are told what man is. That he was at first made holy, in the image of God, that he fell from that state of holiness, and became an enemy to God, and that since the fall, all the imaginations of the thoughts of his heart, are evil and only evil, and that continually.—That the carnal mind is not subject to the law of God, neither indeed can be. And that all mankind were under the wrath and curse of God, and must have been for ever miserable, if they had been left to suffer what their sins deserved. It tells us that God to save mankind, sent his Son into this world to die, in the room and stead of sinners, and that God will save from eternal misery, all that believe in his son, and take him for their Saviour, and that all are called upon to repent, and believe in Jesus Christ. It tells us, that those who do repent, and believe, and are friends to Christ, shall have many trials and sufferings in this world, but that they shall be happy forever, after death, and reign with Christ to all eternity. The bible tells us that this world is a place of trial, and that there is no other time or place for us to alter, but in this life. If we are christians when we die, we shall awake to the resurrection of life; if not, we shall awake to the resurrection of damnation. It tells us, we must all live in heaven or hell, be happy or miserable, and that without end. The bible does not tell us but of two places, for all to go to. There is no place for innocent folks, who are not christians. There is no place for ignorant folks, that did not know how to be christians. What I mean is, that there is no place besides heaven and hell. These two places will receive all mankind, for Christ says, there are but two sorts, he that is not with me is against me, and he that gathereth not with me, scattereth abroad. The bible likewise tells us, that this world and all things in it shall be burnt up—and that "God has appointed a day in which he will judge the world, and that he will bring every secret thing, whether it be good or bad, into judgment—that which is done in secret shall be declared on the house top." Then every thing that every one has done, through his whole life, is to be told, before the whole world of angels and men. There, Oh how solemn is the thought! You and I must stand, and hear every thing we have thought or done, however secret, however wicked and vile, told before all the men and women that ever have been, or ever will be, and before all the angels, good and bad.

Now my dear friends seeing the bible is the word of God, and every thing in it is true, and it reveals such awful and glorious things, what can be more important than that you should learn to read it; and when you have learned to read, that you should study it day and night. There are some things very encouraging in God's word, for such ignorant creatures as we are: for God hath not chosen the rich of this world. Not many rich, not many noble are called, but God hath chosen the weak things of this world, and things which are not, to confound the things that are: And when the great and the rich refused coming to the gospel feast, the servant was told to go into the highways, and hedges, and compel those poor creatures that he found there, to come in. Now my brethren, it seems to me that there are no people that ought to attend to the hope of happiness in another world, so much as we. Most of us are cut off from comfort and happiness here in this world, and can expect nothing from it. Now seeing this is the case, why should we not take care to be happy after death. Why should we spend our whole lives in sinning against God: And be miserable in this world, and in the world to come. If we do thus, we shall certainly be the greatest fools. We shall be slaves here, and slaves forever. We cannot plead so great temptations to neglect religion as others. Riches and honours which drown the greater part of mankind, (who have the gospel,) in perdition, can be little or no temptation to us.

We live so little time in this world, that it is no matter how wretched and miserable we are, if it prepares us for heaven. What is forty, fifty, or sixty years, when compared to eternity. When thousands and millions of years have rolled away, this eternity will be no higher coming to an end. Oh how glorious is an eternal life of happiness! and how dreadful, an eternity of misery. Those of us who have had religious masters, and have been taught to read the bible, and have been brought by their example and teaching to a sense of divine things, how happy shall we be to meet them in heaven, where we shall join them in praising God forever. But if any of us have had such masters, and have yet lived and died wicked, how will it add to our misery to think of our folly. If any of us, who have wicked and profane masters should become religious, how will our estates be changed in another world. Oh my friends, let me intreat of you to think on these things, and to live as if you believed them true. If you become christians, you will have reason to bless God forever, that you have been brought into a land where you have heard the gospel, though you have been slaves. If we should ever get to heaven, we shall find nobody to reproach us for being black, or for being slaves. Let me beg of you my dear African brethren, to think very little of your bondage in this life, for your thinking of it will do you no good. If God designs to set us free, he will do it, in his own time, and way; but think of your bondage to sin and satan, and do not rest, until you are delivered from it.

We cannot be happy if we are ever so free or ever so rich, while we are servants of sin, and slaves to satan. We must be miserable here, and to all eternity.

I will conclude what I have to say, with a few words to those negroes who have their liberty. The most of what I have said to those who are slaves, may be of use to you, but you have more advantages, on some accounts, if you will improve your freedom, as you may do, than they. You have more time to read God's holy word, and to take care of the salvation of your souls. Let me beg of you to spend your time in this way, or it will be better for you, if you had always been slaves. If you think seriously of the matter, you must conclude, that if you do not use your freedom, to promote the salvation of your souls, it will not be of any lasting good to you. Besides all this, if you are idle, and take to bad courses, you will hurt those of your brethren who are slaves, and do all in your power to prevent their being free. One great reason that is given by some for not freeing us, I understand is, that we should not know how to take care of ourselves, and should take bad courses. That we should be lazy and idle, and get drunk and steal. Now all those of you, who follow any bad courses, and who do not take care to get an honest living by your labour and industry, are doing more to prevent our being free, than any body else. Let me beg of you then, for the sake of your own good and happiness, in time, and for eternity, and for the sake of your poor brethren, who are still in bondage, "to lead quiet and peaceable lives in all Godliness and honesty," and may God bless you, and bring you to his kingdom, for Christ's sake, Amen.

PRIMARY SOURCE DOCUMENT

"We Wear the Mask" by Paul Laurence Dunbar

INTRODUCTION The poem "We Wear the Mask" (1896) reflects Paul Laurence Dunbar's dedication to issues of race. Much like W. E. B. Du Bois in *The Souls of Black Folk*, Dunbar suggests that blacks lead a dual existence in American society. While they show one face in their dealings with whites, underneath they hide the true pain and misery of their difficult lives. Sometimes criticized for the lack of racial consciousness implied by some of his other poetry, in "We Wear the Mask" Dunbar clearly demonstrates his concern for the condition of blacks nationwide.

We wear the mask that grins and lies,
It hides our cheeks and shades our eyes,—
This debt we pay to human guile;
With torn and bleeding hearts we smile,
And mouth with myriad subtleties.

Why should the world be overwise,
In counting all our tears and sighs?

Nay, let them only see us, while
We wear the mask.

We smile, but, O great Christ, our cries
To thee from tortured souls arise.
We sing, but oh the clay is vile
Beneath our feet, and long the mile;
But let the world dream otherwise,
We wear the mask!

PRIMARY SOURCE DOCUMENT

Excerpt from *Invisible Man* by Ralph Ellison

INTRODUCTION Ralph Ellison might be labeled a great intellectual simply for the breadth of his output as an essayist and the astonishing perspicacity of his analysis of the African American social and intellectual condition. However, in 1952, Ellison published the novel *Invisible Man,* his answer to all the lore in letters regarding the "Great American novel." The book was composed over more than a decade while Ellison worked a variety of jobs. After its publication, *Invisible Man* was almost immediately canonized and won the National Book Award, though it took five to six years to reach extreme popularity, as the novel was so scathing and visionary it offended many African Americans upon publication. Ellison struggled the rest of his career to produce another great work of fiction. A fire destroyed a work in progress, and then followed a period of coming to terms with the loss of this second novel. After his death, *Juneteenth* was published, a work culled from the pages of a novel clearly intended for completion and publication, but critics contend that Ellison did not have the opportunity to polish the work as only Ellison could have.

Invisible Man is for African American letters what Gabriel García Marquez's masterpiece, *One Hundred Years of Solitude,* is to Hispanic letters. It is a careening journey through the efforts of a man to leave his hometown, educate himself, and find his place in the world. However, the book reads like a surreal collapse of the African American experience, complete with archetypal figures of an "accomodationist" father figure and educator, a Rockefeller-like great white patron, a social theory organization determined to bring equality to the races, a believer who falls into the Sambo-like minstrelsy of personal disillusionment, and finally, an astonishing presage of the Malcolm X type reverend-orator-inciter who seeks to unleash black rage in a violent riot on the streets of New York. In the end, the narrator discovers he is an invisible man and falls literally into the "pit," a New York City manhole, where he decides to remain until he can devise an alternate reality.

This novel, with its repeating double and triple significances, along with Ellison's pitch-perfect tongue-in-cheek oratory and effortless movement through the conventions of the American novelistic tradition, has caused many to label *Invisible Man* one of the greatest novels produced in American letters.

Words, phrases, skipped through my mind; I saw the blue haze again. What had I meant by saying that I had become "more human"? Was it a phrase that I had picked up from some preceding speaker, or a slip of the tongue? For a moment I thought of my grandfather and quickly dismissed him. What had an old slave to do with humanity? Perhaps it was something that Woodridge had said in the literature class back at college. I could see him vividly, half-drunk on words and full of contempt and exaltation, pacing before the blackboard chalked with quotations from Joyce and Yeats and Sean O'Casey; thin, nervous, neat, pacing as though he walked a high wire of meaning upon which no one of us would ever dare venture. I could hear him: "Stephen's problem, like ours, was not actually one of creating the uncreated conscience of his race, but of creating the *uncreated features of his face.* Our task is that of making ourselves individuals. The conscience of a race is the gift of its individuals who see, evaluate, record...We create the race by creating ourselves and then to our great astonishment we will have created something far more important: We will have cre-

Ralph Ellison, author of the 1952 novel *Invisible Man,* is one of the foremost modern American writers. Born in Oklahoma City in 1914, Ellison settled in New York City in the 1930s, becoming part of an artistic community that included Richard Wright, Romare Bearden, and Richmond Barthe. **AP/WIDE WORLD PHOTOS**

ated a culture. Why waste time creating a conscience for something that doesn't exist? For, you see, blood and skin do not think!"

But no, it wasn't Woodridge. "More human"…Did I mean that I had become less of what I was, less a Negro, or that I was less a being apart; less an exile from down home, the South?…But all this is negative. To become less—in order to become more? Perhaps that was it, but in what way *more* human? Even Woodridge hadn't spoken of such things. It was a mystery once more, as at the eviction I had uttered words that had possessed me.

I thought of Bledsoe and Norton and what they had done. By kicking me into the dark they'd made me see the possibility of achieving something greater and more important than I'd ever dreamed. Here was a way that didn't lead through the back door, a way not limited by black and white, but a way which, if one lived long enough and worked hard enough, could lead to the highest possible rewards. Here was a way to have a part in making the big decisions, of seeing through the mystery of how the country, the world, really operated. For the first time, lying there in the dark, I could glimpse the possibility of being more than a member of a race. It was no dream, the possibility existed. I had only to work and learn and survive in order to go to the top. Sure I'd study with Hambro, I'd learn what he had to teach and a lot more. Let tomorrow come. The sooner I was through with this Hambro, the sooner I could get started with my work.

SOURCE: Ellison, Ralph. *Invisible Man.* New York: Random House, 1947.

| PRIMARY SOURCE DOCUMENT |

"Bitter Fruit of the Tree" by Sterling Brown

INTRODUCTION Sterling Brown's extended sonnet "Bitter Fruit of the Tree" provides a deliberate and piercing commentary on the first chapter of Booker T. Washington's *Up from Slavery.* Anxious to assure his white audience of the emancipated slave's good will, Washington repeatedly denied that there was any bitterness among freed people: "no feelings of bitterness against the whites," "long since ceased to cherish any spirit of bitterness," "no feeling of bitterness." Decades beyond emancipation, and well into the era of sharecropping, disenfranchisement, and Jim Crow violence, Brown takes up the word that Washington could not help repeating. In Brown's rendering of it, Washington's hopeful description becomes a prescription: "These are your orders: you *are* not to be bitter."

"Bitter Fruit of the Tree" first appeared in the August 26, 1939, issue of the *Nation.*

They said to my grandmother: "Please do not be bitter,"
When they sold her first-born and let the second die,
When they drove her husband till he took to the swamp-
        lands,
and brought him home bloody and beaten at last.
They told her, "It is better you should not be bitter,
Some must work and suffer so that we, who must, can live,
Forgiving is noble, you must not be heathen bitter;
These are your orders: you are not to be bitter."
And they left her shack for their porticoed house.

They said to my father: "Please do not be bitter,"
When he ploughed and planted a crop not his,
When he weatherstripped a house that he could not enter,
And stored away a harvest he could not enjoy.
They answered his questions: "It does not concern you,
It is not for you to know, it is past your understanding,
All you need know is: you must not be bitter."
And they laughed on their way to reckon the crop,
And my father walked over the wide garnered acres
Where a cutting wind warned him of the cold to come.

They said to my brother: "Please do not be bitter,
Is it not sad to see the old place go to ruin?
The eaves are sprung and the chimney tower is leaning,
The sills, joists, and columns are rotten in the core;
The blinds hang crazy and the shingles blow away,
The fields have gone back to broomsedge and pine,
And the soil washes down the red gulley scars.
With so much to be done, there's no time for being bitter.
Your father made it for us, it is up to you to save it,
What is past is over, and you should not be bitter."
But my brother is bitter, and he does not hear.

The African American Family

ADAPTED FROM ESSAYS BY N'TANYA LEE;
SIDEBAR ESSAYS BY HALLIE S. HOBSON

For no other group in American life is the matter of family life more important than to the Negro. Our very survival is bound up in it.... No one in all history had to fight against so many physical and psychological horrors to have a family life.

—*Dr. Martin Luther King, Jr.*

The African American family in the Americas has one of the most complex and troubling identities of any group in modern times. Many—both people of color and people not identified as such—do not fully realize the psychological impact that goes with a history in which peoples were uprooted from their homes and cultures, then deposited in the New World as slaves. This American slavery was based entirely on the color of the skin of its captives, and was particularly brutal, complete with a numbing range of laws, cultural devices and hysterical myths designed at once to keep the African in the Americas down, or "in their place," and to rationalize the brutal and inhuman behaviors of the society and nation that grew up around it.

Africans who were brought to the United States were subjected to a bizarrely complex system created in order to break down all existing cultural norms, traditions, names—even memory itself. Much history has been written about the extreme efforts that were made by slave holders in the United States, as compared to those in South and Central American and the Caribbean, and the lasting social, economic and psychological effects of that system still resound across stage of our national character. Indeed, in the scope of 450 years of history, many do not recognize just how recent significant advances and freedoms for blacks in the United States truly are. Many scholars today wonder out loud if the most virulent and damaging periods of racial subjugation in the United States in fact came after the Emancipation Proclamation. After the brief hiatus of the Reconstruction in which there were briefly African American congressmen, the nation—and the world—entered a period of a violent and hysterical effort to destroy every shred of self-respect and any sense of belonging for Africans in the New World and Old. In the late nineteenth century, while European scholars and intellectuals investigated, indeed, invented sciences that confirmed the innate superiority of the white race, their counterparts in the United States were weaving an ever-widening maze of laws and codes to keep African Americans apart from all opportunities for advancement. In the history of the United States,

Twentieth-Century African American Poet Sterling Brown (1901–1989)

Sterling Brown was born in Washington, D.C., in 1901, and raised on the Howard University campus. If Paul Lawrence Dunbar was the originator of twentieth-century poetic traditions, Brown was the father of the school that sought to balance great traditions of the English language, trying to blend the poetic concerns of A. E. Housman and W. B. Yeats, with the driving concerns of African Americans seeking to write their own poetic history. Brown was fond of saying "I learned the arts and sciences at Williams; I learned the humanities in Lynchburg, Virginia."

every Emancipation Proclamation, amendment, and piece of civil rights legislation has been met with a flurry of counter legislation and cultural and literal filibustering by those determined to see the old ways remain firmly in place.

With this complex and troubling legacy, African Americans have often slid down the slippery slope of success. While in arts and letters, the argument might be made that the African American people have made some of the most significant contributions to our culture as a whole, the African American family has suffered.

However, Africans in the Americas have always been held up to the yardstick of a western and essentially European sort of success. It is becoming increasingly clear that elements of African culture the early slave holders sought to eradicate have survived and that western European culture in the United States is not nearly as western or European as it seems.

Throughout almost four hundred years of American history, the black family has been the primary social institution in African American life. Black families and family households are where economic survival is organized, gender roles are taught and negotiated, strategies of resistance to oppression are learned, and each individual's relationship to African American identity, culture, and community life is established.

Since the time of slavery, popular and scholarly writing about the black family has been at the center of racial debates about the morality, American-ness, and

Part 1: The Reynolds/Calhoun Family

In the late 1970s, a book and a television series by Alex Haley called *Roots* prompted many African Americans to take an active interest in their ancestors and genealogies. Long before then, my grandmother and great-aunt, the family historians, had begun to recreate the history of our forebears, using only snippets of information: old handkerchiefs, bills of sale, photographs, locks of hair, wills.

My family has since traced back over eight generations into the past: into births, wars, and slavery. This is not always an easy task for an African American family. Records that we take for granted today, like birth and death certificates, marriage licences,

and census records, did not exist for enslaved people. Photographs and letters were scarce. But by using libraries, the memories of family members, and saved artifacts, my family has been fortunate enough to learn about its past.

The oldest known generation of my family is that of my great-great-great-great-great-grandparents, Henry and Sinai Reynolds. Sinai was born a slave in 1777 in Maryland, and her husband, also a slave, was born in 1781 in North Carolina. These two progenitors had eight children, whose lives in many ways show the full range of experience under the peculiar institution. The three eldest children were daughters, but we know little else about them—not even their names. One was sold to a buyer in Mississippi, another was sent to Liberia, while the fate of the third remains unknown. Sinai and Henry bought themselves and four of their remaining children out of slavery, and moved to Chicago in the mid-1850s. One child, Nelley (b. circa 1810), remained a slave in the South, cooking for a white family. Nelley is my great-great-great-great-grandmother.

ABOVE: Sinai Reynolds, who was born in 1777, is shown here in a photograph probably taken in the 1840s. Sinai and her husband Henry were able to sell baked goods and buy themselves and four of their children free. In the 1850s, they moved with these children to Chicago, where they spent the rest of their lives. Henry's death date is not known, but Sinai died in 1869. **MS. HALLIE S. HOBSON**

humanity of African and African American people. In turn, judgments about the black family have been mobilized for use in political debates about whether African Americans "deserve" freedom, constitutional civil rights, and other benefits of U.S. citizenship that white Americans enjoy. The black family has been viciously attacked and passionately defended, for the political stakes have been very high. Ideas about the black family were as central to debates between abolitionists and slaveholders in the mid-nineteenth century as they are to debates about the American welfare state in the late twentieth century.

Unfortunately, most Americans, including historians, have tended to view the family in an extremely narrow way, and this has led to misconceptions about the

black family and, in fact, all American families. As a consequence, the organization of black family life and its role in the survival, resistance, and cultural life of black people in the United States have been obscured in most popular and scholarly writing.

THE MATRIARCHAL VERSUS THE NUCLEAR FAMILY

Since the nineteenth century, friends and foes of the black family have compared it to the so-called traditional or nuclear family, judging it according to its compliance with or deviation from this supposed norm. In the United States, that norm has been seen as white, despite the fact that many white families have never conformed to it. This comparison has shed little light on the reality of African American families, and many misconceptions remain about the history of black family life from slavery to the present. The preoccupation with African American female-headed households and matriarchal families is but one illustration of the limits of such historical discussions.

The matriarchal family is often compared to a norm that has little basis in reality for any racial or ethnic group despite its widespread acceptance. What many consider normal or typical family life is actually a recent ideal that millions strive for and few achieve: the small, two-parent, homeowning suburban family, in which the husband provides economically through work outside the home and the housewife-mother rears the children and maintains domestic order. This ideal family is presented as completely self-sufficient, emotionally and economically—dependent on neither relatives nor the government for survival.

No family actually fits this model. Middle-class families have for years depended heavily on wage-earning mothers, government tax breaks and loan assistance for homeowners, and the help of relatives for child care, emotional support, and financial assistance. Only the wealthiest families have survived without depending on relatives to help with child care, food, and housing, and with finding employment and weathering the emotional difficulties of everyday life. Further, it was largely women's dissatisfaction with attempts at "ideal" family life in the 1950s and early 1960s that produced the modern feminist movement, including black feminism.

Despite the model's unreality, however, the degree to which a social group appears to have achieved this ideal is still taken as a measure of its progress within American society. In particular, whether a household is two-parent or single-parent has become a convenient measure of racial or ethnic-group achievement and character. Thus, the often-cited fact that black families, more often than white, are single-parent is taken as a sign of the deviance, degradation, regression, and even inferiority of African Americans as a group. Such ideas persist despite historical evidence proving that the primary forces shaping family life are not racial or ethnic, but economic, political, and cultural. Scholarship has shown that, given similar social, regional, and economic circumstances, the percentage of black female-headed households has been almost identical to the percentage of white female-headed households throughout American history.

The two-parent family ideal has greatly limited discussion of black family life. Little popular or scholarly attention is paid, for example, to the fact that the dominant family structure among black families has been the extended family network, made up of several interdependent one- and two-parent black family households. While the membership of each household and the relationships among households may change over time, it is this extended family network, with leadership by men and women, that has enabled black families to survive and prosper.

However, even strong extended families and the African American ethos of collective responsibility are no protection against racial discrimination, high unemployment, or the systematic denial of civil rights.

Two features of the slave system are central to understanding the nature of black family life during the period of slavery. For more than two hundred years, slave-owning elites used southern law to control black labor and maximize their profits from that labor. At the same time, and despite their primary economic and legal status as property, black men and women established slave communities and a semiautonomous African American culture, of which extended families—across households, plantations, and state lines—formed the core.

In American chattel slavery, slave owners profited from the ownership of black men, women, and children. Slaveholders sought to make sure that blacks thought of themselves as the property of white masters and as inferior to all whites. The black family system prevented slaveholders from ever being completely successful in this, however, for within the slave system, extended black families and individual family households existed as havens and sites of resistance. Children were socialized into an African American identity that challenged the identity assigned to blacks and existed independently from it.

The fact that slaves could not marry legally was part of a larger reality of the slave system: enslaved black families had no protection under the law. This does not mean that slavery destroyed black families, but it does mean that maintaining family and kinship ties was perhaps the central struggle for slaves. To place the bonds of family over the demands of slave owners was always considered an act of rebellion, and it required courage, skill, and creativity. Parents had no rights to keep, raise, teach, or benefit from the labor of their children. Husbands and wives had no right to see each other, keep house together, or benefit from one another's labor. Mothers and fathers were whipped for trying to protect their daughters from the sexual violence of white masters.

After 1808, a thriving domestic slave trade was developed to replace the Atlantic slave trade. Slaves were sold off to other parts of the country, primarily west and to the Deep South. While some owners valued stable family life among their slaves, many did not. The value slaves themselves placed on their families is attested to by the many who escaped in an effort to find kin that had been sold away.

Part 2: The Reynolds/Calhoun Family
Henry and Sinai Reynolds

From her birth state of Maryland, Sinai was either sold to a buyer in North Carolina or moved there with her owners. In North Carolina, she met her husband, Henry, and bore their three eldest daughters. Emily, Catherine, and possibly Nelley were also born in North Carolina.

Henry and Sinai were owned by a white man named Silas Reynolds. In the mid-1820s they moved with him to the town of Newnan, in Coweta County, Georgia. Here they had their two youngest children, Henry and Felix. Slaves did not usually have family names of their own, but rather took the surnames of their first, longest, or most benevolent owners. Henry and Sinai kept the name of Reynolds when they were sold to William Nimmons in 1832.

Using an arrangement that some slaveholders found profitable, William Nimmons allowed Henry and Sinai to "hire out their time." This meant that they paid their master a certain sum out of their earnings. It also meant that they were responsible for feeding, housing, and clothing themselves and any of their children who remained on the plantation. They were allowed to keep whatever money

The family customs that evolved during slavery allowed enslaved people to maintain their dignity. African American parents and elders imparted values that upheld the authority of all elders in the slave community. In turn, all adults took responsibility for protecting black children. The struggle for autonomous, private space beyond white supervision, control, and power was central in the resistance to slavery and to post-Emancipation forms of oppression like the sharecropping system.

SEE PRIMARY SOURCE DOCUMENTS *Letters from George Steptoe to William Massie, Deed for Sales of 2 Family Members,* and *A Letter from Reverend J. W. C. Pennington to His Family Still in Slavery*

THE MEANING OF FREEDOM

For former slaves, freedom meant first and foremost establishing family ties according to their own cultural systems rather than the demands of slaveholders. In the first days of freedom, they set out on long journeys to find family members lost through the violence and profiteering of the slave system. Thousands of immediate families had been forcibly broken up by the domestic slave trade, and every freedman (or woman) had lost contact with some kin.

Elizabeth Botume, a northern white woman who worked with the freed people in the South Carolina Sea Islands, observed that "these people had a marvelous way of tracing out missing members of their families, and inflexible perseverance in hunting them up." Mamie Garvin Fields recalled how an elderly stranger, whom her family called "Cousin Delia," searched until death for her relatives sold away in slavery: "Delia searched all her life for the family she had lost in Louisiana, but in the meantime she claimed all the people in our two houses kin.... She just lost all her family through slavery. When she died, our people in Charleston had to bury her."

Many, like Cousin Delia, never found their lost kin. Those who did, especially husbands and wives, were anxious to secure legal status for their relationships. Across the country, husbands and wives sought the legal marriage denied them as slaves, which allowed them to establish legal authority over their own children. As the white South scrambled to reassert its control over freed people, hundreds of plantation owners and former slave-

was left. Despite the extra expense, many slaves found this arrangement to their advantage. It allowed them more freedom, as well as a chance to earn and save money. Most importantly, sometimes slaves were allowed to purchase their freedom with the money they had saved.

Under the new arrangement with Nimmons, Henry and Sinai lived in Newnan, where Sinai made baked goods and drinks to sell in the neighborhood. A white resident of Newnan, recalling his youth in the early 1850s, remembered "the old black mammy called 'Aunt Synie' who sold ginger cakes and persimmon beer at a chosen corner on the street." Sinai's baking brought her and Henry enough income to pay their master and to save enough to buy freedom for themselves and four of their children.

Although some masters allowed slaves to hire out their time, the majority of the white community disapproved of the system, since it loosened the bonds of slavery. Cities often imposed fines on owners who were involved in the practice. The other slaveholders in Newnan must have feared that the relative freedom the Reynoldses enjoyed would set a

bad example for their own slaves. In 1839, they filed a formal complaint against Sinai and Henry's owner.

We do not know what action was taken on this complaint, or whether Sinai and Henry had to move back on their master's property. We do know that they continued to bake and to receive some of the profits, which they saved toward their children's manumission. Nimmons seems to have helped the family out by releasing from his service two of the children, Felix and Catherine, in 1852.

Having amassed enough money to purchase themselves, Sinai, Henry, and four of their eight children were free and living in the North before the Civil War. Nelley, still in slavery in Georgia, had been sold to the A.B. Calhoun family. The three eldest sisters had been freed or sold or had died long before.

LEFT: Nelley Calhoun, the daughter of Sinai and Henry Reynolds, was the cook for the Calhoun household. She was the one child who had to remain in the South when the rest of her siblings were bought free and moved north with their parents. Nelley was the mother of Siny Calhoun, whose father, there is reason to believe, was Judge William Ezzard. Nelley was born around 1810. This photograph may have been taken in the 1860s. **MS. HALLIE S. HOBSON**

holders filed claims to apprentice children without legal parents and thus reduce them to working without pay. Legal marriage protected black families from these efforts to reenslave black children.

This new protection under law was a mixed blessing for black mothers, however. Legal marriage qualified black women for child support payments, and if their husbands had left or died during the Civil War, it qualified them for Union army veterans' pensions. However, legal marriage also conferred upon black men a new status as head of house that some used to control the labor, earnings, and household roles of their wives and children—even employing violence, which the law upheld.

The ethos of collective responsibility that was critical to maintaining life and dignity under slavery was extended to the new conditions of freedom. The young, old, or disabled who were unable to work and care for themselves—whether kin or "fictive kin," like the elderly Cousin Delia—were incorporated into rural households and treated as family. Collective responsibility was especially important in the near-slavery of sharecropping, for here survival depended upon the labor, skill, and creativ-

ity of all able members of the household. Every household member had a task that was necessary, and tools were often shared among households—under sharecropping, no one could survive alone.

Sharecropping, like slavery, was an assault on the black family, and as they had done for generations, African Americans struggled at every turn to assert the primacy of family over the needs and demands of white employers. They sought out tenant and sharecropping situations that allowed for the greatest self-direction and autonomy of family life, the least oversight by white people, the least contact between black women and white men, and the greatest opportunities to send children to attend school rather than work in the fields. While plantation owners sought to maintain the power and profits they had known under slavery, freed people strove to organize families on their own terms and for their own benefit.

Every expression of this self-determination brought them into direct conflict with the plantation owners. Black mothers were needed to contribute to the family economy, but rather than work solely for the production of an employer's cash crops, many farmed

Part 3: The Reynolds/Calhoun Family
The Chicago Reynoldses

The Reynoldses—Sinai, Henry, Felix, Emily, Catherine, and Catherine's husband, Adison Gordon—arrived in Chicago in the mid- to late 1850s. We do not know why they chose Chicago to settle in. Many northern states were not friendly to the idea of free blacks taking up residence, and Illinois was no exception. Its sympathies lay with blacks far away in the South in slavery, not the ones in its own cities. From 1848 to 1865, black laws remained on the Illinois books, stipulating high fines and a variety of other measures to discourage blacks from settling in the state.

The black laws were not always seriously enforced, the Reynoldses being a case in point: by 1860 they were living in a house on Griswold Street in the Third Ward of Cook County. Like many families at the time, the Reynoldses took in lodgers to help pay the rent on a large space they would not have been able to afford otherwise. They shared the house with two boarders, a woman and a small child.

Their black neighborhood, surrounded by factories, was located one block away from the Michigan South Railroad tracks. Its buildings were neither fireproof nor clean. Crowded together on half lots,

they held too many people. Mortality rates were high. In 1889, Catherine Gordon wrote a letter to her niece and nephew in Georgia, describing the conditions in which they were living.

The free North offered the family new opportunities as well as new challenges. Their lives were their own and they could earn wages. Like most of the blacks at that time, the Reynoldses made their living as domestics and personal servants. Felix was a barber, Catherine was a seamstress, and Emily kept house. Yet it seems that money was often tight. Keeping the family together was a challenge. Emily and Catherine settled down to make Chicago their home, but Henry Jr. and Felix saw Chicago as just a starting point. They eventually moved and lost touch with the family. In her 1889 letter to relatives in Georgia, Catherine expressed her frustration over the unraveling of the family.

Henry and Sinai probably did not live to see the scattering of the children who had accompanied them north. They died free in Chicago. The date of Henry's death is not known, but Sinai died in 1869. Nelley came up from Georgia to be by her mother's deathbed.

small, independent garden plots that provided food for their families, despite violent opposition from employers. Black fathers sought to establish their homes as havens from the degradation and sexual violence wives and children experienced as domestic workers in white homes, or as field workers under white overseers. Sharecropping parents took their children out of the fields to eat or attend school or simply to help with domestic tasks at home, though they faced economic and physical reprisals for doing so. Black people's oft-spoken desire "not to be worked by nobody" was intimately related to their struggle to maintain and protect black family life.

MIGRATION TO THE CITY

Since the days of slavery, when slaves ran away to freedom following the North Star, sometimes all the way to

Canada, migration has been a central feature of African American life. Significant migration to urban areas began in the decades following Emancipation. With the imposition of Jim Crow segregation, terror, and economic oppression, thousands more headed north. From 1915 on, it became a mass exodus, swelling during the World War I years and continuing well into the 1940s and 1950s. What is now called the Great Migration expanded black northern communities greatly, reshaping black family life.

Migration was in large part a family affair for African Americans, with family networks playing a central role in the transition from rural to city life. Most migrants joined relatives already settled in the city, who provided temporary living quarters, assistance in finding work, and an introduction to the social, religious, and

This photograph shows slaves planting sweet potatoes on the James Hopkinson Plantation, on Edisto Island, South Carolina. The Sea Islands were liberated in the same year the photograph was taken, after which the slaves continued to farm for the Union army. The South Carolina Sea Islands are home to the Gullah people, among whom many West African customs and language patterns still survive. **ARCHIVE PHOTOS, INC.**

political life of the community. Often a father would go north and find work. Once he was settled, he would send for his wife, children, and dependent elders. Letters were exchanged among family members as young and old tested northern waters and sent word home about the new conditions.

Mamie Garvin Fields remembered how she and her family moved from South Carolina to New York City in the early 1920s: "There was hardly any work for anybody. Even then, we were lucky. Bricklayers' Union #1 got word from New York that bricklayers were needed up there right away. Bob packed up and took the Clyde Line ship. I soon followed with the children.... Bob and I had talked everything over carefully first. It's a heavy decision to move somewhere you don't know that's far away from your family and friends. After you decide to give up so much, you still don't know what will happen. But Charleston was very depressed then, and many people were leaving just to look for work." The Fieldses shared an apartment with another family once they arrived in New York.

Consistent with black family patterns since slavery, from the 1920s to the 1960s about 80 percent of black households in northern urban cities contained two parents and children. But households also had to be flexible,

adapting to changing economic and social forces. Housing in the urban North was expensive and in limited supply for black people, and frequently families shared their apartments with a near relative or an unrelated boarder. One historian found that fully one-third of all black urban households between 1915 and 1930 contained a lodger at one time or another. Most married black women worked outside the home, at least occasionally, in order to cover the cost of living and to supplement the low wages paid to black men. Free public schools, available to millions of black children for the first time, allowed them to do so.

In the North, family and extended-kin networks established in the South were adapted to new conditions and continued to provide the foundation for African American life and culture. Children were cared for by members of their extended family—for example, the young Langston Hughes was cared for by his mother, his grandmother, and his grandmother's closest friend, whom he called "Auntie Reed." Newly established churches, social clubs, and self-help associations, which were largely based on networks of kin and friends from hometowns in the South, provided for the economic survival as well as the spiritual and political empowerment of the expanding northern black communities. Migrants

Chaplain William T. Green presides over the marriage ceremony of Florence A. Collins and Corporal William A. Johnson, the first African American couple to marry in the European Theater of Operations. **NATIONAL ARCHIVES AND RECORDS ADMINISTRATION**

commonly made annual visits to the South, thus maintaining multigenerational ties and sustaining the southern roots of African American culture.

While survival continued to depend on collective responsibility, the lack of economic opportunities placed tremendous stress on families. Due to discrimination, even at the peak of wartime work, few black men earned wages high enough to support a family. Some marriages ended, while other family ties were often strengthened. Single mothers depended extensively on their mothers, siblings, and elder kin as well as the kin of their children's fathers, and they often shared resources with friends and fictive kin close to home, a strategy that continues into the twenty-first century.

THE BIDWELLS OF HOLMES COUNTY

The Bidwells of Holmes County, Mississippi, and Chicago, Illinois, give us yet another picture of an African American family's genealogical story recon-

structed. In addition, they illustrate the impact of northern migration on black family life. The Bidwells are independent farmers who, over many generations in both the South and the North, have sustained a vibrant family life and a tradition of community activism. The family elders, Jeff and Jane Bidwell, were born in the 1880s to parents who had been born in slavery. They raised ten children in Holmes County between 1902 and 1924.

The family's first migration north took place in the 1940s, when several Bidwell children, including the eldest, Sylvia, moved north with their families. Sylvia and her husband came to Chicago in 1942 when he got a steady job working on the Illinois Central Railroad. With earnings saved during the war years, they joined with Sylvia's sister's family in 1951 to purchase a building containing several independent apartments. Over the years, that building provided housing for a number of relatives seeking to establish themselves in Chicago. They and

Part 4: The Reynolds/Calhoun Family
Nelley Calhoun, Daughter of Sinai and Henry Reynolds

My great-great-great-great-grandmother Nelley was possibly born in North Carolina and moved to Georgia with the rest of the family. There she was sold to Andrew B. Calhoun, either by Silas Reynolds when he was selling off his slaves in the 1830s, or by William Nimmons at a later date.

Calhoun was born in 1809 in Abbeville, South Carolina. He moved to Newnan, Georgia, in the 1830s and lived on Greenfield Street, the same street William Nimmons lived on. The men had been acquaintances in South Carolina and probably continued their friendship in Georgia. Calhoun served as a witness for Nimmons' will. A young doctor and member of the Georgia legislature, he held eleven slaves in 1850. In the 1860s his household probably grew larger but still would have been considered small. He had a farm that produced corn, cane for syrup and sugar, and livestock for wool. In this household, Nelley served as cook.

Sinai had also been a cook, and Nelley probably learned her trade from her mother. House servants such as cooks and nurses could often spend more time with their children. I believe that Nelley and her mother had an especially close relationship. Working together in the kitchen, the older woman teaching the younger, they would have had time to develop this bond. Ironically, Nelley's cooking skills may have made her a valuable commodity and kept her in Georgia when the rest of the family moved north.

Nelley was married to a slave on the Calhoun plantation, but nothing is known about him. She had two children, Siny and Moses, but Siny was not the child of Nelley's husband. Siny Calhoun was born in 1830 to Nelley and a white man named William Ezzard. "Judge Ezzard," as he is known in my family, was born in 1799, making him about ten years older than Nelley. He served at various times as a senator, judge, and mayor of Atlanta. If people had known that he had a child by a black woman, it would probably have hurt his career. Nevertheless, according to my family, there is no doubt that Judge Ezzard was Siny's father.

ABOVE: The A. B. Calhoun House in Newnan, Coweta County, Georgia. **MS. HALLIE S. HOBSON**

their children joined local churches, social clubs, and self-help groups usually made up largely, if not solely, of migrants from Holmes County.

Two generations after the first Bidwells migrated to Chicago, the family network had grown and established new roots in the North while nurturing old ones "back home." In 1970, half of the Bidwell family resided in Chicago, but 17 percent of living members still resided in their native Holmes County. As longtime, land-owning Mississippians, the elder Bidwells were active in the Civil Rights movement there. The ethic of collective responsi-

bility extended to the needs of the movement, and the Lorenzo Bidwells informally adopted two northern civil rights activists as their own sons. The activists—one of them was Robert Moses, a worker in the Student Nonviolent Coordinating Committee—lived with the Bidwells for more than a year, sharing both family responsibilities and pleasures.

Forty years after Bidwells began moving north, large numbers of them continue to make annual trips home—"every chance you get." Mrs. Peters, for instance, has a new home and takes part in church and community life in Chicago but returns to Holmes County each year to visit with her aging father. During the summer, many children are sent south to live with relatives, in part to solve the dilemma of working parents who cannot afford supervised child care for the summer. Moreover, many Bidwells who have died in cities far from Holmes County have been brought back to be buried with kin.

NEW OPTIONS AND CHALLENGES FOR BLACK WOMEN

Widespread social changes in the last three decades of the twentieth century have had contradictory effects on the lives of black women and black families. On one hand, job opportunities in urban cities have decreased, and the number of poor black families continues to rise. As the number of families who need public assistance has risen, federal and state governments have cut back social welfare programs, thus exacerbating the worsening economic and social conditions.

On the other hand, the expansion of women's civil and reproductive rights, as well as new ideas concerning women's roles in the family and society, have created new economic and social opportunities for black women. Black women have greater access now than ever before to higher-paying, traditionally male jobs (in the postal service, for example), to sales and secretarial jobs that have traditionally gone to white women, to political leadership, and to higher education. In 1970, the majority of black women were for the first time no longer farm laborers or domestic workers. Black women also have greater legal redress for domestic violence, rape, and other forms of male violence. In addition, despite widespread concern about an increase in teen pregnancy, black teen pregnancy has greatly decreased as more women have gained access to family planning information, birth control, and legal abortion.

But family life has dramatically changed: fewer and fewer young black (and white) women are getting married before they have children. Between 1939 and 1959, approximately 18 percent of all black infants were born to unmarried women; by the mid-1980s, 60 percent of black infants were born to unmarried women. Black women now marry at a later age, often after becoming parents; more black women leave unsatisfactory marriages; fewer marry immediately after a divorce or a husband's death. A significant number of heterosexual black women choose not to marry at all, while many black lesbians, acknowledging their sexuality, are building nontraditional families.

With the growth of urban poverty, the resources available to black family networks have been drastically reduced. Millions of two-parent and single-parent families find themselves among the working poor. For some, this has strengthened kinship bonds and exchange relationships. The tradition of sharing responsibility for child-rearing continues and in many cases has intensified. Many children now grow up in a number of different households, depending on fluctuations in the resources available to the adults in their lives. Many elders help raise grandchildren and even great-grandchildren, stepping in for mothers and fathers who are unemployed or who have become parents at too young an age.

For others, however, the continuous lack of basic necessities—sufficient income, health care, child-care support, and the like—has proven too great a challenge. Unable to provide even minimal support and care to their children, some parents are driven to desperate, sometimes illegal measures to maintain their families. This in turn brings the entire family network into conflict with an array of government and private agencies, from social-welfare offices to the criminal justice system, agencies whose representatives may or may not understand the nature of a family's needs. Under these circumstances, black families often prefer to turn to the assistance and support of churches and other community institutions.

Black family networks will continue to respond to social and economic forces with creativity and dignity, with the central purpose of doing better for the next generation.

BIBLIOGRAPHY

Bennett, Lerone. "10 Myths about the Black Family." *Ebony*, August 1986.

Billingsley, Andrew. *Climbing Jacob's Ladder: The Enduring Legacy of African-American Families.* New York: Simon & Schuster, 1992.

Comer, James. *Maggie's American Dream: The Life and Times of a Black Family.* New York: New American Library, 1988.

Fields, Mamie Garvin, with Karen Fields. *Lemon Swamp and Other Places: A Carolina Memoir.* New York: Free Press, 1983.

Gutman, Herbert, *The Black Family from Slavery to Freedom: 1750–1925.* New York: Pantheon, 1976.

Haley, Alex. *Roots: The Saga of an American Family.* Garden City: Doubleday, 1976 (also in video).

Jones, Jacqueline. *Labor of Love, Labor of Sorrow: Black Women, Work and the Family, from Slavery to the Present.* New York: Basic Books, 1985.

Omolade, Barbara. *The Rising Song of African American Women.* New York: Routledge, 1994.

Scapegoating the Black Family. Special issue of *Nation*, July 24–31, 1989.

Stack, Carol. *All Our Kin: Strategies for Survival in a Black Community.* New York: Harper & Row, 1974.

Washington, Mary Helen, ed. *Memories of Kin: Stories about Family by Black Writers.* New York: Anchor, 1991.

PRIMARY SOURCE DOCUMENT

Letters from George Steptoe to William Massie

INTRODUCTION When William Massie married into the Steptoe family in 1814, his father-in-law, James Steptoe, and his brother-in-law, George Steptoe, helped him establish himself as a planter by giving him slaves. Slave families were disrupted in the process, including the family of Edy and "Old Bishop." Edy and their son went to the Massies; Old Bishop remained with the Steptoes.

In 1820, George Steptoe reunited the family on his property, writing several letters to William Massie to arrange the matter, which involved among other things purchasing Edy back and building her a cabin. George Steptoe's letters to his brother-in-law are full of cordial banter. One can detect in them, however, the constant pressure that the members of the enslaved family were applying in their efforts to live together.

George Steptoe to William Massie, Nelson County, May 31 1820

Dear Wm, Your letter of the 29th Inst. is now before me— by which it appears that you are not altogether disposed to accede to the proposition which I had made to you, which was to have old Edy valued— I stated to you that I was willing to take her at whatever any disinterested person would say she was worth, either in cash, or upon a credit of 12 months— You say that your price for her is $275— This, I think is rather high for the times, & (for) a woman of her age—for tho' she may now, be a "Jack of all trades" as you say, yet the time will shortly arrive, when she will be a Jack at none—& when, on the contrary, according to the course of nature, she will be a tax to her Master— She may be a very good crop-hand—& even understand how to apply a clyster—but as I am not particularly in want of a hand of within description at present, these qualifications would not much enhance her value in my estimation— but did I expect to pay for a hand of the latter profession shortly, I should certainly try to get one with younger eyes— But laying aside all joking as I am really in want of a cook—& am not much disposed to stand upon trifles— (if you have any particular objection to having your negro woman valued)—I am willing to give you $250 for her— which I am told by Mr Penn you have said you would take. Would suit me better to take her in the Fall than at present—as I should have to build her a house & am too much engaged at present to go about it—In the meantime you can let me know by the first opportunity whether you will take what I have offered.

George Steptoe to William Massie, Pharsalia,

August 26, 1820

Dear Sir Your letter by mail dated some time ago, was duly received— but as it was only an acceptance of my previous offer I did not think it worth while to reply to it—I have been calculating ever since its reception upon taking old Edy the first of October. Will you want all the money paid down for her when I send for her? or will it make any difference with you about waiting a few months? I dont know but what it will be as convenient to pay for her at that time as any other—If I can collect one twentieth part of what is owing me, it will—But in case I should not—I merely want to know whether it will make the least difference with you? If it will, the money shall be forwarded when I send for her—

George Steptoe to William Massie, Pharsalia,

September 16, 1820

Dear Sir The Bishop after finishing his cabin seems to be a little impatient to see his wife—but urges as a pretext for wishing to go down at this time, that he has a large crop of corn & fodder to save and make sale of—however he seems willing to give away every thing else he has, provided he can bring her away his wife— He had taken up an idea that you were ready & willing to deliver her at any time & insisted upon starting after her—I told him you were not to deliver her before 1st. Oct—& that I could not ask you for her sooner— He has gone down to bring up either his wife or some other plunder—she would be no accommodation to me at this time—but if you have nothing for her to do, & think it proper to accommodate the old man, you can do so—

George Steptoe to William Massie,

Undated

Dear Sir, The old Bishop & his Lady after getting comfortably settled in their old neighborhood, & in a Christian Land—have begun to reflect how much their happyness would be increased by having their only child placed near them—where they could have an opportunity of instilling into him principles of morality & religion and showing him the road to Heaven, & have been applying to me to know whether I could not devise some means of having him sent over from the Heathenish country where he is now living without God& the Gospel, & placed within the reach of salvation. I have told them that I was not in a situation to buy their son—neither did I know what he was worth never having see him, but that I would do anything in my power to save him from destruction— If you have no objection I will give you a reasonable hire for him for one year—& if I like him, I may probably buy him at the end of that time. I had thought that if you were not particularly attached to him, & could hire another hand in your neighborhood in his place, that I would pay his hire. I have none of my own that I could conveniently put in his place, & hope the plan I propose will be acceptable to you.

We are all as well as common & should be glad to see you & yours up this way this Xmas. Give my love to Sally & accept for yourself my best wishes for your health and happyness.

Part 5: The Reynolds/Calhoun Family

In the summer of 1864, Andrew B. Calhoun and some of his slaves left Newnan to visit his son Abner, who had been wounded in the war. Calhoun's daughter Fannie remained at the house in Newnan and wrote to her father, complaining about slaves who had run away to the Yankees. In the same letter, she sent a friendly hello to Nelley's child and grand-child, Siny and Catherine (Kitty), who had accompanied Calhoun on the trip. Calhoun and his slaves were present a few months later when Sherman burned Atlanta. According to family legend, Nelley was ill. They put her on a mattress in a wagon, and everyone escaped to safety.

House servants were often accused of identifying or siding with their owners over their family or friends working in the fields. Slaves were not always open about their feelings, however, and so it is hard to tell whether they were truly attached to their owner's family or only acted that way out of a sense of duty or fear. Nelley and her daughter and granddaughter did remain with the family and performed their duties. It seems that they had won the affection of the white Calhouns—not only did Fannie remember them in her wartime letter, but in 1870 Calhoun deeded the three women a plot of land as a reward for their loyal service.

Yet Nelley's family always remained important to her. Though separated from her mother, father,

---

PRIMARY SOURCE DOCUMENT

Deed for Sales of Two Family Members

INTRODUCTION In 1832, Felix Reynolds was sold by Silas Reynolds to William Nimmons for two hundred dollars, and in 1834 his mother was sold for three hundred dollars. The two sales were recorded together in the Coweta, Georgia County Book of Deeds.

Two Bills of Sale—Georgia: Know all men by these present that I Silas Reynolds of the County Coweta County and State aforesaid for and in consideration of the sum of two hundred dollars to him in hand provide the receipt whereof is hereby acknowledged hath bargained sold and delivered and by these presents doth bargain sell and deliver unto William Nimmons of the County and State aforesaid one negro boy slave by the name of Felix about Eight years of age which negro boy slave Felix he the said Silas Reynolds warrants to be sound and healthy and to him the said William Nimmons his heirs and assigns he the said Silas Reynolds doth warrant and forever defend the right and title thereof. In witness whereof I hath hereunto set my hand and seal this 5th June 1832

> S. Reynolds
> signed sealed and delivered
> in the presence of us
> James Wood
> W F Storey J.P.
> Recorded 1st March 1839
> Batty Mitchell clk

Received of William Nimmons three hundred dollars in full payment of a negro woman by the name of Sina about Sixty years of age which negro woman I warrant the rite and title thereof against myself my heirs Executors administrators or any other person whatever to the said William Nimmons his heirs In Testimony whereof I have hereunto set my hand and seal this 4th day of April 1834

> S Reynolds
> W F Storey JP
> Recorder 1st March 1839
> Batty Mitchell clk

brothers, and sisters when they moved north, she corresponded with them and traveled north to be by her mother's deathbed. The strength of kin ties can also be seen in the family's naming practices. Nelley took the Calhoun name, but she named her daughter Siny for her mother, and both Siny and Moses named children for their aunts and uncles. In this way, like so many enslaved people, Nelley and her children used names to keep family connections and memories alive.

Siny Calhoun had married Preston Webb, and they had had one child, Catherine Webb—or Kitty, as the white Calhouns called her. Not much is known about Preston, but when he died in 1868 at a young age, it left a profound mark on his eight-year-old daughter. Siny gave Catherine an atlas from the year her father died, and in the pages of this volume were pressed his rumpled freedom papers. Catherine kept the atlas in a box on which she inscribed the date of her father's death. This box has been passed down through the generations.

Although A. B. Calhoun had deeded them property in Newnan, Nelley, Siny, and Catherine finally chose not to remain near the people who had owned them. Like many ex-slaves, they moved away from the plantation and into the city. In 1870, they were living on Frasier Street in Atlanta with Nelley's son Moses, his wife, Atlanta, and their children, Lena and Cora. Nelley was working as a laundress and Siny as a hairdresser, and Moses owned a cafe. They must have done quite well, because Catherine attended Atlanta University in 1875 and 1876, and Cora did so in 1882.

When Siny married Joseph Murray, her second husband, in 1880, she and Nelley moved out of her brother's house to Lula, in Hall County, Georgia. They did not remain there long, however, returning to Atlanta, where Nelley lived with her daughter until her death in 1897. Five generations later, her descendants have been scattered around the country and the world, but many of us were born in Atlanta, and we still consider it the family home.

LEFT: Siny Catherine Calhoun was the daughter of Nelley Calhoun and the mother of Catherine Felix Webb. She was born in July 1830 in Newnan, Coweta County, Georgia. Her first husband, Preston Webb, died in 1868. This photograph taken after her second marriage probably dates from the 1870s. **MS. HALLIE S. HOBSON**

PRIMARY SOURCE DOCUMENT

A Letter from Reverend J. W. C. Pennington to His Family Still in Slavery

INTRODUCTION Born into slavery in Maryland in 1807, James W. C. Pennington was first trained as a blacksmith. At the age of twenty, he escaped, leaving behind his parents and numerous brothers and sisters. The Quaker who assisted him in escaping, with whom he spent several months, taught Pennington to read and write, and he went on to become an ordained minister and one of the most distinguished American abolitionists. It was James Pennington who married Frederick and Anna Douglass when Douglass first escaped from slavery.

Though free himself, Pennington was anxious about the family he had left behind in slavery. He worried about them as a son and brother, and also in his new capacity as a Christian minister. In this letter, written to his family after a seventeen-year absence, Pennington expresses the wish that slavery will not prejudice them "against the gospel because it may be seemingly twisted into a support of slavery."

Dearly beloved in bonds,

About seventeen long years have now rolled away, since in the Providence of Almighty God, I left your embraces, and set out upon a daring adventure in search of freedom. Since that time, I have felt most severely the loss of the sun and moon and eleven stars from my social sky. Many, many a thick cloud of anguish has pressed my brow and sent deep down into my soul the bitter waters of sorrow in consequence. And you have doubtless had your troubles and anxious seasons also about your fugitive star.

I have learned that some of you have been sold, and again taken back by Colonel ——. How many of you are living and together, I cannot tell. My great grief is, lest you should have suffered this or some additional punishment on account of my Exodus.

I indulge the hope that it will afford you some consolation to know that your son and brother is yet alive. That God has dealt wonderfully and kindly with me in all my way. He has made me a Christian, and a Christian Minister, and thus I have drawn my support and comfort from that blessed Saviour, who came to preach good tidings unto the meek, to bind up the broken hearted, to proclaim liberty to the captives, and the opening of the prison to

Part 6: The Reynolds/Calhoun Family
The Vanished Sisters

Very little is known about the three eldest daughters of Sinai and Henry Reynolds. According to a brief docu-

ment written by my great-great-grandmother, one was sent to Liberia and another sold farther south. The third has truly been lost in the passage of time.

The daughter who went with six children to Liberia was sent by her owner, who was probably a supporter of the American Colonization Society. The society was started in 1817 by whites who sought to remove free blacks to Africa. They had various motives, both well-intentioned and hostile: to end miscegenation and race mixing, to Christianize Africa, to open profitable trade, and to "uplift the Negro" by giving him a chance to govern himself in his own land. Their main goal, however, was to remove free blacks from American soil.

It was not just whites who supported this movement, however. Many blacks also approved. Slaves and freed blacks would save small amounts of

them that are bound. To proclaim the acceptable year of the Lord and the day of vengeance of our God: to comfort all that mourn. To appoint unto them that mourn in Zion, to give unto them beauty for ashes, the oil of joy for mourning, the garment of praise for the spirit of heaviness, that they might be called trees of righteousness, the planting of the Lord that he might be glorified.

If the course I took in leaving a condition which had become intolerable to me, has been made the occasion of making that condition worse to you in any way, I do most heartily regret such a change for the worse on your part. As I have no means, however, of knowing if such be the fact, so I have no means of making atonement, but by sincere prayer to Almighty God in your behalf, and also by taking this method of offering to you these consolations of the gospel to which I have just referred, and which I have found to be pre-eminently my own stay and support. My dear father and mother; I have very often wished, while administering the Holy Ordinance of Baptism to some scores of children brought forward by doting parents, that I could see you with yours among the number. And you, my brothers and sisters, while teaching hundreds of children and youths in schools over which I have been placed, what unspeakable delight I should have had in having you among the number; you may all judge of my feeling for these past years, when while preaching

from Sabbath to Sabbath to congregations, I have not been so fortunate as even to see father, mother, brother, sister, uncle, aunt, nephew, niece, or cousin in my congregations. While visiting the sick, going to the house of mourning, and burying the dead, I have been a constant mourner for you. My sorrow has been that I know you are not in possession of those hallowed means of grace. I am thankful to you for those mild and gentle traits of character which you took such care to enforce upon me in my youthful days. As an evidence that I prize both you and them, I may say that at the age of thirty-seven, I find them as valuable as any lessons I have learned, nor am I ashamed to let it be known to the world, that I am the son of a bond man and a bond woman.

Let me urge upon you the fundamental truths of the Gospel of the Son of God. Let repentance towards God and faith in our Lord Jesus Christ have their perfect work in you, I beseech you. Do not be prejudiced against the gospel because it may be seemingly twisted into a support of slavery. The gospel rightly understood, taught, received, felt and practised, is anti-slavery as it is anti-sin. Just so far and so fast as the true spirit of the gospel obtains in the land, and especially in the lives of the oppressed, will the spirit of slavery sicken and become powerless like the serpent with his head pressed beneath the fresh leaves of the prickly ash of the forest.

money in hopes of making the journey themselves or buying a membership in the society. Felix Reynolds was a member from 1852 to 1855, as listed in the society's journal, the *African Repository.* He may have joined out of a personal interest in emigrating, or to show support for the cause, or to learn about his missing sister's progress.

Though we do not know when the sister who was sold south went, we know that her fate was a common fear among nineteenth-century slaves, since it meant that they would be sent far away from their families. Masters often raised money by selling their slaves to traders, who moved them to slave markets in the lower South. Some masters took slaves with them to work on new land or secondary plantations farther south. Slaves might even be given away as presents, forced to uproot themselves from their own families and lives. This often happened when a master's children established new plantations on the southern frontier.

The third sister has been lost to us in a sea of possibilities and time. Because of the nature of the institution of slavery, her mother, father, brothers, and sisters might not even have known her fate. Her absence reminds us how tenuous the threads leading to the past can be, and how lucky we are to know what we do know.

Doing genealogical research can be frustrating and rewarding at the same time. At its worst, family history can reveal the gaps and holes in the record. At its best, it reminds us of the individual lives—of mothers, fathers, and children—that came together to create history.

LEFT: Catherine Felix Webb was the daughter of Siny Calhoun, the granddaughter of Nelley Calhoun, and the great-granddaughter of Sinai and Henry Reynolds, the progenitors of an African American family that has traced its lineage back eight generations. Catherine Felix Webb was born in the Calhoun home in July 1860. At the time of this photograph, taken around 1900, she had become the wife of Antoine Graves. **MS. HALLIE S. HOBSON**

There is not a solitary decree of the immaculate God that has been concerned in the ordination of slavery, nor does any possible development of his holy will sanctify it

He has permitted us to be enslaved according to the invention of wicked men, instigated by the devil, with intention to bring good out of the evil, but He does not, He cannot approve of it. He has no need to approve of it, even on account of the good which He will bring out of it, for He could have brought about that very good in some other way.

God is never straitened; He is never at a loss for means to work. Could He not have made this a great and wealthy nation without making its riches to consist in our blood, bones, and souls? And could He not also have given the gospel to us without making us slaves?

My friends, let us then, in our afflictions, embrace and hold fast the gospel. The gospel is the fulness of God. We have the glorious and total weight of God's moral character in our side of the scale.

The wonderful purple stream which flowed for the healing of the nations, has a branch for us. Nay, is Christ divided? "The grace of God that bringeth salvation hath appeared to (for) all men, teaching us that denying ungodliness and worldly lust, we should live soberly, righteously, and godly in this present world, looking for

that blessed hope and glorious appearing of the great God and our Saviour Jesus Christ, who gave himself for us that he might redeem us from all iniquity, and purify unto himself a peculiar people, zealous of good works."—Titus ii. 11–14.

But you say you have not the privilege of hearing this gospel of which I speak. I know it; and this is my great grief. But you shall have it; I will send it to you by my humble prayer; I can do it; I will beg our heavenly Father, and he will preach this gospel to you in his holy providence.

You, dear father and mother cannot have much longer to live in this troublesome and oppressive world; you cannot bear the joke much longer. And as you approach another world, how desirable it is that you should have the prospect of a different destiny from what you have been called to endure in this world during a long life.

But it is the gospel that sets before you the hope of such a blessed rest as is spoken of in the word of God, Job iii. 17, 19. "There the wicked cease from troubling, and there the weary be at rest; there the prisoners rest together; they hear not the voice of the oppressors. The small and great are there; and the servant is free from his master."

Father, I know that thy eyes are dim with age and weary with weeping, but look, dear father, yet a little while toward that haven. Look unto Jesus, "The author and finisher of thy faith," for the moment of thy happy deliverance is at hand.

Mother, dear mother, I know, I feel, mother, the pangs of thy bleeding heart, that thou hast endured, during so many years of vexation. Thy agonies are by a genuine son-like sympathy mine; I will, I must, I do share daily in those agonies of thine. But I sincerely hope that with me you bear your agonies to Christ who carries our sorrows.

O come then with me, my beloved family, of weary heart-broken and care-worn ones, to Jesus Christ, "casting all your care upon him, for he careth for you."—2 Peter v. 7.

With these words of earnest exhortation, joined with fervent prayer to God that He may smooth your rugged way, lighten your burden, and give a happy issue out of all your troubles, I must bid you adieu.

Your son and brother,
Jas. P. Alias J. W. C. Pennington.

The African American Religious Experience

ADAPTED FROM ESSAYS BY IAN STRAKER

THE AFRICAN PAST

The slave trade brought an estimated ten to forty million Africans to the Americas. Among the religions these Africans carried with them were the Yoruba and Bakongo belief systems and Islam. Change in the religious beliefs and practices of these displaced Africans was inevitable, given the altered circumstances of life in the western Atlantic world.

However, in the Caribbean and South America, a number of factors combined to preserve Yoruba and Bakongo religious practices in the forms of Voodoo (Haiti), Santeria (Cuba), and Candomble (Brazil). Perceived similarities between Catholic saints and the *orishas*—deities in African religions—allowed for the worship of African gods under the guise of Christian worship. The high ratio of Africans to Europeans, and a slave population that was constantly replenished by new arrivals from Africa, also contributed to the retention of African religions.

North America proved to be less fertile ground for the cultivation of African-based religions due to a strong Protestant presence and the fact that a much higher percentage of slaves were born in the thirteen British colonies. Still, some African religious practices can be discerned in the African American traditions of conjure

and hoodoo, and particularly in the ring shout, which combines African rhythms and dance-like movements with Christian expressions.

CONVERSION TO CHRISTIANITY: THE GREAT AWAKENING

The nonexclusive nature of African religions made the slave population open to other religious perspectives. This tendency eventually led to the adoption of Christianity during the series of revivals—known collectively as the Great Awakening—that swept the colonies in the latter half of the eighteenth century.

Organized attempts to convert the slaves in North America began as early as 1701 with the formation of the Society for the Propagation of the Gospel in Foreign Parts (SPG), which was the missionary arm of the Church of England. In its efforts to reach slaves, the SPG encountered resistance by slaveholders, who had two major concerns: first, that slaves who were baptized would have to be freed; and second, that sharing church membership with slaves and thus requiring them to learn to read would make them unruly and ungovernable. Early missionaries to slaves tried to convince slave masters that religion would create a more productive and docile work force. Legislation was passed to ensure that baptism and church membership would have no bearing on slave status. Nevertheless, this did not result in more slave conversions, as the staid form of worship and the literacy requirement still proved to be impediments for most slaves.

Success in slave conversions came with the revivals of the Great Awakening and new efforts by converted slaves and by Methodist and Baptist evangelists. The evangelists stressed a personal conversion experience rather than the memorization of catechisms, and their more active worship style appealed to the African American slaves. Preaching was conducted in the language of ordinary people and not the prose of theologically trained scholars. Thus the language of the preacher was more readily understood by both black and white congregants, who were encouraged to participate in worship by praying, singing, exhorting or giving testimony, and even preaching. **SEE PRIMARY SOURCE DOCUMENT** *Letter from a Slave on the Subject of Religion*

Some of the Baptist and Methodist preachers no doubt attracted slaves by their condemnation of slavery. But intense opposition by slaveholders to the mission of these early reformers soon caused them to abandon abolition as an immediate goal and to focus instead on the conversion of both slave and master. Underlying this strategy was the hope that Christian masters would treat their slaves more benevolently.

Some African Americans received licenses to preach and became popular with both black and white audi-

This photograph shows a woman about to be baptized by her pastor. Other members of the congregation are gathered along the shore. This photograph was taken between 1900 and 1906 in the South. **THE LIBRARY OF CONGRESS**

ences. The illiterate preacher Harry Hosier (1750–1806), who often accompanied Bishop Francis Asbury (1745–1816) on his tours of Methodist societies, was praised by the Oxford-trained Thomas Coke (1747–1814) as being "one of the best preachers in the world." By the early nineteenth century, a number of African American women responded to a divine call to preach and became itinerant evangelists, among them Jarena Lee (b. 1783) and Zilpha Elaw (b. circa 1790). Other early African American preachers earned places in history by establishing independent African American churches. **SEE PRIMARY SOURCE DOCUMENT** *Excerpt from* **The Life and Religious Experience of Jarena Lee, A Coloured Lady**

INDEPENDENT AFRICAN AMERICAN CHURCHES

The earliest independent African American church was started between 1773 and 1775 by David George (1743–1810) in Silver Bluff, Georgia. George left Georgia with retreating British forces during the Revolutionary War, moving on to Nova Scotia and later Sierra Leone. In each location he established a black Baptist church. After the war, the church in Silver Bluff, under the leadership of Jesse Galphin, relocated to Augusta as the First African Baptist Church.

While these events were taking place in the South, events in the North were leading to the creation of the first African American denomination. In 1787, African Americans walked out of St. George's Methodist Episco-

pal Church in Philadelphia after one of them, Absalom Jones (1746–1817), was dragged from his knees during prayer for violating the church's segregated seating policy. Jones separated from the Methodists, received ordination in the Episcopal church, and established the St. Thomas African Episcopal Church, the first African American church in that denomination. But others, under the leadership of Richard Allen (1760–1831), remained within the Methodist fold and built the Bethel African Methodist Episcopal Church.

In a number of other cities, black Methodists who refused to tolerate second-class status in a church they had supported with their time, talents, and tithes had also withdrawn from predominantly white churches. In 1816, at a meeting of delegates from several of these groups, a new denomination—the African Methodist Episcopal Church (A.M.E.)—was organized with Richard Allen as its first bishop. In 1821, several other black Methodist groups that were uncomfortable with Allen's leadership formed the nation's second black denomination, the African Methodist Episcopal Zion Church. From their inceptions, these denominations condemned slavery and became advocates for the rights of African Americans.

SLAVE RELIGION

In the antebellum South, slave preachers were implicated in a number of plots and insurrections. The Gabriel Prosser plot in Richmond, Virginia, in 1800 included

Gabriel's brother Martin, a preacher. Denmark Vesey, a free man and A.M.E. class leader in the Charleston, South Carolina, church, was the leader of an aborted plot that resulted in the arrest of 131 Africans and African Americans in 1822. In both incidents, religious meetings were used to help organize a rebellion, and appeals to scripture were made to justify the attack against slavery. In retaliation for Vesey's plot, the local African Methodist church, which had over three thousand members, was burned to the ground and its pastor, Rev. Morris Brown, who was later elected bishop, was forced to flee the state.

The most famous slave rebellion took place in 1831 in Southampton County, Virginia. Its leader was a literate slave preacher named Nat Turner (1800–1831). Observing miraculous signs and hearing the voice of the Spirit directing him to fight, Turner laid plans with five others and struck on August 21. The plotters were joined by about seventy other slaves in a rebellion that saw fifty-seven whites killed before it was crushed. In its wake, the religious activities of slaves were severely curtailed, and slave preachers were prohibited from leading services without white supervision. From these incidents and others, it is apparent that Christianity, contrary to what the slave masters had hoped, did not make slaves more docile or less willing to seek and embrace freedom.

During the Civil War, the first collections of African American spirituals were compiled. Thomas Wentworth Higginson (1823–1911), the commanding officer of one of the Union army's black regiments, wrote down the songs sung by his men, many of whom were newly freed slaves. In his collection, he noted the prevalence of images from Exodus and the Book of Revelation. The story of Moses and the liberation of the children of Israel from Egyptian bondage held special meaning for slaves. The violent images of the Apocalypse and the image of Jesus as a valiant warrior who would conquer the enemies of God were also especially relevant to an enslaved people who turned to God in faith and hope for deliverance from the evils of slavery.

Other whites, like William Kephart, a Union army chaplain, observed the religious life of the ex-slaves and wrote northern sponsors about the "excessive effervescence of emotional feeling" and the lack of theological sophistication among them. Kephart complained that African Americans in Alabama saw Jesus as a physical liberator and not a spiritual one. Similarly, it was reported that Moses was often confused with Lincoln. Although these observations were meant disparagingly, they also reveal that, in their clandestine worship services, slaves made Christianity their own by resisting the interpretations emphasized by their owners, using the Bible selectively with a focus on freedom.

SEE PRIMARY SOURCE DOCUMENT *A Former Slave Discusses the Importance of Religion*

THE ANTEBELLUM NORTH

In the antebellum North, religious African Americans continued to oppose slavery and to fight racism and discrimination. David Walker (1785–1830), a free merchant in Boston, wrote an *Appeal to the Coloured Citizens of the United States* in which he used the Bible to prove that slavery was wrong, to sanction resistance on the part of slaves, and to warn of divine retribution against the United States if the sin of slavery did not cease. Rev. Henry Highland Garnet (1815–1882), who, as a young boy, had escaped slavery with his family and resisted slave catchers in the North, wrote a well-known address in which he urged slaves to violently resist their masters as part of their Christian obligation before God. Other northern churchmen like Samuel Cornish (1795–1859) started newspapers and benevolent organizations for their congregants. **SEE PRIMARY SOURCE DOCUMENT** *Preamble to* Appeal to the Coloured Citizens of the United States *by David Walker*

EMANCIPATION AND THE NADIR

After the Civil War, both black and white missionaries descended on the South to work among the newly freed population, spreading literacy, middle-class values, and "proper" religion. The A.M.E. and A.M.E. Zion denominations expanded into the South and accepted as members some who were both pulled and pushed out of the white Methodist Episcopal Church, South. For not only did some southern black Methodists welcome a chance to affiliate voluntarily with churches that were controlled by African Americans, but a number of southern white churchmen were also uncomfortable having to share church membership with a recently enslaved people whom they would now have to treat as equals. With some assistance from the white denomination, a new church was formed, the Colored Methodist Episcopal Church (now the Christian Methodist Episcopal Church).

The excitement and hopes of the former slaves as they gained their freedom were dashed within a generation. The end of Radical Reconstruction and the rise of disenfranchisement, Jim Crow, lynching, sharecropping, economic uncertainty, and immigration ushered in the era known as "the nadir." During this time, there was renewed interest in Africa as a place where African Americans could thrive without the shackles of discrimination. Some African Americans earnestly debated the prospects of colonizing Africa, and a few did manage to make the arduous journey across the Atlantic. Bishop Henry McNeil Turner (1834–1915), a former Civil War chaplain and member of the Georgia legislature during Reconstruction, used his position as the editor of the A.M.E. publication the *Christian Recorder* to advocate a return to Africa. He received much criticism from other leaders who recognized that African Americans were in many

People outside of a storefront church on Easter Sunday. This 1941 image is the work of Russell Lee, who worked in Chicago as a Farm Security Administration photographer, one of the few who was given an urban assignment. **THE LIBRARY OF CONGRESS**

ways more American than African and had earned a right to share in the wealth and destiny of the United States because of their long years of service and servitude.

Relatively few clergy joined Turner's call for an exodus to Africa, but many did try to understand God's purpose in allowing African Americans to experience the horrors of slavery and its aftermath. Rev. Francis J. Grimke (1850–1937) castigated the white American church for its tolerance of racism but continued to have hope in the power of Christianity to transform the nation and enable African Americans to assume their rightful place.

Many preachers turned to Psalm 68:31—"Princes shall come out of Egypt and Ethiopia shall soon stretch forth her hands unto God"—as a prophecy of African American destiny. Some concluded that through the trials of slavery, African Americans had been exposed to Christianity in order to "redeem" Africa and the world. The Anglican cleric Rev. Alexander Crummell (1819–1898), who was a proponent of this view, spent twenty years in Africa as a missionary. African American theologians like Theophilus Gould Steward (1843–1924) and J. Theodore Holly (1829–1911) concluded that an age dominated by a corrupt, racist Christianity would

soon come to a close and be followed by a new age, in which a pure faith carried by the African race would realize the Kingdom of God on earth.

During this period, African American Baptists founded the National Baptist Convention as a separate black denomination. Five years later, in 1900, Baptist women formed a separate women's convention that worked alongside the Baptist men. Under the leadership of trained women like Nannie Helen Burroughs (1879–1961), the convention supported schools and other educational projects designed to uplift the race. Concern for the negative stereotypes of African American women as immoral—stereotypes that exposed them to a variety of harms—led convention women to emphasize middle-class values as part of their agenda. These women also built on the legacy of Jarena Lee and others by interpreting the Bible in ways that emphasized the important role of women. Inevitably, their efforts presented both a formal, intellectual challenge to the male-dominated church hierarchy and a mirror image of it.

THE URBAN NORTH

With the Great Migration at the beginning of the twentieth century, thousands of African Americans moved to the

In this 1941 photograph, African Americans are worshiping together in a store front Baptist church in Chicago. Black preachers also joined the Great Migration, establishing their own small churches and encouraging members of their old communities to join them in the North. Churches such as this one sprang up throughout the black neighborhoods of northern cities. **THE LIBRARY OF CONGRESS**

North and brought their religious beliefs and practices with them. They swelled the numbers of established black churches, which increased personnel and expanded programs to meet the wide-ranging needs of the newcomers. The Sunday school enrollment of Olivet Baptist Church in Chicago grew to three thousand, and church membership to over eight thousand. The work of the church and its forty-four departments was directed by its pastor, Rev. Lacey Kirk Williams (1871–1940), and five assistant pastors.

Churches were the center of African American social and political life, due largely to the lack of social services available from other sources. Drama clubs, sewing clubs, day-care centers, employment bureaus, and athletic teams were some of the programs that many churches added to their schedule of worship and Bible study. The number of storefront churches grew as migrants who missed the intimacy and leadership opportunities available in their smaller rural churches sought to recreate that atmosphere in the urban North.

Urban life offered African Americans a number of options not available in the premigration South. Dissat-

isfaction with northern ghetto life has been credited with feeding enthusiasm for Marcus Garvey and the Universal Negro Improvement Association (UNIA). A number of African American clergymen supported the UNIA (among them Rev. Earl Little, the father of Malcolm X), which had as its chaplain general Rev. George McGuire, an Episcopal priest who later founded the African Orthodox Church. The UNIA published a *Universal Negro Catechism,* which debunked religious arguments for Negro inferiority and highlighted the role of prominent African Americans, as well as promoting the mission and purposes of the organization.

A number of new African American religious groups arose at the turn of the century, including the Church of God in Christ. This Pentecostal group was founded in Memphis by Rev. Charles H. Mason after he had returned to his church from a trip to the Azusa Street revival in Los Angeles. At the revival, he experienced the gift of speaking in tongues that has become a defining characteristic of Pentecostal churches. Today, the predominantly black Church of God in Christ, with over two million members, is one of the two largest Pentecostal denominations in the world. Smaller groups, like the United House of Prayer under Bishop Charles Emmanuel "Daddy" Grace (1882–1960), the Father Divine Peace Mission Movement, the Church of God/Saints of Christ (Black Jews) led by Prophet William Crowdy (1847–1908), and the Moorish Science Temple (Black Islam) founded by Noble Drew Ali (b. 1886), also sprouted in the urban North and gained a significant number of followers.

SEE PRIMARY SOURCE DOCUMENT *The Autobiography of Omar ibn Said*

ISLAM

The Nation of Islam soon eclipsed the Moorish Science Temple. It is not known whether W. D. Fard, the founder of the Nation of Islam, had any contact with Nobel Drew Ali. In the 1930s, Fard converted and enlisted Elijah Poole (1897–1975), who came to be known as the Honorable Elijah Muhammad and took over the movement after Fard's disappearance in 1934. The Black Muslims taught that white men were devils and that Islam was the true religion of African Americans.

The conversion and rise to leadership of Malcolm X (formerly Malcolm Little) (1925–1965) spurred an increase in the membership and visibility of the Nation of Islam. Conflicts between Malcolm X and Elijah Muhammad, which led to Malcolm's dismissal from the Nation of Islam, are suspected to have also led to his assassination. Malcolm X had adopted a more orthodox form of Islam and was pressing publicly for the human rights of African Americans. Upon the death of Elijah Muhammad, the Nation of Islam split into two factions. Muhammad's son Wallace steered one faction, the interracial American Muslim Mission, toward a more traditional form of Islam. The other faction, the Nation of Islam, has been led by Louis Farrakhan (b. 1933), who continues to espouse the separatist ideas of Elijah Muhammad.

Nation of Islam leaders have consistently faced controversy. When Malcolm X had his falling out with Elijah Muhammad and was ultimately murdered, members of the black community wondered about the involvement of Elijah Muhammad's faction in Malcolm X's assassination. More recently, media organizations historically controlled by whites have targeted the Nation of Islam, in part because its tenets fall outside of mainstream public opinion. Despite these controversies, the Nation of Islam has provided a belief system of "uplift" for disenfranchised African Americans, encouraging a life of intense personal organization, mutual respect, and hard work. The Nation of Islam leader Elijah Muhammad is largely responsible for uniting the disparate threads of Islamic faith within the United States under a powerful

A Farm Security Administration photographer shot this picture of a black congregation leaving church. In the early 1940s it was common for congregations from neighboring churches to join together in revival services. **THE LIBRARY OF CONGRESS**

rubric with a centralized message. In addition, while it has been disparaged in the decades following the civil rights era, there can be no doubt that the organization, personified for a period by the figure of Malcolm X, was a key party in the civil rights struggle.

GOSPEL MUSIC AND RELIGIOUS IDENTITY

Urbanization not only brought about an explosion in the number of religious options available to African Americans; it also brought about new styles of worship. Perhaps the most important of these has been the rise of modern gospel music, credited to the untiring efforts and ingenuity of Thomas Andrew Dorsey (1899–1993), now called "the Father of Gospel Music."

Dorsey was born into a religious family in rural Georgia. At the same time, he was exposed and attracted to blues music and became a popular blues piano player, backing up singers like Gertrude "Ma" Rainey (1886–1939). The death of his wife and child inspired his song "Precious Lord, Take My Hand." This personal crisis, among others, pushed him permanently into the religious-music arena. His songs, which married blues rhythms and chords with religious lyrics, met much resistance in established churches, but Dorsey eventually found a home at Chicago's Ebenezer Baptist Church, under Rev. J. H. L. Smith.

At a Black Muslim rally in New York City on August 6, 1963, Malcolm X holds up a paper for the crowd to see. **AP/WIDE WORLD PHOTOS**

Rev. Smith welcomed a music that was more familiar to some of the newly arrived migrants from the South. Many African American churches in the North had copied European forms of worship, incorporating classical music into their services and leaving behind spirituals and the more lively music and worship styles associated with slavery. The forerunners of this Europeanization were a number of nineteenth-century African American clergymen who had worked to move black worship as far as possible from its slave roots. Prominent among these clergymen was the A.M.E. bishop Daniel Alexander Payne (1811–1893), who railed against the ring shout and "fist and heel worshipers."

Dorsey, from his new base at Ebenezer (and later Chicago's Pilgrim Baptist), set out to promote his music with the singer Sallie Martin (1896–1988). He became a cofounder and first president of the National Convention of Gospel Choirs and Choruses, and through its activities he did much to popularize gospel music. Other gospel music pioneers include Roberta Martin (1912–1969), Clara Ward (1924–1973), Lucie Eddie Campbell (1885–1962), and Rev. William Herbert Brewster (1897–1987). Groups like the Soul Stirrers, the Pilgrim Travelers, and the Swan Silvertones and soloists like Mahalia Jackson (1911–1972), Marion Williams (1927–1994), and Willa Mae Ford Smith became quite popular as they helped move gospel music out of the church and onto the concert stage. In the early 2000s, gospel music is a multimillion-dollar industry that has launched the careers of many rhythm-and-blues and soul artists, including Sam Cooke (1935–1964) and Aretha Franklin (b. 1942).

RELIGION AND THE MODERN CIVIL RIGHTS MOVEMENT

The modern Civil Rights movement had deep roots in the African American church tradition. Dr. Martin Luther King Jr. (1929–1968) was a third-generation Baptist preacher who was well acquainted with African American religious culture. He continually portrayed civil rights (and later, militarism and poverty) as a profoundly moral and religious issue. His emphasis on nonviolence as an active strategy required by a Christian ethic of love helped to establish a firm religious base for the movement.

However, it must not be forgotten that African American clergy had long debated with other African American leaders about the efficacy of nonviolence. Howard Thurman (1900–1981), the dean of the Howard University Chapel, and his wife, Sue Bailey, traveled to India in 1935 to meet with Gandhi (1869–1948), followed in 1936 by Benjamin Mays (1895–1984), the dean of the Howard University School of Religion. Upon returning to the United States, they wrote and lectured about Gandhi and his movement. Although Mordecai Johnson (1890–1976), the president of Howard University, had championed Gandhi as a model for African Americans since the 1920s, his own trip to India did not take place until the late 1940s. King later credited a sermon by Johnson with introducing him to the methods and tactics pioneered by Gandhi.

Themes articulated by King in his speeches echo ideas found throughout the African American religious tradition. For example, in his "Letter from Birmingham Jail," he decried the hypocrisy and impotent faith of white churchmen, as Grimke and others had done generations earlier. Although arguably muted, the voices of Alexander Crummell (1819–1898), J. Theodore Holly, and Theophilus Gould Steward can be heard in King's "I Have a Dream" speech, as he envisions a nation redeemed and transformed by the power of love as practiced by African Americans. On the eve of his assassination, when he spoke of having seen the promised land, King evoked the vivid biblical imagery of the Exodus that has been central to African American religious thought from antebellum days.

The rhythmic and forceful African American preaching style of King and other leaders of the Civil Rights movement, along with the rich African American sacred music traditions adapted to new circumstances, mobilized large numbers of people, black and white. That marriage of preaching style and sacred music became a powerful instrument, trumpeting the message of civil rights and human justice that was the goal of the movement—a message of hope needed to sustain weary warriors who faced violence, brutality, and a host of indignities as part of the ongoing struggle.

It was to be expected that the African American church would play a key role in the modern Civil Rights movement. As noted above, the independent African American church, from its inception, has been in the forefront of the struggle for freedom and equality. There are a number of reasons for this, and an obvious one is that church buildings, owned and operated by African Americans, have been the most available, accessible, and secure spaces for meetings in the African American community. African American preachers, effective public speakers holding the respect and confidence of their church members, have consequently been elected to pub-

More than any other singer, Mahalia Jackson (1911–1972) was responsible for bringing gospel music to a nationwide audience. **AP/WIDE WORLD PHOTOS**

lic office since the days of Reconstruction. Henry McNeil Turner was only one of many mid-nineteenth-century clerics who established patterns followed by twentieth-century pastors and preachers like Adam Clayton Powell Jr. (1908–1972), Walter Fauntroy (b. 1933), William Gray, Floyd Flake (b. 1945), and Jesse Jackson (b. 1941).

Although male preachers have been prominent, there are countless laypersons, both female and male, who have acquired critical skills in public speaking and organization through their nurture in, and association with, the African American church. When private and public secular institutions denied services to persons of color and excluded them from leadership, the African American church filled the need with its own resources. As times have changed, secular institutions have become more inclusive, and a wider variety of African American organizations has been established. The public role of the African American church will thus change, even though the persistence of racism and poverty presents a constant challenge to all African American organizations and people. The church's independence from whites, as well as the relative autonomy of its leadership and finances, continues to make it an ideal instrument for social action on behalf of the community it serves and is served by.

The Reverend Jesse Jackson is known for, among other things, being the first African American to launch a serious presidential campaign. **CORBIS-BETTMANN**

THE AFRICAN AMERICAN PREACHER/ LEADER: JESSE JACKSON AND AL SHARPTON

During the second half of the twentieth century, African Americans found themselves in a continual struggle between the legacy of religious and social traditions and the growing desire to see their leaders make real progress in the nation's two-party political system. This struggle has contributed to the career of the Reverend Jesse Jackson, a savvy and skilled politician who has carried with him, at least in the eyes of the nation's memory, the legacy of having been at Martin Luther King Jr.'s side at the time of his assassination.

It is no mistake—and a very particular element of African American political history—that virtually all of the African American leaders who have captured the nation's attention, particularly those regarded as possible presidential candidates, have been associated with the church. In the age-old puritan dynamic of the nation, prominent African American political figures fell into one of two categories: that of the preacher or that of the revolutionary/criminal, an example of the latter being Black Panther Eldridge Cleaver. Some have gone as far as to speculate that African Americans *will* have a presiden-

tial candidate, but only when a star athlete and national hero along the lines of a Michael Jordan is in the running. There can be no doubt that mainstream America has been willing to embrace only a very select range of African American figures.

This unwillingness on the part of mainstream America brings into perspective an uneasiness that America has with itself, its history, and the collective choices of the nation over the centuries. It has been argued that Jackson, in spite of his qualifications, reminds the electorate of the turmoil and shame of the King years and that period of assassination. Despite his opposition to the views of Malcolm X, Jackson may bring to mind for a certain segment of middle America the tirades of the militant black leader that were broadcast on national television during the 1960s, despite Jackson's efforts over twenty years to free hostages, negotiate peace, and help war-torn nations and peoples in crisis.

Based on election returns, the Reverend Al Sharpton at various times in his career had the ear of more than 85 percent of African Americans and 35 percent of the Democratic voters as a whole in New York City—easily enough

Protestors, including Reverend Al Sharpton (right of center), demonstrate against the killing of Amadou Diallo. Diallo, an unarmed immigrant, was shot at forty-one times by New York City police when they mistook his wallet for a gun. Photograph by Ed Bailey. **AP/WIDE WORLD PHOTOS**

to be a contender in any mayoral race—and still failed to make it onto the national radar of the news media. It is disturbing that a man who has comported himself in an essentially dignified way, while championing the issues that fell on his side of the color line, has been accused of political/religious shilling for the disenfranchised for his own personal gain. All of this makes for a curious indicator of the nebulous and enduring prevalence of racial stereotypes during the twentieth and earlier centuries.

In times of racial injustice and unrest, Sharpton has assumed the role of leader and spokesperson. For example, he led protestors following two infamous cases involving the New York City Police Department. The first concerned Abner Louima, a Haitian immigrant who was brutally sodomized with a toilet plunger in the bathroom of a New York Police Department station house in 1997. Two years later, police shot and killed Amadou Diallo, an unarmed African immigrant who worked two jobs. Officers fired forty-one times at Diallo, who was standing on the front step of his apartment building, striking him with nineteen bullets. Both incidents occurred during the administration of Mayor Rudolph Giuliani, who had won over the public while

launching an all-out assault on so-called "quality of life" crimes (jaywalking, panhandling, and prostitution). The cases of Louima and Diallo served as lightning rods for the sentiment among the city's poorer citizens that the economic good times and the experience of Giuliani's "new New York" heralded by so many, did not extend to them. Following each incident, Sharpton spoke out against the violence to thousands who attended rallies where many contended that the New York City Police Department had a history of abusing and harassing civilians.

It should be pointed out that as Sharpton's career has progressed, he has brought a more dignified and serious tone to his leadership, which has caused the media to struggle with their portrayal of him. For many African Americans it is precisely this type of contradiction that makes for continuing proof that the nation turns a deaf ear where issues of importance to the black populace are concerned. In the late 1980s and early 1990s there was a sense that the nation had failed to come to understand or appreciate the very traditions that underpinned the history of African Americans in the United States. For example, many felt that the subtle reverence with which the media might treat the figure of an Irish priest or policeman certainly did not extend to the figure of a reverend of African American descent who was doing double duty as a public figure and political leader. With the very real changes in the quality of African American life in the second half of the twentieth century, this is a prime example of the subtle and tenacious kinds of prejudicial attitudes so deeply embedded in the fabric of American culture.

BIBLIOGRAPHY

Allen, Richard. *The Life Experience and Gospel Labors of the Rt. Rev. Richard Allen.* Nashville: Abingdon Press, 1960.

Aptheker, Herbert. *American Negro Slave Revolts.* New York: International Publishers, 1987.

Cone, James H., and Gayraud S. Wilmore, eds. *Black Theology: A Documentary History.* Maryknoll: Orbis Books, 1979.

Higginbotham, Evelyn Brooks. *Righteous Discontent: The Women's Movement in the Black Baptist Church, 1880–1920.* Cambridge: Harvard University Press, 1993.

Mullin, Gerald. *Flight and Rebellion: Slave Resistance in Eighteenth-Century Virginia.* New York: Oxford University Press, 1972.

Raboteau, Albert J. *Slave Religion: The Invisible Institution in the Antebellum South.* New York: Oxford University Press, 1978.

Walker, David. *David Walker's Appeal to the Coloured Citizens of the United States.* New York: Hill and Wang, 1995.

PRIMARY SOURCE DOCUMENT

Letter from a Slave on the Subject of Religion

INTRODUCTION Religion has long been understood to be an integral part of African American life. During slavery, religion had many functions and meanings. An agency of social control by white masters, religion was for many slaves a refuge from a hostile world. Slaves were not unaware of this contradiction. Many, in their testimony about slavery, noted that whites used religion in selective ways as a means to shape their workers' behavior. Only limited portions of the Bible were read to slaves—sections that emphasized subservience and docility. But the slaves themselves forged their own unique forms of religion hidden from the watchful eyes of their masters. And as they used religion to help them understand their world, slaves found ways to critique whites' hypocrisy.

This letter was written by a slave to a prominent white preacher in North Carolina. The slave astutely points to the underlying concerns of most masters. Rather than acting as Christians, owners are focused on the money that they can make off of slave labor. For the man writing this letter, such behavior contradicts the meaning of religion.

Wayne County, Ga., 26 June 1821

Master John I want permition if you pleas to speak A few words to you—I hope you will not think me too bold sir, I make my wants known to you because you are, I believe, the oldist and most experienced that I know of in the first place I want you to tell me the Reson you allways preach to the white folks and keep your back to us.

is it because they sit up on the hill we have no chance a mong them there must we be for goten because we cant get near enoughf without getting in the edg of the swamp be hind you. we have no other chance because your stand is on the edg of the swamp, if I should ask you what must I do to be saved, perhaps you would tel me pray let the bible be your gide this would do very well if wee could read I do not think there is one in fifty that can read but I have been more fortunate than the most of the black people I can read and write in my way as to be understood I hopes I have a weak mind about the dutys of religious people If god sent you to preach to siners did he direct you to keep your face to the white folks constantly or is it because they give you money if this is the cause we are the very persons that labor for this money but it is handed to you by our masters did god tell you to have your meeting housis just larg enoughf to hold the white folks and let the black people stand in the sone and rain as the brooks in the field we are charged with inatention it is imposibal for us to pay good attention with this chance in fact some of us scars think we are preached to at all money appears to be the object we are carid to market and sold to the highest bider never once inquire whither you sold to a heathon or christian if the question was put did you sel to a christian what would be the answer I cant tel what he was gave me my prise thats all was interested in Is this the way to heavin if it is there will a good meny go there if not there chance will be bad for there can be many witnesses against them If I understand the white people they are praying for more religion in the world oh may our case not be forgoten in the prairs of the sincear I now leave it to you and your aids to consider or I hope you will reade it to the chearch if you think proper it is likely I never will hear from you on this subject as I live far from you I don't wish you to take any of these things to your self if nothing is due do your god justis in this case and you will doo me the same.

PRIMARY SOURCE DOCUMENT

Excerpt from *The Life and Religious Experience of Jarena Lee, A Coloured Lady*

INTRODUCTION Jarena Lee was born to free parents in 1783 in New Jersey and, like other children of the time, put out to service at a young age. Alone and unguided, Lee nevertheless had a strong sense of right and wrong, but it was not until 1804, at the age of twenty-one, that she experienced Christian conversion. Dissatisfied with the English church, she began to attend services at Richard Allen's Bethel African Methodist Episcopal Church in Philadelphia and soon felt called to preach to the congregation. Richard Allen turned down her request, arguing that women could not preach in the Methodist church.

Undeterred, Lee remained firm in her belief in her own spiritual authority and the spiritual authority of women in general, and in 1818 Bishop Allen finally granted her request. In the years that followed, Lee traveled widely, preaching to audiences of men and women, black and white.

Her *Life and Religious Experience of Jarena Lee, a Coloured Lady*, published in 1836, may well be the first autobiography by an African American woman. It bears strong witness to her own spiritual life and to her belief in the power and effectiveness of women's spirituality.

And it shall come to pass…that I will pour out my Spirit upon all flesh; and your sons, and your daughters shall prophecy.

Joel ii. 28

I was born February 11th, 1783, at Cape May, state of New Jersey. At the age of seven years I was parted from my parents, and went to live as a servant maid, with a Mr. Sharp, at the distance of about sixty miles from the place of my birth.

My parents being wholly ignorant of the knowledge of God, had not therefore instructed me in any degree in this great matter. Not long after the commencement of my attendance on this lady, she had bid me do something respecting my work, which in a little while after, she asked me if I had done, when I replied, Yes—but this was not true.

At this awful point, in my early history, the spirit of God moved in power through my conscience, and told me I was a wretched sinner. On this account so great was the impression, and so strong were the feelings of guilt, that I promised in my heart that I would not tell another lie.

But notwithstanding this promise my heart grew harder, after a while, yet the spirit of the Lord never entirely forsook me, but continued mercifully striving with me, until his gracious power converted my soul.

The manner of this great accomplishment was as follows: In the year 1804, it so happened that I went with others to hear a missionary of the Presbyterian order preach. It was an afternoon meeting, but few were there, the place was a school room; but the preacher was solemn, and in his countenance the earnestness of his master's business appeared equally strong, as though he were about to speak to a multitude.

At the reading of the Psalms, a ray of renewed conviction darted into my soul. These were the words, composing the first verse of the Psalms for the service:

Lord, I am vile, conceived in sin, Born unholy and unclean. Sprung from man, whose guilty fall Corrupts the race, and taints us all.

This description of my condition struck me to the heart, and made me to feel in some measure, the weight of my sins, and sinful nature. But not knowing how to run immediately to the Lord for help, I was driven of Satan, in the course of a few days, and tempted to destroy myself.

There was a brook about a quarter of a mile from the house, in which there was a deep hole, where the water whirled about among the rocks; to this place it was suggested, I must go and drown myself.

At the time I had a book in my hand; it was on a Sabbath morning, about ten o'clock; to this place I resorted, where on coming to the water I sat down on the bank, and on my looking into it; it was suggested, that drowning would be an easy death. It seemed as if some one was speaking to me, saying put your head under, it will not distress you. But by some means, of which I can give no account, my thoughts were taken entirely from this purpose, when I went from the place to the house again. It was the unseen arm of God which saved me from self murder.

But notwithstanding this escape from death, my mind was not at rest—but so great was the labour of my spirit and the fearful oppressions of a judgment to come, that I was reduced as one extremely ill. On which account a physician was called to attend me, from which illness I recovered in about three months.

But as yet I had not found him of whom Moses and the prophets did write, being extremely ignorant: there being no one to instruct me in the way of life and salvation as yet. After my recovery, I left the lady, who during my sickness, was exceedingly kind, and went to Philadelphia. From this place I soon went a few miles into the country, where I resided in the family of a Roman Catholic. But my anxiety still continued respecting my poor soul, on which account I used to watch my opportunity to read in the Bible; and this lady observing this, took the Bible from me and hid it, giving me a novel in its stead—which when I perceived, I refused to read.

Soon after this I again went to the city of Philadelphia; and commenced going to the English Church, the pastor of which was an Englishman, by the name of Pilmore, one of the number, who at first preached Methodism in America, in the city of New York.

But while sitting under the ministration of this man, which was about three months, and at the last time, it appeared that there was a wall between me and a communion with that people, which was higher than I could possibly see over, and seemed to make this impression upon my mind, this is not the people for you.

But on returning home at noon I inquired of the head cook of the house respecting the rules of the Methodists, as I knew she belonged to that society, who told me what they were; on which account I replied, that I should not be able to abide by such strict rules not even one year;—however, I told her that I would go with her and hear what they had to say.

The man who was to speak in the afternoon of that day, was the Rev. Richard Allen, since bishop of the African Episcopal Methodists in America. During the labors of this man that afternoon, I had come to the conclusion, that this is the people to which my heart unites, and it so happened, that as soon as the service closed he invited such as felt a desire to flee the wrath to come, to unite on trial with them—I embraced the opportunity. Three weeks from that day, my soul was gloriously converted to God, under preaching, at the very outset of the sermon. The text was barely pronounced, which was: "I perceive thy heart is not right in the sight of God" [Acts 8:21], when there appeared to my view, in the centre of the heart one sin; and this was malice, against one particular individual, who had strove deeply to injure me, which I resented. At this discovery I said, Lord I forgive every creature. That instant, it appeared to me, as if a garment, which had entirely enveloped my whole person, even to my fingers ends, split at the crown of my head, and was stripped away from me, passing like a shadow, from my sight—when the glory of God seemed to cover me in its stead.

That moment, though hundreds were present, I did leap to my feet, and declare that God, for Christ's sake, had pardoned the sins of my soul. Great was the ecstasy of my mind, for I felt that not only the sin of malice was pardoned, but all other sins were swept away together. That day was the first when my heart had believed, and my tongue had made confession unto salvation—the first words uttered, a part of that song, which shall fill eternity with its sound, was glory to God. For a few moments I had power to exhort sinners, and to tell of the wonders and of the goodness of him who had clothed me with his salvation. During this, the minister was silent, until my soul felt its duty had been performed, when he declared another witness of the power of Christ to forgive sins on earth, was manifest in my conversion.

From the day on which I first went to the Methodist church, until the hour of my deliverance, I was strangely buffetted by that enemy of all righteousness—the devil.

I was naturally of a lively turn of disposition; and during the space of time from my first awakening until I knew my peace was made with God, I rejoiced in the vanities of this life, and then again sunk back into sorrow.

For four years I had continued in this way, frequently labouring under the awful apprehension, that I could never be happy in this life. This persuasion was greatly strengthened, during the three weeks, which was the last of Satan's power over me, in this peculiar manner: on which account, I had come to the conclusion that I had better be dead than alive. Here I was again tempted to destroy my life by drowning; but suddenly this mode was changed, and while in the dusk of the evening, as I was walking to and fro in the yard of the house, I was beset to hang myself, with a cord suspended from the wall enclosing the secluded spot.

But no sooner was the intention resolved on in my mind, than an awful dread came over me, when I ran into the house; still the tempter pursued me. There was standing a vessel of water—into this I was strongly impressed to plunge my head, so as to extinguish the life which God had given me. Had I have done this, I have been always of the opinion that I should have been unable to have released myself; although the vessel was scarcely large enough to hold a gallon of water. Of me may it not be said, as written by Isaiah, (chap. 65, verses 1,2.) "I am sought of them that asked not for me; I am found of them that sought me not." Glory be to God for his redeeming power, which saved me from the violence of my own hands, from the malice of Satan, and from eternal death; for had I have killed myself, a great ransom could not have delivered me; for it is written—"No murderer hath eternal life abiding in him"[1 John 3:15]. How appropriately can I sing—

"Jesus sought me, when a stranger, Wandering from the fold of God; He to rescue me from danger, Interposed his precious blood."

But notwithstanding the terror which seized upon me, when about to end my life, I had no view of the precipice on the edge of which I was tottering, until it was over, and my eyes were opened. Then the awful gulf of hell seemed to be open beneath me, covered only, as it were, by a spider's web, on which I stood. I seemed to hear the howling of the damned, to see the smoke of the bottomless pit, and to hear the rattling of those chains, which hold the impenitent under clouds of darkness to the judgment of the great day.

I trembled like Belshazzar, and cried out in the horror of my spirit, "God be merciful to me a sinner." That night I formed a resolution to pray; which, when resolved upon, there appeared, sitting in one corner of the room, Satan, in the form of a monstrous dog, and in a rage, as if in pursuit, his tongue protruding from his mouth to a great length, and his eyes looked like two balls of fire; it soon, however, vanished out of my sight. From this state of terror and dismay, I was happily delivered under the preaching of the Gospel as before related.

This view, which I was permitted to have of Satan, in the form of a dog, is evidence, which corroborates in my estimation, the Bible account of a hell of fire, which burneth with brimstone, called in Scripture the bottomless pit; the place where all liars, who repent not, shall have their portion; as also the Sabbath breaker, the adulterer, the fornicator, with the fearful, the abominable, and the unbelieving, this shall be the portion of their cup.

This language is too strong and expressive to be applied to any state of suffering in time. Were it to be thus applied, the reality could no where be found in human life; the consequence would be, that this scripture would be found a false testimony. But when made to apply to an endless state of perdition, in eternity, beyond the bounds of human life, then this language is found not to exceed our views of a state of eternal damnation.

During the latter part of my state of conviction, I can now apply to my case, as it then was, the beautiful words of the poet:

"The more I strove against its power, I felt its weight and guilt the more; 'Till late I hear'd my Saviour say, Come hither soul, I am the way."

This I found to be true, to the joy of my disconsolate and despairing heart, in the hour of my conversion to God.

During this state of mind, while sitting near the fire one evening, after I had heard Rev. Richard Allen, as before related, a view of my distressed condition so affected my heart, that I could not refrain from weeping and crying aloud; which caused the lady with whom I then lived, to inquire, with surprise, what ailed me; to which I answered, that I knew not what ailed me. She replied that I ought to pray. I arose from where I was sitting, being in an agony, and weeping convulsively, requested her to pray for me; but at the very moment when she would have done so, some person rapped heavily at the door for admittance; it was but a person of the house, but this occurrence was sufficient to interrupt us in our intentions; and I believe to this day, I should then have found salvation to my soul. This interruption was, doubtless, also the work of Satan.

Although at this time, when my conviction was so great, yet I knew not that Jesus Christ was the Son of God, the second person in the adorable trinity. I knew him not in the pardon of my sins, yet I felt a consciousness that if I died without pardon, that my lot must inevitably be damnation. If I would pray—I knew not how. I could form no connexion of ideas into words; but I knew the Lord's prayer; this I uttered with a loud voice, and with all my might and strength. I was the most ignorant creature in the world; I did not even know that Christ had died for the sins of the world, and to save sinners. Every circumstance, however, was so directed as still to continue and increase the sorrows of my heart, which I now know to have been a godly sorrow which wrought repentance, which is not to be repented of. Even the falling of the dead leaves from the forests, and the dried spires of the mown grass, showed me that I too must die, in like manner. But my case was awfully different from that of the grass of the field, or the wide spread decay of a thousand forests, as I felt within me a living principle, an immortal spirit, which cannot die, and must forever either enjoy the smiles of its Creator, or feel the pangs of ceaseless damnation.

But the Lord led me on; being gracious, he took pity on my ignorance; he heard my wailings, which had entered into the ear of the Lord of Sabaoth. Circum-

stances so transpired that I soon came to a knowledge of the being and character of the Son of God, of whom I knew nothing.

My strength had left me. I had become feverish and sickly through the violence of my feelings, on which account I left my place of service to spend a week with a coloured physician, who was a member of the Methodist society, and also to spend this week in going to places where prayer and supplication was statedly made for such as me.

Through this means I had learned much, so as to be able in some degree to comprehend the spiritual meaning of the text, which the minister took on the Sabbath morning, as before related, which was, "I perceive thy heart is not right in the sight of God." Acts, chap. 8, verse 21.

This text, as already related, became the power of God unto salvation to me, because I believed. I was baptized according to the direction of our Lord, who said, as he was about to ascend from the mount, to his disciples, "Go ye into all the world and preach my gospel to every creature, he that believeth and is baptized shall be saved" [Mark 16:15-16].

I have now passed through the account of my conviction, and also of my conversion to God; and shall next speak of the blessing of sanctification.

A time after I had received forgiveness flowed sweetly on; day and night my joy was full, no temptation was permitted to molest me. I could say continually with the psalmist, that "God had separated my sins from me, as far as the east is from the west" [Ps. 103:12]. I was ready continually to cry,

"Come all the world, come sinner thou, All things in Christ are ready now."

I continued in this happy state of mind for almost three months, when a certain coloured man, by name William Scott, came to pay me a religious visit. He had been for many years a faithful follower of the Lamb; and he had also taken much time in visiting the sick and distressed of our colour, and understood well the great things belonging to a man of full stature in Christ Jesus.

In the course of our conversation, he inquired if the Lord had justified my soul. I answered, yes. He then asked me if he had sanctified me. I answered, no; and that I did not know what that was. He then undertook to instruct me further in the knowledge of the Lord respecting this blessing.

He told me the progress of the soul from a state of darkness, or of nature, was threefold; or consisted in three degrees, as follows: —First, conviction for sin. Second, justification from sin. Third, the entire sanctification of the soul to God. I thought this description was beautiful, and immediately believed in it. He then inquired if I would promise to pray for this in my secret devotions. I told him, yes. Very soon I began to call upon the Lord to show me all that was in my heart, which was not according to his will. Now there appeared to be a new struggle commencing in my soul, not accompanied with fear, guilt, and bitter distress, as while under my first conviction for sin; but a labouring of the mind to know more of the right way of the Lord. I began now to feel that my heart was not clean in his sight; that there yet remained the roots of bitterness, which if not destroyed, would ere long sprout up from these roots, and overwhelm me in a new growth of the brambles and brushwood of sin.

By the increasing light of the Spirit, I had found there yet remained the root of pride, anger, self-will, with many evils, the result of fallen nature. I now became alarmed at this discovery, and began to fear that I had been deceived in my experience. I was now greatly alarmed, lest I should fall away from what I knew I had enjoyed; and to guard against this I prayed almost incessantly, without acting faith on the power and promises of God to keep me from falling. I had not yet learned how to war against temptation of this kind. Satan well knew that if he could succeed in making me disbelieve my conversion, that he would catch me either on the ground of complete despair, or on the ground of infidelity. For if all I had passed through was to go for nothing, and was but a fiction, the mere ravings of a disordered mind, then I would naturally be led to believe that there is nothing in religion at all.

From this snare I was mercifully preserved, and led to believe that there was yet a greater work than that of pardon to be wrought in me. I retired to a secret place (after having sought this blessing, as well as I could, for nearly three months, from the time brother Scott had instructed me respecting it) for prayer, about four o'clock in the afternoon. I had struggled long and hard, but found not the desire of my heart. When I rose from my knees, there seemed a voice speaking to me, as I yet stood in a leaning posture—"Ask for sanctification." When to my surprise, I recollected that I had not even thought of it in my whole prayer. It would seem Satan had hidden the very object from my mind, for which I had purposely kneeled to pray. But when this voice whispered in my heart, saying, "Pray for sanctification," I again bowed in the same place, at the same time, and said, "Lord sanctify my soul for Christ's sake?" That very instant, as if lightning had darted through me, I sprang to my feet, and cried, "The Lord has sanctified my soul!" There was none to hear this but the angels who stood around to witness my joy—and Satan, whose malice raged the more. That Satan was there, I knew; for no sooner had I cried out, "The Lord has sanctified my soul," than there seemed another voice behind me, saying, "No, it is too great a work to be done." But another

spirit said, "Bow down for the witness—I received it—thou art sanctified!" There first I knew of myself after that, I was standing in the yard with my hands spread out, and looking with my face toward heaven.

I now ran into the house and told them what had happened to me, when, as it were, a new rush of the same ecstasy came upon me, and caused me to feel as if I were in an ocean of light and bliss.

During this, I stood perfectly still, the tears rolling in a flood from my eyes. So great was the joy, that it is past description. There is no language that can describe it, except that which was heard by St. Paul, when he was caught up to the third heaven, and heard words which it was not lawful to utter.

My Call To Preach The Gospel

Between four and five years after my sanctification, on a certain time, an impressive silence fell upon me, and I stood as if some one was about to speak to me, yet I had no such thought in my heart. But to my utter surprise there seemed to sound a voice which I thought I distinctly heard, and most certainly understood, which said to me "Go preach the Gospel!" I immediately replied aloud. "No one will believe me." Again I listened, and again the same voice seemed to say, "Preach the Gospel; I will put words in your mouth, and will turn your enemies to become your friends."

At first I supposed that Satan had spoken to me, for I had read that he could transform himself into an angel of light, for the purpose of deception. Immediately I went into a secret place, and called upon the Lord to know if he had called me to preach, and whether I was deceived or not; when there appeared to my view the form and figure of a pulpit, with a Bible lying thereon, the back of which was presented to me as plainly as if it had been a literal fact.

In consequence of this, my mind became so exercised that during the night following, I took a text, and preached in my sleep. I thought there stood before me a great multitude, while I expounded to them the things of religion. So violent were my exertions, and so loud were my exclamations, that I awoke from the sound of my own voice, which also awoke the family of the house where I resided. Two days after, I went to see the preacher in charge of the African Society, who was the Rev. Richard Allen, the same before named in these pages, to tell him that I felt it my duty to preach the gospel. But as I drew near the street in which his house was, which was in the city of Philadelphia, my courage began to fail me; so terrible did the cross appear, it seemed that I should not be able to bear it. Previous to my setting out to go to see him, so agitated was my mind, that my appetite for my daily food failed me entirely. Several times on my way there, I turned back again; but as often I felt my strength again renewed, and I soon found that the nearer I approached to the house of the minister, the less was my fear. Accordingly, as soon as I came to the door, my fears subsided, the cross was removed, all things appeared pleasant—I was tranquil.

I now told him, that the Lord had revealed it to me, that I must preach the gospel. He replied by asking, in what sphere I wished to move in? I said, among the Methodists. He then replied, that a Mrs. Cook, a Methodist lady, had also some time before requested the same privilege; who it was believed, had done much good in the way of exhortation, and holding prayer meetings; and who had been permitted to do so by the verbal license of the preacher in charge at the time. But as to women preaching, he said that our Discipline knew nothing at all about it—that it did not call for women preachers. This I was glad to hear, because it removed the fear of the cross—but not no sooner did this feeling cross my mind, than I found that a love of souls had in a measure departed from me; that holy energy which burned within me, as a fire, began to be smothered. This I soon perceived.

O how careful ought we to be, lest through our by-laws of church government and discipline, we bring into disrepute even the word of life. For as unseemly as it may appear now-a-days for a woman to preach, it should be remembered that nothing is impossible with God. Any why should it be thought impossible, heterodox, or improper, for a woman to preach? seeing the Saviour died for the woman as well as the man.

If a man may preach, because the Saviour died for him, why not the woman? seeing he died for her also. Is he not a whole Saviour, instead of a half one? as those who hold it wrong for a woman to preach, would seem to make it appear.

Did not Mary first preach the risen Saviour, and is not the doctrine of the resurrection the very climax of Christianity—hangs not all our hope on this, as argued by St. Paul? Then did not Mary, a woman, preach the gospel? for she preached the resurrection of the crucified Son of God.

But some will say, that Mary did not expound the Scripture, therefore, she did not preach, in the proper sense of the term. To this I reply, it may be that the term preach, in those primitive times, did not mean exactly what it is now made to mean; perhaps it was a great deal more simple then, than it is now:—if it were not, the unlearned fishermen could not have preached the gospel at all, as they had no learning.

To this it may be replied, by those who are determined not to believe that it is right for a woman to preach, that the disciples, through they were fishermen, and ignorant of letters too, were inspired so to do. To

which I would reply, that though they were inspired, yet that inspiration did not save them from showing their ignorance of letters, and of man's wisdom; this the multitude soon found out, by listening to the remarks of the envious Jewish priests. If then, to preach the gospel, by the gift of heaven, comes by inspiration solely, is God straitened; must he take the man exclusively? May he not, did he not, and can he not inspire a female to preach the simple story of the birth, life, death, and resurrection of our Lord, and accompany it too, with power to the sinner's heart. As for me, I am fully persuaded that the Lord called me to labour according to what I have received, in his vineyard. If he has not, how could he consistently bear testimony in favour of my poor labours, in awakening and converting sinners?

In my wanderings up and down among men, preaching according to my ability, I have frequently found families who told me that they had not for several years been to a meeting, and yet, while listening to hear what God would say by his poor coloured female instrument, have believed with trembling—tears rolling down their cheeks, the signs of contrition and repentance towards God. I firmly believe that I have sown seed, in the name of the Lord, which shall appear with its increase at the great day of accounts, when Christ shall come to make up his jewels.

At a certain time, I was beset with the idea, that soon or late I should fall from grace, and lose my soul at last. I was frequently called to the throne of grace about this matter, but found no relief; the temptation pursued me still. Being more and more afflicted with it, till at a certain time when the spirit strongly impressed it on my mind to enter into my closet, and carry my case once more to the Lord; the Lord enabled me to draw nigh to him, and to his mercy seat, at this time, in an extraordinary manner; for while I wrestled with him for the victory over this disposition to doubt whether I should persevere, there appeared a form of fire, about the size of a man's hand, as I was on my knees; at the same moment, there appeared to the eye of faith a man robed in a white garment, from the shoulders down to the feet; from him a voice proceeded, saying: "Thou shalt never return from the cross." Since that time I have never doubted, but believe that god will keep me until the day of redemption. Now I could adopt the very language of St. Paul, and say that nothing could have separated my soul from the love of god, which is in Christ Jesus [Rom. 8:35–39]. From that time, 1807, until the present, 1833, I have not yet doubted the power and goodness of God to keep me from falling, through sanctification of the spirit and belief of the truth.

My Marriage
In the year 1811, I changed my situation in life, having married Mr. Joseph Lee, Pastor of a Coloured Society at Snow Hill, about six miles from the city of Philadelphia.

It became necessary therefore for me to remove. This was a great trial at first, as I knew no person at Snow Hill, except my husband; and to leave my associates in the society, and especially those who composed the band of which I was one. Not but those who have been in sweet fellowship with such as really love God, and have together drank bliss and happiness from the same fountain, can tell how dear such company is, and how hard it is to part from them.

At Snow Hill, as was feared, I never found that agreement and closeness in communion and fellowship, that I had in Philadelphia, among my young companions, nor ought I to have expected it. The manners and customs at this place were somewhat different, on which account I became discontented in the course of a year, and began to importune my husband to remove to the city. But this plan did not suit him, as he was the Pastor of the Society; he could not bring his mind to leave them. This afflicted me a little. But the Lord soon showed me in a dream what his will was concerning this matter.

I dreamed that as I was walking on the summit of a beautiful hill, that I saw near me a flock of sheep, fair and white, as if but newly washed; when there came walking toward me, a man of a grave and dignified countenance, dressed entirely in white, as it were in a robe, and looking at me, said emphatically, "Joseph Lee must take care of these sheep, or the wolf will come and devour them." When I awoke, I was convinced of my error, and immediately, with a glad heart, yielded to the right way of the Lord. This also greatly strengthened my husband in his care over them, for fear the wold should by some means take any of them away. The following verse was beautifully suited to our condition, as well as to all the little flocks of God scattered up and down this land:

"Us into Thy protection take, And gather with Thine arm; Unless the fold we first forsake, The wolf can never harm."

After this, I fell into a state of general debility, and in an ill state of health, so much so, that I could not sit up; but a desire to warn sinners to flee the wrath to come, burned vehemently in my heart, when the Lord would send sinners into the house to see me. Such opportunities I embraced to press home on their consciences the things of eternity, and so effectual was the word of exhortation made through the Spirit, that I have seen them fall to the floor crying aloud for mercy.

From this sickness I did not expect to recover, and there was but one thing which bound me to earth, and this was, that I had not as yet preached the gospel to the fallen sons and daughters of Adam's race, to the satisfaction of my mind. I wished to go from one end of the earth to the other, crying, Behold, behold the Lamb! To this end I earnestly prayed the Lord to raise me up, if consistent with his will. He condescended to hear my prayer, and to give me a token in a dream, that in due time I should recover my health. The dream was as follows: I thought I saw the sun rise in the morning, and ascend to an altitude of about half an hour high, and then become obscured by a dense black cloud, which continued to hide its rays for about one third part of the day; and then it burst forth again with renewed splendour.

This dream I interpreted to signify my early life, my conversion to God, and this sickness, which was a great affliction, as it hindered me, and I feared would forever hinder me from preaching the gospel, was signified by the cloud; and the bursting forth of the sun, again, was the recovery of my health, and being permitted to preach.

I went to the throne of grace on this subject, where the Lord made this impressive reply in my heart, while on my knees: "Ye shall be restored to thy health again, and worship God in full purpose of heart."

This manifestation was so impressive, that I could but hide my face, as if someone was gazing upon me, to think of the great goodness of the Almighty God to my poor soul and body. From that very time I began to gain strength of body and mind, glory to God in the highest, until my health was fully recovered.

For six years from this time I continued to receive from above, such baptisms of the Spirit as mortality could scarcely bear. About that time I was called to suffer in my family, by death — five, in the course of about six years, fell by his hand; my husband being one of the number, which was the greatest affliction of all.

I was not left alone in the world, with two infant children, one of the age of about two years, the other six months, with no other dependance than the promise of Him who hath said—"I will be the widow's God, and a father to the fatherless" [Ps 68:5]. Accordingly, he raised me up friends, whose liberality comforted and solaced me in my state of widowhood and sorrows. I could sing with the greatest propriety the words of the poet.

"He helps the stranger in distress, The widow and the fatherless, And grants the prisoner sweet release."

I can say even now, with the Psalmist, "Once I was young, but now I am old, yet I have never seen the righteous forsaken, nor his seed begging bread" [Ps. 37:25]. I have ever been fed by his bounty, clothed by his mercy, comforted and healed when sick, succoured when tempted, and every where upheld by his hand.

The Subject Of My Call To Preach Renewed

It was now eight years since I had made application to be permitted to preach the gospel, during which time I had only been allowed to exhort, and even this privilege but seldom. This subject now was renewed afresh in my mind; it was as a fire shut up in my bones. About thirteen months passed on, while under this renewed impression. During this time, I had solicited of the Rev. Bishop Richard Allen, who at this time had become Bishop of the African Episcopal Methodists in America, to be permitted the liberty of holding prayer meetings in my own hired house, and of exhorting as I found liberty, which was granted me. By this means, my mind was relieved, as the house was soon filled when the hour appointed for prayer had arrived.

I cannot but relate in this place, before I proceed further with the above subject, the singular conversion of a very wicked young man. He was a coloured man, who had generally attended our meetings, but not for any good purpose; but rather to disturb and to ridicule our denomination. He openly and uniformly declared that he neither believed in religion, nor wanted anything to do with it. He was of a Gallio disposition, and took the lead among the young people of colour. But after a while he fell sick, and lay about three months in a state of ill health; his disease was consumption. Toward the close of his days, his sister who was a member of the society, came and desired me to go and see her brother, as she had no hopes of his recovery; perhaps the Lord might break into his mind. I went alone, and found him very low. I soon commenced to inquire respecting his state of feeling, and how he found his mind. His answer was, "O tolerable well," with an air of great indifference. I asked him if I should pray for him. He answered in a sluggish and careless manner, "O yes, if you have time." I then sung a hymn, kneeled down and prayed for him, and then went my way.

Three days after this, I went again to visit the young man. At this time there went with me two of the sisters in Christ. We found the Rev. Mr. Cornish, of our denomination, labouring with him. But he said he received but little satisfaction from him. Pretty soon, however, brother Cornish took his leave; when myself, with the other two sisters, one of which was an elderly woman named Jane Hutt, the other was younger, both coloured, commenced conversing with him, respecting his eternal interest, and of his hopes of a happy eternity, if any he had. He said but little; we then kneeled down together and besought the Lord in his behalf, praying that if mercy were not clear gone forever, to shed a ray of softening grace upon the hardness of his heart. He appeared now to be somewhat more tender, and we thought we could perceive some tokens of conviction, as he wished us to visit him again, in a tone of voice not quite as indifferent as he had hitherto manifested.

But two days had elapsed after this visit, when his sister came for me in haste, saying, that she believed her brother was then dying, and that he had sent for me. I immediately called on Jane Hutt, who was still among us as a mother in Israel, to go with me. When we arrived there, we found him sitting up in his bed, very restless and uneasy, but he soon laid down again. He now wished me to come to him, by the side of his bed. I asked him how he was. He said, "Very ill;" and added, "Pray for me, quick?" We now perceived his time in this world to be short. I took up the hymn-book and opened to a hymn suitable to his case, and commenced to sing. But there seemed to be a horror in the room—a darkness of a mental kind, which was felt by us all; there being five persons, except the sick young man and his nurse. We had sung but one verse, when they all gave over singing, on account of this unearthly sensation, but myself. I continued to sing on alone, but in a dull and heavy manner, though looking up to God all the while for help. Suddenly, I felt a spring of energy awake in my heart, when darkness gave way in some degree. It was but a glimmer from above. When the hymn was finished, we all kneeled down to pray for him. While calling on the name of the Lord, to have mercy on his soul, and to grant him repentance unto life, it came suddenly into my mind never to rise from my knees until God should hear prayer in his behalf, until he should convert and save his soul.

Now, while I thus continued importuning heaven, as I felt I was led, a ray of light, more abundant, broke forth among us. There appeared to my view, though my eyes were closed, the Saviour in full stature, nailed to the cross, just over the head of the young man, against the ceiling of the room. I cried out, brother look up, the Saviour is come, he will pardon you, your sins he will forgive. My sorrow for the soul of the young man was gone; I could no longer pray—joy and rapture made it impossible. We rose up from our knees, when lo, his eyes were gazing with ecstasy upward; over his face there was an expression of joy; his lips were clothed in a sweet and holy smile; but no sound came from his tongue; it was heard in its stillness of bliss, full of hope and immortality. Thus, as I held him by the hand his happy and purified soul soared away, without a sign or a groan, to its eternal rest.

I now closed his eyes, straightened out his limbs, and left him to be dressed for the grave. But as for me, I was filled with the power of the Holy Ghost—the very room seemed filled with glory. His sister and all that were in the room rejoiced, nothing doubting but he had entered into Paradise; and I believe I shall see him at the last and great day, safe on the shores of salvation.

But to return to the subject of my call to preach. Soon after this, as above related, the Rev. Richard Williams was to preach at Bethel Church, where I with others were assembled. He entered the pulpit, gave out the hymn, which was sung, and then addressed the throne of grace; took his text, passed through the exordium, and commenced to expound it. The text he took is in Jonah, 2d chap. 9th verse,—"Salvation is of the Lord." But as he proceeded to explain, he seemed to have lost the spirit: when in the same instant, I sprang, as by an altogether supernatural impulse, to my feet, when I was aided from above to give an exhortation on the very text which my brother Williams had taken.

I told them that I was like Jonah; for it had been then nearly eight years since the Lord had called me to preach his gospel to the fallen sons and daughters of Adam's race, but that I had lingered like him, and delayed to go at the bidding of the Lord, and warn those who are as deeply guilty as were the people of Ninevah.

During the exhortation, God made manifest his power in a manner sufficient to show the world that I was called to labour according to my ability, and the grace given unto me, in the vineyard of the good husbandman.

I now sat down, scarcely knowing what I had done, being frightened. I imagined, that for this indecorum, as I feared it might be called, I should be expelled from the church. But instead of this, the Bishop rose up in the assembly, and related that I had called upon him eight years before, asking to be permitted to preach, and that he had put me off; but that he now as much believed that I was called to that work, as any of the preachers present. These remarks greatly strengthened me, so that my fears of having given an offence, and made myself liable as an offender, subsided, giving place to a sweet serenity, a holy job of a peculiar kind, untasted in my bosom until then.

The next Sabbath day, while sitting under the word of the gospel, I felt moved to attempt to speak to the people in a public manner, but I could not bring my mind to attempt it in the church. I said, Lord, anywhere but here. Accordingly, there was a house not far off which was pointed out to me, to this I went. It was the house of a sister belonging to the same society with myself. Her name was Anderson. I told her I had come to hold a meeting in her house, if she would call in her neighbours. With this request she immediately complied. My congregation consisted of but five persons. I commenced by reading and singing a hymn, when I dropped to my knees by the side of a table to pray. When I arose I found my hand resting on the Bible, which I had not noticed till that moment. It now occurred to me to take a text. I opened the Scripture, as it happened, at the 141st Psalm, fixing my eye on the 3d verse, which reads: "Set a watch, O Lord, before my mouth, keep the door of my lips." My sermon, such as it was, I applied wholly to myself, and added an exhortation. Two of my congregation wept much, as the fruit of my labour this time. In closing I said to the few, that if any one would open a door, I would hold a meeting the next sixth-day evening; when one answered that her house was at my service. Accordingly I went, and God made manifest his power among the people. Some wept, while others shouted for joy. One whole seat of females, by the power of God, as the rushing of a wind, were all bowed to the floor at once, and screamed out. Also a sick man and woman in one house, the Lord convicted them both; one lived, and the other died. God wrought a judgment—

some were well at night, and died in the morning. At this place I continued to hold meetings about six months. During that time I kept house with my little son, who was very sickly. About this time I had a call to preach at a place about thirty miles distant, among the Methodists, with whom I remained one week, and during the whole time, not a thought of my little son came into my mind; it was hid from me, lest I should have been diverted from the work I had to, to look after my son. Here by the instrumentality of a poor coloured woman, the Lord poured forth his spirit among the people. Though, as I was told, there were lawyers, doctors, and magistrates present, to hear me speak, yet there was mourning and crying among sinners, for the Lord scattered fire among them of his own kindling. The Lord gave his handmaiden power to speak for his great name, for he arrested the hearts of the people, and caused a shaking amongst the multitude, for God was in the midst.

I now returned home, found all well; no harm had come to my child, although I left it very sick. Friends had taken care of it which was of the Lord. I now began to think seriously of breaking up housekeeping, and forsaking all to preach the everlasting Gospel. I felt a strong desire to return to the place of my nativity, at Cape May, after an absence of about fourteen years. To this place, where the heaviest cross was to be met with, the Lord sent me, as Saul of Tarsus was sent to Jerusalem, to preach the same gospel which he had neglected and despised before his conversion. I went by water, and on my passage was much distressed by sea sickness, so much so that I expected to have died, but such was not the will of the Lord respecting me. After I had disembarked. I proceeded on as opportunities offered, toward where my mother lived. When within ten miles of that place, I appointed an evening meeting. There were a goodly number came out to hear. The Lord was pleased to give me light and liberty among the people. After meeting, there came an elderly lady to me and said, she believed the Lord had sent me among them; she then appointed me another meeting there two weeks from that night. The next day I hastened forward to the place of my mother, who was happy to see me, and the happiness was mutual between us. With her I left my poor sickly boy, while I departed to do my Master's will. In this neighborhood I had an uncle, who was a Methodist, and who gladly threw open his door for meetings to be held there. At the first meeting which I held at my uncle's house, there was, with others who had come from curiosity to hear the coloured woman preacher, an old man, who was a deist, and who said he did not believe the coloured people had any souls—he was sure they had none. He took a seat very near where I was standing, and boldly tried to look me out of countenance. But as I laboured on in the best manner I was able, looking to God all the while, though it seemed to me I had but little liberty, yet there went an arrow from the bent bow of the gospel, and fastened in his till then obdurate heart. After I had done speaking, he went out, and called the people around him, said that my preaching might seem a small thing, yet he believed I had the worth of souls at heart. This language was different from what it was a little time before, as he now seemed to admit that coloured people had souls, whose good I had in view, his remark must have been without meaning. He now came into the house, and in the most friendly manner shook hands with me, saying, he hoped God had spared him to some good purpose. This man was a great slave holder, and had been very cruel; thinking nothing of knocking down a slave with a fence stake, or whatever might come to hand. From this time it was said of him that he became greatly altered in his ways for the better. At that time he was about seventy years old, his head as white as snow; but whether he became a converted man or not, I never heard.

The week following, I had an invitation to hold a meeting at the Court House of the County, when I spoke from the 53d chap. of Isaiah, 3d verse. It was a solemn time, and the Lord attended the word; I had life and liberty, though there were people there of various denominations. Here again I saw the aged slaveholder, who notwithstanding his age, walked about three miles to hear me. This day I spoke twice, and walked six miles to the place appointed. There was a magistrate present, who showed his friendship, by saying in a friendly manner, that he had heard of me; he handed me a hymnbook, pointing to a hymn which he had selected. When the meeting was over, he invited me to preach in a schoolhouse in his neighbourhood, about three miles distant from where I then was. During this meeting one backslider was reclaimed. This day I walked six miles, and preached twice to large congregations, both in the morning and evening. The Lord was with me, glory be to his holy name. I next went six miles and held a meeting in a coloured friend's house, at eleven o'clock in the morning, and preached to a well behaved congregation of both coloured and white. After service I again walked back, which was in all twelve miles in the same day. This was on Sabbath, or as I sometimes call it, seventh-day; for after my conversion I preferred the plain language of the quakers: On fourth-day, after this, in compliance with an invitation received by note, from the same magistrate who had heard me at the above place, I preached to a large congregation, where we had a precious time: much weeping was heard among the people. The same gentleman, now at the close of the meeting, gave out another appointment at the same place, that day week. Here again I had liberty, there was a move among the people. Ten years from that time, in the neighbourhood of Cape May, I held a prayer meeting in a school house, which was then the regular place of preaching for the Episcopal Methodists; after service, there came a white lady of the first distinction, a member of the Methodist Society, and told me that at the same school house, ten years before, under my preaching, the Lord first awakened her. She

rejoiced much to see me, and invited me home with her, where I staid till the next day. This was bread cast on the waters, seen after many days.

From this place I next went to Dennis Creek meeting house, where at the invitation of an elder, I spoke to a large congregation of various and conflicting sentiments, when a wonderful shock of God's power was felt, shown everywhere by groans, by sighs, and loud and happy amens. I felt as if aided from above. My tongue was cut loose, the stammerer spoke freely; the love of God, and of his service, burned with a vehement flame within me—his name was glorified among the people.

But here I feel myself constrained to give over, as from the smallness of this pamphlet I cannot go through with the whole of my journal, as it would probably make a volume of two hundred pages; which, if the Lord be willing, may at some future day be published. But for the satisfaction of such as may follow after me, when I am no more, I have recorded how the Lord called me to his work, and how he has kept me from falling from grace, as I feared I should. In all things he has proved himself a God of truth to me; and in his service I am now as much determined to spend and be spent, as at the very first. My ardour for the progress of his cause abates not a whit, so far as I am able to judge, though I am now something more than fifty years of age.

As to the nature of uncommon impressions, which the reader cannot but have noticed, and possibly sneered at in the course of these pages, they may be accounted for in this way: It is known that the blind have the sense of hearing in a manner much more acute than those who can see: also their sense of feeling is exceedingly fine, and is found to detect any roughness on the smoothest surface, where those who can see can find none. So it may be with such as am, who has never had more than three months schooling; and wishing to know much of the way and law of God, have therefore watched the more closely the operations of the Spirit, and have in consequence been led thereby. But let it be remarked that have never found that Spirit to lead me contrary to the Scriptures of truth, as I understand them. "For as many as are led by the Spirit of God are the sons of God."—Rom. viii. 14.

I have now only to say, May the blessing of the Father, and of the Son, and of the Holy Ghost, accompany the reading of this poor effort to speak well of his name, wherever it may be read. AMEN.

PRIMARY SOURCE DOCUMENT

A Former Slave Discusses the Importance of Religion

INTRODUCTION Elizabeth was born a slave in Maryland in 1766. At age eleven, she was separated from the rest of her family and sent to another plantation some miles away. This event was to have a profound impact on Elizabeth's life. Her loneliness and despair first led her to attempt a clandestine reunion with her mother. Although she managed to spend a few days with members of her family before being returned to her new home, Elizabeth realized that she needed to face a life without them. Having no one else, Elizabeth turned to God for support.

Though Elizabeth received her freedom about twenty years later, she continued to seek comfort and strength in religion. Like many other slaves and free blacks living in the antebellum period, she found a rare comfort in the promise of a better world in the afterlife. Elizabeth's memoir illustrates the importance of religion in the lives of many African Americans who attempted to understand why society forced them into an inferior status.

I was born in Maryland in the year 1766. My parents were slaves. Both my father and mother were religious people, and belonged to the Methodist Society. It was my father's practice to read in the Bible aloud to his children every sabbath morning. At these seasons, when I was but five years old, I often felt the overshadowing of the Lord's Spirit, without at all understanding what it meant; and these incomes and influences coutinued to attend me until I was eleven years old, particularly when I was alone, by which I was preserved from doing anything that I thought was wrong.

In the eleventh year of my age, my master sent me to another farm, several miles from my parents, brothers, and sisters, which was a great trouble to me. At last I grew so lonely and sad I thought I should die, if I did not see my mother. I asked the overseer if I might go, but being positively denied, I concluded to go without his knowledge. When I reached home my mother was away. I set off and walked twenty miles before I found here. I staid with her for several days, and we returned together. Next day I was sent back to my new place, which renewed my sorrow. At parting, my mother told me that I had "nobody in the wide world to look to but God." These words fell upon my heart with pondrous weight, and seemed to add to my grief. I went back repeating as I went, "none but God in the wide world." On reaching the farm, I found the overseer was displeased at me for going without his liberty. He tied me with a rope, and gave me some stripes of which I carried the marks for weeks.

After this time, finding as my mother said, I had none in the world to look to but God, I betook myself to prayer, and in every lonely place I found an altar. I mourned sore like a dove and chattered forth my sorrow, moaning in the corners of the field, and under the fences.

I continued in this state for about six months, feeling as though my head were waters, and I could do nothing but weep. I lost my appetite, and not being able to take enough food to sustain nature, I became so weak I had but little strength to work; still I was required to do all my duty. One evening, after the duties of the day were ended, I thought I could not live over the night, so threw myself on a bench, expecting to die, and without being prepared to meet my Maker; and my spirit cried within me, must I die in this state, and be banished from Thy presence forever? I own I am a sinner in Thy sight, and not fit to live where thou art. Still it was my fervent desire that the Lord would pardon me. Just at this season, I saw with my spiritual eye, an awful gulf of misery. As I thought I was about to plunge into it, I heard a voice saying, "rise up and pray," which strengthened me. I fell on my knees and prayed the best I could the Lord's prayer. Knowing no more to say, I halted, but continued on my knees. My spirit was then taught to pray, "Lord, have mercy on me—Christ save me." Immediately there appeared a director, clothed in white raiment. I thought he took me by the hand and said, "come with me." He led me down a long journey to a fiery gulf, and left me standing upon the brink of this awful pit. I began to scream for mercy, thinking I was about to be plunged to the belly of hell, and believed I should sink to endless ruin. Although I prayed and wrestled with all my might, it seemed in vain. Still, I felt all the while that I was sustained by some invisible power. At this solemn moment, I thought I saw a hand from which hung, as it were, a silver hair, and a voice told me that all the hope I had of being saved was no more than a hair; still, pray, and it will be sufficient. I then renewed my struggle, crying for mercy and salvation, until I found that every cry raised me higher and higher, and my head was quite above the fiery pillars. Then I thought I was permitted to look straight forward, and saw the Saviour standing with His hand stretched out to receive me. An indescribably glorious light was in Him, and He said, "peace, peace, come unto me." At this moment I felt that my sins were forgiven me, and the time of my deliverance was at hand. I sprang forward and fell at his feet, giving Him all the thanks and highest praises, crying, Thou has redeemed me—Thou hast redeemed me to thyself. I felt filled with light and love. At this moment I thought my former guide took me again by the hand and led me upward, till I came to the celestial world and to heaven's door, which I saw was open, and while I stood there, a power surrounded me which drew me in, and I saw millions of glorified spirits in white robes. After I had this view, I thought I heard a voice saying, "Art thou willing to be saved?" I said, Yes Lord. Again I was asked, "Art thou willing to be saved in my way?" I stood speechless until he asked me again, "Art thou willing to be saved in my way?" Then I heard a whispering voice say, "If thou art not saved in the Lord's way, thou canst not be saved at all;" at which I exclaimed, "Yes Lord, in thy own way." Immediately a light fell upon my head, and I was filled with light, and I was shown the world lying in wickedness, and was told I must go there, and call the people to repentance, for the day of the Lord was at hand; and this message was as a heavy yoke upon me, so that I wept bitterly at the thought of what I should have to pass through. While I wept, I heard a voice say, "weep not, some will laugh at thee, some will scoff at thee, and the dogs will bark at thee, but while thou doest my will, I will be with thee to the ends of the earth."

I was at this time not yet thirteen years old. The next day, when I had come to myself, I felt like a new creature in Christ, and all my desire was to see the Saviour.

I lived in a place where there was no preaching, and no religious instruction; but every day I went out amongst the hay-stacks, where the presence of the Lord overshadowed me, and I was filled with sweetness and joy, and was as a vessel filled with holy oil. In this way I continued for about a year; many times while my hands were at my work, my spirit was carried away to spiritual things. One day as I was going to my old place behind the hay-stacks to pray, I was assailed with this language, "Are you going there to weep and pray? what a fool! there are older professors than you are, and they do not take that way to get to heaven; people whose sins are forgiven ought to be joyful and lively, and not be struggling and praying." With this I halted and concluded I would not go, but do as other professors did, and so went off to play; but at this moment the light that was in me became darkened, and the peace and joy that I once had, departed from me.

About this time I was moved back to the farm where my mother lived, and then sold to a stranger. Here I had deep sorrows and plungings, not having experienced a return of that sweet evidence and light with which I had been favoured formerly; but by watching unto prayer, and wrestling mightily with the Lord, my peace gradually returned, and with it a great exercise and weight upon my heart for the salvation of my fellow-creatures; and I was often carried to distant lands and shown places where I should have to travel and deliver the Lord's message. Years afterwards, I found myself visiting those towns and countries that I had seen in the light as I sat at home at my sewing,—places of which I had never heard.

Some years from this time I was sold to a Presbyterian for a term of years, as he did not think it right to hold slaves for life. Having served him faithfully my time out, he gave me my liberty, which was about the thirtieth year of my age.

As I now lived in a neighborhood where I could attend religious meetings, occasionally I felt moved to speak a few words therein; but I shrank from it—so great was the cross to my nature.

I did not speak much till I had reached my forty-second year, when it was revealed to me that the message which had been given to me I had not yet delivered, and the time had come. As I could read but little, I questioned within myself how it would be possible for me to deliver the message, when I did not understand the Scriptures. Whereupon I was moved to open a Bible that was near me, which I did, and my eyes fell upon this passage, "Gird up thy loins now like a man, and answer thou me. Obey God rather than man," &c. Here I fell into a great exercise of spirit, and was plunged very low. I went from one religious professor to another, enquiring of them what ailed me; but of all these I could find none who could throw any light upon such impressions. They all told me there was nothing in Scripture that would sanction such exercises. It was hard for men to travel, and what would women do? These things greatly discouraged me, and shut up my way, and caused me to resist the Spirit. After going to all that were accounted pious, and receiving no help, I returned to the Lord, feeling that I was nothing, and knew nothing, and wrestled and prayed to the Lord that He would fully reveal His will, and make the way plain.

Whilst I thus struggled, there seemed a light from heaven to fall upon me, which banished all my desponding fears, and I was enabled to form a new resolution to go on to prison and to death, if it might be my portion: and the Lord showed me that it was His will I should be resigned to die any death that might be my lot, in carrying his message, and be entirely crucified to the world, and sacrifice all to His glory that was then in my possession, which His witnesses, the holy Apostles, had done before me. It was then revealed to me that the Lord had given me the evidence of a clean heart, in which I could rejoice day and night, and I walked and talked with God, and my soul was illuminated with heavenly light, and I knew nothing but Jesus Christ, and him crucified.

One day, after these things, while I was at my work, the Spirit directed me to go to a poor widow, and ask her if I might have a meeting at her house, which was situated in one of the lowest and worst streets in Baltimore. With great joy she gave notice, and at the time appointed I appeared there among a few coloured sisters. When they had all prayed, they called upon me to close the meeting, and I felt an impression that I must say a few words; and while I was speaking, the house seemed filled with light; and when I was about to close the meeting, and was kneeling, a man came in and stood till I arose. It proved to be a watchman. The sisters became so frightened, they all went away except the one who lived in the house, and an old woman; they both appeared to be much frightened, fearing they should receive some personal injury, or be put out of the house. A feeling of weakness came over me for a short time, but I soon grew warm and courageous in the Spirit. The man then said to me, "I was sent here to break up your meeting. Complaint has been made to me that the people round here cannot sleep for the racket." I replied, "a good racket is better than a bad racket. How do they rest when the ungodly are dancing and fiddling till midnight? Why are not they molested by the watchmen? and why should we be for praising God, our

Maker? Are we worthy of greater punishment for praying to Him? and are we to be prohibited from doing so, that sinners may remain slumbering in their sins?" While speaking these few words I grew warm with heavenly zeal, and laid my hand upon him and addressed him with gospel truth, "how do sinners sleep in hell, after slumbering in their sins here, and crying, 'let me rest, let me rest,' while sporting on the very brink of hell? Is the cause of God to be destroyed for this purpose?" Speaking several words more to this amount, he turned pale and trembled, and begged my pardon, acknowledging that it was not his wish to interrupt us, and that he would never disturb a religious assembly again. He then took leave of me in a comely manner and wished us success. After he was gone, I turned to the old sisters who by this time were quite cheered up. You see, said I, if the sisters had not fled, what a victory we might have had on the Lord's side; for the man seemed ready to give up under conviction. If it had not been for their cowardice, we might have all bowed in prayer, and a shout of victory had been heard amongst us.

Our meeting gave great offence, and we were forbid holding any more assemblies. Even the elders of our meeting joined with the wicked people, and said such meetings must be stopped, and that woman quieted. But I was not afraid of any of them, and continued to go, and burnt with a zeal not my own. The old sisters were zealous sometimes, and at other times would sink under the cross. Thus they grew cold, at which I was much grieved. I proposed to them to ask the elders to send a brother, which was concluded upon.

We went on for several years, and the Lord was with us with great power it proved, to the conversion of many souls, and we continued to grow stronger.

I felt at times that I must exercise in the ministry, but when I rose upon my feet I felt ashmed, and so I went under a cloud for some time, and endeavoured to keep silence; but I could not quench the Spirit. I was rejected by the elders and rulers, as Christ was rejected by the Jews before me, and while others were excused in crimes of the darkest dye, I was hunted down in every place where I appointed a meeting. Wading through many sorrows, I thought at times I might as well be banished from this life, as to feel the Almighty drawing me one way, and man another; so that I was tempted to cast myself into the dock. But contemplating the length of eternity, and how long my sufferings would be in that unchangeable world, compared with this, if I endured a little longer, the Lord was pleased to deliver me from this gloomy, melancholy state in his own time; though while this temptation lasted I roved up and down, and talked and prayed.

I often felt that I was unfit to assemble with the congregation with whom I had gathered, and had sometimes been made to rejoice in the Lord. I felt that I was despised on account of this gracious calling, and was looked upon as a speckled bird by the ministers to whom I looked for instruction, and to whom I resorted every opportunity for the same; but when I would converse with them, some would cry out, "You are an enthusiast;" and others said, "the Discipline did not allow of any such division of the work;" until I began to think I surely must be wrong. Under this reflection, I had another gloomy cloud to struggle through; but after awhile I felt much moved upon by the Spirit of the Lord, and meeting with an aged sister, I found upon conversing with her that she could sympathize with me in this spiritual work. She was the first one I had met with, who could fully understand my exercises. She offered to open her house for a meeting, and run the risk of all the church would do to her for it. Many were afraid to open their houses in this way, lest they should be turned out of the church.

I persevered, notwithstanding the opposition of those who were looked upon as higher and wiser. The meeting was appointed, and but few came. I felt much backwardness, and as though I could not pray, but a pressure upon me to arise and express myself by way of exhortation. After hesitating for some time whether I would take up the cross or no, I arose, and after expressing a few words, the Spirit came upon me with life, and a victory was gained over the power of darkness, and we could rejoice together in His love.

As for myself, I was so full I hardly knew whether I was in the body, or out of the body—so great was my joy for the victory on the Lord's side. But the persecution against me increased, and a complaint was carried forward, as was done formerly against Daniel, the servant of God, and the elders came out with indignation for my holding meetings contrary to discipline—being a woman.

Thus we see when the heart is not inspired, and the inward eye enlightened by the Spirit, we are incapable of discerning the mystery of God in these things. Individuals creep into the church that are unregenerate, and after they have been there awhile, they fancy that they have got the grace of God, while they are destitute of it. They may have a degree of light in their heads, but evil in their hearts; which makes them think they are qualified to be judges of the ministry, and their conceit makes them very busy in matters of religion, judging of the revelations that are given to others, while they have received none themselves. Being thus mistaken, they are calculated to make a great deal of confusion in the church, and clog the true ministry.

These are they who eat their own bread, and wear their own apparel, having the form of godliness, but are destitute of the power.

Again I felt encouraged to attend another and another appointment. At one of these meetings, some of the class-leaders were present, who were constrained to cry out, "Surely the Lord has revealed these things to her" and asked one another if they ever heard the like? I look upon man as a very selfish being, when placed in a religious office, to presume to resist the work of the Almighty; because He does not work by man's authority. I did not faint under discouragement, but pressed on.

Under the contemplation of these things, I slept but little, being much engaged in receiving the revelations of the Divine will concerning this work, and the mysterious call thereto.

I felt very unworthy and small, notwithstanding the Lord had shown himself with great power, insomuch that conjecturers and critics were constrained to join in praise to his great name; for truly, we had times of refreshing from the presence of the Lord. At one of the meetings, a vast number of the white inhabitants of the place, and many coloured people, attended—many no doubt from curiosity to hear what the old coloured woman had to say. One, a great scripturian, fixed himself behind the door with pen and ink, in order to take down the discourse in short-hand; but the Almighty Being anointed me with such a portion of his Spirit, that he cast away his paper and pen, and heard the discourse with patience, and was much affected, for the Lord wrought powerfully on his heart. After meeting, he came forward and offered me his hand with solemnity on his countenance, and handed me something to pay for my conveyance home.

I returned, much strengthened by the Lord's power, to go on to the fulfilment of His work, although I was again pressed by the authorities of the church to which I belonged, for imprudency; and so much condemned, that I was sorely tempted by the enemy to turn aside into the wilderness. I was so embarrassed and encompassed, I wondered within myself whether all that were called to be mouth piece for the Lord, suffered such deep wadings as I experienced.

I now found I had to travel still more extensively in the work of the ministry, and I applied to the Lord for direction. I was often invited to go hither and thither, but felt that I must wait for the dictates of His Spirit.

At a meeting which I held in Maryland, I was led to speak from the passage, "Woe to the rebellious city," &c. After the meeting, the people came where I was, to take me before the squire; but the Lord delivered me from their hands.

I also held meetings in Virginia. The people there would not believe that a coloured woman could preach. And moreover, as she had no learning, they strove to imprison me because I spoke against slavery: and being brought up, they asked by what authority I spake? and if I had been ordained? I answered, not by the commission of men's hands: if the Lord had ordained me, I needed nothing better.

As I travelled along through the land, I was led at different times to converse with white men who were by profession ministers of the gospel. Many of them, up and down, confessed they did not believe in revelation, which gave me to see that men were sent forth as ministers without Christ's authority. In a conversation with one of these, he said, "You think you have these things by revelation, but there has been no such thing as revelation since Christ's ascension." I asked him where the apostle John got his revelation while he was in the Isle of Patmos. With this, he rose up and left me, and I said in my spirit, get thee behind me Satan.

I visited many remote places, where there were no meeting houses, and held many glorions meetings, for the Lord poured out his Spirit in sweet effusions. I also travelled in Canada, and visited several settlements of coloured people, and felt an open door amongst them.

I may here remark, that while journeying through the different states of the Union, I met with many of the Quaker Friends, and visited them in their families. I received much kindness and sympathy, and no opposition from them, in the prosecution of my labours.

On one occasion, in a thinly settled part of the country, seeing a Friend's meeting house open, I went in; at the same time a Friend and his little daughter followed me. We three composed the meeting. As we sat there in silence, I felt a remarkable overshadowing of the Divine presence, as much so as I ever experienced any where. Toward the close, a few words seemed to be given me, which I expressed, and left the place greatly refreshed in Spirit. From thence I went to Michigan, where I found a wide field of labour amongst my own colour. Here I remained four years. I established a school for coloured orphans, having always felt the great importance of the religious and moral agriculture of children, and the great need of it, especially amongst the coloured people. Having white teachers, I met with much encouragement.

My eighty-seventh year had now arrived, when suffering from disease, and feeling released from travelling further in my good Master's cause, I came on to Philadelphia, where I have remained until this time, which brings me to my ninety-seventh year. When I went forth, it was without purse or scrip,—and I have come through great tribulation and temptation—not by any might of my own, for I feel that I am but as dust and ashes before my almighty Helper, who has, according to His promise, been with me and sustained me through all, and gives me now firm faith that he will be with me to the end, and, in his own good time, receive me into His everlasting rest.

PRIMARY SOURCE DOCUMENT

Preamble to *Appeal to the Coloured Citizens of the United States* by David Walker

INTRODUCTION David Walker was born in Wilmington, North Carolina, in 1785, the son of a free mother and an enslaved father who died before he was born. According to the rule that the child followed the condition of the mother, Walker inherited his mother's free status. A witness to the indignities suffered by enslaved people around him, including members of his father's family, Walker also knew through his own experience how the lives of free African Americans were hobbled by racist laws and attitudes. In later years, he raised his voice on behalf of all "colored citizens," both slave and free, in the United States and elsewhere.

Walker left North Carolina as a young man, traveling for a time in the South and finally settling in Boston in 1827. He opened a secondhand clothing shop on the wharves and set about doing what he could to ameliorate the condition of his fellow African Americans—harboring fugitive slaves, contributing money to the anti-slavery cause, and writing for John Russworm's Freedom's Journal. In 1829, he published his *Appeal to the Coloured Citizens of the United States,* the preamble of which is reprinted here.

Nothing like the appeal had ever appeared before. Abolitionists were fired by the sense of outrage it embodied, the excoriating intelligence it displayed on every page, its unremitting exposure of white America's hypocrisy, not just on the issue of slavery but in all racial matters. Those weary of the slow pace of change applauded Walker's call for open rebellion by slaves—among them, Henry Highland Garnet, who renewed the theme in his *Address to the Slaves of the United States of America* (1843). But Walker's appeal terrified southern slaveholders, who demanded its suppression and even put a price of a thousand dollars on Walker's head. Two years later, in 1831, when Nat Turner led a revolt of slaves in Southampton County, Virginia, their fears seemed to come true.

By then, Walker himself had already paid a dear price for his eloquence. In 1830, his body was discovered in the doorway of his shop, the evident victim of poisoning. The circumstances of his death remain a mystery to this day. Many have suggested, though it has never been proved, that he was murdered by proslavery forces in retaliation for his appeal. Despite the fact that Walker was born well after the revolutionary war had ended, William Nell reserved a place for him in his *Colored Patriots of the American Revolution,* in this way honoring the man who is now widely regarded as the first great hero and martyr of black nationalism.

Preamble.

My dearly beloved Brethren and Fellow Citizens.

Having travelled over a considerable portion of these United States, and having, in the course of my travels, taken the most accurate observations of things as they exist—the result of my observations has warranted the full and unshaken conviction, that we, (coloured people of these United States,) are the most degraded, wretched, and abject set of beings that ever lived since the world began; and I pray God that none like us ever may live again until time shall be no more. They tell us of the Israelites in Egypt, the Helots in Sparta, and of the Roman Slaves, which last were made up from almost every nation under heaven, whose sufferings under those ancient and heathen nations, were, in comparison with ours, under this enlightened and Christian nation, no more than a cypher—or, in other words, those heathen nations of antiquity, had but little more among them

than the name and form of slavery; while wretchedness and endless miseries were reserved, apparently in a phial, to be poured out upon our fathers, ourselves and our children, by Christian Americans!

These positions I shall endeavour, by the help of the Lord, to demonstrate in the course of this Appeal, to the satisfaction of the most incredulous mind—and may God Almighty, who is the Father of our Lord Jesus Christ, open your hearts to understand and believe the truth.

The causes, my brethren, which produce our wretchedness and miseries, are so very numerous and aggravating, that I believe the pen only of a Josephus or a Plutarch, can well enumerate and explain them. Upon subjects, then, of such incomprehensible magnitude, so impenetrable, and so notorious, I shall be obliged to omit a large class of, and content myself with giving you an exposition of a few of those, which do indeed rage to such an alarming pitch, that they cannot but be a perpetual source of terror and dismay to every reflecting mind.

I am fully aware, in making this appeal to my much afflicted and suffering brethren, that I shall not only be assailed by those whose greatest earthly desires are, to keep us in abject ignorance and wretchedness, and who are of the firm conviction that Heaven has designed us and our children to be slaves and beasts of burden to them and their children. I say, I do not only expect to be held up to the public as an ignorant, impudent and restless disturber of the public peace, by such avaricious creatures, as well as a mover of insubordination—and perhaps put in prison or to death, for giving a superficial exposition of our miseries, and exposing tyrants. But I am persuaded, that many of my brethren, particularly those who are ignorantly in league with slave-holders or tyrants, who acquire their daily bread by the blood and sweat of their more ignorant brethren— and not a few of those too, who are too ignorant to see an inch beyond their noses, will rise up and call me cursed— Yea, the jealous ones among us will perhaps use more abject subtlety, by affirming that this work is not worth perusing, that we are well situated, and there is no use in trying to better our condition, for we cannot. I will ask one question here. —Can our condition be any worse? —Can it be more mean and abject? If there are any changes, will they not be for the better, though they may appear for the worst at first? Can they get us any lower? Where can they get us? They are afraid to treat us worse, for they know well, the day they do it they are gone. But against all accusations which may or can be preferred against me, I appeal to Heaven for my motive in writing—who knows that my object is, if possible, to awaken in the breasts of my afflicted, degraded and slumbering brethren, a spirit of inquiry and investigation respecting our miseries and wretchedness in this Republican Land of Liberty!!!!!!

The sources from which our miseries are derived, and on which I shall comment, I shall not combine in one, but shall put them under distinct heads and expose them in their turn; in doing which, keeping truth on my side, and not departing from the strictest rules of morality, I shall endeavour to penetrate, search out, and lay them open for your inspection. If you cannot or will not profit by them, I shall have done my duty to you, my country and my God.

And as the inhuman system of slavery, is the source from which most of our miseries proceed, I shall begin with that curse to nations, which has spread terror and devastation through so many nations of antiquity, and which is raging to such a pitch at the present day in Spain and in Portugal. It had one tug in England, in France, and in the United States of America; yet the inhabitants thereof, do not learn wisdom, and erase it entirely from their dwellings and from all with whom they have to do. The fact is, the labour of slaves comes to cheap to the avaricious usurpers, and is (as they think) of such great utility to the country where it exists, that those who are actuated by sordid avarice only, overlook the evils, which will as sure as the Lord lives, follow after the good. In fact, they are so happy to keep in ignorance and degradation, and to receive the homage and the labour of the slaves, they forget that God rules in the armies of heaven and among the inhabitants of the earth, having his ears continually open to the cries, tears and groans of his oppressed people; and being a just and holy Being will at one day appear fully in behalf of the oppressed, and arrest the progress of the avaricious oppressors; for although the destruction of the oppressors God may not effect by the oppressed, yet the Lord our God will bring other destructions upon them—for not unfrequently will he cause them to rise up one against another, to be split and divided, and to oppress each other, and sometimes to open hostilities with sword in hand. Some may ask, what is the matter with this united and happy people? —Some say it is the cause of political usurpers, tyrants, oppressors, &c. But has not the Lord an oppressed and suffering people among them? Does the Lord condescend to hear their cries and see their tears in consequence of oppression? Will he let the oppressors rest comfortably and happy always? Will he not cause the very children of the oppressors to rise up against them, and oftimes put them to death? "God works in many ways his wonders to perform."

I will not here speak of the destructions which the Lord brought upon Egypt, in consequence of the oppression and consequent groans of the oppressed—of the hundreds and thousands of Egyptians whom God hurled into the Red Sea for afflicting his people in their land— of the Lord's suffering people in Sparta or Lacedaemon, the land of the truly famous Lycurgus—nor have I time to comment upon the cause which produced the fierceness with which Sylla usurped the title, and absolutely acted as dictator of the Roman people—the conspiracy of Cataline—the conspiracy against, and murder of Caesar in the Senate house—the spirit with which Marc

Anthony made himself master of the commonwealth— his associating Octavius and Lipidus with himself in power—their dividing the provinces of Rome among themselves—their attack and defeat, on the plains of Phillippi, of the last defenders of their liberty, (Brutus and Cassius)—the tyranny of Tiberius, and from him to the final overthrow of Constantinople by the Turkish Sultan, Mahomed II. A.D. 1453. I say, I shall not take up time to speak of the causes which produced so much wretchedness and massacre among those heathen nations, for I am aware that you know too well, that God is just, as well as merciful! —I shall call your attention a few moments to that Christian nation, the Spaniards— while I shall leave almost unnoticed, that avaricious and cruel people, the Portuguese, among whom all true hearted Christians and lovers of Jesus Christ, must evidently see the judgments of God displayed. To show the judgments of God upon the Spaniards, I shall occupy but a little time, leaving a plenty of room for the candid and unprejudiced to reflect.

All persons who are acquainted with history, and particularly the Bible, who are not blinded by the God of this world, and are not actuated solely by avarice—who are able to lay aside prejudice long enough to view candidly and impartially, things as they were, are, and probably will be—who are willing to admit that God made man to serve Him alone, and that man should have no other Lord or Lords but Himself—that God Almighty is the sole proprietor or master of the whole human family, and will not on any consideration admit of a colleague, being unwilling to divide his glory with another—and who can dispense with prejudice long enough to admit that we are men, notwithstanding our improminent noses and woolly heads, and believe that we feel for our fathers, mothers, wives and children, as well as the whites do for theirs. —I say, all who are permitted to see and believe these things, can easily recognize the judgments of God among the Spaniards. Though others may lay the cause of the fierceness with which they cut each other's throats, to some other circumstance, yet they who believe that God is a God of justice, will believe that Slavery is the principal cause.

While the Spaniards are running about upon the field of battle cutting each other's throats, has not the Lord an afflicted and suffering people in the midst of them, whose cries and groans in consequence of oppression are continually pouring into the ears of the God of justice? Would they not cease to cut each other's throats, if they could? But how can they? The very support which they draw from government to aid them in perpetrating such enormities, does it not arise in a great degree from the wretched victims of oppression among them? And yet they are calling for Peace!—Peace! ! Will any peace be given unto them? Their destruction may indeed be procrastinated awhile, but can it continue long, while they are oppressing the Lord's people? Has He not the hearts of all men in His hand? Will he suffer one part of his creatures to go on oppressing another like brutes always, with impunity? And yet, those avaricious wretches are calling for Peace! ! ! ! I declare, it does appear to me, as though some nations think God is asleep, or that he made the Africans for nothing else but to dig their mines and work their farms, or they cannot believe history, sacred or profane. I ask every man who has a heart, and is blessed with the privilege of believing—Is not God a God of justice to all his creatures? Do you say he is? Then if he gives peace and tranquility to tyrants, and permits them to keep our fathers, our mothers, ourselves and our children in eternal ignorance and wretchedness, to support them and their families, would he be to us a God of justice? I ask, O ye Christians! ! ! who hold us and our children in the most abject ignorance and degradation, that ever a people were afflicted with since the world began—I say, if God gives you peace and tranquility, and suffers you thus to go on afflicting us, and our children, who have never given you the least provocation—would he be to us a God of justice? If you will allow that we are men, who feel for each other, does not the blood of our fathers and of us their children, cry aloud to the Lord of Sabaoth against you, for the cruelties and murders with which you have, and do continue to afflict us. But it is time for me to close my remarks on the suburbs, just to enter more fully into the interior of this system of cruelty and oppression.

PRIMARY SOURCE DOCUMENT

The Autobiography of Omar Ibn Said

INTRODUCTION Many of the Africans who were transported to the Americas were Muslims, though the records of their lives in slavery are few. The *Autobiography of Omar Ibn Said* is one of those scarce records.

Omar Ibn Said, who was born around 1770, studied the Koran for twenty-five years, beginning when he was a boy of six or seven. Around the age of thirty, he had established himself as a trader and Muslim scholar in Futa Tora, south of the Senegal River. In 1807, caught up in the slave trade, he found himself on board a slave ship bound for Charleston, South Carolina, one of the last of those transported to North America prior to the banning of the slave trade. Although Said lived a long life and witnessed Emancipation prior to his death in 1864, he never returned to Africa.

A devout and gentle man, Said became well known in southern circles. Apologists for slavery used Said, or "Prince Moro," as they called him, as proof of the benign nature of the peculiar institution. Prince Moro was regularly portrayed as a royal convert to Christianity. Unwilling to acknowledge the civilization of black Islamic Africa, propagandists also falsified the truth of Said's identity, depicting him as North African—that is, not black African.

None of this was true. Omar Ibn Said was a black African, a common man, and a scholar, and his brief 1831 autobiography reveals him to have kept his Islamic beliefs long after he had been sold into slavery in a Christian country.

In the name of God, the merciful the gracious. —God grant his blessing upon our Prophet Mohammed. Blessed be He in whose hands is the kingdom and who is Almighty; who created death and life that he might test you; for he is exalted; he is the forgiver (of sins), who created seven heavens one above the other. Do you discern anything trifling in creation? Bring back your thoughts. Do you see anything worthless? Recall your vision in earnest. Turn your eye inward for it is diseased. God has adorned the heavens and the world with lamps, and has made us missiles for the devils, and given us for them a grievous punishment, and to those who have disbelieved their Lord, the punishment of hell and pains of body. Whoever associates with them shall hear a boiling caldron, and what is cast therein may fitly represent those who suffer under the anger of God. –Ask them if a prophet has not been sent unto them. They say, "Yes; a prophet has come to us, but we have lied to him." We said, "God has not sent us down anything, and you are in grievous error." They say, "If we had listened and been wise we should not now have been suffering the punishment of the Omniscient." So they confess they have sinned in destroying the followers of the Omniscient. Those who fear their Lord and profess his name, they receive pardon and great honor. Guard your words, (ye wicked), make it known that God is all-wise in all his manifestations. Do you not know from the creation that God is full of skill? that He has made for you the way of error, and you have walked therein, and have chosen to live upon what your God Nasur has furnished you? Believe on Him who dwells in heaven, who has fitted the earth to be your support and it shall give you food. Believe on Him who dwells in Heaven, who has sent you a prophet, and you shall understand what a teacher (He has sent you). Those that were before them deceived them (in regard to their prophet). And how came they to reject him? Did they not see in the heavens above them, how the fowls of the air receive with pleasure that which is sent them? God looks after all. Believe ye: it is He who supplies your wants, that you may take his gifts and enjoy them, and take great pleasure in them. And now will you go in error, or walk in the path of righteousness. Say to them, "He who regards you with care, and who has made for you the heavens and the earth and gives you prosperity, Him you think little of. This is He that planted you in the earth, and to whom you are soon to be gathered." But they say, "If you are men of truth, tell us when shall this promise be fulfilled?" Say to them, "Does not God know? and am not I an evident Prophet?" When those who disbelieve shall see the things draw near before their faces, it shall then be told them, "These are the things about which you made inquiry." Have you seen that God has destroyed me or those with me? or rather that He has shewn us mercy? And who will defend the unbeliever from a miserable punishment? Say, "Knowledge is from God." Say: "Have you not seen that your water has become impure? Who will bring you fresh water from the fountain?"

O Sheikh Hunter, I cannot write my life because I have forgotten much of my own language, as well as of the Arabic. Do not be hard upon me, my brother. —To God let many thanks be paid for his great mercy and goodness.

In the name of God, the Gracious, the Merciful. — Thanks be to God, supreme in goodness and kindness and grace, and who is worthy of all honor, who created all things for his service, even man's power of action and of speech.

From Omar to Sheikh Hunter

You asked me to write my life. I am not able to do this because I have much forgotten my own, as well as the Arabic language. Neither can I write very grammatically or according to the true idiom. And so, my brother, I beg you, in God's name, not to blame me, for I am a man of weak eyes, and of a weak body.

My name is Omar ibn Seid. My birthplace was Fut Tur, between the two rivers. I sought knowledge under the instruction of a Sheikh called Mohammed Seid, my own brother, and Sheikh Soleiman Kembeh, and Sheikh Gabriel Abdal. I continued my studies twenty-five years, and then returned to my home where I remained six years. Then there came to our place a large army, who killed many men, and took me, and brought me to the great sea, and sold me into the hands of the Christians, who bound me and sent me on board a great ship and we sailed upon the great sea a month and a half, when we came to a place called Charleston in the Christian language. There they sold me to a small, weak, and wicked man, called Johnson, a complete infidel, who had no fear of God at all. Now I am a small man, and unable to do hard work so I fled from the hand of Johnson and after a month came to a place called Fayd-il. There I saw some great houses (churches). On the new moon I went into a church to pray. A lad saw me and rode off to the place of his father and informed him that he had seen a black man in the church. A man named Handah [Hunter?] and another man with him on horseback, came attended by a troop of dogs. They took me and made me go with them twelve miles to a place called Fayd-il, where they put me into a great house from which I could not go out. I continued in the great house (which, in the Christian language, they called jail) sixteen days and nights. One Friday the jailor came and opened the door of the house and I saw a great many men, all Christians, some of whom called out to me, "What is your name? Is it Omar or Seid?" I did not understand their Christian language. A man called Bob Mumford took me and led me out of the jail, and I was very well pleased to go with them to their place. I stayed at Mumford's four days and nights, and then a man named Jim Owen, son-in-law of Mumford, having married his daughter Betsey, asked me if I was willing to go to a place called Bladen. I said, Yes, I was willing. I went with them and have remained in the place of Jim Owen until now.

Before [after?] I came into the hand of Gen. Owen a man by the name of Mitchell came to buy me. He asked me if I were willing to go to Charleston City. I said "No, no, no, no, no, no, no, I am not willing to go to Charleston. I stay in the hand of Jim Owen."

O ye people of North Carolina, O ye people of S. Carolina, O ye people of America all of you; have you among you any two such men as Jim Owen and John Owen? These men are good men. What food they eat they give to me to eat. As they clothe themselves they clothe me. They permit me to read the gospel of God, our Lord, and Saviour, and King; who regulates all our circumstances, our health and wealth, and who bestows his mercies willingly, not by constraint. According to power I open my heart, as to a great light, to receive the true way, the way of the Lord Jesus the Messiah.

Before I came to the Christian country, my religion was the religion of "Mohammed, the Apostle of God— may God have mercy upon him and give him peace." I walked to the mosque before day-break, washed my face and head and hands and feet. I prayed at noon, prayed in the afternoon, prayed at sunset, prayed in the evening. I gave alms every year, gold, silver, seeds, cattle, sheep, goats, rice, wheat, and barley. I gave tithes of all the above-named things. I went every year to the holy war against the infidels. I went on pilgrimage to Mecca, as all did who were able. —My father had six sons and five daughters, and my mother had three sons and one daughter. When I left my country I was thirty-seven years old; I have been in the country of the Christians twenty-four years. —Written A.D. 1831.

O ye people of North Carolina, O ye people of South Carolina, O all ye people of America—

The first son of Jim Owen is called Thomas, and his sister is called Masa-jein [Martha Jane?]. This is an excellent family.

Tom Owen and Nell Owen have two sons and a daughter. The first son is called Jim and the second John. The daughter is named Melissa.

Seid Jim Owen and his wife Betsey have two sons and five daughters. Their names are Tom, and John, and Mercy, Miriam, Sophia, Margaret and Eliza. This family is a very nice family. The wife of John Owen is called Lucy and an excellent wife she is. She had five children. Three of them died and two are still living. O ye Americans, ye people of North Carolina—have you, have you, have you, have you, have you among you a family like this family, having so much love to God as they?

Formerly I, Omar, loved to read the book of the Koran the famous. General Jim Owen and his wife used to read the gospel, and they read it to me very much,— the gospel of God, our Lord, our Creator, our King, He that orders all our circumstances, health and wealth, willingly, not constrainedly, according to his power. —Open thou my heart to the gospel, to the way of uprightness. — Thanks to the Lord of all worlds, thanks in abundance. He is plenteous in mercy and abundant in goodness.

For the law was given by Moses but grace and truth were by Jesus the Messiah.

When I was a Mohammedan I prayed thus: "Thanks be to God, Lord of all worlds, the merciful the gracious, Lord of the day of Judgment, thee we serve, on thee we call for help. Direct us in the right way, the way of those on whom thou hast had mercy, with whom thou hast not been angry and who walk not in error. Amen." —But now I pray "Our Father", etc., in the words of our Lord Jesus the Messiah.

I reside in this our country by reason of great necessity. Wicked men took me by violence and sold me to the Christians. We sailed a month and a half on the great sea to the place called Charleston in the Christian land. I fell into the hands of a small, weak and wicked man, who feared not God at all, nor did he read (the gospel) at all nor pray. I was afraid to remain with a man so depraved and who committed so many crimes and I ran away. After a month our Lord God brought me forward to the hand of a good man, who fears God, and loves to do good, and whose name is Jim Owen and whose brother is called Col. John Owen. These are two excellent men. —I am residing in Bladen County.

I continue in the hand of Jim Owen who never beats me, nor scolds me. I neither go hungry nor naked, and I have no hard work to do. I am not able to do hard work for I am a small man and feeble. During the last twenty years I have known no want in the hand of Jim Owen.

African Americans Coming to the Fore of American Identity

If the first half of the twentieth century had represented an excruciating struggle for African Americans, not so much for equality, but for survival and for basic access to the day-to-day opportunities of American life, the second half would be marked with a violent process of rhetoric, followed by riots, followed by legislation, and followed finally by the seeds of change. Over centuries, African Americans had seen the sorts of promises the nation made to them; they had watched as the nation was born with their help, as the Civil War was won with their sacrifices, and as an industrial nation of the first world was created in large part through the sweat of their brows—and always they found themselves locked out of the nation's promise.

The 1950s saw African Americans locked into a pattern of alienation: in the South out-and-out segregation and second-class citizenship; in the North a life spent working in the most menial positions and a cultural identity simultaneously lampooned and commodified from the representations of blacks in films to the phenomenon of the burgeoning beat culture and its interest in the "cool" culture of jazz. At the same time, the first seeds of change had been sown. In a process that would be repeated over and over in American history, African American culture was to be consumed by those on the fringes of society and eventually by elements of the white middle class. Beat poets, African American and white novelists alike, and of course the early years of rock and roll were beginning to bring the two sides of America into increasingly closer contact.

The first trickle of cultural integration came in the 1950s and early 1960s. Artists such as Miles Davis, James Baldwin, and Sidney Poitier had begun to burst onto the national stage. They forced America to realize that African Americans had much to contribute. That said, it was still a bitter, divisive period; by the time African American leaders such as Martin Luther King Jr. and Malcolm X entered the national consciousness and the Civil Rights movement was in full swing, the nation

The Emergence of the Twentieth-Century Preacher/ Leader: Dr. Martin Luther King Jr. (1929–1968) and Malcolm X (1925–1965)

A tradition of African American leadership has grown up out of religious practices that date back to the days of slavery. Slaveholders usually allowed religious (and no other) gatherings. Through the years the connection between politics and religion has remained strong.

This history produced one of the greatest orators and social visionaries in modern history. Martin Luther King Jr. eloquently synthesized the values he found in his Christian faith and the desperate needs for equality and justice in black communities in America.

Malcolm X, another leader who emerged from the same tradition, advocated a different approach to achieving goals. He believed that King's policies of nonviolent demonstration and "engaging the enemy" would be met with a familiar combination of placating words and inaction that African Americans had seen in the United States for more than two centuries. Malcolm X sought to strike fear into the hearts of white America, promising social destruction of biblical proportions and a kind of ongoing psychological terrorism between the black and white races. He also stated in his interactions with other civil rights leaders that his goal was to cause white America to realize they had to capitulate to the reasonable and eloquent requests of the one—Martin Luther King Jr.—or they would have to deal with the violence of the other. In retrospect, there can be little doubt that although King is often celebrated as a great American hero and leader, it is likely that the synergies created by followers of both King and Malcolm X produced some of the results so long sought after during the Civil Rights movement.

would be forced to look at itself in a way that it had struggled to avoid for more than two centuries. ■

The Civil Rights Struggle: From Nonviolence to Black Power

ADAPTED FROM ESSAYS BY SUZANNE SMITH, GEORGE MASON UNIVERSITY

In 1903, the African American scholar and historian W. E. B. Du Bois (1868–1963) declared in his seminal text *The Souls of Black Folk* that "the problem of the Twentieth Century is the problem of the color line."

Du Bois knew that racial segregation had become more entrenched as the nineteenth century drew to a close. In the South, Jim Crow laws had become common throughout the 1880s and 1890s, enforcing racial segregation in public facilities such as railroad cars, restaurants, and hotels. In 1896, the U.S. Supreme Court had upheld the practice of systematic racial segregation in its landmark *Plessy* v. *Ferguson* decision, ruling that "separate but equal" public facilities for African Americans were not discriminatory.

The color line proved to be as problematic in the new century as Du Bois had predicted. In 1909, Du Bois helped found the National Association for the Advancement of Colored People (NAACP). In its first decades of existence, the NAACP organized antilynching campaigns, helped to secure voting rights for blacks, and combated racist practices in America's judicial system. Organizations such as the NAACP and the Urban League assisted African Americans throughout the early twentieth century, a time when many were migrating from the rural South to the urban North and to the West, looking for new opportunities.

As World War II approached, African Americans were increasingly impatient with America's continued practice of forced segregation in the South and de facto segregation in much of the rest of the country, including its defense industries. As soldiers, African Americans were being asked to protect democracy around the world, but they were not treated as equals in the armed forces. On the home front, they faced job discrimination in the wartime economy.

In 1941, A. Philip Randolph (1889–1979) organized the first March on Washington to demand that black Americans be employed in the country's defense industries. In response to the planned demonstration, Presi-

This photograph of labor leader A. Philip Randolph, who was instrumental in organizing the March on Washington in 1963, was taken in the year of the march. Randolph first planned such a march in 1941 when he mounted a campaign to protest job discrimination in national defense work. After President Roosevelt ordered the desegregation of defense industries, Randolph called off the planned march. **AP/WIDE WORLD PHOTOS**

dent Franklin D. Roosevelt (1882–1945) issued Executive Order 8802, which opened up defense industry jobs to blacks, and created the Fair Employment Practices Committee (FEPC). His objective met, Randolph canceled the March on Washington. The episode had proved that the mere threat of collective action by African Americans could be a powerful political tool.

CATALYSTS OF THE MODERN CIVIL RIGHTS MOVEMENT

In post–World War II America, several events acted as catalysts of the modern Civil Rights movement. In the early 1950s, the NAACP's legal team, led by the skillful attorney Thurgood Marshall (1908–1993), began a formal campaign to end segregation in public schools. Culminating with the landmark case of *Brown* v. *Board of Education of Topeka, Kansas.* On May 17, 1954, the

Supreme Court ruled in favor of the plaintiffs, overturning the "separate but equal" doctrine established almost sixty years before in *Plessy* v. *Ferguson.* In their final decision, the justices declared that "in the field of public education the doctrine of 'separate but equal' has no place."

Outside the courtroom, racial tensions in America continued to erupt, with far-reaching consequences. In August 1955, Emmett Till (1941–1955), a fourteen-year-old boy from Chicago, traveled to the Mississippi Delta to visit his relatives. When a rumor began to circulate that Till had whistled at a white woman, he was brutally beaten to death. African Americans across the country followed the trial of Till's accused murderers, which received extensive coverage in the black press. In the end, a local all-white jury acquitted the two defendants. The decision shocked an entire generation of black Americans and inspired a new fight for racial justice.

Martin Luther King Jr. (1929–1968) and the "Letter from Birmingham Jail"

In April 1963, Martin Luther King Jr. and other civil rights leaders began a campaign to desegregate Birmingham, Alabama, widely regarded as the nation's most segregated city. A few days into the campaign, King was arrested, along with hundreds of other demonstrators. From behind bars, King began writing the "Letter from Birmingham Jail," perhaps his most famous essay.

King described the writing of the "Letter" as follows: "This response to a published statement by eight fellow clergymen from Alabama … was composed under somewhat constricting circumstances. Begun on the margins of the newspaper in which the statement appeared while I was in jail, the letter was continued on scraps of writing paper supplied by a friendly Negro trusty, and concluded on a pad my attorneys were eventually permitted to leave me." King later "polished" the letter and published it in his 1963 book *Why We Can't Wait.* "Letter from Birmingham Jail" presents a clear history and description of the nonviolent tactics of the Civil Rights movement, arguing forcefully for immediate action against segregation and racial violence. The statement by his fellow clergy that King was responding to deplored the tensions created by civil rights demonstrations and charged King and others with being "untimely" in their protests. It called upon civil rights activists to wait for a better time and to work for gradual change.

But for King, this was what African Americans could no longer accept. "For years now," he wrote, "I have heard the word 'Wait!' It rings in the ear of every Negro with piercing familiarity. This 'Wait' has almost always meant 'Never.'" So compelling was King's "Letter from Birmingham Jail" that some of the clergy to whom it was addressed eventually joined him in the nonviolent campaign for civil rights.

On December 1, 1955, Rosa Parks (b. 1913), a seamstress and former NAACP secretary, refused to give up her seat to a white passenger on a bus in Montgomery, Alabama. Local police arrested and jailed Parks, who had a reputation as a violator of Jim Crow laws. Her defiance initiated the year-long Montgomery Bus Boycott. The Reverend Martin Luther King Jr. (1929–1968), emerged as the leader of the successful nonviolent campaign that desegregated the city's bus system. By 1957, King had organized the Southern Christian Leadership Conference (SCLC), and the nonviolent struggle to secure the civil rights of all Americans had begun.

THE NONVIOLENT FIGHT FOR INTEGRATION

After the Montgomery Bus Boycott, the civil rights struggle returned to the question of public school desegregation. In 1955, the U.S. Supreme Court ruled that states must comply with the *Brown* v. *Board of Education* decision "with all deliberate speed." In the autumn of 1957, efforts to integrate Central High School in Little Rock, Arkansas, led to the first battle in the South over the federal rulings.

The fight against desegregating Central High was led by the governor of Arkansas, Orval Faubus (1910–1994).

With his blessing, a mob of local protesters confronted nine African American students as they tried to enroll. Forced to intervene, President Dwight D. Eisenhower (1890–1969) sent in federal troops to protect the new students, who became known as the Little Rock Nine.

The Little Rock Nine were finally enrolled, but violent opposition to school desegregation continued throughout the early 1960s. In 1962, James Meredith's (b. 1933) campaign to enter the University of Mississippi led to violence, in which two bystanders were killed by gunfire.

In the face of violent resistance, civil rights activists continued to practice nonviolent civil disobedience in the fight for integration. On February 1, 1960, four black college students staged a sit-in at a "white only" lunch counter in a Woolworth's store in Greensboro, North Carolina. The sit-in movement soon spread to other cities and towns across the South.

In April 1960, three hundred students meeting in Raleigh, North Carolina formed the Student Nonviolent Coordinating Committee (SNCC). SNCC, an independent youth organization, worked with other civil rights groups such as SCLC and the Congress of Racial Equality (CORE) to fight racial injustice. CORE, founded in 1942, organized freedom rides—interracial bus caravans that tested compliance with desegregation rulings in public transportation throughout the South.

As the nonviolent struggle for desegregation grew, the entire nation, not just the South, was forced to address the civil rights question. In April 1963, Martin Luther King and SCLC led a campaign to desegregate public facilities in Birmingham, Alabama. City officials, led by Eugene "Bull" Connor (1897–1973), arrested King and harassed other demonstrators with attack dogs and fire hoses. Newspaper photographs and television coverage of the brutality in Birmingham shocked Americans across the country and tarnished the United States' image abroad.

Civil rights leaders continued to press their case, and at the March on Washington on August 28, 1963, King presented his stirring "I Have a Dream" speech. One year later, on July 2, 1964, President Lyndon Johnson (1908–1973) signed the Civil Rights Act of 1964, the most extensive civil rights legislation ever enacted by Congress. The act outlawed racial discrimination in hotels, restaurants, and all other public accommodations.

CULTURAL STATEMENTS DURING THE CIVIL RIGHTS ERA

African American cultural expression sustained, shaped, and enriched every phase of the civil rights era. In the early years of sit-ins and freedom rides, demonstrators and activists used freedom songs to build solidarity at rallies, to protest racial injustice and violence, and to ward off their fears of violent retaliation. As freedom singer and historian Bernice Johnson Reagon (b. 1942) has said, "When we did those marches and went to jail, we expanded the space we could operate in, and that was echoed in the singing."

At the March on Washington in August 1963, "We Shall Overcome" became the anthem of the struggle for racial equality in America. During the Black Power era of the late 1960s, rhythm and blues songs such as James Brown's (b. 1928) "(Say It Loud) I'm Black and I'm Proud" and Aretha Franklin's (b. 1942) "Respect" also captured the spirit of the times.

Writers, actors, and entertainers also contributed to the civil rights struggle. James Baldwin (1924–1987) defined the central questions of America's racial crisis with insight and passion in the book of essays titled *The Fire Next Time* and in the play *Blues for Mister Charlie*. By the late 1960s, the Black Arts movement was celebrating all forms of African American cultural expression as a means of cultivating racial pride. Poets and writers such as Gwendolyn Brooks (1917–2000), Langston Hughes (1902–1967), Amiri Baraka (b. 1934), Nikki Giovanni (b. 1943), and Dudley Randall (1914–2000) published poetry anthologies and organized art festivals to generate interest

Playwright, actor, and life-long civil rights activist Ossie Davis spoke at the March on Washington in 1963, one of many celebrities present for the occasion. Mr. Davis also delivered the eulogy at the funeral of Malcolm X in 1965. **NATIONAL ARCHIVES AND RECORDS ADMINISTRATION**

in African American arts. The Free Southern Theater, a traveling drama group, performed plays throughout the rural South to educate the public about the black experience and African American history. Entertainers such as Harry Belafonte (b. 1927), Sidney Poitier (b. 1927), Lena Horne (b. 1917), and Dick Gregory (b. 1932) also used their status as celebrities to promote the civil rights cause. **SEE PRIMARY SOURCE DOCUMENT** *Excerpt from* **The Fire Next Time** *by James Baldwin*

POLITICAL EMPOWERMENT AND THE RISE OF BLACK POWER

African American political representation has been one of the central issues of the modern civil rights struggle. Black Americans first held public office during Reconstruction. With the passage in 1870 of the Fifteenth Amendment, they secured the right to vote. These political advances did not last, however. In the South, organizations such as the Ku Klux Klan (first founded in 1866) used violent intimidation to suppress the black vote and keep African Americans from holding office.

By the mid-twentieth century, most blacks in the South were prevented from registering to vote or participating in elections. In 1964, SNCC organized "Freedom Summer," its most extensive campaign to register black voters in Mississippi. White college students from the North and community organizers from rural Mississippi worked together to register voters in a state that had a long history of preventing the black vote.

Fannie Lou Hamer, a leader in the registration campaign, helped organize the Mississippi Freedom Democratic Party (MFDP) to address the needs of the state's black citizens. When the MFDP asked to be seated at the national Democratic convention in Atlantic City, New Jersey, in 1964, the Democratic party refused to recognize the organization. However, its efforts—and its refusal to accept small concessions from Democratic Party leaders—inspired activists nationwide.

The fight to secure political rights for African Americans continued in 1965 in Selma, Alabama. Seeking federal voting rights legislation, SCLC and SNCC chose to focus the campaign on Selma. Once again, nonviolent demonstrations were met with brutal resistance. On what came to be called Bloody Sunday, March 7, 1965, Alabama state troopers attacked demonstrators who were marching peacefully for the right to vote. When James Reeb (1927–1965) and Viola Liuzzo (1925–1965), two white volunteers, were subsequently murdered, pressure increased on the federal government to act. On August 6, 1965, President Johnson signed the Voting Rights Act of 1965 into law.

Passage of the Voting Rights Act, while a clear victory, did not signal an end to tensions in the civil rights struggle. One week after President Johnson signed the voting legislation, riots broke out in Watts, California. During the summers of 1966 and 1967, violent disturbances occurred in cities across the country, including Chicago, Cleveland, Newark, and Detroit. The anger that fueled the riots forced the nation to address racial and economic inequality in America's urban centers. President Johnson appointed the National Advisory Commission on Civil Disorders to investigate the root causes of the violence. In March 1968, the commission proclaimed that the "nation is moving toward two societies, one black, one white—separate and unequal."

The growing complexities of the civil rights struggle ended the unity that had existed in the movement's earlier years. In 1966, Stokely Carmichael took over the leadership of SNCC and announced a new, separatist approach. Promoting the philosophy of Black Power, he expelled most white members from the organization. The Black Panther party, led by Huey Newton (1942–1989) and Eldridge Cleaver (b. 1935), represented an even more

militant radicalism. The black nationalist rhetoric of Malcolm X, who was assassinated in 1965, also inspired many of the new advocates of Black Power.

In his last years, Martin Luther King Jr. continued to express his belief in nonviolent protest while expanding his vision of what constituted justice in American society. King denounced the United States' involvement in the Vietnam War and spoke out against poverty and economic, as well as racial, inequality. On April 4, 1968, King was assassinated in Memphis, Tennessee, only a few weeks before he was to lead a Poor People's March on Washington.

The Civil Rights movement carried on after the death of its most famous leader, but with no simple solutions to the challenges that lay ahead.

BIBLIOGRAPHY

Branch, Taylor. *Parting the Waters: America in the King Years, 1954–63.* New York: Simon & Schuster, 1988.

Carson, Clayborne. *In Struggle: SNCC and the Black Awakening of the 1960s.* Cambridge: Harvard University Press, 1981.

Garrow, David J. *Bearing the Cross: Martin Luther King, Jr., and the Southern Christian Leadership Conference.* New York: W. Morrow, 1986.

Giddings, Paula. *When and Where I Enter: The Impact of Black Women on Race and Sex in America.* New York: W. Morrow, 1984.

Hamilton, Charles V., and Stokely Carmichael. *Black Power: The Politics of Liberation in America.* New York: Random House, 1967.

Malcolm X, and Alex Haley, *The Autobiography of Malcolm X.* New York: Grove Press, 1965.

Moody, Anne. *Coming of Age in Mississippi.* New York: Dial Press, 1968.

Robinson, Jo Ann Gibson. *The Montgomery Bus Boycott and the Women Who Started It: The Memoir of Jo Ann Gibson Robinson.* Knoxville: University of Tennessee Press, 1987.

Weisbrot, Robert. *Freedom Bound: A History of America's Civil Rights Movement.* New York: W.W. Norton, 1990.

Williams, Juan. *Eyes on the Prize: America's Civil Rights Years, 1954–1965.* New York: Viking, 1987.

PRIMARY SOURCE DOCUMENT

Excerpt from *The Fire Next Time* by James Baldwin

INTRODUCTION Published in 1963, *The Fire Next Time* presented author James Baldwin's views on the condition of black people at a critical time in history. The book sold more than a million copies and reinforced the author's reputation as a key figure in bringing to light the struggles of African Americans.

The American Negro has the great advantage of having never believed that collection of myths to which white Americans cling: that their ancestors were all freedom-loving heroes, that they were born in the greatest country the world has ever seen, or that Americans are invincible in battle and wise in peace, that Americans have always dealt honorably with Mexicans and Indians and all other neighbors or inferiors, that American men are the world's most direct and virile, that American women are pure. Negroes know far more about white Americans than that; it can almost be said, in fact, that they know about white Americans what parents—or, anyway, mothers—know about their children, and that they very often regard white Americans that way. And perhaps this attitude, held in spite of what they know and have endured, helps to explain why Negroes, on the whole, and until lately, have allowed themselves to feel so little hatred. The tendency has really been, insofar as this was possible, to dismiss white people as the slightly mad victims of their own brainwashing. One watched the lives they led. One could not be fooled about that; one watched the things they did and the excuses they gave themselves, and if a white man was really in trouble, deep trouble, it was to the Negro's door that he came. And one felt that if one had had that white man's worldly advantages, one would never have become as bewildered and as joyless and as thoughtlessly cruel as he. The Negro came to the white man for a roof or for five dollars or for a letter to the judge; the white man came to the Negro for love. But he was not often able to give what he came seeking. The price was too high; he had too much to lose. And the Negro knew this, too. When one knows this about a man, it is impossible for one to hate him, but unless he becomes a man—becomes equal—it is also impossible for one to love him....

How can the American Negro past be used? It is entirely possible that this dishonored past will rise up soon to smite all of us.... A bill is coming in that I fear America is not prepared to pay. "The problem of the twentieth century," wrote W. E. B. Du Bois around sixty years ago, "is the problem of the color line." A fearful and delicate problem, which compromises, when it does not corrupt, all the American efforts to build a better world—here, there, or anywhere.

SOURCE: Baldwin, James. *The Fire Next Time.* New York: Dial Press, 1963.

The African American Intellectual Experience

ADAPTED FROM ESSAYS BY JONATHAN HOLLOWAY, YALE UNIVERSITY

An intellectual tradition may span many different kinds of inquiry and reveal itself in many different forms of expression. The scientist, artist, writer, teacher, musician, politician, inventor, minister, and even the criminal can be intellectuals, involved in society or detached from it, leaders, followers, or merely uninterested.

The variety of intellectual expression becomes crucial when we consider the history of African American

James Baldwin, who was born in New York City in 1924, the son of southern migrants, was the author of several novels and plays, as well as dozens of essays. Although he spent much of his adult life in Europe, Baldwin returned to New York in 1957 and remained there for the next decade—writing and commenting on the events of the Civil Rights era. **AP/WIDE WORLD PHOTOS**

intellectuals, because racial discrimination often limited their career options and compelled them to unite their creative and political activities. In other words, the particular realities of life for Africans in the Americas gave rise to a very specific intellectual tradition—and very specific types of intellectual leaders. There are a number of primary threads woven through the African American intellectual experience; many of which have their roots in the experience of being uprooted from the African continent and the legacy of bondage and search for freedom. The drive for literacy, the search for identity and the right to shape one's own narrative or history, the poetics of exclusion—these are some of the primary tenets of the literature and ideas grown up out of the African American community in the United States.

While a central and often-times nearly desperate need for self-definition—and the economic and civil rights that should follow—has marked much of the

A radical black activist who began her work in the late 1960s and early 1970s, Angela Davis remains a potent force dedicated to exposing injustice through her writings and lectures.
AP/WIDE WORLD PHOTOS

intellectual experience of African Americans, their "outsider" status and history of disenfranchisement also drove many African Americans to extraordinary heights—extremes of intellectual and artistic achievement. We can only hope that as American history is written, the story will reflect more and more the traditions that African Americans create and perpetuate, and the central role of these ideas in the fabric of the American experience.

THE BEGINNINGS OF THE AFRICAN AMERICAN INTELLECTUAL EXPERIENCE

The history of African American intellectuals begins with the poet Phillis Wheatley (1753–1784). Born in Africa, Wheatley was brought to the United States and purchased by a prominent Boston family. She did not have a "typical" slave experience. Her owners taught her to read and write—skills she mastered with amazing speed. Wheatley dined with her owners and had her own room in the family house. Moreover, when she began to suffer from ill health, the family followed its doctor's advice and sent her to England to recuperate. Along with providing safe passage, Wheatley's owners released her from bondage.

Wheatley's masters were atypical in yet another way. In 1773, they helped her become the first African American to publish a book, *Poems on Various Subjects, Religious and Moral,* but not before they had proved to skeptical publishers that an African slave had the mental capacity to write poetry in the grand English tradition. Indeed, the Wheatleys had to secure written verification of their slave's talents from the governor and lieutenant governor of Massachusetts. Other prominent Bostonians, like John Hancock (1737–1793), also provided support.

The other colonial African American most often cited for his intellectual abilities is the astronomer and mathematician Benjamin Banneker (1731–1806). Born into a Maryland family of freed slaves, Banneker spent most of his life tending the family farm, educating himself in his spare time from borrowed books. He attending school with white and African American children. On the tobacco farm he inherited from his parents, he spent his nights studying the stars.

It was not until Banneker was sixty years old that he began to gain widespread recognition for his abilities. In 1791, he started working on an almanac that incorporated his calculations for solar and lunar eclipses. In the same year, he was chosen to assist in the survey of the Federal Territory, now known as the District of Columbia. After he completed this task, he returned to the family farm and turned his full attention to securing publication of his almanac. Prior to its publication, he sent a copy to slave owner Thomas Jefferson, who was the secretary of state at the time. Banneker produced the almanac for only six years, but the project was quite successful, coming out in twenty-nine separate editions in the United States and England.

Although Banneker was a scientist and Wheatley a poet, these two figures have several important things in common. They both lived most of their lives prior to the Revolutionary War, thus demonstrating that an African American intellectual tradition predates the founding of the United States. Moreover, although they were popular, both were seen as racial oddities by their white contemporaries, who were amazed that a black person could possess the talent needed to write sparkling poetry or compute challenging mathematical formulas.

Perhaps most importantly, neither Wheatley nor Banneker made a career out of agitating for racial progress, a fact that sets them apart from the African American intellectual tradition they helped to establish, which has been characterized by vigorous protest and activist leadership. Did these two early African American intellectuals have an obligation to protest more vigorously against slavery and other forms of social inequality based upon race? Perhaps it was enough that both were masters of their crafts and that, through their mastery, they offered early proof that African Americans were capable of anything.

THE RISE OF THE PREACHER-ACTIVIST: HENRY HIGHLAND GARNET

By 1807, both Wheatley and Banneker had passed away. But their deaths did not spell the end of African American intellectual endeavors. Indeed, this country's early national period was a fertile time for the development of a new type of African American intellectual: the preacher-activist.

It is not surprising that most black intellectuals of the nineteenth century also happened to be religious leaders. After all, preachers often were literate, adept at verbal analysis, and committed to trying to improve the lives of those around them. The rise of abolitionism also played a role in the growing leadership of the African American preacher-activist. Based in church organizations and founded upon Christian belief, the abolitionist movement was in many ways a religious movement, and as it took root in the decades preceding the Civil War, several religious leaders (black as well as white) were catapulted into the spotlight.

Many African American preachers rose to intellectual leadership during the abolitionist era, men like J. W. C Pennington (1809–1875) and Samuel Ringgold Ward. One of the most famous of these spiritual leaders was Henry Highland Garnet (1815–1882). Garnet was born into slavery but gained his own emancipation when he joined his father in an escape to New York City. He received a first-rate theological education and, upon completion of his studies, secured a pastorship in upstate New York, but he was not content to focus solely upon his congregation. Knowing from personal experience the horrors of slavery, he became an outspoken advocate of armed slave resistance. In his 1843 "Address to the Slaves of the United States," delivered at the National Negro Convention in Buffalo, Garnet advised, "You had better all die—die immediately, than live slaves and entail your wretchedness upon your posterity."

Accompanying Garnet's call for aggressive self-emancipation was a philosophy imbued with religious sentiment instructing African Americans how to live their lives. This philosophy is most clearly expressed in Garnet's essay "The Past and the Present Condition, and the Destiny of the Colored Race," in which he asks, "How shall we acquit ourselves on the field where the great battle is to be fought? By following after peace and temperance, industry and frugality, and love to God and to all men, and by resisting tyranny in the name of Eternal Justice." **SEE PRIMARY SOURCE DOCUMENT** *"The Past and the Present Condition, and the Destiny of the Colored Race," by Henry Highland Garnet*

SLAVE, FUGITIVE, ABOLITIONIST, AND LEADER: FREDERICK DOUGLASS

The fight against slavery also propelled fugitive slaves into national prominence, none more famous than

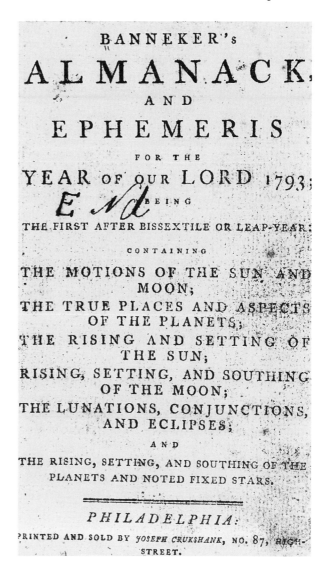

The title page of Benjamin Banneker's almanac, which began publication in 1791. **ARCHIVE PHOTOS, INC.**

Frederick Douglass (1817–1895), perhaps the greatest intellectual leader of the nineteenth century. Like Garnet, Douglass had escaped slavery and was to become a figure in the abolitionist movement. Douglass provides an interesting perspective on the intellectual leader as scholar and political activist. Unlike Garnet, or the African American leaders of the late twentieth century who as often as not have come from a religious background, Douglass was an orator and a manipulator of the political machine. While the two men were different in ways too numerous to count, it might be said Booker T. Washington came out of this tradition. Savvy, an educator and public speaker, Frederick Douglass used the national platform of race and politics, along with the success of his own autobiography to wield considerable clout with various figures in government. Douglass also created a name for himself as a newspaperman, editing and publishing such important periodicals as the *North Star, Frederick Douglass's Paper,* and the *New National Era.* More than any American before him, Douglass filled the role of public intellectual. He devoted his considerable capacities to explicitly political ends, and by so doing paved the way for future generations of African American intellectuals who would do the same.

THE 1890s: DEBATE AND DIVISION AMONG BLACK INTELLECTUALS

The 1890s were an era of profound transition for African American intellectuals. Frederick Douglass, the most prominent African American leader, died in 1895. In the same year, W. E. B. Du Bois (1868–1963), destined to be the most influential African American intellectual of the twentieth century, received his Ph.D., the first black to receive a doctorate from Harvard University. Also in 1895, Booker T. Washington (1856–1915) delivered his "Atlanta compromise" address at the Cotton States and International Exposition, hastening his ascent to national prominence.

A slave until the age of nine, Washington toiled in coal mines as a youth but eventually secured admission to the Hampton Institute of Virginia, where he worked his way through school. Several years after his graduation, Washington founded the Tuskegee Normal and Industrial Institute (1881). The "Tuskegee mission" was to train teachers and workers, and this it succeeded in doing, but only with steady financial assistance from major white corporate philanthropies. Washington was able to secure such assistance because he endeavored to appear and to act unthreatening to white Americans.

The best formulation of Washington's social philosophy remains the Atlanta compromise speech, in which he proclaimed his policy of accommodation to Jim Crow segregation: "In all things that are purely social we can be as separate as the fingers, yet one as the hand in all things essential to mutual progress." Washington urged blacks to improve themselves by pulling themselves up by their own bootstraps and curried favor among whites by accepting social segregation and the denial of political rights. In return for these concessions, Washington became a counsel to corporate executives and even presidents of the United States.

Many prominent black intellectuals did not consider Washington to be a true scholar, despite the fact he was intimately involved in educating African Americans. Rev. Alexander Crummell (1819–1898), for one, entirely disagreed with Washington's advocacy of industrial training. Exceptionally well educated for any person of his time, white or black, Crummell spent the years between 1853 and 1872 in Liberia, fighting to "civilize" the indigenous people. Returning to the United States, he devoted

the rest of his life to "raising" the African American masses via "civilization and culture."

In his final years, probably in response to Washington's Atlanta compromise speech, Crummell sought to create a vehicle for delivering his own moral message. Thus the American Negro Academy was born in 1897, with the mission of fostering the development of African American intellectual talents, improving the quality of black leadership, and guaranteeing that racist propaganda did not go unchallenged. In Crummell's view, Washington's educational and social philosophy was antithetical to the moral and cultural mission of the academy, but the academy's own policies excluded from membership many African Americans who shared this view—women, for example. As forward-thinking and progressive as the academy may have been, it was still very much a reflection of its time.

A protégé of Alexander Crummell and vice president of the American Negro Academy, W. E. B. Du Bois was one of the Booker T. Washington's most unrelenting critics. In 1903, he published his remarkable book *The Souls of Black Folk,* directly challenging Washington's political philosophy. In opposition to Washington's doctrine of self-help, Du Bois advanced the notion that a "talented tenth" of well-educated African Americans would save the black masses. The talented tenth, Du Bois reasoned, had the ability to bring civilization and cultural refinement to black Americans.

Although Du Bois's philosophy appealed to intellectuals for obvious reasons, many of them found it difficult to maneuver around Washington's powerful political machine. Du Bois did his best to implement his own plan of action through organizations like the Niagara Movement (1905–1909) and the National Association for the Advancement of Colored People (NAACP; founded in 1909), both of which he helped establish. But his greatest success as a public intellectual came through his editorship of the NAACP magazine, *Crisis.* From his editorial perch, he routinely advocated positions that he felt African Americans would do well to take. One of his most famous editorials was addressed to black soldiers returning from the battlefields of World War I, where they had made the world "safe for democracy," to the violence of Jim Crow America. Du Bois concluded his editorial with a threat: "We return. We return from fighting. We return fighting." **SEE PRIMARY SOURCE DOCUMENT** *W. E. B. Du Bois and the "Economics of Emancipation"*

THE EDUCATOR AS INTELLECTUAL: ANNA JULIA COOPER

While W. E. B. Du Bois conducted his fights at the national level, Anna Julia Cooper waged her battle for educational improvement at the local level. The only woman who was ever elected to the American Negro

Born into slavery in Virginia in 1856, Booker T. Washington was educated at Hampton Institute, one of the first of the freedmen's schools, and went on to found the Tuskegee Normal and Industrial Institute in Tuskegee, Alabama, where he promoted a Hampton-style curriculum of vocational training. Washington's advocacy of economic progress over political and civil rights earned him the label of "accomodationist," but it also made him one of the most powerful men of his day. **THE LIBRARY OF CONGRESS**

Academy or invited to speak at its conferences, Anna Julia Cooper (1858–1964) was a master educator wholly committed to the profession of teaching. Cooper received her bachelor's and master's degrees from Oberlin College (1884 and 1887), and in 1892 she published a volume of essays, *A Voice from the South,* which emphasized the importance of educated African American women to the future of black America.

Beginning in 1897, Cooper spent the better part of the next four decades working to improve educational opportunities for blacks in the District of Columbia. To that end, she served from 1901 to 1906 as principal of the M Street High School (the second female to hold the position), almost single-handedly turning it into one of the finest high schools for African Americans in the

country. Indeed, M Street, renamed Dunbar High School in 1916, was one of only a handful of black schools whose graduates were not required to take special competency exams for college admission.

Not content with the critically important role she played in the lives of countless District youths, Cooper continued an aggressive public and private push for educational excellence. She pursued further graduate studies of her own at the Guilde Internationale in Paris and at Columbia University, receiving her doctorate from the University of Paris in 1925. She was sixty-seven years old. Five years later, she founded Frelinghuysen University in Washington, D.C., an evening school for blacks working full-time, which offered college-level courses in law and religion. The classes were held at Cooper's home. She

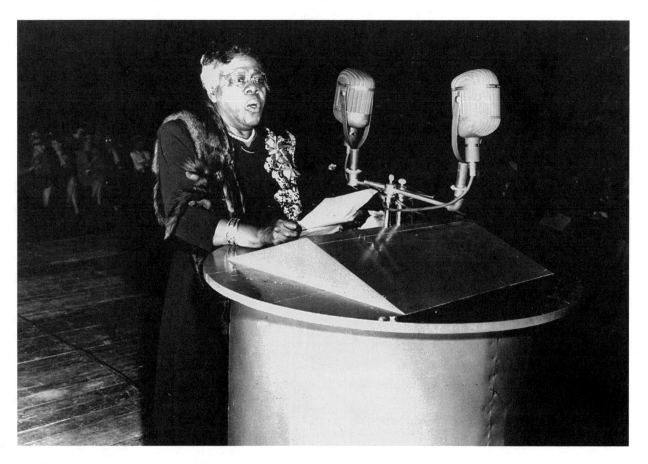

With a dollar and a half and five pupils, Mary McLeod Bethune founded Bethune-Cookman College, Daytona Beach, Florida, in 1904.
CORBIS-BETTMANN

served as the school's president for ten years and its registrar for another ten.

THE BLACK WOMEN'S CLUB MOVEMENT AND THE NATIONAL ASSOCIATION FOR COLORED WOMEN

The 1890s also saw the beginning of the Black Women's Club Movement, which took the lead in battles to improve the daily lives of African Americans, especially women and children. In 1893, Josephine St. Pierre Ruffin (1842–1924) founded the Women's New Era Club, which set up kindergartens for black children in Boston and elsewhere, as well as establishing ties with similar organizations in other cities. In 1895, under Ruffin's leadership, the National Federation of Afro-American Women held its first meetings in Boston to establish a national organization of women's groups, which would lead, in the following year, to the founding of the National Association of Colored Women (NACW).

The NACW functioned as the umbrella organization for numerous black women's groups around the country, setting national policies and agendas in a variety of areas, including improvements in living and working conditions, child-care and early education, and train-

ing and support for young mothers. The association's first chairwoman was Mary Church Terrell (1863–1954), a daughter of newly freed slaves who had risen to civic prominence in Washington, D.C.

Terrell shared with Ruffin, Fannie Barrier Williams of Chicago (1855–1944), and many other women in the club movement a belief in the value of "self-help." Most had entered the middle class through dint of education and effort, a combination which they encouraged other black women to embrace for themselves and their children. They also encouraged black women who were successful to continue to labor for the progress of others. The founding motto of the National Association of Colored Women, "Lifting as We Climb," captured the double mission of those in the club movement: to maintain and advance the economic interests of African Americans through the elevation of the working and middle classes.

Central to the club movement was a strong belief in women's education and the worth of women's work, as moral and spiritual leaders, as mothers and homemakers, and as domestic and industrial laborers. This belief united those in the club movement with other African American women in the first decades of the twentieth century—the noted educator Mary McLeod Bethune

(1875–1955), for example—and also with women like Maria Stewart (1803–1879), Sojourner Truth (1797?–1883), and Frances E. W. Harper (1825–1911), who had been active in the antislavery campaign.

ALAIN LOCKE AND THE NEW NEGRO RENAISSANCE

Having discovered that fighting for their country did not gain them full rights at home, African Americans attempted other forms of advancement during the 1920s. The most famous of these attempts was the cultural philosophy promoted by Alain Locke (1885–1954), the first African American Rhodes scholar and a professor of philosophy at Howard University, in his 1925 book *The New Negro*. With its essays, artwork, poems, and fiction, *The New Negro* celebrated the artistic and cultural movement spreading through Harlem and other major cities. The philosophy that undergirded this movement, popularly referred to now as the Harlem Renaissance or the New Negro Renaissance, was that African Americans could best demonstrate their contribution to the United States via their cultural production.

While many scholars point to Locke's book as the dawning of the New Negro Renaissance, the debate continues as to when that era ended. Because the movement had no specific political agenda, there is also debate about whether and in what way it was successful. Whatever the case, it is clear that the New Negro Renaissance launched the careers of several important African American artists whose work continues to influence American thought and expression: Langston Hughes (1902–1967), Claude McKay (1890–1948), Nella Larsen (1893–1964), Jean Toomer (1894–1967), Zora Neale Hurston (1891–1960), Aaron Douglas (1899–1979), and Countee Cullen (1903–1946), to name a few.

Locke also promoted the rise of a new generation of African American scholars. At Howard University, then the nation's most prestigious black college, Locke urged the recruitment of and then mentored a small flock of African American intellectuals who came of age during the 1930s, people like the sociologist E. Franklin Frazier (1894–1962) and the political scientist—and future Nobel Peace Prize recipient—Ralph Bunche (1904–1971). While a small handful of black Americans had earned Ph.D.s before the mid-1920s, these scholars were part of the first generation of African Americans to receive doctorates in any great numbers. In this respect, they differed from those who preceded them at historically black colleges and universities, to which social custom continued to confine African Americans scholars and teachers.

A WIDENING TRADITION OF INTELLECTUAL LEADERSHIP

The young scholars of this generation were the first modern African American intellectuals, not limited to or

Born in Detroit in 1904, Ralph J. Bunche received a Ph.D. in political science from Harvard University in 1934 and entered government service shortly thereafter, one of the first generation of college-trained African Americans to receive government appointments. Bunche spent many years at the United Nations and was awarded the 1950 Nobel Peace Prize for his efforts as a diplomat in the Middle East. (Photograph by Carl Van Vechten.) **THE ESTATE OF CARL VAN VECHTEN**

defined by theological training like many nineteenth-century African American intellectuals. Furthermore, they were the first African Americans to be recruited to work in administrative positions within the federal government. Starting in the early 1930s, several highly trained African Americans began to take positions as "race advisers" in Franklin D. Roosevelt's (1882–1945) New Deal administration, and many spent much of their working lives in government service. The economist Robert C. Weaver (1907–1997), for example, Roosevelt's first race adviser, eventually became the first black to hold a cabinet position as secretary of Housing and Urban Development under Lyndon Johnson (1908–1973). While we may never know exactly how much influence these race advisers had, we cannot ignore the fact that, from the 1930s on, African American intellectuals were operating from within the political establishment.

Despite their new access to political power, many African American intellectuals preferred to practice their craft within the cloistered walls of the university, and after World War II, teaching opportunities at historically white universities began to be available to black scholars. Most remained at black institutions, but the door had been thrown open to future generations of academics. Interestingly, just as African Americans began to enjoy professional access to major research universities, black ministers became a resurgent force on the national scene. As the fight against slavery had done a century before, the Civil Rights movement now called forth the preacher-activist.

In the 1960s, a new class of intellectuals emerged. Completely secular and rarely holding advanced degrees, these "organic intellectuals" used their cerebral talents to forge new artistic, political, and protest movements. Perhaps the best exemplar of this new tradition is Eldridge Cleaver (b. 1935), Black Panther philosopher, petty criminal, and admitted rapist. Cleaver's brilliant and yet often disturbing masterwork, *Soul on Ice*, much of which was written while he was in prison, reminds us that we cannot accept too limiting a view of who can or cannot be an intellectual.

Much has changed since Phillis Wheatley and Benjamin Banneker astonished the public with their abilities. While we may still be impressed by the intellectual capabilities of some black scholars, we can no longer be surprised, for the African American intellectual tradition now spans nearly three centuries. In the early 2000s, the proliferation of black scholars pushing the envelope of intellectual inquiry, regardless of the form that envelope takes, guarantees that this tradition will continue unabated.

Indeed, some observers believe that we are in the middle of a golden age for African American intellectuals. President Bill Clinton (b. 1946) commissioned Maya Angelou (b. 1928) to write a poem for his inauguration ("On the Pulse of Morning"); the novelist Toni Morrison (b. 1929) has won a Nobel Prize for literature; Rita Dove (b. 1952) has been named the nation's poet laureate; the cultural critic Cornel West (b. 1953) has become an almost permanent fixture on the international lecture circuit; and, in the light of the ascendancy of the Republican Party, neoconservative academics like Thomas Sowell (b. 1930) are in a unique position to affect national policy from inside and outside the government.

BIBLIOGRAPHY

Blackett, R. J. M. *Beating against the Barriers: The Lives of Six Nineteenth-Century Afro-Americans*. Ithaca: Cornell University Press, 1986.

Brotz, Howard. *African-American Social and Political Thought, 1850–1920*. New Brunswick: Transaction, 1992.

Cruse, Harold. *The Crisis of the Negro Intellectual*. 1967. Reprint. New York: Quill, 1984.

Franklin, John Hope, and August Meier, eds. *Black Leaders of the Twentieth Century*. Urbana: University of Illinois Press, 1982.

Litwack, Leon, and August Meier, eds. *Black Leaders of the Nineteenth Century*. Urbana: University of Illinois Press, 1988.

Logan, Rayford, and Michael Winston, eds. *Dictionary of American Negro Biography*. New York: Norton, 1982.

Magill, Frank, ed. *Masterpieces of African-American Literature*. New York: HarperCollins, 1992.

Meier, August. *Negro Thought in America, 1880–1915*. Ann Arbor: University of Michigan Press, 1966.

Meier, August, et al., eds. *Black Protest Thought in the Twentieth Century*. New York: Macmillan, 1971.

PRIMARY SOURCE DOCUMENT

"The Past and the Present Condition, and the Destiny of the Colored Race," by Henry Highland Garnet

INTRODUCTION On February 14, 1848, on the occasion of the fifteenth anniversary of the Female Benevolent Society of Troy, New York, Henry Highland Garnet delivered a speech offering his view of the destiny of black Americans. "The Past and the Present Condition, and the Destiny of the Colored Race" reveals Garnet's thoughts during the years of his greatest fame, in the two decades preceding the Civil War. Reprinted in pamphlet form, it was widely read and discussed during his lifetime.

Though Garnet did not share the anticolonization passion of James Forten or his own contemporary, Frederick Douglass, he does echo their view that African Americans are an inseparable part of the nation: "We are now colonized. We are planted here." And then, in a striking phrase, he adds, "It is too late to make a successful attempt to separate the black and white people in the New World. They love one another too much to endure a separation."

This is a hopeful, even stirring speech, in which Garnet looks back to earlier, and what he sees as outmoded, theories of black inferiority, and forward, past the present enslaved condition of millions of African Americans, to a future of "blessings." "The star of our hope is slowly and steadily rising above the horizon," Garnet asserts. To hasten its ascent, he urges upon his fellow African Americans a Christian program of "peace and temperance, industry and frugality, and love to God, and to all men."

Who is there, after looking at these facts, will question the probability of the assumption, that this republic, and this continent, are to be the theatre in which the grand drama of our triumphant Destiny is to be enacted.

The Red men of North America are retreating from the approach of the white man. They have fallen like trees on the ground in which they first took root, and on the soil which their foliage once shaded. But the Colored race, although they have been transplanted in a foreign land, have clung to and grown with their oppressors, as the wild dry entwines around the trees of the forest, nor can they be torn thence. At this moment when so much feigned hatred is manifested toward us, our blood is mixed with every tribe from Cape Horn to the Frozen Ocean. Skillful men have are themselves to work at analyzation, and yet in many cases they are perplexed in deciding where to draw the line between the Negro and the Anglo Saxon. Whenever our colorless brethren say of themselves, on far do they proclaim our future position. Do they say in proud exultation.

No pent up Utica contracts our powers, The whole boundless continent is ours, in this they bespeak our destiny.

There are those who, either from good or evil motives, plead for the utopian plan of the Colonization of a whole race to the shores of Africa. We are now colonized. We are planted here, and we cannot as a whole people, be re-colonized back to our fatherland. It is no late to make a successful attempt to separate the black and white people in the New World. They love one another too much to endure a separation. Where one is, there will the other be also. Ruth, of the old Testament, puts the resolve of our destiny in our mouths, which we will repeat to those who would expatriate us: "Entreat me nor to leave thee nor return from following after thee, for whither thou goest I will go, and where thou lodgest I will lodge; thy people shall be my people, and thy God shall be my God. Where thou diest there will I die, and there will I be buried. The Lord do so to me, and more; if aught but death part thee and me."

This western world is destined to be filled with a mixed race. Statesmen, distinguished for their forecast, have gravely said that the blacks must either be removed, or such as I have seated will be the result. It is a stubborn fact that it is impossible to separate the pale man and the man of color, and therefore the result which to them is so fearful, is inevitable. All this the wiser portion of the Colonizationists see, and they labor no hinder it. It matters not whether we abhor or desire such a consummation, it is now too late to change the decree of nature and circumstances. As well might we attempt to shake the Alleghanies with our hands, or to burst the rock of Gibralter with our fists. If the colored people should all consent to leave this country, on the day of their departure there would be sore lamentations, the like of which the world has not heard since Rachel wept for her children, and would not be comforted, because they were not. We would insist upon taking all who have our generous and prolific blood in their veins. In such an event, the American church and state would be bereaved. The Reverend Francis L. Hawks, D.D., of the Protestant Episcopal Church, a man who is receiving the largest salary of any divine in the country, would be called upon to make the sacrifice of leaving a good living, and to share the fate of his brethren according to the flesh. The Reverend Dr. Murphy, of Herkimer, New York, a Presbyterian, would be compelled to leave his beloved flock; and how could they endure the loss of a shepherd so eloquent, so faithful and so kind. We should be burdened with that renegade Negro of the United States Senate, Mr. Yulee, of Florida. We should take one of the wives of Senator Samuel Houston. The consort,—the beautiful Cleopatra of his Excellency, R. M. Johnson, late Democratic Vice President of this great nation,—would be the foremost in the vast company of exiles. After we all should return to tread the golden sands of Africa, whether we would add to the morality of our kindred across the deep waters future generations would decide. One thing, I am certain of, and that is, many of the slaveholders and lynchers of the South are nor very moral now. Our cousins of the tribe of Shem are welcome to our deserters. If they are enriched by them they may be assured that we are not impoverished.

On the other continent, the destiny of the colored people will be similar to that of the people among whom they are scattered. Colorphobia is confined almost entirely to the United States and the Canadas. We speak of prejudice against color, but in fact, nothing of the kind exists. The prejudice is against the condition alone. Were not this the case the American feeling would pervade the whole earth.

Many things that there intended for evil to us, will result, I trust, in good. The tyrants have debarred us from the wealth accruing from trade and commerce. This is an evil. But may it not be hoped that we are their juniors in the art of cheating? We have among us some arrant cheats, but it is presumed that but a few will doubt that our white brothers bear off the palm in this department of human depravity. The besetting sins of the Anglo-Saxon race are, the love of gain and the love of power. In many instances, while our services could be dispensed with, we have not been permitted to join the army, and of course have not been killed in the wars. We have been driven from the sanctuaries where our oppressors worship, and it may be that we are not quite as hypocritical as their practices have made them. When the great national account shall be rendered before the tribunal of Justice, the guilt of course must be borne by those who might have had, or who have used the power of the government. There may, therefore, is some good that may come our of this evil. But no thanks to the evil doers. Their works are evil still, the good comes in spite of them.

The old doctrine of the natural inferiority of the colored race, propagated in America by Mr. Thomas Jefferson, has long since been refused by Dr. John Mason Goode, and numerous respectable witnesses from among the slandered, both living and dead: Pushkin in Russia, Dumas in France, Toussaint in Hayti, Banaker, Theodore Sedgwick Wright, and a host in America, and a brilliant galaxy in Ancient History.

There are blessings in store for our patient, suffering race,—there is light and glory. The star of our hope is slowly and steadily rising above the horizon. As a land that has long been covered by storms and clouds, and shaken by thunder, when the storms and clouds had passed away, and the thunder was succeeded by a clam, like that which cheered the first glad morning, and flower and shrub smiled as they looked up to God, and the mountains, plains and valleys rung with joy,—so shall this race come forth and re-occupy their station of renown.

But how shall we hasten on that period? How shall we acquit ourselves on the field where the great battle is to be fought? By following after peace and temperance, industry and frugality, and love to God, and to all men, and by resisting tyranny in the name of Eternal Justice. We must also become acquainted with the arts and sciences, and agricultural pursuits. These will elevate any people and sever any chain.

We must also cherish and maintain national and patriotic sentiment and attachment. Some people of color say that they have no home, no country. I am not among that number. It is empty declamation. It is unwise. It is not logical—it is false.

Of all the people in this wide earth, among the countless hordes of misery, there is not one so poor as to be without a home and a country. America is my home, my country, and I have no other. I love whatever good there may be in her institutions. I hate her sins. I loathe her slavery, and I pray Heaven that ere long she may wash away her guilt in tears of repentance. I love the green-hills which my eyes first beheld in my infancy. I love every inch of soil which my feet pressed in my youth, and I mourn because the accursed shade of slavery rests upon it, I love my country's flag, and I hope that soon it will be cleansed of its stains, and be hailed by all nations as the emblem of freedom and independence.

PRIMARY SOURCE DOCUMENT

W. E. B. Du Bois and the "Economics of Emancipation"

INTRODUCTION The Seventh Annual Conference for the Study of the Negro Problems, which was held at Atlanta University in May 1902, focused on the fate of the black artisan after emancipation. Much of the conference report was written by W. E. B. Du Bois, in his role as both historian and sociologist.

The following sections of the report, entitled "The Ante-Bellum Artisan" and "The Economics of Emancipation," offer a brief but first-rate history of skilled African American workers during slavery and of the obstacles such workers encountered in their search for employment following emancipation.

---

2. The Ante-bellum Artisan. Before the civil war both slaves and free Negroes were artisans to some extent. It is difficult to-day, however, to determine just what proportion could do skilled work and how their work would compare with that of artisans of to-day. We are told that in Virginia:

The county records of the seventeenth century reveal the presence of many Negro mechanics in the colony during that period, this being especially the case with carpenters and coopers. This was what might be expected. The slave was inferior in skill, but the ordinary mechanical needs of the plantation did not demand the highest aptitude. The fact that the African was a servant for life was an advantage covering many deficiencies; nevertheless, it is significant that large slaveholders like Colonel Byrd and Colonel Fitzhugh should have gone to the inconvenience and expense of importing English handicraftsmen who were skilled in the very trades in which it is certain that several of the Negroes belonging to these planters had been specially trained. It shows the low estimate in which the planters held the knowledge of their slaves regarding the higher branches of mechanical work.

As examples of slave mechanics it is stated that among the slaves of the first Robert Beverly was a carpenter valued at (L)30, and that Ralph Wormeley, of Middlesex country, owned a cooper and a carpenter each valued at (L)35. Colonel William Byrd mentions the use of Negroes in iron mining in 1732. In New Jersey slaves were employed as miners, iron-workers, saw-mill hands, house and ship-carpenters, wheelwrights, coopers tanners, shoemakers, millers and bakers, among other employments, before the Revolutionary war. As early as 1708 there were enough slave mechanics in Pennsylvania to make the freemen feel their competition severely. In Massachusetts and other states we hear of an occasional artisan.

During the early part of the 19th century the Negro artisans increased. In the District of Columbia many "were superior mechanics .... Benjamin Banneker, the Negro Astronomer, assisting in surveying the District in 1791" Olmsted, in his journeys through the slave states, just before the civil war, found slave artisans in all the states: In Virginia they worked in tobacco factories, ran steamboats, made barrels, etc. On a South Carolina plantation he was told by the master that the Negro mechanics "exercised as much skill and ingenuity as the ordinary mechanics that he was used to employ in New England." In Charleston and some other places they were employed in cotton factories. In Alabama he saw a black carpenter—a careful and accurate calculator and excellent workman; he was bought for $2,000. In Louisiana he was told that master mechanics often brought up slave mechanics and acted as contractors. In Kentucky the slaves worked in factories for hemp-bagging, and in iron works on the Cumberland river, and also in tobacco factories. In the newspapers advertisements for runaway mechanics were often seen, as, for instance a blacksmith in Texas, "very smart," a mason in Virginia, etc. In Mobile an advertisement read "good blacksmiths and horseshoers for sale on reasonable terms."

An ex-governor of Mississippi says:

Prior to the war there were a large number of Negro mechanics in the Southern States; many of them were expert blacksmiths, wheelwrights, wagon-makers, brick-masons, carpenters, plasterers, painters and shoemakers. They became masters of their respective trades by reason of sufficiently long service under the control and direction of expert white mechanics. During the existence of slavery the contract for qualifying the Negro as a mechanic was made between his owner and the master workman.

Such slaves were especially valuable and formed usually a privileged class, with a large degree of freedom. They were very often hired out by their masters and sometimes hired their own time although this latter practice was frowned upon as giving slaves too much freedom and nearly all states forbade it by law; although some, like Georgia, permitted the custom in certain cities. In all cases the slave mechanic was encouraged to do good work by extra wages which went into his own pocket. For instance, in the semi-skilled work of the Tobacco-factories, the Virginia master received from $150–$200 annually for his slave and the employer fed him; but the slave, by extra work, could earn for himself $5 or more a month. So carpenters sometimes received as much as $2 a day for their masters, and then were given the chance to earn more for themselves. In Texas nine slaves, some of them carpenters, were leased at an average of $280.22 a year and probably earned something over this. If the mechanic was a good workman and honest the master was tempted to allow him to do as he pleased so long as he paid the master a certain yearly income. In this way there arose in nearly all Southern cities a class of Negro clients free in everything but name; they owned property, reared families and often lived in comfort. In earlier times such mechanics often bought themselves and families and became free, but as the laws began to bear hard on free Negroes they preferred to remain under the patronage and nominal ownership of their white masters. In other cases they migrated North and there worked out their freedom, sending back stipulated sums. Many if not most of the noted leaders of the Negro in earlier times belonged to this slave mechanic class, such as Vesey, Nat Turner, Richard Allen and Absalom Jones. They were exposed neither to the corrupting privileges of the house servants nor to the blighting tyranny of field work and had large opportunity for self development.

Usually the laws did not hinder the slaves from learning trades. On the other hand the laws against teaching slaves really hindered the mechanics from attaining very great efficiency save in rare cases—they must work by rule of thumb usually. North Carolina allowed slaves to learn mathematical calculations, but

---

W. E. B. Du Bois (1868–1963)

Born in the Berkshire Hills of Massachusetts in 1868 and educated at Fisk and Harvard Universities and the University of Berlin, W. E. B. Du Bois became one of the greatest American intellectuals of the twentieth century. A prolific writer, he also was a founding member of the National Association for the Advancement of Colored People (NAACP) and for many years the editor of its chief magazine, *Crisis.* Du Bois also helped organize the first Pan-African Conference in 1919, and late in his life emigrated to Ghana, where he became a citizen.

As a young man, Du Bois vigorously opposed Booker T. Washington's championing of economic progress at the expense of civil rights and higher education. In particular, he deplored Washington's emphasis on vocational training as the sole educational model for black Americans. He argued instead for a "talented tenth" of African Americans, trained to the highest standards, who would be in the vanguard of racial leadership and progress.

In his 1903 book *The Souls of Black Folk,* Du Bois included "Of Mr. Booker T. Washington and Others," his most extended critique of Washington's "programme of industrial education, conciliation of the South, and submission and silence as to civil and political rights."

---

not reading and writing; Georgia in 1833 decreed that no one should permit a Negro "to transact business for him in writing." Gradually such laws became more severe: Mississippi in 1830 debarred slaves from printing offices and Georgia in 1845 declared that slaves and free Negroes could not take contracts for building and repairing houses, as mechanics or masons. Restrictions, however, were not always enforced, especially in the building trades, and the slave mechanic flourished.

One obstacle he did encounter however from first to last and that was the opposition of white mechanics. In 1708 the white mechanics of Pennsylvania protested against the hiring out of Negro mechanics and were successful in gettiug acts passed to restrict the further importation of slaves but they were disallowed in England. In 1722 they protested again and the Legislative

Black Intellectuals: Booker T. Washington (1856–1915) and the Atlanta Compromise

Booker T. Washington was famous for having been born to slavery and worked to build himself up, "a self-made man." He was perhaps equally famous for his "accomodationist" stance regarding blacks and the ills of slavery, admonishing those who were angry at the institution itself and former slave owners. In 1895, Booker T. Washington was invited to address the Atlanta International Cotton Exposition. Although Washington had traveled widely and was well known as a speaker and the founder of Tuskegee Institute, this event, which has come to be known as the "Atlanta compromise," brought him into national prominence.

Washington urged his listeners, black and white, to "cast down your buckets where you are." For black southerners, this meant staying put and trying to achieve economic progress in traditional fields of work, such as agriculture, mechanics, and domestic service. For white southerners, it meant using black labor rather than turning to "those of foreign birth and strange tongue and habits," the immigrants who were flooding into the nation.

Washington reminded his white listeners several times of all they shared, historically and economically, with their black neighbors. But he bowed to segregationist fears when he claimed that "in all things that are purely social we can be as separate as the fingers, yet one as the hand in all things essential to mutual progress." Moreover, he seemed to dismiss the struggle for civil rights, especially voting rights, as "artificial forcing."

Although Washington's speech was hailed by whites in both the North and South, it was condemned by many other black leaders as affirming Jim Crow segregation and encouraging violence. As W. E. B. Du Bois wrote, "Is it possible, and probable, that nine millions of men can make effective progress in economic lines if they are deprived of political rights, made a servile caste, and allowed only the most meagre chance for developing their exceptional men? If history and reason give any distinct answer to these questions, it is an emphatic *No*." Du Bois's fears were borne out the next year, when the Supreme Court issued its decision in the case of *Plessy* v. *Ferguson*, ushering in sixty years of legal discrimination.

Assembly declared that the hiring of black mechanics was "dangerous and injurious to the republic and not to be sanctioned." Especially in border states was opposition fierce. In Maryland the legislature was urged in 1837 to forbid free Negroes entirely from being artisans; in 1840 a bill was reported to keep Negro labor out of tobacco ware-houses; in 1844 petitions came to the legislature urging the prohibition of free black carpenters and taxing free black mechanics; and finally in 1860 white mechanics urged a law barring free blacks "from pursuing any mechanical branch of trade." Mississippi mechanics told Olmsted that they resented the competition of slaves and that one refused the free services of three Negroes for six years as apprentices to his trade. In Wilmington, N. C., 1857, a number of persons destroyed the frame work of a new building erected by Negro carpenters and threatened to destroy all edifices erected by Negro carpenters or mechanics. A public meeting was called to denounce the act and offer a reward. The deed was charged upon an organized association of 150 white workingmen. There were similar disturbances in Virginia, and in South Carolina white mechanics about this time were severely condemned by the newspapers as "enemies to our peculiar institutions and formidable barriers to the success of our own native mechanics."

In Ohio about 1820 to 1830 and thereafter, the white Mechanics' Societies combined against Negroes. One master mechanic, President of the Mechanical Association of Cincinnati, was publicly tried by the Society for assisting a young Negro to learn a train. Such was the feeling that no colored boy could find entrance as apprentice, and few workmen were allowed to pursue their calling. One Negro cabinet-maker purchased his freedom in Kentucky and came to Cincinnati; for a long time he could get no work; one Englishman employed him but the white workmen struck. The black man was compelled to become a laborer until by saving he could take small contracts and hire black mechanics to help him. In Philadelphia the series of fearful riots against Negroes was due in large part to the jealousy of white working men, and in Washington, D. C., New York and other cities, riots and disorder on the part of white mechanics, aimed against Negroes, occurred several times.

There were, no doubt, many very efficient slave mechanics. One who learned his trade from a slave writes us an interesting and enthusiastic account of the work of these men:

During the days of slavery the Negro mechanic was a man of importance. He was a most valuable slave to his master. He would always sell for from two to three times as much in the market as the unskilled slaveman. When a fine Negro mechanic was to be sold at public auction, or private sake, the wealthy slave owners would vie with each other for the prize and run the bidding often up into high figures.

The slave owners early saw the aptitude of the Negro to learn handicraft, and fully appreciating what vast importance and value this would be to them (the masters) selected their brightest young slavemen and had them taught in the different kinds of trades. Hence on every large plantation you could find the Negro carpenter, blacksmith, brick and stone mason. These trades comprehended and included much more in their scope in those days than they do now. Carpentry was in its glory then. What is done now by varied and complicated machinery was wrought then by hand. The invention of the planing machine is an event within the knowledge of many persons living to-day. Most of our "wood working" machinery has come into use long since the days of slavery. The same work done now with the machine, was done then by hand. The carpenter's chest of tools in slavery times was a very elaborate and expensive outfit. His "kit" not only included all the tools that the average carpenter carries now, but also the tools for performing all the work done by the various kinds of "wood-working" machines. There is little opportunity for the carpenter of to-day to acquire, or display, genius and skill in his trade as could the artisan of old.

One only needs to go down South and examine hundreds of old Southern mansions, and splendid old church edifices, still intact, to be convinced of the fact of the cleverness of the Negro artisan, who constructed ninetenths of them, and many of them still provoke the admiration of all who see them, and are not to be despised by the men of our day.

There are few, if any, of the carpenters of to-day who, if they had the hand tools, could get out the "stuff" and make one of those old style massive panel doors,—who could work out by hand the mouldings, the stiles, the mullions, etc., and build one of those windows, which are to be found to-day in many of the churches and public buildings of the South; all of which testify to the cleverness of the Negro's skill as artisan in the broadest sense of the term. For the carpenter in those days was also the "cabinet marker," the wood turner, coffin maker, generally the pattern maker, and the maker of most things made of wood. The Negro blacksmith held almost absolute sway in his line, which included the many branches of forgery, and other trades which are now classified under different heads from that of the regular blacksmith. The blacksmith in the days of slavery was expected to make any and everything wrought of iron. He was to all intents and purposes the "machine blacksmith," "horseshoer," "carriage and wagon ironer and trimmer," "gunsmith," "wheelwright"; and often whittled out and ironed the hames, the plowstocks, and the "single trees" for the farmers, and did a hundred other things too numerous to mention. They were experts at tempering edge tools, by what is generally known as the water process. But many of them had secret processes of their own for tempering tools which they guarded with zealous care.

It was the good fortune of your humble servant to have served his time as an apprentice in a general blacksmithing shop, or shop of all work, presided over by an ex-slave genius known throughout the state as a "master mechanic." In slavery times this man hired his own time—paying his master a certain stipulated amount of money each year, and all he made over and above that amount was his own.

The Negro machinists were also becoming numerous before the downfall of slavery. The slave owners were generally the owners of all the factories, machine shops, flour-mills, saw-mills, gin houses and threshing machines. They owned all the railroads and the shops connected with them. In all of these the white laborer and mechanic had been supplanted almost entirely by the slave mechanics at the time of the breaking out of the civil war. Many of the railroads in the South had their entire train crews, except the conductors, made up of the slaves—including engineers and firemen. The "Georgia Central" had inaugurated just such a movement, and had many Negro engineers on its locomotives and Negro machinists in its shops. So it will be seen at once that the liberation of the slaves was also the salvation of the poor white man of the South. It saved him from being completely ousted, as a laborer and a mechanic, by the masters, to make place for the slaves whom they were having trained for those positions. Yet, strange as it may seem to us now, the great mass of poor white men in the South who were directly and indirectly affected by the slave mechanic—

Struggles for African American laborers continued well into the twentieth century. African Americans who joined the March on Washington in 1963 wanted economic opportunities as well as their civil rights. This twin emphasis—on civil rights and job opportunity—has always been part of the Civil Rights movement, uniting twentieth-century activists with free African Americans of the antebellum years. **NATIONAL ARCHIVES AND RECORDS ADMINISTRATION**

being literally forced out of the business, took up arms and fought against the abolition of slavery!

While the poor whites and the masters were fighting, these same black men were at home working to support those fighting for their slavery. The Negro mechanic could be found, during the conflict, in the machine shops, building engines and railroad cars; in the gun factories making arms of all kinds for the soldiers; in the various shops building wagons, and making harness, bridles and saddles, for the armies of the South. Negro engineers handled the throttle in many cases to haul the soldiers to the front, whose success, in the struggle going on, meant continued slavery to themselves and their people. All of the flour mills, and most of every other kind of mill, of the South, was largely in charge of black men.

Much has been said of the new Negro for the new century, but with all his training he will have to take a long stride in mechanical skill before he reaches the point of practical efficiency where the old Negro of the old century left off. It was the good fortune of the writer once to fall into the hands of an uncle who was master of what would now be half a dozen distinct trades. He was generally known as a mill-wright, or mill builder. A mill-

wright now, is only a man who merely sets up the machinery, and his work is now confined mostly to the hanging of shafting, pulleys and belting. In the days of slavery the mill-wright had to know how to construct everything about the mill, from foundation to roofs. This uncle could take his men with their "cross cut saws" and "broad axes" and go into the forests, hew the timbers with which to build the dams across the rivers and streams of water, to erect the "mill house" frames, get out all the necessary timber and lumber at the saw mill. Then he would, without a sign of a drawing on paper, lay out and cut every piece, every mortise and tenon, every brace and rafter with their proper angles, &c., with perfect precision before they put the whole together. I have seen my uncle go into the forest, fell a great tree, hew out of it an immense stick or shaft from four feet to five feet in diameter, and from twenty to thirty feet long, having as many as sixteen to twenty faces on its surface, or as they termed it, "sixteen" and "twenty square." He would then take it to the mill seat and mortise it, make the arms, and all the intricate parts for a great "overshot" water wheel to drive the huge mill machinery. This is a feat most difficult even for modern mechanics who have a thorough knowledge of mathematics and the laws of mechanics.

It is difficult for us to understand how those men with little or no knowledge of mathematics, or mechanical rules, could take a crude stick of timber, shape it, and then go to work and cut out a huge screw and the "Tap blocks" for those old style cotton presses.

To the above testimony we may append reports from various localities. From Alabama we have a report from an artisan at Tuskegee who was 14 or 15 years old at the breaking out of the civil war. The Principal of the Academic Department writes: "He is one of the most remarkable men you ever saw. He is a fine tinner, shoemaker and harness maker, and until the school grew so large held all these trades under his instruction. He is an all-round tinker and can do anything from the repairing of a watch to the mending of an umbrella." This man names 25 Negro carpenters, 11 blacksmiths, 3 painters, 2 wheelwrights, 3 tinsmiths, 2 tanners, 5 masons, and 14 shoemakers in Tuskegee and the surrounding districts before the war. "Tuskegee was a small place" he writes "and you will wonder why such a number of mechanics were there. The answer is this: there were a large number of wealthy white people who lived in the county, owning large numbers of slaves, and there was thus a lot of work all through the country districts; so they were sent out to do the work." Of them in general he says: "The mechanics as a rule lived more comfortably than any other class of the Negroes. A number of them hired their time and made money; they wore good clothes and ate better food than the other classes of colored people. In other words they stood higher in the estimation of the white people than any of the others. A very small number of them were allowed to live by themselves in out of the way houses. All the master wanted of them was to stay on his place and pay over their wages promptly. As a rule a white man contracted for the jobs and overlooked the work. These white men often did not know anything about the trade but had Negro foremen under them who really carried on the work." From Georgia there are two reports:. "Before the civil war all of the artisans in this section of the state were colored men. Their masters compelled some of their slaves to learn these trades so that they could do the necessary work around the plantations." In Marshalville, on the other hand, "There were only two Negro artisans here before the war." From West Virginia comes a report: there were "but two skilled laborers" previous to the war in Bluefield. In Chester, South Carolina, "Before the war there were practically no Negro artisans." Charleston reports: "We have no accurate data to work on, except experiences of ex-slaves, who seem to agree that though the anti-bellum artisan was very proficient, yet he could not be compared in point of intelligent service with the artisan of to-day." From Greenville we learn: "The Negro since the war has entered trades more largely and in more varied lines. He is now in trades not open to him before freedom." In Mississippi one town reports that "Before the war Negroes were not artisans from choice, but many large planters would train some of their slaves in carpentry or blacksmithing for plantation use. Then the Negro did not have to ask, Does this trade pay? Now he does." Another locality says: "Before the war the principal trades were carpentry and blacksmithing and were done by training slaves." In Louisiana "Before and since the war Negroes have built some of the best structures" in New Orleans and Baton Rouge. Olmsted noted many Negro mechanics here. In Texas there were "few if any" Negro mechanics in Georgetown before the war, while in Dallas they did "most of the skilled labor." In Arkansas artisans were few. In Tennessee there were relatively more artisans before the war than now in Nashville, fewer in Murfreesboro and McMinnville and about the same number in Maryville. In the District of Columbia there were many Negro artisans in ante-bellum times, as shown by the directories.

It is not altogether clear from such incomplete reports as to just what the status or efficiency of the ante-bellum artisan was. It is clear that there were some very efficient workmen and a large number who knew something of the various trades. Still, we must remember that it would be easy to exaggerate the ability and importance of the mass of these workmen.

"The South was lacking in manufactures, and used little machinery. Its demand for skilled labor was not large, but what demand existed was supplied mainly by Negroes. Negro carpenters, plasterers, bricklayers, black- smiths, wheelwrights, painters, harnessmakers, tanners, millers, weavers, barrelmakers, basketmakers, shoemak-ers, chairmakers, coachmen, spinners, seamstresses, housekeepers, gardeners, cooks, laundresses, embroider-ers, maids of all work, were found in every community, and frequently on a single plantation. Skilled labor was more profitable than unskilled, and therefore every slave was made as skillful as possible under a slave system."

Here we have, perhaps, the best key to the situation in the South before the war; there was little demand for skilled labor in the rather rude economy of the average slave plantation and the Negro did the most of this. The slave artisan, however, was rather a jack-of-all-trades than a mechanic in the modern sense of the term—he could build a barn, make a barrel, mend an umbrella or shoe a horse. Exceptional slaves did the work exceptionally well, but the average workman was poor, careless and ill-trained, and could not have earned living wages under modern competitive conditions. While then it is perfectly true to say that the slave was the artisan of the South before the war it is probably also true that the average of workman-ship was low and suited only to rough plantation life. This does not, of course, gainsay for a moment the fact that on some of the better plantations and in cities like Richmond, Savannah, Charleston, and New Orleans, there were really first-class Negro workmen who did good work.

3. Economics of Emancipation. Slaves and the low-est freemen were the ordinary artisans of Greece and Rome, save only as the great artists now and then descended from above as sculptors and architects. In mediaeval times mechanics were largely bondsmen and serfs and were purchased and imported just as black car-penters formed a part of the expenses of a Texas emi-grant in 1850. While exceptional mechanics in the mid-dle ages acquired a degree of practical freedom just as the Negro mechanics of the South did, yet they were in earli-er times serfs. Gradually in free communities there arose a class of free mechanics, but in the rural districts and in the households of the lords they still, for many genera-tions, remained serfs. The rise and development of cities gave the freed artisan his chance; there, by defensive and offensive organization, he became the leading factor in the economic and political development of the new city-states. His development was rapid, and about the 14th century a distinction between laborers and masters arose which has gradually grown and changed into our mod-ern problem of labor and capital.

A very interesting comparison between this develop-ment and the situation of the Southern freedmen might be drawn at some length. Even before the war a move-ment of slaves to the cities took place: first of house-ser-vants with the masters' families and then of slave artisans: if the slave was a good artisan he was worth more hired out in the city than on the country plantation. Moreover, the Negro greatly preferred to be in town—he had more

W. E. B. Du Bois founded the National Association for the Advancement of Colored People (NAACP), edited the *Crisis,* and wrote *The Souls of Black Folk.* **THE LIBRARY OF CONGRESS**

liberty, more associates, and more excitement. Probably in time there would have been evolved in the South a class of city serf-artisans and servants considerably removed from the mass of field-hands. It is significant that the Georgia law prohibiting slaves from hiring their time specifically excepted certain of the larger towns.

After emancipation came suddenly, in the midst of war and social upheaval, the first real economic question was the self-protection of freed working men. There were three chief classes of them: the agricultural laborers chiefly in the country districts, the house-servants in town and country and the artisans who were rapidly migrating to town. The Freedman's Bureau undertook the temporary guardianship of the first class, the second class easily passed from half-free service to half-servile freedom. The third class, the artisans, however, met peculiar conditions. They had always been used to working under the guardianship of a master and even though that guardianship in some cases was but nominal yet it was of the greatest value for protection. This soon became clear as the Negro freed artisan set up business for himself: if there was a creditor to be sued he could no

longer bring suit in the name of an influential white master; if there was a contract to be had, there was no responsible white patron to answer for the good performance of the work. Nevertheless, these differences were not strongly felt at first—the friendly patronage of the former master was often voluntarily given the freedman and for some years following the war the Negro mechanic still held undisputed sway. Three occurrences, however, soon disturbed the situation:

(a). The competition of white mechanics.

(b). The efforts of the Negro for self-protection.

(c). The new industrial development of the South.

These changes were spread over a series of years and are not yet complete, but they are the real explanation of certain facts which have hitherto been explained in false and inadequate ways. It has, for instance, been said repeatedly that the Negro mechanic carelessly threw away his monopoly of the Southern labor market and allowed the white mechanic to supplant him. This is only partially true. To be sure, the ex-slave was not alert, quick and ready to meet competition. His business hitherto had been to do work but not to get work, save in exceptional cases. The whole slave system of labor saved him from certain sorts of competition, and when he was suddenly called to face the competition of white mechanics he was at a loss. His especial weakness was the lack of a hiring contractor. His master or a white contractor had usually taken jobs and hired him. The white contractor still hired him but there was no one now to see that the contractor gave him fair wages. Indeed, as the white mechanics pressed forward the only refuge of the Negro mechanic was lower wages. There were a few Negro contractors here and there but they again could only hope to maintain themselves by markedly underbidding all competitors and attaining a certain standing in the community.

What the Negro mechanic needed then was social protection—the protection of law and order, perfectly fair judicial processes and that personal power which is in the hands of all modern laboring classes in civilized lands, viz., the right of suffrage. It has often been said that the freedman throwing away his industrial opportunities after the war gave his energies to politics and succeeded in alienating his friends and exasperating his enemies, and proving his inability to rule. It is doubtless true that the freedman laid too much stress on the efficacy of political power in making a straight road to real freedom. And undoubtedly, too, a bad class of politicians, white and black, took advantage of this and made the reconstruction Negro voter a hissing in the ears of the South. Notwithstanding this the Negro was fundamentally right. If the whole class of mechanics here, as in the Middle Age, had been without the suffrage and half-free, the Negro would have had an equal chance with the white mechanic, and could have afforded to wait. But he saw himself coming more and more into competition with men who had the right to vote, the prestige of race and blood, the advantage of intimate relations with those acquainted with the market and the demand. The Negro saw clearly that his industrial rise depended, to an important degree, upon his political power and he therefore sought that power. In this seeking he failed primarily because of his own poor training, the uncompromising enmity and apprehensions of his white neighbors and the selfishness and half-hearted measures of his emancipators. The result was that the black artisan entered the race heavily handicapped—the member of a proscribed class, with restricted rights and privileges, without political and social power. The result was of course that he was enabled to maintain himself only by accepting low wages and keeping at all hazards the good-will of the community.

Even here however he could not wholly succeed. The industrial conditions in the country were rapidly changing. Slowly but surely the new industrial South began to arise and with it came new demands on the mechanic. Now the Negro mechanic could not in the very nature of the case meet these demands; he knew how to do a few things by rule of thumb—he could build one of the rambling old-fashioned southern mansions, he could build a slave shanty; he could construct a rough sugar hogshead and resole a shoe; in exceptional cases he could do even careful and ingenious work in certain lines; but as a rule he knew little of the niceties of modern carpentry or iron-working, he knew practically nothing of mills and machinery, very little about railroads—in fact he was especially ignorant in those very lines of mechanical and industrial development in which the South has taken the longest strides in the last thirty-years. And if he was ignorant, who was to teach him? Certainly not his white fellow workmen, for they were his bitterest opponents because of strong race-prejudice and because of the fact that the Negro works for low wages. Apprenticeship to the older Negro mechanics was but partially successful for they could not teach what they had never learned. In fact it was only through the lever of low wages that the Nergo secured any share in the new industries. By that means he was enabled to replace white laborers in many branches, but he thereby increased the enmity of trades-unions and labor-leaders. Such in brief was the complicated effort of emancipation on the Negro artisan and one could not well imagine a situation more difficult to remedy.

African Americans in the Sciences

ADAPTED FROM ESSAYS BY DR. JAMES JAY

The story of black American participation in the sciences, in medicine, and in invention is like so much of

Born into slavery in 1864, George Washington Carver became the first African American to graduate from Iowa State College, in 1894. Carver spent many years on the faculty of Tuskegee Institute, where he pioneered the development and use of products from a variety of agricultural staples, including potatoes, peanuts, and pecans. **FISK UNIVERSITY LIBRARY**

African American history in the United States, a mixed tale of achievement and exclusion, of progress and denied opportunities. While black Americans achieved notable early success as inventors, their participation in science and medicine has been historically hampered by discrimination that has limited their access to many of the nation's best schools and science programs.

Individual excellence is a necessity for success in science and medicine, as it is in any endeavor. But these fields also typically require group efforts, whether in the form of laboratory assistance or peer review. During the 1800s, the common view among the majority population in America was that blacks were deficient in the mental faculties needed to succeed in science and medicine. Educational opportunities were denied to them, and many able individuals simply were not given the chance to train and succeed as doctors and scientists. Inventors, on the other hand, tend to work and act alone. For this reason, black inventors enjoyed relatively good success in the several decades immediately following the Civil War, a level of success that far exceeded that of their counterparts in science and medicine.

With one notable exception, the early breakthroughs made by black physicians came in the first half of the twentieth century, when they were practicing in all-black

Daniel Hale Williams began his career as a surgeon at South Side Dispensary in Chicago, a city with only three other black surgeons. Aware of the limited opportunities for African Americans in the medical field, he organized Provident Hospital in 1891 where he performed one of the first open-heart surgeries recorded. **CORBIS-BETTMANN**

medical facilities. Black achievements in mathematics, science, and engineering, by contrast, have been more conspicuous during the second half of the twentieth century, as doors have been opened for the training of black scientists and as the attitudes of their white peers have become more receptive.

ACHIEVEMENTS IN INVENTION AND MEDICINE IN THE NINETEENTH CENTURY

Black inventors flourished during the 1880s and 1890s, although several black Americans were noted much earlier for their inventions. Better known as a self-taught astronomer and mathematician, Benjamin Banneker (1731–1806) is also credited with inventing a striking clock in 1752. Two of the earliest patent holders among black inventors were J. Hawkins and N. Rillieux (1806–1894). In 1845, Hawkins was awarded patent number 3,973 for his gridiron, while Rillieux received patent number 4,879 in 1846 for the development of an evaporating pan for refining sugar.

The black inventors who are most often cited made their contributions between 1880 and 1900. Indeed, black

inventors were more conspicuous during those years than they are now, more than a hundred years later. Lacking formal academic training, they were not deterred by the negative attitudes of teachers who doubted the intellectual ability of the former slaves and their children.

Two of the most prolific inventors, in terms of their recorded patents, were Elijah McCoy (1843–1929) and Granville T. Wood (1856–1910). Born in Canada to a fugitive slave couple, McCoy invented numerous devices for automatically lubricating locomotive engines and other machinery. More than twenty-five patents were recorded for him between 1882 and 1892. A free-born Ohioan, Granville Woods (1856–1910) held at least twenty-five patents covering various electrical devices, all recorded between 1884 and 1903.

The 1890s also witnessed the medical achievements of Daniel Hale Williams (1856–1931). Williams founded Provident Hospital in Chicago in 1891 when he was denied the right to practice at other hospitals, and there, two years later, he became the first man to perform open-heart surgery when he repaired a knife wound. Like the black inventors who flourished at the same time and like the black physicians who would come after him, Williams was able to execute his idea in large part because his white peers did not impede him. Had he been on the staff of another hospital, he would probably have been denied the opportunity to attempt open-heart surgery.

GRADUATE TRAINING IN THE SCIENCES PRIOR TO 1900

Father Patrick Francis Healy (1834–1910) became the first American black to earn a Ph.D. when the University of Louvain in Belgium conferred this degree on him in 1865. Although his degree was not in a scientific field, there are two aspects of his life that are relevant here. First, he was born near Macon, Georgia, during the time of slavery, and only by going abroad could he receive the advanced training that he sought. Second, no American university offered the Ph.D. degree in 1865. Father Healy, who served as president of Georgetown University from 1873 to 1883, was able to find employment that fit his academic qualifications in large part because of his religious affiliation. This was not a possible course for most of the early black scientists.

Edward A. Bouchet (1852–1918) became the first black to receive a Ph.D. degree in science in 1876, when Yale University granted him a doctorate in physics. He was also the first black American to be initiated into Phi Beta Kappa. In several respects, Bouchet was unlike most black scientists who earned the Ph.D. degree over the next fifty years: he was born in a northern city (New Haven, Connecticut) and received his bachelor's degree from Yale rather than one of the historically black colleges or universities. Furthermore, he did his graduate training in a physical, rather than a life or biological, science.

Unlike Father Healy, Bouchet was unable to obtain employment that matched his academic achievement. One might assume that, with a Ph.D. in physics from Yale, Bouchet would have found many doors open to him, but this was not the case. He held a federal civil service position in St. Louis, taught at a high school in Ohio, taught at the Institute for Colored Youth in Philadelphia for over twenty-five years, and served on the faculty of Bishop College in Texas. He is remembered by Yale University through the annual Bouchet Lecture and Prize.

By 1900, only one other black American had joined Bouchet in gaining a graduate degree in science. Most blacks lived in the racially segregated South at this time, and slavery had been abolished only thirty-five years earlier. The elementary and high school training of blacks took place in all-black schools that were staffed with teachers who had no science training to speak of, so it is understandable that few black scientists emerged during this period. However, two things occurred in the 1880s and 1890s that would have a positive impact in the early decades of the 1900s.

A HALF-CENTURY OF SCIENTIFIC TRAINING IN BLACK INSTITUTIONS

Most private black colleges were established in the decades before 1900. Not only did they provide college training, but many also had high school departments that assisted in the preparation of students for college. Because they were private, they were not restricted by state laws from hiring whites, and for this reason they were able to develop excellent faculties. With teachers who were themselves better prepared, the quality of the graduates from these institutions began to improve, and with an increased pool of better-trained college graduates, the numbers of blacks who entered scientific fields slowly began to increase during the first two decades of the 1900s.

During the first thirty years of this century, the historically black colleges and universities took the lead in the scientific training of black undergraduates. The first black American to receive a doctorate in chemistry (1916) was a graduate of Fisk University, and the second to receive a Ph.D. in physics (1918), following Bouchet, was also a Fisk alumnus. In fact, the private black institutions were the leading source of undergraduate training for black Americans in all fields of science until 1950, when the publicly supported black colleges and universities began to catch up.

The importance of this cannot be overestimated. Most black Americans were southerners, and black southerners were unable to attend the white colleges and universities of the segregated South. Without the training offered in the black colleges and universities, there would have been far fewer black scientists during those years.

Matthew Henson (1866–1955) and the Journey to the North Pole

On April 6, 1909, an American expedition became the first in history to reach the North Pole. The expedition was led by the well-known explorer Commander Robert E. Peary. At his side was Matthew Henson, an African American who had accompanied him on every one of his expeditions since 1888.

Born in Maryland in 1866, Matthew Henson began traveling at a young age, signing on as a cabin boy "on board a vessel bound for China." Before the age of twenty, Henson had become an "able-bodied seaman" and world traveler. He met Peary in 1888, when Peary was at the beginning of his career as an explorer, and for the next twenty-three years, the two men traveled together. They undertook several Arctic expeditions during that time, finally reaching the North Pole in 1909. Henson recorded the details of their journey to the pole in his 1912 memoir *A Negro Explorer to the North Pole*.

Henson was a stirring role model for African Americans of his time. As the Negro explorer Herbert Frisby wrote, "Matthew Henson was the greatest hero in my life." In his foreword to Henson's memoir, Booker T. Washington spoke of him as one who offered hope and encouragement to "a race which has come up from slavery."

ABOVE: The explorer Matthew Henson is shown here. Commander Robert E. Peary and Henson reached the pole on April 6. **CORBIS-BETTMANN**

ERNEST E. JUST AND WILLIAM A. HINTON

During the first decades of the twentieth century, two black men in particular achieved distinction as scientists. Ernest E. Just (1833–1941), one of the best known of the black biological scientists, was born in Charleston, South Carolina, in 1883. Rather than attend a black college in his native state, he went to Dartmouth College in New Hampshire, where he received his bachelor of science degree in 1907. After teaching for a time at Howard University, he took a doctorate from the University of Chicago in 1916 and rejoined the faculty of Howard University when he could not find employment elsewhere.

Just spent many summers pursuing research on marine invertebrates at the Woods Hole Marine Laboratory in Massachusetts. As a young instructor at Howard, he had met Jacques Loeb (1859–1924), then a prominent scientist at the Rockefeller Institute in New York City, and the two became close friends. It was in fact Loeb who nominated Just for the first Spingarn Medal of the National Association for the Advancement of Colored People (NAACP) in 1914. However, in his later research at Woods Hole and his thesis research for the University of Chicago, Just began to question one of Loeb's widely held hypotheses about fertilization among marine invertebrates. Not only did he challenge his friend; during the years 1919–1920 he also disproved Loeb's hypothesis through careful experimentation. It was this work that established Just among marine embryologists, although, as one might imagine, it did not make him popular among Loeb's followers.

Like many black musicians of the time, Just went to Europe to pursue his work and found a warmer reception there for his research and ideas than he did in his own country. The last dozen or so years of his life were spent in Germany, France, and Italy. While most professional societies did not admit blacks to their membership in the 1920s, Just not only held memberships in several but was appointed to the editorial boards of three well-known journals. The success Just enjoyed in being admitted to professional societies was not shared by most black scientists, however. The all-black National Institute of Science was founded because blacks were not allowed to join in the American Association for the Advancement of Science (AAAS). Similarly, the National Medical Association and the National Dental Association were formed by black physicians and dentists respectively because the American Medical Association and the American Dental Association were closed to them.

Among black physicians and medical researchers during the early 1900s, William A. Hinton (1883–1959) stands out in several ways. He received a medical degree from Harvard in 1912 and became the first black member of the medical school faculty when he was appointed instructor in 1915. Hinton's medical accomplishments were in the area of syphilis diagnosis and treatment. His laboratory test for the detection of syphilis, the Hinton test, was the official method used by the Massachusetts Department of Health laboratories throughout the l920s and 1930s. Hinton was also the first black physician to publish a textbook (*Syphilis and Its Treatment*, 1936). He was offered the Spingarn Medal but declined because of his modesty. In 1953, he retired from Harvard with the title of emeritus professor.

DAVID H. BLACKWELL AND PERCY L. JULIAN

Although black scientists in all disciplines encountered difficult circumstances in the first half of the twentieth century, without doubt the mathematicians faced the greatest challenges. As late as the 1950s, the Mathematical Association of America did not welcome blacks. Not until 1925 did a black American receive a Ph.D. in mathematics. This distinction is held by Elbert F. Cox, who earned his doctorate from Cornell in that year. The first black women to earn doctorates in mathematics were Evelyn Boyd Granville Collins (Yale, 1949) and Marjorie L. Browne (Michigan, 1949).

For blacks who wished to pursue advanced training in mathematics, the choice of a graduate school was crucial, for the prevailing view in some mathematics departments was that blacks did not have what it took to do Ph.D. work in mathematics. Those who did enter mathematics programs had to be very cautious about who they chose as their major professor. With the wrong professor, they might find themselves being nudged into mathematics education programs, advised to quit mathematics altogether, or simply washed out of the program. Unfortunately, this prejudice, along with a similar prejudice against women in the field, still exists even into the early 2000s on some campuses. Between 1925 and 1994, it is estimated that about two hundred black Americans earned Ph.D. degrees in mathematics, including about thirty women.

One of the most distinguished black mathematicians to emerge during this period was David H. Blackwell (b. 1919), a specialist in statistics and game theory. A native of Centralia, Illinois, Blackwell received his bachelor of science degree in 1938 and his Ph.D. in mathematics in 1941 from the University of Illinois, the latter when he was only twenty-two years old. He taught at several black colleges before going to the University of California at Berkeley. Blackwell became the first black mathematician to be admitted to the Institute for Advanced Studies at Princeton University in 1941, at a time when Princeton did not yet accept black students. (He was followed a year later by J. Ernest Wilkins, a black mathematician who received his Ph.D. at the age of nineteen from the University of Chicago.) In 1965, Blackwell became the first black member of the National Academy of Sciences, an honor that is second only to the Nobel Prize. In addition to a textbook on statistics, Blackwell published *Theory of Games and Statistical Decisions* (1980).

Like Ernest Just, the chemist Percy L. Julian (1899–1975) was born in the South (Montgomery, Alabama) but went north—to DePauw University in Indiana—for his college training. As was the case for a fair number of blacks during this period, Julian felt he needed to go abroad for his doctorate, which he received in 1931 from the University of Vienna. His alma mater, DePauw, would not hire him after he received the Ph.D., and although the Institute of Paper Chemistry in Appleton, Wisconsin, offered him a job, he was forced to turn it down because the city ordinances forbade "housing a Negro overnight." Like most black scientists during this period, Julian taught for a while at black colleges, but he finally chose not to spend his years in academic jobs. A top-notch organic chemist, Julian landed employment with a chemical company, where he pioneered the development of several synthetic hormones. He was the first to effect the total synthesis of physostigmine, used in the treatment of glaucoma, and he also developed a low-cost method for synthesizing a form of cortisone. The holder of 105 patents, he later formed his own company, Julian Laboratories, near Chicago, and eventually sold it to a major pharmaceutical firm. Percy Julian was the second black to become a member of the National Academy of Sciences, after David Blackwell.

BLACK SCIENTISTS DURING WORLD WAR II

World War II had a dramatic impact on the lives of black Americans in general, and black scientists in particular. The search for employment in northern defense industries brought many black southerners north, while the GI Bill for veterans provided returning black soldiers with funds for educational training. Relatively large increases in the numbers of black Americans holding science doctorates occurred throughout the 1940s.

Black physicians and scientists also made significant contributions to their country's efforts in World War II. Among the physicians, Charles Drew (1904–1950) established himself as a world authority on the preservation of blood plasma, and he is now remembered as the father of the blood bank—although it was the British government, not his own, that asked for his advice on preserving blood plasma. Many of the techniques and procedures developed by Drew and people working with him were adopted by medical communities both inside and outside of the military.

Hildrus A. Poindexter (1901–1979), who received his medical degree from Harvard and his Ph.D. in bacteriology from Columbia, was the only black tropical disease specialist on military duty during the war. When General Douglas MacArthur learned of Poindexter's

Charles Drew's work on blood-plasma storage and transfusion saved thousands of lives during World War II. For a short time Drew served as medical director of the American Red Cross blood bank program and assistant director of blood procurement for the National Research Council. He resigned the posts after the military issued a directive to the Red Cross that blood supplies for Caucasians and non-Caucasians needed to be kept separate. **AP/WIDE WORLD PHOTOS**

expertise, he asked that Poindexter be assigned to his forces in the South Pacific. Following military service, Poindexter spent time in a number of foreign countries trying to combat tropical diseases of all types. His autobiography, *My World of Reality,* was published in 1972.

The Manhattan Project, which developed the atomic bomb, recruited the best scientists from around the country, among them at least two blacks, William J. Knox Jr. (1904–1995) and J. Ernest Wilkins Jr. (b. 1923). Knox, a chemist, was a section leader of the project at Columbia University from 1943 to 1945, while Wilkins, a mathematician and physicist, was a member of the project at the University of Chicago from 1944 to 1946.

NEW OPENINGS ON SEVERAL POINTS

The most important event to occur in the decades following World War II was the integration of educational institutions in the South and Southwest. The desegregation of schools formerly closed to black Americans, which began in the mid-1950s, should have had a noticeable impact on the number of blacks training in the sciences. However, the results were mixed.

In 1954, the University of Oklahoma became the first of these institutions to grant a Ph.D. to a black in a science field, followed a year later by the University of Texas at Austin. Significant improvements were also made in science education at the state-supported black colleges and universities. For this reason, and because they paid higher salaries than most of the private black institutions, they began to attract science faculty of high quality. During these years, public institutions such as Southern University, Tennessee State, and North Carolina A&T began to supplant Fisk and Morehouse as training grounds for young black scientists. The emergence of the black female scientist from the shadow of her male counterpart also occurred during the 1960s. However, in spite of the end of legal segregation in the sections of the country where most blacks resided, notable increases in the numbers of black scientists did not occur, and some reasons for this will be noted later in this essay.

During these decades, the major scientific and professional societies were not only opened to blacks, but some also elected blacks to various offices and journal positions. Harold E. Finley, a parasitologist at Howard University, served as vice president of the American Society of Protozoologists (1963–1964) and later as president (1966–1967), and in 1971 he was elected president of the American Microscopical Society. Paul B. Cornely (b. 1906) of Howard University was elected president of the American Public Health Association for 1969–1970. Samuel M. Nabrit (b. 1905), a zoologist and former president of Texas Southern University, was appointed by President Lyndon Johnson to the U.S. Atomic Energy Commission in 1966.

One of the noted black scientists active during these two decades was the chemist W. Lincoln Hawkins (1911–1992). Hawkins grew up in Washington, D.C., and earned his Ph.D. from McGill University in Montreal in 1938. From 1942 to 1976, he was employed by Bell Laboratories in New Jersey, where he was assistant director of the Chemical Research Laboratory at the time of his retirement. The holder of at least fourteen patents, Hawkins was the first black American elected to the National Academy of Engineering. He was the coinventor of a plastics process that extends the life of telephone cables for over fifty years.

Prior to the 1970s, about one-third of all doctorates awarded to black Americans were in chemistry, but in the 1970s notable changes began to occur. The number of blacks training as engineers increased, as did the number of black female scientists. In the early 2000s, of the hundred or so blacks awarded doctorates in math, science, or engineering each year, only about fifteen are chemists. Engineers account for ten to twelve doctorates each year, and these come at the expense of degrees in chemistry, while more than half of all black scientists continue to work in the fields of health and medicine and the life, biological, and agricultural sciences. Some "firsts" have occurred, however: Charles E. Anderson received his doctorate in meteorology from MIT in 1960,

Benjamin F. Peery (b. 1922) a doctorate in astronomy from Michigan in 1962, and James C. Christopher a doctorate in geology from Ohio State in 1959.

SUCCESSES AND DISAPPOINTMENTS

Although some interesting milestones were achieved by black scientists and physicians during these years, they must be balanced with the disappointments. Among the bright spots have been the recognition of black scientists by their peers, as reflected in appointments to key positions and election to key offices in scientific societies. For example, the engineer John Slaughter (b. 1934) was named director of the National Science Foundation in 1980, and in 1991, the physicist Walter Massey was named to the same post. Massey (b. 1938) later became president of the American Association for the Advancement of Science. Henry A. Hill (1915–1979) was elected president of the American Chemical Society in 1977, and several black physicians have served as president of the American Public Health Association.

Black scientists and physicians have also been involved in advances made by the U.S. space program during the 1980s and 1990s. Of the black astronauts who have flown missions, two are physicians, including a woman, and two are scientists—the aerospace engineer Guion Bluford (b.1942) and the laser physicist Ronald McNair (1950–1986). (McNair was a crew member of the ill-fated Challenger mission of 1986.)

The first black member of the astronaut corps, the late Robert H. Lawrence Jr. was a scientist. He was born in Chicago in 1935, received his Ph.D. in physical chemistry from Ohio State University in 1965, and was admitted to the astronaut corps the same year. He died in 1967 from injuries suffered in an airplane crash. Among the scientists currently employed by the National Aeronautics and Space Administration (NASA) is the aeronautical engineer George R. Carruthers (b. 1939), who has designed a lunar-surface ultraviolet (UV) camera and spectrograph, space telescopes for the Apollo 16 mission, and various detectors for UV and other radiation.

The biggest disappointments during the 1990s have been the decrease in the number of blacks entering math, science, and engineering fields and the scarcity of black males in particular. With the legal barriers to college and graduate education long removed, one might presume that blacks would be knocking down the doors to enter these fields, but this is not the case. The largest number of doctorates awarded to American-born blacks in a single year was 130 in 1978. The last year that black males exceeded black females studying math, science, and engineering was 1979.

The year 1972 saw the first American-born black females earn the Ph.D. degree in physics and engineering, and in the late twentieth century around 60 percent of all black Americans earning doctorates in math, science, and engineering are women. Of all persons receiving doctorates in these areas from American universities in the 1990s who designate themselves as black, between 65 and 70 percent are foreign-born, with Nigerians accounting for nearly one half. Foreign-born students tend to pursue training in engineering and the physical sciences at much higher rates than their American-born counterparts. Why are these numbers, especially for black males, so dismal? And what might be done to turn the situation around?

To this writer, there does not appear to be any single or simple answer to these questions, but here are some of the factors that bear on the situation:

1. Lack of discipline: Success and excellence in science demand discipline, a quality which, as many have observed, modern youth seem to lack.

2. The lure of sports: It is often said that more black youngsters would pursue science careers if they could be assured the money and publicity awarded to professional athletes.

3. Poor attitudes: Some black students, at both the high school and college level, simply do not study much, believing they will get into college or graduate school or secure a job, whatever they do, simply because they are black. This "I'm black, so I'll get a chance" attitude does not work in science, which is neutral with respect to race, ethnicity, and gender.

4. Negative influences: These include academic counselors who steer blacks away from careers in science, as well as so-called friends and family members who discourage students from pursuing "white" fields instead of becoming a "real doctor" (physician), lawyer, or teacher. It should be noted here that American-born blacks earn doctorates in education at a much higher rate than any other ethnic group.

5. "Black English" and "black culture": Students who cannot function in Standard English are likely to have problems in any discipline that is written in English. The unwillingness or inability to correctly pronounce a technical word puts one at a distinct disadvantage, since the meaning of the word is often implicit in its correct pronunciation. The adherents of what is sometimes referred to as "being and speaking black" are sure to have a more difficult time in a scientific field.

6. Black role models: It is often said that more black students would enter science if they had black role models. With the end of racial segregation in schools, it is true that black students see relatively fewer black teachers. However, even in large northern cities, where the public school population, including teachers, is often more than 90 percent black, the public schools are not producing students who pursue careers in science.

Whatever the reasons for the fact that so few blacks elect careers in science, the prospects for the immediate future do not seem bright. In spite of interventionist efforts such as the Minority Biomedical Research Program and the Minority Access to Research Careers Program, both of which are funded by the National Institutes of Health, the number of American blacks earning doctorates each year in mathematics, science, and engineering will probably remain essentially unchanged into the early 2000s.

Up to and through the 1960s, the typical black scientist was a male born in a small town in a southern state, a graduate of one of the historically black colleges and universities, and more likely than not in a math, physical science, or engineering field. In the 1990s, this profile has changed. As the twenty-first century begins, the typical American-born black scientist is a female with a doctorate in a life, health, or medical science field who is not necessarily of southern origin and did not necessarily study at one of the black institutions. If the current trend continues, the typical black male scientist will be foreign-born, especially in engineering, mathematics, and the physical sciences.

The question is not whether more blacks can or should become scientists; it is, rather, why more do not.

BIBLIOGRAPHY

Bedini, Silvio A. *The Life of Benjamin Banneker.* New York: Charles Scribner & Sons, 1972.

Black Achievers in Science. Chicago: Museum of Science and Industry, 1988.

Burt, McKinley. *Black Inventors of America.* Portland: National Book Co., 1969.

Carwell, Hattie. *Blacks in Science: Astrophysicist to Zoologist.* Hicksville: Exposition Press, 1977.

Driver, Paul J. *Black Giants in Science.* New York: Vantage Press, 1973.

Haber, Louis. *Black Pioneers of Science and Invention.* New York: Harcourt, Brace, Jovanovich, 1970.

Jay, James. "Black Americans in the Sciences." In *Minorities in Science.* Boston: Plenum Press, 1977.

Klein, Aaron E. *Hidden Contributors: Black Scientists and Inventors in America.* Garden City: Doubleday, 1971.

Manning, Kenneth R. *Black Apollo of Science: The Life of Ernest Everett Just.* New York: Oxford University Press, 1983.

McKissack, Patricia, and Frederick McKissack. *A Proud Heritage: African-American Inventors.* Brookfield: Millbrook Press, 1994.

Newell, Virginia K., et al. *Black Mathematicians and Their Works.* Ardmore: Dorrance, 1980.

Poindexter, Hildrus A. *My World of Reality.* Detroit: Balamp Publishers, 1973.

Sammons, Vivian O. *Blacks in Science and Medicine.* New York: Hemisphere Publishing, 1990.

Taylor, Julius H. *The Negro in Science.* Baltimore: Morgan State College Press, 1960.

American labor unions have had a long history of excluding black workers from their membership and from the trades they represent. By the mid-twentieth century, however, African Americans, especially in the major industries, had taken their place in union ranks, and their presence translated into vigorous union support for the Civil Rights movement of the 1950s and 1960s. These demonstrators were photographed at the 1963 March on Washington. **NATIONAL ARCHIVES AND RECORDS ADMINISTRATION**

African American Labor History

ADAPTED FROM ESSAYS BY ERIK ARNESEN, YALE
UNIVERSITY/BRANDEIS UNIVERSITY

From the arrival of the first slaves in Virginia in 1619 to the present, African Americans have formed an important part of the American working class. Whether as slaves or as free men and women, they have performed a wide range of tasks vital to the building and sustaining of the nation's economy.

Yet blacks often found themselves possessing few economic resources of their own, restricted to lower sectors of the economy, and shut out from better-paying jobs. Despite their tremendous achievements in the economic realm, black Americans have faced a long history of racial discrimination at the workplace and in the job market. Throughout the course of American history, African Americans—both individually and collectively—have challenged with varying degrees of success the limits placed on their economic opportunity.

SLAVERY
A driving force behind the growth of chattel slavery in North America was white Americans' need for labor, par-

ticularly on the farms and plantations of the South. White slaveholders exploited African and African American slaves in order to expand agricultural production and enrich themselves.

The first slaves in Virginia in the seventeenth century were put to work cultivating tobacco. Slaves in South Carolina and Georgia in the late seventeenth and eighteenth centuries labored on large rice plantations. By the beginning of the nineteenth century, the rise of "King Cotton" ensured that the majority of slaves would work on the cotton plantations rapidly extending westward from the eastern seaboard states through Alabama, Mississippi, Louisiana, and Texas.

Not all slaves were agricultural laborers. On large plantations, some black women worked as cooks, domestic servants, midwives, and nurses. Skilled male artisans worked as carpenters, ship builders and caulkers, and iron molders, while some unskilled male slaves were leased to individuals and companies to lay railroad tracks, dig canals, and mine coal or salt.

Not all slaves were confined to the South, either. Until northern states passed gradual emancipation laws in the late eighteenth century, slaves also labored as freight handlers and teamsters on the docks and in the streets and

This multigenerational family of sharecroppers posed for a photograph around 1939. The children were expected to work at the harvest along with their elders. **THE LIBRARY OF CONGRESS**

warehouses of such cities as Philadelphia, Boston, and New York. They also worked in ropewalks and shipyards, on farms and plantations, and even on ships.

THE EMANCIPATED BLACK WORKER: SHARECROPPING

The Civil War that ended slavery in the South did not produce economic equality for the four million freed men and women. During the Reconstruction era (1866–1877), emancipated slaves encountered greatly restricted economic opportunities.

Southern white legislators passed so-called black codes in 1865 and 1866 that barred blacks from working in skilled jobs, and while the North quickly outlawed black codes, white craftsmen aggressively resisted the entrance of black workers into their trades. Most ex-slaves, while formally free, continued to work as dependent, landless agricultural laborers on cotton, sugar, and rice plantations. Their strong desire to secure their economic independence through land ownership was thwarted by a number of factors: the federal government's failure to support land reform, black people's

deep economic deprivation, and the refusal of white landowners to sell property to blacks.

By the 1870s, a system of sharecropping had emerged that granted black workers a small degree of day-to-day independence from white control while at the same time guaranteeing their continued economic subservience to more powerful white property owners. In exchange for the use of land, tools, seed, and fertilizer, black families planted and harvested their crop. At year's end, they paid substantial rent plus interest, or turned over a large portion of the crop to the landowner.

Some blacks managed to escape oppression by migrating west or north. In some cases, people saved enough to purchase small plots of land. But the sharecropping system remained dominant well into the twentieth century. Only in the 1940s and 1950s did the mechanization of southern agriculture destroy the system, rendering a large sharecropping population economically unnecessary.

Black workers also faced discriminatory employers and fellow workers in the North, where the black population remained small in the decades following the Civil

War. Most black northerners were excluded from skilled or factory jobs and confined to the ranks of unskilled common labor or domestic service.

ISAAC MYERS AND BLACK LABOR AFTER THE CIVIL WAR

An organized labor movement emerged after the Civil War in response to growing industrialization, but it was largely hostile or indifferent to the needs and desires of the freed people. As a result, black workers in many cities organized their own unions or associations to represent their members' interests.

In Baltimore, Maryland, for instance, Isaac Myers (1835–1891), who had been born to free parents in 1835, defended his fellow black ship caulkers who lost their jobs when white workers—many of them demobilized Confederate soldiers—went on strike to demand the firing of black shipyard workers. In 1866, Myers helped to found the Chesapeake Marine Railway and Dry Dock Company, a black owned and operated company that gave employment to hundreds of unemployed black shipworkers before it finally closed in 1883.

Since white unions excluded blacks as members, Myers vigorously advocated all-black unions. He saw them as a way of increasing black workers' power and also of fostering eventual alliances with white trade unions. When the all-white National Labor Union refused to admit black organizations into membership, Myers in 1869 founded and led the short-lived Colored National Labor Union, a federation of recently formed associations of black ship caulkers, longshoremen, hod carriers, and other laborers.

But Myers's optimism about the possibility of an alliance between black and white workers did not survive the depression of the 1870s; by 1881, he had concluded that the prejudice of white labor against blacks was simply too strong: "Everywhere," he wrote, "the white trades union prohibits the admission of colored men as members." As long as these organizations were effective, he argued, black mechanics would "gradually drop into obscurity and the grave."

Despite the hostility of white trade unionists, some black workers continued to form unions to protect and improve their wages and working conditions and to gain access to work in a discriminatory job market.

During the 1880s, the Knights of Labor—a national body composed of thousands of local "assemblies"—opened its doors to black members, on the grounds that all workers, regardless of race, should have equal rights and should work together to further the interests of the "producing classes." After the collapse of the knights in the late 1880s and early 1890s, the dominant organization of workers was the American Federation of Labor (AFL), an association of skilled craft unions.

The AFL proved less open than the Knights of Labor to black workers, as well as to other minorities and women. In most cases in which white craft unions excluded blacks from membership, the AFL took no action against them. Nor did the AFL do much to organize black workers in unorganized industries.

In the 1910s, the radical Industrial Workers of the World (IWW) challenged the AFL. In contrast to the AFL's "craft unionism," which organized workers according to their craft, the IWW advocated "industrial" unionism, whereby all workers in a given workplace would join the same union. The IWW also promoted the overthrow of capitalism and the formation of an alliance of all workers, regardless of race.

In the timber camps of Louisiana and East Texas and on the docks of Philadelphia, the Wobblies, as IWW members were called, successfully organized black and white workers and fought aggressively for their members' rights. Repression by employers and the government, however, ended the IWW's influence during and after World War I.

THE RISE OF BIRACIAL UNIONISM

White trade unions' long record of racial exclusion and discrimination created considerable skepticism and even hostility among large numbers of blacks toward the union movement. In the late nineteenth and early twentieth centuries, black workers tended to organize separately from their white counterparts—a process known as "biracial unionism." Given the pervasiveness of segregation by the end of the nineteenth century, few whites or blacks proposed organizing integrated locals. Instead, all-black locals and all-white locals formed, sometimes competing for jobs and benefits, sometimes cooperating.

On the docks of New Orleans in the 1880s, and again from 1901 to 1923, for example, black and white longshoremen and cotton yardmen belonged to separate unions, but they agreed to divide available work equally between blacks and whites, to abide by identical rules and accept the same wages, and to present a united front in all union-management negotiations. Similarly, in the coal fields of Alabama in the 1880s and 1890s, black and white locals of the Knights of Labor and the United Mine Workers jointly represented miners of both races.

Black labor activism targeted the exploitative conditions, low wages, and harsh or discriminatory treatment faced by African American workers. Like their white counterparts, blacks participated in a wide range of labor conflicts and upheavals. In 1887, nine thousand black sugar workers joined the Knights of Labor to challenge planters and militiamen in an unsuccessful showdown in the sugar parishes of Louisiana. In 1892, thousands of blacks joined with white workers in a general strike that temporarily shut down New Orleans.

The World War I era witnessed several large-scale strikes: by black dock workers along the Gulf coast, by black female laundry workers in Mobile and Little Rock, by black coal miners in Alabama and West Virginia, and by black phosphate miners in Florida. During this period, associations of African American railroad workers—including porters, dining car workers, locomotive firemen, brakemen, and yard switchmen—lodged literally thousands of protests with managers and federal officials, calling for an end to race-based differences in pay, promotion, and job assignment.

If biracial unionism offered advantages to black workers in some cases, at other times it locked blacks out of better jobs. Members of AFL "auxiliary unions," which enrolled black workers excluded from more powerful white locals, were often forced to pay dues to white officers and received little protection in exchange. Only in the 1940s did black workers' protests and U.S. court decisions put a legal end to discriminatory auxiliaries that denied black workers equal rights.

White trade unions' long record of racial exclusion and discrimination created considerable skepticism and even hostility among large numbers of blacks toward the union movement.

THE RISE OF THE BROTHERHOOD OF SLEEPING CAR PORTERS

The 1930s witnessed two crucial developments in the history of black labor. The first was the rise to prominence of the Brotherhood of Sleeping Car Porters (BSCP), led by the charismatic black radical A. Philip Randolph (1889–1979). The BSCP was formed in 1925 by disgruntled employees of the Pullman Company, which manufactured and operated luxurious sleeping cars for long-distance train travel. The BSCP called for a reduction in the number of hours that porters had to work each month, increases in pay, a grievance procedure that protected employee rights, official recognition of the BSCP as the legal bargaining agent for Pullman porters, and collective bargaining between the company and the union.

From the start, the BSCP confronted numerous obstacles. A powerful opponent, the Pullman Company conducted a well-financed antiunion campaign: it hired spies, sponsored its own loyal "company union," and disciplined and fired union activists and supporters. The BSCP, in contrast, had little money to pursue its union drive and was opposed by many black ministers and newspaper editors, who argued that it jeopardized black jobs.

The tide began to turn in the 1930s. Under dedicated and able leadership, the BSCP received the backing of the AFL, won over the support of black leaders, and took advantage of a more prolabor attitude in government. Sweeping a government-conducted union election in

The Brotherhood of Sleeping Car Porters played an important role in the advancement of African American workers' rights. The union demanded better pay for employees and shorter hours while championing civil rights issues. In this 1947 photo, Fred "Kid" Wright starts his 56th year as the nation's oldest Pullman porter. **CORBIS-BETTMANN**

1935, the BSCP finally won a contract from the Pullman Company in 1937. Porters' wages and working conditions improved significantly, and the BSCP became the leading African American union in the nation.

From the 1930s through the 1960s, BSCP locals were extremely active in civil rights activities in the North and South. BSCP members and leaders fought against segregation laws and practices, funded court challenges to Jim Crow segregation, spoke out constantly against racial oppression, and regularly challenged the AFL's racist policies toward black workers.

SEE PRIMARY SOURCE DOCUMENT *"Pullman Pass" by Michael Harper*

THE CONGRESS OF INDUSTRIAL ORGANIZATIONS

The second important development in black labor history during the 1930s was the formation of the Congress of Industrial Organizations (CIO). The AFL had refused to

Labor units saw little combat during World War I. They were responsible for loading, moving, and unloading war material. This crew loads drums onto a boat in New Orleans, Louisiana. **THE LIBRARY OF CONGRESS**

commit itself to organizing production workers in basic industries such as auto, steel, farm equipment, rubber, and meat packing. It had also refused to embrace the strategy of industrial unionism. In 1935, several unions broke away from the AFL to form a rival labor federation, the Congress of Industrial Organizations (CIO). The CIO took the position that all workers in a given factory or industry—regardless of their specific tasks or skills, race, ethnicity, or sex—ought to belong to a single organization. The new CIO conducted extensive organizing campaigns in the late 1930s and 1940s, winning victories that produced substantial gains for their members.

Success in unionizing the auto, steel, meat packing, and other basic industries required the support and active involvement of African American workers. Failure to recruit black support would guarantee the loss of any union drive, and the CIO, unlike the AFL, actively sought black participation. But the "approach to the Negro was not dictated solely by expediency," concluded the black social scientists Horace Cayton and St. Clair Drake in 1945, "for the CIO was, in a sense, a crusading movement also."

The rise of industrial unions affiliated with the CIO did not end discrimination in the labor market. In many cases, southern locals were more conservative and racist than their northern counterparts. Some unions, usually those with left-wing leadership, like the Farm Equipment Workers' Union or the United Packinghouse Workers of America, earned a good reputation on issues of racial equality. Others, like the United Steelworkers of America, were sharply criticized for failing to protect black workers or advance their interests.

African American laborers' struggle for racial equality, then, took place in both the workplace and the union hall.

BLACK LABOR IN THE NATION'S DEFENSE INDUSTRIES

During the World War I years, labor shortages occurred in the North as a result of the military draft, the cutoff of European immigration to the United States, and an expanding wartime economy. These factors, combined with an agricultural crisis and continued racial oppression in the South, produced an unprecedented Great Migration that brought half a million black southerners to industrial centers like Chicago, Detroit, and New York.

Because of the demand for labor, black men and some black women broke the color bar in employment, securing unskilled or semiskilled factory jobs for the first

The shopkeeper James Roberts, of New York City, displayed the fact that his was "A Negro Enterprise" on his shop window. With the Great Migration and the development of black urban communities, such signs proliferated. The "Don't buy where you can't work" campaign of the 1920s actively encouraged black consumers to give their trade to black-owned businesses, which employed black workers and thus supported black urban communities. **CORBIS-BETTMANN**

time. Although the end of the war in late 1918 produced high rates of black unemployment, an expanding economy in the 1920s contributed to an even greater migration of southern blacks to the North. Black economic advancement remained slow, however. When the Great Depression of the 1930s ended and the economy geared up for World War II, black workers were hired only as a last resort.

In 1941, A. Philip Randolph and others pressured the government to take a stand against employment discrimination in the defense industry and elsewhere. Their protests resulted in an executive order desegregating the defense industry and the creation of the Fair Employment Practices Committee (FEPC) to investigate charges of discrimination. But the FEPC had no enforcement powers. Some companies and industries voluntarily

complied with its orders to hire African Americans. Others, such as the railroad industry and its all-white unions of locomotive firemen and brakemen, continued to bar black employment.

RECENT EVENTS
The labor movement has experienced hard times since the 1970s. Increasingly hostile employers, competition from corporations using cheap labor overseas, deindustrialization, and government policies that favor employers—these factors have all taken their toll on union membership, which has dropped significantly in recent decades. Yet black Americans who are union members—in industrial and in government jobs—continue to earn higher wages and experience better working conditions than their nonunion counterparts.

Even as the union movement has declined, there have been some notable success stories. The rise and growth of Hospital Workers' Local 1199 has dramatically transformed a once poorly paid sector in one of the nation's fastest growing industries. A politically and racially progressive organization, Local 1199 became an important "civil rights" union in the 1960s, raising the living standards and improving the working conditions of its largely minority membership.

Black protests and the passage of civil rights laws in the 1960s and 1970s made employment discrimination illegal. Along with affirmative action and antipoverty programs, these contributed somewhat to the breakdown of racial barriers in the job market. But a stagnating economy in the 1970s and a conservative political reaction in the 1980s and 1990s have weakened the enforcement and efficacy of both laws and programs.

A black middle class—including teachers, civil servants, politicians, doctors, lawyers, and corporate executives—has expanded dramatically since the 1960s, but a large percentage of urban blacks remain trapped in poverty. In a process known as "capital flight," corporations have moved hundreds of thousands of high-wage factory jobs from America's urban centers to suburban and rural areas and abroad to Mexico and Asia. The resulting deindustrialization has devastated the nation's inner cities, drying up the employment opportunities once available to urban black workers.

BIBLIOGRAPHY

Anderson, Jervis. *A. Philip Randolph: A Biographical Portrait.* New York: Harcourt Brace Jovanovich, 1972.

Arnesen, Eric. "Following the Color Line of Labor: Black Workers and the Labor Movement before 1930." *Radical History Review* 55 (1993): 43–87.

———. *Waterfront Workers of New Orleans: Race, Class, and Politics, 1863–1923.* Urbana: University of Illinois Press, 1991.

Barrett, James R. *Life and Work in the Jungle: Chicago's Packinghouse Workers 1894–1922.* Urbana: University of Illinois Press, 1987.

Brazeal, Brailsford R. *The Brotherhood of Sleeping Car Porters: Its Origin and Development.* New York: Harper & Brothers, 1946.

Grossman, James. *Land of Hope: Chicago, Black Southerners, and the Great Migration.* Chicago: University of Chicago Press, 1989.

Halpern, Rick. "Race, Ethnicity, and Union in the Chicago Stockyards, 1917–1922." *International Review of Social History* 37 (1992): 25–48.

Harris, William H. *Keeping the Faith: A. Philip Randolph, Milton P. Webster, and the Brotherhood of Sleeping Car Porters, 1925–37.* Urbana: University of Illinois Press, 1977.

Honey, Michael K. *Southern Labor and Black Civil Rights: Organizing Memphis Workers.* Urbana: University of Illinois Press, 1993.

Kelley, Robin D. G. "'We Are Not What We Seem': Rethinking Black Working-Class Opposition in the Jim Crow South." *Journal of American History* 80 (1993): 75–113.

Nelson, Bruce. "Organized Labor and the Struggle for Black Equality in Mobile during World War II." *Journal of American History* 80 (1993): 952–88.

Pfeffer, Paula F. *A. Philip Randolph, Pioneer of the Civil Rights Movement.* Baton Rouge: Louisiana State University Press, 1990.

Rachleff, Peter. *Black Labor in Richmond, 1865–1890.* Urbana: University of Illinois Press, 1984.

Roediger, David R. *The Wages of Whiteness: Race and the Making of the American Working Class.* New York: Verso, 1991.

Spero, Sterling D., and Abram L. Harris. *The Black Worker: The Negro and the Labor Movement.* 1931. Reprint. New York: Atheneum, 1969.

Starobin, Robert S. *Industrial Slavery in the Old South.* New York: Oxford University Press, 1970.

Stein, Judith. "Southern Workers in National Unions: Birmingham Steelworkers, 1936–1951." In *Organized Labor in the Twentieth-Century South*, ed. Robert H. Zieger. Knoxville: University of Tennessee Press, 1991.

PRIMARY SOURCE DOCUMENT

"Pullman Pass" by Michael Harper

INTRODUCTION In this poem, Michael Harper reflects on the history and experience of African Americans who worked in the Jim Crow era and calls attention to the thinly veiled hostilities that have characterized the "separate but unequal" culture of twentieth century. Describing the experiences of a Pullman porter, the poem pays tribute to African oral traditions, touching on the value of memory and personal history.

He was eighty-seven
when I photographed
him, straight up
in the natural light
of his fifty-year
gold service Pullman's
pass, Twentieth Century Limited,
and claimed he was there
when Rockefeller and Vanderbilt
agreed on the merger
at the US Hotel
in Saratoga Springs;
he'd been a jockey then—
the Skidmore girls
would count the hairs
on his smooth skin
while he told them stories
in any direction or position.

He told this dime story
once about Rockefeller
giving out new dimes
in the parlor car
relaxing from his dinner.

"I'll put these with the others,"
Henry said to Rockefeller;
"How many of these do you have?"
and so Henry went back to his locker
and brought back a cigar
box with a rubber band around it,
and opened up the lid.
Rockefeller turned to his lawyer-
accountant and said to count
the dimes in the box
and write out the check
for the amount,
a dollar for a dime.

Henry had a soft voice;
he roadsided every cavern
and watering hole when he rode
on his pass;
 he bought his wife
a farm with that Rockefeller
check: $2600,
a lot of acreage
for a black man
who feigned reading and writing;
straight back, tall as an arrow,
and pretty walking out the US
Hotel, where he had friends.

Segregated then at the Hotel:
wouldn't let no white people work there.

SOURCE: Harper, Michael S. "Pullman Pass," in *Healing Song for the Inner Ear.* University of Illinois Press, 1985. Copyright © 1985 by University of Illinois Press. All rights reserved. Reproduced by permission.

The Art of African Americans

ADAPTED FROM ESSAYS BY MARY KORDAK, YALE UNIVERSITY

Despite the troubling legacy of slavery and the violent attempt on the part of slaveholders to erase the culture and identity of Africans brought to the Americas, it is clear that African Americans have added to the foundation of every element of American culture, from the highbrow to the low.

African Americans suffered behind the Western contention that art and refinement were best represented in the European model, especially in painting, sculpture, and ceramics. Traditionally, African Americans have excelled in whatever style of art they have attempted. Many art historians and the public are coming to new perceptions of "what good art is," and perhaps most importantly, realizing that the roots of great American art run deep. We are coming to a new appreciation of the hybrid history of American artistic traditions. Much like in the case of rock-and-roll or rhythm and blues—musi-

Richmond Barthe's powerful sculpture *Blackberry Woman* honors the labor of generations of African American women. Barthe was born in Bay St. Louis, Mississippi in 1901, the son of free Creoles of African, French and Native American descent. He moved to Chicago in 1924 to study at the Art Institute, joining Archibald Motley and other African American artists who were students there. **THE LIBRARY OF CONGRESS**

cal traditions that grew out of African rhythmic sensibilities—painters and artisans considered to be American masters today have had to deal with European traditions, but at their best have struck out toward the frontiers of an unexplored artistic world.

Unlike others who came to America, the Africans arriving through the slave trade arrived with no material possessions. These men, women, and children, sold into slavery dressed only in odd bits of clothing, shackles, and chains, were survivors of the Middle Passage across the Atlantic. Luck, good health, and mental tenacity had brought them this far, and they would need all this and more to adjust to life in the colonies. As they learned a new language and adapted to another culture with a value system different from what they had known, the precious memories of their former lives and of their African homelands, families, and friends would sustain them and nourish their art for generations to come.

AFRICAN AND AFRICAN AMERICAN SLAVE ARTISANS

Africans brought to America in the slave trade came from large cities as well as small towns. They had been kings, priests, lawmakers, warriors, doctors, and farmers. Some had also been highly skilled artisans: sculptors expert at carving wood, ivory, and stone; metalworkers who knew how to work gold, brass, and copper; potters and basketmakers; textile workers who wove cloth and painted designs on fabric.

From such materials, they made objects for religious purposes, but also the practical items needed for daily life. Transported to America, they continued to exercise their skills. In the objects they fashioned for their own and others' use, the slave artists and artisans would give lasting form to their memories and knowledge.

The majority of Africans sold into servitude in the early years became field hands on farms and plantations throughout the South and in some parts of the North. As the colonials became more self-sufficient, however, and began to make more of the things they needed rather than importing them from England, the need for skilled artisans and craftspeople grew. Before long, whites realized that among the slave population were highly skilled artisans whom they could put to work constructing buildings, fabricating tools, weaving, making furniture, and performing many other tasks requiring a degree of expertise.

However, it was the diversification of agriculture and industry after the American Revolution that propelled increasing numbers of blacks out of the fields and into the workshop. By the early nineteenth century, black artisans were represented in every known trade and craft in America. Because most slave owners kept detailed records of their human property, the documentation regarding early slave artisans is extensive. Although it was not widely acknowledged until the twentieth century, such documentation confirms that not all slaves were confined to the unskilled labor of field work. Some held skilled and semiskilled jobs.

By the end of the eighteenth century, many whites, and even some free blacks, owned slave artisans. These artisans were a source of income, for the master owned not only the slave, but also the slave's skill, as well as the product he or she made—and like other commodities, slaves could be rented or their services sold.

When Isaiah Thomas published *A History of Printing in America* in the early nineteenth century, he included mention of a slave who, as early as 1724, had established a reputation as an artist and printer. The slave belonged to Thomas Fleet, the owner of a successful printing business in Boston, who readily affirmed the slave's importance as the one "who cut on wooden blocks, all the pictures which decorated the ballads and small books of his master." This same slave artisan and printer, whose name remains unknown to this day, had two sons, Caesar and Pompey, also mentioned in Thomas's *History* as excellent artisans and printers.

It was not unusual for slaves to negotiate with their masters for freedom. As free men with marketable skills, they could open their own businesses. Thomas Day (c. 1801–1861), a cabinetmaker and wood finisher from the Charleston area, may have been such a person. Day ran a flourishing business between 1820 and 1840, and the original designs of his beautifully crafted furniture are highly prized today.

THE RECOVERY OF EARLY AFRICAN AMERICAN ARTISTS

Art historians now know that African Americans excelled as visual artists, successfully mastering the skills of drawing, printing, painting, and sculpting just as white artists did in the early years of America's history. But this was not always known. Paintings and other objects of art change hands through time and are often unsigned. They cannot tell us by themselves the names or racial identities of the artists who made them. It has taken years of painstaking research to discover the names of many of the early African American artists. At every turn in the research, there have been problems to overcome as well as unexpected surprises. In the early 2000s, while the names of most early slave artisans and folk artists remain unknown, art historians have discovered the names of some of the slaves and free blacks who worked in the fine arts as long ago as the late eighteenth century.

Some of them were "limners," as the early portrait painters were called. As a rule, limners had little if any formal artistic education. More often than not, they were itinerant sign painters who traveled from place to place, finding work wherever they could. Whatever their race, limners rarely signed their pictures. In order to identify them, art historians have had to rely on journals, diaries, payment receipts, and similar records preserved by the families they painted. Such documents rarely identify the race of the artist, however, and because the achievements of black limners received little mention in other sorts of documents, it has been even more difficult to determine their identities.

The lack of family documents for African American artists has also made the work of art historians more difficult. Such documents—birth and marriage certificates, family letters, diary entries, art dealers' and museum records—help to identify who made a particular work of art and to keep track of its location through time. But most eighteenth- and nineteenth-century African American artists have left no such paper trail. Their birth and death dates are unknown, their family histories fragmented and unreliable. Since most were never exhibited in museums or private galleries until well into the twentieth century, institutional records are also lacking.

This charming painting of a Baltimore lady and her five children was only recently identified as the work of the African American limner Joshua Johnston. Papers of Mrs. Everette, the lady in the painting, were found that called the painter "J. Johnson." The brass tacks clearly visible along the back of the couch are one of Johnston's "signatures." Some eighty portraits from the late eighteenth and early nineteenth centuries have now been identified as Johnston's work. He was probably self taught, although he may have been a slave or a servant to a skilled artist at some time in his life. **MARYLAND HISTORICAL SOCIETY**

Finally, the recovery of late eighteenth- and early nineteenth-century black artists has been hampered by the scarcity of their works. Though we know his name, we know of no surviving works by Robert Douglas, for example, and only a few by Eugene Warburg, John G. Chaplin, and Annie E. Walker. All of these problems come together in the case of the limner Joshua Johnston (1765–1830), the probable maker of a series of splendid portraits from the late eighteenth and early nineteenth centuries. For a long time, the maker of these portraits was known only as the "brass tacks" artist, because his paintings often contained furniture decorated with rows of brass upholstery tacks. Some of the paintings had remained in the Baltimore families for whom they were made, preserved into the twentieth century along with persistent family rumors that the painter had been an African American—a "slave who painted," "a very bright black young man." In one such family, the painter was said to have been a "William Johnson," the slave of another limner whose name had been forgotten. As was so often the case with early portraits, the works of this painter were unsigned, though one of them, entitled *Mrs. Everette and Her Children,* was identified in a family will as the work of a "J Johnson."

In 1942, a descendant of one of the Baltimore families set about verifying the family legend of the African Ameri-

can painter. In the 1817 Baltimore city directory, he discovered, listed among the "Free Householders of Color," a "Joshua Johnston, portrait painter." This proved to be—and has remained to this day—the sole piece of written evidence pointing to Joshua Johnston's race. His name appears in other Baltimore records—church documents, numerous city directories, petitions, and the like—but he is never again identified by race. Nevertheless, Joshua Johnston is regarded as an African American artist and one of the finest of the early portrait painters.

Occasionally, one or two well-placed clues have led art historians to the recovery of one of these elusive early artists. Scipio Moorhead, a slave from Massachusetts, engraved the two known portraits of the slave poet Phillis Wheatley (1753–1784), who left two clues about his identity in her work. The first is her poem entitled, "To S. M., a Young African Painter, on Seeing His Works." The second is a copy of the 1773 edition of Wheatley's *Poems on Various Subjects, Religious and Moral* bearing an inscription in Wheatley's hand. It reads, "Scipio Moorhead, Negro servant to the Rev. John Moorhead of Boston whose genius inclined him that way." Thanks to these clues, art historians have been able to determine that Moorhead executed the Wheatley portraits, that he was a slave in the Moorhead family, and that he was

Richmond Barthe, shown here with Lincoln bust in 1944, was the first African American sculptor to be elected to the National Academy of Arts and Letters. **AP/WIDE WORLD PHOTOS**

instructed in drawing and painting by Sarah Moorhead, the Reverend Mr. Moorhead's wife and herself an amateur artist.

Why is it important to know for certain whether an early artist was African American? For many reasons. It allows us to understand the ways in which early black artists responded to the world around them. What did it look like to them? What did they choose to represent? What were the secret "signatures," like Joshua Johnston's "brass tacks," which they used to identify their art? It also gives us a better idea of the working lives of early black artists—where they lived, how they went about finding customers, how much they were paid, how others responded to their work. Perhaps most importantly, however, the recovery of these early artists provides inspiration to present-day African American artists, assuring them that they are part of a tradition stretching back in time to the nation's beginnings.

ART EDUCATION FOR AFRICAN AMERICANS

Historically, African American artists have had to overcome the same basic obstacles as white artists, but their efforts have been complicated by racism and prejudice. From the early to mid-nineteenth century, African Americans were denied entry to art schools, where a for-

mal study of art could be undertaken, and only rarely were they able to study with practicing white artists. Robert Douglas and Eugene Warburg, who wanted to study with practicing artists—and could afford to pay for lessons—had to go to Europe to find people willing to teach them. Apprenticeships to engravers and lithographers were a surrogate form of art school for both Grafton T. Brown (1841–1918) and Patrick Reason (1817–?), who learned the rudiments of drawing while working as printers.

Lacking access to formal training, some aspiring artists taught themselves how to draw, copying from the prints of works by academically trained European artists. But some forms of art, like sculpture, require a knowledge of materials and methods that is hard to master on one's own. The sculptor Mary Edmonia Lewis (1848–1909), for example, had trouble finding artists willing to work with her. Fortunately, she had the financial support of her older brother, the encouragement of African American artists like Edward Bannister (1828–1901), and the friendship of women like Lydia Maria Child (1802–1880), who provided Lewis with introductions to friends who commissioned works from her.

African Canadian painter Robert Duncanson was an exception in this respect. Born in upstate New York in 1823, he was raised in Canada, where he received in Canadian public schools the education that would have been denied him in the United States. In 1841, he settled in Cincinnati in order to pursue his artistic training, and soon came to the attention of Cincinnati's thriving art community. One of the best of the nineteenth-century American landscape painters, Duncanson achieved recognition and respect in his lifetime, especially in Canada, where he relocated during the Civil War.

ART EDUCATION ABROAD

After the Civil War, a number of black artists took advantage of opportunities to travel to Europe, where they continued their study of art by visiting the great museums and taking courses at the British and French academies. These experiences in the Western art traditions made it even more difficult to distinguish the work of black artists from that of their white counterparts. Even when the subject matter of their work contained references to race or racial issues, it was virtually impossible to identify the race of the artist. Moreover, blacks were popular subjects for white artists like Eastman Johnson (1824–1906), William Sidney Mount (1807–1868), and Winslow Homer (1836–1910), while black artists routinely painted pictures without any clear reference to black subject matter.

While it was sometimes difficult to distinguish the work of black artists from that of other artists, their experience was unique in one important way. Whatever the nature of their work, people simply did not acknowledge them as artists. Edward Mitchell Bannister's *Under the Oaks* won the gold medal at the 1876 Centennial Exposition, but when he went to accept his prize, he was refused entry. Those making the awards refused to believe the winner was an African American.

Some African Americans who traveled abroad to study never returned to America, where overt racism made it impossible for them to live as they wished. This was the case with Mary Edmonia Lewis, who endured racial attacks, both overt and subtle, while a student at Oberlin College and later as a Boston resident. Eventually, she settled in Rome among a group of expatriate female artists that included the sculptors Harriet Hosmer (1830–1908) and Anne Whitney (1821–1915), finding in Italy a more congenial atmosphere for her artistic temperament and alternative lifestyle.

Henry O. Tanner (1859–1937), perhaps the best-known late nineteenth-century African American artist, also expatriated and settled in Paris. He studied briefly with Thomas Eakins (1844–1916) at the Pennsylvania Academy, until a malicious racist prank on the part of his white schoolmates caused him to leave the academy, never to return. During the formative phase of what came to be known as the New Negro Movement, Tanner (1859–1937) was selected by Alain Locke (1886–1954) to head a new school of African American art. He refused the honor, however, preferring to stay in Europe, where he was less conscious of the racism that had so frustrated him in America. Tanner became an influential role model for young African American artists studying abroad. His studio was always open to them, and he gave generously of his time, encouraging them in whatever way he could. Although Tanner never left Paris to participate in the New Negro Movement, he contributed to it in his own way.

THE NEW NEGRO MOVEMENT, OR THE HARLEM RENAISSANCE

During the first decades of the twentieth century, the Great Migration brought African American artists and aspiring artists together in cities across the North. The result was the birth of the New Negro Movement, or the Harlem Renaissance, which sought to encourage racial pride, solidarity, self-help, and education among black city dwellers.

Among its leaders was Alain Locke, a Harvard-educated philosopher, the first black Rhodes scholar, and one of the foremost African American intellectuals of the twentieth century. A contemporary of W. E. B. Du Bois (1868–1963), Marcus Garvey (1887–1940), and James Weldon Johnson (1871–1938), Locke was a major force behind the New Negro Movement. It was Locke who urged African American artists to look across the Atlantic to their African ancestral homeland, where they would discover not one but many artistic legacies.

Aaron Douglas Jr. is one of the artists who gained prominence during the New Negro Movement (Harlem Renaissance). His works portrayed a positive, noble image of African Americans. **GIBBS MUSEUM OF ART/CAA**

Locke's championing of the African arts was part of a philosophy known as "Negritude," a forerunner of "Afrocentricity." According to this philosophy, if blacks learned the truth about their African ancestry, if they studied the ancient civilizations, history, and art of their forebears, they would come to understand the contributions Africans had made to the world. Such knowledge would in turn become a source of collective pride, a building block for future generations. African art, in particular sculpture, was already an important influence in the work of modern European artists, who discovered in it "a mine of fresh *motifs* … a lesson in simplicity and originality of expression." Locke felt that black art would exert an even greater influence on the work of black artists, "the blood descendants, bound to it by a sense of direct cultural kinship."

Artists within the New Negro Movement generally responded with enthusiasm to the call "to look back to their African heritage." Some gained a new inspiration and self-understanding through an appreciation of the land of their black ancestors. They took Locke's exhortation to heart, and using African crafts, folklore, and traditional culture as their spiritual models, they produced fine art, literature, and music, proving conclusively that they were capable of achievements in the high arts. They remained largely unaware, however, of the centuries-old legacy of African and African American artists and artisans in the United States, whose achievements were still unrecognized in the 1920s and 1930s.

Aaron Douglas Jr. (1899–1979) is the artist most closely associated with the New Negro Movement. The stylized designs and African themes of his paintings gave the movement a "look" that continues to identify it to this day. The painters Palmer Hayden (1890–1973) and Archibald Motley (1891–1928) also came to artistic maturity at this time, vividly recording the life of the burgeoning black urban centers.

Other artists, though not formally affiliated with the New Negro Movement, came to be associated with it through their work. Jacob Lawrence (1917–2000), whose parents came north in the Great Migration, was still a boy when the New Negro Movement began, but as an adult he would chronicle the time in a series of paintings called *The Great Migration.* Horace Pippin (1888–1946), in his small paintings of interior scenes, depicted the lives of people who were part of the age. By comparison to the sophisticated and urbane work associated with the New Negro Movement, Pippin's paintings seem more in the folk art tradition, but he achieved a large measure of success in the 1930s and 1940s, and his paintings, like those of Jacob Lawrence, are highly valued in the early twenty-first century.

SUPPORT FOR BLACK ARTISTS: HARMON FOUNDATION AND WPA

In 1928, the first all–African American exhibition of art, sponsored by the Harmon Foundation, was held at International House in New York City. It included work by Archibald Motley (1891–1928), Aaron Douglas Jr. (1899–1979), Augusta Savage (1892–1962), Sargent Johnson (1887–1967), James Porter (1905–1970), James Latimer Allen, and Hale Woodruff (1900–1980). For many years afterward, the foundation held annual exhibitions of black art, but the depression years of 1928 to 1933 were critical ones. Many black artists who are well known today might not have survived as artists without the keen interest and financial support of William Harmon (1862–1928) and the foundation during this time.

The Harmon Foundation exhibitions traveled around the country from city to city, making the art of black Americans more visible and accessible to the nation as a whole. The foundation established community art centers where children and adults could receive instruction and artists could have the use of expensive equipment such as printing presses. The foundation also offered cash prizes to the winners of its annual competitions, and in one form or another continued its support of Negro artists until it ceased operations in 1976.

When the U.S. Treasury Department established the Works Project Administration (WPA) in 1933, American artists of all colors received support from the federal government for the first time. Commissioned to create works of public art, they painted murals in post offices, airports, schools, libraries, and hospitals in communities across the nation. In this massive artistic outreach by the Roosevelt Administration, the WPA brought art to people who would not ordinarily have had access to it.

Many African Americans matured as artists during the WPA years, and with federal support they were able to achieve distinction in their fields. Hale Woodruff, John Biggers (1924–2001), Lois Mailou Jones (1905–1998), and others went on to head art departments in black colleges around the country. The printmaker Robert Blackburn (b. 1920), today the holder of a MacArthur Foundation fellowship, founded his own printmaking studio with WPA support. James Porter (1905–1970), Charles White (1918–1979), Elizabeth Catlett (b. 1919), Romare Bearden (1911–1988), William H. Johnson (1901–1970), Malvin Gray Johnson (1896–1934), Richmond Barthe (1901–1989), Dox Thrash (1892–1965), and the abstract expressionist Norman Lewis (1909–1979), among others, established their reputations as artists during these years.

FOLK ART

In traditional African societies, the visual arts were closely associated with religious practices and rituals. Sculpture, carving, and weaving served to teach people religious concepts and remind them of the importance of certain rituals. When African religious practices were outlawed in America, however, the visual component that accompanied these practices fell into disuse. Seeking to protect the limited freedom that Christianity gave them, Africans adopted the Protestant ban on religious imagery.

Early on in colonial America, the skills and craft traditions of Africans became combined with those of Europeans, but the African impulse did not entirely disappear. Without the religion and ritual that had been the basis of their art, Africans tended to focus on the secular, using their skills to fashion utilitarian and folk art. The African connection was expressed in objects with specific uses, such as walking sticks, or in objects imbued with special significance, such as face jugs, although the meaning such objects held for slaves remains unclear. Carved wooden bowls, furniture, iron work, and numerous decorative items made use of the designs and motifs found in traditional African artifacts.

The techniques and methods of fabrication used by Nellie Mae Rowe (1900–1982), James Hampton (1909–1964), William Edmondson (1882–1951), and other modern black folk artists are similar to those used by Africans. African American folk art combines a variety of media, with artists using assemblage and collage techniques to literally build their art. Graphic artists such as Bill Traylor (1854–1947), Sister Gertrude Morgan (1900–1980), and Mary A. Bell used paint, graphite, and crayon and frequently combined words and text with

Augusta Savage's sculpture *The Harp* was commissioned for the 1939 New York's World Fair. It was inspired by James Weldon Johnson's and J. Rosamond Johnson's hymn "Lift Every Voice and Sing." The song is often referred to as the "Negro National Anthem" for its inspiring message of faith and perseverance. Although Savage's plaster sculpture was destroyed shortly after the fair, the song remained a fixture in the Civil Rights movement and was eventually adopted as the NAACP's official song. **UPI/CORBIS-BETTMANN**

overlapping images to create a multilayered space on a flat, two-dimensional surface.

African American folk sculpture is carved with simple tools or constructed from wood, stone, aluminum foil, or iron. Africans believed that reflective materials—bits of shiny stone, copper, brass, and glass—would enhance the spiritual nature of an object. By incorporating bottle caps, aluminum, tin, and other reflective materials in their art, African American folk artists have maintained, perhaps without realizing it, stylistic links to African art.

Do the shiny reflective materials used by modern African American folk artists serve the same spiritual purpose as they did for Africans? The African American folk artists would never try to explain why they reach for

a particular object, shape, or color, any more than they would try to explain the origins of their art. But many offer a simple but profound explanation for what they do as artists, asserting that they are merely the vehicles of God; God is the artist, and they are his instrument of visual and spiritual communication. This spiritual connection or impulse has been constant in the folk art of African Americans for almost four hundred years, and it continues to inform the work of present-day native, visionary, and folk artists.

CONTEMPORARY AFRICAN AMERICAN ARTISTS

Since the 1960s, a younger generation of black Americans has been making another strenuous effort to under-

The African American artists Romare Bearden and Charles H. Alston served together in the 372nd Infantry Regiment stationed in New York City. In this photograph, the artists are discussing *Cotton Workers,* a painting by Bearden. Alston, a noted artist in his own right, was one of Bearden's first art teachers and also his cousin. **NATIONAL ARCHIVES AND RECORDS ADMINISTRATION**

stand their African heritage: painters like Barkley Hendricks (b. 1945), Richard Yarde (b. 1939), Deborah Muirhead, and Jonathan Green; mixed-media artists like Faith Ringgold (b. 1930), Howardena Pindell (b. 1943), Lorna Simpson (b. 1960), Betye Saar (b. 1926), and Allison Saar (b. 1956); sculptors like Martin Puryear (b. 1941), Renee Stout (b. 1958), and Willie Birch (b. 1942); as well as artists who are difficult to classify, like Fred Wilson (b. 1954) and Adrian Piper (b. 1948). Their art and that of others has grown more self-conscious as they have endeavored to understand the meanings and spirtual significance that are the heart of traditional African art. As a result, they have learned to understand and appreciate the visual art traditions of their black ancestors and to synthesize those traditions with Western modes of perception and presentation, creating unique works of American art.

Contemporary black artists display a determination to work despite the irritating racism that continues to exclude them from major museum collections and prominent galleries. The confusion and guilt over what constitutes appropriate subject matter and content—which may have frustrated earlier artists—is being

resolved through education, self-knowledge, and an understanding of black history, freeing black artists to confidently pursue their own personal artistic inclinations without denying their race.

As black men and women who make art, present-day artists must confront many of the same obstacles that hampered, but did not hinder, earlier African American artists. In the work of their forerunners, African American artists in the early 2000s find guides for their own intense and sometimes painful self-examination, without which there cannot be artistic expression or growth.

Clearly, we are on an eternal seesaw of American values, one day celebrating, the next demonizing African and black American values. While the binary black versus white thinking that has characterized American identity for four centuries runs deep, it is clear that this equation is becoming more and more difficult to maintain. What of the changing face of the country, particularly in young Americans? Is it possible that, as the United States discovers its multicultural self, we are traveling back toward the multiple and contradictory faces of reality

The African American Urban Artist: Rap, Graffiti, and the Painting of Jean-Michel Basquiat (1960–1988)

In the early 1980s, the young artist Jean-Michel Basquiat burst onto the New York art scene. Many have characterized him as the first great African American artist in the tradition of modern art luminaries such as Pablo Picasso or Jackson Pollock. While this ignores such talents as Romare Bearden and others, Basquiat's tremendous success did herald the appearance of an African American artist who was creating a wholly unique visual language. It was a means of expression not necessarily born of American folk traditions, but rather, on the one hand an intuitive sensibility for the tastes of the largely white and European New York and international art culture and on the other a visual language unique to Basquiat's Caribbean and African American perspective.

Basquiat's painting came out of the urban New York culture of the clubs in the early 1980s, as well as the burgeoning rap culture. Basquiat complained bitterly of the racism he suffered and found questions often loaded with a subtext involving his role as a successful black artist during interviews. As a result, though he came out of the graffiti scene, he sought to distance himself from that label and the implications that seemed to go with it. Still, he counted among his friends the likes of Freddy Braithwaite (better known as Fab 5 Freddy) and Toxic, both young graffiti artists of color. Basquiat's work exploded onto the scene while he was still in his early twenties, after a series of shows in alternative venues. The artist's jagged, skeletal figures, African mask-like portraits, and arcane iconography of scrawled words made him at once an undeniably powerful and unique artist and a lightning rod for the "primitivism in art" dialectic that had been a recurring theme in modern art since the Cubist images of Picasso and Matisse.

Indeed, many complained that Basquiat had been created, that he was a product of mass marketing, polished and presented by the doyennes of the art world in order to line their own pockets. This view, casting the artist both as somehow unskilled and victim, conveniently glosses over the fact that Basquiat himself longed for fame and made a concerted campaign to win over the New York art scene over the course of half a decade. It was precisely the sort of commentary that characterized his experience as a young, talented, black artist, and in some ways he received as much criticism from the black art world because of his disdain for the label of "black artist." Put simply, his was a success that drew criticism from any and all sides.

The truth, however, is that Jean-Michel Basquiat was as media savvy and as calculating in his efforts to present his vision as any young art star, and that, in the end, the artist was consumed by his own campaign. In the late years of his career, he suffered from tremendous doubts as to his talent, fueled by the persistent presentation of the artist as some kind of "affirmative action" mascot of the art world. He ultimately died of a drug overdose, feeling alone and openly talking about never painting again. Many have speculated that the artist felt increasing desperation as a fascinated and critical public came to expect the young artist to constantly outdo his previous work. Whether intentional or not, there is no question his death was the result of the same forces that made him an international star in the first place, and is a frightening cautionary tale as to the pressures and costs artists of colors must endure if they wish to succeed at its highest levels.

once celebrated in the traditional African cosmogonic belief systems? Is it possible that we might be on the tapering end of the half millennia of negative values traditionally ascribed to African Africans? There is still an infinite amount of work to be done. However, if there is any one thing that historical and sociological study teaches us, it is that those who believe in themselves lead the lives worth living. And perhaps even more importantly, they are the ones who continue to push the American equation forward, creating a history we can be proud of. Perhaps even one day we will throw the old equation out, in favor of a better one: an equation that equals an American reality that all Americans will wake up to every day.

BIBLIOGRAPHY

Bearden, Romare, and Harry Henderson. *A History of African-American Artists: From 1792 to the Present.* New York: Pantheon, 1992.

Black Art, Ancestral Legacy: The African Impulse in African-American Art. Dallas: Dallas Museum of Art, 1989.

Driskell, David. *Hidden Heritage: Afro-American Art, 1800–1950.* San Francisco: Art Museum Association of America, 1985.

Harlem Renaissance: Art of Black America. New York: Studio Museum in Harlem.

Honour, Hugh. *The Image of the Black in Western Art: From the American Revolution to World War I.* Houston: De Menil Foundation, 1989.

Livingston, Jane, and John Beardsley. *Black Folk Art in America: 1930–1980.* Jackson: University of Mississippi Press, 1982.

McElroy, Guy C. *Facing History: The Black Image in American Art, 1710–1940.* San Francisco: Bedford Arts, 1990.

Perry, Regenia A. *Free within Ourselves: African-American Artists.* Washington: National Museum of American Art, Smithsonian Institution, 1992.

Porter, James A. *Modern Negro Art.* Washington: Howard University Press, 1992.

Vlach, John Michael. *Back of the Big House: The Architecture of Plantation Slavery.* Chapel Hill: University of North Carolina Press, 199.

The Close of the Twentieth Century and Beyond

ESSAYS BY GABRIEL BURNS STEPTO

At the tail end of the Civil Rights movement, a new promise was present in American society for peoples of color. Much of the segregationist infrastructure in place since the beginning of American slavery had been dismantled. Where a range of legislation had stood before, ensuring that African Americans might never rise above a certain level, there was a new body of legislation effectively trying to promote just the opposite. Antidiscrimination laws had been drafted for many areas of American society. These laws essentially were designed to prevent, and even redress, the cultural habits of racism bred for centuries into the American social system.

Nevertheless, the same tendencies—the same age-old battles—were a nearly constant presence in the lives of African Americans in the 1970s and 1980s. In the media and the halls of power, the rhetorical and political tug-of-war over race was played out nearly every day. For many, a key example was the issue of affirmative action. This policy was designed to address the lack of access African Americans experienced, for example, in the workplace and in private schools and universities. In many ways, affirmative action accomplished essentially the same thing as the antidiscrimination legislation, but it did so while taking a more activist stance. Because of their proactive nature, affirmative action programs have drawn wild criticism from conservatives and opponents on the right, who contend that such plans are unconstitutional. That said, there can be no question that the affirmative action policies of the 1980s and early 1990s made for a sea change in the way universities recruited their student bodies. And while many elements of the affirmative action initiative have been struck down, not only did the policy help to greatly expand the ranks of African Americans and other minorities in the coveted programs of the top universities, but it also seems to have changed the way university administrations view the very process of selecting their student bodies.

For many, it is not difficult to see the same old forces at work, striking down the legislative efforts designed to promote African Americans even as they are written into law. The same forces that fought back against the gains of Reconstruction with black codes and Jim Crow and the gains of each Constitutional amendment and each piece of civil rights legislation with counterlegislation, will, it seems, always be around in the United States. That said, there were many elements of progress at the tail end of the twentieth century that were encouraging—indeed, encouraging in ways that suggest real progress was made during the period of the civil rights struggle and in the years after. This is, of course, an issue that arouses intense debate, with people on different sides of the color line and with different shades of African America interpreting the gains in different ways. Looking a little below the surface, however, there are signs suggesting that important changes began taking place in the last decades of the twentieth century. That said, if American history has taught us anything, it is that the struggle for opportunity in the United States is constant and that gains should never be taken for granted because there are always forces that are eager to return things to the ways they were before.

THE RISE OF "CLASSISM" WHERE RACIAL DIVISION STOOD BEFORE

One of the principal, and in many ways most befuddling, elements of the struggle for equality and opportunity in the second half of the twentieth century was a subtle shift in the terms by which racism and discrimination were perceived, measured, and addressed. During the civil rights era there was little doubt that the nation had a history of racial injustice and that the dismantling of that infrastructure of legislation and social and cultural norms was a goal on which most could agree. As African Americans began to live in a more integrated society and had arrayed before them at least the promise of various opportunities, concerns about the treatment of African Americans began shifting away from the obvious wrong of racial discrimination toward the more nebulous iniquity of class discrimination.

Class discrimination is one of the most difficult elements of social inequality to address, much less undo, because the fact of poverty, the fact of the haves and have-nots, is at the heart of the capitalist system. Mainstream America is wary to critique this system, much less point to it as the cause of some of the inherent racial ills in the nation's history.

Although antidiscriminatory legislation sought to address the legacy of segregation and disenfranchisement, the economic picture for people of color in the United States in the last quarter of the twentieth century was disturbing. A disproportionate number of African American adults, and an even more disproportionate number of black children, lived below the poverty line. There was also the much-cited fact that one in four African American males was either in prison or had at some time in his life been incarcerated, a fact that led to a host of related and equally troubling statistics. The ongoing reality of institutionalized segregation, whereby African Americans males were nearly ten times as likely as their white counterparts to be in prison, with their labor supporting state coffers rather than their own families, provided a disturbing insight into the quality of life for African Americans in the United States.

Perhaps even more troubling was that these facts were echoed by aspects of the psychological profile of African Americans. Many observers have noted the rapid advance of immigrants of color from the Caribbean, South America, and even Africa. For example, Colin Powell (b. 1937), the secretary of state under George W. Bush (b. 1946), is of Caribbean ancestry and has stated that he always believed that if he worked hard he could advance as far as his talents would allow. This conviction is not held by all African Americans, particularly those living in poverty, and sociologists cite this as evidence of a potentially crippling set of psychological attitudes that are being passed on from generation to generation. Indeed, the implications are very troubling. Such attitudes can affect the readiness of African Americans to compete in the career marketplace, and they lead to the propensity of black Americans to view themselves as guilty before the fact or as having committed some unnamed social wrong. With this kind of psychological anxiety always around the next corner, many sociologists and historians have pointed out the negative impact of these factors on everything from the quality of daily life to the life expectancy of African Americans. Whatever the case may be, there can be no question that many blacks in the United States feel an ongoing sense of rage and frustration at the limitations of their own experience and the sense of collective wrongs perpetrated against their ancestors—wrongs made worse by the lack of any real reparations for the cultural crime of slavery, whether of a financial or moral nature. Indeed, that the

In the last three decades of the twentieth century a new kind of black intellectual began to appear in the United States. While firmly rooted in the traditions of protest and the struggle for justice, the novelist John Edgar Wideman (b. 1941) has sought to address a world of wrongs—but not with the easy prose of political protest. Drawing comparisons to author James Baldwin, Wideman has dealt with social and political issues in such novels as *The Lynchers* and *Philadelphia Fire.* (Photograph by Jerry Bauer.) ©JERRY BAUER

notion of reparations is viewed as suspect or even ridiculous by many white Americans is itself a sort of barometer of the gulf that continues to stand between the black experience and that of white America.

So it is that many African Americans at the end of the twentieth century felt an inherent conflict between their ambition to advance and their sense of community and belonging. Indeed, the cultural reality is one in which black traditions, such as "uplift," protest, and religious leadership, have themselves been stigmatized, rather than celebrated, and the only way to participate in the promise of the American dream is to renounce the cultural identity and collective history of the African American experience.

THE REAGAN AND BUSH YEARS

During the administrations of Presidents Ronald Reagan (b. 1911) and George H. W. Bush (b. 1924), African Americans encountered a somewhat bizarre catalog of policies that, while couched in seemingly innocuous language, did a great deal to freeze and even retard their progress. During the 1980s, a record number of black

Few rival the business empire of Oprah Winfrey (b. 1954), whose syndicated talk-show became a national sensation in the mid-1980s. A powerhouse in television, film, publishing, and many other sectors of the market, Winfrey's Harpo organization has been synonymous with success. **AP/WIDE WORLD PHOTOS**

Americans were unemployed and incarcerated. The welfare rolls swelled, creating what many categorized as simply a new form of second-class citizenship, one that kept people of color scrambling from check to check, often in spiraling conditions of poverty and substance abuse. President Reagan's now-debunked "trickle-down economics" promised to create wealth in the upper-middle and upper classes, thereby creating an economy in which jobs would flourish and the rest of the nation would be provided for. Given the historical psychology of the nation, the disproportionate distribution of wealth among nonminorities, and the stigmatized image of blacks and black culture as one consisting of criminals, addicts, nonattendant fathers, and teen and/or single black mothers—to name some of the most prevalent and enduring stereotypes of African Americans—it should not come as a surprise that these Republican administrations presided over a painful era for blacks in the United States. That said, one of the more troubling elements of this period is that so many Americans look back on it as an era of national prosperity and even one of noble and/or heroic values in the national leadership.

Culturally, while the groundwork was being laid for the cultural changes of the 1990s and beyond, the situation had not improved much. In the early 1960s, Sidney Poitier (b. 1927) had become the first African American to

win an Academy Award for lead actor, but it would be nearly forty years before that feat would be duplicated in the year 2002. The simple fact is that the 1980s were a period characterized by the changing and perhaps the refining of stereotypes of who black Americans were—but the images presented in television, film, and radio were stereotypes of broad, easy strokes, nonetheless. An example of this lack of real progress is the television series *The Jeffersons,* which ran from 1975 to 1985 and which was a spin-off from *All in the Family* (in which the comic tension and release centered around an exasperated working-class Irish American complaining bitterly about blacks, Jews, Hispanics, and other ethnic groups infringing on the world he knew). *The Jeffersons* presented a black man who had prospered in the laundry business but who still had the values of his origins—an impoverished, penny-pinching environment—and, like the show's model, an oftentimes openly racist view of the world.

During the 1970s and early 1980s virtually all television commercials presented the potential consumer with a white male, family, couple, or child as the face of products' consumers. During this period the first of the "buddy" commercials appeared, in which working-class men, a white man with his black coworker, might be presented as the face of the product in question. It was during this period that the notion of the "token" or accompanying African American gained traction and cachet in the parlance of the nation. As a rule, there were no commercials that presented a black male or female where no white was present. There were virtually no black celebrities pitching products, with the possible exception of actor-comedian Bill Cosby (b. 1937).

In essence, this situation reflected the perceived financial reality of the marketplace. While of course African Americans were consuming products, they were not considered a viable enough market sector to warrant the production of commercials, and the marketing executives assumed—and thereby promoted—a reality in which consumers would not readily turn to a product represented by an African American spokesperson.

In the arts, the situation was sometimes better when an insulated venue was involved. The 1980s saw, for example, the plays of August Wilson (b. 1945) and the painting of Jean-Michel Basquiat (1960–1988). These artists, however, continued to face the daunting racial reality when it came to the acceptance and promotion of their work. The question always lingered: despite their success, was the art celebrated in part *because* they were African American? Nevertheless, this period was also the testing ground that produced the artists, entertainers, and musicians who forever changed both the perception of African Americans and the perception of American culture around the world. The greatest example is most likely the "King of Pop," Michael Jackson (b. 1958). The moniker echoes that of "the King," Elvis Presley

(1935–1977), and it is not ingenuous to compare the wild international popularity of Jackson and his music with the phenomenon of Presley in the days when network television stations cropped the bottom half of the screen in order to protect viewers from his gyrating hips. When Jackson performed his famous "moonwalk" it was literally history in the making, and unlike the black musical stars that had gone before him, Jackson catapulted into the stratospheres of superstardom, with all the attendant wealth and media circumspection that had to date been afforded to only the most mainstream of cultural superstars.

It could be argued that while the Civil Rights movement had worked to tear down the walls of overt discrimination, it was not any moral imperative but rather money—and the awesome success of such entertainers as Jackson—that began to create a new cultural reality in the United States. That said, there was a sense during these years that there was a new cultural rubber-stamping that occurred with these megastars. As Spike Lee's film, *Do the Right Thing* (1989), suggested, an Italian American in the Bedford-Stuyvesant section of Brooklyn might have had as a favorite singer, Michael Jackson, and as a favorite athlete, Michael Jordan (b. 1963), yet have simultaneously continued to hold views of African Americans as dishonest, dangerous people—qualities of character that were the exact opposite of those he associated with his black cultural heroes. In many ways, this goes back to the issues of classism versus racism in the changing American society: A black American with an inordinate amount of wealth and the attendant social status was, in effect, made temporarily and honorarily white.

THE CLINTON YEARS

In contrast to the numbing realities of life for African Americans during the Reagan and Bush years, the 1990s brought the beginnings of a change in African Americans' social realities. There was almost a sense that the Republicans had been looking backward, working to hold onto a version of race relations in the United States that pertained to the 1950s and early 1960s. Meanwhile, however, much had been changing, and by the time William Jefferson Clinton entered office in 1993, there was a groundswell of the already changed and the ready to be recognized and a subsequent momentum that caught the nation unawares, creating one of those moments where history and national identity seem to turn on a dime.

From the first moment Clinton took office, he promised that his cabinet "would look like America does" and went on to appoint a range of African Americans, Hispanics, and women to important positions. This was in complete contrast to the preceding administrations: While Bush had paid lip service to the values of

Bill Clinton (b. 1946) speaks with friend and adviser Vernon Jordan (b. 1935) after an announcement at the White House that Treasury Secretary Robert Rubin would resign from his post. A successful lawyer and civil rights activist in the 1960s, Jordan had considerable pull in the president's policy and staffing decisions even though he did not hold an official position in the Clinton administration. **AP/WIDE WORLD PHOTOS**

diversity, he had kept himself cloistered in an old boy's network of conservatives and various captains of industry. Clinton in his first years in office created a bedrock of support, turning to Wall Street, Hollywood, the unions, and the leaders of various minority groups. History will likely show that many of Clinton's overtures to the African American leadership and people were at times cosmetic. For many he will be forever remembered for the compromises he made, by which some in the African American community felt profoundly betrayed. He signed into law the legislation that effectively put into motion welfare reform, jettisoning hundreds of thousands from the welfare rolls, and to some degree he ignored the black leadership when it came to the critical battles of his presidency. There can be no doubt, however, that during the eight years of the Clinton presidency the nation underwent dramatic changes in regard to the lives of African Americans, their image in American culture, and their sense of self.

The causes of these changes are manifold, and not as easy to identify or obvious as they might seem at cursory glance. As mentioned above, a national leadership that seemed intent upon giving African Americans their place in the national spotlight and treating with gravity issues that involved minorities, along with an oratory of inclusion that on more than one occasion recalled the ennobling tones of Abraham Lincoln's second inaugural

Jackie Robinson (1919–1972), who began playing professional baseball for the Brooklyn Dodgers in 1947, paved the way for the entry of African Americans in all professional sports. **ARCHIVE PHOTOS, INC.**

address, had the effect of framing the national debate on race in a light that had perhaps never been seen in the country's entire history. During the period of scandal and the "criminalizing of political difference" that began with the investigation into a failed Arkansas savings and loan and culminated during the president's second term with the investigation of an affair between the president and a subordinate, Clinton almost invariably had the support of African Americans. Indeed, the vitriol with which his critics parsed the president's testimony and examined the details of his personal life looked quite familiar to many black Americans. The president's poor origins in southern Arkansas, his inclination to turn to the Reverend Jesse Jackson (b. 1941) in times of personal crisis and prayer, and even his personal appetites and his attitude toward sexuality—all of these seemed to recall that "other" that various elements of the political hierarchy in the nation had sought to banish, discredit, and "keep in its place" during each and every era of American history.

AFRICAN AMERICAN SPORTS FIGURES AT THE CLOSE OF THE CENTURY

During the 1980s and 1990s, the nation saw an explosion of black talent in a range of sports. While major league baseball had seen Jackie Robinson (1919–1972) win the National League Most Valuable Player Award in 1949, by the mid-1990s the sport had a roughly equal number of black and white players, with the player ranks disproportionately weighted toward the Latin American ballplayers, who excelled in the sport. In other major sports (with the exception of hockey), this trend had gone much further than it had in baseball. Basketball and football had become sports where, for all intents and purposes, all but a few players were people of color. Because of the will to win and the desire of owners to fill their stadiums and make profits, sports had simply turned to whoever performed best. As a result, even the sports that were traditionally white and that had been born out of the tradition of leisure and entitlement, such as golf, saw the arrival of superstar players of color, such as Tiger Woods (b. 1975).

THE EMERGENCE OF BLACK SUPERSTARS IN HOLLYWOOD

In 2002 African Americans won Academy Awards for both best actor (Denzel Washington [b. 1954]) and best actress (Halle Berry [b. circa 1968]). This stood in dramatic contrast to previous decades, in which only one African American, Sidney Poitier, had ever won for best actor, and none had ever won for best actress. The long-overdue event was certainly in large part a result of the clearly extraordinary performances of Washington and Berry. As always with award shows, however, politics played at least a small role, with the industry realizing it was both shameful and ridiculous, considering the breadth of talented African American actors out there, that none had won a lead actor Academy Award for more than four decades.

That said, those four decades were characterized by a range of stereotypical limitations on the roles that black actors were offered. Beyond the infamous reality of the 1960s, 1970s, and 1980s, in which African Americans almost always found themselves limited to the roles of street thugs, the parts that followed were often of the action variety. There are a number of African American actors who have made incredible strides in finding more complex and humanizing roles. Washington, Samuel L. Jackson (b. circa 1948), Angela Bassett (b. circa 1958), Will Smith (b. 1968), Cuba Gooding Jr. (b. 1968), Jada Pinkett Smith (b. circa 1971), Wesley Snipes (b. 1962), Ving Rhames (b. 1961), and Berry are actors who, beyond being able to hold their own in terms of the Hollywood money machine, have also managed to find roles originally conceived for whites or simply written without the usual baggage of preconceptions as to which roles are "right" for African Americans. Nevertheless, the list is clearly very thin where black women actors are concerned, and even for these privileged few it is a constant battle to find quality scripts.

There can be no doubt that Hollywood is opening up. As is the case with television, the American public seems to have a very healthy appetite for talented young African American performers who at once entertain and, perhaps, at the same time assuage some guilt regarding the troubled relationship between the races. America has always had an appetite for its own dark side, as witnessed in film noir, gangster films, and thrillers. Much the way tongue-in-cheek urban sidemen (often with Italian or Irish ethnic overtones) were a staple of the films of the 1930s, 1940s, and 1950s, African Americans are coming to occupy a very regular place in the narratives Americans consume. Nevertheless, as long as the major players in Hollywood's studio system and those who produce films continue to be people of other ethnic backgrounds, African Americans will continue to suffer from the traditional "black/white" dialectic, and Americans will continue to get a picture of black America that is not without racist or at least prejudicial overtones.

In music, the successes of Michael Jackson were followed by a generation of African American superstars, male and female. By the time rap and hip-hop had exploded across the nation (and the world), not only was mainstream American popular culture dominated by the music of African Americans, but that music was also acting as a vehicle out of impoverishment and as an expression of those origins.

Some would argue that the consumption of black culture as "popular music" by a white mainstream audience goes as far back as the music itself does, and there can be no doubt that the appropriation of black culture by the mainstream is a staple of the troubled rapport between the two sides in American society. Even so, the late 1980s and 1990s did see those two sides begin to blur. Within the hip-hop community, there was the emergence of African American media moguls. There was the explosion of African American athletes, not as sheer examples of physical prowess, but as role models and figures of fascination for the nation as a whole. There was the rise of African American actors and entertainers and the accompanying stories about their families, their homes, and children, not to mention the appearance of a fourth television network committed in large part to programming portraying blacks. In a society in which Hollywood, sport, and the pursuit of fame have become largely equated with that other holy grail of American values, the "pursuit of happiness," the viewing public's attention is focused on those African American stars who have managed to distinguish themselves in their careers. These advances, while not ubiquitous, were affecting the lives of African Americans in many areas of the country, particularly the coastal and major metropolitan regions, and they had begun to slowly change the tenor of the perception of "mainstream" America.

The comedian Eddie Murphy (b. 1961) started to achieve fame on *Saturday Night Live,* creating a range of characters that often provided pointed commentary on the troubled relationship between the races. As his career progressed, he became an actor and a major box office draw, not only as a lead actor, but one of the few who could be counted on to draw over $100 million per film. **AP/WIDE WORLD PHOTOS**

TELEVISION AND THE NEW AMERICAN CULTURE

There were even more powerful changes going on below the surface of American society in the last years of the twentieth century. As a result of these changes, the improving quality of life for African Americans was not entirely cosmetic or experienced only by those in positions of power. In the early and mid-1990s, for the first time in their sixty-year history, the standards and practices departments of the major television networks instituted a new set of guidelines governing the content and language of national programming. This development provides an example of a key point: that it was not moral imperatives but rather the sheer force of the capitalist machine and its drive for profits that did more to advance a changing reality for blacks in America around the end of twentieth century than any other thing. As a result of newly institutionalized and refined systems of polling, the major television networks began to promote a series of values that were far more positive for African Americans. The same data that enabled programming to venture to the edge of indecency (using words such as *ass* and *suck*) also told the executives that programs that showed

Secretary of State Colin Powell (b. 1937) and National Security Adviser Condoleezza Rice (b. 1954) seated on either side of President George W. Bush (b. 1946). **AP/WIDE WORLD PHOTOS**

minorities in a positive light had a marked advantage over other programs. The people who enforced an unspoken code of national morality, stipulating, for example, that cigarettes be smoked only in scenes of stress or in a clearly negative light and that bad characters receive a moral retribution by plot's end, were demanding a new presentation of blacks in the media that in many ways turned the old stereotypical world (present right up until the preceding decade) on its head. Executives rushed to create shows that showed "edgy" African Americans living decent family lives in which positive moral conclusions were reached by the end of each episode. This was a new spin on *The Cosby Show* of the 1980s, a show that clearly must be largely responsible for showing the executives that African American family life could garner high Nielsen ratings and advertising dollars. Now blacks were present across the board in the vast majority of "docudramas" as a proportionate representative of an integrated and heroic team, and the newer networks (namely Fox) played with police dramas in which the majority of the cast were either people of color, other minorities, or women. During this period the number of black celebrities and near-celebrities skyrocketed.

At the same time the representation of African Americans in advertising was completely different from that of the 1970s and early 1980s. The "buddy" commercials were still there, but it was not always entirely clear, however, who was the buddy, the white or black figure—or perhaps both!—one for each market sector being courted. More revealing was that African American housewives, mothers, and families were often pictured on their own, representing a product clearly meant to be consumed across the racial spectrum. It was not uncommon to find major national brands advertised through multiyear campaigns in which the sole spokesperson was an African American. These changes represent an astonishing shift in the national perception of African Americans. Working-class white people are presented as having comfortable daily relations with their black counterparts, and for youth markets the images of blacks and whites are often those of people who do not distinguish whatsoever on the basis of race (provided all are of the same class denomination). More to the point, one has to wonder about what effect this bombardment of images of easygoing race relations, not to mention the wit and sarcasm at the troubling issues of the American racial past that is sometimes featured in the advertising, is having on those areas of middle America where a lack of integration, or even various casual and not-so-casual forms of segregation, have persisted.

THE 2000 CENSUS AND DAWNING OF A MULTIRACIAL AMERICA

In the year 2000, a painstaking new census was completed, and the implications were readily apparent to all who chose to look. Among other findings, the heart of the new census lay in the image of a multiracial America very different from the notion of the "melting pot" at the turn of the previous century. Essentially the melting pot referred to an America in which many groups were in contact with one another. The new census described an America in which those culturally and ethnically mixed groups had already produced one or more generations of offspring and readily identified themselves as belonging to all of their ethnic origins. First and foremost, the census suggested that around the year 2020 "white" Americans would be outnumbered by "minority" Americans, in effect making whites the minority. The reality, however, was a little more startling that that. The previous decades had always encouraged the divisions of "white," "black," "Native American," and so on. This census, however, showed not only the growth of groups of people of color but also an unwillingness among even "white" Americans to be collectively lumped as such. The last decades had seen a change in the way in which Americans named themselves, and many now identified with a primary source of ancestry, such as "Italian American" or "Irish American." Perhaps most important was the explosion of the groups who considered themselves as "mixed-race" or "other." The stigma attached to being of mixed ancestry had, apparently, begun to lessen, or even been forgotten, and millions now recognized and celebrated multiple ancestries, rather than categorizing themselves with more convenient labels. Census workers admitted that if the questions had been asked in a way that recognized more groups, or had been phrased more euphemistically (instead of using the terms "mixed-race" and "other," which were themselves not present on earlier censuses), the number of people who identified themselves as having multiple ancestries might have been far greater. In the end, of course, the result of the census is determined by the way the questions are asked.

Whatever the case, there can be no question that, as the nation destigmatizes the notion of race and the "politically correct" language of identity becomes further institutionalized, all of the ideas of America that have dominated public and political discourse over previous centuries, and even previous decades, are being rapidly reevaluated. This can only be good for African Americans, because "the dualism of the white folk mind," as the novelist Ralph Ellison described the binary black and white approach to American identity, has over the centuries consistently aligned African Americans with the negative end of that equation. This is no small thing. If there is anything the careful study of American history shows us, it is that the mechanisms that have enforced the disenfranchisement of black America are not so simple as some prejudicial attitude taken up one day and just as easily discarded the next. Rather, they ride in lockstep with the currents of Western civilization, dating back to Enlightenment values of day and night, light and dark, black and white, and good and evil, and before that to the human animal's most primitive fears.

So where are we in the early twenty-first century? Is it possible that, as America discovers its multicultural self, we are in fact traveling back toward the multiple and contradictory faces of reality once celebrated in the traditional African cosmogonic belief systems? Is it possible that we might be on the tapering end of the half millennia of negative values ascribed inherently to Africans and Africans in the New World? There can be no doubt that there is much work to be done. That said, if there is any one thing all of the historical and sociological study teaches us, it is that those who believe in themselves, whether they must simply ignore or even lie to themselves about the forces arrayed against them, are the ones who lead the lives worth living. And perhaps even more importantly, they are the ones who continue to push the equation forward, creating a history we can be proud of and a history that is itself slowly turning things around.

BIBLIOGRAPHY

Collins, Patricia Hill. *Black Feminist Thought: Knowledge, Consciousness, and the Politics of Empowerment.* Boston: Unwin Hyman 1990; revised 10th anniversary edition, New York: Routledge, 2000.

Davis, Angela. *Women, Race and Class.* New York: Random House, 1982.

Fanon, Franz. *Black Skin, White Masks.* New York: Grove Press, 1967.

Kelley, Robin D. G. *Yo' Mama's Disfunktional!: Fighting the Culture Wars in Urban America.* Boston: Beacon Press, 1997.

Malcolm X and Alex Haley, *The Autobiography of Malcolm X.* New York: Grove Press, 1965.

List of Contributors

Erik Arnesen, Yale University/Brandeis University

Emily Bernard, Smith College

Lori Brooks, Berea College

Allison Epstein

Rob Forbes, Gilder Lehrman Center

Kimberly Goff-Crews

Adam Green, Yale University

Hallie S. Hobson

Jonathan Holloway, Yale University

Dr. James Jay

Mary Kordak, Yale University

N'tanya Lee

Anthony Miles

Laura Mitchell, University of California

Edward Pavlic, University of Wisconsin

Patrick Rael, Bowdoin College

Carlo Rotella, Boston College

Marcy Sacks, Albion College/Hamilton College

Barbara Savage, University of Pennsylvania

Stacy Shorter

Suzanne Smith, George Mason University

Gabriel Burns Stepto

Ian Straker

Cynthia Young

Index

Page numbers in italics indicate illustrations. A term associated with an illustration may also be covered in the text on the same page as the illustration. Following terminology in the text, the index uses both "black" and "African American." See separate index for more direct access to primary source documents.

54th Massachusetts Volunteers, 16–17, 19, 173
Final Call, 232
Finley, Harold E., 424
Fire, 231
The Fire Next Time (Baldwin), 49, 401, 402–403
First African Baptist Church, 5, 369
First Kansas Colored Volunteers, 16, 18
First Louisiana Native Guards, 16
First South Carolina Volunteers, 16, 173
Fisk Jubilee Singers, 20, *21,* 324
Fisk University, 20, 277, 421
Fitzgerald, Ella, 38, 332
Flake, Floyd, 375
Flipper, Henry O., 24, *25*
Florida, 21, 28
  See also Deep South
Floyd, Eddie, 326
Folk art, 438–439
Folkways, 333–336
For colored girls who have considered suicide when the rainbow is enuf (Shange), 342
Ford, Barney, 216
Ford, Gerald, 56
Fort Pillow massacre (1864), 18
Forten, Charlotte, 16, 174
Forten, James, 8, 9, 10
Foster, Andrew "Rube," 33
Fourteenth Amendment, 20, 21, 47, 194, 247–249
  primary source document, 262–263
  See also Plessy v. *Ferguson*
"Foxy Lady" (Hendrix), 52
Frank Johnson Band, 8
Franklin, Aretha, 330, 374, 401
Franklin, John Hope, 63
Fraternities/sororities, 29, 30
Frazier, E. Franklin, 409
Frazier, Joe, 54
Frederick Douglass's Paper, 112
Free African Society, 6, 7, 102
Free black legal status
  antebellum era, 8, 9, 11, 15, 162
  colonial era, 3, 75–76, 90, 91
  See also Voting rights
Free blacks
  abolitionism and, 7, 11, 102, 112–113, 160
  American Revolution and, 90–91, 100
  antebellum era, 100, 101–102
  colonial era, 2, 3, 4, 6, 70–71, 89–90
  colonial era land grants, 2
  colonization movement and, 113
  War of 1812 and, 8
  See also Free black legal status; *specific people*
"Free jazz," 328

Free Soil Party, 13, 113
Free Southern Theater, 401
Freedmen, 20, 173–174, *201, 202, 247*
  black press and, 229
  education, 275
  Freedmen's Bureau, 19, 194, *199*
  primary source documents, 198–200
  See also Reconstruction era
Freedmen's Bureau, 19, 194, *199,* 275
Freedom Riders, 41, 42, 48, 401
Freedom's Journal, 9, 102, 112, 228
Freedomways, 232
Freeman's Advocate, 228
Frelinghuysen University, 407–408
Fremont, John C., *170,* 171
Frisby, Herbert, 421
"From Dakto to Detroit: Death of a Troubled Hero" (Nordheimer), 304–311
Frontier, 213–228
  African American cowboys, 22, 214–215, *214,* 217–219
  black laws, 8
  Buffalo Soldiers, *184,* 215, 295
  California, 6, 15, 215
  Estevanico, 1
  Exoduster movement, 24, 215–216, 219–228
  explorers, 7, 13, 213–214
  primary source documents, 217–228
  Spanish colonization, 1, 213
  See also Slavery, expansion of
The Fugitive Blacksmith (Pennington), 166–168
Fugitive Slave Act (1850), 13, *131, 132*
  abolitionism and, 114, 115
  contraband and, 171
  Garner escape and, 15
  kidnapping and, *168*
Fugitive slave laws
  Burns case, 14, 163
  Chesapeake area colonies, 1, 2, 92–93
  Christiana Riot (1851), 14
  Constitution and, 6, 101
  Ellen and William Craft and, 13
  late eighteenth century, 7
  repeal (1864), 18
  Runaway Slave Act (Virginia), 2, 92–93
  See also Fugitive Slave Act (1850)
Fugitive slaves, *135, 138, 140*
  Canada migration, 10, 13
  contraband, 16, *19,* 171–172, *171, 172,* 185–188, *275*
  escape narratives, 13, 113, 114, 152, 163
  Latimer, 12
  maroons, 75, 155
  primary source documents, 168–169
  Tubman, 13, 31, 174–175
  Underground Railroad, 10, 113, 138
  See also Fugitive slave laws
Fuller, Blind Boy, 325

Fuller, Hoyt, 232
Fuller, Willie, *297*
Furness, Henry, 28

G

"Gag rule," 11
Gage, Frances D., 161–162
Gaines, Lloyd, 39
Galphin, Jesse, 369
Gang Starr, 330
Gangsta rap, 331, 335
Garner, Erroll, 56
Garner, Margaret, 15, 62
Garnet, Henry Highland
  abolitionist activities, 12, 102
  African Free School, 6
  colonization movement and, 113, 174
  education of, 11
  government service, 25
  intellectual tradition and, 405
  Liberty Party and, 13
  life of, 9, 25, 129
  primary source documents, 128–133, 410–412
  religion and, 370
  Thirteenth Amendment and, 19–20
Garrison, William Lloyd, 10, 111
  black abolitionists and, 13, 112, 113
  Canterbury School and, 280
  Civil War and, 19
  primary source documents, 127–128
Garvey, Amy Jacques, 231
Garvey, Marcus, 31, 33
  death of, 40
  imprisonment, 34, 35
  Negro World, 32, 231
  primary source documents, 239–243
  religion and, 372
Gates, Henry Louis, Jr., *344*
Gaye, Marvin, 58, 332
Gayle v. *Browder,* 248–249
Gell, Monday, 156
George, David, 5, 369
Georgia, 22, 155, 159, 274
  See also Deep South; Low country region colonies
Gershwin, George, 38
Ghana, kingdom of, 67, *68*
Ghost, 61
Gibson, Althea, 47
Gilbert, Olive, 161
Gillespie, Dizzy, *38,* 62, 327, 329
Gilpin, Charles, 33
Giovanni, Nikki, 341, 342, 401
Gladys Hampton Houses, 65
Glory, 64
"Go Down, Moses," 323, 334
Go Tell It on the Mountain (Baldwin), 49

Primary Source Document Index

This index provides access exclusively to primary source documents and their introductions. For coverage outside of the primary source documents and their introductions, see separate index.